SECRET WRITING

SECRET WRITING

Keys to the Mysteries of Reading and Writing

by Peter Sears

Teachers & Writers Collaborative
5 Union Square West, New York, N.Y. 10003

Secret Writing: Keys to the Mysteries of Reading and Writing

Funding for this publication has been provided by the New York State Council on the Arts and the National Endowment for the Arts.

Teachers & Writers Collaborative programs and publications are also made possible by funding from American Broadcasting Companies, Inc., American Can Company Foundation, American Stock Exchange, Chemical Bank, Consolidated Edison Company, General Electric Foundation, Long Island Community Foundation, Mobil Foundation, Inc., Morgan Guaranty Trust Company, Morgan Stanley, New York Foundation for the Arts' Artists-in-Residence Program (supported by funds from the National Endowment for the Arts), New York Telephone, The New York Times Company Foundation, Henry Nias Foundation, Overseas Shipholding Group, Inc., Pisces Foundation, Helena Rubenstein Foundation, and The Scherman Foundation.

Teachers & Writers Collaborative
5 Union Square West
New York, N.Y. 10003

Library of Congress Cataloging-in-Publication Data

Sears, Peter.
  Secret writing.

  Bibliography: p. 159
  Summary: Discusses secret writing, ciphers, and the processes of creating and deciphering secret or difficult languages. Includes thinking and writing exercises.
    1. Cryptography—Juvenile literature. 2. Ciphers—Juvenile literature. 3. Language and languages—Juvenile literature. [1. Cryptography. 2. Ciphers. 3. Language and languages] I. Title.
Z103.3.S4 1986   001.54'36   86-5893
ISBN 0-915924-86-2

Printed by Philmark Lithographics, N.Y.C.
Second Printing

Permissions

Thanks

I want to thank Ron Padgett, the editor of this book. First, for the basics: clarify, condense, and restructure, the lucidity services all good editors provide. Ron Padgett contributed much more: he added, questioned, provoked, and created. And what a jolly, supportive taskmaster! The fun is what I will remember most. My gratitude centers here, on the pleasure of our writing this book.

I also want to thank my friend Christopher MacMillan, another fine writer and editor, for making me aware of the importance of secret writing. This book grew out of that awareness.

To my sister Missy and my brother Jay

Table of Contents

A Note to Everyone: About the Exercises

Throughout this book there are exercises. Some are thinking exercises, some are thinking and writing or drawing exercises. They're all self-explanatory.

Each exercise is numbered. "Exercise 2.1" means that it's in chapter 2 and it's the first one in that chapter. "Exercise 3.5" means that it's in chapter 3 and it's the fifth one in that chapter. And so on.

At the end of each exercise there's a symbol, like this: •. I put it there as a stop sign, to remind you to stop reading and to start thinking about your response. If you run the stop sign, you'll skid right into my response to the exercise. Yes, in most cases my response is right beneath the exercise question, because in writing this book I became a student too.

It's better for you if you stop and think of your own response before you read mine. Your response will usually be different from mine. That's fine. Most of the exercises ask questions that don't have just one correct answer. For instance, some of them ask for your opinion, and your opinion is as good as anyone else's (including mine).

So remember: when you see the • symbol, you're supposed to stop and think (and sometimes write or draw) before you continue reading.

A Note to Students

This book is about secret language and the secrets of language. One kind of secret language is codes. Ciphers are another. The book starts with codes and ciphers. First we find out about the language of codes and ciphers, and then we see what codes and ciphers tell us about our own language. Secret writing tells us a lot about English. It tells us how we make English and other languages. We then use this information to decipher hard passages of English.

Then we look at other kinds of languages, not just other written languages like Hebrew and Chinese, but languages of pictures and numbers too. Egyptian hieroglyphs and arithmetic. Comics and traffic signs. There is a lot of odd stuff in this book: cattle brands, petroglyphs, tap dancing, symbols, Indian sandpainting, computer graphics, and slang. Why all these? Because they are language systems: they are ways to communicate meaning.

The last three chapters of the book are about trying to communicate with aliens. This, I think, is the most interesting question about language. What do you think? We have already sent messages into space. Did you know that? We will look at a space message that scientists have sent, and then we will decide what message we think should be sent into space.

Throughout the book there are exercises so that you can try out your ideas about the material. I do the exercises too. At least I try to. These aren't the kind of exercises you can get wrong. We just try out our own ideas about deciphering and inventing language systems.

I've had a lot of fun writing this book. I hope that comes through to you.

A Note to Teachers and Parents

This book grew out of an article I wrote for *Teachers & Writers* magazine, "Teaching Language by Invention." The article, in turn, came from years of teaching English and wondering how to interest students in language, for I have long been convinced that *the way language is made* should be the fundamental subject of an English course. Most textbooks, unfortunately, are not written to interest students in how language is made. Instead, English textbooks state and demonstrate the principles of proper English usage. They are basically reference books with exercises. I wanted to do an interesting schoolbook about language, with English at the center.

I scrambled about, borrowing from here and there, inventing some exercises of my own. I found that my students responded to language-making exercises because the activity touches their imaginations. The best of these exercises were developed from specific examples. These examples required some figuring out before inventing one's own language system. Thus the basic idea of this book: decipher the language example and then invent one's own system based on it.

Collecting good exercises and doing a sensible book are two very different matters. This I learned the hard way, through one false start after another. Thanks, though, to help from teachers and students, I managed to assemble what I like to think is a coherent sequence natural to student thinking.

The book begins with secret writing (chs. 1-2). Students like codes and ciphers. I use secret writing to demonstrate how regular writing works: codes and ciphers reveal the foundation of English.

The second part of the book (chs. 3-6) presents the elements of this foundation of English—and of other languages for that matter. The basic elements of language I call "conventions." The five conventions of language are 1) a series of basic elements, 2) a notion of spacing, 3) use of direction, 4) establishing meaning through sequencing, and 5) use of signaling devices for further clarifying of meaning. I show that by altering these conventions one can disguise meaning: these disguises take the form of codes and ciphers. On the other hand, one can communicate clearly by following the conventions.

The third part of the book (chs. 7-12) uses this knowledge of the five conventions of language to figure out hard passages in English, from the Middle English of Chaucer to the experimental modern writing of Joyce and Cummings. These exercises provide deciphering challenges for the reader, not abstract literary questions.

The fourth part of the book (chs. 13-16) is an examination of other kinds of language. I apply the conventions of language to systems of numbers and picture-writing to see if they are languages too. Traffic signs and comic books are among the surprising subjects of these chapters.

This fourth section of the book is a preparation for the fifth and final part (chs. 17-19): the sending of a message into space, which is an interesting issue of language and one that students take to readily. Students examine the messages we have sent out and then decide on their own messages. Before inventing their own, however, they have quite a challenge in deciphering the messages sent out by scientists. And so do I.

However far the subject matter of the book may range, the central question throughout is how people create a means to communicate reliably. The book is laced with exercises in deciphering and language making, the breaking and making of language, with the emphasis on the systematic nature of language.

Whatever exercise I ask the students to do, I usually do too — or say why I don't. Thus, there is no need for teachers using the book to do any additional work. The book requires no special preparation. Nor are there any answers in the back. All the questions are dealt with openly, on the spot. It is all self-explanatory. It gives you the opportunity to become a student yourself.

I respond to the exercises not with the distant grandeur of objective authority but, instead, as a student might, with everything from enthusiasm to utter frustration. I participate like this, directly, to encourage students to participate. I hope my example will give them confidence to engage their own ideas fully. This approach is ultimately more important to me than the novelty of the subject matter.

I have found that students are most engaged by language study that calls upon them to make language. As long as students regard language as a rigid body of opaque, restrictive rules, they're not going to be very interested. But draw them into seeing language as something that people have created and that they themselves can create, and their attitude toward the study of English will change dramatically.

I believe this book will work as either a regular text or a supplementary text. To claim that a book will work as a supplementary text—without teacher supervision—sounds, admittedly, arrogant if not foolhardy. Still, having experimented with these exercises in the classroom, I feel sure that secret writing can be used this way, and used well.

Naturally, though, the book will work better with your support. However encouragingly I manage to write, it is not enough to prevent some students from second-guessing themselves and needing reassurance or a nudge. Students often express this need by asking a question. Your help is useful then.

Finally, is there a kind of student for whom the book is particularly helpful? I raise this question because many books for students are fashioned for a student of a particular level; content that is supposedly too hard or too easy is ruled out. I wonder if such categorizing responds to the needs of real students. I question whether this focusing actually helps students and teachers. An editorial approach that limits student interest and imagination is overly prescriptive. So I have established only one boundary: a minimal vocabulary level. Difficult words in this book are followed by a synonym in parentheses. Otherwise, the effectiveness of the book is not limited to students of a particular ability. The many open-ended exercises will take truly able students as far as they want to go. Likewise, the average student—if there is such a creature—will have plenty of occasions for success and stimulation. And most important, there is nothing about this book to make a student feel stupid. The weakest of students can feel as much at home in it as the gifted student. Engagement is a matter of interest, not ability.

I am concerned more about attitude than ability. I intend to motivate *all* students, irrespective of ability. A bright student can become just as bored as a less able student, and a bright student too can hold back or feign disinterest, if only for peer acceptance. Less able students see themselves as having little choice about their attitude toward learning because success is so often the only permission for showing interest. So I make sure that the book fully supports the hesitant student, either the one who lacks confidence and accepts meager accomplishment all too readily, or the one who has been so unsuccessful that the only posture to assume is aggressive disinterest. This book, I believe, will engage the most hesitant student.

CHAPTER 1

Hangman

Have you ever met a person who makes and breaks codes? I haven't. At least I don't think I have. But you know, if you were a professional codemaker or codebreaker and somebody asked you what you did for a living, you probably wouldn't say. You might not be allowed to, and you might not want to. Perhaps you would dodge the question by replying, "Oh, I work for a company" or "I work for the government." Your job might involve guarding valuable information. You might have the responsibility of conveying valuable information to key people.

EXERCISE 1.1
Imagine you are a professional codemaker and a company hires you to protect a valuable formula. How would you do it and what would you want to know in order to maximize protection? •
(Think of your answer before you read mine.)

My response to Exercise 1.1
I would make up a code, memorize it, enter the formula in code in a computer under a false heading, and tell as few people at the company as possible. How to maximize protection beyond that would depend on all sorts of things about the company.

I had thought that people who work with codes just tried out different ideas to make a code or to break a code. Then I found out that these people have their tools, like everybody else. One tool the codebreaker has is the Frequency Table. This "table" lists how frequently the letters of the alphabet appear in words. I can't imagine how many words must be used to figure out the sequence of most frequently used letters of the alphabet, but there really is such a list.

1

I learned about the Frequency Tables the hard way. Do you know the game Hangman? If you don't know the rules, here they are. It takes two people to play Hangman. One person thinks of a word of at least six letters and which is not a name. This person draws the same number of spaces as there are letters in the word—for example, for the word "hockey" six spaces, as well as a gallows, above the spaces:

— — — — — —

The other person starts guessing letters, one at a time. If the guess is correct, the person who knows the word puts the letter in the right place—for example, the guess *E:*

— — — — **E** —

If the person guessing says a letter that is *not* in the word, the other person draws a leg. Another wrong guess means another leg. Then the wrong guesses go: body, one arm, the other arm, the neck and, finally, the head. That means hanged. So the person guessing letters has to guess all the letters, or the word itself, before guessing seven wrong letters, because the seventh letter is the head.

Governor Padgett's Variation: In Hangman, write down the missed letters too. If you get hanged, you can get a last-minute reprieve if you can arrange the missed letters into a word. This introduces a new strategy into the game—a safety net, so to speak.

I knew only that it is a word-guessing game when a friend of mine asked me if I wanted to play. I said, "Sure." My friend said, "Give me a really hard word, one that I don't know the meaning of, and make it as long as you want. I bet you I can guess it."

No way, I figured. I picked a long word I found in the dictionary: CONCATENATION, which means "a linked series or chain." I was sure he wouldn't guess it. I made the thirteen spaces for the letters.

My friend guessed six correct letters before he guessed a letter *not* in the word. I couldn't believe it! He guessed in order, *E T A O N I.* So he had

_ **O N** _ **A T E N A T I O N**

All he had to guess was the *C* and he would have it. But he didn't know the word, so how could he guess the right letter?

He guessed *S* and got a leg. He guessed *R* and got another leg. He guessed, in order, *H*, *L*, and *D*. All wrong. He had two legs, the body, and two arms. If he missed again, he would have the neck — and one more miss after that would mean he was hanged.

He guessed *C*. He won. I was mystified.

Later he told me about the Frequency Table. Here it is. The letters are listed in the order of their frequency. A group of letters means that the frequency of the letters is approximately the same.

E   T   AO   NIS   R   H   L   D   CU   FPMWYBG   KQXJZ

Knowing the Frequency Table was only half of my friend's trick. The other half was to trick me into giving him a *long* word to guess.

EXERCISE 1.2
Can you see why a long word makes the Frequency Table more valuable? •

My response to Exercise 1.2
The longer the word, the more chances there are for the most common letters to appear.

It was my turn. I had the sequence of letters my friend had guessed, but when I asked him to give me a word, I forgot to specify a *long* word. He gave me a six-letter word. I guessed as he had, in order, *E T A O N I*. The fourth letter was *T*. None of the other letters was in the word. I had two legs, the body, and two arms. Two more wrong guesses and I was hanged. I guessed *R*. The first letter was *R*.

R _ _ T _ _

EXERCISE 1.3
What letter do you think I should have guessed next? •

My response to Exercise 1.3
My friend had guessed *H*, *L*, and *D* before guessing *C*, but should I guess these consonants when I hadn't yet established the vowel or vowels? No, I figured. I guessed *U*.

No *U*. I didn't know what to do. I guessed *D*. No *D*. I was hanged. Can you guess the word? If I had been lucky and guessed *H* instead of *D*, I would have had

R H _ T H _

3

EXERCISE 1.4

Now what would you guess? •

The word is "rhythm." My friend had stumped me with a simple word. At least it sounds simple. It is easy to say and it is a common word. But its spelling isn't simple at all.

EXERCISE 1.5

What word do you think would be hard? It has to have at least six letters and may not be a name like "Dallas" or "Melvin." •

My response to Exercise 1.5

A word that looks simple but might be hard is "through." It is short, has only one syllable, and the letter combinations are tricky, I think. However, the letters are pretty common.

EXERCISE 1.6

What word do you think looks like it would be hard because it is uncommon and long, but, with the help of the Frequency Table, might not be hard at all? •

My response to Exercise 1.6

You already know the word I came up with: "concatenation."

Playing Hangman is like trying to break a code. Hangman is easier, though, because the other person has to tell you if the letter you guess is in the word and has to put the letter in the right place if it is. If you are trying to break a code, no one tells you if you are right or wrong. Instead, you have to try new ideas. If you get a possible solution to a word, then you try out the letters in other words. Also you may have other information that will help you.

For example, let's say you intercept a coded message that appears to be a six-letter word, and you have reason to believe that the word is the name of a major city in the Northeast. In looking at the coded word, you see that the second letter and the fifth letter are the same. So you have:

$$\underline{} \quad \underline{} \quad \underline{} \quad \underline{} \quad \underline{} \quad \underline{}$$

same

EXERCISE 1.7

What do you think the word is? •

My response to Exercise 1.7
There is a pretty good chance that the word is "Boston."

The word is composed of the letters *B, o, s, t,* and *n.* Most of these letters are pretty common, high up in the Frequency Table. If you have enough other messages in this code to establish what you think is a fairly reliable frequency sequence, then you can see if the first letter of the coded word (*B,* here) is fairly uncommon, at least in comparison to the others.

A professional codebreaker has a list of the frequency of the letters of the alphabet and also lists of the frequency of certain combinations of letters.

EXERCISE 1.8
Can you think of a common combination of letters? •

My response to Exercise 1.8
Common combinations of letters are "ing," "tion," and "ed." Knowing common letter combinations and the Frequency Table helps a professional codemaker invent a good code. For example, if the codemaker wants to enter a valuable formula in a computer under a key word, the codemaker would be smart to pick a word that is not easily guessed. A good word might be one that does not include common letters or common letter combinations. The seven most common letters are, as you know from the Frequency Table, *E T A O N I S.* Let's rule these out, along with the three most common letter combinations, and think of a word to be the key word for the codemaker.

EXERCISE 1.9
Would ruling out the seven most common letters also rule out the three most common letter combinations? •

My response to Exercise 1.9
Yes, ruling out the seven most common letters would rule out the three most common letter combinations because each of the three letter combinations include at least one of the seven most common letters.

EXERCISE 1.10
Can you think of three words of at least six letters that do not include any of the seven most common letters? •

My response to Exercise 1.10
Three such words are "church," "chubby," and "frumpy."

Does "frumpy" count? Is it in the dictionary? I'm not sure—but I don't want to check because I don't know if I can think of another word. With only *u* of the vowels (I'm not counting *y*), finding a word with these letters is hard. I guess this is the kind of information that codemakers discover quickly.

Still, wouldn't it be great to be able to hide messages! Finding a word for entering a valuable formula on a computer is one thing. What I would like better is being able to send a message to a friend so other people couldn't read it, even if they found it. I am not as interested in hiding as I am in disguising my meaning. How about you? Have you ever fooled around with secret writing? Have you and a friend ever invented a code so that you could exchange messages without anyone else knowing what you are saying?

EXERCISE 1.11
What would you use secret writing for? You don't have to say. Just think about it. •

That is what the next chapter is about, secret writing.

CHAPTER 2

Secret Writing

Can you read this?

TEEM EM TA HCNUL

Reading it forwards doesn't make sense. How about reading it backwards?

LUNCH AT ME MEET

This doesn't make sense either, but we are getting somewhere. We now have four words. Just the sequence of words doesn't make sense. Can we make sense out of the four words by rearranging the sequence?

Maybe you just look at the four words and come up with a sensible sequence. Maybe you try out all the possible combinations. One way or the other you are going to come upon the possibility

MEET ME AT LUNCH

You have not only solved the problem, but you have also confirmed a fact of the English language: English reads from left to right. That is obvious to you. Yet that is not true of all languages. In the next chapter we are going to look more into what codemaking tells us about the English language.

For now, let's look again at the secret message TEEM EM TA HCNUL. To hide the meaning of the message, the codemaker simply reversed the order of letters in each word. That's all. Nothing else.

EXERCISE 2.1
Can you think of another way to make the message secret? •

My response to Exercise 2.1
Another way to make the message secret is to write all the words together.

You probably thought of this way and other ways, too. If you write the words together, you would have

TEEMEMTAHCNUL

That's certainly harder to read, and in using this idea we confirm another fact about the English language: we indicate the end of a word by leaving a space before beginning the next word. This fact is obvious too.

Another way to make the message harder to read is to make up another alphabet and write the message in this new alphabet.

A B C D E F G H I J K L M N O P Q R S T U V W X Y Z
R M G K Z J Q C W E P Y B U T H L A V X D N I F O S

In my new alphabet the secret message looks like this:

XZZBZBXRCGUDY

That is harder to read than the way it was before.

EXERCISE 2.2
Make up your own secret alphabet and write the message in it with all the reverse-spelled words written together. •

Let's summarize what we have done to make the message MEET ME AT LUNCH hard to read:

1. Reversed the order of the letters in each word;
2. Written the words together;
3. Written the message in an invented alphabet.

What we have done may be, in your opinion, not very complicated, but pretend you don't know our method. Would you be able to figure out the meaning? I couldn't.

Just for the fun of it, read your coded message aloud a few times. Pretend, as you say it aloud, that it really is *your* language, the language you speak all the time. Notice how this makes you "feel" different.

Now say the message in English. Can you describe how it "feels" to speak English, your own language?

Notice, by the way, that in normal talk we don't leave spaces between the words, the way we do when we write. Why don't we leave spaces between words when we talk?

Finally, when you said the coded message aloud, did it remind you of a foreign language? Which one? Or does it make you think of a language from outer space?

We have written a secret message. You might call it a coded message.

Many people think of code as the way to make a message secret, and code is the word we use for any secret writing. Actually, though, there are three ways to make a message secret:

Code
Cipher
Stenography

Stenography is the hiding or concealing of a message.

Invisible ink is a method of stenography. Have you ever used "invisible ink"? It's easy. Instead of regular ink, use lemon juice or milk. When it's dry, heat the paper over a flame or light bulb (but be careful that you don't burn yourself or the paper). The heat will cause what you've written to emerge, in brown letters.

Another way to write invisibly is with a typewriter. Insert a piece of paper with a piece of carbon paper on top. Type directly onto the back of the carbon paper. What you type will appear on the paper underneath, but you won't be able to read it until you take it out of the machine and remove the carbon sheet.

A third way to write invisibly is with a word processor. Of course you have to know how to use the word processor first. To write invisibly with it, just turn off the monitor, so you won't be able to peek at what you've written.

EXERCISE 2.3

Using any of these three methods, try an experimental writing technique called "freewriting." There is only one rule for freewriting: write as fast as you can, nonstop, for a set period of time, such as five minutes. You can write *anything*, as long as it's words and you keep going without stopping. Don't worry about spelling or neatness or grammar. Just try to make your hand write words as quickly as your mind thinks them.

When you've finished, bring out the invisible writing by heating up the invisible ink, by taking the carbon sheet off, or by turning the monitor on. •

Are there any words you didn't remember writing? Did you write anything you didn't expect to write? If the answer is yes, it shows that you are able to write things you didn't know you could, things that were "hidden" from you.

Stenography is a method for making a message secret, but it is not a method of secret writing. There are two methods of secret writing:

1. *Cipher* is the method of secret writing in which *the individual letters* are jumbled or replaced by other letters, or numbers, or symbols.

2. *Code* is a method of writing in which *a group of letters* or numbers is substituted for syllables, words, phrases, or sentences.

"Code" and "cipher" sound a lot alike, so let's look at an example. To make the message MEET ME AT LUNCH hard to read, we jumbled the letters by writing each word backwards and running them together. And we replaced each letter with something else from the alphabet we invented. So we did what the definition of "cipher" says.

What we did is called "enciphering." You *encipher* a message when you make it secret by the cipher method. When you figure out the meaning of an enciphered message, you *decipher* it.

EXERCISE 2.4
What do you think the words might be for writing a message in code and for figuring out a message in code? •

My response to Exercise 2.4
When you make a message secret by putting it in code, you *encode* the message. When you figure out the meaning of an encoded message, you *decode* it.

So, the cipher method has two possibilities: jumbling the letters (which is called "transposition"), and substituting a letter, number, or symbol for each letter (which is called "substitution"). The code method has only one method, substitution, but you can substitute one or a group of letters or numbers or a combination of them for a syllable, a word, a phrase, or a sentence. In a sense, you can do anything you want to make figuring out the encoded message as hard as possible.

Let me show you an example in which I restrict the options to using only one or more numbers for each word.

MEET	7
ME	314
AT	88
LUNCH	13

So, MEET ME AT LUNCH becomes 7 314 88 13.

EXERCISE 2.5
Which do you think is the more effective method of secret writing, the cipher method or the code method? •

EXERCISE 2.6
Which of the two methods do you think involves less information to

write down, lug around, and protect? •

Code may be more effective than cipher for making a message hard to figure out, but it certainly involves more information to write down, lug around, and protect. With the cipher method, you need only establish instructions for transposing (scrambling) the letters and, if you want, a different alphabet. But with the code method, you have to encode all the words you are going to need either as a word, phrase, or sentence. That's not the sort of thing someone is going to memorize easily. In fact, professional codemakers usually write information in what is called a "codebook."

The codebook is larger than what you probably imagined because the example of a code you have here is pretty simple. The example is simple because each word has only one coding. The code can be made even harder, and often is, by establishing two or three *different* ways to encode certain words. This is done to prevent the use of the principle of the Frequency Table (which you read about in Chapter 1).

For example, the word ME in the message MEET ME AT LUNCH might be encoded as 10 or 46 besides 314 as it is in the encoded message. So you would have three ways to encode the message:

7 10 88 13
7 46 88 13
7 314 88 13

Then, what if you go ahead and add two further ways to encode the word AT? Suddenly, you have many ways to encode a simple, four-word message. Think what possibilities might come up for encoding a much longer message! And remember, I encoded only each word. What if for a longer message we had also encoding for certain syllables, phrases, and sentences? That would become very complicated to encode, much less to decode.

Yet people do this for a living, not just making up codes but trying to break them! Many codemakers are also codebreakers, too.

EXERCISE 2.7
Do you think you might like this kind of work? •

EXERCISE 2.8
Make up your own coded version of MEET ME AT LUNCH in which you mix letters and numbers and have at least two ways to encode one of the four words. •

EXERCISE 2.9

Write a brief conversation between two spies. Then go back and encode their words. Read it aloud to friends and watch their reactions. •

CHAPTER 3

Conventions

You have enough information now about ciphers and codes to send a secret message to a friend. This same information can also help you to understand the English language. Maybe that doesn't make sense, but remember, a code or cipher is based on a language. Your codes and ciphers are based on English. When you make a coded or enciphered message, you alter the language in order to hide your meaning. So if we look at what we did with the enciphered message of MEET ME AT LUNCH, we will be able to spot basic facts about English.

Many of these facts you already know because you know English. You may even know every one of the facts. But once we add them all up and look at them, you may find that you actually know more about language than you thought.

For example, when we invented a secret alphabet to make the enciphered message of MEET ME AT LUNCH even harder to read than it already was, we invented a new use for what is primary to any language: an alphabet. Our alphabet is the basis of our language. That is obvious. We form all our words from the letters of the alphabet. So every language must have an alphabet, right?

Wrong. We have basically the same alphabet as many other languages, such as Spanish. And there are other alphabets: the Russian language has a different alphabet from ours. But there are languages that have no alphabet.

EXERCISE 3.1
Can you think of a way to invent a language without an alphabet? •

If a language doesn't have an alphabet, it still has to have something to begin with. It must have some sort of elements from which various meanings are made. Every language has a series of basic elements. So the question is, what sort of series of basic elements can that be, if it is not an alphabet?

Chinese is a language with another kind of series of basic elements, and Chinese isn't the only one. But the others are like Chinese in that they begin with pictures, not letters. English is one of many "alphabet languages." Chinese is one of many "picture languages."

Chinese is composed of "characters." Each character represents a thing or an idea. Here is the character for "sun" and the character for "moon." Put these two together and you have the character for "bright."

Sun 日 and moon 月 together mean "bright." 日月

Pretty good, huh? Here are some others.

Woman 女 and child 子 together mean "good." 好

Brain 田 and heart 心 together mean "think." 思

An eye 目 on two legs 儿 means "to see." 見

So a Chinese character can have either just one part, like the character for "sun," or it can have two parts, like the character for "see," or more.

This combining of parts to make a Chinese character resembles our combining of letters to make a word. It also resembles our combining of words to make a new word. For example, we combine "basket" and "ball" to make "basketball." But if you see a letter in our alphabet being the equivalent of a one-part Chinese character, then there is a big difference between Chinese and English. A one-part Chinese character has a meaning. "Moon" is an example. But a letter in our alphabet doesn't necessarily have a meaning. In fact, the only letters that do are *A* as in "a book" and *I* as in "I sent you a message" and maybe *O* as in "O great chief...." Our letters are not pictures of ideas.

Now you can see why the Chinese language is sometimes called "picture writing" or "idea writing."

EXERCISE 3.2

Can you invent two of your own one-part characters and what each means? •

My response to Exercise 3.2
My two one-part characters are

sky ⌒
water ∿∿∿

14

EXERCISE 3.3

Can you invent your own two-part characters and explain how each is made? •

My response to Exercise 3.3

Here are my two two-part characters.

Basket ⊔ and ball ○ together mean "basketball." ⊟

Play ⟩⟨ and laugh — together mean "fun." ⟩⟨̄

Every language begins with a series of basic elements, whether alphabetic or pictorial. That is our first property of language. Let's see if we can figure out another one from what we did to encipher the message MEET ME AT LUNCH. Do you remember another method we used to make the message harder to read? We ran all the words together.

TEEM EM TA HCNUL became TEEMEMTAHCNUL

What we did tells us another fact about English: in English we leave a space between words to indicate the end of one word and the beginning of another. The same is true in Chinese. "Sun" by itself has one meaning, but when it is combined with "moon," the meaning becomes "bright." If, on the other hand, a space is left between the two characters, they mean "sun" and "moon."

So we have two facts about our language:

1. A series of basic elements
2. A space between words

There is another basic fact of language to be seen in our enciphering of the message MEET ME AT LUNCH.

Before we started tinkering around to try to make the message harder to read, it had already been enciphered into TEEM EM TA HCNUL. In solving this puzzle, I said that you had also established a fact about English, that English reads from left to right. Not all languages read from left to right. Arabic and Hebrew for example, read the opposite way, from right to left. Here is an example from Hebrew.

ןולח דיל הבשי איה
to the window   next   sat   she

The Hebrew way of writing would be like writing

ℲↃИU⅃ TA ƎM TƎƎM

15

EXERCISE 3.4
Do you think this is harder to read than TEEM EM TA HCNUL? •

My response to Exercise 3.4
No, I think it is easier to read. It is easier for me anyway because some of the letters point the way to read it, from right to left.

The fact that Hebrew reads from right to left and that English reads from left to right establishes a *third* property of language, *direction*.

We have been looking at the direction on the horizontal. There is also the vertical. How do we read English? Obviously, we read from top to bottom. But which do we do first, read from top to bottom or from left to right?

Sure, we read first from left to right and then from top to bottom. We read across one line from left to right, and when we come to the end of the line we go down to the next line, and on down the page, as you're doing now.

But do all languages read the same? Whether they begin on the left side or the right side, do they read across the page and then down—or up—or do they do it another way? Take a look at the Chinese in figure 1.

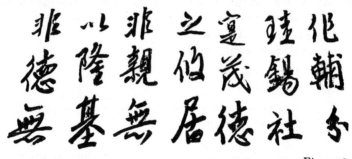

Figure 1

EXERCISE 3.5
Which way do you think you read this, in a horizontal direction or a vertical direction? What is your guess? •

Wouldn't you know it, you don't begin on the horizontal as you do in English. Instead you begin on the vertical. You read classical Chinese from top to bottom. And you don't begin on the left. You begin on the right. So you read down the page in columns, and the columns go from right to left. (To get in step with the modern world, the Chinese are now trying to change their system. We'll see how well it works.)

16

Try to imagine what a traditional Chinese book looks like. Chinese books are backwards from ours. The front of the book is where you would find the back of an English book.

Direction in Chinese is very different from direction in English. Still, each language has its own simple pattern of direction. So direction is to be added to our list of conventions of the language.

1. Series of basic elements
2. Space between words (or "word pictures")
3. Direction (horizontal and vertical)

Just these three conventions of language provide all sorts of possibilities for beginning to invent a language. For example, for the first convention you could use the English alphabet. Then for the second convention, instead of spacing, you might use a hyphen, as is done sometimes in code (18-472-812-397). Then for the third convention (direction), you might begin on the right and move across the page to the left, as in Hebrew, but instead of moving from top to bottom, you might choose to go from bottom to top.

Following those directions, the message MEET ME AT LUNCH. I HAVE SOMETHING VERY IMPORTANT TO TELL YOU. DO NOT BRING ANYONE WITH YOU would look like this:

BRING-ANYONE-WITH-YOU
VERY-IMPORTANT-TO-TELL-YOU-DO-NOT
MEET-ME-AT-LUNCH-I-HAVE-SOMETHING

If we scrambled a few of the letters and perhaps dropped the hyphens, this new language would look more like a code or a cipher than a language. But isn't that the point about codes and ciphers? They *are* languages. The difference is that a code or cipher is meant to *hide* the meaning, whereas a language such as English or Chinese is meant to *convey* the meaning. The difference is in purpose, not in the way they are made. Codes and ciphers, like English and Chinese, are developed from the same three conventions: series of basic elements, spacing, and direction.

CHAPTER 4

Sequencing

We have identified three conventions of language, three ways by which people make language. As important as these three conventions are, they are not enough to make a language as sophisticated as the English language that you know. You know a lot about English that goes well beyond these three conventions.

Perhaps we can spot other conventions in the message MEET ME AT LUNCH. When we first saw this message, it had been enciphered into TEEM EM TA HCNUL. To decipher it, we first read it backwards: LUNCH AT ME MEET. We then saw that the meaning of the message was MEET ME AT LUNCH.

EXERCISE 4.1
What did we do when we changed LUNCH AT ME MEET to MEET ME AT LUNCH? •

My response to Exercise 4.1
We put the words in their proper sequence.

Did you phrase your answer differently? You may have—with just as good an answer—for there are lots of ways to say "proper sequence." You may have said that the change in the sequence of words was to make the words go together correctly. Or, to make the relationship of the four words clear. Or, to make the meaning clear. Or, to make sense out of the words. The point is that there is a definite connection between the meaning and the sequence of the words.

A word has its individual meaning. This is the meaning you find in the dictionary. A word has further meaning. This is the meaning it gains by being put together with other words in a particular sequence. Like what, for example? Like a sentence. A sentence is a series of words that communicate a meaning. How? By the sequence of the words. The sequence creates a series of relationships among the words. Each relationship creates a meaning. All the relationships of all the words in the sentence add up to the overall meaning of the sentence. If we want to change its meaning, we can change either a word or the location of one of the words already in the sentence. If we are given a bunch of words and asked how they might go together, we try to find a sequence for the words that creates an overall meaning.

When we are little kids, we often learn words one at a time and say them one or two at a time. As we get older and go to school, we deal less with words one at a time than we do with groups of words sequenced to make a meaning. We get so used to sequencing words to say or write what we mean that we make these sequences in our minds very quickly. For example, when you saw LUNCH AT ME MEET, you probably changed this sequence very quickly to MEET ME AT LUNCH because that is the arrangement that makes sense of the four words. What else could the four words mean? Right? The question of the proper sequencing of the four words may have struck you as being so easy that it was no question at all. That's because you are good at sequencing words. It makes sense to sequence words. Sequencing words is the way we create the meanings we want to communicate.

This message sentence is short enough for us to see the proper sequence of the words very rapidly. A longer sentence of scrambled words would require more time to set the words in a sequence in which all the words relate to one another clearly. The point, though, is not how easy it is to sequence a few words or how hard it is to sequence many words, but instead that there is an overall meaning for words that comes from their sequencing. LUNCH, AT, ME, and MEET gain an overall meaning once we sequence them MEET ME AT LUNCH.

Sequencing is basic to language. It is another fundamental way to make meaning, and therefore, another convention of language. In grammar the word for sequencing is "syntax." Syntax is the orderly relationship of words that makes them make sense.

Our list of conventions now looks like this:

Convention	Use of the convention in English
1. Basic series of elements	1. The alphabet
2. Spacing	2. Space between words
3. Direction	3. Left to right, top to bottom
4. Sequencing	4. Syntax

By the age you start to study the sequencing of words in a sentence, sequencing is so natural to you as a convention of language that you are rarely if ever asked in school to sequence a series of words to make a clear, overall meaning. Instead, you are asked to learn the way the words function to *make* this clear relationship. You learn how sentences are built from the way words are classified. This classification appears alongside the word in a dictionary: noun, verb, pronoun, adjective, adverb, conjunction, and interjection. These classifications are called "parts of speech."

Yes, this is grammar. And perhaps now you can see why grammar can seem boring. You already know your language not only because you know the meanings of words but also because you know the conventions of language. You know, for example, that overall meaning for a group of words is created by sequencing the words. You know this even if you have never heard the idea expressed, because you know it through experience. So when you meet grammar in school, you can't help but wonder what the point is of all of these strange terms.

But knowing grammar does help to make meaning clear. It helps with sequencing by supplying a way to explain how the sequencing works. With a short sentence, such as the one we have been working with, there is little need for a way to explain why the words are sequenced as they are. But, as you know, a longer sentence can become confusing. If you are writing a longer sentence and can't be sure whether or not you are conveying the meaning you want, a knowledge of grammar comes in handy. This knowledge allows you to check out the various relationships of the words of the sentence. You might find that rearranging the sequencing conveys your meaning more directly.

Grammar helps by first supplying a part of speech of a word. Grammar helps even more in checking the *usage* of the word in the sentence. Let's take the four words of the message. "Me" is a pronoun; "meet" is (usually) a verb; "at" is a preposition; and "lunch" is (usually) a noun.

For example, the word "at" (a preposition) introduces a prepositional phrase. That is what a preposition does. A prepositional phrase requires, in addition to a preposition, a noun or pronoun as the object of the preposition. This fancy statement simply means that only two of the remaining words can directly follow "at."

EXERCISE 4.2
Which two of the remaining three words ("meet," "me," and "lunch") can directly follow "at"? •

My response to Exercise 4.2
"Me" and "lunch" can directly follow "at."

20

Grammar doesn't tell us *which* of the two words, though. *That* we figure out by checking the possibilities of meaning. But grammar does tell us something else about the sequencing of these four words. A basic idea of sequencing is that words that go together are *placed* together. Grammar supports this sensible idea. We already know, for example, that grammar says that the word "at" must be followed by either "me" or "lunch." Does grammar tell us anything about the sequencing of the other words?

The most general way that grammar expresses how we sequence words to make sense is like this: a simple sentence has two parts, the subject and the predicate; the words that make up the subject usually come first, the words that make up the predicate come next.

There is not much to the subject of MEET ME AT LUNCH. We know that the sentence means "You are to meet me at lunch." The subject is "you (understood)." This means that it is understood that the subject of the sentence is the "you" being addressed. When we state this meaning as a command, we leave out the "you" and simply say, " Meet me at lunch."

EXERCISE 4.3
Do any of the four words go with the "you" (understood) subject, or do they all belong to the predicate of the sentence? •

My response to Exercise 4.3
All the four words belong to the predicate of the sentence.

If all the words belong to the predicate, what determines the sequence of words in a predicate? Usually the verb comes first. That is "meet." If "meet" comes first, which comes next—"me" or the phrase "at lunch"? "Me" comes next. The pronoun "me" is the object of the verb "meet." The object of the verb comes next after the verb. That is the way we sequence verb and object in a sentence. Any phrase comes afterwards.

Why make up such rules? Because the rules help us to understand *how* the words function in the sentence, so that when we write or say complicated sentences that we've never written or said before, we have a way of checking to see if they are arranged well.

The part of grammar that is most important for figuring out the sensible sequencing of a group of words is not the part of speech of a word but the *usage* of a word. Knowing the part of speech may be the first way to identify a word, but it is general. Usage, on the other hand, is exact. Usage is what you want to figure out about a word. For example, in the sentence "I will take you to the movies," both "I" and "you" are the same part of speech, pronoun. But their usage is different. "I" is the subject of the sentence, so it comes at the beginning of the sentence. "You" is the object of the verb "take," so it comes in the predicate after the verb. The usage of "I" and "you" determines its location in the series of words.

This connection between the usage of a word and the location of the word in a sentence is the way a sentence *usually* works. First the subject, then the predicate.

But this pattern may vary. For example, take the sentence "The door slammed suddenly." It is just as short as "Meet me at lunch," and, like it, no matter how scrambled the words are, you would be able to sequence them in a meaningful way pretty quickly. But that doesn't mean that the only sequence of the four words is "The door slammed suddenly."

EXERCISE 4.4
Is there any other way to sequence the four words "the door slammed suddenly"? •

My response to Exercise 4.4
Yes, the four words may also be sequenced like this:

> The door suddenly slammed.
> Suddenly the door slammed.

Can this be true? May the word "suddenly" be moved around to two other locations in the sentence? Doesn't the usage of the word determine its location in a sentence? Yes, but only in general. The pattern is only that, a pattern. So it is flexible, not ironclad.

But "suddenly" is an adverb — right? — that modifies (changes the tone of) the verb "slammed." So it is in the predicate of the sentence. "In the predicate" could mean after the verb or before the verb. Therefore, "The door suddenly slammed" is all right. But putting "suddenly" at the beginning of the sentence — how does that make sense?

EXERCISE 4.5
How is it that "suddenly" may be placed at the beginning of the sentence? •

My response to Exercise 4.5
You may place "suddenly" at the beginning of the sentence if you want to.

That may sound like a pretty flimsy answer, but it is true.

EXERCISE 4.6

Can you think of any reason why you might want to place "suddenly" at the beginning of the sentence? •

My response to Exercise 4.6

Placing the word "suddenly" at the beginning of the sentence makes the sentence more dramatic.

Yes, placing "suddenly" at the beginning gives the sentence more tension. The placement also makes "suddenly" the most noticeable word in the sentence. This may be precisely what the person who wrote the sentence wants.

EXERCISE 4.7

Try moving the adverb in the following sentences to the front of each sentence, and then decide for yourself if that word both gains greater emphasis and adds more tension to the meaning of the sentence.

> He slipped slowly into the quicksand.
> She angrily stormed into the room.
> The fire swept rapidly up the wall. •

Whatever your decision with each sentence, it is good to know for your own writing that you have some choice as to where you locate your words. If there is a word you want to give emphasis to, you may put it at the beginning of the sentence. If that doesn't work, you may arrange the sequence of the words some other way to focus attention on the word you want to be most noticed. You have this flexibility.

Not every word can go anywhere, however. Even the word "suddenly," which, as you have seen, may go in three different places in the sentence, cannot go in a fourth location: you can't write (except in creative writing) "The suddenly door slammed." Why not? Because it doesn't make sense. Why doesn't it make sense? Because placing the word between "the" and "door" makes the word "suddenly" appear to modify "door." It is right next to "door" and preceded by "the" just as we might write "the big door" or "the blue door." But we know that "suddenly" modifies "slammed." So, to place it between "the" and "door" is just confusing.

This example of where "suddenly" won't go illustrates the only rule about moving a word around in a sentence. Can you guess what this rule is?

EXERCISE 4.8

Can you guess what the only rule is about moving a word around in a sentence? •

My response to Exercise 4.8

The only rule is that you may move a word around in a sentence as long as the placement of the word does not confuse the word's usage, because each word's usage must be clear to make the sentence clear.

Let's take a last look at lunch. There is one question about MEET ME AT LUNCH that we have not dealt with. That is, why can't we sequence the words this way: AT LUNCH MEET ME?

EXERCISE 4.9

Is it possible to sequence the sentence AT LUNCH MEET ME? •

My response to Exercise 4.9

It is perfectly all right to sequence the sentence AT LUNCH MEET ME.

Then why don't we? We don't because we don't. I am not trying to sound clever. We don't sequence the words this way because we don't have any reason to. Our language is a curious combination of rules and flexibility. Sometimes it all boils down to plain old common sense.

CHAPTER 5

Signaling Devices

Did that last chapter on sequencing become pretty complicated? Have we gone as far as we can in identifying conventions of language? No, there is one more convention. Look at these:

    MEET ME AT LUNCH
    MEET ME AT LUNCH.

EXERCISE 5.1
What is the difference between these two sentences? •

My response to Exercise 5.1
There is no difference in the words. The difference is that the second sentence has a period at the end of it.

The addition of a period does not seem like much here because it certainly doesn't help us further to understand the statement. But what about the following sentence?

    SHE IS PRETTY TALL AND SHY

EXERCISE 5.2
Can you say for sure what this sentence means? •

Here is another:

    I LOVE PIZZA CHARLIE

EXERCISE 5.3
Can you say for sure what this sentence means? •

These two sentences illustrate how we can use little marks to make our meaning exact. The little marks we call "punctuation." They are small, apparently of minor significance, but if neither of these sentences has yet been punctuated, then we can't be sure of their meanings. Both sentences have two possible meanings, and the difference in each case is large.

EXERCISE 5.4
Can you figure out the two possible meanings of the first sentence? •

It can be punctuated in two ways:

SHE IS PRETTY TALL AND SHY.
SHE IS PRETTY, TALL AND SHY.

(Actually, it can be punctuated a third way:

SHE IS PRETTY, TALL, AND SHY.

This third way is only a variation of the second in that it doesn't change the meaning from the second version. The period isn't the issue, obviously. The comma after PRETTY is the issue.)

EXERCISE 5.5
What is the difference in meaning between the first and second versions of the sentence? •

My response to Exercise 5.5
The difference is in the word "pretty." The first version of the sentence means that she is fairly tall and shy. The meaning of the second version is that she is three things: pretty and tall and shy. The big difference is, obviously, that the second version says that she is attractive, whereas the first version makes no mention of whether or not she is attractive.
Say the sentences out loud each way. Notice the pause. That's the comma. How about the second sentence?

EXERCISE 5.6
What does I LOVE PIZZA CHARLIE mean if the only punctuation is a period at the end of the sentence? •

My response to Exercise 5.6
I LOVE PIZZA CHARLIE with a period at the end means that the speaker loves a fellow called Pizza Charlie.

A statement of love is important. It is important to the speaker and it may be important to Pizza Charlie. But what if the speaker had an altogether different meaning in mind?

EXERCISE 5.7
What is the other possible meaning of this sentence? •

EXERCISE 5.8
How do you "mark" the sentence to convey this meaning clearly? •

My responses to Exercises 5.7 and 5.8
You place a comma after PIZZA to make sure that the reader doesn't think you might mean some sort of nickname PIZZA CHARLIE but, instead, that PIZZA is what the speaker loves and CHARLIE is the person being told.

    I LOVE PIZZA, CHARLIE

A comma is used to set off a word in what is called "direct address"—when someone is talked to and his name is used in the sentence. That is the punctuation rule that applies to this sentence. Here are two other examples of the comma in direct address.

    CHARLIE, I LOVE PIZZA.
    HEY, CHARLIE, I LOVE PIZZA.

Do you remember back in EXERCISE 5.3 when I asked you if you could say what the sentence I LOVE PIZZA CHARLIE means without saying that it means either this or that? At that time you might have been one step ahead of me and thought to yourself, "If this sentence were written not just in capital letters but in both capital letters and small letters, I could then say for sure what the sentence means." If you thought of this, you are very smart—and if you didn't think of it but can figure it out now, you are no slouch of a thinker. Let's look at the sentence in small letters (or what is called "lower case"):

    i love pizza charlie

EXERCISE 5.9
Can you see what is wrong with the sentence? •

My response to Exercise 5.9
The "i" should be capitalized because that is the way we write it, and besides it begins the sentence. And "charlie" should begin with a capital C because the word is a name.

All right. So we have

I love pizza Charlie.

EXERCISE 5.10
If that is all the capitalizing that the sentence needs in order to be written correctly, what does the sentence mean? •

My response to Exercise 5.10
The sentence means that the speaker is telling Charlie that he or she loves pizza.

EXERCISE 5.11
How do we know that the speaker is telling Charlie that he or she loves pizza and is not saying that he or she loves a fellow called "Pizza Charlie"? •

My response to Exercise 5.11
We know that the "Charlie" is just "Charlie" and not "Pizza Charlie" because the *p* of "pizza" is not capitalized. If the speaker had meant "Pizza Charlie" as a nickname, then the *p* would have been capitalized.

Perhaps you noticed that I caught myself in a trap by asking the question in EXERCISE 5.11. I *had* to capitalize "pizza" at the end in order to write the question correctly if it was meant as part of Charlie's name.
Now look at these two sentences:

I like the jazz.
I like The Jazz.

EXERCISE 5.12
What is the difference in meaning between these two sentences? •

My response to Exercise 5.12
The first sentence means that the speaker likes "the jazz," as in jazz music. The second sentence means that the speaker likes a group called "The Jazz."

Let's see what we have figured out here. We have seen that punctuation and capitalization are other ways we can use to indicate our meaning clearly when we write. By using punctuation and capitalization we signal to our reader how to read what we have written. "How to read"

28

means the same as "how to understand." I call punctuation and capitalization "signaling devices." Our fifth and last convention is *signaling devices*.

Here — at last! — is our *complete* list of the conventions of language.

Convention	Use of the convention in English
1. Basic series of elements	1. The alphabet
2. Spacing	2. Space between words
3. Direction	3. Left to right, top to bottom
4. Sequencing	4. Syntax
5. Signaling devices	5. Punctuation and capitalization

The rules for capitalization are much simpler than the rules for punctuation. You know this all too well, right? The reason is obvious, isn't it? With capitalization there are only two choices: either you capitalize or you don't. On the other hand, there are so many different ways to punctuate. The period, the question mark, the exclamation mark, the comma, etc. The comma has enough different usages to give you a headache if you try to get them into your head all at once. Then there are quotation marks, parentheses, underlining, the ellipsis, the virgule, the apostrophe, the colon, the semicolon, the hyphen, and the dash. There are even two kinds of quotation marks, single and double. And there are two kinds of parentheses, but they don't say that. They just tell you that there are "brackets." I like brackets. I don't use them, but I like them. I don't have them on my typewriter, though.

Speaking of a typewriter, have you ever looked closely at one to see how many "marks" there are. Besides the letters and the numbers (0 through 9) and a way to make capital letters, there are 22 marks, and I have only a regular Smith-Corona electric typewriter. All I need is four more marks and I would have enough to make up an alphabet for writing cipher messages.

! @ # $ % ¢ & * ( ) _ - + = " ' : ; ? / . ,

That is 22 marks. How many of these do you know? How many of these are punctuation marks? Do you think these marks might be good for inventing a cipher for sending a secret message?

EXERCISE 5.13
You have probably already seen some of these marks used in comic strips. What, exactly, do you think the guy in figure 2 is saying? •

Figure 2

To some degree these are international symbols. You could print this square in France or Argentina or Israel and the readers would be able to make their own translations, just as you have. Modern poets have also used punctuation and typographical symbols in new ways. In Ron Loewinsohn's poem, the semicolon takes on a new life:

SEMICOLON; for Philip Whalen

Semicolon ; like the head & forearm of a man swimming, the arm in foreshortened perspective, his head looking
away ; his mouth's open in exaggerated O inhaling on
the other side, his wrist's bent just about to re-enter the surf
   ; water   dripping   from   the   fingertips   ;   semicolon

Or a whole row of them

; ;

swimming off to Catalina

Normally in reading aloud, we don't pronounce the semicolon; we just pause. (Read that sentence aloud and you'll see what I mean.) But what about in Loewinsohn's poem?

EXERCISE 5.14
How would you read aloud the semicolons in Ron Loewinsohn's poem? •

My response to Exercise 5.14
Hmm. If I were reading before an audience, I think I'd try to "act out" the semicolon, maybe by pointing to my head (on the "semi") and then crooking my arm (on the "colon"). Then when I got to the row of them I

might make an abbreviated swimming motion.

If I were reading onto a tape, say, with no audience, then acting it out wouldn't help. I'd have to do it all with my voice. I might get brave and read the row of semicolons as "splash splash splash splash splash" and so on. The more I think about it, the more I see that this poem was written for the eye, not the ear.

Maybe there is such a thing as "eye poetry," poetry that only the eye can fully enjoy. What do you think? Do you think that "eye poetry" is limited because it appeals basically to one sense? What about "ear poetry?" This would be poetry that appeals only to the ear. A poem is sounds and rhythms. Perhaps you have heard someone say, "I like the sound of the poem; I don't care what it says." Maybe poetry is music first and meaning second. What do you think? The eye? The ear?

EXERCISE 5.15
Do you have any thoughts about "eye poetry" and "ear poetry?" •

In Belgian poet Paul de Vree's poem about April in Paris, the parentheses flutter around like birds:

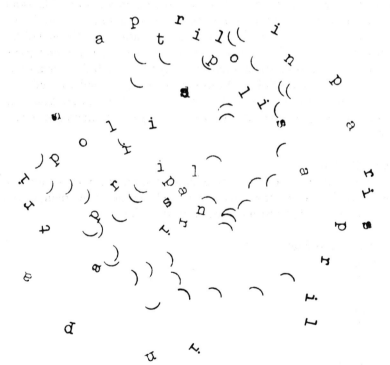

EXERCISE 5.16

How would you read Paul de Vree's poem aloud? •

My response to Exercise 5.16
I think I'd get some people to read it with me, in chorus, with everyone saying "April in Paris" at random times and in fluttery voices, to make it light and airy and jumbled, the way it is on the page. I'd hope the flutteriness would give a feeling similar to that of the parentheses in the poem.

If these questions seem hard, try this one: Who invented the question mark? I've asked this question of many writers and teachers. Not a single one knew the answer. Ask your teacher, and watch the stunned expression.

The question could be rephrased and made larger: What is the history of punctuation? It turns out that our system of punctuation has been in effect for only around 400 years. In ancient times the words tended to be all run together with no punctuation, though there were paragraph divisions. Occasionally there was *some* punctuation: in a 3rd-century B.C. text, for instance, the double point (:) served as a period. The single point, placed high on the line, also indicated a period. The same point, placed in the middle of the line, indicated a comma. "Our" comma appeared around the 9th century. But it wasn't until the end of the 15th and beginning of the 16th centuries that our system of word separation and punctuation was standardized (by the great Italian printers of that time). It's odd, isn't it, to think of something so small and ordinary as a comma being invented? It's odd to think how punctuation has changed in the past, and how we never imagine it changing in the future.

EXERCISE 5.17

If you were asked to design new punctuation marks, what would you make them look like? Make up a new period, comma, semicolon, colon, exclamation point, question mark, and parentheses. •

My response to Exercise 5.17

. = ✓
, = ❭
; = ⋎
: = ⩕
! = ⩑
? = ⱸ
( ) = ⊢ ⊣

32

Now write or copy a paragraph or two, using your new system of punctuation marks, and see how it looks.

CHAPTER 6

The Bridge to Deciphering

You now have the five conventions of language. You can take on the challenge of deciphering. You will be better off, though, if you look at some examples, not just for the practice but also to see if there is a principle involved, a principle that will help in deciphering.

Your task in deciphering is to figure out the meaning of a passage. You may decipher a good part of it but be temporarily stumped by the one remaining part. How, then, will you go about trying to decipher the one remaining part? Will you take it out of the passage and look at it separately? Perhaps. But more likely you will think about what it might mean *in relation to* the meaning you have already established. For example, for a missing word in a sentence, you will think about what the word could mean in the sentence, right?

Let's say you're reading a book about baseball. But a dog took a bite out of a page, so that one word is missing from it. It says, "The mighty slugger slammed the ball over the fence, a home_____." That's easy, right? But it's easy only because you know the *context* here is baseball.

Now let's take away the context entirely. Imagine that you find a piece of paper with only "a home_____" on it: you wouldn't know how to finish it. There are too many possibilities. A home owner? A home-made pie? A home economics teacher? A home entertainment center? A homeland? You see how important the context is. The context gives us a better idea of what the words mean.

Perhaps you have heard the phrase "out of context." For example, a person who has been quoted may complain that his or her meaning did not come across clearly because the quoted sentence had been lifted "out of context." What does this complaint mean? It means that the sentence by itself does not mean what it may appear to mean. Instead, so the complaint goes, its meaning is clear only *in context*, in relation to the rest of the passage or statement.

Again let's try out the principle that the way you understand meaning is by understanding the context. Here is your example, a bit harder than the baseball example: you are trying to decipher a statement in which you have figured out all but the last two words, and you know that the next-to-last word is some form of the verb "stammer" or "stutter":

The girl is so beautiful that she reduces the boy to a _____   _____.

What then can you tell *from the context* (from the location of the missing words in the sentence)? You know that the next-to-last word is some form of the verb "stammer" or "stutter." That it might be some other form makes sense *in context* because the next-to-last word isn't going to be a verb. It couldn't be, with "to a" coming before it. Instead, the next-to-last word has to modify the last word, which in grammatical terms is called the object of the preposition and has to be a noun or a pronoun. The four words together, "to a _____   _____" form a prepositional phrase. In short, the next-to-last word is probably either "stammering" or "stuttering." So we have

The girl is so beautiful that she reduces the boy to a stuttering _____.

The last word is likely to be "fool" or something like that. You can check out this possibility against what comes before or after this sentence. If your deciphering of these two words still makes sense, then you can be sure that you are on the right track.

For me to explain this line of reasoning, I used terms from grammar. That doesn't mean, though, that you had to know the grammatical terms to follow the reasoning. As a matter of fact, you don't even need the reasoning to come up with the same answer for the words. You might have just guessed them. The context makes good guessing possible. The context suggests what the last two words are. To put this another way, you can figure out the two words "in context," and not by means of grammatical analysis.

There is an advantage to knowing grammar, though: you have a way to explain step by step what *kind* of words are likely to be the missing words. By "kind" I mean that the next-to-last word is not likely to be a regular form of the verb but, instead, a form with "ing," which makes the word into an adjective modifying the last word.

Working in context takes a lot more than a good capacity to analyze the possible forms of words or, what in grammar is called their part of speech and usage. More important than a knowledge of grammar is a feel for the language. This sensitivity to language helps you to comprehend what the intended meaning of the passage is. For example, let's say that you have worked out the sentence we have been discussing to mean:

> The girl is so beautiful that she reduces the boy to a stuttering fool.

And then someone challenges you by claiming that your deciphering of the sentence is ridiculous because no one could, just by her beauty, change someone into a "stuttering fool."

EXERCISE 6.1
How would you reply to this criticism of your deciphering? •

My response to Exercise 6.1
I would say that the criticism is foolish because the criticism is based on a misunderstanding of the sentence.

Would you say something like this? Do you agree with the criticism? Do you agree with my defense against the criticism?

The problem with the criticism is that it takes the phrase "stuttering fool" literally. What is wrong with this approach? Everything. The sentence doesn't mean that the boy was literally changed into a "stuttering fool." And certainly not permanently, whatever the change. The point of the sentence is how the girl's beauty affected the boy's behavior. "Stuttering fool" is an exaggeration in order to emphasize the point. The phrase gives the sentence its punch. In fact, you *expect* the phrase or something like it to follow the verb "reduced." This expectation is an example of sensitivity to language. Given the context of the sentence, the last two words are likely to be as strong as possible. "Stuttering fool" is a much more expected and appropriate ending to the sentence than, say, "a state of nervous confusion." Look how flat it would be with those words:

> The girl is so beautiful that she reduces the boy to a state of nervous confusion.

Clear? Yes. But graphic? No.

The principle of context applies not only to picking the appropriate phrase for a sentence, as we just did, but also in working with the multiple meanings a word can have. For example, say you have figured out a sentence this far:

> She is a _____ _____.

And you think the fourth word might be "good." You don't have to decide now, nor does it make much sense to, until you decipher what the

36

next word might be. If you have no hint for the next word, you would do well to go on to the next sentence to see if figuring out this sentence might shed some light on the two missing words in the previous sentence. Let's say that the next sentence is about all the swimming races she has won. Then the last word of the previous sentence might be "swimmer." Or, say the next sentence is about how trustworthy and helpful she is. Then the last word of the previous sentence may be "friend."

"Swimmer" and "friend" are very different. Could, then, "good" be the next-to-last word in either case? If it could, would its meaning be the same in both sentences?

EXERCISE 6.2
Would "good" have the same meaning in "good swimmer" and "good friend"? •

My response to Exercise 6.2
No, "good" would not have the same meaning in the two sentences. In the first sentence it would mean "capable." In the second it would mean "loyal."

The meaning of "good" changes from one sentence to the next. The meaning of "good" in each case is clear, nevertheless, by the context. Once we know that the last word is "swimmer," we know that "good" means "capable." Once we know that the last word is "friend," we know that "good" means "loyal."

How does this help your deciphering? You may decipher a word and be puzzled by it because you are thinking of only one of its meanings. Don't worry. Wait until you decipher the *other* words in the passage— then see if the word makes sense with another meaning.

This is pretty easy, isn't it? I'm glad, because explaining the different meanings a word can have is difficult sometimes. For example, how would you like to try to differentiate the meaning of "good" in the following three expressions, assuming there is a difference?

good luck
good going
good night

Knowing the subtle changes in meaning a word may have, depending on its context, helps you in deciphering precisely the right word, even if that word is a very little and apparently not very important one.

EXERCISE 6.3

Can you fill in each blank with a different word that, nevertheless, makes good sense?

good _____ baseball
good _____ toast
good _____ little kids
good _____ a sandwich
good _____ nothing

My response to Exercise 6.3

The first is "at." The second is "on." The third is "to." The fourth is "on." The fifth is "for."

There may be another series of words, each different, that answers the question. For example, the third could be "with" just as easily as "to." The second could be "with" also. And a sports announcer could be "good on baseball," which would have a different meaning, obviously, from "good at baseball."

The point, though, is that a change in the little word, no matter how unimportant it may seem, causes a change in meaning of the phrase. For example, there is a definite difference in meaning between "good on bread" and "good in bread." There is also a difference in meaning between "good to little kids" and "good with little kids," but this difference is not as easy to explain. It's more subtle. Still, the difference in meaning among the five phrases may be so distinct in your estimation that you would say that the little words actually *change* the meaning of "good" from one phrase to another. For example, "good to little kids" and "good with little kids" may be close in meaning, but that doesn't mean that the meaning of "good" is the same in both phrases. "Good to little kids" means "kind" or "nice to little kids," whereas "good with little kids" means, for example, that the person works well with little kids.

To make this point clear, here are three more phrases, each of which takes a different word, but in these cases, the little word does *not* alter the meaning of "good."

good _____ the circumstances
good _____ my standards
good _____ the highest expectations

EXERCISE 6.4

What words would you place in the blanks? •

38

My response to Exercise 6.4
The first is "under." The second is "by." The third is "beyond."

In these three phrases, the meaning of "good" does not change much, if at all. Basically, the meaning of "good" stays the same throughout all three. Another way to express this consistency of meaning is to say that the word that follows "good" in each case — "under," "by," and "beyond" — does not change the meaning of "good." This makes this group of three phrases different from the preceding group of five phrases involving the word "good" because there the meaning of "good" is changed by the word that follows it. To recognize this difference requires some sensitivity to language, and this sensitivity comes in very handy in deciphering.

If you read often, you become familiar with the way people phrase ideas. This familiarity comes in handy in deciphering work, too. For example, to form a phrase, the word "circumstances" often takes "under" before it, as in "under the circumstances." The phrase "under the circumstances" is no fancy, special phrase. It's pretty common. Similarly, the word "standards" often takes the word "by" before it to form a phrase, and "expectations" often takes "beyond" in front of it.

If you read a lot, you have probably run across these phrases. This familiarity allows you to think quickly of what a missing word might be in a particular context. For example:

> The weather was terrible for opening night of the play; _____ these circumstances, we started fifteen minutes late in order to allow people time to get there before the curtain went up.

The missing word here is "under." If the phrase is familiar to you, you will think of "under" pretty quickly. If it is not familiar to you, you might grope around for some time, trying to decide what word should go there.

Context is where your knowledge of the conventions of language comes in very handy. And when you are good at working in context, then you can be sure that you will be good at deciphering. Context is your bridge to deciphering.

CHAPTER 7

Deciphering Difficult English

If the conventions of language are all I have cracked them up to be, then we might as well test them against something really challenging.

Let's go back in English writing to the seventeenth century. That's 300 years ago. Any writing then is hard enough for us now, but I am picking the hardest I can find—so hard that you won't run across it in school until college. The writing is especially hard because the writer, a scholar in many languages, used his language knowledge in writing the book. He did whatever he could to elevate his subject, to make his subject sound important. The book was one of the most ambitious in all of English literature—ambitious in that he tried to write a book unlike any that had been written before. He succeeded. And no one has written one like it since.

The purpose of the book, as the author states, is to "justifie the wayes of God to men." Not only is this a big subject, some of the words are spelled oddly.

EXERCISE 7.1
Which words in the line are spelled differently from the way we spell them? •

My response to Exercise 7.1
The two words are "justifie" and "wayes," which we spell "justify" and "ways."

To warm up for this deciphering exercise, you can get a feeling for the writing by reading these opening lines of the book:

1 Of Man's First Disobedience, and the Fruit
2 Of that Forbidd'n Tree, whose mortal tast
3 Brought Death into the World, and all our woe,
4 With loss of Eden, till one greater Man
5 Restore us, and regain the blissful Seat,
6 Sing Heav'nly Muse, that on the secret top
7 Of Oreb, or of Sinai, didst inspire
8 That Shepherd, who first taught the Chosen Seed,
9 In the Beginning how the Heav'ns and Earth
10 Rose out of Chaos:

And we haven't even reached a period yet! What is this? It is strange, like nothing else written in the English language. The author intended it to be like nothing else written in the English language. Here is how it goes on:

10 Rose out of Chaos: Or if Sion Hill
11 Delight thee more, and Siloa's Brook that flowd
12 Fast by the Oracle of God; I thence
13 Invoke thy aid to my advent'rous Song,
14 That with no middle flight intends to soar
15 Above th' Aonian Mount; while it persues
16 Things unattempted yet in Prose or Rime.

In that last line, line 16, the author even says that this writing is supposed to be unique: "Things unattempted yet in Prose or Rime." "Rime" means poetry. Prose is any writing other than poetry. The author goes on to say:

17 And chiefly Thou O Spirit, that dost preferr
18 Before all Temples th'upright heart and pure,
19 Instruct me, for Thou know'st; Thou from the first
20 Wast present, and with mighty wings outspred
21 Dove-like sat'st brooding on the vast Abyss
22 And mad'st it pregnant: What in mee is dark
23 Illumin, what is low raise and support;
24 That to the highth of this great Argument
25 I may assert Eternal Providence
26 And justifie the wayes of God to men.

This part ends with the line quoted earlier in which the author states his purpose for writing the book.

This is a sample of what you are going to take on. If this isn't hard, I don't know what is. *Everything* is hard about it. The words are hard, the sentences are hard, and the subject matter is hard. Still, I am curious what — if anything — is clear to you within these first 26 lines.

EXERCISE 7.2

What, if anything, comes across in these first 26 lines? Do you have *any* idea what the author is saying? •

EXERCISE 7.3

What about the beginning? What do you think the author means by "Man's first Disobedience"? Are you helped at all by the next phrase "the Fruit of that Forbidd'n Tree"? •

Perhaps the next two lines help (lines 3 and 4). Apparently, the "tast(e)" of this "Fruit" "Brought Death into the World, and all our woe," and caused the "loss of Eden."

Is the subject clear now? The Garden of Eden. Adam and Eve. The sin of eating the apple. The Devil tempted Eve to disobey God's order; when she did, God expelled Adam and Even from the Garden of Eden, from Paradise. Now mankind had to suffer and die.

Perhaps you recognize this as the Biblical story of the Fall of Man. Thus, the title of this book, *Paradise Lost*. Perhaps you also recognized "That Shepherd, who first taught the chosen Seed" (line 8) as Christ. It seems that the author intends to retell the story of the Bible. But the author claims no special knowledge. Instead, he asks God to help him in his writing.

EXERCISE 7.4

Do you see a place where the author asks God to assist him? •

My response to Exercise 7.4

One place is line 17, "And chiefly Thou O Spirit, that dost preferr/ Before all Temples th'upright heart and pure,/ Instruct me." The author asks God to "instruct" him so that he can "justifie the wayes of God to men" (line 26).

Declaring one's subject right at the beginning and asking God for assistance was the custom for beginning an important book. The Greek writer Homer did this; Homer wrote *The Odyssey* and *The Iliad*. These books are called "epics." The author of *Paradise Lost* intended to write an epic. He invoked (asked for) God's help in telling the story of the Fall of Man.

27 Say first, for Heav'n hides nothing from thy view
28 Nor the deep Tract of Hell, say first what cause
29 Moved our Grand Parents in that happy State,

30 Favour of Heav'n so highly, to fall off
31 From their Creator, and transgress his Will
32 For one restraint, Lords of the World besides?

I have shown you the first 32 lines of *Paradise Lost* to give you a feeling for what you are going to try to decipher. The language is special, but it is still English. Before trying to decipher a group of lines, let's see first how closely the author sticks to the conventions of English.

1. The alphabet we know;
2. The words are spaced apart;
3. The lines read from left to right and top to bottom;
4. The words are sequenced to create an overall meaning;
5. Punctuation and capitalization are present.

But the author's language is *not* the English language as we know it.

EXERCISE 7.5
What to you is the biggest difference? How would you describe what makes the author's language hard? •

My response to Exercise 7.5
What I think is the hardest about this writing is the sentences. Not the strange words, not the old-fashioned feeling, not the high and mighty tone, but the sentences. They are long and complicated. I get lost. What is the author trying to do? Confuse me?

EXERCISE 7.6
Does your answer to Exercise 7.5 relate in any way to the conventions of language? •

My response to Exercise 7.6
Yes, there is a connection to the conventions of language. The fourth convention, sequencing. We sequence words in order to make sense, to make a clear overall meaning. This author seems to sequence words in as complicated a way as possible. If what he is writing is so important, then why can't he get his ideas straightened out enough first to deliver them in a way we can understand? I'm willing to try—but not if he is just going to make me feel stupid.

Perhaps you are sympathetic with my complaint. The writing is hard, no doubt about it. The sentences are long and complicated. One wonders how anyone could write this way in the first place. Here is how it happened. The author—John Milton—was a scholar. He studied many languages and he especially liked the ancient languages, Greek and Latin. In fact, he *wrote* in Greek and Latin. He wrote in Italian too. When he conceived of writing *Paradise Lost*, he wanted to establish a language that would be fitting to his subject.

What's wrong with his own language? Milton did not think much of the English language of his time, the seventeenth century. His dislike was directed against his contemporary writers, in particular the poets, for their dependence on rhyme. Milton called this dependence "the modern bondage of Rimeing." He called rhyme "the Invention of a barbarous Age, to set out wretched matter and lame meeter, grac'd indeed since by the use of some famous modern Poets, carried away by Custom." Milton regarded the subject matter of the literature of his time as "wretched" because it didn't aspire to great purpose. He regarded the literature of his time as also lacking in real music because the writing was confined to "lame meeter."

"Meeter" is "meter." The word means a specific rhythmic pattern of stressed and unstressed syllables. Here is an example that I made up; the half circles above syllables indicate unstressed syllables, and the diagonal lines indicate stressed syllables. ("Stressed" means emphasized, "unstressed" means not emphasized.)

I came | to see | what you | had done

and looked | around | and ate | a bun.

Each line is composed of four units of an unstressed syllable and a stressed syllable. It is a hard way to write and hold the reader's interest. This kind of writing can become so singsongy that the reader doesn't pay much attention to what is actually being expressed. Milton felt that set rhythm (the "meeter") was "lame" and the rhyme added only "a jingling sound of like endings."

To find another way to write, Milton went back to ancient writers whose work he loved. These writers didn't rhyme and their rhythms were, to Milton's ear, not as confining. He modeled his English on their writing and called it "English Heroic Verse without Rime as that of Homer in Greek and Virgil in Latin." In a sense then, Milton invented his own English language. So he *did* have his reasons for writing in a different way.

EXERCISE 7.7

If you were going to write a very important book, would you consider inventing a new kind of English for the book? •

My response to Exercise 7.7
This is an interesting question because, on the one hand, I might feel that inventing a new kind of English is going too far. I might lose even a curious reader. The gamble is not good. On the other hand, writing is experienced first as language. To put this idea another way, the first thing you experience in reading is the language itself; you get a feeling from the language before you get a strong sense of the content. If this is true, then perhaps considering changing the language in some ways is a good idea for certain subjects. The changed language is your signal to the reader of your special purpose. The question then becomes how far to go in altering the language. When does a possibly good idea become, in practice, a bad idea? This question is one that writers think long about.

We have seen enough of Milton's language to identify some characteristics. Most noticeable, I think, is the sentence structure. Milton's sentence structure is based on Latin sentence structure, which is different from English sentence structure. Even if you haven't studied Latin, you can appreciate from Milton's writing that Latin sentence structure can sound complicated.

EXERCISE 7.8
What other feature of Milton's language do you notice as different from normal English? •

My response to Exercise 7.8
Milton capitalizes a lot of words that we do not capitalize in modern English.

In modern English, we capitalize proper nouns (such as names of people, places, and organizations), but in ancient languages, more than just proper nouns were capitalized. Milton may have drawn on ancient languages as his model for capitalizing. You may have guessed that he increased the capitalizing in order to bring emphasis to more words. Look at the capitalizing in just the first three lines:

> Of Man's First Disobedience and the Fruit
> Of that forbidd'n Tree, whose mortal Tast
> Brought Death into the World and all our woe,

Capitalizing the first letter of each line of poetry is a custom of poetry still practiced by many poets today.

Another characteristic of Milton's "invented" English, his "heroic verse," is to replace the letter *e* with an apostrophe. This characteristic may have been the one you had in mind in reply to Exercise 7.8. Here are some examples.

forbidd'n (line 2)
Heav'nly (line 6)
Heav'ns (line 9)
th' (line 15)

EXERCISE 7.9
What does this dropping of the *e* do to the word? •

My response to Exercise 7.9
Dropping the *e* reduces that syllable.

"Forbidd'n" (in line 2) no longer has three complete syllables, but two and a partial one. You might say that the word now has two and a half syllables. Milton does this so much that we can assume that he has a purpose. He is affecting the way we read the words. He is affecting the rhythm of the line. He is trying to set the rhythm of the language the way he *wants* us to read it, to feel it. This technique is used by other writers. Mark Twain, for instance, used it to represent American slang in *The Adventures of Huckleberry Finn*.

Let's summarize the characteristics we have established of Milton's "invented" (altered) English language.

1. Complicated sentence structure (difficult syntax)
2. Increased capitalization
3. Replacing the letter *e* with an apostrophe

Add the problem of old-fashioned spelling and we have ourselves quite a challenge.

Now let's try to decipher some of this. We will go from where we left off in Book I of *Paradise Lost*.

33 Who first seduc'd them to that foul revolt?
34 Th'infernal Serpent; hee it was, whose guile
35 Stirrd up with Envy and Revenge, deceiv'd
36 The Mother of Mankinde; what time his Pride
37 Had cast him out from Heav'n, with all his Host
38 Of Rebel Angels, by whose aid aspiring
39 To set himself in Glory above his Peers,
40 He trusted to have equaled the most High

3. Now connect all or many of your sentences, using connecting words such as "and," "but," "thus," "because," "of whom," "although," "despite," and so on. You'll probably be creating the run-on sentences that teachers dislike in essays, but what you're writing isn't an essay.

4. If it doesn't sound enough like Milton, take some phrases and sentence parts and move them to another spot in the piece, but not so far away that the reader won't have any idea what they mean.

5. If you and other classmates are doing this, you might put all the descriptions together, to form a description of a superhell. (If you don't like the subject matter, change it to a description of any kind of heaven. Be forewarned, though, that through the ages writers seem to have found it easier to describe a hell than a heaven.) •

CHAPTER 8

Using Deciphering Techniques to Crack Another Language: Part I

I'm going to give you a passage in an old language, one you have probably never seen before. At first it may look like a code or a cipher, but it is really a language, and you're going to "crack" it. I'll help by giving you the meanings of some of the words.

Remember what you have learned from your deciphering work in the previous chapter. Remember too what you have learned about working in context. Use your logic and your imagination. Don't be afraid to guess. Treat it as a guessing game. I think you may be surprised by what you can do.

Here are four lines in the language:

1 Whan that Aprill with its shoures soote
2 The droghte of March hath perced to the roote
3 And bathed every veyne in swich licour,
4 Of which vertu engendred is the flour;

Let's see what we can discover about this by applying what we know about the conventions of language. How about the first convention? Do you recognize a familiar series of basic elements, and are these elements pictorial or alphabetical? Alphabetical, right? Secondly, what about spacing? Are groups of basic elements set off from one another by spacing? If so, then we have words as we know them. Next is direction. In which direction does it seem that we are to read the four lines? If we can figure out the direction, then we can go after the meaning of the words. Only then can we figure out if the words have been set in a particular sequence in order to create an overall meaning as we do in English. And the fifth and last convention, signaling devices. Is there any use of capitalization and punctuation or anything that resembles these devices?

EXERCISE 8.1
List the five conventions to the left, and to the right list the way the conventions appear to be used in this language. •

My response to Exercise 8.1

Convention	**Usage**
1. Basic series of elements	1. The alphabet
2. Spacing	2. Space between words
3. Direction	3. Left to right, then top to bottom
4. Sequencing	4. ?
5. Signaling devices	5. Capitalization, punctuation

The language resembles English, doesn't it? Let's see if the resemblance to English goes beyond the conventions.

EXERCISE 8.2
Do you recognize any of the words? •

My response to Exercise 8.2
Yes, I recognize about half of them, maybe more, and some of the others look like English words, but they are spelled differently.

All right, let's make a list of the words we recognize.

Line 1   that, Aprill, with, its
Line 2   The, of, March, to, the
Line 3   And, bathed, every, in
Line 4   of, which, is, the

How does this list compare to the list of words you recognize? I'm going to take the four lines and italicize all the words in the list above.

Whan *that Aprill with its* shoures soote
The droghte *of March* hath perced *to the* roote
And bathed every veyne *in* swich licour
Of which vertu engendred *is the* flour.

Are there other words here you think you might know? Are there words that look like English words enough to guess at them? Not everyone is going to pick the same, but I bet we agree on some of them.

EXERCISE 8.3

Which words in these four lines resemble words in English? •

My response to Exercise 8.3
Here are my picks:

Line 1	"Whan"	resembles "when"
	"shoures"	resembles "showers"
Line 2	"droghte"	resembles "drought"
	"hath"	resembles "has"
	"perced"	resembles "pierced"
Line 3	"veyne"	resembles "vein"
	"licour"	resembles "liquor"
Line 4	"flour"	resembles "flour" and "flower"

EXERCISE 8.4

Did I pick any words you didn't? Did you pick any words that I didn't? •

The words that I picked seem to make sense in context. So I am going to go with them as a reasonable guess at this point. You pick the ones you think are reasonable guesses. Then insert them in the lines and read the lines over to yourself. See if any other words, words that I haven't mentioned, suggest a meaning.

As I read over the lines, other words come to mind. I am not as sure of these, but here they are, my second group:

Line 1	"soote"	resembles "soot"
Line 3	"swich"	resembles "switch"
Line 4	"vertu"	resembles "virtue"
	"engendred"	resembles "engendered"

That last one, "engendered," may not be one you go along with, it may not be a common word to you, but "engender" is an English word. It means "to give," as in "The writer engendered his hero with great strength."

EXERCISE 8.5

Did you pick any of my second group of words in your list? •

EXERCISE 8.6

What do you think of the words in my total list, namely the two bunches of the words that I think resemble English words? •

The best way to try out the words on your list and the words on my list is to test them *in context*. That means, as you know, to try out the words in the actual passage and see if they make sense. In using this method we are assuming that the writing was intended to make sense. Therefore, if we substitute a word and it does not make sense, we can figure, at least for the time being, that our word is wrong.

First, let's see how many of the words in the four lines are already covered. Here they are, either italicized (as words we know) or in bold type (for words that resemble words in English):

> **Whan** *that Aprill with its* **shoures soote**
> *The droghte of March* **hath perced** *to the* **roote**
> *And bathed every veyne in* **swich licour**
> *Of which* **vertu engendred** *is the* **flour;**

Working off of my list, every one of the words is either a word we know in English or a word that resembles a word in English. So let's see if we can figure out what these lines are saying.

EXERCISE 8.7
What do we know that line one is about and what more can we guess? •

My response to Exercise 8.7
We know that line one is about "April" and it looks as if it's about "April showers."

EXERCISE 8.8
What do you make of the whole line? Can you decipher it? •

My response to Exercise 8.8
Line one reads: "When that April with its showers soot."

EXERCISE 8.9
Does that deciphering (translation, interpretation) make sense? •

My response to Exercise 8.9
Not really. Some of it makes sense. It appears that you don't need the "that," but "soot" doesn't make any sense, unless "shoures soot" means "showers of soot." Although that makes sense grammatically, it does not make sense in context because there is no mention of fire or smoke or factories. On the contrary, the line seems to be about the coming of spring.

So the problem of the meaning of "soot" has to wait. It can't be solved in

the context of the line because the suggested meaning, through the resemblance of "soote" to our word "soot," doesn't work in the context. Yet
the meaning might be revealed by our working on the other lines. So
let's go on to line 2:

The droghte of March hath perced to the roote.

If "hath" is "has," and "perced" is "pierced," and "roote" is "root," then
we have

The drought of March has pierced to the root

So the first two lines look like this

When April with its showers ___?___
The drought of March has pierced to the root

What we have here is a literal deciphering or translation. That means a
word-by-word replacing (with "that" left out of line 1). A literal deciphering is a big step forward, but it is not the whole matter. The question remains as to whether or not the literal deciphering makes sense.

EXERCISE 8.10
Does the literal deciphering of the first two lines make sense? •

My response to Exercise 8.10
The lines sound as if they make sense, but something is wrong. They
don't really make sense.

Perhaps the answer lies with the meaning of "soote." So let's have the
meaning. "Soote" is an old word meaning "sweet." Say "oo" out loud.
Notice that your lips are almost saying "w." So the phrase is "with its
showers sweet," and since our normal sequencing of words places the
adjective before the noun it modifies, we would say "with its sweet
showers."
   Does that help? Well, sure, it helps, but it doesn't solve the problem of
the *overall* meaning of the two lines. The problem is one of syntax. That
means the same as saying the problem is one of the relationships of the
words. Specifically, the problem is what is doing the piercing. Is it
"April with its sweet showers" or "the drought of March?"

EXERCISE 8.11
What does common sense tell you is the answer to the question of what is
doing the piercing? •

My response to Exercise 8.11

"The drought of March" doesn't pierce something "to the root" unless it means to deplete the water supply to the extent that the root can't reach any water. That makes sense within itself, but the other way makes better sense for these two lines. That is, the "April showers" pierce "the drought of March" "to the root" by dropping so much rain water that the water sinks all the way down to the roots. The meaning here is literal, right to the roots of plants and trees. There is also a figurative (suggested) meaning: the "April showers" pierce "the drought of March" to *its* root. The meaning here is that the rain is so strong and plentiful that the earlier drought is totally ended. I like the way the literal and figurative meanings work easily together. Anyway, following this interpretation of the first two lines, we have

> When April with its sweet showers
> has pierced the drought of March to the root.

Ah, now that seems to make sense. To solve this problem, we had to figure out the relationship of the parts. We did so by common sense. We figured out the relationship in context. To make a sensible relationship of the parts, we had to rearrange the parts. This kind of deciphering work we are familiar with. It is the fourth convention, sequencing. The relationship of the parts of a sentence is determined first by sequencing and second by rules of grammar. Sequencing and grammar work together to indicate the overall meaning.

Let's go on to the next two lines:

> And bathed every veyne in swich licour
> Of which vertu engendred is the flour.

Let's try it with the words I listed:

> And bathed every vein in switch liquor
> Of which virtue engendered is the flower.

That doesn't work very well, does it? Well, we tried. Now what can we do? At least "And bathed every vein" looks pretty good. Since the subject of the verb "bathed" we know is "April showers," then "vein" could be a vein of the ground (or perhaps of a leaf). The word "vein" makes the ground sound like a body, but that may be the writer's purpose. Ground, receiving spring rain, is like a body coming back to life. Spring is the season of life beginning again.

But what about "swich licour"? Is the water "switching to liquor" as it mixes with the roots of plants and animals? That doesn't make much sense. And "liquor" is a depressant, and not a particularly healthy one.

57

Does the next line help? We know that something happens to the flowers. We expect that the meaning involves the blossoming of spring. The meaning of "engender" (to give) supports this idea. Perhaps the rain water gives something to make the flower, or the rain water helps the flower to appear. But what does "virtue" have to do with it? Is it a "virtue" that the rain helps the flower? That sounds a little strange, doesn't it?

We certainly established the general subject of the coming of spring, and we have a lot of the words of the four lines, but without the meaning of "swich licour" and "vertu" we can't go much further. So here they are:

"swich licour"   means "such moisture"
"Of whose vertu"   means "by whose power"

So the critical words are "swich" meaning "such" and "vertu" meaning "power." Let's see what we have:

And bathed every vein in such moisture
By whose power engendered is the flower.

Again, as with the first two lines, the overall meaning doesn't come clear with a literal translation. So let's guess that the problem is the same as the one we encountered in the first two lines, the problem of sequencing.

EXERCISE 8.12
Is there another way to sequence the words in the two lines? •

My response to Exercise 8.12
There is no problem with sequencing in the third line. The problem is with the fourth line. What about sequencing it like this:

By whose power the flower is engendered.

This sequencing is better, isn't it? Now the line makes sense. "Engendered" means here "given strength" or "given life." So let's see what the four lines look like in our deciphering:

When April with its sweet showers
Has pierced the drought of March to the root
And bathed every vein in such moisture
By whose power the flower is engendered.

I am wondering if you noticed why we had the sequencing problem in lines two and four. Any ideas? Look again at the original four lines. Do you notice anything about the line-ending words?

58

EXERCISE 8.13

Do you have any idea of what caused the sequencing problem in lines two and four? •

My response to Exercise 8.13

The rhyme caused it. The writer moved the parts of the sentence around in order to make the lines rhyme in pairs. Lines 3 and 4 aren't that obvious a rhyme, but probably the words rhyme when you say them.

That's right — unless, of course, the sequencing was normal to the language of its author's time.

CHAPTER 9

Using Deciphering Techniques to Crack Another Language: Part II

These last few chapters may have been pretty hard or perhaps pretty slow. I don't know. Deciphering isn't easy. But you are getting the hang of it, so let's try some more. I bet it's easier. Here are the next lines of what we were working on in the last chapter.

5 Whan Zephirus eek with his sweete breeth
6 Inspired hath in every holt and heeth
7 The tendre croppes, and the yonge sonne
8 Hath in the Ram his halve cours yronne,

These four lines break into two parts at the comma in line 7. Let's look at the first part.

EXERCISE 9.1
Which words in the first part do we already know from English? •

My response to Exercise 9.1
We know: with, his, in, every, and, the, tendre.

EXERCISE 9.2
What other words can we add to this list either because we have learned them from the previous lines we deciphered or because they closely resemble words in English? •

My response to Exercise 9.2
From the previous lines we know that

"whan" means "when"
"hath" means "has"

And the following words closely resemble words in English:

"sweete"   resembles "sweet"
"breeth"   resembles "breath"
"heeth"   resembles "heath" (land without trees)
"croppes"   resembles "crops"

EXERCISE 9.3
What words does that leave in this first part? •

My response to Exercise 9.3
The remaining words are: Zephirus, eek, holt.

I don't expect you to know that they mean. I didn't know them until someone told me:

"Zephirus"   means "the west wind"
"eek"   means "also"
"holt"   means "wooded land"

So what do we have? Let's see.

When the west wind with his sweet breath
Inspired has in every wooded land and heath
The tender crops. . . .

"Inspired" means here literally "breathed into."

EXERCISE 9.4
How would you rearrange the sequencing of words in this first part? •

My response to Exercise 9.4
I would rearrange the sequencing this way:

Also, when the west wind with his sweet breath
Has breathed into the tender crops in every
Wooded land and heath,

That sounds pretty clear and sensible. All right, let's move along to the second part

. . . and the yonge sonne
Hath in the Ram his halve cours yronne

Instead of making our list of known words and words resembling words in English, let's just go for it. You probably have guessed that "yonge sonne" is "young sun," that "halve" is "half," and that "yronne" is "run." So what do we have?

EXERCISE 9.5
How would you decipher this second part? •

My response to Exercise 9.5
This second part comes out this way:

> ...and the young sun
> has in the Ram his half course run,

and this literal deciphering can be changed to:

> ...and the young sun
> has run his half course in the Ram.

Fine, but what does it mean? Here you deserve some help. "Ram" refers to Aries, the first sign of the Zodiac. "Halve cours" means the second half of the sun's course, which falls in April, the time of spring. The line describes where the sun is at this time of year.

All right, that wasn't too hard. Here is some more:

> 9 And smale foweles maken melodye
> 10 That slepen al the nyght with open ye
> 11 (So pricketh hem Nature in hir corages)

There are many new words here, but I think you can guess some of them. Try. Go ahead and take a shot at lines 9 and 10.

EXERCISE 9.6
What do you make of lines 9 and 10? •

My response to Exercise 9.6
Here is how I decipher them:

> And small fowl make melody
> That sleep all the night with open eyes

That sounds pretty good. It certainly makes sense. How does it compare with your version?

Line 11 is harder—but maybe not so hard if you know the two pronouns:

62

"hem"   means "them"
"hir"   means "their"

"Hir" looks like "her," but it means "their." "Corages" looks like "courage," doesn't it? And the meaning is close. "Corages" means "hearts." So line 11

(So pricketh hem Nature in hir corages)

means

(So pricketh them Nature in their hearts)

That literal translation can be changed to

(So nature urges them in their hearts)

"Nature" is urging the birds to "maken melodye." So all these lines are about spring and the return of life. Now we will see the effect of spring on some of the people:

12 Thanne longen folk to goon on pilgrimages
13 And palmeres for to seken straunge strondes
14 To ferne halwes, kowthe in sondry londes

Pretty hard? Harder than the lines before? Let's see what we can figure out. The words we know are:

folk, to, on, pilgrimages (line 12)
And, for, to (line 13)
To, in (line 14)

That's not a whole lot, but perhaps we can do some guessing. If "whan" means "when," then "thanne" might be "then" (and not "than"). "Goon" is probably not our word "goon" (a stupid person) because in context that doesn't make sense. The word "goon" may just be a form of the verb "go" because that would make the last three words of the line "go on pilgrimages," which makes good sense. What about "straunge"? Couldn't it be "strange"? And what about "sondry"? It could be "sundry" or "various." And "londes" might be "lands." Let's try these.

Then *longen* folk to go on pilgrimages
And *palmeres* for to seek strange *strondes*
To *ferne halwes, kowthe* in *various lands*

I have italicized the words we haven't tried to guess. I bet you would guess "longen" if the line were written this way:

Thanne maken folk longen to goon on pilgrimages

63

"Longen" means "to long for." "Palmeres" is just another word for "pilgrims." "Strondes" means "shores." "Ferne halwes" are "distant shrines," and "kowthe" means "known." So these lines can be deciphered like this:

> Then folks long to go on pilgrimages
> and pilgrims seek strange shores
> of distant shrines known in various lands

So, overall, we have a description of spring as the time when people think of going on a pilgrimage, and the more experienced pilgrims head out on longer journeys to far away, holy places.

Here are the last five lines we are going to decipher:

15 And specially from every shires ende
16 Of Engelond, to Caunterbury they wende,
17 The hooly blisful martir for to seke
18 That hem hath holpen whan that they were seeke.

Let's italicize the words we know:

And specially from every shires ende
Of Engelond, *to* Caunterbury *they* wende,
The hooly blisful martir for to seke
That hem hath holpen *whan that they were* seeke.

EXERCISE 9.7
What other words here can you guess at? Can you guess at *all* the remaining words? •

My response to Exercise 9.7
I will try to guess at all the remaining words.

"specially"	means "especially"
"shires"	means "some sort of place"
"Engelond"	means "England"
"Caunterbury"	means "Canterbury," (a place)
"wende"	means "wend, go"
"seke"	means "seek"
"holpen"	means "hope"
"seeke"	means "sick"

Pretty good. A couple of little things. "Shires" is more specific than "some sort of place." It means "district." It is used today in England with this meaning and often appears at the end of a place name (such as Berkshire). "Holpen" does not mean "hope" but "help." And the word

64

underlined earlier, "blisful," doesn't mean "blissful" but "blessed." (There is no way you could have known that.) So let's try these lines.

> And especially from every shires end
> of England, to Canterbury they wend (or go)
> to seek the holy blessed martyr
> who has helped them when they were sick.

This completes the deciphering of nineteen lines in another language. See how much of what we have done has stayed with you. Try reading the whole thing through in the original language.

> Whan that Aprill with his shoures soote
> The droghte of March hath perced to the roote
> And bathed every veyne in swich licour
> Of which vertu engendred is the flour;
> Whan Zephirus eek with his sweete breeth
> Inspired hath in every holt and heeth
> The tendre croppes, and the yonge sonne
> Hath in the Ram his halve cours yronne,
> And smale foules maken melodye
> That slepen al the nyght with open ye
> (So priketh hem Nature in hir corages),
> Thanne longen folk to goon on pilgrimages,
> And palmeres for to seken straunge strondes
> To ferne halves, kowthe in sondry londes;
> And specially from every shires ende
> Of Engelond, to Caunterbury they wende,
> The hooly blisful martir for to seke
> That hem hath holpen whan that they were seeke.

How did you do? I'll bet it was a lot easier this time through. Can you read a lot more of this language than when you started? Did you decipher more of these lines than you thought you might be able to? Even if you can't remember a word here or there, you can still pick up on the general meaning, right? I'll bet you would have deciphered even more if it hadn't been for those sequencing problems. These problems might not have been there had the writer not chosen to write in rhyme.

And what about this old language anyway? Any idea what it is? It is called "Middle English." And yes, there is a form of English that preceded it. And yes, it is harder. But this is hard enough, right? Well, maybe not. Maybe you think now, after your deciphering, that it isn't so hard after all.

The writer's name is Geoffrey Chaucer. He is writing about the people who went on a pilgrimage to Canterbury, England. His book, *The*

Canterbury Tales, is divided up into different people's stories. The lines you deciphered are the first 18 of "The General Prologue," the introduction to the book.

At the time Chaucer wrote the book, most works of literature were written in Latin. That's right, Latin, because Latin was the language of the church, and the church was the place of learning and culture. Or in French, the language of the court. To write literature in "the common language" was a rather radical thing to do.

Chaucer has been "translated" into modern English, but I like the way his Middle English looks. It looks authentic. Here's a final section, for you to try on your own, just for the heck of it. See how much comes through on a first try.

> Bifil that in that seson on a day
> In Southwerk at the Tabard as I lay,
> Redy to wenden on my pilgrymage
> To Caunterbury, with ful devout corage,
> At nyght was come into that hostelrye
> Well nyne and twenty in a compaignye,
> Of sondry folk, by aventure yfalle
> In fellaship, and pilgrimes were they alle
> That toward Caunterbury wolden ride.

See if your school or public library has recordings of Middle English. It sounds great.

CHAPTER 10

Dropping One Convention

Can you read these lines?

> . . . they might as well try to stop the sun from rising tomorrow the sun shines for you he said the day we were lying among the rhododendrons on Howth Head in the gray tweed suit and his straw hat the day I got him to propose to me yes I first gave him the bit of seedcake out of my mouth. . .

Is it hard? If you have a problem with it, what is the problem? Does the writer conform to the conventions of English?

EXERCISE 10.1
Which convention or conventions of English does the writer break? •

My response to Exercise 10.1
The writer breaks only one convention, signaling devices. The writer does not capitalize or punctuate.

Actually, the writer does capitalize once ("Howth Head," the name of a place).

Here is how the passage goes on:

> . . . first I gave him the bit of seedcake out of my mouth and it was leapyear like now yes 16 years ago my God after that long kiss I near lost my breath yes he said I was a flower of the mountain yes so we are flowers all a woman's body yes that was one true thing he said in his life and the sun shines for you today yes that was why I liked him because I saw he understood or felt what a woman is and I knew I could always get round him. . .

I love this writing. It is from *Ulysses*, a novel by James Joyce, an Irish writer. Published in 1922, the book was, and still is, a source of controversy. It is a particularly challenging book you are not likely to see until a literature course in college. The novel is the story of one day in the lives of two men, and the final chapter, from which this passage comes, is told by the wife of one of the two men. About ten lines later the final chapter ends like this:

> . . . and big wheels of the carts of the bulls and the old castle thousands of years old yes and those handsome Moors all in white and turbans like kings asking you to sit down in their little bit of shop and Ronda with the old windows of the posadas glancing eyes a lattice hid for her lover to kiss the iron and the wineshops half open at night and the castanets and the night we missed the boat at Algeciras the watchman going about serene with his lamp and O that awful deepdown torrent O and the sea the sea crimson sometimes like fire and the glorious sunsets and the figtrees in the Alameda gardens yes and all the queer little streets and pink and blue and yellow houses and the rosegardens and the jessamine and geraniums and cactuses and Gibraltar as a girl where I was a flower of the mountain yes when I put the rose in my hair like the Andalusian girls used or shall I wear a red yes and how he kissed me under the Moorish wall and I thought well as well him as another and then I asked him with my eyes to ask again yes and then he asked me would I yes say to yes my mountain flower and first I put my arms around him yes and drew him down to me so he could feel my breasts all perfume yes and his heart was going like mad and yes I said yes I will Yes. . .

I think that's wonderful writing. What do you think?

EXERCISE 10.2
Do you think the dropping of the signaling devices helps or hinders the impact of the passage? •

My response to Exercise 10.2
My opinion is that the dropping of the signaling devices helps the impact of the passage because the words flow more quickly. The phrases roll one on top of the other, like waves of the sea; and I think the writer wants this effect. It makes the ending more dramatic.

EXERCISE 10.3
Try an experiment in writing something like this ending of *Ulysses*. Write a description in which you drop the signaling devices of punctuation and capitalization. You might want to write about a scene or event that was particularly exciting or filled with action. First, choose the thing you're going to write about, and then write very quickly, without stopping to think. Let the pencil or pen do the thinking, on paper. Write this way for a minimum of five minutes. Remember, don't use any punctuation or capitalization. •

Is this fun to do? Do you like what you came up with? Does the dropping of signaling devices help your piece of writing? If you are writing action, you certainly increase the speed of your narrative by dropping the signaling devices.

EXERCISE 10.4
Do you think that dropping signaling devices in poetry is the same as it is in fiction? •

My response to Exercise 10.4
No, I don't think so, because a poetry line ends before the righthand margin. In poetry the line endings are a sort of punctuation, a pause. The poet can end a line at the end of a sentence or phrase and that way avoid the confusion that may arise from dropping signaling devices.

If a poet uses very simple phrasing and generally ends the lines at the end of a sentence, the absence of signaling devices is no problem for the reader. Here is an example:

[From "Tall Tale of the Tall Cowboy"]

How they buffaloed both sides
How they gave them bullets to bite
How they swallowed hard
when the Great Cowboy laughed on TV
How the Great Cowboy waved his hand
and disappeared over the horizon
How he walked softly and carried a big nuke
How he brandished it like a hunting rifle
How the President of Mexico gave him a great stallion
How he tried to mount it as the cameras rolled
How he slung his hunting rifle behind him and swung up
How the people hid in their houses
How the hot sun beat down on the mined land of the world
How the swinging-door saloons stood empty and silent
How the natives were restless and beat their drums
in the concrete jungles of the world

The poem is by the contemporary Californian poet Lawrence Ferlinghetti. This is the middle section of the poem.

EXERCISE 10.5
What exception does the poet make to the dropping of signaling devices? •

My response to Exercise 10.5

The poet capitalizes the first word of the line when the word is "How." Many of the lines begin with "How." The poem is actually a series of "How" clauses. Can you guess whom the poem is about? It's probably about President Reagan. The poem is political satire. The poet is poking fun at what he believes the President did wrong. As light as the poem is, the poet may very well be dead serious. This is what makes satire interesting. The contrast between the tone of a satirical poem and its intention is often striking. Here is how the poem goes on and finishes:

> How the Indians said How Come instead of How
> How the Indians hid in the hills
> How the Great Smiler smiled no more on TV
> How he came on his great white stallion
> propped up from behind with a big stick
> How he stood tall in the saddle
> and looked straight into the cameras
> How the old hands hid in the old corrals
> How the deputies deputized themselves
> and took to the roofs
> How the people trembled in their houses
> How they thought it was the final shootout
> How a great hush fell upon the plazas of the world
> How the Great Cowboy put on one black glove
> How his eyes narrowed and his hand reached behind him
> How suddenly there was nowhere to hide
> How suddenly there was no turning back
> How suddenly it was High Noon

Do you know why "High Noon" is capitalized? Do you know your movies? How about famous cowboy movies? *High Noon* is a famous cowboy movie. "High Noon" refers in the movie to the time of the final gunbattle in which Gary Cooper takes on the bad guys. The movie is a classic— but here in the poem the name of the movie has a frightening suggestion. Put the idea of the President of the United States as the "Great Cowboy" together with the idea of "High Noon" and you've got yourself a shootout that goes well beyond a corral in the west. It means world war. Lawrence Ferlinghetti is dead serious in his satirical poem "Tall Tale of the Tall Cowboy."

EXERCISE 10.6

Does the dropping of the signaling devices (with the exception of capitalizing "How") make the poem harder to read than if the signaling devices were included? •

My response to Exercise 10.6
No, I don't think so. There is nothing complicated about the sequencing of the words; therefore, the overall meaning of each "How" is clear.

EXERCISE 10.7
Write your own "How" poem, beginning each new thing with a capitalized How. Don't use periods at the ends of the lines. Have the poem build up to something that's just about to happen, then stop right there. •

How about this next poem? Does it make sense?

But I Loved My Grandma

A sweet pea
stuck in each grass-stained ear
sneaks up barefoot
behind
soapsuds Grandma
with a dead-fly
flyswatter
swats her topknot
hard hard hard
take that
for not frying
doughnuts
you promised me
and that
for not telling
about
Jesse James
and this
for being so
old old old

The first time you read this poem, you can tell that a little kid is swatting grandma's "topknot," but beyond that fact the poem may be a little confusing. Even though the words are simple, the poem isn't easy to read, at least not in the beginning. I mean, how can "a sweet pea" "sneak up barefoot"? And what's a "dead-fly flyswatter"?

EXERCISE 10.8
What do you think a "dead-fly flyswatter" is? •

My response to Exercise 10.8
A "dead-fly flyswatter" could be a flyswatter with a dead fly still stuck to it.

If so, it's gross, sure, but it's true that sometimes the fly sticks to a flyswatter when you swat it.

EXERCISE 10.9
What do you make of the "sweet pea" sneaking "up barefoot"? •

My response to Exercise 10.9
This question is harder. I think it is a little kid with "a sweet pea stuck in each grass-stained ear" who "sneaks up barefoot." The little kid is the grandson.

If this explanation makes sense, then the first four lines would normally read like this:

> With a sweet pea
> stuck in each
> grass-stained ear
> the boy sneaks up barefoot

I added "with" at the beginning and "the boy" in line 4. I'm sure the poet Dave Etter could have added those words or any other to make these lines clearer. He chose not to. Why? To move the poem along more rapidly and make it more interesting. Certainly the details gain more notice this way. But it's chancy. That's what poets do, take chances with language. It is part of the fun of experimenting with words. That doesn't mean, though, that it always works. That's up to the reader. What do you think? I'm not asking about only the first time you read the poem. The second time counts just as much, if not more.

By the way, I'm making a calculated guess that the kid in the poem is a boy.

The question of clarity doesn't stop with the first four lines. The two lines we have already mentioned—"with a dead-fly flyswatter"—may be confusing. What is a "dead-fly flyswatter" and who has it? The little kid has the flyswatter; that becomes obvious as we read on. Yet when these two lines appear in the poem, they come right after "Grandma," so it may sound like "soapsuds Grandma with a dead-fly flyswatter." If this is a problem of clarity, isn't it cleared up right away, though, by the next line, "swats her topknot"? Doesn't it have to be the little kid swatting the Grandma's topnkot with the flyswatter? If you agree, then this part of the poem works because it is both clear and vivid.

My favorite spot in this poem is the word "this" in the third-to-last line. Such a simple, everyday word, but the way it appears here, I love it. Line 12 ("take that") and line 16 ("and that") set up the expectation that if there is to be another one, it will be introduced by "and that." But the poet writes "and this." A very small change from "that" to "this," but for me the change to "this" makes the last action the most immediate and the most important of the three. Which it is—"and this for being so old old old."

Which brings up another question about this poem: why the little kid swats his grandma. Is he mean? Doesn't he like her? The poet says in the title "But I loved my grandma." So maybe our question should be, how can the poet love his grandma and keep swatting her topknot? What do you think? Well, maybe he swats her *because* he loves her. Does that make any sense? What do you think?

Perhaps the question is not how he can swat her and say he loved her but why he swats her "for being so old old old."

EXERCISE 10.10
Why would he swat her "for being so old old old"? •

My response to Exercise 10.10
The only reason I can see why he would swat her "for being so old old old" is that he doesn't want her to be so old, but there is nothing he can do about it.

Perhaps the little boy wants his grandma to be younger so that she can play more with him, or maybe he knows down deep that his grandma doesn't have long to live. Young kids have a particularly hard time with the realization that someone they love is not going to be alive much longer. You probably know this. Adults have a hard time with this realization, too.

I like this poem. I like the way it takes me from light, funny thoughts to serious, loving thoughts — and it does so very quickly. What I especially like about this poem is that I feel these thoughts directly from the scene. The poet doesn't tell me what to feel. If he did, the poem would be ruined. I like the poem the way it is. Sure, I have to do a little work to understand the scene fully, and there are different ways to interpret the meaning, particularly at the very end. But I think that this openness of interpretation makes the poem stronger, not weaker. What do you think?

CHAPTER 11

Dropping More Than One Convention

Dropping the convention of signaling devices is taking a chance, but not a very big chance, for signaling devices is the last of the five conventions. But to drop, in addition, one or more of the other conventions, now that is really taking a chance. The writer whose work we are going to look at here did just that. His name is E. E. Cummings. He was a contemporary of James Joyce. These two writers are two of the most important innovators of the modern movement in literature. This movement does not have an official beginning date or ending date, but it is generally thought of as the period between World War I and World War II (roughly between 1910 and 1940). Literature since World War II has been called, for lack of a better name, "contemporary literature."

E. E. Cummings wrote poems, plays, novels, and essays. He is best known for his poems. What is not commonly known is that he was also a painter. He loved to paint and he painted a lot. He was attracted to the possibilities for visual experiment that the typewriter affords.

Beautiful

is the
unmea
ning
of(sil

ently)fal

ling(e
ver
yw
here)s

now

Can you read this? It's tricky, isn't it? But read through it a couple of times; I bet you catch on. Try again. The words start coming together, right? The poem no longer appears as strange as it may have at first. Do you like it? It's interesting, anyway, isn't it?

A good way to make sure you understand the words is to write the poem out as prose; that is, all the way out to the righthand margin.

EXERCISE 11.1
Write the poem out as prose. •

My response to Exercise 11.1
"Beautiful is the unmeaning of silently falling everywhere snow."

That takes some of the fun out of it, doesn't it? But at least we are sure we have the words right.

EXERCISE 11.2
Write the poem in its two parts, first the part not in parentheses and, second, the part in parentheses. •

My response to Exercise 11.2
The part not in the parentheses is "Beautiful is the unmeaning of falling snow." The part in parentheses is "silently everywhere."

Now let's see how Cummings experimented with the conventions of English.

EXERCISE 11.3
How did Cummings treat the conventions of English in his poem "Beautiful?" •

My response to Exercise 11.3
At first, it looks as if Cummings ignored the conventions of English altogether, but when you look more closely you see that he experimented with almost every convention in a particular way. He uses the alphabet and he sets off at least some of the words with a space on either side. Other words he does not; he breaks them up and runs them together. So with the second convention he is already experimenting. As to the third convention, the poem reads, as in normal English, from left to right and from top to bottom, but the lines are so short that the poem seems to

read basically from top to bottom. As for sequencing, the fourth convention, you can't exactly call this normal English. The part not in parentheses reads as a normal English sentence, "Beautiful is the unmeaning of falling snow," with the obvious exception of the made-up word "unmeaning." But once you add the words in parentheses, the sentence becomes a little strange. Whereas there is nothing strange about modifying falling with "silently" placed before it, it is very strange to modify "snow" with "everywhere" before it. But still, we know what it means. "Everywhere snow" does make sense. As for signaling devices, he does capitalize the title "Beautiful," but he doesn't put a period at the end. Instead, he uses parentheses twice in a way that almost creates a second part of the poem.

It sounds as if Cummings retained the alphabet but experimented with the other four conventions.

EXERCISE 11.4
Do you think the break with any one convention is more important than the breaks with the other conventions? •

My response to Exercise 11.4
As much as he experimented with direction, sequencing, and signaling devices, I think that the most important breaking with the conventions of English is the breaking with the convention of word formation. The breaking up of the words into groups of letters and a single letter is what makes the poem hard to read, at least at first.

EXERCISE 11.5
Do you think the breaking up of words in the first half of the poem is as hard to grasp as it is in the second half of the poem? •

My response to Exercise 11.5
No, I don't think so. The way he breaks up "everywhere" in the second half is harder than any word-breaking in the first half.

"Everywhere" is spread out over four lines. The first two lines of the word are broken at the syllables, as we normally break a word and add a hyphen at the end of a line of prose. "Ever" is broken between the *e* and the *v*, and the second syllable is left as a line. But the third syllable, *y*, is not kept separate. Instead, it is directly followed, without a space, by the *w* of "where." How do we read *yw*? There is no common sound for *yw.* Then, instead of "where," we read "here" on the fourth line of "everywhere." This only makes the word less clear.

Therefore, Cummings is not only breaking up words but he is doing so in an "unconventional" way. The conventional way is to break the word between syllables. For example, the word "hyphen," if it is to be broken at the end of a line, would be broken between the *y* and the *p* to keep the two syllables intact: "hy-phen."

Every word that Cummings breaks up he does so in this non-syllabic, unconventional way. These words are "unmeaning," "silently," "falling," "everywhere," and "snow." You might think that the *way* he breaks up these words is more important than the fact that he breaks them. For example, wouldn't the first four lines of the poem be easier if they read like this:

> is the
> unmean
> ing
> of(si

The only changes here are making the second syllable of "unmeaning" complete and making the first syllable of "silently" complete.

EXERCISE 11.6
Does the poet also run words together? •

My response to Exercise 11.6
It looks as if he does, but the only space he drops is before beginning parentheses and after an ending parenthesis. For example, in the line "ently)fal" there would normally be a space between the parenthesis and the *f*. This seems like such a little change, but its effect on the page is pretty big.

The exercises up to this point have been about the poet's experimenting with the conventions of language. The poem is generally considered a big departure from normal English. The reasons for this view are pretty obvious, aren't they? But your knowledge of conventions allows you to say precisely in what way the poet broke from the conventions. Perhaps this understanding leads you to conclude that this poem is not such a big departure from the conventions of English. On the other hand, even with your understanding, you may feel that this poem is a radical departure.

EXERCISE 11.7

How big a departure from the conventions of English do you judge this poem to be? •

This question is finally a matter of opinion because you are attaching importance to what the poet did differently from the conventions of English. I am going to leave this question with you and go on to what the poet is actually expressing. That way we will have a context for the experimenting. Having a context provides us with a purpose for the poem. This we need in order to evaluate the altering of the conventions.

We are helped in thinking about what the poet is expressing in the poem by the fact that the poem is a statement, "Beautiful is the. . . ." And the statement is noticeable for the arrangement of the words in the sentence. The normal sequencing of words would be a reversal of the actual ordering. The sentence would *end* with "is beautiful." The way the poet has sequenced the words suggests that he wants to express something about the nature of beauty.

EXERCISE 11.8

Do you see the poet expressing an idea about beauty? •

My response to Exercise 11.8

I have no way of telling exactly what the poet has in mind, but judging by what he says I certainly notice the word "unmeaning." It jumps out of the sentence. The word conveys the idea that the scene of the snow falling is just that; it doesn't possess a symbolic meaning outside of itself. Yet it is beautiful. More specifically, the scene is beautiful *for* its "unmeaning." So the poet could have said "Beautiful is silently falling everywhere snow." By adding "the unmeaning of" after "is" the poet seems to be emphasizing that beauty is not a matter of meaning, but is, on the contrary, a matter of something else entirely.

That makes sense. Cummings certainly emphasizes that beauty is not a matter of meaning. But what then is it a matter of? Well, let's consider a scene which we notice as being beautiful. We can experience this scene as an idea. Ideas come to us in words, so we might actually say to ourselves, "This scene is beautiful." But there is another way. We are so captivated by the beauty of a scene that we are totally absorbed by it. We don't bother to think about it at the time. We don't need to, for we know intuitively (by intuition, by feeling), and we don't want to because we don't want to interrupt our experience with thinking. The first kind of experiencing of beauty is abstract, intellectual, conceptual. It occurs within our minds. The second kind is immediate, direct, engrossing. It occurs between us and the scene itself, as a feeling. Perhaps this second kind of experience of beauty is what the poet is expressing.

EXERCISE 11.9
Do you see anything in the poem that suggests that the poet favors the immediate experience, the felt experience, rather than the thought-about experience? •

My response to Exercise 11.9
Yes, the last word of the poem, "now." It is immediate.

EXERCISE 11.10
Do you see anything else that expresses immediacy? •

My response to Exercise 11.10
The "here" on the previous line. "here" and "now" is about as immedi-ate as you can get.

The "here" and "now" at the end of the poem certainly suggest that Cummings wanted to express the immediacy of the experience of beau-ty. He even skipped a line to set off "now" as the last word. Besides, the words aren't added to the poem as ideas. Instead, they emerge directly from the description of the scene. "Here" comes right out of "every-where," and "now" comes right out of "snow." "Here" and "now" are a part of the actual scene.

EXERCISE 11.11
Do you think the way Cummings brings notice to "here" and "now" proves that his purpose is to express the immediacy of the experience of beauty? •

I leave that up to you and ask you about something else in the poem. Did you notice the parentheses? Do they suggest any sort of pattern to you? They suggest one to me. If you draw a line connecting all the parenthe-ses, you get a waving line, which suggests to me the motion of falling snow. This may be accidental, but I doubt it. The poems seems, from what we have discussed so far, to be a very carefully crafted thing. Ob-viously, the short lines give the poem a vertical shape that suggests fall-ing. Why not then a motion within the shape? It would be a nice addi-tion to the poem, wouldn't it?

79

If the poet was this thoughtful and clever and careful and imaginative about every detail of the poem—and my guess is that he was, for remember, he was a painter too—then we have to ask why he broke up the words as he did. We have two reasons already. The first is to highlight "here" and "now." The second is to make the poem basically vertical. These reasons account for breaking up the words in general. They do not, however, account for breaking them up specifically in a non-syllabic fashion. What is gained, for example, by writing "unmea/ning" instead of "unmean/ing?" This is an important question about the poem because although it appears to be only a detail, it is critical to his most important break from the conventions of English.

EXERCISE 11.12
What, if anything, do you think is gained or lost by the non-syllabic breaking of the words? •

My response to Exercise 11.12
This is a hard question. It's puzzling because it would seem that he could accomplish what he wanted by breaking the words in the conventional way, the syllabic way. But he didn't, and perhaps we should assume, at least for the time being, that he had a purpose in mind, a purpose beyond just making the poem puzzling.

The poem is certainly more puzzling for the way he broke up the words. So why not ask what he gains by making the poem more puzzling? Well, it takes us longer to figure out what he is saying. Once we do, though, the poem is suddenly clear, at least what it says. So what has Cummings gained by creating such an experience of the poem for us, an experience of puzzlement to sudden clarity?

I think the poet wants to involve us in what he is saying. I think he wants to create an experience for us. I think he wants the particles of the poem, the broken words, to reassemble in our heads. He obviously wants us to like the poem better for the way it is written. That means the same as enjoying our experience of reading the poem. And if we enjoy reading the poem, perhaps we see the scene in a fresh, new way. Every poet wants to use the language so that it seems new and fresh because what the poet is expressing comes across directly, powerfully.

EXERCISE 11.13
Do you think the scene of the falling snow is more vivid for the way Cummings uses the language?

If your answer is "yes," then the poet has succeeded in doing exactly what the poem says. He has created for you an imaginative experience of the snow falling. This imaginative experience does not contain ideas. It is simply an imaginative experience that you have enjoyed. And isn't this precisely what the poem says, that beauty is an experience, not an idea? The snow isn't beautiful because of some way we can think about it. It is beautiful because that is how we experience it. We don't think about it being beautiful. It just *is* beautiful. We feel it. The experience is direct, powerful, clear, immediate. We don't need anybody to give us reasons why it's beautiful. We know it is beautiful.

EXERCISE 11.14

What do you think of what I have offered as a reason for the poet's non-syllabic way of breaking the words, namely that the poet wants the poem to be somewhat confusing at first in order to create for us an experience that demonstrates what he is saying in the poem about beauty? •

I want to leave this question with you. It's heady. The following discussion may help you form an opinion on this question.

Perhaps the easiest way to figure out what you really think about this poem is to consider how it would be if it had been written according to the conventions of English. For example:

> Beautiful
>
> is the unmeaning
> of silently falling
> everywhere snow

Or pulling back even farther to the conventions of English:

> Beautiful
>
> is the lack of meaning of snow
> falling silently everywhere

EXERCISE 11.15

Do you like either of these better than the poet's version? Why or why not? Perhaps you have another way that you prefer to the poet's version. •

My response to Exercise 11.15
I like the first one better than the second one, but I like the poet's version

best. Here is another version I like, though:

Beautiful

is silently
falling
everywhere
snow

But this version isn't really a variation on the poem because it removes the phrase "the unmeaning of." Still, the best way to see what you really think of the imaginative technique that Cummings came up with is to try it out yourself. Looking closely at his poem is fine for appreciating the possibilities of visual experimenting on a typewriter. But the best way to test the possibilities is to fool around with them yourself.

EXERCISE 11.16
Write a one-sentence description and break with any convention of English you choose to in order to highlight your meaning. •

EXERCISE 11.17
How do you like your poem? What conventions(s) did you choose to break? Do you think your poem is too confusing for a reader to understand? Or do you think it is more interesting and enjoyable for the way you chose to write it? •

The "Beautiful" poem is called an "ideogrammatic" poem. An "ideogram" is the picture of an idea, or an idea picture. This poem is ideogrammatic in that Cummings uses visual (or pictorial) ways to express an idea. As a painter, Cummings was particularly aware of the pictorial dimension of a poem, so it's only natural that he wrote many ideogrammatic poems. Here's another ideogrammatic poem by Cummings:

l(a

le
af
fa

ll

s)
one
l

iness

Can you read this? It's harder, isn't it? Cummings certainly pushed the technique further than in the poem "Beautiful." "Beautiful" is one sentence, whereas here you don't even have a sentence. But that deosn't mean you can't read it.

EXERCISE 11.18
What is outside the parentheses and what is inside the parentheses? •

My response to Exercise 11.18
The word "loneliness" is outside the parentheses, and "a leaf falls" is inside the parentheses.

The poem is just an image of an idea. "A leaf falls" is an image of "loneliness." The poem is set vertically, like "Beautiful," for the same reason, to set off a falling effect. The poem is different, though, for the way the poet uses parentheses.

EXERCISE 11.19
How is the poet's use of parentheses different in this poem from his use of parentheses in "Beautiful?" •

My response to Exercise 11.19
In this poem he sets the parentheses within a word. This he did not do in "Beautiful."

The poet's use of parentheses is more unconventional in this poem.

EXERCISE 11.20
Why do you think Cummings uses parentheses in such a unique way in this poem? •

My response to Exercise 11:20
He is probably trying to draw the image and the idea as close together as he can.

Cummings is not only an innovative poet, a poet who likes to experiment with the language, but he is also a very clever, playful poet. For example, he has a trick up his sleeve in this poem. He uses the idea of *oneness* to enhance the effect of loneliness. Take a look at how many times the idea of *one* appears in the poem.

EXERCISE 11.21
How many times does the idea of one appear in this poem? •

My response to Exercise 11.21

The idea of one occurs in the first line with the first *l* of "loneliness." The *l* by itself looks like a 1 (the number one). The idea of one occurs again in the first line with the *a*. The idea occurs again in line 2 with the *l* and twice in line five with the two *l*'s. It occurs in line 7 with the word "one," and again in line 7 if you bring down the *l* from the first line, past the parentheses, and join it up with the word "one," which makes "lone." The next line, the next-to-last of the poem, has another *l* in it, and the last line completes the word "loneliness." Also, the whole poem looks like a one, coming down in almost exactly the same width to the bottom, "iness," which is longer, like the base of a one. Now I don't know if you would count all these, but if you do you would have the idea of one occuring nine times. That's nine times in nine lines. Does *that* make another *one*?

Pretty clever. Too clever? The poem is certainly an image of its meaning. You may even feel that the poem is more of a picture than it is a group of words.

EXERCISE 11.22

Do you like the poem more or less for being more ideogrammatic than "Beautiful?" Which poem do you prefer? •

Cummings certainly pushed this technique a long way. I really like the way lines 3 and 4 are a mirror image of one another, as if the leaf is floating back and forth, and then how the next line, the two verticals, speeds up the descent.

If you had seen this poem first, I wonder if you could have read it. It might have appeared at first glance to be indecipherable, unreadable. But we know that it isn't, and we can see, with our understanding of conventions, exactly what Cummings did to make the poem visually interesting. Perhaps you would have seen this without your understanding of conventions, but maybe not as quickly, and you might not have been as sure that you were right.

EXERCISE 11.23

Pick a single word (such as "incredible") and write down the first part of it. Then interrupt it by opening a parenthesis, like this:

In(

Then write the part that goes inside the parentheses; for example:

In(
the d
og s
poke
Eng
lish
)

Then add the rest of the original word:

In(
the d
og s
poke
Eng
lish
)credible

Instead of making it a skinny poem, you could do a fatter version, as in:

Ou(just as I dropped the brick on my bare feet the books fell off the top shelf onto my head and you swung around and knocked my glasses off)ch!

Or you could use multiple parentheses to keep opening parentheses inside parentheses, like Chinese boxes:

I (((my hair is blond ((the wheat is ripe (my uncle was in the Navy) and waving)) and long))) laugh.

Give it a try. •

CHAPTER 12

Indecipherable Literature

You might think the second poem by E. E. Cummings is as far as some-one can go in fooling around with the conventions of language and still try to make something interesting, something that people will want to read again. But there is another kind of writing that makes even this second poem look pretty simple, yet once you figure it out, it too is really easy.

> 'Twas brillig, and the slithy toves
>   Did gyre and gimble in the wabe:
> All mimsy were the borogoves,
>   And the mome raths outgrabe.

Does this make any sense at all? What are these words? Are they English? Are they hiding meaning behind them? Is this some sort of code or cipher? Is this secret writing?

EXERCISE 12.1
Read the four lines aloud a couple of times, until it's easy to say the words. Don't read them in a bored or flat tone of voice: put some dramatic expression in it.

Then ask yourself: now do the lines have a slightly different feeling for you? •

Perhaps you know these lines. They are from "Jabberwocky," by Lewis Carroll, who wrote *Alice in Wonderland*. They are nonsense. They are also famous nonsense. So maybe there is a difference between good nonsense and bad nonsense. I will leave that up to you, but one thing is certain about these lines from "Jabberwocky": they sure create a mood. But how can they do that if they are nonsense? This is a pretty good question, and you can answer it. Use your understanding of the conventions of English. These lines may be nonsense, but that doesn't mean Lewis Carroll ignored the conventions of English altogether. Perhaps he created the mood through a careful use of the conventions. Does that mean we can decipher the lines? What do you think? Let's see.

EXERCISE 12.2
Did Lewis Carroll follow any of the conventions of English in writing these lines from "Jabberwocky"? •

My response to Exercise 12.2
Yes, he did. He used the alphabet. He made words by leaving a space before and after each word. He set the lines so that they read from left to right and then from top to bottom. He sequenced the words—at least he seems to have—in a way that creates some sort of overall meaning, or maybe it is better to say feeling. And he used signaling devices; he punctuated and capitalized.

So one could say that Lewis Carroll used all five conventions. That doesn't mean that you can read it and figure out a meaning. It just means that the lines read as English or like English.

EXERCISE 12.3
Then what makes these lines hard to decipher? •

My response to Exercise 12.3
Obviously, the words themselves make it hard to read. He made up words. They aren't in the dictionary.

Yes, Lewis Carroll made up words. He made up so many words that either the lines are just for fun or are in some sort of code. But he didn't make up *all* the words. As a matter of fact, did he make up even half of the words in these four lines? No, he didn't. He made up 11 words, and there are 23 words in these four lines. The exact number isn't the point, obviously. It is the effect he creates by the words he did make up.

EXERCISE 12.4
Did he make up the more important or the less important words? •

My response to Exercise 12.4
In terms of our being able to understand the meaning, he made up the more important words.

It's hard to say much more than "more important" words without trying to figure out what the lines may mean. So instead of taking on that problem first, let's look at the words he did not make up, to see what kind of words they are.

Let's look at the first line. The words he didn't make up are "'twas" (an old form of "it was"), "and," and "the." In the second line the regular English words are "did," "and," "in," and "the." Look at the regular words of lines 3 and 4. What sort of words do you have in the four lines? What do you want to call them? The little words? The extra words? How about the helping words, or the secondary words? Actually, there aren't many.

EXERCISE 12.5
How many regular English words are used in the four lines? •

My response to Exercise 12.5
Seven, counting "'twas" as one.

Are these seven, regular English, little words enough to tie together the four lines so that they really do resemble English? Let's see. Let's look at the first line. The made-up words are "brillig," "slithy," and "toves." Let's try to ask two questions of these words at the same time. What do the words sound like, and what sort of word are they likely to be? In other words, does the sound of the word suggest an English word, and what is the grammatical function of each word?

EXERCISE 12.6
Try the sound association question out on the three made-up words (*brillig, slithy, toves*) of line 1: what do they sound like? What do they suggest? •

My response to Exercise 12.6
The sound of "brillig" doesn't suggest a particular word in English to me. If anything, it's the sound a frog might make, but I probably think of that because "toves" sounds like "toads." The mood of the four lines makes me read "brillig" as if it means something like "misty" or "spooky." "Slithy" sounds like "slimy."

You may have different answers to Exercise 12.6, but let's use the ones I offered, in order to check out what sort of words fit grammatically.

EXERCISE 12.7

What sort of word can "brillig" be? To use the language of grammar, what part of speech can "brillig" be? •

My response to Exercise 12.7

"Brillig" can be either an adjective, as in "'twas misty," or a verb, the main verb of a phrase like "'twas finished."

I vote for the adjective because of the feel of the word and because its second syllable doesn't suggest to me a verb.

EXERCISE 12.8

How about "slithy toves?" What parts of speech could they be? •

My response to Exercise 12.8

I think "slithy" is an adjective, like "slimy," and "toves" is a noun, like "toads."

Can you see reasons to support these guesses? Do adjectives usually come before nouns or after nouns? Before. Right. Besides, the *y* ending of "slithy" suggests that it's an adjective, like "bumpy," "sleepy," and "sleezy." How about "toves?" Sure, perhaps there are some adjectives ending in *s*, but *s* is the common way to make a plural in English. So the percentages favor "slithy" being an adjective and "toves" being a noun. That doesn't mean they are. It means that we *read* them that way. Lewis Carroll is using more than sound-resemblance to suggest a meaning for his made-up words; he is using the fourth convention of sequencing, too. He is *also* using the way we spell in English, particularly the ending of our words.

EXERCISE 12.9

What parts of speech are "gyre " and "gimble" likely to be? •

My response to Exercise 12.9

"Gyre" and "gimble" are likely to be verbs because they are preceded by "Did," which appears to be their helping verb as in "Did jump and jangle" or "Did gyrate and gambol."

"Gyre" is actually an English word. It is a noun, but for it to be a noun here it would have to be a collective noun as in "He made trouble." But look what would happen to "gyre" and "gimble" if each word ended in *s*.

EXERCISE 12.10

If we added an *s*, what part of speech would "gyres" and "gimbles" appear to be? •

My response to Exercise 12.10

"Gyres" and "gimbles" would appear to be nouns, as in "Did jumps and cartwheels."

We can be sure that "wabe" is a noun because of "in the" that precedes it. Why? Because "in" is a preposition and a preposition takes either a noun or a pronoun to complete a prepositional phrase.

EXERCISE 12.11

Then why can't "wabe" be a pronoun? •

My response to Exercise 12.11

"Wabe" can't be a pronoun because it is preceded by "the." For "wabe" to be a pronoun the phrase would have to be "in wabe" as in the phrase "in them" or "in it." We don't say "in the them" or "in the it."

All right, how about the third line? If "borogoves" is a noun — and it sure looks like one with that final *s* — then "mimsy" must be. . .what? The only part of speech it can be is an adjective, as in "All cozy were the. . . ." What are these "borogoves" anyway, some sort of fantastic beavers?

These first three lines are pretty easy for figuring out possibilities for the parts of speech of the made-up words. At least they are easy compared to the fourth line. Here we have only two regular English words and they appear together at the beginning of the line. Then we have three made-up words in a row. You see what happens when you leave out the little, helping words? Trouble. This is hard. But let's try.

Let's try "mome" and "raths" together. Well, "raths" has an *s* at the end of it, so it could be a plural noun like "rats" or "rafts" (but not "wrath"). But verbs end with *s* sometimes too. How about "screams" or "rants"?

EXERCISE 12.12

Why can't "raths" be a verb like "screams" or "rants"? •

My response to Exercise 12.12
Because those verbs are in the present tense and the three lines before are in the past tense — "'Twas," "Did gyre and gimble," and "were."

EXERCISE 12.13
If, then, "raths" can't be a verb and is a noun, what is "mome"? •

My response to Exercise 12.13
"Mome" is probably an adjective because the common place for an adjective is before the noun when an adjective and noun are written together. Also, "mome" is preceded by "the."

The "the" is important here. Take it out and for "And mome raths outgrabe" you could have "madly rats scamper." But with "the" in the line where it is, "mome" must be an adjective because you can't say "And the madly rats scamper" if "madly" is meant to be an adverb rather than an adjective.

EXERCISE 12.14
If "mome" is an adjective modifying the noun "raths," then what is "outgrabe"? •

My response to Exercise 12.14
"Outgrabe" is a verb.

"Outgrabe" is a wonderful made-up word because it looks like "out grab" and sounds like "out grave," neither of which really makes sense, but which certainly convey a mood.

"The Jabberwocky" is nonsense. Nonsense is not meant to be deciphered. This poem cannot really be deciphered. But that doesn't mean we don't get some sort of meaning from it even if the meaning is primarily one of mood. (As Alice said in Wonderland, "Somehow it seems to fill my head with ideas — only I don't exactly know what they are!") Not only that, we can and did figure out how the words work together. We couldn't have done it without the little, helping English words because they act as the glue to hold the made-up words together. Sound association helped us, too. And sound is a very important part of the pleasure that Lewis Carroll has created for us.

As we found out, the suggested meaning or meanings of the words do not come from sound alone. It also comes from the relationships of the words. From these relationships we can figure out what part of speech each word is or probably is. The sequence of the words is important to our deciphering work. So is the way the words were written, especially the endings, because then we could use grammar to help us. Working with all these possibilities—sound, sequence, spelling, and grammar—is to work *in context.* Remember?

EXERCISE 12.15
Remove from Carroll's four lines the words

> brillig
> slithy
> toves
> gyre
> gimble
> wabe
> mimsy
> borogoves
> mome
> raths
> outgrabe

and replace them with new nonsense words you make up and which have the same number of syllables as the words they replace. For example, "brillig" could be replaced by "hodo." (Optional: make your version use rhyme or off-rhyme, the way Carroll's does.) •

My response to Exercise 12.15
'Twas goonig and the fritty javes
  Did grink and gruddle in the flangs:
All sloozy were the gidderraves
    And the groon crads zopjang.

EXERCISE 12.16
Make a list of nonsense words, some short, some medium, some long. Use them in a sentence. •

My response to Exercise 12.16
Porf, deducamify, ot, zurt, othebon, murty, semblam, tor, hame, leated. Sentence: To deducamify the porf I had to tor the leated othebon, semblam the ot, and hame the murty zurt.

EXERCISE 12.17
Use your nonsense sentence as the opening of a story or short prose sketch.

Let the sentence kind of float around in your head. See what it makes you think of. (Mine makes me think of a worker in a factory in the future or in another galaxy, explaining how he (it?) repaired a machine. •

CHAPTER 13

Difficult Language

Are the deciphering techniques you have good enough to crack any kind of difficult writing? I wish it were true, but it isn't. Some kind of writing is simply too hard to decipher by the kind of effort that we have been making. And if I didn't tell you that, it wouldn't be fair. It's also important to give you some examples so that you'll know when to expect problems.

EXERCISE 13.1
How would you describe the kind of writing that would be, as far as you are concerned, the hardest to decipher, to understand? •

My response to Exercise 13.1
I think the hardest kind of writing would be full of lots of big words discussing a subject I know nothing about.

Yes, writing that demands a lot of knowledge about a particular subject would be hard for the average person to decipher fully. And the more specialized the field, the more difficult the writing will be.

But does language that is very hard to understand occur only in books? What I mean is, is difficult language always formal? Is it based on what you can learn only in school, for example? What about slang? I'll bet you know some words of slang that your parents, for example, don't know. Slang is not just new words; sometimes slang is a new meaning given to an old word.

EXERCISE 13.2
Can you think of a regular word that has been adopted by young people to express high approval? For example, what might you substitute for "wonderful" in the sentence "That is wonderful!"? •

My response to Exercise 13.2

The word I am thinking of is "awesome." It is a regular word I have heard used in this way lately.

Did you pick a different word? There are many — and they keep changing. Slang is always changing. Slang words rise and fall in popularity like a popular song. Some slang words and phrases do last. And slang develops differently in different areas. For example, if you moved to a different part of the country, you might hear different slang, so different that you couldn't understand it.

Slang is a special language, just as is the language of a particular field of study. Slang is at one pole of special language. Learned language is at the other pole. One is informal, the other is formal. The hardest new language to decipher is at either of the two poles of language: the informal (like slang) and the formal (like language in a book of a specialized field of study).

For example, the phrase "in your face" and the word "interface" would be hard to understand unless you had particular knowledge. In the sentence "I am going to shoot the ball in your face," it sounds as if the speaker is going to hit the other person with the ball. But "in your face" doesn't mean that. This usage of the phrase comes from basketball. The speaker is challenging the other person. No matter how closely the other person guards the speaker to prevent him or her from shooting, the speaker is contending that he or she is not only going to get the shot off, but do so by going right through or over the other person, and to score, too. The phrase is meant to challenge, obviously, but not to threaten the other person.

"In your face" is an example of informal language. "Interface" is formal language. "Interface" is a new word from computer terminology that is used often in business. In the sentence "We should interface with the new group," do you know what "interface" means? If not, the meaning of this sentence may not be clear. As in "in your face," the word "face" is the noticeable part of "interface." But what could it mean?

The meaning of the word isn't precise. "Interface" means "to relate to," but that isn't very clear either. In the example above, "interface" means to talk with and get to know, to establish a relationship.

If you are not around people who use the word "interface," you are not likely to know its meaning. Therefore, if you were to come across it first in written form, you would have difficulty understanding it, even if the context were helpful. The same is true for "in your face." If you are not around people using the phrase, you are not likely to know its meaning.

But of the two—"interface" and "in your face"—the slang term is probably going to be easier to understand because, as a rule, slang is more suggestive than formal language. Formal language tends to be abstract. For example:

> Gestalt psychology has demonstrated that we may know a physiognomy by integrating our awareness of its particulars without being able to identify these particulars, and my analysis of knowledge is closely linked to this discovery of Gestalt psychology.

This passage is hard. We are told that "Gestalt psychology"—whatever that is—has apparently "demonstrated" something, and the writer's "analysis of knowledge is closely linked to this discovery," whatever it is. But do we really understand what the writer is saying? Not likely. Some of the words here may be unfamiliar. But more important, what is the writer talking about? We need to know what the writer's subject is and then what he or she is saying about it. Sure, we are told the subject in the first two words, "Gestalt psychology." But what is that?

EXERCISE 13.3
Say you run across a passage about a special subject, such as Gestalt psychology, and you want to see if you can decipher the passage. What can you do? •

My response to Exercise 13.3
You can look the term up in the dictionary.

In this case, you could look up both words separately and then see if under "Gestalt" there is any mention of "Gestalt psychology." The dictionary is a good tool for this kind of detective work, or "research." Not only scientists perform research, but also anyone who looks for additional information about a particular topic.

EXERCISE 13.4
Can you think of another tool for "researching" the meaning of "Gestalt psychology?" •

My response to Exercise 13.4
Another research tool is the encyclopedia.

You are likely to find more about Gestalt psychology in an encyclopedia than in a dictionary.

There are other things you can do, too. If the writing comes from a magazine, check the start of the article. Read the title and the first couple of paragraphs. This may help. Flip through the magazine to get a sense of the other articles. Then read the last couple of paragraphs of the article. If the passage comes from a book, turn to the front. Try reading its preface. If you can make any sense of the preface, you may gain information that will help clarify the meaning of the passage you are trying to decipher.

Some writing, like that in the newspaper, is meant to be easy for just about everybody to read. Other writing is meant to be easy and clear only to some people, because the writer is writing for an audience that already knows a lot about the topic at hand. To understand a medical textbook, you have to know first a lot about biology and chemistry. Technical books on computer science sound like gibberish until you learn about computers. When you try to read difficult, specialized books, don't be discouraged: you aren't stupid, you just don't yet have the background knowledge necessary to understand them.

Once you have the background knowledge of a subject, you might go on and make important discoveries. Why not? Who says you can't? Or you might push the subject into new areas. Take computers, for example. When they first came out, we saw only numbers and letters on the screen. Who would have thought of pictures? Who would have thought of making a computer that you could program to make pictures?

Someone did. Someone experimented with computers to see if a computer could be adapted to make pictures, and from this experimenting came computer graphics. That is the name of the new field of making pictures with computers. These pictures make computer arcade games look terrific.

A new field develops its own language. Just as each sport has its own special terms — official and unofficial — so does computer graphics. So does microelectronics. So does biotechnology. These are all new fields. Between the time you began school and the time you finish school, more new fields will develop. You may go into a field of work that doesn't exist today. This is why your teachers insist that the most important thing to do in school is to learn to think — and the second is to learn to express yourself clearly. Think clearly, read well, and write clearly — that's what counts. Then you can take on any specialized language, even ones that don't exist yet.

But does that mean that you should automatically respect all special writing of a formal kind? You learn in school to respect writing that sounds important, that sounds learned and serious. But this doesn't mean that all specialized writing is for real. Some writers may be bluffing. They may just want to *sound* good. They may want to impress their readers, without committing themselves to saying anything specific. They use fancy phrases to disguise their lack of content. As long as they are good at handling the special language, they figure that they can get away with saying next to nothing. So you don't have to assume that everything that looks impressive is genuine. Just because a piece of writing may sound learned and profound, that doesn't mean it really is. So challenge the writing. Look at it closely. Try to get past the special vocabulary and see what, if anything, the writer is actually saying. The less the writer seems to be saying, the more suspicious you should become.

Good writers have been reminding us for many years that overblown writing is just a disguise. The modern English writer George Orwell is well known for his novels *1984* and *Animal Farm*; he deserves credit too for his essay "Politics and the English Language." In this essay, Orwell cites examples of vague, pretentious writing in science, business, education, art, politics, and psychology. Orwell claims that "this mixture of vagueness and sheer incompetence is the most marked characteristic of modern English prose, and especially of any kind of political writing." To get his point across, Orwell cites a well-known verse from Ecclesiastes in the Bible:

> I returned and saw under the sun, that the race is not to the swift, nor the battle to the strong, neither yet bread to the wise, nor yet riches to men of understanding, nor yet favour to men of skill; but time and change happeneth to them all.

And then Mr. Orwell rewrites this passage in a parody (making fun) of modern overblown English:

> Objective consideration of contemporary phenomena compels the conclusion that success or failure in competitive activities exhibits no tendency to be commensurate with innate capacity, but that a considerable element of the unpredictable must inevitably be taken into account.

A wonderful word for the phony kind of writing that is creeping more and more into our life is "gobbledygook." Stuart Chase uses this word as the title of an essay in which he takes up where Orwell left off. Chase makes fun of pretentious language by "translating" passages of it, or, you might say, deciphering it. For example:

A New Zealand official made the following report after surveying a plot of ground for an athletic field:

"It is obvious from the difference in elevation with relation to the short depth of the property that the contour is such as to preclude any reasonable development for active recreation."

Seems that the plot was too steep.

An office manager sent this memo to his chief:

"Verbal contact with Mr. Blank regarding the attached notification of promotion has elicited the attached representation intimating that he prefers to decline the assignment."

Seems that Mr. Blank didn't want the job.

EXERCISE 13.5

Can you write a short, clear sentence and then rewrite it in a long, vague way? Overdo it. Have some fun. Write it so badly that you are sure that no one would ever take it seriously. You might be surprised, though. •

My response to Exercise 13.5

Here is my short sentence: "You may not go because I say so." And here is the same sentence rewritten in overblown language:

> Because of my recognition of what is and is not most beneficial to your maturation as a young person who cannot yet critically discriminate, you may not attend the social occasion of dubious merit.

If you would like to have a little checklist against bad writing, George Orwell offers a good one in his essay:

1. Never use a metaphor, simile, or other figure of speech which you are used to seeing in print.
2. Never use a long word where a short one will do.
3. If it is possible to cut a word out, always cut it out.
4. Never use the passive [voice] where you can use the active [voice].
5. Never use a foreign phrase, a scientific word or a jargon word if you can think of an everyday English equivalent.
6. Break any of these rules sooner than say anything outright barbarous.

These rules, written in 1945, just after World War II, will do just fine today.

CHAPTER 14

Ciphers Invented by Writers

UG2! UIdwo 10Bbzug
8bo ub oguoo 23 ub
UGO UVdwo bg o=kv
∧2bz bg UGO #hzo
bz ózuGoθ 12Ró

Can you read this? It's in Middle English. Dirty trick, huh? I can't read it either. Maybe I could if I spent days on it. You probably could too. But at least we have heard of the person who wrote it, Geoffrey Chaucer. Do you remember him? Do you remember your deciphering of a passage from Middle English? It began, "Whan that Aprill with its shoures soote," the first line to the *Prologue to the Canterbury Tales* (Chapter 8). Chaucer wrote other things, too. He was interested in ciphers. He made up his own cipher alphabet. It's used in the cryptogram above. "Cryptogram" means "secret writing." "Crypt" means "secret" and "gram" means "writing."

Another writer of the Middle Ages, Roger Bacon, an English monk, wrote in *Secret Works of Art and the Nullity of Magic* (what a title!), "A man is crazy who writes a secret in any other way than one which will conceal it from the vulgar." (The word "vulgar" refers here to ignorant people.) In this book written in the mid-1200s, Bacon listed seven ways to disguise written meaning systematically.

Are Bacon and Chaucer the only writers to work with ciphers? No, writers have always been fascinated by codes and ciphers, just as many

100

mathematicians have. Do you recall deciphering the poem "Jabberwocky" in Chapter 12? Lewis Carroll wrote the poem, as you know, as well as *Alice's Adventures in Wonderland* and *Through the Looking Glass*. Both a writer and a mathematician, Lewis Carroll invented a cipher, which he published anonymously in 1868. Here it is (fig. 3).

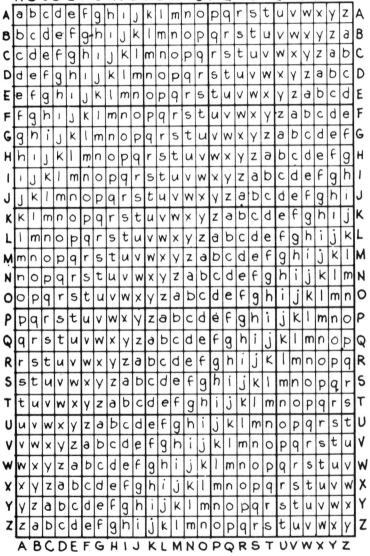

Figure 3

The first row along the top, under the line, is the alphabet in its regular order of letters. Each row that follows is the alphabet shifted one position to the left. Therefore, the second row starts with *b* and the third with *c* and so on. The cipher does require a "key word," though. A "key word" is the word used to begin enciphering or deciphering a cipher message—it helps *unlock* the mystery. Lewis Carroll, in his explanation of the cipher, used the word VIGILANCE to illustrate the cipher method with the message MEET ME ON TUESDAY EVENING AT SEVEN. The key word is written above the message, repeated as often as necessary.

V I G I L A N C E V I G I L A N C E V I G I L A N C E V I

M E E T M E O N T U E S D A Y E V E N I N G A T S E V E N

The first letter of the enciphered message becomes *V* because it is above the first letter of the actual message, *M*. So you go to the column of the cipher grid (called a "matrix") under *V*. Then you move down the *V* column until you come to the row marked *M* (capital *M* outside the lines on both the right and left side). The letter here at the meeting of column *V* and row *M* is *h*. So *h* is the first letter of the cryptogram.

Try the second letter. The second letter of the message is *E*. The letter above it in the key word VIGILANCE is *I*. So go to column *I*. Then down to row *E*. The letter there is *m*.

EXERCISE 14.1
Can you encipher the first three words, MEET ME ON, in Lewis Carroll's cipher? •

My response to Exercise 14.1
The first three words MEET ME ON become hmkb xe bp.

The entire message MEET ME ON TUESDAY EVENING AT SEVEN is hmkb xe bp xpmylly rxiiqto lt fgzzv.

How would someone decipher this? Without knowing the key word and the idea behind the cipher matrix, I don't know how someone would begin to decipher the message.

Writers have not only invented ciphers and codes, they have put them in their books. In 1852, Thackeray put a cipher in his novel *The History of Henry Esmond*. Jules Verne began *Voyage to the Center of the Earth* with a three-step cryptogram. Rudyard Kipling put a cipher in "The First Letter," one of the stories in the *Just So Stories* for children. Here is Kipling's own drawing (fig. 4).

Figure 4

Kipling says that the strange signs are magic letters, but they are a substitution cipher spelling out THIS IS THE STORY OF TAFFIMAI, ALL WRITTEN OUT ON AN OLD TUSK.

Deciphering work is like detective work; you have to figure out the scheme and then work through the details. So detective stories are a natural place for codes and ciphers to appear. And the great detective hero is a master of cryptanalysis, of course. Figure 5 shows a cryptogram in *The Adventures of Sherlock Holmes* by Sir Arthur Conan Doyle.

Figure 5

Here is the passage from the book about this "Dancing Man" cipher:

> "Why, Holmes, it is a child's drawing," cried Dr. John Watson when he first saw the above figures penciled on a page torn from a notebook. But Sherlock Holmes recognized it immediately as a substitution cipher. The message is AM HERE ABE SLANEY. The little flags mark the end of words.
>
> "I am fairly familiar with all forms of secret writing," Holmes declared, "and am myself the author of a trifling monograph upon the subject, in which I analyze one hundred and sixty separate ciphers..."

Have you ever heard the expression "Who knows what evil lurks in the hearts of men? The Shadow knows"? The Shadow was a mysterious, crime-fighting hero of a popular comic strip in the 1930s, which later became a radio show. Created by Maxwell Grant — pseudonym (false name) for Walter Gibson — the Shadow was ingenious with ciphers. Look at figure 6 for one from the story "The Chain of Death."

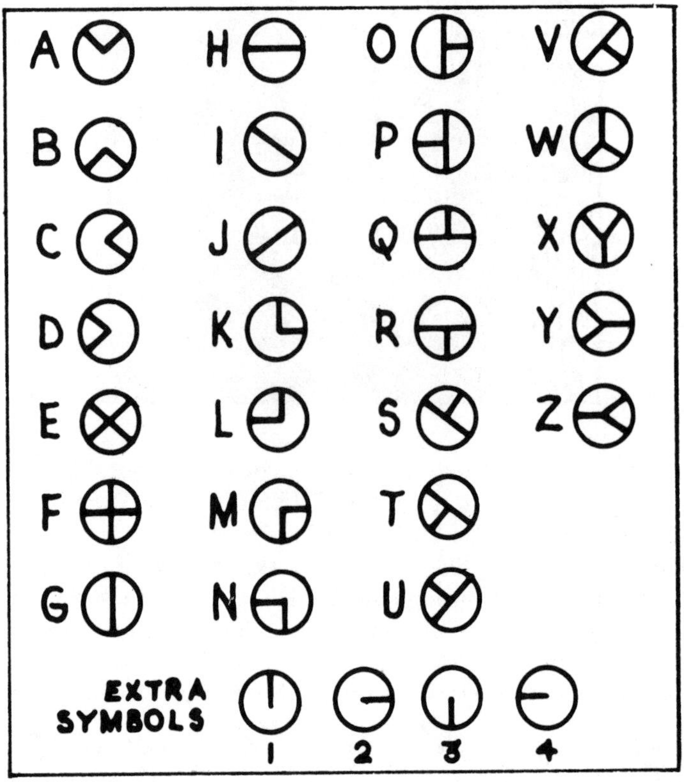

Figure 6

Do you see the four "extra symbols" at the bottom? Do you see how each one is pointing differently? Inserting an extra symbol in a cryptogram means that the reader is to turn the cryptogram in that direction to continue reading. An extra symbol may be inserted anywhere. For example, the word "help" would read

104

Right? Now let's put an extra symbol in the middle. Let's put extra symbol #3 ⊘ between the *e* and the *l*. When we do, the letters that come after the extra symbol are changed in position. Extra symbol #3, with its line pointing down, means that the next letters are to be turned downward, which is half way around the circle. "Help" would then read

EXERCISE 14.2

Can you encipher the word GOLD in this cipher and insert an extra symbol half way through and change the last two letters accordingly? •

My response to Exercise 14.2

This is GOLD with the extra symbol #2, which calls for a quarter turn clockwise.

In the modern novel *Darkness at Noon* by Arthur Koestler, the story opens with the main character Rubashov being imprisoned. Rubashov hears a tapping on the wall of the cell next to him. The tapping goes 2, pause, 5, long pause, 3, pause, 2, long pause, 4, pause, 3. Rubashov guesses that this is a message. 2-5 3-2 4-3. What does it mean? The way the numbers are paired up may give you a hint about the cipher. Write the numbers one through five down the left column. Then write the same numbers, one through five, along the top, from left to right. Then, beginning in the upper lefthand space, write the alphabet down the first column, then the second column, and so on. With 25 spaces you have to leave out one letter because the alphabet contains 26 letters. I will leave out the letter J.

EXERCISE 14.3

Can you make this cipher? •

My response to Exercise 14.3
Here is the cipher, following the instructions above:

	1	2	3	4	5
1	A	F	L	Q	V
2	B	G	M	R	W
3	C	H	N	S	X
4	D	I	O	T	Y
5	E	K	P	U	Z

Each letter has a pair of numbers. The first number is the one from the lefthand column. The second number is from the series across the top. For example, the pair of numbers for *R* is 2-4. The pair of numbers for *K* is 5-2. The pair of numbers for *Y* is 4-5. This cipher is called the "Checkerboard Cipher." It is also called the "quadratic alphabet." Now let's see if we can decipher the message sent to Rubashov through the wall of his cell.

EXERCISE 14.4
Can you figure out the message 2-5 3-2 4-3? •

My response to Exercise 14.4
The message spells out W-H-O.

EXERCISE 14.5
If you wanted to reply with only your first name, what would you tap on the cell wall? •

My response to Exercise 14.5
I would tap out 5-3 5-1 4-4 5-1 2-4 to spell P-E-T-E-R.

Speaking of tapping: do you know how tap dancing began? In 1746 there was a slave rebellion in the Carolinas. The Blacks used drums to call each other to march. When the rebellion was put down, a law was enacted making it illegal for Blacks to play drums. So the Blacks cleverly used foot tapping as a secret way of communicating, and this evolved into tap dancing.

Codes and ciphers appear frequently in literature, from the short stories of O. Henry to the mysteries of Agatha Christie. Perhaps you could think up a story that revolves around figuring out a secret message. The writer who made this popular is Edgar Allan Poe. His most famous story of this kind is "The Gold Bug." Do you know it? An amateur naturalist sketches a gold-colored bug on a piece of parchment and, in showing it to his friend, holds it near a fire, which reveals a death's-head on the parchment. Intrigued, he searches more. A cryptogram (secret message). The story involves his deciphering the cryptogram and finding a pirate's treasure. Here is the cryptogram.

```
53‡‡†305))6*;4826)4‡.
)4‡);806*;48†8¶60))85
;1‡(;:‡*8†83(88)5*†;46
(;88*96?;8)‡(;485);5
*†2:*‡(;4956*2(5*–4)8¶
8*;4069285);)6‡‡;1
(‡9;48081;8:‡1;48†85
;4)485†528806*81(‡9;48
;(88;4(‡?34;48)4‡;161
;:188;‡?;
```

The cryptogram, a substitution cipher in invisible ink written without word divisions by the pirate Captain Kidd, says

A good glass in the bishop's hostel in the devil's seat—forty-one degrees and thirteen minutes—northeast by north—main branch seventh limb east side — shoot from the left eye of the death's-head — a beeline from the tree through the shot fifty feet out.

Poe, one of the first outstanding American writers, deserves recognition as the person who popularized cryptology (the study of secret writing) in the United States, not only for his stories but for the challenge he gave the public to send him any cryptogram to solve. He sent out this challenge in 1839 through the newspaper for which he worked, *Alexander's Weekly Messenger* in Philadelphia. The newspaper was swamped with mail. Poe solved one cryptogram after another — and never revealed how he did it. Once he said he would tell, then said he wouldn't. Better for business I guess. Poe became famous as a cryptologist. He claimed, "It may be roundly asserted that human ingenuity cannot concoct a cipher which human ingenuity cannot resolve." So far Poe has not been proven wrong.

Do you keep a diary? If so, is it secret? If you don't keep a diary or journal, do you think you might some day? Since a diary is the most personal kind of writing, the question naturally arises as to how private you want to keep it. Sure, you can hide it, but an even safer means is, of course, secret writing.

EXERCISE 14.6
Assuming you kept a diary, would you use secret writing? •

My response to Exercise 14.6
I don't keep a diary, but if I did, I would write only parts in secret writing, because it would take so long to write it all in code or cipher. But I would encipher random passages at the beginning so that if someone

found it and read it and deciphered the early, enciphered passages, he or she would not assume that later enciphered passages were particularly personal, or should I say juicy? Pretty clever, huh? Probably not.

Do you think there is such a thing as the most famous secret diary, among those that have been found and deciphered? Well, there is. At least in literature, and there is proof: the diary of Samuel Pepys, published in 1825, has been in print ever since. The diary is included in many literature and English history courses.

The diary was written long before it was published. Samuel Pepys kept his diary from 1660 to 1669, writing 3,000 pages in shorthand. Shorthand had just been invented, so only a few people knew about it. Besides, Pepys told only a few people that he was writing a diary. At his death, the diary stayed at Magdalene College in England for about 20

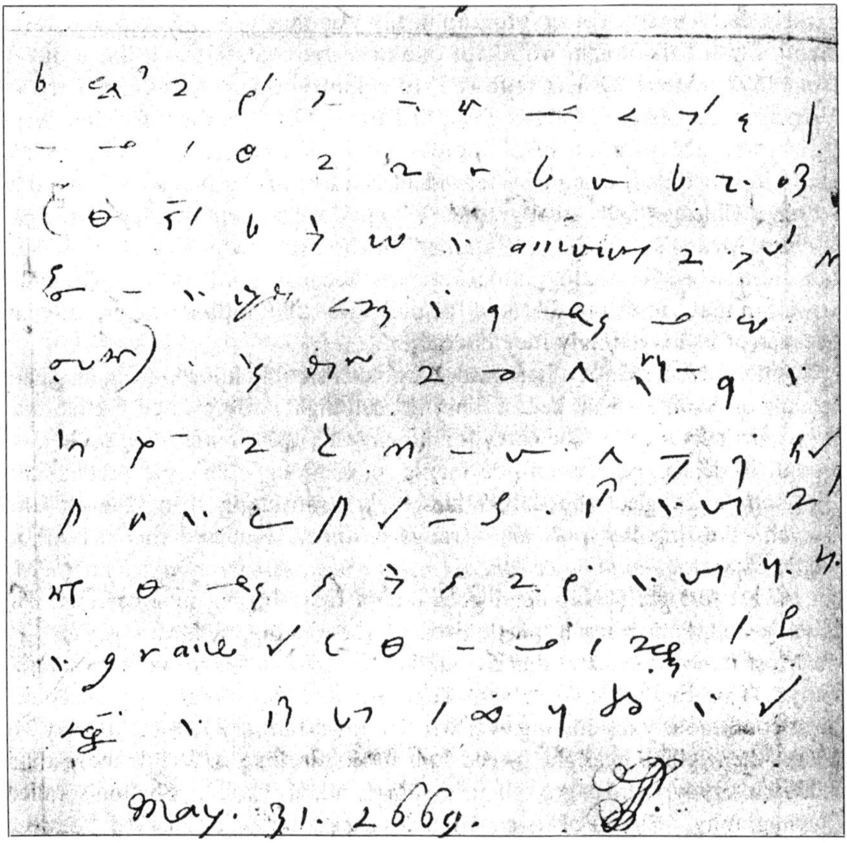

Figure 7

years, untouched. Then the master of the college, who had known Pepys, decided to look at it for what it might add to contemporary English naval history, for Pepys had held positions in the Navy. The college master couldn't read it, so he gave it to someone who might be able to, who struggled with a few pages, and handed it on to an undergraduate at another college. The young man spent about 12 hours a day for three years, deciphering the entire diary.

Figure 7 is a page from the diary written in shorthand. The value turned out not to be for naval history but for the intimate portrait of an interesting person.

Perhaps the most bizarre tale of writing and cryptology is a story of someone trying to prove that the alleged writer did not in fact write the works attributed to him. How does one try to do this from looking only at the work itself? One would look for some sign of the actual writer giving away his identity in the book itself.

There is a single, most famous effort of cryptological detective work to prove that the works attributed to one man were actually written by another, under a pseudonym. And the reason for this fame is partly due to the writer. Which writer in the English language would attract the most attention for such a claim? The most famous writer in English, naturally — William Shakespeare. Wouldn't it be something to prove that Shakespeare was not Shakespeare after all, but someone else? Here is a passage from a diary written in 1882, here in the United States:

> "I have been working. . . at what I think is a great discovery I have made, to wit: a cypher in Shakespeare's plays. . . asserting Francis Bacon's authorship of all plays. . . I am certain there is a cypher there, and I think I have the key; all this cannot be accident."

("Cypher" is an earlier spelling of "cipher.") The writer is Ignatius Donnelly, a colorful American political figure from Minnesota who served in the House of Representatives. Voted out of office in 1878, Donnelly turned to writing about his two pet theories: the existence of Atlantis and the catastrophic prehistoric collision of the earth with a comet. In 1882 appeared his book on Atlantis in which he asserted that the lost continent existed and was the actual Garden of Eden! The book was immensely popular, and the next year his collision-theory book appeared.

Prior to these publications, Donnelly had heard of the idea that the plays of Shakespeare had actually been written by Francis Bacon, a contemporary of Shakespeare's. Donnelly began reading the plays, looking for clues, looking especially for possible ciphers of the name Francis Bacon. Thus began his great ambition, *The Great Cryptogram*. Figure 8 is

computations	word number	page and column	plaintext
$516-167 = 349-22b$ & $h = 327-30 =$			
$297-254 = 43-15b$ & $h = 28$	28	75:2	Shak'st
$516-167 = 349-22b$ & $h = 327-248 = 79.$			
$193-79 = 114+1 = 115+b$ & $h = (121)$	(121)	75:1	spur
$516-167-349-22b$ & $h = 327-254 = 73-$			
$15b$ & $h = 58. \ 498-58 = 440+1 = 441$	441	76:1	never

Figure 8

an example of the computations for his book. As impressive as these figures may appear, Donnelly did not take the time, unfortunately, to explain them fully. Maybe that tells you something. The book flopped. It didn't sell. Worse, cryptologists made mince meat of Donnelly's "proofs."

Undaunted, Donnelly went to Europe to lecture on his cause. He even wrote another book on the subject. It went nowhere, and in the next year, as a vice-presidential nominee, Donnelly went down to resounding defeat in McKinley's election.

There are some twists to this story. As soundly as Donnelly's argument was refuted, the idea that Shakespeare is a pseudonym has not died out. Perhaps this says more about how wonderfully nutty people are and how famous Shakespeare really is than about how credible Donnelly's idea is.

CHAPTER 15

Numbers and Pictures

In the last chapter we saw ciphers and codes made out of all sorts of things. Lewis Carroll's was made out of the letters of the alphabet. Arthur Koestler's "checkerboard cipher" was made out of numbers. The "Dancing Man" and the Shadow's cipher in "The Chain of Death" were made out of pictures. Later we're going to be looking at a special message sent in numbers and pictures.

But are numbers a language? Do they have the conventions of language we identified earlier?

- A series of basic elements? Yes: 1, 2, 3, 4, 5, 6, 7, 8, 9, 0 are the basic elements that all numbers are made of.

- Spacing? Yes. A space in the middle of the number 46 makes it 4 and 6.

- Direction? Of course: 96 is not the same as 69.

- Sequencing? Yes, for subtraction and division anyway. The sequencing of, say, 8-5 and $12 \div 3$ is important. In addition and multiplication, though, the sequencing can go in either direction: $5 + 4$ is just as good as $4 + 5$; likewise 7×6 and 6×7.

- Signaling devices? Yes. The $+$, $-$, $\div$, $\times$, and $=$ are like punctuation, telling us how to treat the material next to them.

But what about pictures? Can we talk about pictures as language? Are pictures a system of meaning too?

We have seen how pictures can be used in making ciphers. The "Dancing Man" cipher and the Shadow's cipher in the story "The Chain of Death" are examples we saw in the previous chapter. So if a cipher can be made out of a picture, why not a clear language system? Let's look around us. Is there a picture language that we see every day if we live in a town or a city? How about traffic signs?

EXERCISE 15.1
Do traffic signs use pictures to express their meaning? •

My response to Exercise 15.1
Yes, some traffic signs are pictures or partly pictures.

Some traffic signs are just words. Can you think of one? "STOP" is always spelled out as a word. How about numbers? Some traffic signs are just numbers — for instance, to indicate a change in speed limit. And some traffic signs are combinations of letters and pictures.

EXERCISE 15.2
Do you happen to know the meaning of this sign? •

My response to Exercise 15.2
This sign means "railroad crossing."

Some signs are just pictures.

EXERCISE 15.3
Do you know what these signs mean?

   •

My response to Exercise 15.3
The first sign means "two-way traffic." The second means "merge from the right." The third means "pavement narrows."

None of these three signs uses either words or numbers. Do you think that these signs are as easily understood as word signs or number signs? Perhaps not. But just because a sign uses letters, that doesn't mean it is clear to everybody. For example, do you know the meaning of PED XING? It means "pedestrian crossing." Can you imagine someone saying, "I'll meet you at the ped xing"? And what about the sign SLOW CHILDREN? Do you think that this sign works well? I mean, is it clear?

I don't think so. It is meant to convey the message "Drive slowly, look out for children" or "Go slow, children nearby." But it doesn't say that. By reducing the words to just two, "slow" and "children," the meaning is unclear. I think it could be improved by substituting a picture of children for the two words.

Do you have a favorite sign? My favorite is for "Deer in the area." Have you seen it? The sign is just a picture of a deer leaping. I would like to see one for bears. Then again, maybe I wouldn't. I wonder if there is one somewhere for elephants.

Think of traffic signs and traffic signals. Do they form a language? What do you think? They do form a system whereby drivers and pedestrians are told what they may do and what to be on the alert for. Would you call this system a language? Maybe a language must do more than convey information.

A kind of picture that is like a sign is called a "symbol". Here are three symbols.

EXERCISE 15.4
Do you happen to know what these three symbols mean—or, I should say, stand for? •

My response to Exercise 15.4
The first sign stands for woman. The second for peace. The third for man.

What is the difference between a sign and a symbol? A sign is meant to convey a piece of specific information. Symbols don't deal with information. A symbol stands for an idea. The meaning of a symbol is larger and more general than the meaning of a sign.

To have a language of symbols we would need a lot of them so that we could move them around to cover a large range of meaning. In other words, we would need a *system* of symbols just as we have a system of traffic signs and signals to cover all driving situations.

Let's look at another group of marks that look like signs and symbols.

EXERCISE 15.5
Does this series look like a good candidate for a pictorial language? •

My response to Exercise 15.5
This series looks like a pretty good possibility for a pictorial language because some of its parts look as if they could be pictures of something. That's the point. Do they or do they not look like pictures of something? If you think that they look more like numbers or letters than they look like pictures of something, then you would *not* call this series a good candidate for a pictorial language.

But what if some look like pictures and some look like letters or numbers? Well, that's a problem. But just because something looks like a letter or number doesn't mean it can't be a picture of something, right? So then the question is, what does the thing represent?

Do you happen to know what these figures are? You are not likely to know unless you are familiar with cattle raising. These figures are cattle brands.

Brands have names as well as owners. Here are the three brands and their names:

Pitchfork J   Bar 96   Open AZ

EXERCISE 15.6
Take a guess at the names of the three brands below. •

My response to Exercise 15.6
I will give it a try. The first might be called the Double C. The second might be called the Fancy J. And the third might be called the Horseshoe B.

The real names of these three brands, it turns out, are the C Bar C, the Quarter Circle J, and the Lazy SB. I like my names better. How about you? Do you like your names better than the real ones?

I also like the combination of the brand and the name.

EXERCISE 15.7
Pick any one of the last six brands and explain the connection between the brand and the name. •

114

My response to Exercise 15.7
I will pick the Lazy SB. The S is turned a little on its side, and leaning against the *B* as if it's "lazy." The *B* is clearly a *B*.

EXERCISE 15.8
If you had a ranch, what would you name it, and what would its brand look like? •

My response to Exercise 15.8
Maybe I'd call it the Hidden PS. The brand would look like this:

Cattle brands are not a pictorial language. They are a pictorial system of meaning, like traffic signs, but they are not a language. That doesn't mean that we couldn't use them to invent a pictorial language. (To do so, though, we might choose to use those brands that look the least like numbers or letters.)

We've already talked about a real pictorial language, way back in chapter 3. Chinese is a pictorial language. It began with pictures representing ideas. These pictures are called "characters." Each character has a meaning. Then there are ways to vary the meaning of a character. Here is an example. This is the character for "man."

"Big" comes from "man." "Big" is "man" with a horizontal line through the top, like a man with his arms stretched out, as if to say, "That fish was *this* big."

大

Add a horizontal line above "big" and you get "heaven":

It's as if "big" plus "above" equals "heaven."

You begin with a character, and then you make additions to the character to develop other, new meanings. This is a good way to develop a pictorial language, don't you think?

Once you are told the meaning of the three characters as "man," "big," and "heaven," you can see the progression. The change from one character to another makes sense. That doesn't mean, though, that every Chinese character visually resembles its meaning. Anyway, how would you draw heaven with a few lines? But the base character—the one for "man"—possesses more of a visual resemblance to its meaning than the other two do.

To get a feel for this way of developing new meanings by making certain additions to a character, let's take these three characters and assign our own meanings.

EXERCISE 15.9
Can you make up a sequence of three new meanings for the three characters 人 大 天 ? •

My response to Exercise 15.9
Here is my sequence of three meanings for these characters.

| walking | work | generous |

My guess is that your sequence of three meanings is different from mine, and perhaps considerably different. I say that because we all have our own associations with pictures. By that I mean that simple, line pictures such as these can easily suggest different things to different people.

It is pretty easy, I think, for each of us to look at a simple line drawing and make an association with an idea. It is also pretty easy to begin with an idea and make a simple, line drawing to represent it. What is hard, though, is to make a simple, line drawing and give it a meaning that will be recognizable by everyone else. The other hard thing to do in pictorial languages is to make drawings for abstract ideas.

Ancient Chinese is clearer to us than modern Chinese because Ancient Chinese is closer to simple pictures. Figure 9 gives some examples.

	Ancient	Modern
Sun	⊖	日
Moon	⅁	月
Woman	𠨏	女
Water	𛰫	水
Eye	👁	目
Stone	石	石
Hand	手	手
Gate	門	門
Cart	車	車
Street	彳	行

Figure 9

Aren't the ancient characters easier to recognize than the modern ones? Why didn't the Chinese people keep the ancient characters? Language, like everything else, goes through changes. Once the ancient characters were established and everyone knew them, then they weren't just pictures anymore. The characters became Chinese writing. So they changed just as our own writing changes,from the time we are little kids in school learning how to write to the time when we are adults. Do you remember how you wrote your name when you first learned to write? You sign

117

your name differently now, don't you? Well, that is natural change. Your writing evolves, changes, over time. A language does the same.

A language evolves not only in the way it looks but also in the way it makes meanings. We mentioned before the problem of making a character for an abstract meaning. It isn't hard to make a character for a concrete thing, like man, but what do we do to represent "love" or "freedom?" These are abstractions.

The Chinese have a wonderful method for representing ideas. Here is an example. Perhaps you can figure it out before being told. You know the character for "man," right? Here is the character for "eye":

Here is the combination of the characters for "man" and "eye":

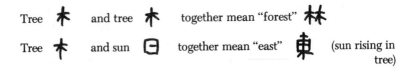

EXERCISE 15.10
What do you think this combined character means? •

My response to Exercise 15.10
Perhaps "man" and "eye" mean "look."

That's close. Actually, the two characters together mean "see." (The point is not really what the answer is because the answer is just a guess.) The point is that the Chinese *combined* characters to make a new meaning. This method is much like our combining words to make a new word, such as combining "basket" and "ball" to make "basketball." Here are two other combined or two-part characters.

Tree 木 and tree 木 together mean "forest" 林

Tree 木 and sun 日 together mean "east" 東 (sun rising in tree)

I like these combinations. They tell me something about how the Chinese people think. And you may have already figured out that two-part

118

characters aren't the only additional way the Chinese people developed new characters for new meanings. They also developed three-part and four-part characters.

Chinese differs from English not only in being a pictorial language (instead of an alphabetical language) but also in the way it applies the other conventions. Most noticeable to us is the direction. Classical Chinese is written not across the page, but down the page, and you begin reading at the far right-hand column, not the far left-hand side as we do in English. The convention of direction is applied in Chinese in almost directly the opposite way as it is applied in English. The front of a Chinese book is where we would normally go to find the back of a book in English. This makes sense when you realize that in Chinese you are reading the columns from right to left, instead of from left to right.

A pictorial language that you may have come across in your studies of ancient civilizations is Egyptian. The ancient Egyptian civilization was one of the greatest the world has known, and the language of this civilization began as pictorial. The pictorial element in ancient Egyptian is the hieroglyph ("sacred carvings," because in ancient Egypt writing was the exclusive right of the priests) and the system of writing is called "hieroglyphics."

What is particularly interesting about Egyptian hieroglyphics is that what began as pictures also developed into an alphabet. That may sound strange. Chinese and other Asian pictorial languages did not develop into an alphabetical language. The Egyptians had a reason, though, to make a connection between the hieroglyphs and particular sounds. Figure 10 shows the classical Egyptian alphabet, used in ancient Egypt for 3,000 years.

The sounds, as you can see, correspond to the sounds of many of the letters of our alphabet. (Some experts believe that the formation of our alphabet goes back all the way to the Egyptians.) Some of our letters are not present in the Egyptian alphabet, and some of their sounds cannot be represented by one letter of our alphabet. As you study other languages, you will find that there are sounds that are hard to represent with the letters of our alphabet because the sound is not common to English. But the sounds are not what is most noticeable to us about the classical Egyptian language. Instead, it's the fact that the sound is represented by a picture of a thing or a creature. At the same time, these symbols can also stand for whole words!

Letters of our alphabet may have had a pictorial source, way, way

Classical Egyptian Alphabet

HIEROGLYPH	OBJECT DEPICTED	SOUND
	vulture	a
	foot	b
	placenta	ch
	hand	d
	arm	e
	horned viper	f
	jar stand	g
	twisted flax	h
	reed leaf	i
	snake	j (dj)
	basket	k
	owl	m
	water	n
	mat	p
	hill	q
	mouth	r
	folded cloth	s
	pool of water	sh
	loaf of bread	t
	tethering ring	tch
	quail chick	u or w
	two reed leaves	y
	door bolt	z

Figure 10

back in time. But we don't think of them as pictorial. We think of them as being only letters, namely something visual that stands for a sound.

EXERCISE 15.11
Can you write your name in classical Egyptian? (If a letter in your name is missing in the classical Egyptian language, then you simply leave it out.) •

My response to Exercise 15.11
Here is my name (Peter) in classical Egyptian.

Egyptian hieroglyphic writing could be written in *either* direction—left to right or right to left—*and* in vertical columns. Talk about an open approach to the convention of direction! But wouldn't this freedom cause all sorts of problems? I can't see how it wouldn't. I wonder how long it took for people to read a short passage.

Hieroglyphic writing wasn't deciphered by Europeans until the discovery of the Rosetta Stone, a rock with glyphs in three languages—all saying the same thing.

Just as Chinese developed from its ancient characters to its modern characters, so did Egyptian. Hieroglyphics are pictures of ideas. They take some time to draw. A practical question about a language is how rapidly a person can write it. Simple marks can be done more quickly than pictures. So, for the purpose of speed, Egyptian hieroglyphic writing changed. It became simpler. This means that it became less pictorial too.

The second stage of Egyptian writing is called "hieratic." It is about half way between hieroglyphics and the final stage, called "demotic." You can see in figure 11 that some of the hieroglyphs changed so much that their pictorial origin vanished.

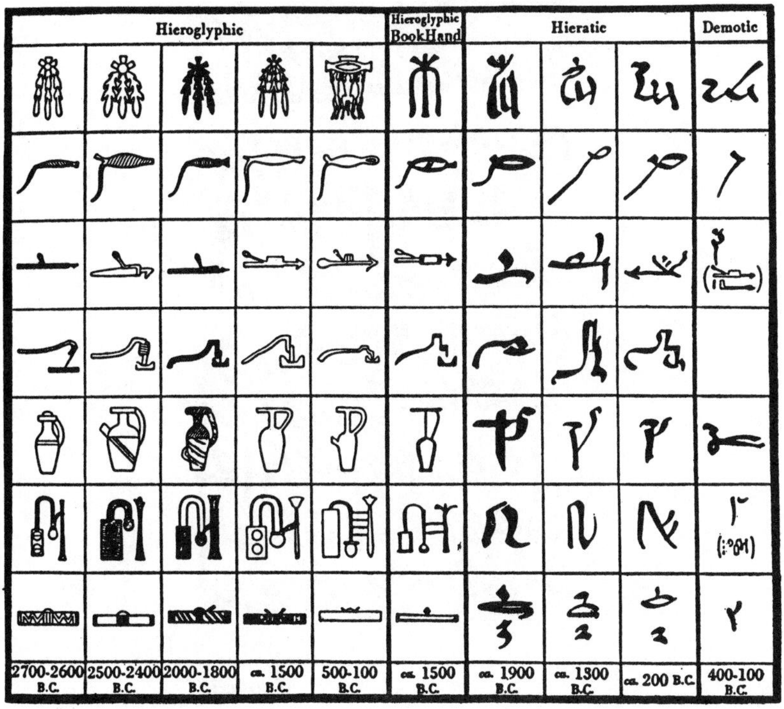

Hieroglyphic					Hieroglyphic BookHand	Hieratic			Demotic
2700-2600 B.C.	2500-2400 B.C.	2000-1800 B.C.	ca. 1500 B.C.	500-100 B.C.	ca. 1500 B.C.	ca. 1900 B.C.	ca. 1300 B.C.	ca. 200 B.C.	400-100 B.C.

Figure 11

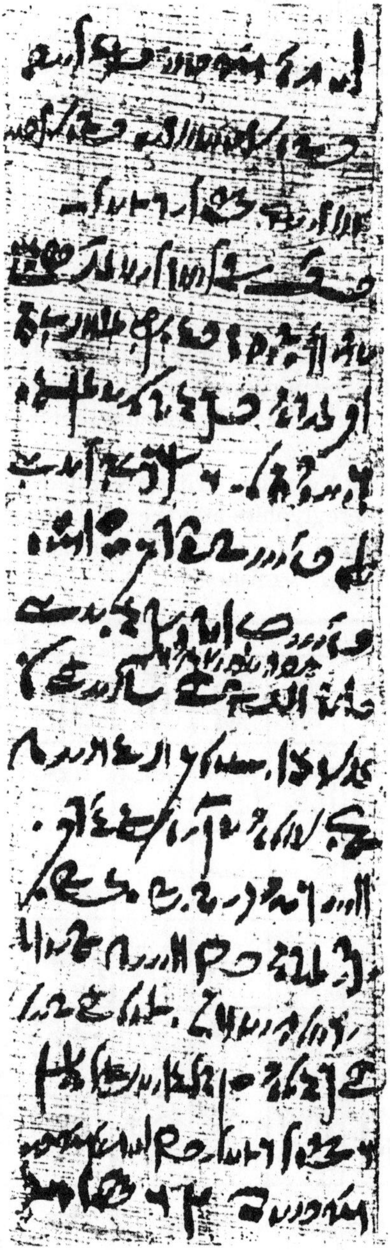

Figure 12

You might have expected only three columns, one for hieroglyph, one for hieratic, and one for demotic. There are more columns because in the first two stages of Egyptian writing there was more than one way to make the figure. The first stage—hieroglypics—was the most elaborate. There are five columns here for five different ways to make the hieroglyph.

EXERCISE 15.12
What do you make of the fact that there are five columns for hieroglyphics, three for hieratic, and one for demotic, and one for hieroglyphic book hand? •

My response to Exercise 15.12
The decreasing number of columns suggests that the Egyptians gradually simplified their language, probably for practical reasons.

In figure 12 is a passage of demotic writing from 270 B.C.

The demotic ("of the people") form came about partly because of the invention of papyrus (the ancestor of paper) and the use of a brush and ink to write with. No longer did words have to be carved in stone. Handwriting was of course quicker and more fluid than carving.

CHAPTER 16

Paintings, Petroglyphs, and Comics

It is easy to forget that written languages can look beautiful. We call the art of beautiful handwriting "calligraphy," an art form taught, for example, in art school and college. Students learn how to make the letters of different alphabets, ancient and modern, as well as the characters and figures of pictorial languages.

That we regard writing as something that can be done artistically may go all the way back to our prehistoric ancestors, who drew and cut pictures and designs on the walls of the caves they lived in, long before there was any kind of writing, much less writing that was systematic enough to be called a language.

The caves most famous for their prehistoric wall paintings are in France, but I would like to show you other cave paintings (figs. 13, 14, 15), from caves in the Sahara Desert.

The Sahara Desert may not seem like a probable place to find prehistoric cave paintings, but 8,000 years ago the land was laced with rivers and plentiful with wildlife. These caves, called Tassili-n-Ajjer, contain at least 800 paintings. The caves are regarded by some experts as the greatest natural museum of prehistoric painting in the world.

You don't have to go half way around the world to find ancient paintings and petroglyphs (stone carvings). Right here in the United States the prehistoric peoples who preceded the native American Indians left their art carved and painted on smooth rock faces, caves, and boulders. Figure 16 shows one of Bighorn sheep in Monument Valley, Arizona. Many Indian paintings and petroglyphs are, like this one, realistic. But not all were: figure 17 shows an old Indian painting done by the Chumash Indians in southern California.

The fact that this painting appears to be a hodgepodge of images and symbols suggests that it was not meant to tell a specific story or convey information. But what does it mean? Some researchers believe that

Figure 13

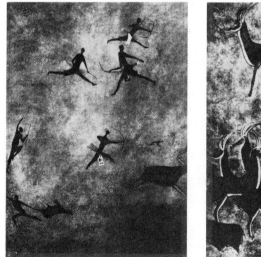

Figure 14

Figure 15

Figure 16

Figure 17

Figure 18

much Indian rock art was not intended to be organized or narrative or informative, but was meant to do only one thing: gain spiritual power by invoking through pictures the spirits of sacred animals. How else would you try to explain the 170-foot-long figure (fig. 18) cut into the desert gravel near Blythe, California? Such an immense figure, fully visible only from high above the desert, must have been intended for a special purpose. But what?

EXERCISE 16.1
What do you think? Nobody knows, so your idea is as good as anyone else's. •

My response to Exercise 16.1
I have no idea, other than the spiritual power theory. Strange and fascinating paintings and petroglyphs exist throughout the country, and their varying ages show that for centuries the ancient people of this land made such images for reasons other than telling stories.

How important this art was becomes clear when we realize that these peoples had no written language. They expressed themselves in storytelling, music, and dance, but rock art was their only fixed, permanent means of expression. It was the closest thing they had to written language.

Once the people are able to read this kind of pictorial shorthand — once they understand its conventions, much like the conventions of written language — an artist can convey much meaning in a fairly simple drawing. Would such a drawing be realistic? Perhaps. Perhaps not. It might be a mixture of realistic and abstract parts. However it is done, its meaning will extend way beyond what the painting appears to be. Here is an example:

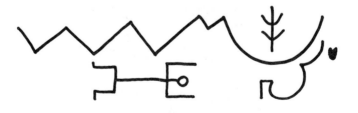

EXERCISE 16.2
Do you recognize any parts of this drawing? •

127

My response to Exercise 16.2
There is a human figure on its side and, above it, what looks like mountains or water, and, to the right, a tree.

These parts of the drawing seem fairly clear. But what about the other parts? They don't look like anything, do they? And what does the whole drawing mean?

In *Book of the Hopi,* Frank Waters explains:

> The old chief Salavi is pictured horizontally to show that he has passed away. The jagged line above him denotes water, which ends in a spring to the right, and out of this grows the spruce tree into which he transformed himself at death. The arms or branches of the spruce are upraised because the spruce is holy, the most magnetic of all trees, its branches forming a throne for the clouds to rest upon. The symbol below represents Salavi's lifeline; it rises at birth from Mother Earth, extends horizontally at ground surface during his life span, sinks down at death, and then comes back in spirit form into the roots of the spruce directly above. The footprint is the mark of the people on their migration.

This is a wonderful explanation of the meaning of the drawing. It is actually a story, and looking back and forth from the explanation to the drawing is interesting. But to figure out the meaning without the explanation would be impossible. Without intimate knowledge of Hopi culture, this drawing remains indecipherable.

At least it's *one* drawing. Imagine if it weren't clear that a group of pictorial elements were meant to be viewed as parts of a whole. For example, figure 19 shows another Hopi drawing. Three pictorial elements with no evident connection to one another form this one picture. It could just as well be three separate parts of a code or ciphers.

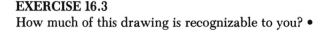

Figure 19

EXERCISE 16.3
How much of this drawing is recognizable to you? •

128

My response to Exercise 16.3
Only one element, the human figure, is recognizable to me. The other two look like abstract designs.

The other two elements do appear to be abstract designs, but, according to Frank Waters, they aren't. The element in the upper left is a cloud reflected in water below, and the row of repeating patterns along the bottom is four waves of water. So each of these is a stylized, abstract drawing of something real. But this is just the beginning of the problem. Just because these two abstract-looking parts come from something real, that doesn't mean they are there just to represent real things. Instead, they may be symbolic. In other words, in the drawing they may stand for something else.

This is precisely what they do in this drawing. The four waves represent "the four migration routes to be completed by the Water Clan." That is symbolic.

This kind of drawing deserves its own term. Perhaps "symbolic pictures" is a sensible name because even though these pictures contain realistic parts, each part of the picture, realistic or abstract, stands for something else. In other words, each part is symbolic. This greater complexity means more of a problem to us in trying to figure out its meaning. But what about looking at this difficulty in the opposite way? Couldn't this greater complexity mean greater richness in meaning?

Do you think these symbolic drawings resemble a language? In some ways they do, and although I think of these drawings as being as powerful to the Hopi as our language is to us, I wouldn't call them "writing," because there is one important difference between drawings and written languages: the third convention of language, direction. A written language must have direction, but what about a drawing?

EXERCISE 16.4
Is there direction in a symbolic drawing? Is it clear that we are supposed to start looking at a drawing in one place and then move in a certain direction to the other parts of the drawing? •

My response to Exercise 16.4
No, we do not look at a drawing this way.

No, there is no convention of direction in a drawing. In fact, part of the pleasure of looking at a drawing is looking at whatever part you want in whatever sequence you want.

This difference may be important for making a distinction between these drawings and written languages, but it is not important to the general similarity between these drawings and pictorial languages. There is, after all, a natural connection between symbolic drawings and pictorial languages (such as Chinese or classical Egyptian). And one thing is certain about symbolic drawings: they are a powerful way for a people to express themselves.

Rather than being set against one another, writing and pictures often team up in popular ways. Obviously, many books and magazine articles include drawings or photographs. Here, the writing is usually primary, the pictures secondary. In other publications, the drawing is primary and the writing is secondary.

EXERCISE 16.5
In what sort of publication is the drawing primary and the writing secondary? •

My response to Exercise 16.5
A publication in which drawing is primary and the writing is secondary is comics (fig. 20).

EXERCISE 16.6
Would you like to do the next page of the story in figure 20? Take it anywhere you want. •

I am going to leave this up to you, but I hope you give it a try, even if you don't consider yourself a great artist. I want you to see how unimportant the words might be if you are presenting action. I wouldn't be surprised if your story line were clear without any words.

Yet what is essential to the clarity of the story is the sequencing. If you couldn't sequence your drawings, you would have a much harder time telling your story. Notice in this comic page how specific the sequence is. There is no uncertainty about the sequence. And why is the sequence so clear? Because it is based on the second convention, direction. Once the direction is set, sequencing is easy to establish. The clarity of comics is based as much on the conventions of written languages as it is on the clarity of the drawings themselves.

Let's go back to the Sahara Desert one more time. In the prehistoric cave drawings some of the figures have round heads and seem to be wearing strange suits, as in figure 21.

Figure 20

Figure 21

What does the figure on the left look like to you? People who study pre-historic drawings have not been able to agree on what this figure is supposed to be. One person has come up with an interesting theory: Erich von Daniken proposes in his book *Chariots of the Gods* that this figure, and others like it, are realistic, that they are astronauts from another planet who visited earth sometime in the prehistoric past. He shows similar pictures from the art of other prehistoric peoples to support this claim. Take another look at the prehistoric cave painting. Decide for yourself. Your thinking will launch you into the final part of this book.

CHAPTER 17

The Most Interesting Question About Language

What is the most interesting question about language? What do you think? I think that sending a message into space is the most interesting language question. What would we say? How would we say it?

Sending a message into space is the subject of these final chapters. We are going to do two things: we are going to try to decipher a message that *has* been sent into space, and we are going to make up our own message.

Figure 22 shows a picture of the first message sent into space by humans. It was first sent in 1974 from the Arecibo radio telescope in Puerto Rico. A radio telescope is not something you look through, it's more like a transmitter and receiver of electromagnetic waves, like radar. The Arecibo is the largest radio telescope in the world. The message continues to be sent.

EXERCISE 17.1
What do you make of the message? Can you decipher any of it? •

My response to Exercise 17.1
The space message is a strange-looking thing, all those little squares. If it is a code or a cipher, I have no idea how to read it. I don't know where to start. About two-thirds of the way down in the middle is something that looks like a human figure, though.

Are you having the same problems I am? Do you think that that is a human figure? If it is, the language system of the message is pictorial. But then, what are the other parts? What are they pictures of? I don't see any other pictures. Do you?

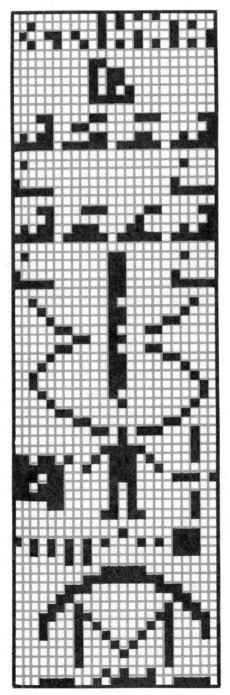

Figure 22

Maybe they are not *all* pictures. Maybe only a part of the message is pictorial. In other words, could the language system of the space message be part pictorial and part something else, maybe a code or a cipher?

EXERCISE 17.2
What do you think? Do you think the message might be part pictorial and part something else? •

My response to Exercise 17.2
I don't know. Maybe that isn't a figure at all. Nothing else in the message looks like a picture to me.

Maybe we can't get much farther this way. Let's try another approach. Let's think about what *we* would put in a message to be sent into space.

EXERCISE 17.3
What would you include in a message to be sent into space? •

My response to Exercise 17.3
I would put information about the earth and about human beings, and I would put some sort of a greeting so that the message would be taken as friendly.

Whatever we decide to include in our message, we face a hard problem: how do we represent our content? Do we use pictures? Do we use a written language like English? Do we use numbers? Do we use something else? It depends on what we want to say, I suppose. Think about what you want to say. Then think about how you are going to say it.

Can you say it with pictures? If you can, you can send a message that is totally pictorial.

If you can't say it with just pictures, then you have to figure out how to express it. To put this another way, if your message is to include words, you have to think about how to make words understandable to intelligent life in space.

The same would be true if you want to include numbers in your message: you would have to include some way for the numbers to be understood, unless you think that intelligent life somewhere out there in space could understand our numbers and our writing without some sort of explanation. Maybe they could.

Think what that would be like. Could you understand a message in

135

Chinese? And what if Chinese were a language that no one on earth spoke? If no one on earth knew the language of a message we received from space, how could we tell that the message was actually a message, much less figure out how to read it?

We have to keep in mind that our languages are things we human beings have invented. Our languages may seem commonplace to us, but we don't know that there are alphabets or numbers out in space. So if we use one of our languages, we have to think about helping other intelligent life decipher our message.

This is a hard problem. And there is no definite solution to it either. Even if we figure out a way to indicate the language of the message, will there be enough space in the message to include the explanation of the language? Even then, how do we indicate that one part is the explanation and the other part is the actual message? This *is* a hard problem, no doubt about it.

Still, let's go ahead and make up our own message. Where do we start? Let's start with the message the scientists are sending out from the Arecibo radio telescope. At this point we may not be able to figure out what this message says, but that doesn't mean we can't use the basic form of it for our own message. Besides, by using the same form the scientists did, we can compare our message with theirs.

Do you see all those little black squares? I am counting the squares and the spaces between them to figure out the physical dimensions of our message. I come up with 23 blank and darkened squares across, and from top to bottom I come up with 73 squares. So we have a message whose dimensions are 23 × 73 squares. Whatever we make that fits into this form would fit what is now going out into space.

EXERCISE 17.4
Draw a rectangle of 23 spaces across and 73 spaces down. •

Now *you* decide what to put in it. If you want to make your message entirely pictorial, you darken in the squares to make whatever picture you want to.

I happen to like the idea of including a human figure. I want to include a woman and a man. So I will have two human figures in mine. Do you want to include a human figure?

I also want to include a message. I mean a message of words. I am not going to write the words. I mean, I am not going to write letters in the squares. Instead, I am going to make up a cipher for the letters of the alphabet.

136

EXERCISE 17.5

Can you think of a way to make up a cipher for the alphabet? •

My response to Exercise 17.5
I hope you have worked out your own way. Here is mine.

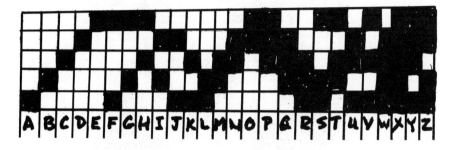

I need 26 different combinations of blank and darkened squares in order to represent the alphabet completely. So I write the alphabet from left to right and then start building up combinations of blank and darkened squares until I have a different combination for each letter.

If you were to include a message with words, what would you say? There are so many different things to say, aren't there?

I want to say FROM PLANET EARTH   MAN AND WOMAN and then, separately   PEACE.

EXERCISE 17.6

Can you write your own message of words in your own cipher? I suggest making it short. •

My response to Exercise 17.6
Figure 23 shows my message in words in the cipher I just showed you. I put it in the message form along with the figure of a man and a woman.

My message is made up of two language systems, one pictorial and the other alphabetical. How about yours? Is yours made up of one?   Or two? Or three? Or more?

As simple as I like to think my message is, I wonder if intelligent life out there in space could make anything out of it. Could they tell that one part is pictorial and the other is alphabetical? They *could* tell that

Figure 23

one part is pictorial if they had seen a human being, but what chance is there of that?

And what would they make of the alphabetical part? What would they think those darkened and blank squares mean? Perhaps the message would be clearer if I included the alphabet. I mean the cipher for the alphabet. I could put the cipher of the alphabet along the top, above the message in words.

Then again, maybe it would be better to include a picture of the earth and the sun. Maybe I could indicate somehow that earth is the third planet from the sun. Is that a good idea?

I would also like to include water because it is basic to life on earth. I could include H_2O. But then I would have to make a cipher for 2. This is becoming complicated. I certainly couldn't add all of these possibilities; there wouldn't be room.

I wonder if it is possible that intelligent life could develop elsewhere in the galaxies and develop so far as to be able to receive and send space messages and yet *not* have a written language—or neither a written nor a numerical language. That's a strange question, I suppose. The answer is probably no. But then again, who is to say? If you are sure that the answer must be no, then you are stating your belief of how important language is to intelligent life.

EXERCISE 17.7

Think about this question of sending a message into space. Then look at the message you worked out. How would you change yours, if at all? Either write out your changes or make a new message, using the form the scientists did who conceived the message going out from the Arecibo radio telescope. •

I like thinking about my own message. I hope you enjoy thinking about yours. Still, I'm curious about the message the scientists have sent out. I want to know what it means.

CHAPTER 18

Deciphering Our Space Message

We have worked on deciphering the Arecibo space message. I think we deserve some more help with the meaning of the space message. Look at figure 24. Perhaps it will help us understand the meaning of the space message.

EXERCISE 18.1
Does this diagram help you to understand the space message better? If so, how? •

My response to Exercise 18.1
Yes, it helps because of the words. I know some of the words, but not all. We were right about the human figure, labelled here "earthling." The solar system right below it is meant to be pictorial, too. I didn't recognize it before. I like the way the earth is lifted up a little bit out of the horizontal line of planets and placed right under "earthling." But this image of the solar system isn't as clear as the image of the human figure. Do you agree? You don't have to, you know. "Arecibo" is a word I know because I know about the radio telescope in Puerto Rico from which the

140

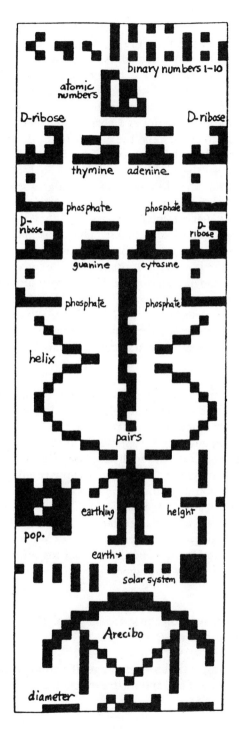

binary numbers 1-10
atomic numbers
D-ribose   D-ribose
thymine   adenine
phosphate   phosphate
D-ribose   D-ribose
guanine   cytosine
phosphate   phosphate
helix   pairs
earthling   height
pop.
earth→
solar system
Arecibo
diameter

Figure 24

message is being sent. Still, without including the words "radio tele-scope" the designation "Arecibo" doesn't help all that much. The figure above "earthling" marked "helix" is the double helix of DNA, the chem-ical substance basic to transmitting our characteristics from generation to generation. The double helix is pictorial too, like the telescope, but if you don't know about genetics as a part of the general field of biology, you are not going to understand the picture of the double helix of DNA, even with the word "helix" next to it. To make it as clear as possible, I would identify it as "the double helix of DNA." So, for the pictorial parts of the message, we have the earthling, the solar system, the telescope, and the double helix. But "pop" (population), "height," and "diameter" are obviously all measurements. Therefore, they represent numbers, right? But I can't read these numbers. They must be in some sort of ci-pher or code, maybe something like the way I worked out a cipher for the alphabet in the last chapter, remember? But maybe we have some help here with these measurements: The "binary numbers 1-10" across the top might be the cipher or code we need. The "atomic numbers" be-low it and all the scientific terms ("D-ribose," "trymine," "adenine," etc.) might be written in binary numbers. What do you think? You need some knowledge of chemistry to understand this upper part of the mes-sage.

That's a long answer. And this is rough going. The space message isn't simple, even with the additional help of this diagram. I am having an easier time with the pictorial parts than the non-pictorial parts. I figure that the rest of the message is represented in the binary numbers 1-10. But beyond this I can't go, not without more help, because I don't know the binary number system. I don't even know if what I am looking at across the top *are* actually binary numbers or if they're the binary num-bers in some kind of cipher or code. So I am in a fix. Here I am, given the explanation, at least a partial explanation, and I still can't read the space message! What about someone in space? What about you? Given this explanation and what I have said about my effort to figure it out, what do you make of the message?

EXERCISE 18.2
What do you now make of the space message? Do you have any of the problems that I am having? •

As I keep looking at the space message, it reminds me more and more of beaded Indian belts and Indian drawings. I am thinking of a Navaho sandpainting (fig. 25).

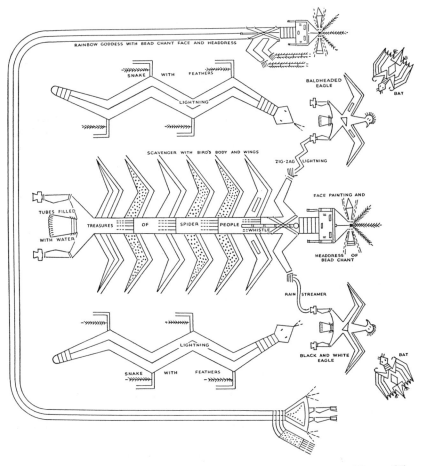

Figure 25

This Navaho sandpainting is entirely pictorial, but that doesn't mean it is simple. It isn't simple. Much meaning is packed into the picture—so much meaning that unless you are Navaho or have studied these sandpaintings and the Navaho culture, you would have little chance of understanding the intended meaning.

Think of the problem you have trying to "see" the full meaning of this sandpainting. Then try to imagine the problem someone way out there in space, in another galaxy, might have trying to understand the pictorial parts of our space message.

EXERCISE 18.3

What do you think of sending pictorial parts in our space message? Do you think it is just as good as any other method? •

My response to Exercise 18.3

I don't know how I feel about it. I still like the idea of making at least a part of our space message pictorial, and I also like the idea of including some words. But as to which method (which language system) might be better, I have no idea, and I don't know how anyone could decide. The question remains theoretical—doesn't it?—until we actually get a reply to our actual message and then ask about it.

We have done a lot of work trying to decipher the space message. It's like trying to translate a foreign language, or maybe *two* foreign languages at the same time. We need more help. Here is another "translation" of the space message, another diagram (fig. 26). Perhaps this one will shed some light on the problems we have been having. At least *I* have been having.

EXERCISE 18.4

Does this diagram make the space message any clearer? •

My response to Exercise 18.4

It sure does. The explanations are more complete than in the previous diagram. Also, the substituting of "1" (one) for each dark square and "0" (zero) for each light square allows me to see the binary numbers better.

But I am still not sure I understand. My problem begins with the binary numbers. I don't know what "binary numbers" are, and the dictionary doesn't tell me much more than that they are made up of 0's and 1's only.

Then there's the problem of how to read the ones in the illustration. To read the numbers at the top, do I keep the page straight up and down, as usual, or do I have to turn it sideways? And further down, around the outline of the human being, the numbers are arranged straight up and down, "normally," but at the bottom they look upside down. What gives?

The caption in *Scientific American* (where these diagrams come from) explains that the message has to be turned in three different directions to read the numbers. I wonder why. It seems pointlessly confusing.

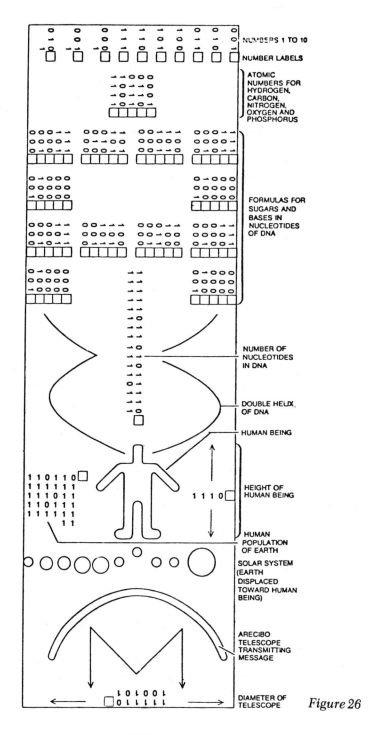

NUMBERS 1 TO 10

NUMBER LABELS

ATOMIC NUMBERS FOR HYDROGEN, CARBON, NITROGEN, OXYGEN AND PHOSPHORUS

FORMULAS FOR SUGARS AND BASES IN NUCLEOTIDES OF DNA

NUMBER OF NUCLEOTIDES IN DNA

DOUBLE HELIX OF DNA

HUMAN BEING

HEIGHT OF HUMAN BEING

HUMAN POPULATION OF EARTH

SOLAR SYSTEM (EARTH DISPLACED TOWARD HUMAN BEING)

ARECIBO TELESCOPE TRANSMITTING MESSAGE

DIAMETER OF TELESCOPE

Figure 26

145

If having to turn the message in three different ways to read the binary numbers is confusing, we can improve the message. Can you figure out a way to write the numbers in only one direction? Can you combine this change with whatever scientific information from the actual message that you want to keep in yours? You can keep whatever else you decided on including yourself, as long as there is room.

EXERCISE 18.5
Re-do your message or do a new one, keeping the numbers in only one direction. Can you do this? •

My response to Exercise 18.5
My revised space message is in figure 27.

This message is a combination of my previous message and the actual message the scientists sent out. I included the binary numbers; the atomic numbers for hydrogen, carbon, nitrogen, oxygen, and phosphorus; the formulas for sugars and bases in nucleotides of DNA; and the number of nucleotides in DNA. (I don't know what all these are, but I've been told they're important, so I put them in.) I did not include the double helix of DNA or anything below it with the exception of the human figure, to which I added the figure of a woman and the verbal message from my original message: FROM PLANET EARTH and MAN AND WOMAN and PEACE.

I decided to include much of the scientific data because the scientists knew what they were doing, I figured. I picked the scientific data that I thought was the most important. I included all numbers so that they could be written in only one direction. I ran the binary numbers from top to bottom down the upper left side, then arranged the scientific data listed in binary numbers nearby. I then had room left for the man and the woman figure and the verbal message, but I did not have room to include the cipher for the alphabet that I worked out in the last version of the message.

I like this new message because it contains both scientific data and my own personal material. But I don't really think the scientific data and my personal material blend very well. What do you think? I don't know how to make the combination work any better.

What nags me is that the actual message does not include anything we might call a greeting. The message is purely scientific information. What about the people of the earth? What do they have to say? How are

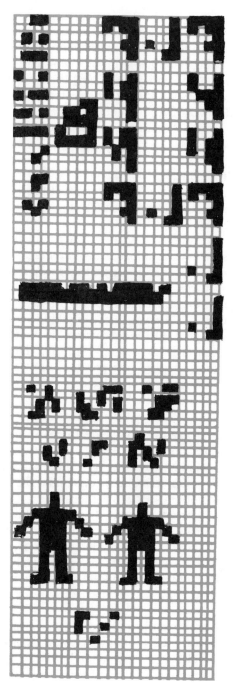

Figure 27

they represented in this message? Aren't we trying to communicate people-to-people (or life-to-life)? I don't like the idea of us here on earth being thought of simply as fact senders. I want more for us.

My objection is based on my belief that the written language is the universal language. I don't think that scientists would agree with this opinion. Scientists would probably contend that mathematics is the universal language, and that therefore our message into space should be basically in numbers.

EXERCISE 18.6

What do you think about this argument about the universal language? Do you think the space message should be basically mathematical, verbal, or even pictorial? •

The problems we have examined in this chapter *assume* that the space message is visual. But is it? Is the signal that the Arecibo telescope sends out basically a picture?

The *Scientific American* caption below figure 26 began: "Arecibo message in pictures. . . ." Do you notice anything here? Why isn't it just "The Arecibo message"? Why are the words "in pictures" added? What do you make of the words "in pictures?" Is it that the message is in some other form and then *changed* into pictures? How can that be? But I guess it's true. What we have been looking at are *pictures* of the message. Here (fig. 28) is the actual message.

We had enough problems before. Now things are even more difficult. And the caption says the message is supposed to be "decoded by breaking up the characters into 73 consecutive groups of 23 characters each and arranging the groups in sequence one under the other, reading left to right and top to bottom." How would we ever figure this out for ourselves? Or, more important, how would other life in the universe figure this out? The scientists didn't explain this part. In any case, this arrangement follows the conventions of language and mathematics as we know them. Each group of 23 characters is arranged one under the other, just as we set lines of writing, and the lines are to be read from left to right.

We come all this way to the message being sent into space and meet again what we started with, the conventions of language. The message is to be read from left to right and top to bottom. I guess the scientists figure that our convention of direction for reading language is as good as any other one.

148

```
0 0 0 0 0 0 1 0 1 0 1 0 1 0 0 0 0 0 0 0 0 0 0 0 1 0 1 0 0 0 0 0 1 0 1 0
0 0 0 0 0 0 1 0 0 1 0 0 0 1 0 0 0 1 0 0 0 1 0 0 1 0 1 1 0 0 1 0 1 0 1 0 1
0 1 0 1 0 1 0 1 0 1 0 0 1 0 0 1 0 0 0 0 0 0 0 0 0 0 0 0 0 0 0 0 0 0 0 0 0
0 0 0 0 0 0 0 0 0 0 0 0 0 0 1 1 0 0 0 0 0 0 0 0 0 0 0 0 0 0 0 0 0 0 0 0 0
1 1 0 1 0 0 0 0 0 0 0 0 0 0 0 0 0 0 0 1 1 0 1 0 0 0 0 0 0 0 0 0 0 0
0 0 0 0 0 0 0 1 0 1 0 1 0 0 0 0 0 0 0 0 0 0 0 0 0 0 0 0 0 0 1 1 1 1 1 0
0 0 0 0 0 0 0 0 0 0 0 0 0 0 0 0 0 0 0 0 0 0 0 0 0 0 0 0 0 0 1 1 0 0 0 0
1 1 1 0 0 0 1 1 0 0 0 0 1 1 0 0 0 1 0 0 0 0 0 0 0 0 0 0 0 1 1 0 0 1 0
0 0 0 1 1 0 1 0 0 0 1 1 0 0 0 1 1 0 0 0 0 1 1 0 1 0 1 1 1 1 1 0 1 1 1 1 1
0 1 1 1 1 1 0 1 1 1 1 1 0 0 0 0 0 0 0 0 0 0 0 0 0 0 0 0 0 0 0 0 0 0 0 0 0
0 1 0 0 0 0 0 0 0 0 0 0 0 0 0 0 0 0 1 0 0 0 0 0 0 0 0 0 0 0 0 0 0 0 0 0 0
0 0 0 0 0 0 0 0 0 1 0 0 0 0 0 0 0 0 0 0 0 0 0 0 0 0 0 1 1 1 1 1 1 0 0
0 0 0 0 0 0 0 0 0 1 1 1 1 1 0 0 0 0 0 0 0 0 0 0 0 0 0 0 0 0 0 0 0 0 0 0
0 0 1 1 0 0 0 0 1 1 0 0 0 0 1 1 1 0 0 0 1 1 0 0 0 1 0 0 0 0 0 0 0 1 0 0 0
0 0 0 0 0 0 1 0 0 0 0 1 1 0 1 0 0 0 0 1 1 0 0 0 1 1 1 0 0 1 1 0 1 0 1 1 1
1 1 0 1 1 1 1 1 0 1 1 1 1 1 0 1 1 1 1 1 0 0 0 0 0 0 0 0 0 0 0 0 0 0 0 0 0
0 0 0 0 0 0 0 0 1 0 0 0 0 0 0 1 1 0 0 0 0 0 0 0 0 0 1 0 0 0 0 0 0 0 0 0
0 0 1 1 0 0 0 0 0 1 0 0 0 0 0 1 0 0 0 0 0 1 1 0 0 0 0 0 0 0 0 0 0 0 0 0
1 1 1 1 1 1 0 0 0 0 1 1 0 0 0 0 0 1 1 1 1 0 0 0 0 0 0 0 0 0 1 1 0
0 0 0 0 0 0 0 0 0 0 0 1 0 0 0 0 0 0 0 1 0 0 0 0 0 0 0 1 0 0 0 0 0 1
0 0 0 0 0 1 1 0 0 0 0 0 0 1 0 0 0 0 0 0 1 1 0 0 0 0 1 1 0 0 0 0 0 0
1 0 0 0 0 0 0 0 0 0 1 1 0 0 0 1 0 0 0 0 1 1 0 0 0 0 0 0 0 0 0 0 0 0 0 0
0 1 1 0 0 1 1 0 0 0 0 0 0 0 0 0 0 0 1 1 0 0 0 1 0 0 0 0 1 1 0 0 0 0 0
0 0 0 0 1 1 0 0 0 0 1 1 0 0 0 0 0 0 1 0 0 0 0 0 0 0 1 0 0 0 0 0 0 1 0 0 0
0 0 0 0 0 0 1 0 0 0 0 0 1 0 0 0 0 0 0 1 1 0 0 0 0 0 0 0 0 1 0 0 0 1 0 0 0
0 0 0 0 0 1 1 0 0 0 0 0 0 0 1 0 0 0 1 0 0 0 0 0 0 0 1 0 0 0 0 0 0
1 0 0 0 0 0 1 0 0 0 0 0 0 1 0 0 0 0 0 0 1 0 0 0 0 0 0 1 0 0 0 0 0 0
0 0 0 0 0 1 1 0 0 0 0 0 0 0 1 1 0 0 0 0 0 0 1 1 0 0 0 0 0 0 0
0 1 0 0 0 1 1 1 0 1 0 1 1 0 0 0 0 0 0 0 0 0 1 0 0 0 0 0 0 1 0 0 0 0
0 0 0 0 0 0 0 0 0 1 0 0 0 0 0 1 1 1 1 0 0 0 0 0 0 0 0 0 0 0 1 0 0 0
0 1 0 1 1 1 0 1 0 0 1 0 0 1 1 0 1 1 0 0 0 0 0 0 1 0 0 0 1 1 1 0 0 1 0 0 1 1 1
1 1 1 1 0 1 1 0 1 0 0 0 1 1 0 0 0 0 0 1 1 0 1 1 1 1 0 0 0 0 0 0 0 0 0 1 0
1 0 0 0 0 0 1 1 1 0 1 1 0 0 1 1 0 0 0 0 0 1 0 1 0 0 0 0 0 1 1 1 1 1 1 0 0
1 0 0 0 0 0 1 0 1 0 0 0 0 0 1 1 0 0 0 0 0 1 0 0 0 0 0 1 1 0 1 1 0 0 0
0 0 0 0 0 0 0 0 0 0 0 0 0 0 0 0 0 0 0 0 0 0 0 0 0 0 0 0 0 1 1 1 0 0
0 0 0 1 0 0 0 0 0 0 0 0 0 0 0 0 1 1 1 0 1 0 1 0 0 0 1 0 1 0 1 0 1 0 1
0 1 0 0 1 1 1 0 0 0 0 0 0 0 0 0 1 0 1 0 1 0 1 0 0 0 0 0 0 0 0 0 0 0
0 0 1 0 0 0 0 0 0 0 0 0 0 0 0 1 1 1 1 0 0 0 0 0 0 0 0 0 0 0
0 0 0 1 1 1 1 1 1 1 1 0 0 0 0 0 0 0 0 0 0 0 0 1 1 1 0 0 0 0 0 0 0 1 1 1
0 0 0 0 0 0 0 0 0 1 1 0 0 0 0 0 0 0 0 0 1 1 0 0 0 0 0 0 1 1 0 1 0 0
0 0 0 0 0 0 0 1 0 1 1 0 0 0 0 0 1 1 0 0 1 1 0 0 0 0 0 0 0 1 1 0 0 1 1 0 0
0 0 1 0 0 0 1 0 1 0 0 0 0 0 1 0 1 0 0 0 1 0 0 0 1 0 0 0 1 0 0 1 0 0 0 1
0 0 1 0 0 0 1 0 0 0 0 0 0 0 1 0 0 0 1 0 1 0 0 0 1 0 0 0 0 0 0 0 0 0 0
0 1 0 0 0 0 1 0 0 0 0 1 0 0 0 0 0 0 0 0 0 0 0 1 0 0 0 0 0 0 0 0 0 1 0 0
0 0 0 0 0 0 0 0 0 0 1 0 0 1 0 1 0 0 0 0 0 0 0 0 0 1 1 1 1 0 0 1 1
1 1 1 0 1 0 0 1 1 1 1 0 0 0
```

Figure 28

149

We have done a lot of work to decipher the scientists' space message. Let's make a list of what has to happen for the message to be received *and* understood. Here is my list:

1. There must be someone or something out there to receive it;
2. The message must be regarded as a message, as an intentional communication by an intelligence;
3. The message must be clearly and completely recorded;
4. The recipient must get the idea to divide the total number of signals ("characters") up into 73 series of 23 characters;
5. These series of 23 characters must be set one under the other;
6. Each series must be read from left to right;
7. The binary numbers must be regarded as the code for understanding much of the rest of the message;
8. The coded numbers must be read from one of three different directions;
9. It must be recognized that not only scientific data can be so represented, but also pictorial parts;
10. The relationship among the coded parts and between the coded parts and the pictorial parts must be recognized (for example the relationship between the picture of the human being and the height of the human being).

You may not come up with all these conditions, and you might come up with some of your own. In any case, there are a lot of conditions. Are there too many?

EXERCISE 18.7
What do you think? Is there a chance of this space message ever being deciphered if it is received? •

This is a very important question to think about. It is critical to communication with other life in the universe, unless, of course, we manage to create a means to travel far beyond our own solar system, or the other life comes to us. As much as we talk about our own space traveling, what captures our imagination even more is the idea of other life coming here to earth. What are your thoughts on this subject?

EXERCISE 18.8
Do you think there is life existing elsewhere in the universe, intelligent life that we might be able to communicate with? •

I wonder what the scientists have to say about this question.

CHAPTER 19

Communicating with Aliens

If you've thought about the questions in the previous two chapters, you have done pretty much all you can to figure out the meaning of the space message and how it is supposed to work. Now, here in the last chapter, you are going to hear from the scientists who made the message. Then you are going to be in a good position to assess their work. And they will tell you what they think of the possibility of communicating with other intelligent life in the universe.

Let's go right to the most important question: could intelligent life develop elsewhere in the universe? Carl Sagan and Frank Drake, who wrote the article about the space message, say:

> From our knowledge of the processes by which life arose here on earth we know that similar processes must be fairly common throughout the universe. Since intelligence and technology have a high survival value it seems likely that primitive forms on the planets of other stars, evolving over billions of years, would occasionally develop intelligence, civilization, and a high technology.

On the basis of what they see as a common pattern for the way in which life might develop anywhere, scientists Sagan and Drake are arguing here for the possibility of life developing elsewhere in the universe. They are arguing on the basis of probability. They try to go farther:

> There might be a kind of biological law decreeing that there are many paths to intelligence and high technology, and that every inhabited planet, if it is given enough time, will arrive at a similar result.

I love the way they snuck "every inhabited planet" in there. But these scientists aren't kidding. Listen to this:

> It is obviously a highly uncertain exercise to attempt to estimate the number of such civilizations. The opinions of those who have considered the problem differ significantly. Our best guess is that there are a million civilizations in our galaxy at or beyond earth's present level of technological development.

A million!

EXERCISE 19.1

What do you think of Sagan and Drake's ideas? •

My response to Exercise 19.1

I don't really know, but I admit that their argument about a possible kind of pattern for the development of life seems pretty sensible. Still, the problem with their argument is that it is about the pattern of developing, not about the beginning of life. I think that the beginning of life elsewhere is more questionable than the pattern it might follow.

Let's see what these two scientists say about sending and receiving signals.

> If they [these other civilizations] are distributed randomly throughout space, the distance between us and the nearest civilization should be about 300 light years. Hence any information conveyed between the nearest civilization and our own will take a minimum of 300 years for a one-way trip and 600 years for a question and response.

From this line of thinking it makes sense to conclude:

> It seems to us quite possible that one-way messages are being beamed at the earth at this moment by transmitters on planets in orbit around other stars.

And what do these scientists think of our capacity to communicate?

> We on earth now possess all the technology necessary for communicating with other civilizations in the depths of space. Indeed, we may now be standing on a threshold about to take a momentous step a planetary society takes but once: first contact with another civilization.

This sounds great, but what about practical problems? To begin with, what about receiving such a signal? Aren't there many many possible transmission frequencies, too many possible "stations" to tune into? How are we supposed to guess which frequency a signal might come in on? Here is what Sagan and Drake have to say:

> To intercept such signals we must guess or deduce the frequency at which the signal is being sent, the width of the frequency band, the type of modulation and the star transmitting the message. Although the correct guesses are not easy to make, they are not as hard as they might seem.

(Would someone who knows about radio transmissions please explain "frequency band." Thank you.)

What about actually looking for the signal? Now *there* is a very practical problem. Their idea:

When we actually search for signals, it is not necessary to guess the exact bandwidth, only to guess the minimum bandwidth. It is possible to communicate on many adjacent narrow bands at once. Each such channel can be combined to yield the equivalent of a wider channel without any loss of information or sensitivity. The procedure is relatively easy with the aid of a computer.

EXERCISE 19.2
What do you think of what Sagan and Drake have to say about finding a signal coming in from somewhere in the universe? •

My response to Exercise 19.2
I don't know much about radio frequencies. What I understand sounds pretty good to me. Still, clearly, it is basically guesswork.

Do the scientists have any ideas about how such a message might be sent?

> One method of transmitting information, beginning simply and progressing to more elaborate concepts, is pictures.

So the scientists cite pictures as the simplest way to send a message to us. That's interesting. We raised this question in chapter 17. Do you remember? We chose between pictures, numbers, and words, or a combination of two or perhaps all three.

EXERCISE 19.3
Are you surprised that the first way the scientists mention is pictorial? •

My response to Exercise 19.3
Yes. I would have thought that they would choose numbers as the first kind of language for sending a message.

What question is most important to these two scientists? "The real question is not how, because we know how; the question is when." By "when" Sagan and Drake mean "how soon," and they believe that pooling our resources might lead to making contact with other life in the universe "within the lifetime of most of those [people] alive today."

EXERCISE 19.4
Do you think that "when" is the most important question? •

My response to Exercise 19.4
No, I don't think that "when" is the most important question, but I like the positive and imaginative attitude of these two scientists.

Another message was sent out before this radio transmission. It was of a different kind. It was on two engraved plaques attached to a spaceship. Here in figure 29 is a picture of one of the two identical plaques.

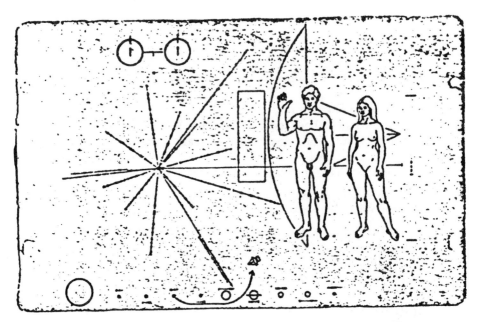

Figure 29

Sagan and Drake included this picture in their article in *Scientific American.* Here is what they say about this previous space message:

> We have sent another kind of message: two engraved plaques that ride aboard Pioneer 10 and Pioneer 11. These spacecraft, the first artifacts of mankind that will escape from the solar system, will voyage forever through our galaxy....
>
> Identical plaques for each vehicle were designed by us and Linda Salzman Sagan. Each measures six by nine inches and is made of gold-anodized aluminum.

Sagan and Drake call these plaques "cosmic greeting cards." Do you like the term? Maybe it is a little corny, but I like it because it feels friendlier than the previous message we looked at.

But what about the plaque as a message? Do you like it? Is it clearer than the other message?

EXERCISE 19.5

How do you like this message? Do you prefer it to the previous one, the radio transmission? •

My response to Exercise 19.5

I prefer this one because it conveys a feeling of welcome. Both human figures are drawn, rather than made out of squares, and the male figure seems to be waving, as if saying hello. I like that.

EXERCISE 19.6

What do you make of its meaning, other than the two human figures? How much more of the message makes sense? •

My response to Exercise 19.6

The only other part of the message that I can be sure about is the line of the sun and the planets that runs along the bottom. I like the little line marking the path of the spaceship. The rest of the message is unclear to me. My guess is that the rest of the message contains information about the origin of the space flight and about life on earth.

Here is what the scientists say about the contents of the message on the plaques.

> These engraved cosmic greeting cards bear the location of the earth and the time the spacecraft was built and launched. The sun is located with respect to 14 pulsars. The precise periods of the pulsars are specified in binary code to allow them to be identified.

EXERCISE 19.7

Do you understand the explanation so far? •

My response to Exercise 19.7

No, I don't. I see "the location of the earth" in respect to the other planets and the sun, but in only this way. I don't understand how the sun is located "with respect to 14 pulsars" because I don't know about pulsars, and I don't see either binary code representation of numbers or a code key of the binary code. In short, I don't get much out of the explanation thus far.

The scientists go on to say:

Since pulsars are cosmic clocks that are running down at a largely constant rate, the difference in the pulsar periods at the time one of the spacecraft is recovered and the periods indicated on the plaque will enable any technically sophisticated civilization to deduce the year the vehicle was sent on its epic journey. Units of time and distance are specified in terms of the frequency of the hydrogen spin-flip at 1,420 megahertz.

"The hydrogen spin-flip at 1,420 megahertz" sounds great, but I don't have the foggiest idea what it means.

And how long will these plaques last? Will they rust gradually and fall apart? The scientists say:

These plaques are destined to be the longest-lived works of mankind. They will survive virtually unchanged for hundreds of millions, perhaps billions of years in space. . . . They will show that in the year we called 1973 there were organisms, portrayed on the plaques, that cared enough about their place in the hierarchy of all intelligent beings to share knowledge about themselves and others.

Well, you have seen the plaque and read the scientists' comments. What do you think? Do you like the message? Do you like how it was represented on the plaque?

EXERCISE 19.8
What is your final assessment of the plaque message? •

My response to Exercise 19.8
I preferred it to the previous message originally, but now that I realize that I can't understand about half of the message, even after reading the scientists' explanation, I am not so sure.

A plaque on a spaceship allows us to use pictures, numbers, or words, or any combination of them. Besides, we don't have to deal with little squares; we can simply draw or write whatever we want. I prefer that to working with a radio transmission.

EXERCISE 19.9
Design the plaque for the next space flight out of our solar system. Explain its contents and explain why you chose to include what you did. •

My response to Exercise 19.9
I am going to leave this project entirely up to you and add only a final, personal comment.

As I started to type this chapter, I turned off the television set. The movie *Close Encounters of the Third Kind* was just beginning. I had seen this movie and had liked it.

After typing for a while, I went out to play basketball with some friends. During the game I thought again of the movie. This didn't help my concentration on the game. When I came home, I wanted to take a little break before resuming my typing. I flicked on the television. The movie was just ending.

A remote landing strip in a mountain has been prepared for the arrival of the spaceship. The landing strip is brilliantly lit. As the spaceship descends, the humans send out their welcoming signal. Pictures? Numbers? Words? No, the message is a series of musical chords. (The chords are from a piece by the modern Hungarian composer Bela Bartok.) The chords are played slowly at first — and then, as the spaceship draws near, faster and faster. The humans wait. The silence is huge.

From the spaceship comes the reply, a repeating of the chords of music—the first real communication between the earth and its visitors, the first sign of recognition of human beings by aliens. The final exchange between one of the scientists there and the apparent head of the visitors from space is the scientist's making a series of gestures with his right hand that correspond to the chords, and the alien's repeating the gestures with its right hand.

I love this ending. Not only is it lovely, peaceful, and simple, but the chords and the corresponding hand gestures don't *mean* anything. I mean, they don't stand for anything else. They are not a code, they are not binary numbers. They are just sounds and gestures. They stand for nothing beyond themselves. They convey no information. Yet, to me, they are just right. They are all that is needed, and more would be too much. In that simple exchange is embodied the profound importance of the "encounter" for both the human race and the visiting race.

Sitting there at my desk, I realized why I had been thinking about the movie. I had been thinking about the ending, this communication through sound, through music.

As you know, throughout these final chapters about communicating with aliens, I have expressed my uneasiness with the messages we have sent into space, insisting that these messages present the human beings as senders of information rather than intelligent life gesturing in a friendly way to other intelligent life. To argue my point, I had cited the absence of words in the messages because words can carry the very meaning that I see as missing from our present messages. What the movie showed me, and showed me in my memory of it before I realized it consciously, is that I had forgotten music.

Perhaps music is the universal language, not mathematics. Music is mathematically based and it certainly can be a clear gesture of welcome. Perhaps that is why Carl Sagan and Ann Druyan selected the "world's great music" and put it on discs sent into outer space.

In a visual message, such as the plaque, music is obviously not a possibility, although a hand gesture is. But how about a radio transmission? Do you think music is a good idea for a radio transmission? I love the idea of a sound floating through interstellar space. I don't know if it is possible because I know little about radio transmission, but if it is, all we would need to receive—to know that there is other life—is an echo.

Books and Magazines Consulted

Books

Brier, Bob. *Ancient Egyptian Magic*. New York: William Morrow & Co., 1980.

Chase, Stuart. *The Tyranny of Words*. New York: Harcourt Brace, 1959.

Gardner, Martin. *Codes, Ciphers and Secret Writing*. New York: Dover, 1972.

Gaur, Albertine. *A History of Writing*. New York: Scribner's, 1984.

Kahn, David. *The Codebreakers*. New York: Macmillan, 1967.

Orwell, George. *Shooting an Elephant and Other Essays*. New York: Harcourt Brace Jovanovich, Inc., 1974.

Polyani, Michel. *The Tacit Dimension*. New York: Doubleday, 1967.

Reichard, Gladys A. *Navajo Medicine Man Sandpainting*. New York: Dover, 1977.

Steindorff, George and Seele, Keith C. *When Egypt Ruled the East*. Chicago: University of Chicago Press, 1942.

Waters, Frank. *Book of the Hopi*. New York: Ballantine Books, 1977.

W Wor H. Watson Co. Attleboro

C M Robbins Attleboro. arm bird

Encyclopedia of
American Silver
Manufacturers

*"Grand Baroque" sterling flatware by
Wallace International. (Photo courtesy of
Wallace Silversmiths)*

Encyclopedia of
American Silver
Manufacturers

Third Edition Revised

Dorothy T. Rainwater

Schiffer Publishing Ltd

77 Lower Valley Road, Atglen, PA 19310

Front Cover:

Tureen made by Meriden Britannia Company about 1878 and "Clovis" ladle by Forbes Silver Company, 1898. Both are silverplate. (Photo courtesy of International Silver Company)

Published by Schiffer Publishing Ltd.
77 Lower Valley Road
Atglen, PA 19310
Please write for a free catalog.
This book may be purchased from the publisher.
Please include $2.95 postage.
Try your bookstore first.

Acknowledgments

This book could never have been written without the generous help of others. My deepest debt of gratitude is to Edmund P. Hogan of the International Silver Company who opened up the historical files to me and allowed me to draw freely from notes compiled by the late Wm. G. Snow. Mr. Hogan also has been unfailing in his encouragement and friendship.

A special note of thanks is due Kenneth K. Deibel, Dallas, Texas, for the loan of scarce and important research materials.

My sincere thanks go to Dr. Elliot A.P. Evans, Orinda, California, for notes about California silversmiths derived from his as yet unpublished material.

For biographical notes about some Boston silversmiths I am deeply indebted to J. Herbert Gebelein of that city.

The generosity of Charles A. McCarthy, Seattle, Washington, in supplying photographs from which I drew a number of the marks is exceeded only by his enthusiasm for the entire project. Both are much appreciated.

My warmest thanks and deepest appreciation go to the following librarians, representatives of silver manufacturers and collectors: A. Abrahamsen, John Arcate, James Avery, Swift C. Barnes, Fred M. Birch, John R. Blackinton, Patricia Blanchard, Mrs. H. Batterson Boger, RADM J. F. Bowling, USN, RET., Helen K. Butler, Louis Cantor, Nathalie Caron, Elizabeth T. Casey, Nancy F.Chudacoff, Bert Cohen, C.F.W. Coker, David M. Doskow, CMDR Frederick F. Duggan, Jr., Bernice Egbert, William Felker, George Fina, Michael C. Fina, Mrs. Olin M. Fisk, Mrs. Leonard I. Freedman, Paul A. Frey, George F. Gee, German Embassy, Herman W. Glendenning, Mrs. J.A. Greeley, Mrs. Mildred T. Guisti, Albert T. Gunner, Virginia Gunner, Margaret Smith Gunster, Robert Haftel, Nancy L. Harvey, Bruce A. Hauman, K.J. Herman, Beulah D. Hodgson, R.W. House, Rufus Jacoby, D. Wayne Johnson, K. Kovvalski, Charles Lamoureaux, Joan B. Lehner, Joseph McCullough, James D. McPherson, Helena Matlack, Mrs. William B. Mebane, Harold A. Milbrath, Dwane F. Miller, Mrs. Hester Miller, John G. Miller, Mrs. J.C. Mitchell, Dr. James Mitchell, B.J. Murphy, Dan Nagin, Helen Norris, Leonard E. Padgett, Don Parker, Enoch Pratt Free Library, Mrs. John H. Prest, Mrs. J.O. Randahl, Jr., Shirley Robertson, George S. Rogers, W.E. Rooks, Virginia Schmid, Stephen Schuldenfrei, Edwin Sellkregg, R. Champlin Sheridan, Jr., Jules Silverstein, Stanley S. Smith, Mrs. Clyde H. Smith, Charles C. Stieff II, Rodney G. Stieff, Peter J. Texier, Ernest T. Thompson, Jr., Le Roy Timmer, L.R. Titcomb, Albert S. Tufts, Ruth Van Meter, Mrs. Bert Welch, Rufus F. Wells, Elizabeth Willard, Harold Wolfson and Roland H. Wordwell.

Most of all, I am indebted to my husband, Ivan, who through the years has traveled thousands of miles with me, walked the halls of countless museums, tape recorded innumerable interviews and photographed thousands of silver articles and their marks to assist me, all with unfailing cheerfulness and good humor.

"Beauvoir" sterling flatware by Wallace International. (Photo courtesy of Wallace Silversmiths)

Contents

Acknowledgments
to Third Edition

The addition of new material to this third edition would not have been possible without the assistance of the following: Elenita C. Chickering, Etna, New Hampshire; Frances Downing, Assistant Curator of Decorative Arts, New York Historical Society; Dr. Elliot A.P. Evans, Orinda, California; Betty Grissom, Peoria, Illinois; Edgar W. Morse, San Francisco, California; Noralynn Naughton, Customer Service, Gorham Division of Textron, Inc.; Patrice Phillips, Director, Public Relations, Reed & Barton Silversmiths; A. Christian Revi, Hanover, Pennsylvania; Barbara L. Shaw, Publicity Manager, Oneida, Ltd.; Don A. Soeffing, New York City; Joseph F. Spears, Alexandria, Virginia; Rodney G. Stieff, Chief Executive Officer, Kirk-Stieff; Eileen Terrill, Lunt Silversmiths; Michele Tinker, Advertising, Wallace-International; Bennett W. Trupin, Norwalk, Connecticut; Ruth Van Meter, Yucaipa, California and Russell H. Weldon, Vice President Marketing Service, World Tableware International. Also Robert C. Gill, Gahanna, Ohio; John R. McGrew, Hanover, Pennsylvania; Charles C. Williams, Washington, D.C.

Special appreciation is due Mrs. Alden Redfield, Columbia, Missouri, for the photographic reproductions of trademarks and information concerning Redfield & Rice and related companies.

Diana Cramer, editor of SILVER has been most generous in giving permission to reprint marks and other material from that magazine.

Once again, Edmund P. Hogan, Meriden, Connecticut, has been unfailing in giving freely of information concerning the many changes in ownership of silver manufacturing companies. His enthusiasm and knowledge have made this book possible. His is a very special friendship.

I wish to thank Nancy and Peter B. Schiffer, Schiffer Publishing, Ltd. without whose guidance and encouragement this book could not have been completed.

My particular thanks go to attorney Daniel P. Mannix, V, West Chester, Pennsylvania, for legal advice.

And, as always, my husband, Ivan, has endured the disruption of household affairs without complaint.

Author's Preface

The identification and dating of American silver presents problems because, unlike England and a few other countries, no official stamps or date letters were used. Nor, was there ever established a guild hall for keeping records. Therefore, it is only through the identification of maker's marks and trademarks that the names of silversmiths and manufacturers can be traced.

The *manufactur* of silverware in the United States began about 1842. Prior to that time there were no real factories in this country. Almost all the silver was custom made with the buyer dealing directly with the silversmith. With the rise of manufactured goods, a new relationship of manufacturer-wholesaler-retailer-consumer developed. Many of these wholesalers and retailers had their own marks put on articles made for them or to be sold by them exclusively. In addition, there were some manufacturing companies who made nickel silver wares that were sold "in the metal" for plating by jobbing firms who then stamped them with their own or with retailers' marks. For the purpose of identification some of these trademarks are included. Many manufacturing jewelers also made various types of silver products. Some of the jewelry marks included in this book appear on silver articles and may, or may not, also be stamped "STERLING." The products of some foreign firms appear in such large quantities in this country that they have also been included. Most of them registered their trademarks in the United States Patent Office.

The first major effort to collect American silver manufacturers' trademarks was the publication in 1896, by the JEWELERS' CIRCULAR (now the JEWELERS' CIRCULAR-KEYSTONE) of *Trade-Marks of the Jewelry and Kindred Trades*. This was followed by editions in 1898, 1904, 1909, 1915, 1943, 1950, 1965, 1969, and 1973. Many of the trademarks illustrated here are from the 1896-1915 editions and are reproduced by the permission of the former Editor, Donald S. McNeil. Other trademarks were obtained from the United States Patent Office records, from silver and jewelry manufacturers, from old company catalogs, from actual pieces of silver and from photographs.

A number of trade journals and their related directories and indices are the principal source of trademarks and dates used in this book. The dates given are those of the various editions and are not to be construed as actual dates a particular company was in business unless specifically stated. To simplify the listings the following abbreviations are used:

AHR: American Horological Review
JBG: Jewelers' Buyers Guide
JC: Jewelers' Circular
JC&HR: Jewelers' Circular & Horological Review
JC-K: Jewelers' Circular-Keystone
JC-W: Jewelers' Circular-Weekly
JKD: National Jewelers' Trade and Trade-Mark Directory
JR: Jewelers' Review
JW: Jewelers' Weekly
KJI: Keystone Jewelers' Index
KS: The Keystone
NJSB: National Jewelers' Speed Book

How to Use This Book

There are many tradenames used which do not include the name of the company concerned, these and brand names are grouped together in a separate section with the name of the company following. To locate the company that used the brand name DIAMOND EDGE, for instance, consult this alphabetical listing and find that it was used by the Shapleigh Hardware Company.

Most of the trademarks have letters or words giving at least a clue to the letter of the alphabet with which the company name begins; a few do not. These are grouped together in the back of the book with the company name and are also illustrated within the regular company listing.

Very few of the trademarks illustrated in this volume appear *exactly* as they do when actually stamped on a piece of silver. Allowance must be made for imperfect stamping, and very often, for simplification of the stamped mark. Many of the illustrations are from printed sources and show more detail than is possible when stamped on silver. Varying angles of light on a mark can cause it to have a different appearance also.

Lettering for some of the marks drawn from actual specimens was sometimes done by the author with Artype, Prestype or similar grapic art products.

Alphabetized Listing
of Manufacturers

A

ABBOTT SILVERSMITHS, INC.
New York, New York

Listed JBG 1957-61 as manufacturers of silverware.

ALBERT ABRECHT
Newark, New Jersey
also ABRECHT & COMPANY
also ABRECHT & SULSBERGER

Listed in the Jewelers' Weekly in 1896 as Abrecht & Sulsberger. Listed in JC as Abrecht & Co., 1896-1904; succeeded by Albert Abrecht before 1915. Manufacturers of sterling and plated silver, gold chains, pendants, scarf pins and brooches. Last listing found was 1936-37.

 A & S

ACADEMY SILVER CO. (Showroom)
New York, New York

Listed JBG 1951-1961 as manufacturers of silverware.

ACME SILVER COMPANY
Toronto, Ontario, Canada

Manufacturers of silverplated wares c. 1885. Liquidated May 2, 1893. Sold to W.K. George and others who formed the Standard Silver Co., Toronto Ltd., later part of the International Silver Company of Canada Ltd.

ACME SILVER PLATE CO.
Boston, Massachusetts

Reported to have made plated silverware c. 1885. Not listed in U.S. Patent Office records.

C.C. ADAMS
Brooklyn, New York

"C.C. Adams, one of the largest and most prominent retail jewelers houses of Brooklyn, N.Y. have gone into the hands of a receiver. Stockholders are Sarah F. Adams, Cushing Adams, and Geo. S. Adams. The business was founded by the late Caleb Cushing Adams in 1887. He died Dec. 13, 1893, and since then the business has been in charge of his son, Cushing Adams." (JC 12-30-1896, p. 18)

The name is found impressed on flatware.

ADAMS, CHANDLER & CO.
Brooklyn, New York

Manufacturers of fine plated wares. They advertised in the *Watchmaker & Jeweler*, Nov. 1869, p. 43, a patent tilting ice water pitcher.

"John P. Adams (of Adams, Chandler & Co.), brother of Caleb Cushing Adams of Brooklyn, was recently deceased." (JCW, 2-7-1894, p. 6)

ADAMS & FARNSWORTH
Boston, Massachusetts

George Edward Adams and John C. Farnsworth were associated in the jewelry and silversmithing business from 1844 through 1848 (no directories available 1849-53), after which time Farnsworth was listed alone until 1857.

The firm began in 1839 under the name A.L. (Aaron L.) Dennison who was listed as an importer of watches. (It was Dennison who, in 1846, visited the Springfield Armory in Massachusetts and was impressed by the mass production or "interchangeable system" used there in the manufacture of weapons. Four years later he and others applied the same principles when they launched the American Horologe Co. in Roxbury, which eventually became the Waltham Watch Co.) By 1843 the firm had become A.L. Dennison, Adams & Co., jewelers, silversmiths and watchmakers. From 1846 to 1848 the firm name was Adams & Farnsworth.

GEORGE C. ADAMS
Baltimore, Maryland

Listed in the 1864 Baltimore City Directory as a silversmith.

ADAMS & SHAW
New York, New York
Newark, New Jersey

Caleb Cushing Adams president, was born in Newburyport, Massachusetts, March 25, 1833. He received his education at the famous colonial institution, Dummer Academy. While still a boy he started his business life in the employ of Joseph Moulton, an old jeweler in Newburyport. At the age of about 17 he went to New York City and became a salesman for Ball, Black & Co. where he remained about three years. His next post was Columbus, Georgia where he established a jewelry store. He sold his interest in a little more than a year and returned to New York in a position with Roberts & Bro. In 1858 he joined the Gorham Company as a traveler.

Thomas Shaw, head of the manufacturing, had learned electroplating at Elkington's of Birmingham, England, and came to America about 1860. He settled first in Providence, Rhode Island, where he worked for the Gorham Company, which was then trying to break into the trade in electroplate. In connection with Tiffany & Company Shaw formed the manufacturing company of Thomas Shaw & Company. By 1876 it was listed as Adams & Shaw. There was a notice (JC&HR, August 1876, p. 99) of the opening of the Adams & Shaw sample offices at No. 1 Bond St., New York City, for wholesale orders of sterling and electroplate. Following a fire in the Waltham Building, the factory moved to Newark, New Jersey and located at Park Street, corner of Mulberry, 1878-1880.

Both Adams and Shaw were skilled designers and both had worked for the Gorham Company. For 18 years Adams was the predecessor of Edward Holbrook as general manager there. Each had relatives associated in silversmithing. John P. Adams, brother of C.C. Adams, was owner of Adams, Chandler & Co., jewelers of New York City. Shaw had a son, Frank, also a fine designer, whose promising career was cut short.

In 1880 the Adams & Shaw Company was bought out by Dominick & Haff (Obit of Isaac Mills, JC&HR, 3-6-1895, p. 15). Their flatware patterns and dies were acquired from John R. Wendt & Co., New York, and eventually passed to Dominick & Haff. Following the closing of Adams & Shaw, Adams was connected with Leroy W. Fairchild & Co., and became buyer for N. Matson & Co., Chicago, Illinois. After about a year he became a partner in the Eugene Jaccard Jewelry Co., St. Louis, Missouri. In 1886 he again returned to New York City and formed the firm of C.C. Adams & Co., soon one of the leading jewelry firms there. He remained head of this firm until his death December 13, 1893.

The Carpenter's (see *Tiffany Silver*) findings concerning the disposition of Adams & Shaw was as follows: "The Adams & Shaw operation was absorbed into Tiffany & Co., probably in the 1880s, with Mr. Shaw becoming superintendent of the Tiffany plant."

WM. ADAMS
New York, New York

"William Adams, silversmith, New York City. Listed in directories there 1840-51. He was an Alderman (Ass't. 1840-42 and Alderman 1847-48). He learned the silversmith trade from Pierre Chicotree, Adams died about 1860." (JC&HR 8-5-1896)

In 1841 Adams reproduced the 46" mace of the House of Representatives, the original having been destroyed by fire when the British burned the Capitol in 1814.

WILLIAM ADAMS, INC.
New York, New York
Birmingham, England

Advertised that they are "Master craftsmen since 1854." (JC-K March 1966 p. 78 Importers of English Sheffield silverplate. Manufacturers of antique English silver and Sheffield plate.

In 1932 and 1950 registered a trademark in this country for which they claimed use since Dec. 1, 1899.

ADELPHI SILVER PLATE CO.
New York, New York

First record, 1890. Listed in the Jewelers' Weekly in 1896. Out of business between 1904-1915. John Schimpf & Sons, proprietors. They designed and made gold, sterling and plated silver holloware. Advertised "sterling silver mountings for cut glass a specialty."

ADIE BROTHERS, LTD.
Birmingham, England

Registered trademark in this country for flatware and holloware made of or plated with precious metal. Filed Sept. 1, 1948. Now part of British Silverware Ltd.

ALLAN ADLER, INC.
Los Angeles, California

Allan Wilbur Adler was born May 8, 1916 in Hamilton, Montana, son of August Martin Adler and Daisy Beatrice Fox. The family soon moved to Burbank, California where he grew up and became a successful home builder. On March 24, 1938 he married Rebecca Blanchard, daughter of Porter Blanchard (q.v.) Blanchard taught his sons-in-law silversmithing. Adler became skilled in all phases of silversmithing and began his own business in 1939. He was joined by his brother Kenneth. The business was later expanded into wholesale marketing servicing such stores as Marshall Field, Neiman-Marcus and B. Altman Co.

Adler's flatware patterns include Chinese Key, Modern Georgian, Round End, Starlit, Sunset and Swedish Modern. The Adler line also includes holloware, gift items, key rings and an extensive line of jewelry.

All pieces are marked ALLAN ADLER with the trademark of a square formed of "A's" or a double "A A."

AHRENDT & TAYLOR CO., INC.
Newark, New Jersey

First listed as Ahrendt & Kautzman; succeeded by Wm. G. Ahrendt and became Ahrendt & Taylor Co., Inc. between 1922-

36. Not listed after 1943. Manufacturers and distributors of sterling silver novelties.

AKRON SILVER PLATE CO.
Akron, Ohio

"Akron Silver Plate Co., Akron, Ohio, in hand of receivers." (JC&HR 6-8-1898, p. 16)

ALBANY SILVER PLATE CO.
See Barbour Silver Co.
See International Silver Co.
See I.J. Steane Co.

ALBANY SILVER PLATE CO.
TRIPLE PLATE.

ALBERT BROS.
Cincinnati, Ohio

Wholesale jewelers who advertised that their silverplated holloware patterns were made especially for them. (JC&HR 11-6-1895, p. 35)

C.A. ALLEN
Chicago, Illinois

Specialized in plating pieces "in the metal" manufactured by others. Said to have been in the wholesale business from 1887 to c. 1900.

T.V. ALLEN CO.
Los Angeles, California

Listed as manufacturers of silver medals and trophies in 1931.

ALLSOPP-STELLER, INC.
Newark, New Jersey

The following company names were found:

Wordley, Allsopp & Bliss Co., Inc.	1915 JC
(Allsopp-Bliss Co. successors)	
Allsopp & Allsopp	1927 KJI
Allsopp-Bliss	1927 KJI
Allsopp Bros.	1927 KJI
Allsopp-Bliss Co.	1931 NJSB
Allsopp Bros.	1931 NJSB
Allsopp-Steller, Inc.	1943-1973 JC-K

Listed as manufacturers of sterling novelties.

 (On sterling novelties)

ALVIN CORPORATION
Providence, Rhode Island
See Gorham Corporation

Organized as Alvin Mfg. Co., in Irvington, New Jersey by Wm. H. Jamouneau in 1886. Jamouneau was president until his retirement in 1898. A note in JC&HR (4-19-1893, p. 44) states that "The Alvin Mfg. Co., has been changed to the Alvin-Beiderhase Co., Wm. H. Jamouneau, Henry L. Leibe and George B. Beiderhase all of Newark, incorporated to manufacture metal, plated and other goods and novelties." In 1895 the Alvin factory was moved from Irvington, New Jersey to Sag Harbor, Long Island. It was purchased by Joseph Fahys & Co., watch-case manufacturer in 1897 and operated as a branch of that firm c. 1898-1910. The name of the company was changed to the Alvin Silver Co. in 1919. They were makers of sterling silver flatware, holloware, dresserware, silver deposit ware and plated silver flatware. Certain assets, dies and patterns were purchased by the Gorham company in 1928 and the name changed to the Alvin Corporation. It still functions as a division of the Gorham company.

In addition to the manufacture of electroplated wares by the old methods, the Alvin company patented (January 5, 1886) a new process for depositing pure silver on both metalic and non-metallic surfaces. The first articles produced in this country by the process were cane and umbrella handles. In this process, the article was first coated with silver and afterwards a part of the coating was cut away, thus exposing the base, as in pierced work.

CHRONOLOGY

Alvin Mfg. Co.	1886-1893
Alvin-Beiderhase Co.	1893-1919
Alvin Silver Co.	1919-1928
Alvin Corporation	1928-present

ALVIN

ALVIN STERLING

SHERWOOD SILVERPLATE

STEGOR SILVERPLATE

SILVERPLATE

ALVIN-BEIDERHASE CO.
New York, New York
See Alvin Corp.

Made Official World's Fair souvenir spoons for the Columbian Exposition held in Chicago 1893-94.

AMERICAN RING CO.
Waterbury, Connecticut

Manufacturers of plated silverware c. 1920.

AMERICAN SILVER CO.
Bristol, Connecticut
See Holmes & Tuttle Mfg. Co.
See International Silver Co.

Established in 1901 as successor to Holmes & Tuttle Mfg. Co. and Bristol Brass & Clock Company. Bought by International Silver Co. in 1935.

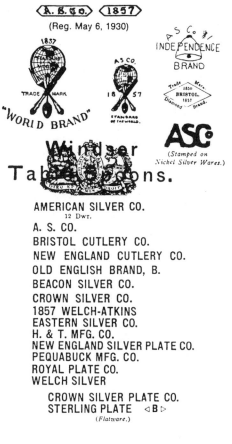

AMERICAN SILVER CO.
12 Dwt.

A. S. CO.

BRISTOL CUTLERY CO.

NEW ENGLAND CUTLERY CO.

OLD ENGLISH BRAND, B.

BEACON SILVER CO.

CROWN SILVER CO.

1857 WELCH-ATKINS

EASTERN SILVER CO.

H. & T. MFG. CO.

NEW ENGLAND SILVER PLATE CO.

PEQUABUCK MFG. CO.

ROYAL PLATE CO.

WELCH SILVER

CROWN SILVER PLATE CO.

STERLING PLATE ◁B▷
(Flatware.)

AMERICAN SILVER COMPANY

Wallingford, Connecticut

See also World Tableware International

The American Silver Company was established in 1983 to acquire World Tableware International (WTI) (q.v.) from Insilco Corporation by A. Reed Hayes and Robert Bartlett, Jr. Hayes became WTI's president and Bartlett, executive vice president and chief financial officer.

They took the name American Silver from the name of a company which was once part of International Silver Company. Although AMSCo is technically a newly-formed corporation, the American Silver Company name has appeared frequently in the history of Connecticut silversmithing. Originally founded in 1851 as Holmes & Tuttle in Bristol, the company was purchased by Bristol Brass & Clock Company in 1857. In 1901 the name was changed to American Silver Company, and it was operated continuously under this name as a unit of Bristol Brass & Clock Company until 1935 when the company was purchased by International Silver Company.

American Silver was an active trademark of International Silver Company for many years thereafter and, the American Silver name was originally used in connection with a number of WTI's current products. Their products are distributed only in the foodservice industry.

AMERICAN SILVER PLATE CO.

See Simpson, Hall, Miller & Co.

AMERICAN STERLING CO.

Naubuc, Connecticut

See F. Curtis & Co.

See Thomas J. Vail.

See Williams Bros. Mfg. Co.

Successors to the Curtisville Mfg. Co. in 1871 when they took over the property of Thomas J. Vail, manufacturer of German silver and plated ware. In business till 1880 when it was bought by James B. and William Williams and the name changed to Williams Bros. Mfg. Co.

AMES MFG. COMPANY

Chicopee, Massachusetts

Nathan Peabody Ames and James Tyler Ames, founders of the Ames Mfg. Co., in 1829, began with the production of swords and sabers, many of which were presentation pieces for such eminent figures as Ulysses S. Grant and Zachary Taylor.

It was at the Ames company that the process of electroplating was introduced into the United States, according to Chicopee historian, Ted M. Szetela. His account says that Charles R. Woodworth, an artist employed by Ames, was the pioneer plater of the country. They made silver services for the leading hotels of the country. Among the elaborate plated silverware they exhibited at the New York World's Fair, 1853-54, were a wine cooler, a sword and standing salt cellar.

James T. Ames became head of the company after the death of his elder brother in 1847.

In 1853, the company added the manufacture of bronze statuary becoming the first company in the United States to cast bronze statues. The bronze doors of the United States Capitol in Washington, D.C., were cast at Ames from designs by Thomas Crawford, American sculptor. These were commissioned in 1853. The East doors were installed in 1868 and the West doors in 1905. Both doors are made up of panels which depict scenes of important events in American history.

During the Civil War, Ames became the largest producers of light artillery and third largest supplier of heavy ordnance.

James T. Ames retired in 1874 and was succeeded by his son-in-law, Albert C. Woodworth. The company was later owned by Emerson Gaylord and James C. Buckley and went out of business in 1920. It is thought that they discontinued the manufacture of silverplate wares about 1872. The silverplate aspect of the business is believed to have been transferred to the Meriden Britannia Company while the sterling and bronze departments were transferred to Providence where the Gorham Company developed them in later years. No records in the Meriden Britannia Company offices substantiate this.

AMITY SILVER INC.,

Brooklyn, New York

Manufacturers of sterling silver c. 1950.

AMSTON SILVER CO., INC.
Meriden, Connecticut
    Manufacturers of sterling and plated wares. Listed 1965 JC-K as a division of Ellmore Silver Co. Out of business c. 1960. Flatware dies purchased by Crown Silver Co., Inc.

STERLING   FINE SILVER PLATE

ANCHOR SILVER PLATE CO.
Muncie, Indiana and St. Paul, Minnesota
    Listed in 1898 and 1904 JC. Listed in 1909 JC as out of business.

ANCHOR SILVER PLATE CO.
(On Quadruple Plate.)

INDIANA BRAND
(On Triple Plate.)

ANCHOR BRAND
(On High Grade Novelties.)

ANCHOR SILVERWARE CO.
Oswego, New York
    "The company formerly known as the Seliger-Toothill Novelty Company will hereafter be known as the Anchor Silverware Co. The former was a stock company incorporated in New Jersey with head offices in Newark and factory in Oswego, N.Y." (JC&HR 11-11-1896, p-6).

ANCO SILVER CO.
New York, New York
    Manufacturers of sterling silverware c. 1920-1927.

DAVID ANDERSEN
Oslo, Norway
    Established in 1876 as retail and manufacturing firm by David Andersen. Especially noted for filigree work and enamel. Firm presently directed by sons, grandson and great grandson. Distributed in the U.S. by the Norwegian Silver Corporation.

L.D. ANDERSON JLY. CO.
Reading, Pennsylvania
    In business c. 1910. Louis D. Anderson was listed in the Reading City Directories from 1914-1939 as a manufacturer of jewelry and souvenir spoons. Listed again 1941-44. No further listing and no record of store.

L. D. A.

ANDOVER SILVER COMPANY
Andover, Massachusetts
    Manufacturers of silverplate c. 1950.

ANDOVER SILVER PLATE CO.
See R. Wallace & Sons Mfg. Co.

APOLLO SILVER CO.
New York, New York
See Bernard Rice's Sons
    Succeeded by Bernard Rice's Sons before 1899. Sterling dies now owned by Garden Silver Co.

ARCHIBALD-KLEMENT CO., INC.
Newark, New Jersey
    Successor to C.F. Kees & Co. c. 1909. No record after 1922. Trademark used on sterling and gold lorgnettes.

ARGENTUM SILVER COMPANY
New York, New York
    Listed 1958 JBG and 1965-73 JC-K. Recent inquiry returned by post office as undeliverable.

DEKRA

ARISTON SILVERSMITH CORP.
New York, New York
    Listed 1931 NJSB as manufacturers of sterling silver holloware.

JAMES R. ARMIGER
Baltimore, Maryland
    Successors to Justis & Armiger in 1892. Armiger was born in Baltimore in 1835. He received his training as a watchmaker from his foster father, John F. Plummer, jeweler. Was later employed by Canfield Bros. & Co., Baltimore. During the early part of the Civil War he moved to Magnolia, Harford

County, Maryland, remaining there only a year. He returned to Baltimore and once again entered the employ of Canfield, where he remained until May 1, 1878 when he went into partnership with John C. Justis, the firm succeeding Justis & Co. This partnership continued for 14 years when Justis retired and Armiger conducted the business until his death February 23, 1896 in a fire that destroyed his home.

According to an article in the JCW (2-5-1919) the Armiger company was a direct descendant of the B. Larmour & Co., in business in Baltimore at least as early as 1869. This article states that in 1874 the Larmour firm was succeeded by W.M. Justis and was styled Justis & Co. A few years later James R. Armiger became associated with the business and it was then known as Justis & Armiger. This was succeeded by James R. Armiger in 1892 and was incorporated as the James R. Armiger Co. in 1896. It continued to be listed in Baltimore City Directories in 1936.

ARROWSMITH SILVER CORP.
Brooklyn, New York

Listed as manufacturers of sterling silver c. 1960-66. Succeeded by Garden Silversmiths Ltd.

A.R.S. STERLING
Boston, Massachusetts

Partnership of Frederick J.R. Gyllenberg and Alfred H. Swanson at 514-516 Atlantic Avenue, Boston, in 1926. Gyllenberg was a member of the Handicraft Shop of Boston and on Atlantic Avenue shared facilities with Swanson, Leinonen and son. Gyllenberg, following the 1930s depression entered the automobile service business with a garage in Islington, Dedham, Massachusetts.

F.G.
A.R.S.
STERLING
6 3 5

ART CRAFT PRODUCTS CO.
Sycamore, Illinois

Listed 1927 KJI as manufacturers of art metal novelties; silver deposit ware and silverplated holloware.

ART MFG. CO.
Meriden, Connecticut
See International Silver Co.

Name used on sterling silver match boxes.

ART METAL STUDIOS
Chicago, Illinois

Founded by Edmund Boker (b. 1886; retired 1977) and Ernest Gould (1884-1954) as the Chicago Art Silver Shop in 1912. It became the Art Silver Shop in 1918 and changed to Art Metal Studios, the name under which it still operates. Boker and Gould came to this country from Hungary in 1907 where they had received their training in a Budapest factory. Boker did the designing and Gould executed the designs. During the depression of the 1930s they began the production of wholesale jewelry manufacturing under the name Art Metal Studios. Marshall Field & Company and Lord & Taylor were among the department stores which carried their line including key chains, money clips and perfume funnels. They also made beautiful handmade silver jewelry and bronze jewelry inset or overlaid with sterling ornamented with pierced or applied monograms.

ART STAMPING & MFG. CO.
Philadelphia, Pennsylvania

Listed in 1909 JC as manufacturers of sterling and plated silverware. No record after 1915.

A. S. & M. CO.

ART STERLING SILVER CO., INC.
New York, New York

Their 1968 catalog says "Manufacturing & Importers of Fine Sterling Silver." About half the catalog is devoted to Judaica. Some other articles made by Weidlich Sterling Company.

ARTCRAFT SILVERSMITH CO., INC.
New York, New York

Listed with manufacturers of sterling holloware 1927 KJI and 1931 NJSB.

ARTCRAFT
STERLING

ASSOCIATED SILVER CO.
Chicago, Illinois

Listed 1915 and 1922 JC, 1922, 1931 KJI as manufacturers of plated silver flatware.

SILVERSEAL

YOUREX

H.F. ATKINSON & CO.
Baltimore, Maryland
   Listed in Baltimore City Directories 1887-1889 under plated silverware.

ATTLEBORO CHAIN CO.
Attleboro, Massachusetts
   Listed in JC 1909-1915. Trademark used on sterling dresserwares.

ATTLEBORO MFG. CO.
Attleboro, Massachusetts
   Listed in JC 1898-1915, as manufacturers of sterling silver novelties. Out of business before 1922.

(Novelties.)

AULD CRAFTERS, INC.
Columbus, Ohio
   Manufacturers of pewterware.

AURORA SILVER PLATE CO.
Aurora, Illinois
See Mulholland Bros., Inc.
   Organized under charter from Illinois Legislature in 1869 when the city's industries were few in number and the population of the city was only 10,000. It employed 65 people at the start. The company was an important factor in the development of the city. Its rolling mill was "the only one west of Cincinnati" at that time. They made plated silver flatware and holloware. Succeeded by Mulholland Bros., Inc. in 1919.
   Built on Stolph's Island, the business was founded by J.G. Stolph (president for several years). Charles L. Burphee, Daniel Volintine, George W. Quereau, A.N. Shedd, D.W. Young, Charles Wheaton, Samuel McCarty, M.L. Baxter, William Lawrence, William J. Strong and James G. Barr.

AVERBECK & AVERBECK
New York, New York
   "Manufacturers of Easter spoons, book marks, paper cutters, etc." (Adv. JCW 3-30-1898, p. 14)

JAMES AVERY, CRAFTSMAN, INC.
Kerrville, Texas
   James Avery taught design at the Universities of Iowa, Colorado and Minnesota from 1946-54. He first set up shop with a small investment and built a workbench and a few hand tools, and "with a few scraps of silver and copper set up shop in a garage near Kerrville, Texas." For three years he worked alone and in 1957 hired his first employee. Today there are more than 125 designers, craftsmen, management and support personnel. Their work is primarily jewelry of gold and sterling silver, much of it handcrafted and with a sculptural look. Their outstanding line is their Christian jewelry, all of it symbolic and inspirational.

1869
AURORA SILVER PLATE M'F'G. CO.
12 Dwt.
(Flatware.)

B

J.A. BABCOCK & CO.
New York, New York

"J.A. Babcock & Co., manufacturers of silver plated ware, have dissolved. The business is continued by Wm. Tuscano under the style of the Knickerbocker Mfg. Co." (JC&HR 2-7-1894, p. 94)

BACHRACH & FREEDMAN
New York, New York

Listed in 1896 JC under sterling silver. Succeeded by E. & J. Bass in 1900.

BAILEY, BANKS & BIDDLE CO.
Philadelphia, Pennsylvania

CHRONOLOGY

Bailey & Kitchen	1832-46
Bailey & Company	1846-78
Bailey, Banks & Biddle	1878-94
Bailey, Banks & Biddle Co.	1894-present

On September 20, 1832 Joseph Trowbridge Bailey and Andrew B. Kitchen formed a partnership under the firm name of Bailey & Kitchen for the manufacture and sale of silverware, jewelry and kindred articles and began business at 136 Chestnut Street, Philadelphia.

Mr. Kitchen died in 1840 but the business was continued under the same name until 1846, when E.W. Bailey, formerly of Maiden Lane, New York, the brother of J.T. Bailey, and Jeremiah Robbins and James Gallagher formed a new partnership under the name of Bailey & Company and continued business at the same location until 1859 when they constructed a new building at 819 Chestnut St.

Joseph Trowbridge Bailey, II entered the business in 1851 and was admitted into partnership at the age of twenty-one in 1856. His father died March 15, 1854.

In 1878 Joseph T. Bailey, II, George Banks of J.E. Caldwell & Co. and Samuel Biddle of Robbins, Clark & Biddle, formed a partnership under the name of Bailey, Banks and Biddle. Mr. Biddle retired in 1893 and on March 2, 1894 the business was incorporated with J.T. Bailey, II as president, Charles W. Bailey as vice-president and treasurer and Clement Weaver as secretary.

In 1903 and 1904 a new modern 10-story building was erected at 1218-20-22 Chestnut Street with a floor space of 76 x 230 feet and an eight-story factory.

In old City Directories the firm was listed primarily as jewelers but from 1839 through 1846 they were listed as jewelers and silversmiths. Brief mentions in old trade journals tell about the factory buildings (1868) and new buildings (1903-04) but they neglected to say whether these factories were for the manufacture of jewelry or silverware. George Sharp is known to have made silver for them and much of it is found bearing his personal stamps as well as "Bailey & Co."

In 1871 Bailey & Company published their *History of Silver, Ancient and Modern.* This is a 54-page booklet measuring about four by six inches. There is only one illustration of a Bailey & Company article but on p. 21 there is the statement, "The advent of Messrs. Bailey & Company, in the year 1832, with new and improved machinery, created quite a revolution in the art of manufacturing silverware. They immediately took the lead in this department of industry which they have steadily maintained.

"They claim the distinction, and without cavil, of having first introduced silver of the full British standard of 925-1000 the American standard being but 900. The advantage of raising the standard are that it prevents the importation from abroad, and especially from British workshops, for purchasers are assured by a guarantee of receiving silver, pure as that stamped by the English government. Besides, the quality of the silver renders the article more brilliant, whiter, and more susceptible of a higher finish, and obviates discoloration from exposure."

And on a later page, "Messers Bailey and Company, formerly Bailey & Kitchen, as old and reliable manufacturers of Silverware for the past *forty years*, desire, in connection with the foregoing interesting sketch, to direct especial attention to the following list of articles with prices appended." Eighteen pages of price lists follow.

Silverplate ware received attention also for toward the back of the brochure we find, "PLATED WARE—Of our own manufacture, of every style, constantly in store and warranted equal to any sold in this country. Guaranteed in every particular. Information sent upon inquiry."

"Born in Philadelphia, July 10, 1844, Samuel Biddle began his career by buying

the business of Thomas G. Garrett, silversmith, and forming the firm of Clark & Biddle. Later this firm was changed to Robbins, Clark & Biddle. Subsequently, in 1878, Mr. Biddle became a member of Bailey, Banks & Biddle, a house established in 1832 by Joseph Trowbridge Bailey, Grandfather of Charles Weaver Bailey, the present head of Bailey, Banks & Biddle." (Obituary, JCW March 12, 1919, p. 63.)

ROSWELL & B.M. BAILEY
Woodstock, Ludlow & Rutland, Vermont

In 1837-72 with partners, Parmenter & Parker, made silverware. The Baileys' apprentices made doll-size spoons as evidence of their craftsmanship and were allowed to sell them for their own profit for 25¢ each.

Roswell Bailey established his own large shop in 1839 and kept a dozen journeymen and apprentices busy. He was in business until 1875.

BRADBURY M. BAILEY
Ludlow and Woodstock, Vermont

A brother-in-law of Roswell Bailey of Woodstock, he worked as a silversmith in Ludlow before moving to Rutland in 1852. Closed his business in 1885. Born 1824-died 1913.

BAIRD-NORTH CO.
Providence, Rhode Island

Advertised that they manufactured and sold direct to the user. Advertised 200 page free catalog in 1912. Basically they were distributors.

BAKER-MANCHESTER MFG. CO.
Providence, Rhode Island
See Manchester Silver Co.

A short-lived concern in operation from c. 1914-1915 to the early 1930s. Manufacturers of sterling silver fancy flatware, souvenir spoons, holloware and novelties.

BALDWIN & CO.
Newark, New Jersey
CHRONOLOGY

Taylor, Baldwin & Co.	c. 1825-41
Baldwin & Co.	c. 1841-69

Manufacturing jewelers around 1840-69. Established by Isaac Baldwin, formerly with Taylor, Baldwin & Co. c. 1825-41. (He had also been a partner with James M. Durand in Baldwin & Durand c. 1845-50.)

After the death of Isaac Baldwin, the business was continued by his son, Wickliffe. Sold to Thomas G. Brown in 1869.

BALDWIN, FORD & CO.
New York, New York
See Cohen & Rosenberger
See Ford & Carpenter

Listed in the 1896 JC as Baldwin, Ford and Co. Succeeded by Ford & Carpenter before 1904. They, in turn, were succeeded by Cohen & Rosenberger before 1915. Baldwin, Ford & Co., whose factory was in Providence, Rhode Island, advertised that they made "the only one piece stud in the market," patented May 6, 1884.

BALDWIN & JONES
See Shreve, Crump & Low Co., Inc.

BALDWIN & JONES

BALDWIN, MILLER CO., INC.
Indianapolis, Indiana

First established in 1883. Manufacturers, wholesalers and jobbers of silverware, jewelry, clocks, and appliances. Their early trademarks have been found on souvenir spoons. Still in business.

B. M. CO.
Not used after 1915

B. & M.
Present trademark

BALDWIN & MILLER INC.
Newark, New Jersey

Manufacturing silversmiths. They manufacture sterling and pewter holloware, novelties and special trophy items—cups, trays, etc., to order.

The company was founded by Fred W. Miller, Sr. and Milton Baldwin. It began as a partnership in 1920 supplying retail stores with special order sterling silver holloware and stock items. Following Mr. Baldwin's death in 1939 the Miller family purchased all stock in the business. The firm is now in the third generation and is still in the hands of the Miller family.

Not related to Baldwin, Miller Co., Indianapolis, nor to Baldwin & Co., Newark.

B & M
(On sterling and on pewter)

BALDWIN SILVER CORP.
New York, New York
  Listed JBG 1957-61 as manufacturers.

BALL, BLACK & COMPANY
New York, New York
See Black, Starr & Frost, Ltd.
  Successors to Ball, Tompkins & Black in 1851. Partners were Henry Ball and William Black. In the 1860s they bought Reed & Barton wares "in the metal" and operated their own plating establishment. Succeeded by Black, Starr & Frost in 1876.

EDWARD BALL CO.
New York, New York
  Manufacturers of sterling silverware. Listed JKD 1918-19 as silversmiths.

BALL, TOMPKINS & BLACK
New York, New York
See Black, Starr & Frost, Ltd.
  Successors to Marquand & Co. in 1839. Partners were Henry Ball, Erastus O. Tompkins and William Black. Succeeded by Ball, Black & Co. in 1851.

THE BALLOU MFG. CO.
Attleboro, Massachusetts
  Manufacturers of gold, gold-filled and sterling silver jewelry, materials and findings. Listed in JC 1915 and 1922; JKI 1927.

BALTES-CHANCE CO., INC.
Irvington, New Jersey
  Manufacturers of sterling silver novelties. First record found in early 1920s. Succeeded by Baltes Mfg. Co. before 1927.

BALTIMORE NICKEL PLATING WORKS
Baltimore, Maryland
  Listed in Baltimore City Directories 1874-1886 as silverplaters.

BALTIMORE SILVER CO.
Baltimore, Maryland
  Listed in Baltimore City Directories 1906-1908 as silverplaters. Successors to Baltimore Silver Plating Co.

BALTIMORE SILVER PLATE CO.
Baltimore, Maryland
See Balt. Silver Plating Co.
  Listed in Baltimore City Directories as silverplaters 1894-1907. Succeeded by Baltimore Silver Plating Company.

BALTIMORE SILVER PLATING CO.
Baltimore, Maryland
  In business from 1905-1907 as successors to the Baltimore Silver Plate Company which was first listed in 1894. Succeeded by the Baltimore Silver Co.

BALTIMORE SILVERSMITHS MFG. CO.
Baltimore, Maryland
See Heer-Schofield Co.
See Schofield Co., Inc.

BALTIMORE STERLING SILVER BUCKLE CO.
Baltimore, Maryland
  Listed c. 1900-1904 at the same address as the Baltimore Sterling Silver Co.

BALTIMORE STERLING SILVER CO.
Baltimore, Maryland
See Stieff Co.

C.A. BAMEN
Boston, Massachusetts
  Listed as specialist in plating c. 1860.

BANCROFT, REDFIELD & RICE
New York, New York
See Bernard Rice's Sons

In the 1860s they purchased Reed & Barton wares "in the metal" and operated their own plating establishment. Predecessors of Redfield & Rice, Shepard & Rice and Bernard Rice's Sons.

BARBOUR BROS. CO.
Hartford, Connecticut
See Barbour Silver Co.
See I.J. Steane & Co.

Samuel L. Barbour, of Chicago, moved to New Haven, Conn. about 1881-82, to join his brother Charles who was in business there. They marketed the plated silverware produced by I.J. Steane & Co. Succeeded by Barbour Silver Co. in 1892.

BARBOUR HOBSON CO.
Hartford, Connecticut
See Barbour Silver Co.

The Barbour Hobson Company was organized in 1890 for manufacturing sterling silver. The interests of I.J. Steane, the Barbour Bros. Co. and the Barbour Hobson Co. were so nearly identical that it was thought best to unite them and the Barbour Silver Co. was the result.

BARBOUR SILVER CO.
Hartford, Connecticut
See International Silver Co.

When the Barbour Silver Co. was organized in 1892 by Samuel L. Barbour, Isaac J. Steane and J.L. Daigleish, they succeeded I.J. Steane & Co., Barbour Hobson Co. and Barbour Bros. Co. In August of 1893, they took over at least some of the machinery and stock of the Hartford Silver Plate Co., organized in 1882 and believed to have been carried on for a short time under the name of Hartford Silver Co.

When the International Silver Co. was formed in 1898, Samuel L. Barbour, who had been active head of the Barbour Silver Co. for several years, continued as manager of that branch (known as Factory "A") and was made a director of the new company and remained in that capacity for several years after the plant was moved to Meriden to the buildings formerly occupied by the Meriden Silver Plate Co.

Samuel L. Barbour was born in Norwalk, Conn., about 1865 and died in San Francisco, Nov. 11, 1925. He was identified with A.I. Hall & Son.

One of the original companies to become part of the International Silver Co. in 1898.

The "half circle" trademark first used in 1921 but not registered until 1923.

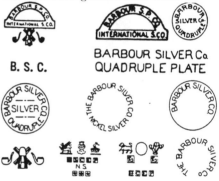

BARDEN, BLAKE & CO.
Plainville, Massachusetts
See Chapman & Barden

B. B. & CO.
STERLING.

BARKER BROS. SILVER CO., INC.
New York, New York
See Ellis-Barker Silver Co.

Sterling and plated silver wares; wholesaler and importer. Registered trademark Feb. 10, 1935 for silverplated holloware and flatware for table, toilet, or ornamental use. Claims use since Oct. 1, 1934.

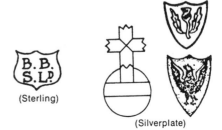

(Sterling)

(Silverplate)

C.E. BARKER MFG. CO.
New York, New York

Manufacturers of sterling (?) and plated silverware. First listed in JC in 1896. Out of business before 1915.

JAMES MADISON BARLOW
Salt Lake City, Utah

Barlow was born in Georgetown, Kentucky on July 9, 1812. He and his father, Thomas, became famous for their many inventions, a cradling harvester, the Barlow knife, a locomotive, a cannon and an instrument used in the study of astronomy.

Barlow, traditionally, is referred to as Utah's pioneer silversmith. Also, according to tradition, Henry Barlow, James' grandfather, and the earliest of the Barlows to arrive in Kentucky, was also a gold and silversmith.

Whether in search of wealth, or just to turn his back on his wife, cousin Betsey Barlow, he left in 1850 to join the Latter Day Saints in Salt Lake City. His Kentucky family refused to join him. He then married a widow with three children in 1851. She died soon afterwards and he married again late in 1852 and again in 1856. The two later marriages were to sisters, Susanna and Electa Mott, domestics in the home of Brigham Young.

Barlow's first work in Utah was in fixing and extracting teeth, mending watches and clocks and making a small amount of custom jewelry. This work in precious metals established his reputation as a fine craftsman. Utah's first silver tableware was the coin spoons he made. According to tradition, these spoons were given to Brigham Young for use in his Beehive House.

In 1860 Barlow was asked by Young to design and mint five dollar gold pieces. A temporary mint was set up in his jewelry shop. Between February 28 and March 8, 1861, 472 coins with a face value of $2,360 were stamped by Barlow and his assistant Douglas Brown.

Twelve silver cups he made in 1867 for communion service in the new "Great Tabernacle" were his best known works. For 25 years the congregation received communion in them. Soon after 1900 the cups were presented to a local congregation which used them until the influenza epidemic of 1918. They are now part of the pioneer relics exhibited in the LDS Church Museum in the Temple Square, Salt Lake City.

GEORGE BARRETT
Baltimore, Maryland

Listed in the Baltimore City Directories 1873-1898 as silverplaters (electroplate). Successors to Barrett & Rosedorn who were first listed in 1871 as silversmiths.

BARRETT & ROSENDORN
Baltimore, Maryland

Listed 1871-1872 as silversmiths and silverplaters. Succeeded by George Barrett in 1873.

H.F. BARROWS & CO.
North Attleboro, Massachusetts

Organized by Henry F. Barrows and James Sturdy in 1851 under the firm name of Barrows & Sturdy. Sturdy withdrew and the business became H.F. Barrows & Company. They acquired Ripley & Gowen Company, Inc., Attleboro, in 1968. Barrows Industries manufactures the R.L. Griffith lines of charms and earrings. Their emblematic division, the Williams & Anderson Company, makes service awards, medals, etc.

Barrows are manufacturers of sterling silver and gold-filled 10k and 14k gold jewelry. They began a line of religious medals and symbols c. 1965. In 1969 E.N. Riley assumed ownership of H.F. Barrows.

A stone marker at the present factory site in North Attleboro marks the spot where American jewelry making began in 1789.

H.F.B. & CO.	Sterling.

E. & J. BASS
New York, New York

Manufacturers of sterling silver wares, sterling silver deposit wares and plated silver and jewelry. In business from 1890-c. 1930.

"E. & J. Bass, New York manufacturers of silver novelties, announce they have purchased from Reeves & Browne, Newark, N.J., the entire outfit of tools and dies used in the manufacture of silver novelties and

have purchased the dies, tools, trademarks, etc., of Bachrach & Freedman." (JC-W 5-9-1900, p. 33)

N. BARSTOW
Providence, Rhode Island
Successors c. 1904 to Barstow & Williams.

BARSTOW & WILLIAMS
Providence, Rhode Island
See N. Barstow Co.

About 1880 Nathaniel Barstow began the manufacture of jewelry and in 1888 Walter S. Williams joined him to create the firm of Barstow & Williams. They added the manufacture of silver novelties to their line which then formed a complete line of jewelry and silver ornaments. Apparently Williams dropped out because by 1904 the firm name was once again N. Barstow & Co.

E. BARTON & COMPANY
New York, New York
See Black, Starr & Frost, Ltd.

In business 1815-1823. Partners were Erastus Barton and Isaac Marquand.

BASCH BROS. & CO.
New York, New York

Listed in 1904 JC under sterling silverware. Out of business before 1915.

THE BASSETT JEWELRY CO.
Providence, Rhode Island

Manufacturers of sterling silver and gold jewelry. Listed in JC 1896-1943.

They took over the plant and stock of Kent & Stanley in 1894.

J.C. BATES
Northfield, Vermont

Advertised in 1859 and 1860 that he sold watches, jewelry, silver clocks, toys and fancy goods.

BATES & KLINKE, INC.
Attleboro, Massachusetts

Established in 1919 as a die cutting and jobbing firm by Harold Bates and Oscar F. Klinke. Both were accomplished die cutters who served their apprenticeship before World War I. After serving in the army, they started business in November, 1919. The company was incorporated in 1929. The company gradually moved into the jewelry business. They now manufacture convention and special jewelry and souvenir spoons, mostly of sterling silver.

BATTIN & CO.
Newark, New Jersey

Listed in JC 1896-1922. Manufacturers of 14k and sterling silver match boxes, cigarette cases, eyeglass cases, belt buckles and pocket knives. KJI 1927.

BAY STATE JEWELRY & SILVER-SMITHS CO.
Attleboro, Massachusetts

Patent No. 104,012. Registered April 27, 1915. Application filed October 20, 1914. Serial No. 82,010. Trademark used continuously since August 1, 1914. For jewelry and precious metal ware; silver novelties, match boxes, purses, dresserware, cigarette cases, vanity cases and coin holders. Filed by Carrie L. Saart, Treasurer.

BAY STATE SILVER CO.
North Attleboro, Massachusetts

In business 1890-93. Made bracelets and novelties. (JC-W 4-13-1898, p. 28)

BEAUCRAFT INC.
Providence, Rhode Island

Listed 1950-65 as manufacturers of sterling novelties.

Registered trademark 1948 for costume jewelry. Claims use since Aug. 5, 1947.

BECHARD MFG. CO.
Chicago, Illinois

Manufacturers of plated wares c. 1943-45.

BECHT & HARTL, INC.
Newark, New Jersey

Manufacturers of sterling silver c. 1935-50.

ERNST GIDEON BEK, INC.
Pforzheim, Germany
See Binder Bros., Inc.

Manufacturers of sterling silver, gold and platinum mesh bags. Prior to World War I, Bek's was represented in the United States by Binder Bros., Inc. Following the war, Binders purchased the Bek stock from the alien custodian. The German company is thought to be still in operation. Pforzheim is the center of the German silver industry.

BELKNAP HARDWARE & MFG. CO.
Louisville, Kentucky

Silverplate flatware with their imprint was sold. Identical patterns bore the imprint of the Rockford Silver Co. and were probably made by the Williams Bros. Co. The Belknap Co. is still in business.

BELL BROS.
Ogdenburg, New York

"Bell Bros. silver ware factory, Ogdensburg, N.Y. has been sold. Purchasers are Messrs. Tucker & Parkhurst, Concord, N.H." (JC-W 3-3-1898, p. 17)

GEORGE BELL CO.
Denver, Colorado

Retail jewelry company. Listed in JC 1904-1922. Their trademark was found on souvenir spoons.

O.E. BELL COMPANY
Cincinnati, Ohio
See Cincinnati Silver Co.

Founded in 1892 as the Cincinnati Silver Company. O.E. Bell was general manager in 1898 and took over the company in 1899. They were manufacturers of plated silver holloware and novelties. Out of business c. 1900.

BELL TRADING POST
Albuquerque, New Mexico

A division of Sunbell Corporation. In business since 1932. Manufacturers of sterling silver, tuquoise, copper and nickel silver jewelry and souvenir spoons.

W. BELL & COMPANY
Rockville, Maryland

Founded in 1950 by Walter Bell. For several years operated as a catalog source for high-quality, high-value gift items and premiums. Sales efforts formerly directed primarily toward businesses and organizations. In 1971 their marketing activities were expanded and services extended. Twenty-one showrooms are scattered throughout the country.

Besides sterling, silverplate and pewter is made by several outstanding firms under their own names and trademarks, they also market WARWICK sterling silver and SOMERSET silverplated holloware in exclusive designs made for them by various manufacturers.

Warwick (Sterling Silver)

Somerset (Silver Plated Holloware)

BENEDICT MFG. CO.
East Syracuse, New York

Organized in 1894 with M. Stewart Benedict as president. Incorporated in 1902 and reorganized in 1906 as T.N. Benedict Mfg. Co. Their principal business at the start was silverplated holloware and they continued this line of goods which was adapted to household purposes and gradually included a line of holloware for hotel and restaurant use. Later they added a line of holloware plated on a nickel silver base, and a variety of equipment for soda fountains, including flatware. In 1910 they established a branch factory in Canada. They continued to produce lines mentioned above until 1942 when much of their plant facilities was converted to war work. Out of business in 1953.

In the consolidation of January 1912, they absorbed the Hamilton Silver Mfg. Co. of New York, the Benedict Dunn Co., Bridgeport, Connecticut, and the Benjamin Clark Silver Co., Ottawa, Illinois (founded 1890). Most of these factories were moved and merged with the East Syracuse plant.

BENEDICT PERIOD PLATE
GEORGIAN
CHIPPENDALE
BERKELEY
INDESTRUCTO
M. S. BENEDICT QUADRUPLE PLATE
(Above on silverplated holloware)

REVERE
STANDISH
(Above on pewter)

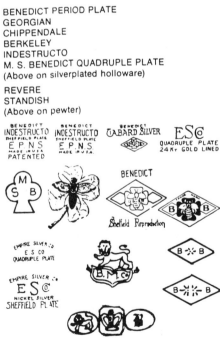

BENEDICT & MCFARLANE CO.
Bridgeport, Connecticut

"The Benedict & McFarlane Co. has been organized to manufacture silverplated flatware. The company gets its name from M.S. Benedict of the M.S. Benedict Mfg.

Co., Syracuse; and F.H. McFarlane, treasurer and manager of the Bridgeport Silver Plate Co. of Norfolk, Virginia. The Benedict Mfg. Co. will purchase the entire outfit of the new company." (JW 10-4-1899, p. 9)

BENEDICT-PROCTOR MFG. CO.
Trenton, Ontario, Canada

Listed 1920 to present as manufacturers of plated silverware.

T.N. BENEDICT
East Syracuse, New York
See Benedict Mfg. Co.

BENNETT-MERWIN SILVER CO.
New Milford, Connecticut
See Merwin-Wilson Co., Inc.

U.S. Patent No. 91,548, May 13, 1913, registered for use on plated silver flat, hollow and tableware.

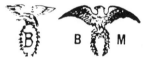

WM. BENS CO., INC.
Providence, Rhode Island

Listed 1915-c. 1920 as manufacturers of sterling silver dresser-ware.

JOHN DEAN BENTON
Providence, Rhode Island

Listed as a jeweler in city directories of Providence, Rhode Island 1855-1858 and 1862; Wilmington, Delaware 1864-1870 and Philadelphia, Pennsylvania 1874-1877.

Among the silver articles for which he became famous were the gold and silver models of railroad locomotives. He is thought to have made 13 such models, among them the *Daniel Webster* for the Philadelphia, Wilmington & Baltimore Railroad, the *Charles Morgan*, made in 1866 and now in the Marine Museum of Fall River, Massachusetts. He also built gold models of the ironclads *Monitor* and *Roanoke* and a gold and silver model of the steamer *Commonwealth*. Of the 13 known models, only seven, or possibly eight, are

known to be still in existence, some of them thought to have burned in the fire which destroyed the Crystal Palace in New York.

FREDERICK BERENBROICK
Weehawken, New Jersey

Established c. 1840 at 15 John Street (New York?) by Frederick Berenbroick, the pioneer maker of filigree in the United States. In 1858 the business was taken over by his nephew, Gottlieb Berenbroick, who made filigree and silver jewelry and novelties at 78 Duane St. In 1889, at death of Gottlieb, the business was taken over by Berenbroick& Martin, Frederick Berenbroick and Max Martin. Max Martin retired in 1919 and Frederick Berenbroick continued. The last listing found was 1935. He manufactured reproductions of old Dutch, English and French silverware.

ODO BERGMANN
Baltimore, Maryland

Listed in Baltimore City Directories 1897-1900 under silverware, solid and plated.

BERNDORF METAL WORKS
Berndorf, Austria
(Arthur Krupp)

Manufacturers of plated silverware c. 1910. No record after 1915.

SAMUEL E. BERNSTEIN
New York, New York
See National Silver Co.

Founded in 1890 and succeeded by the National Silver Company in 1904.

BEVAN & CO.
Baltimore, Maryland

Listed in 1872 Baltimore City Directory as silverplaters.

BIGELOW, KENNARD & COMPANY, INC.
Boston, Massachusetts

The firm began in 1830 when John Bigelow opened a jewelry store near the head of State Street in Boston. Soon afterwards he was joined by his brother, Alanson Bigelow, and the firm name was changed to John Bigelow & Company. Later Abraham O. Bigelow, brother, and M.P. Kennard, William H. Kennard and F.P. Bemis became members of the firm and the name was changed to Bigelow, Kennard & Company. They moved to Boylston Street in 1869, which at the time was considered the southerly limit of the business district and friends predicted disaster.

Alanson Bigelow died in 1884, Abraham O. Bigelow and M.P. Kennard retired from the firm, both of them dying a few years later. Bemis died, leaving then Alanson Bigelow, Jr., who was joined in 1895 by his son, a third Alanson Bigelow. Another son, Homer Lane Bigelow, became a member of the firm in 1899, retiring a few years later, at which time Reginald C. Heath, a son-in-law, was admitted. The business was incorporated in 1912 and went out of business in January 1922.

I. BIGGERS SILVER CO.
Taunton, Massachusetts

Manufacturers of silverplated novelties c. 1895.

I. BIGGERS SILVER CO. TAUNTON

BIGGINS—RODGERS CO.
Wallingford, Connecticut

Founded May 18, 1894 to manufacture sterling, silverplated and metal goods. Founders were Henry E. Biggins, president, former superintendent of Hartford Silver Plate Co., Frank L. Rodgers, treasurer, descendant of Joseph Rodgers, of Joseph Rodgers & Sons, well-known English firm and Henry B. Hall, secretary, formerly with R. Wallace & Sons. They purchased the machinery of the Hartford Silver Plate Co. and installed it in their new factory building. Succeeded by Dowd-Rodgers Co., c. 1915-20.

D

BINDER BROS. INC.
New York, New York

Prior to 1919, Binder Brothers Incorporated were the exclusive American agents for Ernst Gideon Bek, Inc., Pforzheim, Germany. To their knowledge the Bek Company is still doing business in Germany today.

Since 1919, when Binder Brothers Incorporated purchased the Ernst Gideon Bek stock from the alien custodians who had taken it over during World War I,

Binder has manufactured, imported and had made up exclusively under its own trademark, jewelry, watchbands, sterling novelties, etc.

JAMES BINGHAM
Philadelphia, Pennsylvania

Listed from 1896 to c. 1910 as manufacturer of sterling silverware and jewelry.

FRED M. BIRCH CO., INC.
Providence, Rhode Island

Manufacturer of gold filled and mens' sterling jewelry only from 1959 to 1971. Have since diversified and are now making ladies' gold filled and sterling lockets, crosses, pins, etc.; also brass items.

BIRMINGHAM SILVER CO., INC.
Yalesville, Connecticut

Successors to Goldfeder Silverware Co. Manufacturers of sterling silver and silverplate.

". . . Sol Goldfeder—newly married and with $150 in his pocket—launched a small silver holloware company anyway. He still recalls his first order. 'It was $30, may be $31. We sold it to M.A. Cohen & Sons.' The sale was a good omen. Soon Goldfeder owned a prospering factory in Brooklyn. In 1957, after 25 years there, his firm, now named Birmingham Silver Co., shifted operations to Yalesville, CT. Now the firm has added a New York address." (JC-K July 1974, p. 223)

(Sterling & silverplate)

(Silverplate)

BIXBY SILVER CO.
Providence, Rhode Island

Listed in JC as manufacturers of sterling silverware 1896-c. 1909.

B. S. C.

SPE ET LABORE

BLACK, STARR & FROST, LTD.
New York, New York

CHRONOLOGY

Marquand & Co.	1810
Ball, Tompkins & Black	1839
Ball, Black & Co.	1851
Black, Starr & Frost	1876
Black, Starr, Frost-Gorham Inc.	1929
Black, Starr & Gorham, Inc.	1940
Black, Starr & Frost, Ltd.	1962

Black, Starr & Frost traces its history to Marquand & Paulding who began their partnership in Savannah, Georgia in 1801. Several related firms were established in Savannah, New Orleans and New York. For a complete account see *The Silversmiths of Georgia*, by George Barton Cutten.

The present firm does not manufacture items but uses the trademarks shown.

B S & F

Black Starr

Black, Starr & Frost Ltd

R. BLACKINTON & CO.
North Attleboro, Massachusetts

Founded in 1862 by Walter Ballou and Roswell Blackinton in North Attleboro, Massachusetts and was owned and operated by members of the same two families for many years. The original trademark was used till c. 1900. Their products have consisted mostly of sterling silver and 14 karat gold novelties, flatware, holloware and dresserware, with a small amount of costume jewelry.

Bought by Wells, Inc. Attleboro, Mass. June 1967. About 1965-66 their *Marie Louise* flatware pattern was sold to the U.S. State Department for use in all United States embassies throughout the world.

PONTIFEX
(On dresserware)

MARIE LOUISE
(On dresserware)

(*Nethersole Bracelets.*)

W. & S. BLACKINTON CO.
Meriden, Connecticut

Founded in 1865 by the Blackinton brothers who specialized in gold jewelry.

Acquired by the Ellmore Silver Co. in 1938. While owned by Ellmore, operations expanded to include plated silver holloware. Production was curtailed during World War II and resumed with new lines in 1945. Independently owned since 1961. Incorporated between 1961-65. Purchased by Raimond Silver Mfg. Co., Meriden, Connecticut in 1966 and moved to Chelsea, Massachusetts.

W. & S. Blackinton

BLACKSTONE SILVER CO.
Bridgeport (Stratford), Connecticut

Started by E.H.H. Smith, formerly of Meriden, Connecticut, when he did business alone or under the name E.H.H. Smith Silver Co. The firm went into receivership April 12, 1914 and was reorganized as Blackstone Silver Co. It was backed to some extent by Albert Pick & Co., Chicago, for whom it had been making hotel ware. The Blackstone Silver Co. was sold in 1943 to Bernstein (of National Silver Co.?)

CHARLES BLAKE
Baltimore, Maryland

Silverplaters listed in Baltimore City Directories as Charles Blake 1868-1876, and as Charles W. Blake 1877-1886.

JAMES E. BLAKE CO.
Attleboro, Massachusetts

The Manufacturing Jeweler (10-25-1894) called James E. Blake one of the "pioneer silversmiths of Attleboro." It commented on the increased use of silver for useful and ornamental purposes and credited the firm of Blake & Claflin as being one of the most successful in its efforts in that direction. James E. Blake, senior partner, was born in Chicopee Falls, Massachusetts in 1851. In 1879 he was married to a daughter of C.H. Sturdy, a member of the old firm of Sturdy & Bros. & Co., manufacturing jewelers, established in Attleboro in 1859. In 1880 he joined the Sturdy firm and the following year entered into partnership with Edward P. Claflin, the foreman of the old firm, and Albert W. Sturdy, one of the Sturdy brothers under the firm name of Blake & Claflin. Blake & Claflin thus succeeded to the business of Sturdy Bros. & Co. About 1889 the firm began the manufacture of articles in silver, match boxes being among their first products. Various other novelties were added from time to time. In 1898 James E.

Blake, William H. Blake and Lefferts S. Hoffman filed papers of incorporation under the name James E. Blake Co. The firm name continued to be listed until 1936.

On January 31, 1905 they were granted a patent (No. 44,102) for the manufacture of sterling silver and silver inlaid with 14k gold cigarette and vaniety cases, match boxes, men's belt buckles and pocket knives.

Their factory building is now occupied by Bates & Klinke.

PORTER BLANCHARD
Calabasas, California

Silversmiths and pewterers. Specialists in restoration and handwrought flatware and holloware. Designers of pewter wares for Lewis Wise. Porter Blanchard learned silversmithing from his father, George Blanchard.

E.A. BLISS CO.
Meriden, Connecticut
See Napier Company

Founded in 1875 by E.A. Bliss and J.E. Carpenter in North Attleboro, Massachusetts when they took over the Whitney & Rice Co. where Bliss had been a traveling salesman: succeeded by E.A. Bliss in 1883. Moved to Meriden, Connecticut in 1890. Began the manufacture of sterling silver in 1893. Succeeded by Napier-Bliss Co., c. 1915.

(Stamped on Nickel Silver Wares.)

Used on World's Fair souvenirs, Chicago, 1893 (U. S. Patent 18,479, September 30, 1890.)

L.D. BLOCH & CO.
New York, New York

Manufactured plated silver novelties c. 1920.

BONTON
B
SILVERPLATE

BLUE RIBBON SILVER MANUFACTURERS, INC.
New York, New York

Max Sherman, Brooklyn, New York received Design Pat. No. 62,036, March 6, Blue Ribbon Mfgrs. Sept. 13, 1921. He also received Design Pat No. 62,036, March 6, 1923, for fruit basket, pierced design; not assigned.

J.C. BOARDMAN & CO.
S. Wallingford, Connecticut

The company was founded in 1950 by Joseph C. Boardman. Originally located in New Haven, Connecticut and moved to Wallingford, Connecticut in 1962. They originally manufactured silverplated novelties and unweighted (no artificial weight such as pitch or plaster of Paris) sterling holloware. Boardman was one of the first American manufacturers to recognize the revival of pewter in 1956 and today manufactures America's most complete pewter line—more than 300 items. Today they also continue to make the finest quality sterling holloware. With the increased price of silver, the temptation to weight the product is something to which all but a few in the industry have succumbed. Although the name is the same, they are not direct descendants of the Thomas and Sherman Boardman line.

"The J.C. Boardman Co.,...will be adding sterling flatware to its line by acquiring a Rhode Island Company.

"The Boardman Co...has purchased the Manchester Silver Co. of Providence, R.I.

"Besides the newly acquired rolling mills (needed to produce thinner strips of silver for flatware) and drop hammers, Boardman has obtained the rights to all the Manchester patterns.

"The Boardman Co. is perhaps best known to the general public for its famous silver trophies including those for the Super Bowl, Wimbledon and U.S. Open tennis tournaments and the Miss America Pageant." (*Record-Journal*, Meriden, Ct., 26 November 1985). J.C. Boardman Co. bought the F.B. Rogers Co. in 1985.

LUTHER BOARDMAN & SON
East Haddam, Connecticut

The company was founded by Luther Boardman in the 1820s; became L. Boardman & Son between 1840-44 and went out of business about 1905.

Luther Boardman was born at Rocky Hill, Connecticut, December 26, 1812. He was apprenticed to Ashbil Griswold at Meriden, Connecticut, where he learned the britannia trade. In 1833 he worked for Burrage Yale at South Reading, Massachusetts and became owner of the shop in 1836. In 1837 he returned to Meriden and married Lydia Ann Frary. In 1838 he worked for Russell & Beach at Chester, Connecticut and later made britannia spoons in his own shop there. In 1842 he moved to East Haddam, Connecticut. Most of his work after this time was silverplated britannia.

In 1864 his son was made a partner and the name of the firm changed to L. Boardman and Son which was continued for some time after his death in 1887. In 1866 a new plant was built for making nickel silver, silverplated spoons. The business was discontinued shortly before the death of Norman S. Boardman in 1905.

L. BOARDMAN & SON

Z. BOSTWICK
New York, New York

Zalmon Bostwick advertised in *The New York Mercantile Register* 1848-49 as "successor to Thompson," and that he "Would inform the public generally that he has made extensive preparation for the manufacture of SILVER WARE, in all its branches..." Listed in New York City Directories 1851-52.

F.L. BOSWORTH CO.
Minneapolis, Minnesota

Founded 1900. Jobbers and wholesale jewelers. They bought wares "in the metal" from manufacturers and plated them in their own shop. Succeeded by P.M. Vermaas c. 1915. Vermaas was president when Bosworth died in 1914.

BOTT SILVERSMITHS, INC.
New York, New York

Listed 1961 JBG as manufacturers of silver wares.

D.C. BOURQUIN
Port Richmond, New York

Founding date not known. Listed in JC 1904, under sterling and jewelry. Out of business before 1909. Trademark identical to Wortz & Voorhis.

BOWLER & BURDICK CO.
Cleveland, Ohio

Listed in JC 1904-1922. Wholesaler whose trademark was found on souvenir spoons. In business before 1890.

JACK BOWLING
Philadelphia, Pennsylvania

Silversmith, designer and lecturer on silver and silver work. His own works are included in the permanent collections of the Honolulu Academy of Arts and the Library of Congress. He has won numerous awards for excellence and is noted especially for his handwrought ecclesiastic silver.

Admiral Bowling, while still a lieutenant, gained an international reputation as an engraver and print maker but found rough seas unsuitable for the pursuit of these skills. He turned then to metal work and started with the handiest material—tin cans, and soon graduated to gold and silver. He made a silver ladle while at sea on an anti-submarine patrol in 1943 and was impressed with the time and patience required. It was then that he selected his "turtle" maker's mark, chosen because of its significance that "slow and steady does it."—a most appropriate symbol on hand-wrought silver. The two stars were added on his promotion to Rear Admiral and retirement from the Navy in 1947. In addition, he engraves "jack bowling— philadelphia" and the date of completion on finished articles when suitable. This is not a stamp but an actual signature.

The turtle mark used with 14k, 10k on gold; with STERLING on silver.

WM. N. BOYNTON
Manchester, Iowa

Registered trademark June 27, 1882 for manufacture of gold, silver and plated ware. This is essentially the same trademark used by the United States Jewelers' Guild until c. 1904. This latter mark was also used by J.H. Purdy & Co., wholesale and retail jeweler in Chicago, listed c. 1896- 1924. It was also used by others who belonged to the Guild.

BRAINARD & WILSON
Danbury, Connecticut

Listed 1909-1922 in JC under plated silver wares.

B. & W.

(On Silver Plated Art Ware.)

W.J. BRAITSCH & CO.
Providence, Rhode Island

Silversmiths before 1895. They were manufacturers of sterling dresserware. In 1898 they introduced a new type of dresserware of 14k gold plate which they guaranteed to wear ten years. An ingot of gold was welded to an ingot of gun metal, both were then rolled into sheets of the desired thickness and then made into backs for brushes, mirrors, trophies, etc. They were hand chased and either a gold or gold plated shield was inserted. The process was somewhat related to the "Old Sheffield Plate" process. Out of business before 1922.

E.P. BRAY & DAUCHY
New York, New York

Advertised in *Harper's Weekly* (12-4-1858) as "agts., Manufacturers... We *Manufacture and Plate* our own Ware, and are thus enabled to offer...Coffee, Tea, and Hot Water Urns... Liquor, or Cordial Stands; Magic perfumery and Cigar Stands with Thermometer attached; Magic Castors and Egg Stands combined; complete with Cups and Spoons; Fillagree (sic!) Card and Sugar Baskets; Wine Syphons; Champagne and Hock Bottle Holders; New Style French 3 and 4 Ring Breakfast Castors, & c. & c."

RAYMOND BRENNER, INC.
Youngstown, Ohio

Registered trademark for sterling silverware, silverplated holloware, flatware and table cutlery. Claims use since August 29, 1949.

CHAS. C. BRIDDELL, INC.
Crisfield, Maryland
See Towle Silversmiths

Started in business c. 1900 and originally made oyster knives and other seafood tools and implements for the watermen who worked the lower Chesapeake Bay area. In

1905 the firm registered the trademark "Carvel Hall" to be used on cutlery, machinery and tools. The name, Carvel Hall, was chosen many years ago by a designer for the company who was visiting Annapolis. While there, he noticed the elegant designs on the massive doors of the Carvel Hall Hotel and returned to Crisfield with the suggestion that the name be used on the line of knives being made by the firm. They now make a dozen lines of dinner knives and carving knives. Carvel Hall is now a Division of Towle Silversmiths.

BRIDE & TINCKLER
New York, New York

Wholesalers of sterling silverware and jewelry. Listed JC 1896-1922.

BRIDGEPORT SILVER CO.
Bridgeport, Connecticut

In business in 1880. President, James Staples; sec-treas., superintendent, Samuel Larkin. About 1882 there was a report that they were to merge with the F.B. Rogers Silver Co. Business continued until 1884 or longer.

BRIDGEPORT SILVER PLATE CO.
Bridgeport, Connecticut
Lambert's Point, near Norfolk, West Virginia

Incorporated January 15, 1891 with George A. Leonard of Boston as president; treasurer, F.H. MacFarlane; sec., Thomas F. MacFarlane. Moved to Lambert's Point, near Norfolk, West Virginia in 1898 although in 1910 there was a MacFarlane Mfg. Co. listed in the Bridgeport Directory. In 1894 there was a Bridgeport Silver Plate Co., probably controlled by MacFarlane. In 1913 there was a firm, MacFarlane, Brothers Mfg. Co. In August 1913 the deeds, tools, etc., were given to the Newfield Silver Co.

BRINSMAID
Burlington, Vermont

CHRONOLOGY

Pangborn & Brinsmaid	1833-43
J.E. Brinsmaid & Brothers	1843
Brinsmaid & Bros.	1843-1850
Brinsmaid, Brother & Co.	1850-1854
James E. Brinsmaid	1854-1884
Brinsmaid & Hildreth	1854-1902

The Brinsmaid name has been connected with silversmithing in Burlington since c. 1795 when Abram Brinsmaid, from Great Barrington, Massachusetts, settled there. His three sons, James Edgar, Sedgwick Swift and William Bliss, set up in business in 1843 at the old stand of Pangborn & Brinsmaid under the name J.E. Brinsmaid & Brothers, a name soon shortened to Brinsmaid & Bros. Sedgwick left the partnership in 1850 and the two remaining brothers took into partnership Chester Hildreth under the new firm name of Brinsmaid, Brother & Co. In 1854 James Edgar announced that he was opening his own business as successor to Brinsmaid, Brother & Co. William Brinsmaid and Chester Hildreth went into business together under the name of Brinsmaid & Hildreth. Both new firms claimed to be successors to Pangborn & Brinsmaid, Brinsmaid & Bros. and Brinsmaid, Bros. & Co. James E. Brinsmaid retired in 1884. Brinsmaid & Hildreth business continued until 1902 when it was sold to Nelson A. Bero.

A. Brinsmaid B & H

Brinsmaid's B ⊙ D Brinsmaid

Brinsmaid & Hildreth

BRISTOL BRASS & CLOCK CO.
Bristol, Connecticut
See American Silver Co.
See International Silver Co.

Organized in 1856. They furnished Holmes & Tuttle with their metal. Successor to Holmes & Tuttle Mfg. Co. in 1857. In 1901 became The American Silver Co. which was bought by International Silver Co. in 1935. Bristol Brass & Clock Co. owned the entire stock of American Silver Co. until 1913 when a distribution of stock was made.

Makers of silver tableware, solid and plated. Patent 26,297, March 26, 1895.

1857 WELCH-ATKINS
NEW ENGLAND SILVER PLATE CO.
H. & T. MFG. CO.
WELCH SILVER.
ROYAL PLATE CO.

BRISTOL MFG. CO.

Attleboro, Massachusetts

Founding date not known. They were manufacturers of plated silverware, cut and plain glass. Succeeded by Bristol Silver Co. c. 1895.

SILVEROIN
Novelties

GERMAN SILVER
(On Mesh Bags.)

BRISTOL SILVER COMPANY

Attleboro, Massachusetts

Successors to Bristol Mfg. Co. Out of business before 1915.

(Sterling Finish.)

BRISTOL SILVER CORP.

Taunton, Massachusetts

See Poole Silver Company, Inc.

BRITANNIA ARTISTIC SILVER

See M.T. Goldsmith

BRITANNIA ARTISTIC SILVER

BRITANNIA METAL CO.

See Van Bergh Silver Plate Co.

BRODGERS SILVER CO.

Taunton, Massachusetts

The trademark shown here has previously been attributed to a "Brodgers" Silver Company. It is actually the trademark of F.B. Rogers Silver Company of Taunton, Massachusetts, successor to the West Silver Company.

THOMAS F. BROGAN

New York, New York

Listed JC 1896-1930 under sterling silverware and jewelry.

D.L. BROMWELL, INC.

Washington, D.C.

Founded in 1873 by James Bromwell as a small silver and nickel-plating plant. Wet cells were used for the electroplating process, but the buffing wheels that were used to develop the gleaming finish employed a huge mastiff dog, named Cleo, as the motive power. So well did Cleo love the work that it was a problem getting the dog out of the wheel when his efforts were no longer needed. An old-style gas engine was installed later to replace Cleo's power potential, but it broke down periodically and Cleo was allowed to return to the beloved wheel.

James Bromwell's shop, which was capable of making or repairing almost anything, soon became the popular refuge of inventors, who would bring their problems there to be solved. One inventor was trying to develop a gramaphone at about the time Edison was perfecting his. While working with the inventor on the basis of a coated cylinder to retain the sound impressions, James discovered how to plate babyshoes with precious metals, a branch of the business which is still active.

Requests for repair and replacement of antique door knockers, fireplace andirons, fenders and fire tools led to new fields and the development of a bewildering array of metal products spread the fame of the establishment all over the country.

In 1907 James Bromwell died, and his son, Dwight, took over the business. His own son, Berton also began to learn the business, but his interests were in its administration. In 1924 the firm was incorporated under its present name. It is presently operated by the fourth generation of Bromwells. They no longer do their own plating and now specialize in fireplace fixtures.

J.T. BROMWELL

Baltimore, Maryland

Listed in the Baltimore City Directories 1881-1888 under the name T.T. Bromwell, silver plater; listed 1889 as Bromwell Plating Works; 1898-1901 as John T. Bromwell and 1902-04 as Bromwell Plating Works.

BRONZART METALS CO.

New York, New York

Listed among manufacturers of silver c. 1940.

BRONZART

BROOKLYN SILVER CO.

See Schade & Co.

"Satin finish" on plated silver patented in 1870 by James H. Reilly.

BROOKLYN SILVER PLATE CO.
Brooklyn, New York

In business c. 1890. "Brooklyn S.P. Co. Quadruple Plate" mark used on napkin rings made by E.G. Webster & Son c. 1895-1900.

BROWER & RUSHER
New York, New York
See Walter S. Brower

Listed in New York City Directories 1837-1842 as retailers for S.D. Brower; Hall, Hewson & Co.; Hall, Hewson & Brower.

WALTER S. BROWER
Albany, New York

CHRONOLOGY

Carson & Hall	1810-1818
Hall & Hewson	1818-1829
	1842-1847
Hall, Hewson & Co.	1839-1842
	1847-1850
Hall, Hewson & Merrifield	1845
Hall, Hewson & Brower	1849-1850
Hall & Brower	1852-1854
Hall, Brower & Co.	1854
S.D. Brower & Son	1850
Walter S. Brower	1850

The history of the Walter S. Brower company of Albany, New York can be traced to Carson & Hall (Thomas Carson & Green Hall, 1810-1818); Hall & Hewson (Green Hall & John D. Hewson, listed in City Directories 1818-1829; 1842-1847); Hall, Hewson & Co. (Green Hall, John D. Hewson and S. Douglas Brower, listed in the City Directories 1839-1842; 1847-1850);

Hall, Hewson & Merrifield (Green Hall, John D. Hewson & Thomas V.Z. Merrifield, in business c. 1845); Hall, Hewson & Brower (Green Hall, John D. Hewson & S.D. Brower listed in the City Directory 1849-1850); Hall & Brower (Green Hall & S. Douglas Brower & Co. (Green Hall and S.D. Brower, listed in City Directories after 1854); S.D. Brower & Son (S.D. Brower & Walter S. Brower, in business around 1850) and finally Walter S. Brower, who began around 1850 in Albany. Walter S. Brower was the son of S. Douglas Brower, who had been apprenticed to Hall & Hewson before setting up his own shop in Troy, New York in 1834. S. Douglas retired to a farm temporarily and then returned to silversmithing with the firm of Hall, Hewson & Brower c. 1849-50. Father and son were in business together soon afterwards. Walter S. Brower retired in 1898.

BROWN & BROS.
Waterbury, Connecticut

Established in 1851. They originally produced brass and German silver. September 21, 1875 they registered a patent for brass, German silver and plated silver goods. In 1874 they engaged LeRoy S. White, who had been with Rogers & Brother for 17 years and earlier with Hartford Mfg. Co., to start making silverplated flatware. The business continued for about ten years but was not too successful and the entire business discontinued in 1884 or 1885. No successor of their silverplated line was recorded. In 1886 Randolph and Cough took over the plant but evidently did not continue making silverplated flatware.

THOMAS G. BROWN & SONS
New York, New York

CHRONOLOGY

Hinsdale & Taylor	1807-1817
Taylor, Baldwin & Co.	1817-1841
Baldwin & Co.	c. 1840-1869
Thomas G. Brown	1869-1881
Thomas G. Brown & Sons	1881-c. 1915

Manufacturers of some sterling goods for Gorham Mfg. Co., which were so marked.

"Justus Verschuur, for several years connected with the Alvin Mfg. Co., is now connected with Thomas G. Brown & Sons." (JC&HR 3-18-1896, p. 24)

"William A. Brown, New York, formerly of Thomas G. Brown & Sons, and Frederick T. Ward, formerly of Cox, Cooper, Ward & Young, have formed a partnership and started in business to manufacture high class novelties in sterling silver." (JC&HR 3-25-1896, p. 24)

"This concern started in Newark c. 1801-02 and has been in existence for 98 or 99 years, thus outdating all others." (Letter from T.G. Brown & Sons, JC-W 5-16-1900, p. 52)

The sons were Thomas B. and William A. Brown.

(Goods made for Gorham Mfg Co.)

THOMAS J. BROWN
Baltimore, Maryland

"Listed in Baltimore City Directories 1867-1874 as a goldsmith and silversmith. The company name was changed to Thomas J. Brown & Son in 1875 and continued under this listing through 1883.

BROWN & SHARP
Warren, Rhode Island
Pawtucket, Rhode Island
Providence, Rhode Island

Brown & Sharp, established in 1804 by David Brown, jeweler and silverware, in Warren, Rhode Island. When business failed he traveled through the valley of the Connecticut and ground razors and fine cutlery. He also carried with him silverware of his own manufacture. He followed this itinerant occupation for 3 years. In 1828, he moved from Warren, Rhode Island to Pawtucket, Rhode Island and five years later, in 1833, formed a co-partnership with his son Joseph P. Brown and not long afterwards founded in Providence the establishment which became incorporated in 1868 as Brown & Sharpe Mfg. Co. still in business in 1919." (JC-W 2-5-1919)

BROWN & WARD
New York, New York
See Thomas G. Brown & Sons

Listed JC 1896 under sterling silver. Out of business before 1904.

BROWNE, JENNINGS & LAUTER
New York, New York
See Jennings & Lauter

BRUN-MILL CO.
Pittsfield, Illinois

Manufacturers of plated silverware c. 1920.

FRED BUCHER
Baltimore, Maryland

Listed in Baltimore City Directories 1877-79 as a goldsmith and silversmith.

BUCK SILVER COMPANY
Salamanca, New York

Listed as Buck Silver Company c. 1900-1914 when it became Buck Plating Co. Out of business before 1922. According to an unidentified newspaper clipping dated 1908, they made an extensive line of plated holloware.

BUCKER & ROHLEDER
Baltimore, Maryland

Listed in Baltimore City Directories 1901-04 as silverplaters.

SILAS E. BUCKER
Baltimore, Maryland

Listed in Baltimore City Directories 1907-13 as a silverplater.

CALEB H. BURGESS
Baltimore, Maryland

Listed in 1864 Baltimore City Directory as a silverplater. Listed as Caleb H. & John Burgess 1865-1883—Caleb H. Burgess 1884-89.

JOHN BURGESS
Baltimore, Maryland

Listed in 1864 Baltimore City Directory as a silverplater.

OWEN D. BURGESS
Baltimore, Maryland

Listed in Baltimore City Directories 1894-1899 as a silverplater.

CHAS. B. BYRON CO.
New York, New York

Successors to Bryon & Vail Co. before 1909.

BRYON & VAIL CO.
New York, New York
See Chas. B. Byron Co.
Succeeded by Chas. B. Byron Co. Founding date not known. Manufacturers of sterling silverware, gold and platinum cigarette and vanity cases, match boxes and powder boxes.

C

J.E. CALDWELL
Philadelphia, Pennsylvania
"Jewelers, silversmiths and antiquarians since 1839," according to advertisements. The *Jewelers' Circular-Weekly* (2-5-1919) says that J.E. Caldwell was founded in 1832. No documentary evidence has been found to support this. Their first advertisement appeared in 1893 in the *United States Gazette* on June 20.

James E. Caldwell took in his son, J. Albert Caldwell, and he in turn took in his son, J. Emott Caldwell. The original J.E. Caldwell was a watchmaker.

In 1843 Caldwell had James M. Bennett as a partner and the firm was then known as Caldwell & Bennett. Bennett left the firm in 1848 and the name was changed to J.E. Caldwell & Company which it remains today. James Caldwell died in 1881 and was succeeded by his son, J. Albert Caldwell, who ran the business until his death in 1914.

J. E. C. & CO.

CAMDEN HALL INC.
New York, New York
Importers. Listed JC-K 1964 in New York; no further listing.

J.D. CAMIRAND & CO.
Montreal, Canada
Manufacturers of plated silver c. 1920.

MADE OF
J D CAMIRAND
& CO
MONTREAL

A. CAMPBELL
Chicago, Illinois
Listed in Chicago City Directories 1853-1855 as a silverplater.

ARCHIBOLD CAMPBELL
Baltimore, Maryland
Listed in 1864 Baltimore City Directory as a silverplater.

JAMES J. CAMPBELL
Baltimore, Maryland
Listed in Baltimore City Directories 1874-1877 as silverplaters.

SAMUEL K. CAMPBELL
Baltimore, Maryland
Listed in 1864 Baltimore City Directory as a silverplater.

CAMPBELL-METCALF SILVER CO.
Providence, Rhode Island
Founded by Ernest W. Campbell and Joseph M. Metcalf. Campbell was born in Providence, Rhode Island April 11, 1860. Studied art at Brown University. Started in silver manufacturing business as a designer and superintendent at "one of the prominent Providence silver manufactories" (probably Gorham). Metcalf was born in Brooklyn, Connecticut in 1861 and received his education in Providence. His first business experience was as a salesman for a drug firm. Campbell and Metcalf joined together under the name Campbell-Metcalf Silver Company in 1892 to manufacture sterling silver goods.

"The Campbell-Metcalf Silver Co. was adjudged insolvent." JC&HR 6-8-1898, p. 17) In 1900 Campbell designed silverware for W.H. Manchester Co.

CANADIAN JEWELERS, LTD.
Montreal, Quebec
Manufacturers of silver deposit ware 1912-1923. Successors to Hemming Mfg. Co.   DEPOS-ART

CANADIAN WM. A. ROGERS CO., LTD.
Toronto, Canada
See Oneida Silversmiths
See Wm. A. Rogers Co.

"HEIRLOOM"   RP   Wm. A. Rogers
"WM. A. ROGERS"

✠ W. R. ☒   1881 (R) ROGERS (R) A1

CANFIELD & BROTHER
Baltimore, Maryland
Ira B. Canfield and William B. Canfield, silversmiths in Baltimore c. 1830.

CANFIELD BRO. & CO.
Baltimore, Maryland
Ira B. Canfield, Wm. B. Canfield and J.H. Meredith. Importers and manufacturers of watches, jewelry and silverware, "Albata & Plated ware." Listed in Baltimore City Directories 1850-81. Succeeded by Welsh & Bro.

CANTERBURY SILVERSMITHS, INC.
Brooklyn, New York
    Manufacturers of sterling and plated wares.

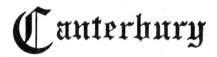

Trademark filed Nov. 12, 1948; use claimed since February 1946. For use on silverplated and sterling silver holloware, namely, serving trays, bread trays, water pitchers, food serving dishes, table platters and plates.

1950 trademark on sterling and plated wares.

OSCAR CAPLAN & SONS
Baltimore, Maryland
    Silversmiths, established 1905.

CALBERT MFG. CO.
New York, New York
    Listed JC 1915 as manufacturers of plated silver. Out of business before 1922.

GONDOLA SILVER

DAVID CARLSON
Gardner, Massachusetts
    Listed KJI 1927 as manufacturer of hand-wrought sterling silverware.

CARON BROS.
Montreal, Canada
    Listed in JC as manufacturers of metal products and jewelry. Their trademark has been found on souvenir spoons. In business 1901-1931.

CARPENTER & BLISS
North Attleboro, Massachusetts
See Napier Company
    Began business as Carpenter & Bliss in 1875 in North Attleboro, Massachusetts. Succeeded by E.A. Bliss Co. in 1883.

M.W. CARR & CO., INC.
West Somerville, Massachusetts
    Listed from c. 1920 to the present as manufacturers of bag frames, dorine boxes, vanity cases, match boxes, jewel boxes, Dutch reproductions, pewterware, photo frames and other novelties.

CARR CRAFT

SANDERS W. CARR
Baltimore, Maryland
    Listed in 1876 Baltimore City Directory as a silverplater. Succeeded by W.S. Carr & Co. in 1877.

W.S. CARR & CO.
Baltimore, Maryland
    Successors to Sanders W. Carr, silverplater, first listed in 1876 Baltimore City Directory. In business through 1886.

JOHN CARROW
Philadelphia, Pennsylvania
    In business about 1884.

JOHN CARROW. PHILA. QUAD. H.W.M.

CARTER-CRUME CO.
Niagara Falls, New York
    Listed in the Niagara Falls City Directory as the earliest manufacturers of salesbooks in this country. Succeeded by American Salesbook Co., now Moore Business Forms, Inc.
    They were also listed in the 1898 JC as manufacturers of plated flatware.
    These two trademarks were registered at the U.S. Patent Office for use on plated flatware.
    The Niagara Silver Co. (Wm. A. Jameson, manager) was a branch of Carter-Crume.

EXTRA {COIN SILVER NC12} PLATE

U.S. Patent 30,185, June 15, 1897 to be used on spoons, forks, knives and plated flatware.

RSMC

U.S. Patent 30,962, December 14, 1897, to be used on blades of knives, shanks of spoons and forks.

H.A. CARY CO.
    "H.A. Cary formerly of Phelps & Cary Co. has gone into business for himself. Incorporated at Albany (New York) Friday. They will engage in the business of silversmithing." (JC-W 6-6-1900, p. 34)

LEWIS CARY
Boston, Massachusetts

Silversmith c. 1820. One of his apprentices was Newell Harding.

CASTLE SILVER CORP.
New York, New York

Manufacturers of silverplated wares c. 1950.

CATTARAUGUS CUTLERY CO.
Little Valley, New York

In 1904 advertised "Manufacturers of fine cutlery since 1876." No record after 1910.

YUKON SILVER
98-100 FINE.

CELLINI CRAFT, LTD.
Chicago, Illinois

Founded by Ernest Gerlach as The Cellini Shops in 1914 and named for the celebrated Renaissance goldsmith, Benvenuto Cellini. Gerlach had received his training as metalsmith in the Craft Shop at Marshall Field & Company. He served in the Navy during WWI and left the shop in charge of Wilhelmina Coultas. Following the war, his brother, Walter, who had studied jewelry making at the Chicago Art Institute, joined him. Hans Gregg and William Conrad, both from Germany, and other European jewelers and silversmiths joined the firm.

During the Depression it was necessary to find a less expensive medium for their work than silver. In 1934 Walter Gerlach and Hans Gregg established Celline Craft, Inc. and added a line of holloware and flatware called Argental, made from an aluminum alloy. This soon replaced their handwrought jewelry and silver as their principal product.

In 1957 the Randahl Company bought Cellini Craft and moved the workshop to Skokie, Illinois. The Randahls sold their patterns and designs to Reed & Barton in 1965 where a few of the original Cellini silver designs continued to be made. In 1969 the Randahl Company purchased the Cellini Shop and discontinued its custom workshop. The retail part is still in operation.

CENTRAL STERLING CO.
Brooklyn, New York
See J. Wagner & Son, Inc.

Discontinued between 1909-14.

CENTURY SILVER MFG. CO.
New York, New York

Listed 1927 and 1931 KJI as manufacturers of silverplated wares.

CHAPIN & HOLLISTER CO.
Providence, Rhode Island

Listed in JC 1915-22. Manufacturers of gold, silver and gold-filled knives and jewelry.

C. & H. Co.

CHAPMAN & BARDEN
Attleboro, Massachusetts
See Barden, Blake & Co.

C. & B.

CHARTER COMPANY
See International Silver Company

Trademarks used on sterling reproductions of early Colonial silver. Made in the Barbour Silver Co. plant c. 1930-33. When that division was closed, the Charter line was moved to the sterling division in Wallingford. Discontinued about 1942.

BENJAMIN K. CHASE
Rutland, Vermont

Went into business in 1869 as a silversmith and jeweler after serving as a captain in the Union Forces in the Civil War. Advertised gold and silver goods and watches.

JOHN CHATTELLIER
Newark, New Jersey

Manufacturer of sterling cigar, cigarette and clock cases, razor sets, jewel, match and cigarette boxes, picture frames and watch cases.

CHELTENHAM & CO., LTD.
Sheffield, England
See National Silver Co.

CHICAGO MONOGRAM STUDIOS
Chicago, Illinois

Listed 1922 JC as manufacturers of sterling, 10, 12 and 14k gold buckles, belt and trouser chains. Successors to Chicago Monogram Jewelry Works. William Nicholls registered their Silvergrams trademark in 1948 and claimed that it had been in use since Oct. 23, 1947. It was for monograms in the form of initials made of, or plated with precious metal, to be attached to automobiles.

CHICAGO SILVER CO.
Chicago, Illinois

Listed in business c. 1925-1950 as manufacturers of sterling silverware.

CHICAGO SILVER PLATE COMPANY
Chicago, Illinois

Founded in 1868 and a year later moved to Aurora, Illinois and renamed the Aurora Silver Plate Company (q.v.)

SAMUEL CHILD & CO.
Baltimore, Maryland

Listed in Baltimore City Directories 1868-1886 as silverplaters.

CHRISTOFLE
Paris, France

Founded in 1839 by Charles Christofle. He was the founder of the plated and gilded silverware industry of France. He bought up all the French electroplate patents then extant and started his own silver and gold plating industry. Later he branched out into sterling and gold wares. Workmanship of the Christofle firm has always been outstanding. The firm is still considered one of the leaders in world silver design. They are represented in the U.S. by Christofle at Baccarat, New York.

July 9, 1949 Christoflle filed application for a trademark in the U.S. to be used on gold and sterling silver flatware and holloware.

CHURCH & ROGERS
See Rogers Brothers

LOREY CHURCHILL
Baltimore, Maryland

Listed in Baltimore City Directories 1864-1868 as a silverplater.

CINCINNATI SILVER CO.
Cincinnati, Ohio
See O.E. Bell Co.

FREDERICK H. CLARK
Newark, New Jersey

Listed in JC 1915 as manufacturer of sterling silverware. Out of business before 1922.

GABRIEL D. CLARK
Baltimore, Maryland

Silversmith in Baltimore 1830-1896, associated with James A. Foxcroft 1831-1839 in the firm of Foxcroft & Clark. Born 1813—died 1896.

G. D. CLARK

CLARK & NOON
Newark, New Jersey

First listed in JC as W.F. Cory & Bros., Newark, New Jersey in 1896. Clark & Noon are listed as successors in 1915 and not listed after 1922. Makers of sterling silverware and 14 and 18k gold jewelry.

BENJAMIN CLARK SILVER CO.
Ottawa, Illinois
See Benedict Mfg. Co.

CLIFF SILVER CO.
New York, New York

They advertised (*Antiques*, Nov. 1929, p. 407) that they specialized in "Reproducing by hand sterling or Sheffield Plate." The ad says "Established 1905."

CLIMAX MESH BAG CO.
Newark, New Jersey

Listed in JC in 1915. Out of business before 1922.

COBB, GOULD & CO.
Attleboro, Massachusetts
See Wallace Silversmiths
See Watson Co.

Founded in 1874 in Attleboro, Massachusetts. Succeeded by Watson & Newell in 1894; the Watson Company in 1919 and Wallace Silversmiths in 1955.

HERBERT COCKSHAW, JR.
New York, New York

Listed in 1904 as Howard & Cockshaw; Herbert Cockshaw successor in 1915 and Herbert Cockshaw, Jr. in 1936-37 in the Jobbers' Handbook.

CODDING BROS. & HEILBORN
North Attleboro, Massachusetts

Codding Bros. & Heilborn were manufacturers of silver novelties, founded in 1879 in North Attleboro, Massachusetts. In 1882 their business was burned out and they erected a new factory that same year. Leo A. Heilborn was admitted to the firm in 1891. In 1895 the members of the firm were Arthur E. Codding, James A. Codding, Edwin A. Codding and Leo A. Heilborn. C.A. Vanderbilt (q.v.) was in charge of the domestic trade office from 1893. "Codding Bros. & Heilborn, Providence, incorporated for the manufacture and selling of jewelry and silverware and novelties." (JC 4-28-1897, p. 28) The firm went out of business in May 1918.

C. B. & H.
STERLING.

D.D. CODDING
North Attleboro, Massachusetts

Listed in JC in 1896 as manufacturers of sterling silverware. Out of business before 1904.

STERLING
D. D. C.

See page 233 for additional information.

COHANNET SILVER CO.
Taunton, Massachusetts

Catalog published 1896. Illustrated candlesticks, fern dishes, shaving mugs, tea sets, pickle casters with glass inserts, etc.

A. COHEN & SONS CORP.
New York, New York

Founded in 1911 by Hyman J. Cohen, Samuel Cohen, Harry Cohen and Abraham Cohen. They are the largest wholesale jewelry distributors in the world catering

to the retail jewelers. A division of Cohen-Hatfield Industries, Inc. Wholesalers of sterling and silverplated holloware and flatware which is produced under contract for them.

CROSBY KRANSHIRE

L.H. COHEN
New York, New York

Listed in the Jeweler's Weekly 1896 as manufacturers of sterling silverware. Listed in JC 1904. Succeeded by L.H. Cohen Co., Inc. between 1909-1915. Last listing was in 1922.

COHEN & ROSENBERGER
New York, New York

Listed in JC as Baldwin, Ford & Co. 1896; Ford & Carpenter in 1904 and Baldwin, Ford & Co. 1915-1943. Advertised imitation pearls, novelty jewelry and beads. Listed in sterling silver section until 1943.

S. COHEN & SON
Boston, Massachusetts

A jobbing concern that specialized primarily in plating about 1856.

J.J. COHN
New York, New York

Listed in Jewelers' Weekly, 1896 in sterling section. Also listed in JC 1896, leather goods.

L. COHN
Baltimore, Maryland

Listed in 1868-69 Baltimore City Directory as a silverplater.

WILLIAM H. COLE & SONS
Baltimore, Maryland

Listed in 1895 Baltimore City Directory. Advertised plated silverware.

ALBERT COLES & CO.
New York, New York

New York silversmiths. Listed in city directories from 1836 to 1880. The factory was at 6 Liberty Place. This was a large factory and the silver was sold to numerous retailers who, in turn, stamped their own names on pieces that Coles had actually manufactured. Coles was succeeded in

business by Morgan Morgans who, in turn, sold out to Geo. W. Shiebler in 1876. Coles' spoon designs were continued by the Shiebler company for many years, some of them being quite popular as late as 1895. From 1880 until his death November 27, 1885, Coles was listed only at his residence, 225 West 39th St.

Albert Coles advertised in 1848-1849, "All kinds of silver knives and forks constantly on hand." And, again in 1856, "Albert Coles & Co., manufacturers of silverware, butter, fish, fruit & dessert knives, spoons, etc. always on hand and made to order—6 Liberty Place."

COLONIAL SILVER COMPANY, INC.
Portland, Maine

Successor to the Stevens Silver Co. in 1899. They were manufacturers of plated silverware and pewter. Gold and silver and nickel plating done to order. In business until 1943.

COLONIAL SILVER CO.
(Nickel Silver Hollowware)

(Plated holloware)

(On white metal)

COLONIAL SILVER CO.
(White Metal Hollowware)

COLUMBIA MFG. CO.
Gowanda, New York

"The Columbia Mfg. Co. of Gowanda, New York has been incorporated with a capital stock of $15,000 for the purpose of manufacturing plated ware. The company will at once begin constructing a factory." (JW 6-1-1892)

COLUMBIA SILVER CO.
Brooklyn, New York

Listed 1957-61 JBG as manufacturers of silver.

COLUMBIA SILVERSMITHS
New York, New York

Listed 1957-61 as manufacturers of silver.

COMMONWEALTH SILVER CO.
Los Angeles, California

Manufacturers of sterling silverware 1905-c. 1920.

CONCORD SILVERSMITHS, LTD.
See Ellmore Silver Co., Inc.

Began as Concord Silver Co., in 1925 using the old Durgin factory. In 1939 a new concern was organized under the name of Concord Silversmiths, Ltd., and bought the plant, machinery, tools of the Concord Silver Co., then in bankruptcy. They were to manufacture heavy sterling flatware only. In September of 1942 they discontinued the manufacture of sterling for the duration of the war. Ellmore Silver Co. took over the business and produced their patterns. Dies purchased by Crown Silver Co.

CONTINENTAL MFG. CO.
New York, New York

Listed 1927 KJI as manufacturers of silverplated flatware and holloware.

CONTINENTAL SHEFFIELD SILVER CO.
Brooklyn, New York
See Continental Silver Co.

CONTINENTAL SILVER CO.
New York, New York

The Continental Silver Co. of New York and the Continental Sheffield Silver Co. are related. The former being the sales office of the latter. Listed as manufacturers of plated silver holloware on nickel silver base c. 1920 to 1950.

JOHN COOK
New York, New York
See Theo. Evans & Co.

John Cook, foreman for Wm. Gale & Son, 1855, patented a design for "Table-Set for Silver and Plated Ware," Design Patent No. 3384, February 23, 1869. Partner with Theo. Evans in Theo. Evans & Co.

Attributed

P.A. COON SILVER MFG. CO.
Syracuse, New York

Manufacturers of plated silverware. Successor to Albert G. Finn Silver Co. between 1904 and 1909. Out of business before 1915.

CORNELIUS & COMPANY
Philadelphia, Pennsylvania

Christian Cornelius, born in the Netherlands, arrived in Philadelphia in 1783. He began working as a silversmith in 1810, became a silver plater and patent lamp manufacturer in 1825 and later operated under the name of Cornelius & Company. He left a dynasty of lampmakers who worked late into the 19th century. One of their c. 1875 catalogs shows that they were influenced by the Gothic Revival designs of Charles Eastlake.

In 1857 in the *Annals of Philadelphia*, John F. Watson wrote that "Mr. Cornelius now makes the most elegant mantel and hanging lamps; his manner of succeeding in that, and in silverplating, is a very curious history, and would deserve to be told at great length."

CORONET SILVER CO., INC.
Brooklyn, New York

Manufacturer of silverplated wares c. 1950.

CORONET

CORTLAN & CO.
Baltimore, Maryland

Listed in Baltimore City Directories 1868-1870 as silverplaters.

W.F. CORY & BRO.
Newark, New Jersey
See Clark & Noon

Y STERLING.

Not used after 1904

S. COTTLE CO.
New York, New York
See Howard Sterling Co.

Established 1865. I.N. Levinson, President. H.S. Morris, Sec'y-Treas. Makers of 14k gold and sterling silver novelties. Not listed after 1920.

S. Cottle invented the machine for making a collar button which became the specialty of Howard & Son about 1880.

"S. Cottle, manufacturer of paper knives, pen trays, penwiper stands, letter files, candlesticks, mounted inkstands in sterling silver, etc. Shubael Cottle retired in 1878 and the firm continued as Hale & Mulford. Six years later L.J. Mulford retired and Seth W. Hale & Co. succeeded. This firm continued two years, at which time Mr. Hale assumed the management of *The Jewelers Circular*." (JC&HR 2-4-1894, p. 4) (This account does not agree with the listings which continue as S. Cottle Co. until c. 1915.

₵

M.A. COURTRODE
New York, New York

Listed JKD 1918 as silversmiths.

COWLES MFG. CO.
Granby, Connecticut
See International Silver Co.
See Rogers Brothers

Rev. Whitfield Cowles began silverplating in 1843. After he died his son, William B. Cowles, continued the experiments. In 1845 the Cowles Mfg. Co. was organized

with Asa Rogers, James H. Isaacson and John D. Johnson. They used German silver as the base for their silverplated wares. In business only a few years.

The Cowles' business led to the first real development in commercial silverplating in this country.

ROYAL COWLES
Cleveland, Ohio

Royal Cowles set up shop as a silversmith in the 1840s. In 1849 he took Joseph R. Albertson of Fellow, Wadsworth & Co., of New York into partnership. This partnership lasted for nine years after which each set up his own; the jewelry firm of Cowles & Company being formed in 1857. The other member of the firm was Homer Goodwin. Cowles continued in business until 1889 when he moved to New York City. He died there in 1897.

Royal Cowles was the son of Ralph Cowles who was a well known surveyor and county auditor. Some confusion has arisen, presumably because father and son had the same initials and the same address. William G. Rose, in his history of Cleveland substantiates that the silversmith's name was Royal, not Ralph.

About 1861 George Cowell and his son, Herbert, started a jewelry business, H. Cowell & Co., and took over the business of Royal Cowles. In this way, one of Cleveland's largest and most exclusive jewelry stores had its beginning in the business of one of the city's early silversmiths.

W.I. COWLISHAW
Boston, Massachusetts

Cowlishaw was in business at least as early as 1898 and was known especially for his pewter reproductions of early pieces which were made by the traditional methods of casting and spinning.

He was succeeded by Morton Wheelock c. 1930. Wheelock continued to use the Cowlishaw name but changed the mark to a shield with the name enclosed. He made newer forms rather than reproductions and continued the business until the 1940s. Pieces marked with small circular mark with initials "W.I.C." and an eagle. (Used c. 1898-1930)

(Used c. 1930-c. 1940-45)

COYWELL SPECIALTY CO.
New York, New York

Listed in 1915 JC as manufacturers of sterling silverware. Out of business before 1922.

COYWELL
PLATNOID

CRAIG SILVER CO.
Bridgeport, Connecticut

"A concern operating under the name of Craig Silver Co. has been in existence in Bridgeport for some time." (JW 6-6-1894)

CRAIGHEAD SILVER PLATE CO.
Bridgeport, Connecticut

"The report of the receiver is that employees of the defunct concern received only 7 percent of the money they earned." (JC&HR 12-4-1895, p. 17)

CRESCENT SILVERWARE MFG. CO., INC.
Port Jervis, New York

Founded in 1922 in New York City. Moved to Port Jervis, New York in 1939. Manufacturers of silverplated holloware and during their early years also made pewter and chrome-plated items. For the past forty years have made only silverplated holloware. At the present time they manufacture about 450 different items. They took over the Knickerbocker Silver Co.

Sold to Samuel Kirk & Son. Inc. in 1977.

CRESCENT

CROMWELL PLATE CO.
Cromwell, Connecticut
See Barbour Silver Co.
See I.J. Steane & Co.

Organized in 1881 to manufacture a variety of silverplated wares. Sold to I.J. Steane & Co. before 1885.

CROWN MFG. CO.
North Attleboro, Massachusetts

Listed in 1915 JC as manufacturers of plated silverware. Out of business before 1922.

C. M. C.

CROWN SILVER CO., INC.
Brookline, Massachusetts

Listed 1936-37 Jobber's Handbook and 1950 JC-K as manufacturers of plated wares.

CROWN SILVER INC.
New York, New York

The Hasselbring Silver Company, founded in Brooklyn about 1890 by John Hasselbring; the Revere Silver Company, successor to Revere Silversmiths Inc., founded in Brooklyn about 1914 and the Wolfenden Silver Company, successor to J.W. Wolfenden Corporation became divisions of the Crown Silver Inc. in 1955. Manufacturers of sterling silver wares. They own the dies of Amston Co. and bought the F.M. Whiting Co. dies for sterling flatware when the Ellmore Silver Co. went out of business in 1960.

CROWN SILVER PLATE CO.
Bristol, Connecticut
See American Silver Co.

CROWN SILVER PLATE CO.
New York, New York
See J.W. Johnson

"There is no longer any Crown Silver Plate Co. but J.S. Johnson stamps this name on plated silver ware." (JC&HR 4-17-1898, p. 23)

CROWN SILVER PLATE CO.
Toronto, Ontario

Listed in JC 1909-15. Out of business before 1922.

H.C. CULMAN
Honolulu, Hawaii

Listed JC 1909. Out of business c. 1917. Manufacturing jewelers. Trademark found on Hawaiian souvenir spoons.

H. C.

J.F. CURRAN & CO.
New York, New York

Silverplaters c. 1860-1900.

CURRIER & ROBY
New York, New York
See Elgin Silversmith Company

Currier & Roby, New York silversmiths, was headed by Ernest M. Currier. It was founded in 1900 when Currier was 33 years of age. It was incorporated in 1901. They specialized in the reproduction of antique silver holloware and flatware, mostly English and American. Currier was also the author of *Marks of Early American Silversmiths*, published posthumously, two years after his death in 1936.

Currier & Roby succeeded in George A. Henckel & Co. (q.v.) in 1940 and they, in turn, became a division of Elgin Silversmith Co., Inc. (q.v.) which went out of business in 1976.

There are in existence a number of small sketches that are dated as early as 1895 but are believed to have been done by Currier since Roby was chiefly a silversmith and not a designer. It is possible that Currier and Roby met as early as 1885 when Currier would have been only 18 years old, and possibly served his apprenticeship as a designer. Roby was 23 years old and already a silversmith foreman.

Harry E. Roby was born at Concord, New Hampshire on June 6, 1862, son of Harrison A. Roby and Sophronia (Sarbent) Roby. He was apprenticed to William B. Durgin (q.v.) and then entered the employ of J. B. & S. M. Knowles (q.v.) and later with the Van Sant Co. (Vansant) (q.v.) of Philadelphia. In 1885 he moved to Newburyport, Massachusetts as silversmith foreman for the A.F. Towle & Son Co. (q.v.) where he remained until 1890. That year he became superintendent of the Wendell Mfg. Co. (q.v.) of Chicago where he remained until 1900. For a short time he was head of the sample making department of the Towle Mfg. Co. (q.v.) of Newburyport, Massachusetts and in 1901 with E.M. Currier established Currier & Roby in New York to make sterling holloware.

Currier was an authority on early American silver and had one of the largest collections of marks in the United States. His collection of record drawings of antique silver along with his photograph collection was also the largest known outside of the large museum collections.

The United States Amateur Championship Gold Trophy, made about 1925, is considered Currier's masterpiece. The design was inspired by the classical period of the Renaissance, a high standing urn made entirely of 18k gold. After the completion of Currier's drawings for the trophy, someone tampered with the design. An action which met with his disfavor. It was with much reluctance that he completed the project and after it was finished, the shop drawings, molds, patterns and

templates disappeared from the shop. Their only record is an 8" x 10" black and white photograph. The trophy itself is in the museum vault of the U.S. Golf Association in New Jersey and recently was used in the competition each year, photographed with the winner and returned to the vault. It is now permanently on display in the museum Golf House.

(a)

C R (b) STERLING

(c)

(d)

(e)

Currier & Roby Trademarks: (a) Trademark used on all silver and gold articles made by Currier & Roby. (b) Probably C&R original trademark used when organized in 1901. We recall this C&R mark with lion's head within broken rectangle drawn by hand on early working drawings of that date. (c) Typical art-deco hand drawn ornament (one of several designs) as used on the front cover of 4x6 promotional booklets by Currier. (d) Signature of E.M. Currier occasionally found on the back of sketches, sometimes accompanied by a rubber stamp of Currier & Roby, Silversmiths, with address. (e) Trademark used on copyright 5x7 promotional quatrefoil folders by Currier. (SILVER May-June 1983 by permission)

CURTIN & CLAKE HARDWARE CO.
St. Joseph, Missouri
Listed in JC 1909-22 as silverplaters.

C C C

CURTIS & DUNNING
Burlington, Vermont
Lemuel Curtis and Joseph N. Dunning advertised that their "silver spoons are made from crowns, without the least alloy." In partnership 1822-32.

F. CURTIS & CO.
Connecticut
See American Sterling Co.
See Williams Bros. Mfg. Co.
Frederick and Joseph S. Curtis, brothers who manufactured German silverware, spoons and spectacles in Hartford, moved to Glastonbury. The first notice of the partnership appeared January 24, 1848. Company offices remained at Hartford while manufacturing operations were begun at Curtisville—that section of Glastonbury which today comprises a part of Naubuc. The company name was changed to Curtisville Mfg. Co. "The Memorial History of Hartford County" states that at Curtisville was manufactured the first German Silver in America. The silver-white metal, an alloy of copper, zinc and nickel, was hauled by wagon to Waterbury and there rolled to the desired thickness (*Retrospect,* A publication of the Historical Society of Glastonbury, No. 10, Feb. 1948.)

H.H. CURTIS & CO.
North Attleboro, Massachusetts
The earliest record found was a Patent Office registration of the trademark in the name of Curtis and Wilkinson, November 3, 1891, to be used on jewelry, table and flatware. The company was sold at auction in May 1915.
Note that the trademark is similar to those of the W.H. Glenny & Company and the Waldo Foundry.

H. H. C. CO.
(German Silver Bags.)

JAMES CURTIS
Chicago, Illinois
Listed in 1854-1855 Chicago Directory as a silverplater.

CURTISVILLE MFG. CO.
Connecticut
See American Sterling Co.
See F. Curtis & Co.
See William Bros. Mfg. Co.
See Thomas S. Vail

Successor to F. Curtis & Co. of Hartford and Glastonbury. F. Curtis & Co. was reorganized on September 18, 1854 under the name Curtisville Mfg. Co. with Charles Benedict as President and R.F. Fowler, Sec. and Treas. By 1857 the locale was called Curtisville and had its own postmaster. In 1859, Thomas J. Vail assumed the Presidency and the Curtis family no longer appeared in the Hartford listings.

D

DAMAKS REFINING CO.
New York, New York

Manufacturers of sterling holloware c. 1950.

THE DANFORTH COMPANY
See Merwin-Wilson Co., Inc.

DANIEL AND ARTER GLOBE NEVADA SILVER WORKS
Birmingham, England

The Daniel and Arter Globe Nevada Silver Works produced great quantities of flatware bearing their trademarks and various tradenames which included the word "silver." These terms refer to alloys, none of which contain any silver, though some were plated with it.

ALUMINUM SILVER
ARGENLINE
BURMAROID
INDIAN SILVER
JAPANESE SILVER
LAXEY SILVER
NEVADA SILVER

WILLIAM G. DeMATTEO
Bergenfield, New Jersey

The late William G. deMatteo (1895-1980) was born in Italy and came to this country as a boy. He was first interested in medicine but made a chance visit to a silversmith's shop in New York City which changed his life's direction. He was apprenticed at Reed & Barton's New York shop in 1911. He went into business for himself in 1919, and, in 1921, moved his shop to Bergenfield, New Jersey. He worked there until he retired in 1968.

During that period he produced literally thousands and thousands of hand wrought pieces of holloware: trays, tea sets, centerpieces, etc. Also included were silver and gold chalices used by churches all over the world, silver surgical instruments and silver plates for bone replacement following surgery. All of his silver objects were his own original designs.

A major contribution to the silversmiths' art was the thorough training he gave to his son, William L. deMatteo (q.v.)

His marks: deM Studio, D in a wheel and DEMATTEO.

WILLIAM L. DeMATTEO
Alexandria, Virginia

William deMatteo is a Master Silversmith. The term "master" and the tradition it represents are quickly disappearing. He apprenticed to his father (q.v.), the premier silversmith of his generation in New York, who passed on to him the skills of the Master Craftsman and a love for the remarkable properties of silver and gold.

After leaving his father's studio he became the Master Silversmith at Colonial Williamsburg. In 1979 with his long-time partner, Philip Thorp, and his son, Chip, he founded Hand & Hammer. While at Colonial Williamsburg deMatteo supervised the interpretation of silver craftsmanship to hundreds of visitors daily, trained apprentices in his shop, and produced many variations of silver in reproductions of 18th century work as well as in modern sculptural forms.

DeMatteo has made special gifts for many of the important foreign leaders, including a matching set of riding crops for Queen Elizabeth II and Prince Philip; a miniature tea service for Queen Elizabeth the Queen Mother to be given to Princess Anne; and gifts for King Baudoin of the Belgians, King Hussein of Jordan and the presidents of several countries.

Among his noteworthy accomplishments was a hand-hammered replica of a silver Town Crier's bell, presented to the late Sir Winston Churchill as the symbol of the

Williamsburg Award for outstanding achievement in advancing the principles of liberty and human freedom.

In 1973 he created an adaptation of an 18th century inkwell in the form of a globe. This creation took about 200 hours work and perhaps a hundred thousand hammer blows. It was presented to former President Nixon by the White House Correspondents Association.

During his career, deMatteo has been commissioned to design and fashion unique sterling silver gifts for every President since John F. Kennedy.

Hand & Hammer has specially developed hundreds of jewelry designs for the museum merchandising programs at the Smithsonian Institution, Colonial Williamsburg, Boston Museum of Fine Arts, Art Institute of Chicago, National Trust for Historic

Preservation and more than 50 other museums.

Hand & Hammer's Collection also includes handmade Christmas ornaments based on motifs and designs found in America's important museums. Most are of sterling silver while some are crafted in pewter.

Phi Beta Kappa has designated Hand & Hammer sole supplier of their keys to their initiates. They also have many important corporate and commercial customers. These include Tiffany & Co.; AT & T, for whom an abstract sculpture was designed to mark the company's 100th anniversary; the Masters' Golf Tournament; Mass Mutual Insurance Company; Lord & Taylor; The Horchow Collection and many others.

The American Institute of Architects awarded deMatteo its Craftsman Medal for high achievement in the field of industrial arts and in 1975 he became the first American silversmith to be honored by an Associate Membership in the Goldsmiths' Company in London.

William L. deMatteo's mark: deM as recorded at the Goldsmiths' Company in London.

DART CRAFTSMAN CORP.
New York, New York

Manufacturers of silverplated novelties c. 1950.

A. DAVIS CO.
Chicago, Illinois

Successors to M.C. Eppenstein & Co. before 1904. Out of business shortly afterwards.

R. COIN   R. SPECIAL

DAVIS & GALT
Philadelphia, Pennsylvania

Registered U.S. Patent No. 22,275, January 3, 1893 for manufacture of sterling silverware. Patent Office records show this trademark in use since July 21, 1888. Listed in JC 1896-1915. Out of business between 1915-22.

Junius H. Davis and Charles E. Galt first listed in 1889 as Davis & Galt in the Philadelphia City Directory. In 1887 and 1888 the Directories list Junius H. Davis as a silversmith with no associate. The 1880 Directory lists Hamilton & Davis (Matthew F. Hamilton and Junius H. Davis) as silversmiths.

Adaptation of an 18th century inkwell in the form of a globe. Made by William L. deMatteo and presented to former President Nixon by the White House Correspondents Association. (Photo courtesy of William L. deMatteo)

"Davis & Galt have dissolved partnership." (JC&HR 5-30-1894, p. 30)

"Wm. Linker of Davis & Galt, has returned from a successful business trip." (JC&HR 3-4-1896, p. 25) Apparently, the company itself continued for some time after the partnership was dissolved. Charles E. Galt was related to the Galt family (See Galt & Bro.) in Washington, D.C. He was mentioned in a Dec. 19, 1902 newspaper item about the Washington Galts as being deceased. Junius H. Davis was associated with M.F. Hamilton in the firm of Hamilton & Diesinger.

DAWSON COMPANY MANU-FACTURERS
Cleveland, Ohio

DAWCO

Organized in the middle 1920s by Irwin H. Dawson to make fraternity, school, and other special pattern jewelry and allied products. These include plaques, pins, emblems, medals, trophies and some other items of sterling silver, gold plate and other metals. Sterling silver plaques with crests and trademarks thereon are one of their specialties.

JAMES J. DAWSON CO.
New York, New York

Listed in JC 1904 in plated silverware section. Out of business before 1915.

NORTH AMERICA

DAY, CLARK & CO.
Newark, New Jersey
New York, New York

Manufacturers and distributors of sterling and jewelry. The trademark was first used in 1895. Last record found was 1935.

E.L. DEACON JEWELRY CO.
Denver, Colorado

Listed in JC 1909; Eugene L. Deacon, successor before 1915 with address given as Los Angeles, California.

E. L. D.
(Souvenir Spoons.)

DECOREX INDUSTRIES, INC.
Meriden, Connecticut

Formed by the merger of the Rockwell Silver Co. (q.v.) and Silver City Glass Co. April 19, 1978. Manufacturers of sterling silver decorated crystal items.

I.N. DEITSCH
New York, New York

Listed in JC 1904-15 as manufacturers of sterling silverware. No records after c. 1920.

DEITSCH BROS.
New York, New York

Patent Office records show they were manufacturers of leather articles with sterling silver mountings, September 8, 1896. Listed in JC 1896-1922.

DELAWARE SILVER CO.

Found on grape design sterling and plated flatware of c. 1895-1900.

DELAWARE SILVER CO.

DELLI SILVERPLATE
San Francisco, California

Succeeded by Leonard Silver Mfg. Co. 1974.

DEPASSE MFG. CO.
New York, New York

Manufacturers of sterling silver deposit and gold encrusted glassware. Listed in JC 1909-15. Succeeded by Depasse, Pearsall Silver Co. before 1922.

DEPASSE, PEARSALL SILVER CO.
New York, New York

Successors to Depasse Mfg. Co. between 1915-1922. Last record was 1935.

DERBY SILVER CO.

Derby (Originally called Birmingham).
Connecticut
See International Silver Co.

Founded in 1873 by Edwin N. Shelton, Watson J. Miller and Thomas H. Newcomb, silverplaters of holloware. They made decorative wares of sterling silver.

U.S. Patent No. 15,642, June 26, 1888, registered by Watson J. Miller and Henry Berry for M & B sterling trademark to be used on forks, spoons, tea sets, brushes, mirrors and pitchers.

One of the original companies which formed the International Silver Co. in 1898.

Sterling mark not used after about 1895. Another Derby Silver Co. mark c. 1900-1904 had the anchor & crown with Derby Silver Co., Derby, Conn. around the edge.

Their first few years were largely devoted to the production of flatware as they had purchased from the bankrupt Redfield & Rice concern their tools and material. They gradually dropped flatware and started silverplated holloware which continued under the direction of Colonel Watson J. Miller who came from New York in 1879. They put out a large line of plated dresserwares. The factory continued to operate in Birmingham (Derby) until July 1933 when it was consolidated with other plants in Meriden.

(Pewter Holloware)

ALDEN
(Pewterware)

M & B. STERLING

The "half circle" trademark was first used in 1921 but not registered until 1923.

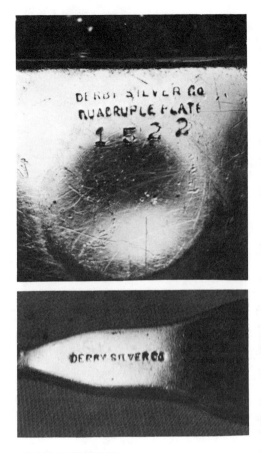

ADAM DEUPERT
Baltimore, Maryland

Listed in Baltimore City Directories 1875-1882 as a gold and silversmith (gold leaf).

DIAMOND SILVER CO.
Lambertville, New Jersey

In business in the 1930s. Clipping from the *Lambertville Beacon*, New Jersey (1-4-1949) says that the Diamond Silver Co. is now part of Ekco Products Co., Chicago, Illinois. (Nickel silver and silverplated flatware)

MISS SARAH B. DICKINSON
Niagara Falls, New York
See Mrs. Sarah B. Dickinson Wood
See Thomas V. Dickinson

THOMAS V. DICKINSON
Buffalo, New York
See Mrs. Sarah B. Dickinson Wood

U.S. Patent No. 19,905, registered July 21, 1891 for silver, flat and tableware. The mark is the same as that used by Mrs. Sarah B. Dickson Wood.

RICHARD DIMES COMPANY
South Boston, Massachusetts

Founded in 1908, according to one account and in 1923 by another. Sold to the King Silver Company in October 1955, which was acquired by Rogers, Lunt & Bowlen (Lunt Silversmiths) soon afterwards. They made sterling silver holloware and flatware and the trademark is registered with the U.S. Patent Office, No. 755,049, by Rogers, Lunt & Bowlen for use on sterling holloware and novelty items.

Manchester Silver Company in 1955 or 1956 acquired the tools, dies and rights to the flatware patterns formerly produced by Richard Dimes. Richard Dimes in 1890 started the holloware room of the Towle Mfg. Co. He later went to Frank W. Smith Co. and finally started his own business.

AUGUST DINGELDEIN & SON
New York, New York

Factories in Hannau am Main and Idar, Germany. Manufacturers of handmade sterling holloware. Listed in Keystone 1931 as manufacturers in New York.

DINGLEDEIN STUDIO INC.
Cape Girardeau, Missouri

"Silversmiths since 1852" according to advertisement in 1977 catalog.

DIRIGO DISTRIBUTING CO.
New York, New York
See Dirilyte Co. of America

DIRIGOLD

DIRILYTE COMPANY OF AMERICA, INC.
Kokomo, Indiana

Began in 1926 under the tradename DIRIGOLD. Their wares are of gold color, not plated, but solid metal developed in Sweden. Objection to the name was raised by the U.S. Patent Office as it implied that gold was included in its composition when there was none. In 1937 the name was changed to DIRILYTE. Both flatware and holloware are still being made. Since 1961 a process called Bonded Protection has been used to protect the finish which is tarnish free but loses its luster in the dishwasher. Dirilyte made prior to 1961 may have this finish applied at the factory.

DIRKSEN SILVER FILIGREE CO.
Freeport, Illinois

Founded by Gerritt Dirksen, born Emden, Germany, 1818. Though a silversmith by trade when he and his wife came to this country c. 1844 they settled on a farm in Ridott Township, Illinois. Several years later they moved to Freeport where he established a grocery business and was first listed in the city directories in 1872. In the back of the store Dirksen set up a small silversmith shop where he created many pieces of filigree ware. By 1890 the silverware business had prospered so that the grocery line was terminated and the entire two-story frame building converted into a silver filigree factory. This business was given a tremendous boost by the World's Columbian Exposition held in Chicago 1893-94. Gerritt and his two sons designed, made and exhibited some very elaborate pieces in a booth at the Fair. The elder son, John, a jewelry salesman, sold the Dirksen line with his other merchandise and Richard D., the younger son, assisted his father and eventually managed the shop. The elder Dirksen's work was more delicate than that of his son or the other employees. The 1900-01 city directory lists the firm as Dirksen Silver Co. (G. and R.D. Dirksen). The following year R.D. Dirksen is listed as proprietor. The elder Dirksen died in 1903. Demand for the delicate filigree work lessened and in 1905 the company closed. Dirksen filigree silver is plentiful in the Freeport, Illinois area and the pieces are included in the collections of the Stephenson County Museum.

D. S. F. CO.

J. DIXON & SONS
Sheffield, England

Established in 1806 by James Dixon as silversmiths and were among the first in Britain to manufacture "Old Sheffield Plate" and britannia wares. They were the leading makers of the britannia and silver-plated wares imported into this country in the period from the 1830s to the 1860s. At least one large American firm frankly

copied Dixon designs as fast as they reached this country. Registered U.S. Patent No. 14,806 for the manufacture of silver, nickel-silver, britannia and plated goods, Oct. 11, 1887. In 1930 the Dixon firm took over the goodwill of William Hutton & Sons. Dixon's is now run by fifth generation descendants of the founder.

PLATED SILVER STERLING SILVER

JAMES M. DIXON
Chicago, Illinois

Listed in 1854-55 Chicago Directory as a silverplater.

DODGE, INC.
Los Angeles, California

Listed in city directories 1940s to present in Chicago, Dallas, Los Angeles, Miami and Newark, as manufacturer to whole-saler. Sterling and silverplate.

(Sterling)   (Silverplate)

WILLIAM WALDO DODGE, JR.
Asheville, North Carolina

He was born in Washington, D.C. on February 6, 1895, son of William W. Dodge and Mary Amelia Parker Dodge. Attended Princeton University and later graduated from the Massachusetts Institute of Technology in Architecture in 1916; Masters Degree from MIT. Spent a year and a half at Oteen Military Hospital and Gaylord Sanitarium recovering from combat disabilities. There he learned to make hand-wrought silver. Married Margaret Wheeler in 1921 and taught in Asheville. Opened a shop there to make handwrought silver. Practiced architecture as William Waldo Dodge, Jr. A.I.A. His major silver works were for country clubs and rifle associations for annual trophies. One of his better known commissions was the Mayflower Cup now in the Archives and History exhibit in Asheville. He died there February 21, 1971.

HAND WROUGHT SILVER

DOMINICK & HAFF
New York
See Reed and Barton

CHRONOLOGY

Wm. Gale & Son	1821
Gale & North	1860
Gale, North & Dominick	1868
Gale, Dominick & Haff	1870
Dominick & Haff	1872
Dominick & Haff, Inc.	1889

The firm of Dominick & Haff was established by H. Blanchard Dominick, descendant of George Dominick, French Huguenot, who came to this country in 1740 and Leroy B. Haff who first entered the silversmithing business in the retail department of William Gale in 1867. In their early days they devoted themselves to the manufacture of small silverwares and became especially noted for their vinaigrettes, chatelaines and other fancy articles. Following a disastrous fire in 1877, they moved to a new factory and began to manufacture all kinds of articles in silver. Other moves were necessitated by the growing firm which eventually manufactured a general line of silverware.

The complicated inter-relationships of silversmiths and silver manufacturing is amply demonstrated by the history of Dominick & Haff whose beginnings can be traced back to William Gale & Son, silversmiths in New York in 1821. The succession of firm names was Gale & North; Gale, North & Dominick; Gale, Dominick & Haff; and in 1872 Dominick & Haff. William Gale had been an apprentice of Peter & John Targee, silversmiths in New York (John Targee, w. 1797-1841; Peter Targee, w. 1809-11; together, 1809-16), who had succeeded to the business of John Vernon, New York silversmith (w. 1787-1816). In 1879 Dominick & Haff bought out the business of Adams & Shaw (which had been founded about 1873 by Caleb Cushing Adams, for 18 years the general manager of the Gorham Company, and Thomas Shaw, an Englishman employed by the Gorham Company, until in connection with Tiffany & Company, he formed the manufacturing firm of Thomas Shaw & Company) the tools, fixtures, and patterns that related to the manufacture of silverware (the rest went to the Whiting Mfg. Co.), and which Adams & Shaw had previously purchased from John R. Wendt & Company, of New York. Dominick & Haff, was in turn, sold to Reed & Barton in 1928 and consolidated with that firm. There

were also connections with the McChesney Company, formed in 1921 by Samuel D. McChesney whose brother was Wm. F. McChesney, treasurer and later president of Dominick & Haff. At the death of Samuel D. McChesney, his business was taken over by Dominick & Haff. What was left of that business was acquired by Reed & Barton in 1928.

D. & H.

DORLING COMPANY OF AMERICA, INC.

Jenkintown, Pennsylvania

Registered trademark for use on flatware. Claims use since August 24, 1949.

DORST CO.

Cincinnati, Ohio

Successors (?) to Jonas, Dorst & Co. in business 1896. Manufacturers and retailers of sterling and plated silverware, and jewelry. Succeeded c. 1940 by Dorst Jewelry Co. which is still in business.

STERLING SILVER

LENORE DOSKOW, INC.

Montrose, New York

Founded in 1934 by Lenore and David Doskow. All pieces are designed by Leonore Doskow and made under her supervision. The company moved from New York City in 1942 and occupied its own building in Montrose, New York. They manufacture sterling and gold jewelry and novelty items. The line today comprises two thousand sterling silver pieces ranging from boxes to yoyos. Concentration is on the unusual— sets of measuring spoons, cookie cutters, melon scoops, collar stays, toothpicks, sport jewelry, desk accessories, etc.

 LEONORE DOSKOW
HANDMADE STERLING

DOWD-RODGERS CO.

Wallingford, Connecticut

Listed in the City Directory 1915/16-1937. Not listed in 1939. Directories published every two years. Jobbers of plated silverware. Listed as manufacturers of silverplated wares 1922 KS.

TRADE **D** MARK

Sugar bowl and creamer by Dominick & Haff, dated 1901. (Photo courtesy Diana Cramer, Editor SILVER)

DROBENARE BROS. INC.

New York, New York

Listed directories 1960s through 1973 as manufacturers of sterling silver.

THE DUHME COMPANY

Cincinnati, Ohio

Herman Duhme was born in Osnabruck, Hanover, Germany, June 14, 1819, the son of Herman H. and Margaret Duhme. Herman H. Duhme came to the United States August 1834 and brought his family. He was accompanied by some 100 other emigrants, the voyage being made from Bremen to New York in a small vessel chartered by Duhme. They settled in Ohio in a colony at Springfield. Young Herman Duhme was then 15 years of age. He began his business life with Griffith Foos whose wife took a motherly interest in him, teaching him English and social usage.

In 1840 Herman Duhme moved to Cincinnati and became a salesman in a dry goods store but a year later accepted a position in a jewelry store. He saved his money and three years later opened a small store which later expanded to become one of the largest jewelry stores in the midwest. It had its own manufacturing plant. The company continued after his death August 21, 1888. In 1896 the firm name was changed to The Duhme Jewelry Company. By 1899 there were two Duhme firms listed—one the Duhme Brothers, operated by Frank and Herman, sons of Herman, Sr. and The Duhme Jewelry Company, run by Herman and Oscar Keck. The Duhme Brothers was last listed in 1904 city directories; The Duhme Jewelry Company continued until 1910.

The Duhme Jewelry Company was incorporated January 22, 1898 for the manufacture of gold and silver articles. A notice in the *Jewelers Circular* (1-26-1898) states that "The Duhme Company have purchased the mfg. concern of Neuhaus, Lakin & Co. and will remove the plant to their building and begin the mfg. of sterling silver." Four months later there was a note that "The Kecks are in full possession of Duhme firm. Duhmes to open again under the name Duhme Bros." About 1893 the title of the firm was again changed to The Duhme Company and this listing continued in the city directories until 1907.

RUFUS DUNHAM

See Stevens and Smart
See New England Silver Co.

Made britannia and plated ware 1863-1875. In 1877 the company became Rufus Dunham & Sons and continued this same name until 1883 with sons Joseph S., Charles A. and John associated with the firm. In 1894 Joseph S. formed the New England Silver Company.

DUNKIRK SILVERSMITHS, INC.

Meriden, Connecticut

Successors c. 1945-50 to Gold Recovery & Refining Corp.

BENEDICT DUNN

See Benedict Mfg. Co.

L.F. DUNN

Niagara Falls, New York

Registered U.S. Patent No. 10765 for the manufacture of knives, forks and spoons, Dec. 4, 1883. Not listed in City Directory (1886 Directory is the earliest available).

CARBON

DURAND & COMPANY

Newark, New Jersey

CHRONOLOGY

James M. Durand	1838
Durand & Annin	1852
Durand, Carter & Co.	1859
Durand & Co.	1864
Durand & Co., Inc.	1892-1919

The firm of Durand & Co., manufacturing jewelers and silversmiths 1838-1919, was a culmination of seven successive generations of manufacturing jewelers. The Durand name is a very old one, dating back to 1100 A.D. in France and Italy; Durante being the Italian spelling of the name of which "Dante" is a corruption.

For many generations the Durands were identified with the artistic side of the jewelry trade as watchmakers, engravers, jewelers and silversmiths, sometimes one man being proficient in all these. Dr. Jean Durand, the Huguenot progenitor of the Durand family in America, was born in France in 1667 and came to this country in 1685. He died in Derby, Connecticut in 1727. His son, Samuel, born in Derby in

1713, was the first of the Durands in America to engage in jewelry manufacturing. He left Derby in 1740 for New York where he stayed for ten years as a farmer, watchmaker and jeweler. In 1750 he moved to Newark and then to South Orange where he died in 1787. John Durand, son of Samuel, was a jeweler and watchmaker. During the Revolutionary War he was highly praised by George Washington for his skill in repairing field glasses. John Durand's son, Henry, was a manufacturer of jewelry, silverware and crystals for watches. James Madison Durand, son of Henry Durand, founded the firm of Durand & Co. in 1843. He learned his trade with Taylor & Baldwin of Newark. From 1820 to 1840 he was engaged as an engraver, engine turner, watchcase maker and jeweler. His son, Wickliffe Baldwin Durand, became head of the partnership in 1880. Harry Durand entered the partnership in 1882 as purchaser and became secretary and treasurer. Harry Durand, Jr. was interested in the selling end of the business. Wallace Durand was associated with his father and brothers in the firm and became its president in 1892. Perhaps the best known of the Durand family was Asher Brown Durand (1796-1886) who was first an engraver. He later took up the engraving of plates from which pictures were printed. Many of these are in the National Portrait Gallery, the most famous one being Trumbull's "The Signing of the Declaration of Independence." From 1835 he devoted his time to painting, mainly landscapes, and with Thomas Cole is credited with founding the Hudson River school of painting.

Among the many items made by the Durand company were scarfpins, silver links, studs, collar buttons, brooches, pendants, necklaces, lorgnettes, vanity cases, purses, mouchoir bags, rings, vest chains, cigarette cases and other novelties.

DURGIN & BURTT
St. Louis, Missouri
See F.A. Durgin
Listed in St. Louis City Directory 1859-60 as manufacturers of silver and plated silverware.

F.A. DURGIN
St. Louis, Missouri
Founded by Freeman A. Durgin in St. Louis in 1858. The 1859-1860 St. Louis Directory lists him as a member of the firm, Durgin & Burtt. From 1863-1888 he was in business for himself. From 1888-1911 he

was a salesman for the Jaccard jewelry firm. It has not been definitely established that he was actually a manufacturer of silver and plated silverware as he advertised, or whether he was a wholesaler or retailer for others. Much silver, especially flatware, is found with his name.

F. A. DURGIN
ST. LOUIS

WM. B. DURGIN CO.
Concord, New Hampshire
Providence, Rhode Island
See Gorham Corporation
Founded in 1853 by William B. Durgin in Concord, New Hampshire. Durgin had been born in Compton Village, New Hampshire in 1833 and left his mountain home at the age of 16 to seek his fortune in Boston. He apprenticed himself to Newell Harding. On completion of his apprenticeship he set himself up in business in Concord. He soon purchased the tools of two jeweler-spoonmakers of that town. Not long afterwards he also bought the tools of a retail jeweler in Claremont, New Hampshire. His initial order was given by Carter Bros., then in business in Concord and later in Portland, Maine. This order was for six sets of teaspoons. During his early days as a spoon maker, Durgin would make up a lot of spoons and pack them in a handsatchel or small trunk and start out with a horse and wagon to sell them, sometimes taking old silver in barter. Durgin was noted for the fine quality of his silver spoons and was soon able to set up a shop which grew rapidly into a factory which made sterling flatware, gold, silver and plated tableware, jewelry and similar articles. The Durgins, father and son, continued in the business until their deaths, both in 1905, in which year the ownership passed out of the family. It was purchased by the Gorham Company but continued to operate in Concord until 1931 when it was moved to Providence, Rhode Island.

DISCOVERY
(Discontinued.)
CROMWELL
WATTEAU

FAIREAX

DURHAM SILVER CO.
New York, New York
Listed in directories in the 1950s and 60s as manufacturers.

JOSEPH DYAR
Middlebury, Vermont

Advertised from 1822 through 1845 that his table and tea spoons, cream and salt spoons, sugar tongs, thimbles and gold beads were of first quality and workmanship. He was born in 1804 and died in 1851.

E

EAGLE SILVER CO.
Providence, Rhode Island

Listed in Providence City Directories 1922-1953 as manufacturers of silver novelties. Owners—Memelaus Sava and Ignatius H. Findan. Manufactured sterling silver cigarette cases, vanity cases, whiskey flasks, match safes, 14k gold inlaid and onyx inlaid wares.

E.S.C.O.

EAGLE SPOON COMPANY
Bridgeport, Connecticut

"Articles of association of the Eagle Spoon Company were filed in Bridgeport last week. The purpose of the association is to manufacture and sell all kinds of personal property, including spoons and forks and other flatware. Stockholders are William H. Waterman, Hartford; George C. Edwards and C.A. Hamilton, Bridgeport; and James G. Ludlum and Thomas B. Lashar." (JC-W 5-30-1900, p. 47) Succeeded by Housatonic Mfg. Co.

EAGLE STERLING CO.
Glastonbury, Connecticut

Successors to W.L. & H.E. Pitkin July 1, 1894. Organized in 1894 by William H. Watrous and others to manufacture silverware. Listed in 1896 JC in plated silver section. Out of business before 1904.

GEORGE EAKINS
Philadelphia, Pennsylvania

Advertised in *Jewellers, Silversmiths & Watchmakers*, December 1877 as "Mfg. of silver plated ware and dealer in cut glass bottles."

EARLY AMERICAN PEWTER CO.
Boston, Massachusetts

Advertised in the 1940s.

EASTERLING COMPANY
See Westerling Company

(Used since December 1944)
(Sterling silver flatware and holloware)

EASTERN CAROLINA SILVER CO.
Hyattsville, South Carolina

EASTERN CAROLINA SIL. CO.

Made silverplated holloware c. 1900.

EASTWOOD-PARK COMPANY
Newark, New Jersey

Manufacturers of exclusive designs in sterling silverware, dresserware, novelties, mesh bags and jewelry for the wholesale trade.

Listed JC 1909-1915. Out of business before 1922.

ECCLESIASTIC SILVERSMITHS
Wallingford, Connecticut

"International Silver Company sold its Ecclesiastic division to Ecclesiastic Silversmiths, a new company in Wallingford, Connecticut. The new company will be a division of Lamson-Goodnow Mfg. Co., which is affiliated with Voos Industries, Inc. (JC-K April 1979, p. 144)

Dissolved on April 10, 1981.

ECKFELDT & ACKLEY
Newark, New Jersey

Listed in 1896 Jewelers' Weekly in sterling silverware section. Listed 1898-1915 JC as jewelers. Last record found c. 1935.

EDSON MFG. CO.
New York, New York
Newark, New Jersey

"The Edson Mfg. Co., New York, was incorporated Feb. 16, 1893 for the manufacture of silver novelties with a factory in Newark. Franklin Edson, Sr., president; Albert E. Coon, sec. & treas., and Henry T. Edson, Manager." (JC&HR 3-1-1893, p. 28)

EDWARDS, HORTON & EDWARDS
Chicago, Illinois
   Silversmiths c. 1850.

EISENBERG-LOZANO, INC.
New York, New York
See Samuel Kirk & Son
See Kirk International
   Founded by Arthur Eisenberg and Neal Lozano in 1953. Purchased by The Kirk Corporation in 1970 after the deaths of the founders.

WM. J. EISENHARDT
Baltimore, Maryland
   Listed in Baltimore City Directories 1887-1888 as a silverplater.

M. EISENSTADT JEWELRY CO.
St. Louis, Missouri
   M. Eisenstadt Company (Wholesale distributors of silverware and jewelry). Founded in 1853 by Michael Gabriel Eisenstadt. First appeared in St. Louis directory in 1866. From 1904 is listed as M. Eisenstadt Manufacturing Co., and from 1908 on they are listed as manufacturers of jewelry, jobbers of watches and importers of diamonds in the 1920s, 1930s and 1940s they are listed as M. Eisenstadt Mfg. Co. and they are still in business as M. Eisenstadt, wholesale jewelry.

(Plated silver holloware)

   Their logo of a capital E sitting on a carpenter's square—the "E on the square," stood for straight-forward, honest dealings and has been used by the firm since the 1880s. (JC-K May 1982)

ELDRIDGE & CO.
Taunton, Massachusetts
   Listed in Taunton City Directories from 1800-1884 as silver manufacturers "at Britanniaville, near R.R. crossing Reed & Barton."

ELECTROLYTIC ART METAL CO.
Trenton, New Jersey
   Listed in JC 1915 with manufacturers of sterling silverware. No record after 1920.

ELEDER-HICKOK CO.
Newark, New Jersey
See Hickok-Matthews Co. Silversmiths
   Originally Lebkuecher & Co.; the name was changed by law to F.A. Lester after 1915 and was taken over by the Eleder Co. in 1918. By 1922 it had become the Eleder-Hickok Co. It merged with the Matthews Company after 1931 to form the Hickok-Matthews Company, manufacturers of sterling silver novelties.

WM. R. ELFERS CO., INC.
New York, New York
   Listed in 1931 NJSB and KS as manufacturers of sterling silver holloware, candlesticks, vases, salt and pepper shakers, sherbet compotes, centerpieces, etc.

ELGIN-AMERICAN MANUFAC-TURING COMPANY
Elgin, Illinois
   Began business in 1887. An undated Elgin-American catalog in the writer's possession (wtih illustrations of souvenirs engraved "Remember the Maine" and desk calendars dated January 1898) includes flatware of plated silver, smoking sets, jewel cases, bracelets, dresser sets, match safes and novelties.
   Registered U.S. Patent No. 103,053, March 16, 1915 for manufacture of silverware.
   Became a division of Illinois Watch Case Company before 1950. Observed their 65th anniversary in 1952. This is the last record found.

On plated silver knives about 1898

ELGIN SILVERSMITH CO., INC.
New York, New York
See Redlich & Co.

Founded by two partners, Ludwig & Redlich, and operated under that name until 1892 when Mr. Ludwig sold his interest to three of his old employees and it became Redlich & Co., Inc. It was taken over by Elgin Silversmith Co., Inc. in 1946. Products are sterling flatware, holloware and 14k goldwares. The Redlich trademark has not been changed and is still used by the firm to the present day. Currier & Roby is now a Division of Elgin Silversmiths.

(Sterling)

ELKINGTON & CO., LTD.
Birmingham, England

George Richards Elkington was apprenticed at 14 to his two uncles, Josiah and George Richards to learn silverplating. This was in 1815 and the silverplating process he learned was "close plating"—hammering thin layers of silver over base metal, with adhesion being by soldering. His cousin, Henry Elkington, joined him about 1829-30 in the making of small articles. They were constantly doing research towards better methods of gilding base metals. Between 1836 and 1839 the firm of G R & H Elkington took out various patents, including one for "electrogilding." Therefore, they are usually credited with the invention of electroplating. John Wright discovered the need for cyanide of potassium in the plating solution and submitted his process to the Elkington company who embodied it in their patent of 1840. This process was available to other manufacturers on a royalty basis. A third partner, Josiah Mason was admitted in 1842 and the firm became Elkington, Mason & Company. Beginning then, their electroplate was marked with "E & Co." in a shield, and "E M & Co" in three separate shields, together with their company date letters. Mason left the firm about 1859 but his initial was not dropped from the marks until 1864. The Crown, long used as part of many silverplaters' marks, was dropped from Elkington's "E & Co" mark in 1896.

In 1963 Elkington and Mappin & Webb merged to form British Silverware Ltd. Soon afterwards they acquired Walker & Hall, Adie Bros., and Gladwyn Ltd. Prod-

ucts of all four firms are now sold under the Elkington name.

Through changes in Elkington's trademarks it is possible to date their products with reasonable accuracy. They first used "E & Co., crowned" within a shield and ELEC TRO PLATE. In 1842 a series of numbers was added to the trademark. The numbers ran from 1 to 8 with the number 6 being reversed. In 1849 letters of the alphabet were substituted for the numbers, beginning with the letter K. A new series of letters began in 1865 with a change in the trademark. Letters B, C, and J were omitted. The letter Q was not used by the sheet department and used on only part of the cast articles. The letter Q as well as R was used from 1900 onwards. Both numbers and letters are enclosed within shapes that aid in their dating.

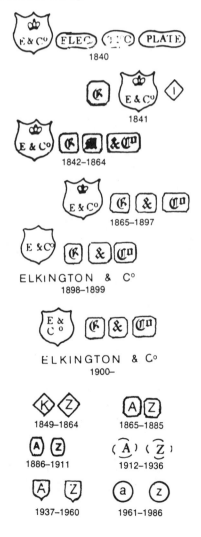

54

ELLIS SILVER COMPANY, INC.
New York, New York
See Ellis-Barker

Established in New York c. 1900 as a branch of Ellis & Co., Birmingham, England.

ELLIS-BARKER SILVER COMPANIES
Birmingham, England
New York, New York

The Ellis-Barker Company can trace its history to a partnership c. 1820 by partners Barker and Creed. It became Barker Bros. (William and Matthias Barker) c. 1860. Encouraged by their success in England, they opened an American branch in 1897 (Samuel Buckley & Co., New York) where a full line was introduced. Among the pieces offered were trays, candelabra, candlesticks, plates, urns and bottlestands. These articles were copper, heavily electroplated with silver and mounted with handles, borders and edges of sterling silver. In 1921 Barker Bros. was joined by Levi & Salamon, specialists in dresserware and by Potosi Silver Co., spoon and fork makers. In 1931 they purchased the Ellis Silver Co. (Ellis & Co., Birmingham, being the parent) and the firm has been known since then as Ellis-Barker. They are noted especially for their beautiful reproductions of antique silver.

A 1978 advertisement says "Division of Towle."

FOR SILVER AND ELECTROPLATED TRAYS, WAITERS, CANDLESTICKS, CANDELABRA, DINNER SETS, FLOWER-STANDS, COFFEE AND TEA SERVICES, VASES, WINE-COOLERS, TEA-URNS, INK-STANDS, DECANTER-STANDS, DINNER-PLATES, MEAT-DISHES, ENTRÉE DISHES, BOTTLE-STANDS, CAKE-BASKETS, SIPHON-HOLDERS, BOWLS, JUGS, TEA-CADDIES, BOXES, FRUIT-STANDS, AND FRUIT-BASKETS.
Claims use since October 1906.

FOR TRAYS, WAITERS, CANDLESTICKS, CANDELABRA, DINNER SETS, FLOWER-STANDS, DINNER-PLATES, BOTTLE-STANDS, VASES, TEA AND COFFEE SERVICES, WINE-COOLERS, TEA-URNS, INK-STANDS, DECANTER-STANDS, MEAT-DISHES, CAKE-STANDS, SIPHON-HOLDERS, FRUIT STANDS AND BASKETS, BOWLS, JUGS, TEA CADDIES, BOXES, AND ENTRÉE-DISHES. ALL MADE OF PRECIOUS METALS OR PLATED WITH PRECIOUS METALS.
Claims use since August 1912.

FOR CAKE-BASKETS, CRUETS, CUPS, DISH-COVERS, MEAT-DISHES, ENTRÉE-DISHES, EGG-FRAMES, TEA AND COFFEE SERVICES, WINE-COOLERS, INKSTANDS, LIQUOR-FRAMES, MUSTARD-POTS, MUFFINEERS, SALT-CELLARS, SAUCE-BOATS, SOUP-TUREENS, SIPHON-STANDS, SWEET-DISHES, TEA-URNS, TOAST-RACKS, TEA-CADDIES, TRAYS, VASES AND WAITERS, ALL MADE OF SILVER OR PLATED WITH SILVER.
Claims use since November 1912.

FOR SILVER-PLATED HOLLOWARE.
Claims use since 1912.

FOR SILVER PLATED HOLLOWARE AND FLATWARE.
Claims use since Mar. 2, 1932.

J.E. ELLIS & CO.
Toronto, Canada

James E. Ellis moved from Liverpool, England, to Canada in 1848 and was associated with Rossin Bros. until 1852. He bought into that business that year. Ellis' son joined him in 1862. The firm name became J.E. Ellis & Co. in 1877 when M.T. Cain became a partner. It continued until 1901 when it was sold at auction.

P.W. ELLIS
Toronto, Canada

In business c. 1876 as a partnership of Philip W. Ellis and Matthew C. Ellis (nephews) of Toronto silversmith James E. Ellis). The company was incorporated in 1901; liquidated in 1928 and taken over by Birks.

They were importers and wholesalers of watches, clocks, sterling and plated silverware, china and cut glass, artware, jewelry, diamonds, tools, materials and supplies.

SOVEREIGN PLATE
(Nickel Silver)

P. W. ELLIS   STERLING

ELLMORE SILVER CO., INC.
Meriden, Connecticut
See Concord Silver Co.
See G.H. French & Co.
See Frank M. Whiting Co.

Founded c. 1935 by I.A. Lipman who rented space in the old C.F. Monroe factory and took over F.M. Whiting Co. of N. Attleboro, G.H. French & Co., New York and Concord Silversmiths, Ltd., Concord, New Hampshire about 1939. Whiting had been making sterling flatware and some holloware. French made novelties and dresserware. With these lines added, the Ellmore company increased production and established branch offices in New York, Los Angeles and Chicago. The W.S. Blackinton Co. became a division of the Ellmore co. in the 1940s. The Ellmore Co. went out of business in 1960. The Blackinton Co. was purchased by Raimond Silver Mfg. Co., Meriden, Connecticut, in 1966 and moved to Chelsea, Massachusetts. The sterling flatware dies of the Whiting Company were bought by the Crown Silver Co., New York. It is believed that they are no longer being used.

(Used since 1950)

ARNOLD ELTONHEAD
Baltimore, Maryland
Listed as a silversmith in the 1850 census. Born Pennsylvania.

EMPIRE ART METAL WORKS
New York, New York
Listed 1909 JC in plated silver section.

EMPIRE CRAFTS CORP.
Newark, New York
Manufacturers of silverplated flatware 1930s to 1950s. Later controlled by Oneida Silversmiths.

(Silverplate)

(Sterling)

EMPIRE SILVER PLATE CO.
Brooklyn, New York
Advertised in 1896 JW and JC&HR as manufacturers and importers of silver-plated holloware. Last record found 1931.

ENGLISH SILVER MFG. CORP.
Brooklyn, New York
See Leonard Silver Mfg. Co.
Manufacturers and importers of silver-plated wares from c. 1950. Still in directories.

ENTERPRISE PLATING WORKS
Baltimore, Maryland
Listed in Baltimore City Directories 1894-1916 as silverplaters.

M.C. EPPENSTEIN & CO.
Chicago, Illinois
See A. Davis & Co.
Earliest record found was Patent Office Registration No. 24,525, April 17, 1894 for use on plated silver tableware. Succeeded by A. Davis & Co. c. 1904.

R. COIN.

GEORGE C. ERICKSON
Gardner, Massachusetts
George Erickson was born in Sweden and came to this country when six months of age. He served his apprenticeship under Arthur J. Stone (q.v.) where he developed into a master craftsman in the production of sterling silver flatware. In 1932 Erickson bought from the heirs of the late David Carlson, the shop which Carlson had run for several years and even during the Depression days was able to build a successful business. His first mark "G. C. E." used in 1932 was soon changed to "Erickson Sterling." Also, during the 1930s George Erickson and Herman Glendenning joined together and made silver using the mark "Erickson Handwrought." In 1971 Glendenning set up his own shop. Erickson's grandson, Peter, is continuing to make flatware.

ETON SILVER INC.
Glendale, New York
Listed directories from the 1960s to the present as manufacturers and importers.

EUREKA MFG. CO.
Taunton, Massachusetts

Listed directories from the 1950s through the 1960s as manufacturers of silverware.

EVANS & ANDERSON
Newark, New Jersey

Horace B. Anderson and Theodore Evans, silversmiths, worked 1864-c. 1866. Listed Newark City Directory as "Evans and Anderson, Successors to Henry Evans. Dealers in Clocks, Watches, Jewelry, etc., and manufacturers of Sterling silver wares." Succeeded by Horace B. Anderson and operated under his name.

EVANS & ANDERSON

EVANS CASE CO.
North Attleboro, Massachusetts

Listed in the 1920s as D. Evans Case Co. Still in business as a division of the Hilsingor Corp., Plainville, Massachusetts.

THEO. EVANS & CO.
New York, New York

"Theodore Evans was the son of Henry Evans. He succeeded his father as Evans & Anderson (1864-66), in New York City. Theo Evans & Co. (Theo. Evans and John Cook) since 1855." (JC&HR 6-30-1897, p. 33)

"An old-time silversmithing house was that of Theodore Evans & Co. who started business in 1855 at 6 Liberty Place, New York. The firm was composed of Theodore Evans and John Cook. Mr. Evans was a salesman for Wm. Gale & Son from 1850 to 1855, while Mr. Cook was foreman for the same firm, but in '55 they joined forces and started for themselves, soon doing a large southern business in flat and hollow wares. They manufactured many of the old patterns: Plain, Tipped, French Thread, Plain Thread, Oval Thread, Mayflower, Shell, Grape, as well as a patented one named Ribbon...Many of their goods are still extant in the south.

"In 1865 the firm name was changed to Evans & Cook, Jas. E. Johnson having been admitted as a special partner. In 1869 Mr. Evans retired and John Cook continued for several years. In their prosperous days everything in their line, from a thirty inch tray to a salt spoon, could be found in their safes, and in no instance was a piece issued which was not up to the standard at that time—that of New York coins. They lost heavily through the war, as most of the silverware houses did, the south before the war being fond of luxuries." (JC&HR 6-30-1897, pp. 33-34)

T. EVANS & CO.

F

OTTO G. FABER
Baltimore, Maryland

Listed in Baltimore City Directories 1895-1910 as a silversmith, goldsmith and jeweler. Some of his pieces bear a marked similarity to designs made by Samuel Kirk & Son.

WILLIAM FABER & SONS
Philadelphia, Pennsylvania

Silversmiths and silverplaters 1828-1887.

FAHYS WATCH-CASE CO.
New York, New York

Listed in 1896 as Jos. Fahys & Co.: 1922 as Jos. Fahys & Co., Inc. Design patents Nos. 32,914, July 10, 1900 and 38,583, May 28, 1907 for spoons, forks or similar articles were taken out by Fred Habensack, Sag Harbor, New York and assigned to the Fahys Watch-Case Co.

FAIRCHILD & CO.
New York, New York

CHRONOLOGY

Randall & Fairchild	1837
LeRoy W. Fairchild	1843
LeRoy W. Fairchild & Co.	1867
L.W. Fairchild	1873
L.W. Fairchild & Sons	1886
LeRoy Fairchild & Co.	1889
Fairchild & Johnson	1898
Fairchild & Company	1919

Founded in 1837 as Randall & Fairchild. In 1843, known as LeRoy W. Fairchild; 1867-1873 as LeRoy W. Fairchild & Co.; 1873-1886 as L.W. Fairchild; 1886, L.W. Fairchild & Sons; 1889 it was incorporated as LeRoy Fairchild & Co.; in 1896 Harry P. Fairchild bought out the business and in 1898 he formed the corporation of Fairchild

& Johnson. In 1919 it was known as Fairchild & Co., and went out of business c. 1922. Makers of sterling silverware.

F

L. W. FAIRCHILD & CO.

FAIRCHILD & JOHNSON CO.

LEROY C. FAIRCHILD CO.
New York, New York

"Leroy C. Fairchild Co., manufacturers of gold pens and novelties recently incorporated. Directors are Julia L.M. Fairchild, W. Clifford Moore and Leonard S. Wheeler. They purchased the machinery, tools, etc. used by the defunct Leroy W. Fairchild & Co. Leroy C. Fairchild, president of the old company, is now is charge of the new corporation's selling and manufacturing departments. (JC&HR 6-9-1897, p. 23)

FARBER BROS.
New York, New York

Manufacturers and jobbers of plated silver holloware c. 1920-1950. Now a division of LCA Corp.

Silvercraft

(On silverplated holloware)

FARRINGTON & HUNNEWELL
Boston, Massachusetts

Silversmiths 1835-85. Great quanties of flatware turn up with their (Star) F & H (Star) trademark, often accompanied by the mark of another as retailer.

Attributed

lion passant

head?

FEDERAL SILVER COMPANY
New York, New York

Listed from c. 1920 to 1961 as manufacturers of sterling and plated wares.

The trademark at right appears under the name Jones & Woodland, Newark, New Jersey in 1896-1915 JC and 1950 JC-K.

(On silverplate)

(On sterling)

W.J. FEELEY CO.
Providence, Rhode Island

One account says that the company was founded in 1875 by Michael Feeley. Another says it was established by W.J. Feeley in 1875 and incorporated in 1892. According to this account, W.J. Feeley was born in Providence, January 19, 1855 and learned the trade of silversmithing from Knowles & Webster; worked several years as a journeyman before beginning business on his own account.

They were manufacturers of gold and silver ecclesiastical goods. City Directories list the company from 1875 to 1920 as manufacturing jewelers and silversmiths. Listed in 1936-1937 Jobbers' Handbook.

ALBERT FELDENHEIMER
Portland, Oregon

U.S. Patents registered April 28, 1891 and January 1892 for sterling souvenir flatware and jewelry. Became A. & C. Feldenheimer between 1896-1904. Last record c. 1904.

FRANCES FELTEN
Winstead, Connecticut

Pewterer, currently in business.

FENNIMAN CO.
New York, New York

Listed JC 1915 in sterling silver section. Out of business before 1922.

PETER FERRARI
Baltimore, Maryland

Listed in Baltimore City Directories 1887-89 as a silverplater.

FESSENDEN & COMPANY
Providence, Rhode Island

CHRONOLOGY

Whiting, Fessenden & Cowan	1858
Wm. P. Fessenden & Co.	1860
Fessenden & Company	1860

In April 1858 William B. Fessenden who had at one time been a member of the firm of Whiting, Fessenden & Cowan, moved to Providence and established a silverware factory there. He took into partnership his son, Thomas F. and started as Wm. P. Fessenden & Co., in the manufacture of fancy flat and staple hollowares. In 1860 the father sold out his interest to his son and retired. Soon afterwards, Thomas took Giles Manchester as partner, who remained in charge of the manufacturing department until his death in 1886. In 1876, Silas H. Manchester, a brother of Giles, joined the firm and later became a partner and assumed management. Silas Manchester became sole owner about 1895. On his death in 1905 the company was incorporated. It continued to be listed in business until 1922.

925 STERLING 1000

MARSHALL FIELD & CO.
Chicago, Illinois

Began business in 1864 as Farwell, Field & Company. In 1865 the company became Field, Palmer & Leiter; Potter Palmer sold out his interests in 1866 and the firm name became Field, Leiter & Company. Marshall Field became sole owner in 1881 and gave the firm its present name.

Marshall Field's was one of the first large department stores to have many articles stamped with trademarks registered for its own use. U.S. Patent No. 146,536, September 6, 1921, was registered for their use on silverware, both sterling and plated.

An advertisement in a 1966 Chicago(?) paper read as follows: "Silver is a glittering thread interwoven with the history of Britain. The ancient craft of the English silversmith has been regulated by Royal Ordinances and Acts of Parliment since the late 12th century. Since 1935, the Marshall Field & Company hallmark has been registered at the Worshipful Company of Goldsmiths in London. In all the world, we are one of the few non-British companies privileged to have our own shield put on silver made for us in England. This mark of quality distinguishes a pattern of silver flatware made expressly for Field's in England."

(Used since June 1935)
(On sterling silver table articles)

FIFTH AVENUE SILVER CO., INC.
Taunton, Massachusetts

The company was founded September 1948 by Manuel J. Andrade of Taunton, a spinner by trade. It was first named the Pilgram Silver Company, that name being soon changed because of a conflict with a tradename already in use. The name was changed to Prospect Silver Company in the early 1950s but was again changed to Fifth Avenue Silver Company. In 1960 the company changed ownership and was incorporated. The new owners are Leon J. and Mildred A. Bunk and Frank and Joanna Todorsky. Mr. Bunk is general manager and president. From the beginning the company has been manufacturers and wholesale distributors of silverplate and pewter hollowares.

5 TH AVE SILVER CO. SILVER PLATED	5 TH AVE SILVER CO. SILVER ON COPPER

LEXINGTON PEWTER
(On pewter)

HARVEY FILLEY & SONS
Philadelphia, Pennsylvania

FILLEY & MEAD
Philadelphia, Pennsylvania
See John O. Mead

FILLEY, MEAD & CALDWELL
Philadelphia, Pennsylvania
See John O. Mead

FILLKWIK CO.
Attleboro, Massachusetts
See Shields Inc.

MICHAEL C. FINA CO., INC.
New York, New York
Founded December 1935 by Rose Fina and Michael C. Fina. Manufacturers and wholesalers of sterling and silverplate holloware.

WILLIAM C. FINCK CO.
Elizabeth, New Jersey
Listed in JC 1896-1904. Out of business before 1915. Manufacturers of sterling silverware. Among their products were sterling souvenir spoons.

$\frac{925}{1000}$ STERLING

FINE ARTS STERLING SILVER COMPANY
Morgantown, Pennsylvania
Founded in Philadelphia in 1944 by Jerry N. Ashway. They are sole distributors of six sterling flatware patterns manufactured by the International Silver Company and distributed through direct sales.

The company was moved from Philadelphia to Morgantown, Pennsylvania in 1972.

The founder and board chariman, aged 66, died November 1973 at his home in Glenside, Pennsylvania.

Moved to Jenkintown, Pennsylvania in 1977. Out of business in September 1979.

tiny diner

(Used since January 24, 1949 on children's tableware)

ALBERT G. FINN SILVER CO.
Syracuse, New York
See P.A. Coon Silver Mfg. Co.
Manufacturers of plated silverware. Founding date not known. Listed JC 1904. Succeeded by P.A. Coon Silver Mfg. Co. between 1904-1909.

**ALBERT G. FINN SILVER CO.
CRESCENT SILVER CO.**

TRADE-MARK

FISHEL, NESSLER & CO.
New York, New York
See Majestic Mfg. Co.
Manufacturers of sterling silver and rhinestone-set jewelry, platenoid rhinestone-set jewelry, plated jewelry and card jewelry. Registered U.S. Patent No. 23,016 for use on jewelry, May 16, 1893. Last listing found was 1936-1937.

"Established over 45 years." (Adv. KJ 1931)

FISHEL NESSLER CO.,
184 Fifth Ave.,
NEW YORK.

(This trademark also found with "J. O.-N. Y." on the center strip.)

FISHER SILVERSMITHS, INC.
Jersey City, New Jersey
New York, New York
Successors to M. Fred Hirsch Co. Manufacturers of sterling and silver plated flatware and holloware since 1936 or earlier. Still in business.

No longer manufacturing.

(On sterling)

FISHER, COLTON & KINSON
Montpelier, Vermont
"Fisher, Colton & Kinson, silverplaters, Montpelier, Vermont, have sold out to Fisher & Colton." (Jeweller, Silversmith & Watchmaker, Nov. 1877)

FLAGG & HOMAN
Cincinnati, Ohio
See Homan Mfg. Co.

(Pewter)

W.L. FLETCHER
South Chatham, Massachusetts
Pewterer, currently in business.

FLORENCE SILVER PLATE CO.
Baltimore, Maryland

Listed in Baltimore City Directories 1894-1942 as silverplaters. No City Directories available 1942-1955.

FOOT & COLSON
Chicago, Illinois

Listed in 1854-1855 Chicago Directory as silverplaters. In 1856 Foot was listed as working alone.

E.B. FLOYD
Burlington, Vermont

Worked as late as 1868 in coin silver.

FORBES SILVER CO.
Meriden, Connecticut

See International Silver Co.

Organized in 1894 as a department of Meriden Britannia Co. for holloware silverplating. One of the original companies which formed the International Silver Co.

(This mark sometimes used with the words SHEF-FIELD REPRODUCTION.)

FORD & CARPENTER
New York, New York

See Cohen & Rosenberger.

Succeeded Baldwin, Ford & Co. between 1896 and 1904 and were succeeded by Cohen & Rosenberger before 1915.

E

BEN FORMAN & SONS, INC.
New York, New York

In directories 1950s and 1960s as manufacturers of silverwares.

FOSTER & BAILEY
Providence, Rhode Island

See Theodore W. Foster & Bro. Co.

Theodore W. Foster and Samuel H. Bailey. Succeeded by Theodore W. Foster & Bro. Co.

THEODORE W. FOSTER & BRO. CO.
Providence, Rhode Island

Established January 1, 1873 under the name White & Foster. Walter E. White had been listed previously as a jeweler from 1869-1872. The name was later changed to White, Foster & Co. and in 1878 when White withdrew, the name became Foster & Bailey. (S.H. Bailey) In May 1898 the company was incorporated under the name Theodore Foster & Bros., Co. They were among the largest manufacturers of jewelry and sterling silver goods in Providence. Among the goods were gold filled, electroplated and sterling silver vanity cases, cigarette cases, clock cases, ecclesiastical goods, cigar and cigarette holders, knives, medals, pens and pencils, photo frames, dresserware and candlesticks for which U.S. Patent 28,069, April 17, 1896 was registered. This last listing continued until 1951.

F. & B.

J.F. FRADLEY & CO.
New York, New York

In 1867 or 1868, J.F. Fradley who had completed his apprenticeship as a chaser in the silverware factory of Wood & Hughes, opened a small workshop and began doing chasing for the trade. He soon had a staff of 25-30 chasers in his employ.

In 1870 he opened a small factory for the production of gold-headed canes. This venture was so successful that in 1873 he moved to larger quarters and added all kinds of silver novelties to his productions. The business was incorporated in 1890. Fradley retired in 1902 but the firm continued under the same name with Geo. F. Fradley, a son of the founder. The last record found was 1936. Among the articles made were 14k gold and sterling silver cane and umbrella handles; 14k dresserwares and novelties; sterling photo frames, vases, desk accessories and other novelties.

TRADE MARK

AUG. C. FRANK CO., INC.
Philadelphia, Pennsylvania

Founded in 1894 by a German-born engraver, August Conrad Frank. As his two sons, Herman and Edwin, grew up he taught them engraving and brought them into the company. In 1942 the business was made a partnership with the father and two sons under the Aug. C. Frank name. Today, Edwin Frank is the only survivor. The senior Frank died Oct. 31, 1946 at the age of 83, and the eldest son, Herman, died May 24, 1966 at the age of 68. The present firm was incorporated May 1, 1971.

The Frank company had a fine tradition of excellent medallic work in the Philadelphia area. Custom medals, sports awards, badges, advertising coins and plaques were produced.

On September 15, 1972 the Frank company medal division was purchased by Medallic Art Company of Danbury, Connecticut. The dies, medal presses and other equipment were immediately moved to their Danbury, Connecticut factory. The purchase did not include the non-medallic business of the Aug. C. Frank firm, which will continue in other areas in which it engages, including plastic thermomolding, light metal stamping and their tool and die business.

(Trademark shows the motif of a hand-operated medal screw press.)

THE FRANKLIN MINT
Franklin Center, Pennsylvania

The Franklin mint was founded in 1963 by Joseph M. Segel and has become the world's largest and foremost private mint. It is the principal operating division of the Franklin Mint Corporation and the only non-government mint in the United States that produces legal tender for foreign countries. It is best known for its many series of commemorative and art medals, which are usually struck in sterling silver and issued in limited editions.

The Franklin Mint specializes in *proof-quality* coins and medals. *Proofs* bear the "FM" mark and are characterized by flawlessly minted detail on a brilliant, mirror-like background and are highly prized by collectors everywhere.

The Franklin Mint is the official minter for many important series of commemorative medals such as those for the Bicentennial Council of the Thirteen Original States, the White House Historical Association, Postmasters of America, the National Governors' Conference, the National Audubon Society and the United Nations.

In 1973 they entered the field of signed art prints with the formation of the Franklin Mint Gallery of American Art. Early in 1974 they began the publication of luxury editions of books of proven literary importance and the creation of limited edition sculptures of fine pewter. On July 10, 1973 they dedicated the Franklin Mint Museum of Medallic Art which houses a most complete collection of Franklin Mint issues.

Their extensive sculpturing and engraving staff is augmented by more than 100 distinguished sculptors working in their own studios, thus making the Mint an important patron of the arts and largely responsible for the modern renaissance in medallic art.

FRANKLIN SILVER PLATE COMPANY
Greenfield, Massachusetts
See Lunt Silversmiths

Incorporated in Greenfield, Massachusetts in 1912. Ceased operations between 1920-22. They were manufacturers of plated silver holloware. The trademark was taken over by Rogers, Lunt & Bowlen (Lunt Silversmiths) c. 1922, but with minor exceptions has not been used.

FRARY & CLARK & SMITH
Meriden, Connecicut

In business c. 1850-65. Merged with Landers & Smith in 1865 to form Landers, Frary & Clark.

PETER FREDERICK
New Orleans, Louisiana

Listed in New Orleans city directories as a silversmith in 1871.

FRENCH & FRANKLIN
North Attleboro, Massachusetts

Listed in Jewelers' Weekly, 1896 as manufacturers of sterling silverware.

G.H. FRENCH & CO.
North Attleboro, Massachusetts
See Ellmore Silver Co., Inc.

Earliest record found c. 1920. Manufacturers of sterling silver novelties, cigarette and vanity cases, cups and tableware. Succeeded by Ellmore Silver Company, Inc., between 1935-43.

FRIED, MILLS & CO. INC.
Irvington, New Jersey

Listed in JC 1915 in sterling silver section. Last record found c. 1935.

FRIEDMAN SILVER CO., INC.
Brooklyn, New York
See Gorham Corporation

Creators of fine holloware since 1908. Bought by the Gorham Corporation in 1960.

Much of their holloware bore pastoral Dutch designs.

FORD & TUPPER
New York, New York

Patrick Ford, Jonas C.H. Tupper and Ford & Tupper are listed at the same addresses for the following years in the New York City Directories.

Ford, Tupper & Behan; silverware and jewelry (William J. Behan) 609 Broadway	1866-1868
Ford & Tupper, Jeweler 609 Broadway	1869
Ford & Tupper, silver 789 Broadway	1870-72
Ford & Tupper, silver 787 Broadway	1872
Ford & Tupper, silver	1873-75

BENJAMIN FROBISHER
Boston, Massachusetts

Benjamin Frobisher was a silversmith and jeweler. Though britannia wares are generally thought not to have been made in this country until 1835 or afterwards, according to the late Carl Dreppard, Frobisher advertised them as early as 1829.

FERD. FUCHS & BROS.
New York, New York

Ferdinand Fuchs and his brothers came to this country from Germany about 1835. They were in business first in Boston and later moved to New York. The firm was composed of Ferdinand and Rudolph Fuchs and was established in 1884 for the manufacture of sterling silverware. Richard Fuchs was sales representative in Baltimore, Philadelphia and the West. Piérre Joseph Chéron designed some of their wares. They were out of business before 1922.

FUCHS & BEIDERHASE
New York, New York

Founded by Rudolph Fuchs and George B. Beiderhase in 1891. Makers of sterling holloware, cups, napkin rings, dresserware, library articles and novelties. Succeeded by Alvin Mfg. Co. before 1896.

"Rudolph Fuchs, president of Fuchs & Beiderhase, silversmiths, died Thursday morning. Only 34 years old he had been connected with the silverware business for 18 years. He served his apprenticeship with B.D. Beiderhase & Co., New York and was afterwards connected with Adams & Shore (Shaw?), Dominick & Haff and J.F. Fradley & Co. When he left the latter firm in 1884 he went into partnership with his brother under the firm name of Ferdinand Fuchs & Bro. The partnership was dissolved in 1891, and Mr. Fuchs and Mr. Beiderhase formed the firm of Fuchs & Biederhase, incorporated last April. Mr. Fuchs was president." (JC&HR 1-18-1893, p. 5)

G

JOHN GAILLISSAIRE
Baltimore, Maryland

Listed in Baltimore City Directory as silverplater in 1864.

GALE & HAYDEN
New York, New York

William Gale and Nathaniel Hayden are recorded in New York city directories from 1846 to 1850 as retailers of silverware. Gale had formerly been associated with Jacob Wood and Jasper W. Hughes. After the dissolution of the firm of Gale & Hayden, he continued to deal in silverware with his son William Gale, Jr. while Hayden became a banker.

Some of the flatware sold by them bears marks of Gale & Hughes. Gale & Hayden obtained Design Patents #149 and #150, September 11, 1847 for flatware.

WM. GALE
New York, New York
See Gorham Corporation
See Graff, Washbourne & Dunn

William Gale was born in Orange County, New York of native parents on April 5, 1799. He died December 17, 1867. His son, William Gale, Jr., was born in 1825 and became a partner with his father after reaching his maturity.

William Gale invented and patented a process for making spoons with ornamental patterns. This entailed cutting the ornament on rollers, both the upper and lower rollers being cut with the pattern. This made the production of pattern spoons much less expensive than the former method of hand hammering patterns by the use of dies. During the fourteen years Gale controlled this patent he became the largest manufacturer of spoons in the country. The process was superseded by the mechanical perfection of the drop hammer, spoons then being made from flat dies, the upper and lower dies containing the ornament. Shaped dies were a still later development.

GALT & BRO., INC.
Washington, D.C.

CHRONOLOGY

James Galt	1802-47
M.W. Galt & Bro.	1847-79
M.W. Galt, Bro. & Co.	1879-92
Galt & Bro.	1892-34
Galt & Bro. Inc.	1934-present

James Galt moved from Georgetown to Alexandria in 1802 and established his business which included the making of watches, and later fine silver pieces.

In 1847 James Galt died and ownership of the business passed into the hands of M.W. Galt and William Galt, his sons. Among their patrons were Abraham Lincoln and Jefferson Davis. In 1879 William Galt withdrew from the firm. The following year M.W. Galt retired and turned over to Norman Galt, grandson of the founder, the responsiblity for maintaining the prestige and respect which the House of Galt had earned. He was assisted by Henry C. Bergheimer.

About 1900, Galt and Brother was chosen to execute a bowl which was presented to Postmaster Charles Emory Smith for his efforts in establishing a rural mail system. This piece of work brought a special congratulatory note from President Roosevelt in 1902, the one hundredth anniversary of Galt and Brother.

In 1908 Norman Galt died and Henry C. Bergheimer became the first the manage the business without bearing the founder's name. That year they began automobile delivery service. In 1923, Henry C. Bergheimer died and the management was carried on under William H. Wright. In 1934 Galt & Brother was incorporated when Norman Galt's widow, Edith Bolling Galt Wilson (Mrs. Woodrow Wilson), turned the firm over to the employees.

U.S. Patent No. 19,421, May 5, 1891. Portrait of Christopher Columbus, a copy of M. Maelia's engraved picture of Columbus published by Joseph Delaplaine, Philadelphia and later given to the U.S. Navy Department.

U.S. Patent No. 20,488, December 8, 1891. Landing of Columbus. Facsimile of the famous painting later placed in the U.S. Capitol.

Both trademarks were used on gold, silver and plated silver articles, presumably of the souvenir type.

The George and Martha Washington medallions were registered trademarks for use on souvenir spoons conceived by M.W. Galt. The first of these was a ladle that was an exact facsimile of the Washington ladle preserved in the National Museum, with the addition of the Washington medallion stamped in the bowl.

GALT & BRO.

ALBERT J. GANNON
Philadelphia, Pennsylvania

The Philadelphia City Directory lists Albert J. Gannon as a salesman in 1905; as a silversmith between 1906-1910 and lists Albert J. Gannon Company silversmiths from 1911-1914. This is the last listing.

GARDEN SILVERSMITHS
New York, New York

Listed in directories 1960s and in 1973 JC-K. Successors to Arrowsmith Silver Corp. They own the dies for sterling silver wares formerly made by Apollo and Bernard Rice's Sons.

GARRETT & SONS
Philadelphia, Pennsylvania

In the 1860s they purchased Reed & Barton wares "in the metal" and operated their own plating establishment.

GEBELEIN SILVERSMITHS
Boston, Massachusetts

Gebelein Silversmiths was founded by George C. Gebelein who was born near Bayreuth, Bavaria, in 1878 and was brought to this country when a year old so his training was entirely American. He was apprenticed at the age of 14 to Goodnow & Jenks (q.v.). He concluded his apprenticeship in November 1897 and went to work for Tiffany & Company in their new (1895) factory at Forest Hills, New Jersey. He returned to New England to work for William B. Durgin (q.v.) in 1900 before starting out for himself as a member of The Handicraft Shop of Boston at the end of the year 1903, then setting up the shop of his own at the foot of Beacon Hill in 1909 where it remained until forced to move in 1968.

Besides making fine reproductions and adaptations, Gebelein was a collector and dealer in old American and European silver, becoming a recognized authority on silver. He was one of the early recipients of the medal for excellence presented by the Society of Arts and Crafts of Boston. The Williamsburg Communion set is one of his best-known productions.

His son, J. Herbert Gebelein, followed him in the silversmithing craft and is usually noted for the excellence of his work. After the father's death in 1945, the company was incorporated under family directorship as Gebelein Silversmiths Inc.

The customary marking on sterling silver from 1908-09 has been:

1. Incised surname without outline;
2. Incised name in cut-cornered rectangle;
3. Small surname (raised capitals in rectangle) STERLING (and usually) Boston.

In some instances, in emulation of the Colonial practice, this last mark was struck without STERLING unless the customer preferred it. More cases of the omission of the STERLING mark occurred since the addition of another stamp (about 1929) enclosing the name Gebelein in oval cartouche. Used mostly in its largest of three sizes, this mark was intended in general to go on entirely handfashioned pieces.

Other marks:
1904-08 G or GG (incised) with H anvil S (raised in outline) Year STERLING or COIN.
In 1908 G or GEBELEIN H anvil S.
From 1908 GEBELEIN (in cut-cornered rectangle, incised) (2 sizes; continued in use).
From 1909 GEBELEIN (incised, no outline) STERLING Boston (incised) (medium and small continued in use).
Another old stamp GEBELEIN (raised letters in rectangle).
A small G (for marking small areas) (incised in Old English—Gothic text capitals).

The mark above includes a G, the outline beaded at top, bottom and sides. Not used on solid silver as a rule but on work in metals other than gold and silver such as the specialty of Gebelein, hand-hammered silver-lined copper bowls, or some few silver-plated or pewter specialties.

STERLING GEBELEIN BOSTON

(On hand-forged special order flatware, forks and spoons)

GELSTON & GOULD
See Gould & Ward

GEM SILVER CO.
See International Silver Co.
Trademark of Wilcox Silver Plate Co. for dresserware and several flatware patterns.

GEM SILVER CO.

GENOVA SILVER CO., INC.
New York, New York
Manufacturers of sterling silver c. 1950.

ARTHUR R. GEOFFROY
New York, New York
Listed in JC 1896 as manufacturer of sterling silverware. Out of business before 1904. Advertised as maker of wares in sterling silver for the trade only.

GERITY PRODUCTS, INC.
Toledo, Ohio
Their advertising reads, "Custom platers since 1898."

GERMAN SILVER
See Holmes & Edwards

GEORGE E. GERMER
Boston, Massachusetts
George E. Germer was the son of a Berlin jeweler and was born in 1868. Even before his apprenticeship, he showed a love of silver. Otto Gericke of Berlin, was his teacher and from him he learned chasing and modeling. He came to the United States in 1893 and for nearly 20 years worked in New York, Providence and Boston. After 1912 he worked independently, producing mostly ecclesiastical silver.

During his latter years, he moved his shop to Mason, New Hampshire and produced more silver for churches, some of which is now in museums.

MICHAEL GIBNEY
New York, New York
Michael Gibney was listed in the New York City Directories 1836-45 and 1849-51. He was issued the first Design Patent for a flatware design in this country (Design Patent No. 26, Dec. 4, 1844). Pieces in this pattern are marked "Ball, Black & Co.," "Ball, Thompkins & Black," with a "Y" or completely unmarked. Gibney was also issued other Design Patents. One, *Tuscan* (Design Patent No. 59, July 10, 1846) was designed at the request of E.K. Collins, noted shipbuilder, who wished to equip a new vessel with a silver service with "a pattern different from the old ones then prevailing." The order was placed through Marquand & Co. It was later marketed by them and eventually became one of the first standard patterns issued by the Whiting Mfg. Co.

Gibney was a designer for the trade as well.

F.S. GILBERT
North Attleboro, Massachusetts
Listed JC 1904 as manufacturer of sterling silverware. Out of business before 1915.

STERLING **G**

GILBERTSON & SON
Chicago, Illinois
In business in the 1920s as silversmiths, platers and finishers, mesh bag repairers and electroplaters.

GINNELL MFG. CO.
Brooklyn, New York
Listed in JC 1915-22 as a manufacturer of sterling silverware and jewelry.

G. MFG. CO.

GLASTONBURY SILVER CO.
Chicago, Illinois

Listed in JC 1922-1950 as manufacturers of plated silver flatware and holloware. Between 1931-1950 the company name became Glastonbury, Inc.

ARROW PLATE
(On plated flatware)

GEE-ESCO

R. GLEASON & SONS
Dorchester, Massachusetts

Began with Roswell Gleason who was a tin worker in 1822. He was first listed as a pewterer about 1830. He was noted for the extremely fine quality of his work. This quality was carried over into britannia work later when the business became one of the largest and most important in Dorchester. After 1850 their products were mostly silverplated. The business closed in 1871.

Used on plated silver. Attributed to Manhattan Silver Plate Co. in 1904 JC.

HERMAN W. GLENDENNING
Gardner, Massachusetts

Herman W. Glendenning is a silversmith. As a young boy he lived across the street from Arthur J. Stone (q.v.) whose shop he entered in 1920 to learn silversmithing. He was first instructed in making flatware, forging with a three or four pound hammer. He then progressed to holloware which he still prefers as there is more variety in its design and execution. When he was judged proficient, he was permitted to put his "G" under the Stone trademark and eventually attained his goal of "Master Craftsman."

After Stone's retirement. Mr. Glendenning became the designer and producer of holloware at the Erickson Shop (q.v.) where he worked for about thirty-five years. In 1971 he retired from the Erickson Shop but is currently teaching a young man silversmithing with the view to having him take over the business, including tools and patterns.

Glendenning Sterling Handwrought
(Used since 1955)

W.H. GLENNY & CO.
Rochester, New York

Wholesale and retail silverware and jewelry. Note similarity of trademark to that of The Waldo Foundry, Bridgeport, Connecticut, and H.H. Curtis & Co., North Attleboro, Massachusetts.

ESTABLISHED 1876

W.H. GLENNY, SONS & CO.
Buffalo, New York

"W.H. Glenny Sons & Co., was established in 1840 in Buffalo, New York, as a crockery and glassware business. Branch stores were opened in St. Paul, Elmira and Rochester. St. Paul and Elmira stores closed several years ago but the Buffalo and Rochester stores continued until 1898 and were operated by the sons. At the time of closing of the entire business it was operated by William H. Glenny, Bryant B. Glenny, W. Henry Glenny and Francis Almy and William Keagey." (JC&HR 2-2-1898, p. 23)

They were wholesalers of silverware, including souvenir spoons stamped with their trademark.

FRANCES M. GLESSNER
Chicago, Illinois

She was briefly a student under Madeline Wynne and later studied with A. Fogliati, metalsmith associated with Hull House. She was a socialite, Mrs. John A. Glessner, who fitted out her conservatory as a metal shop. She made silver bowls, inkstands, salt cellars, hat pins, necklaces and jars which she gave to friends and family. She received commissions to make silver platters for wedding gifts. Her silver was marked with a G enclosing a bee—the latter reflecting her other interest—bee-keeping. She continued working in silver until c. 1915.

GLOBE ART MFG. CO.
Newark, New Jersey
Listed in JC 1915-1922 as manufacturers of sterling silver and plated silverware.

GLOBE SILVER CO.
New York, New York
Listed in directories 1957-61 as manufacturers.

JACOB GMINDER
Baltimore, Maryland
Listed as a silverplater 1867-1901 in Baltimore City Directories.

GODINGER SILVER ART CO., LTD.
New York, New York
"Godinger Silver Art Co. Ltd. has moved to 37 W. 26th St. New York City. The new quarters comprise 15,000 sq. ft.—more than three times the space occupied at the firm's former address at 45 W. 45th St.

"Adjacent to the office and showroom is a new factory where most of Godinger's handcrafted silver holloware and pewter merchandise is manufactured. In addition to special order work, retail jewelers are encouraged to use the firm's personalized merchandising program: products are supplied gift boxed and printed with the store's logo.

"Godinger will exhibit its new copyrighted designs for 1975 at the Atlantic City China and Glassware Show, as well as the Spring RJA Show in January." (JC-K Dec. 1974)

ALEXANDER GOLDMAN
New York, New York
Listed directories 1920s and 1930s as manufacturer of sterling holloware, sterling religious articles.

GOLD RECOVERY & REFINING CORP.
New York, New York
Manufacturer (?) of sterling and silverplate c. 1940-45. Succeeded by Dunkirk Silversmiths, Meriden, Connecticut.

GOLDFEDER SILVERWARE COMPANY, INC.
Yalesville, Connecticut
Established in 1932. Manufacturers of silverplated hollowares, namely candelabra, trays, water pitchers, champagne buckets, vegetable platters, combination platters, lazy susans, punch bowls and cups, tea sets, sugar and creamers, tea kettles and gravy bowls.

Trademark issued to Sol Goldfeder, New York. Succeeded by Birmingham Silver Co.

(Used since Jan. 1, 1947)

GOLDMAN SILVERSMITHS CO.
New York, New York
Manufacturers (?) of sterling silver articles c. 1940-45.

M.T. GOLDSMITH
Brooklyn, New York
Established in 1864 by Marcus Goldsmith as Goldsmith Brothers Smelting & Refining Company, Lexington, Kentucky. In 1882, his sons, Moses and Simon, succeeded to the business and in 1884 moved to Chicago. In 1909, the New York branch was opened by Simon. They were known as leaders in smelting and refining gold, silver and platinum. Listed by JC as out of business in 1909.

BRITANNIA ARTISTIC SILVER

GOLDSMITH'S COMPANY OF CANADA, LTD.
Toronto, Canada
Listed in JC 1915-1922 in the plated silver section.

NICKELITE SILVER
SHEFFIELD CUTLERY

GOLDSTEIN & SWANK CO.
Worcester, Massachusetts
Listed in JC 1915-1922 as makers of plated ware, jewelers and special order work.

Became Goldstein, Swank & Gordon before 1936. This is the last record found.

JEREMIAH GOMPH
Utica and Albany New York
Spoonmaker Albany 1855-1862; Utica 1862- c. 1865. He later became a jeweler. (JCW 2-5-1919)

GOODBY MFG. CO.
San Francisco, California

Listed in the 1931 JKI as special order work in silver holloware and gold ware; gold and silver plating, repairing and refinishing.

A.E. GOODHUE
Quincy, Massachusetts

In 1950 JC-K and 1957 JBG under sterling and silverplate.

GOODNOW & JENKS
Boston, Massachusetts

Successors to Kennard & Jenks. They were established in 1893 to manufacture and sell sterling silverware. Walter R. Goodnow, formerly of Bigelow, Kennard & Co., was a financial partner only. Barton Pickering Jenks, son of the gifted designer Lewis E. Jenks of Kennard & Jenks, received his degree in architecture from M.I.T. about 1890 after beginning his college career for a year at Harvard.

Goodnow & Jenks were the principal silverware manufacturers of their time in Boston, concerned mainly with holloware. In 1904 or 1905 Jenks resigned and went to work for Wm. B. Durgin Co.

One of the senior silversmiths at Goodnow & Jenks was George F. Hamilton, Irish-born 1831, who arrived in Boston as a boy where he served his apprenticeship with Charles West (also possibly with Newell Harding whose Court Avenue address was nearby). Hamilton had been with Haddock & Andrews (Henry Haddock, 1811-92, apprenticed to Moses Morse, Boston; Henry Andrews, 1809-93) and with Haddock, Lincoln & Foss, before going with Goodnow & Jenks. When Goodnow & Jenks closed, Hamilton went with the Tuttle Silver Co.

Another silversmith at Goodnow & Jenks was Adolph Krass, born in Westphalia, Germany, in 1833. He came to this country at the age of about twenty and was first employed by Ferdinand Fuchs & Bros. (q.v.). It was Krass from whom George C. Gebelein (q.v.) obtained special attention during his apprenticeship at Goodnow & Jenks August 1893 to November 1897.

GOODWILL MFG. CO.
Providence, Rhode Island

Listed 1927 KJI as manufacturers of flatware, dresserware and holloware.

FREDERICK GORDON
Baltimore, Maryland

CHRONOLOGY

George B. Gordon	1864-79
Gordon & Company	1880-94
F.S. Gordon	1894-97
Frederick Gordon	1898-99

Silverplaters.

GORHAM CORPORATION
Providence, Rhode Island
(Division of Textron)

CHRONOLOGY

Gorham & Webster	1831-1837
Gorham, Webster & Price	1837-1841
J. Gorham & Son	1841-1850
Gorham & Thurber	1850-1852
Gorham & Company	1852-1865
Gorham Mfg. Company*	1865-1961
Gorham Corp.	1961-present

*Or Lion and Anchor

Jabez Gorham, founder of the Gorham Corporation, was born in Providence, Rhode Island in 1792 and at 14 began his seven year apprenticeship to Nehemiah Dodge. After serving his apprenticeship, he formed a partnership with Christopher Burr, William Hadwen, George C. Clark and Harvey G. Mumford about 1815-1818 at which time he purchased his own shop to manufacture small items and became known for his "Gorham chain," unequaled at the time.

With Stanton Beebe he made jewelry until 1831 with Henry L. Webster, formerly with Lewis Cary in Boston, joined the firm to make silver spoons. The firm name was changed to Gorham & Webster. In 1837, the firm was called Gorham, Webster & Price. When Gorham's son, John joined the firm in 1841, the name was changed to Jabez Gorham & Son. John Gorham quickly recognized the advantages of machinery and as a result the Gorham Company was among the first to introduce factory methods to augment hand craftsmanship in production of silverware. He designed and made much of the machinery himself if none was available to suit his purposes.

In 1850, three years after Jabez Gorham retired, the company name was Gorham & Thurber. By 1852, it was Gorham & Company. The firm was chartered by the Rhode Island Legislature as the Gorham Manufacturing Company in 1863 and

organized as a corporation in 1865. In 1868, they abandoned the coin silver standard (900/1000) and adopted the sterling standard of 925/1000 fine silver. At the same time, the familiar trademark—a lion, an anchor and a capital G—was adopted for use on all sterling articles. Ecclesiastical wares of gold, bronze, stone, wood and sterling were added in 1885. *L'art nouveau* designs of the talented English artist, William Christmas Codman, were added under the name "Martelé" in the late 19th century.

The Gorham Company has employed other silver designers who became well known in their own right. Among them were Erik Magnussen (q.v.) and Thomas J. Pairpoint (q.v.).

By 1863 the company decided to use its facilities for making electroplated silverwares using nickel silver as the base. Made entirely of nickel silver, these wares were processed by the same general methods used in making sterling silverware, even to the use of silver solder in assembling the component parts. The tooling and die work occupied about two years so that it was not until 1865 that the first of their silverplated line was marketed. They ceased production of their silverplated flatware May 1, 1962 but their silverplated holloware continues to be an important part of their output.

Holding companies were chartered in New York during 1906 and 1907 for the purpose of acquiring the Whiting, Durgin and Kerr companies. These corporations in the order of their formation were known as the Silversmiths Stocks Company and The Silversmiths Company. In the reorganization of the Company in 1924, the Silversmiths Company was purchased, its assets taken over and the company dissolved. The Gorham Company then operated as subsidiary divisions, the Whiting Mfg. Co. (moved to Providence in 1925); William B. Kerr Company, (moved to Providence in 1927); and William B. Durgin Company, (moved to Providence in 1931).

About 1913 the Gorham interests expanded to include the Mt. Vernon Company Silversmiths, Inc. which had resulted from the merging of the Roger Williams Silver Company of Providence, Rhode Island, the Mauser Manufacturing Company of Mt. Vernon, New York and Hayes & McFarland of New York City.

The Alvin Silver Company was acquired in 1928 and its title changed to The Alvin

Corporation. It products are made at the Providence plant though it functions as an organization separate from The Gorham Company.

The Gorham retail store at 5th Avenue and 47th Street in New York merged with Black Starr and Frost in 1929 under the new firm name of Black, Starr and Frost-Gorham Inc. In 1962 The Gorham Company sold its interest and the name became Black, Starr & Frost, Ltd.

In 1931 the McChesney Company of Newark, New Jersey was purchased and its tools and dies moved to Providence.

The Quaker Silver Company of North Attleboro, Massachusetts was purchased in 1959, the Friedman Company of Brooklyn, New York in 1960 and Graff, Washbourne & Dunn of New York in 1961. The Gorham Company was sold to Textron, Inc. in 1967.

At all periods the Gorham Company has been noted for the fine quality of its die work as well as superior design and fine finishing of all products.

Gorham's familiar trademark was registered (#33,902) Dec. 19, 1899 at which time it was stated that it had been in use since January 1, 1853. The Gorham Company now states that this trademark was used as early as 1848 and that from 1848 to 1865 the lion faced left rather than right.

NEWPORT STERLING
TWINKLE STERLING
VOGUE

BANQUET PLATE
ELMWOOD PLATE

SUFFOLK SILVERPLATE (Tradename used with Gorham's silverplate mark and METROPOLITAN MUSEUM REPRODUCTION)

STERLING
(Sterling silver)

The Athenic trademark was used on articles that are Art Nouveau in feeling but Greek in inspiration. Sterling silver is combined with other materials.

A.	1868		1885		1902		1918
B.	1869		1886				1919
C.	1870		1887		1903		
D.	1871		1888		1904		1920
E.	1872		1889		1905		1921
F.	1873		1890		1906		1922
G.	1874		1891		1907		
H.	1875		1892		1908		1923
I.	1876		1893		1909		1924
J.	1877		1894		1910		
K.	1878		1895		1911		1925
L.	1879		1896		1912		1926
M.	1880		1897		1913		1927
N.	1881		1898		1914		1928
O.	1882		1899		1915		1929
P.	1883		1900		1916		1930
Q.	1884		1901		1917		1931

Holloware year markings have been used since 1868. Letters of the alphabet A through Q were used from 1868 through 1884 at which time symbols were adopted for each year until 1933 at which time they were discontinued. In January 1941, year markings were resumed on sterling holloware except lower priced items.

During 1933 year marks were discontinued.

1932   1933

January 1941 year marking was resumed on sterling holloware except lower priced items.

1941

The square frame indicates the decade of the 40s. The numeral indicates the year of the decade.

The pentagon indicates the decade of the 50s. The numeral indicates the year of the decade.   1950
1951

The hexagon indicates the decade of the 60s. The numeral indicates the year of the decade.

1960   1961

The heptagon indicates the decade of the 70s. The numeral indicates the year of the decade.

1970   1971

This marking will be used only on heavy sterling items such as tea sets and on specially made sterling items for individual consumers. The Christmas items such as the Snowflake will be back stamped with a four digit numeral to indicate the year of production.

At one time flatware was made in as many as five different weights for the same pattern. The letters below are those used to indicate these weights:

T   for Trade   H   for Heavy
M   for Medium   EH   for Extra Heavy

Regular weight had no marking. Gorham archival records are now at the John Hay Library, Brown University. Open to researchers by appointment.

JOHN T. GOSWELL
Baltimore, Maryland
    Listed in Baltimore City Directories 1864-1868 as silverplaters.

GOTHAM SILVER CO., INC.
New York, New York
    Manufacturers of plated silver holloware c. 1920. Last record found was 1950.

WEAR-WELL

GOULD, STOWELL & WARD
Baltimore, Maryland
    James Gould A. Stowell, Jr., William H. Ward, silversmiths and dealers in jewelry. Advertised silverware made to order. Listed in Baltimore City Directory 1855-1856.

GOULD & WARD
Baltimore, Maryland
    James Gould and William H. Ward were successors to Gelston & Gould, silversmiths, c. 1810-1820. Became Gould, Stowell & Ward, c. 1855.

GRAF & NEIMANN
Pittsburgh, Pennsylvania
    Manufacturers of silverware c. 1900.

Gorham mark on the back of the "Lady Washington" pattern showing the 1876 date. (Photo by H. Ivan Rainwater)

No. 9,420, August 1, 1876) This was the only design patented that year. (Photo by H. Ivan Rainwater)

72

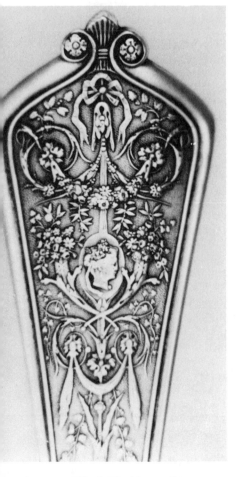

Close-up of "Lady Washington" pattern. This elegant pattern appears to be scarce. (Photo by H. Ivan Rainwater)

Martelé ewer and tray designed by William C. Codman for the Gorham Company. A graceful expression of Art Nouveau. (Photo courtesy of Gorham Corporation)

GRAFF, WASHBOURNE & DUNN
New York, New York
See Gorham Corporation

The predecessors of Graff, Washbourne & Dunn may be traced back to William Gale who was active in silversmithing in New York in 1833. He was followed by the firm of Wm. Gale & Son, then Gale, Wood & Hughes, and Wood & Hughes. In 1899, Wood & Hughes sold their factory to Graff, Washbourne & Dunn who at once incorporated. Charles Graff was president, designer and factory manager. Clarence A. Dunn was vice-president and treasurer, also manager of the business and general executive. William L. Washbourne was secretary and in charge of sales. Graff died in 1931 and Washbourne in 1941. Dunn acquired the stock of both and in 1942 became sole owner and then sold his entire holdings, including the corporate name to Harrison W. Conrad, who became president and Eugene Rossi, who became treasurer. The company was purchased by the Gorham Corp. in 1961. Graff, Washbourne & Dunn were makers of sterling silver holloware and novelties.

GRANAT BROS., INC.
San Francisco, California

Registered trademark for use on silver flatware, silver services, jewelry and novelties made wholly or partly of precious metal. Published Dec. 6, 1949. Granat Bros. bought Shreve, Treat & Eacret in 1941. Is now owned by Bailey, Banks & Biddle.

Granat
(Used since Aug. 1, 1929)

R.B. GRAY & COMPANY
San Francisco, California

Listed in S.F. city directories 1855-1872 as retailers and manufacturers of jewelry and silverware. Robert Gray, in 1868, was described as one of the "most extensive manufactories of silver ware in this city..."

GREATREX LTD.
New York, New York

Trademark registered May 29, 1951 for use on sterling silver, silverplated and silver mounted flatware and holloware.

(Used since 1947)

GREEN-SMITH CO.
Denver, Colorado
See Frederick L. Smith

GREGG SILVER CO., INC.
Taunton, Massachusetts

Manufacturers of silverplated holloware c. 1950.

F.L. GREGORY
Niagara Falls, New York

Listed in the 1886 Niagara Falls Directory as makers of silver and plated silverware.

CHARLES W. GRESHOFF
Baltimore, Maryland

Gold and silversmith. Listed in Baltimore City Directories 1888-1898.

FRANCIS A. GRESHOFF
Baltimore, Maryland

Gold and silversmith. Listed in Baltimore City Directories 1864-1885. Succeeded by Frances A. Greshoff & Son in 1887. This listing continued through 1894.

GRIFFON CUTLERY WORKS
New York, New York

Began business before 1904 as Silberstein, Hecht & Company, soon succeeded by A.L. Silberstein and has been Griffon Cutlery Works since 1915.

GRIFFIN SILVER PLATE CO.
Elgin, Illinois

"The Griffin Silver Plate Co.'s factory, Elgin, Illinois, has started up with a small force of hands." (JC&HR 2-1-1893, p. 17)

ED. GRONEBERG
Baltimore, Maryland

Listed in 1855-1856 Baltimore City Directory as a manufacturer and dealer in fine gold jewelry and silverware.

GROSJEAN & WOODWARD
New York, New York

Their partnership was listed in Boston in 1840. Charles Grosjean and Eli Woodward were silversmiths in New York from 1852 to 1862. Charles Grosjean was a silversmith in Würtemberg, Germany. He came to New York in 1836 and died on January 30, 1865. Their "G & W" mark is to be found on many silver articles sold through Tiffany & Co., around 1852-53.

Charles Grosjean (son?) designed and patented the Tiffany Indian Dance spoons February 10 and 17, 1885 as well as several full line flatware patterns of theirs.

LEWIS GUIENOT
Baltimore, Maryland
Listed in Baltimore City Directories 1870-1877 as a gold and silverplater.

A.T. GUNNER MFG. CO.
Attleboro, Massachusetts
Albert T. Gunner was born January 23, 1897, in Wallingford, Connecticut, second son of Charles R. and Etta (Simmons) Gunner.

He attended public school in Providence, Rhode Island and Attleboro, Massachusetts, and, in 1919, took night courses in Accounting in New York City.

On July 5, 1912, he went to work to learn a trade as a spinner at the Watson Company in Attleboro, Massachusetts. Later he worked for F.W. Whiting Company in North Attleboro as foreman of the Spinning Department.

In 1918 he enlisted in the Army and was stationed in New York City with the Chemical Warfare Service. He was a Sergeant at the end of the war.

He then went to work as a metal spinner for the Gorham Company in New York City. Upon leaving that company, he was employed by Graff, Washbourne & Dunn as a spinner.

In 1920 he returned to Attleboro and started his own business for the manufacture of sterling silver holloware. It has been in operation ever since.

In 1921 Mr. Gunner married Grace Elizabeth Mahler of New York City.

An ancestor by the name of Gunner, who was in the agricultural business was given an order by the King of England in 1660 to supply cannon for the army. In recognition for this, he received the coat of arms which has been passed down in the family. The Latin inscription on it says, "We are known by our deeds." In Birmingham, England, there is a Gunner's Lane named after this ancestor.

H

J.H. FERD. HAHN
Baltimore, Maryland
Listed 1899-1911 Baltimore City Directory as a silverplater and metal worker.

HALL BROS. & CO.
Pittsburgh, Pennsylvania

H. B. & Co.

Wholesale and retail outlet in business c. 1910-1915.

HALL, BOARDMAN CO.
New York, New York
Philadelphia, Pennsylvania
Hall, Boardman & Company and its successor, Hall and Boardman, are listed in the Philadelphia and New York City Directories from 1845 through 1856 as makers of britannia wares. The New York firm apparently was solely a retail outlet.

HALL, ELTON & CO.
Wallingford, Connecticut
See International Silver Co.
See Maltby, Stevens & Curtiss
See Watrous Mfg. Co.
In 1837 Deacon Almer Hall, William Elton and others formed the firm of Hall, Elton & Co. for the manufacture of German silver flatware and britannia ware. In 1890 the company was purchased by Maltby, Stevens & Curtiss which was in turn purchased by Watrous Mfg. Co. In 1898 they were one of the original companies to become part of the International Silver Co.

Registered U.S. Patent, January 20, 1873 for use on flatware.

They made britannia spoons at least until 1875.

(German Silver Flatware.)

WILBUR B. HALL
Meriden, Connecticut
Specialist in silverplated peppers and salts, napkin rings, cups and other small articles. He was the son of Lewis Hall,

superintendent of Wilcox Silver Plate Co. The business started in 1886 and continued for about 50 years. *(Meriden Journal, Anniversary Issue, April 17, 1936)*

HALLMARK SILVERSMITHS, INC.
New York, New York

An advertisement by Hallmark appeared in the *Saturday Evening Post* in 1917. The Hunt Silver Co., Inc. and Hallmark Silversmiths, Inc., merged in 1954 to form Hunt-Hallmark Co. Officials, Carl K. Klein, Joseph C. Hirsch and Irving L. Hirsch.

HALLMARK

CHARLES W. HAMILL & CO.
Baltimore, Maryland

Charles W. Hamill, manufacturer of silverplated wares was born in Baltimore, Maryland, March 2, 1845. After eleven years working for someone else he entered business for himself in 1876 with ten employees. His business increased rapidly so that by 1878 he had 40 employees. The company was listed in Baltimore City Directories from 1877 to 1884 inclusive.

C.A. HAMILTON
Waterbury, Connecticut
See Rogers & Hamilton

U.S. Patent No. 13,289 May 11, 1886 was registered by Charles Alfred Hamilton, president of Rogers & Hamilton, for the manufacture of spoons, knives, forks, ladles, cheese-scoops, tea sets, casters, pitchers, waiters and napkin rings.

HAMILTON & DIESINGER
Philadelphia, Pennsylvania
See M.F. Hamilton & Son

Hamilton & Diesinger were successors c. 1895 to Hamilton & Davis (Matthew F. Hamilton and Junius H. Davis) listed in Philadelphia City Directories in 1880. Davis was associated briefly with Charles E. Galt in the firm of Davis & Galt (q.v.). Hamilton & Diesinger were manufacturers and retailers of both sterling and silverplated wares. The partnership was dissolved in

1899 when Hamilton's interest were bought out by Diesinger. Hamilton and his son then opened their own business under the name M.F. Hamilton & Son (q.v.). In 1900 Diesinger sold what remained of the Hamilton & Diesinger business to Gimbel Bros.

HAMILTON & HAMILTON, JR.
Providence, Rhode Island

Registered U.S. Patent Office, No. 49,473, February 6, 1906.

This manufacturing jewelry business was established January 1, 1871 by R.S. Hamilton, R.S. Hamilton, Jr., and George C. Hunt. They began the manufacture of ladies' jewelry sets, lace pins and gentlemen's chains—all of solid gold. Six months later they began the manufacture of rolled plate chains. They advertised that they were the first makers of gold filled chains. April 27, 1886 they registered a patent for jewelry, chains, trimmings, cuff buttons, bracelets, lockets, cigarette holders and cases, knives and novelties. Listed from 1921-1935 as Hamilton & Hamilton Jr., Inc. Ralph S. Hamilton is still listed as a manufacturing jeweler not associated with a particular firm. "Hamilton & Hamilton began in 1870 as Hamilton & Hunt. The firm became Hamilton & Hamilton in 1883." (JW 3-30-1892)

"Ralph Spence Hamilton, senior member of Hamilton & Hamilton, Jr., died at the residence of his son, Ralph H. Jr., early Tuesday. He was born in St. Louis, Missouri, June 14, 1829. When quite young his parents moved to New Orleans. At age nine he accompanied his parents to Jamaica, where his father became interested in the cultivation of sugar and owned extensive plantations. Here he remained until about 16 years of age, when he started out for himself. He went to New York and apprenticed himself to learn the jewelry business. He adopted his pursuit from the interest which had been manifested in watching the native Indians of Jamaica fashion ear-rings and other trinkets out of metal by the crude method of hammering. Having concluded his apprenticeship, he went to Attleboro in the early 60's where he engaged in business for himself. In 1870 he removed to this city (Providence) and with J. Hunt formed the well known concern of

that period, Hamilton & Hunt, which began the manufacturing business on a small scale on Potter Street. The business grew rapidly and new and larger quarters had to be obtained, and the firm removed to 226 Eddy St. where it remained for more than a decade.

"The firm of Hamilton & Hunt was dissolved by mutual consent early in 1883, and on July 10 of that year the firm of Hamilton & Hamilton, Jr. was organized, Mr. Hamilton taking his eldest son, Ralph S. Hamilton, Jr. into partnership with him. The business increased steadily so that when the Enterprise Building was erected in the Spring of 1888 the factory was removed to the new building." (JC&HR 2-8-1893, p. 14)

★ H&H

★ H&H

HAMILTON MINT
Arlington Heights, Illinois

The Hamilton Mint was organized in 1972 by a group of men with experience in art and minting who chose to found a new private mint specializing in medallions, ingots, plates and art forms honoring man's most noteworthy accomplishments in graphic arts and sculpture.

Their first major offering was announced August 1972 and was a series of three plates adapted from Picasso paintings in the National Gallery of Art, Washington, D.C.

M.F. HAMILTON & SON
Philadelphia, Pennsylvania

Successors to Hamilton & Diesinger before 1904 and out of business before 1909.

HAMILTON MFG. CO.
Chicago, Illinois

"The Hamilton Mfg. Co., Chicago, incorporated Wednesday to manufacture silverware with C. Van Allen Smith, Arthur R. Wells and Frederick H. Gade." (JC&HR 5-1-1895)

HAMILTON MFG. CO.

HAMILTON SILVER MFG. CO.
New York, New York

Absorbed by T.N. Benedict Mfg. Co., in 1912 and moved to East Syracuse, New York.

HAMILTON SILVER MFG. CO. O.
New York

JAMES B. HAMLIN
North Bridgton, Maine

Pewterer. Currently in business.

HAMMERSMITH & FIELD
San Francisco, California

John A. Hammersmith and Hampton S. Field were listed in city directories from at least 1899 to 1908 but had terminated before 1915. Attributed to their shop are trophies for the K.T. Conclave and some souvenir spoons with the seal of the State of California on the handle.

HAMPSHIRE SILVER CO.
New York, New York

In directories c. 1950s through 1960s as manufacturers.

HAMPTON ROADS CUTLERY CO.
Norfolk, Virginia

Listed in JC 1915 and JKI 1918-19 as Hampton Roads Silver Company, manufacturers of silverplated ware and table cutlery.

HAND AND HAMMER
Alexandria, Virginia
See William L. deMatteo

A.H. HANLE, INC.
New York, New York
See Hanle & Debler, Inc.

Silversmith. Also listed as pewterer.

HANLE & DEBLER, INC.
New York, New York

Founded in 1933 by Adolf Hanle, from a family of silversmiths. He was trained as a spinner near Stuttgart, Germany. He worked from 1929 to 1932 for Samuel Kirk & Son, Inc. as a spinner. Let out for lack of work along with five other spinners, he went to New York City and started the firm of Hanle & Debler, Inc. His partner, Debler, retired in 1935 at which time the firm name became A.H. Hanle, Inc. It was operated as a small family business.

Hanle's products, reflecting Adolf Hanle's European background, are clean and tend toward the contemporary. More

recently, colonial reproduction styles have met with success. Hanle products are offered in both polished and satin finishes.

In June 1971 the firm was purchased by The Kirk Corporation.

HANNON & SMITH

See Studio Silversmiths

NEWELL HARDING & COMPANY
Haverhill & Boston, Massachusetts

Newell Harding (b. 10-20-1796, Haverhill, Mass.) was a silversmith. He was apprenticed to his brother-in-law, Hazen Morse. He went into business for himself in 1822. Under his own name and later as Newell Harding & Co., he made plain spoons in a factory in Court Street, Boston. The firm had a high reputation and did considerable business. Harding sold his business to Ward & Rich in 1832. Ward retired in 1835 and Obadiah Rich continued it until 1849 when he also retired.

Ensko *(American Silversmiths & Their Marks III)* credits Harding with introducing power to the rolling of silver.

Gibb *(The Whitesmiths of Taunton)* identifies the Harding company as one of those who operated its own silverplating establishments and purchased goods "in the metal."

HARPER & McINTIRE CO.
Ottumwa, Iowa

Silverplaters c. 1920.

HAR-MAC

HARRINGTON & MILLS
Baltimore, Maryland

Listed in Baltimore City Directories 1868-1874 as silverplaters.

R. HARRIS & CO.
Washington, D.C.

Established in 1874-1876. Manufacturing jewelers and silversmiths according to their catalog E, published c. 1898. No trademark but the company name. Still in business.

THOMAS B. HARRIS
New Orleans, Louisiana

Listed as silversmith in New Orleans city directory in 1871.

HARRIS & SCHAFER
Washington, D.C.

Listed in the Washington, D.C. Directories 1880-1938 as Harris & Schafer, Jewelers.

Edwin Harris was born in Charles County, Maryland in 1831. Educational facilities were limited at that time, so at a very early age he went to work in the store of Galt Bros. of Washington. He was taken into partnership in 1870 and remained there in that capacity for nine years. He then sold his interest and started a store of his own.

Charles A. Schafer, the junior partner, was born in Boonsboro in Washington County, Maryland. He moved to Washington, D.C. when ten years of age. He attended both Gonzaga College and Georgetown University. He entered the employ of Galt Bros. in 1849 and remained with that firm for thirty years, mastering the jewelry making and watchmaking business. When Harris opened his own store, Schafer chose to join him as a partner.

Trademarks were registered at the U.S. Patent Office in 1891 and 1892 for gold, sterling silver and plated silver flat and tableware. These trademarks were used on souvenir silver. It is doubtful if Harris & Schafer did any manufacturing themselves. They were noted, however, for the fine quality of silver, jewelry, watches, diamonds, artwares and crystal and glassware they sold. Much of it was imported from the finest houses in Europe.

HARRISON & GROESCHEL
New York, New York

Listed in JC 1896 in sterling silver section. Out of business before 1904.

LUCIUS HART MFG. CO.
New York, New York

Lucius Hart is listed in New York City Directories 1828-1850. The earlier listings are in connection with Timothy Boardman, pewterer, under the name Boardman & Hart. By 1850 the Boardman name was dropped and the listing was Lucius Hart, Britannia Ware Manufacturer. After 1863 the listing was Lucius Hart & Company. During the 1860s Hart bought many of Reed & Barton's wares "in the metal" and operated his own plating establishment in New York.

R.H. & A.W. HART

Brooklyn, New York
Silverplaters c. 1860.

HARTFORD HOLLOWARE CO.

Hartford, Connecticut

Reportedly, an off-shoot by some workmen previously in business with other Hartford silverware companies. In operation c. 1888-1901.

HARTFORD MANUFACTURING CO.

Hartford, Connecticut
See Bernard Rice's Sons

Organized September 23, 1854 by E.W. Sperry. Listed in city directories 1854-62 inclusive. The 1863 Hartford directory does not contain the Hartford Mfg. Co. but on March 23, 1863 the Hartford Plate Co. was organized to make German silver goods with Sperry listed as a member of the firm. The Hartford Plate Co. was organized by Redfield & Rice of New York.

HARTFORD SILVER PLATE CO.

Hartford, Connecticut
See Barbour Silver Co.
See International Silver Co.
See I.J. Steane Co.

Listed in Hartford City Directories from 1882 through 1894. Each listing accompanied by a half or full page advertisement.

The 1882 listing says they were manufacturers of fine electroplated holloware. Incorporaters: James G. Batterson, E.N. Welch, Henry C. Robinson, W.H. Post, Jonathan Goodwin, James L. Howard and Rush P. Chapman.

They advertised "Everything in silver plate." Absorbed by Barbour Silver Co. in 1893 which became part of the International Silver Co. in 1898.

"The Hartford Silver Plate Co. are engaged in refinishing and replating the beautiful candelabra of the White House, Washington, D.C." (JC&HR) 9-21-1892, p. 30)

HARTFORD STERLING COMPANY

Philadelphia, Pennsylvania
See I.J. Steane Co.
See Tennant Company
See Phelps & Cary Co.

Successors(?) to the Tennant Co., New York, 1900.

The Philadelphia City Directories list the Hartford Sterling Company from 1901-1924. In 1901 and 1902 the listing refers to foreign plated ware. Subsequent listings are for plated ware. The 1907-1912 Directory lists Isaac J. Steane (probably Isaac J. Steane, Jr.), president, Arthur B. Wells, secretary and Jacob S. Hecker, treasurer.

"The Hartford Sterling Co. has purchased the plant and business of Phelps & Cary Co. of New York and also Jacob S. Hecker & Co. . mfgrs. of silver plated holloware. H.A. Cary went into business for himself." (JC-W 7-4-1900, p. 23)

The firm was listed at 5th & Baltimore Ave., Lansdowne, Pennsylvania as manufacturers of sterling and silverplated holloware in the 1931 Keystone.

The upper trademark is identical to those of The Tennant Co. and Phelps & Cary Co., with the exception of the initials in the shield.

HARVEY & OTIS

Providence, Rhode Island

Manufacturing jeweler and silversmith. Listed JC 1896 to present.

H-O

HASKELL, BEECHER & CO.

Baltimore, Maryland

Listed in Baltimore City Directories 1885-1886 as silverplaters.

HENRY C. HASKELL

New York, New York

Listed in JC in sterling silver and jewelry sections 1896-1904. Out of business before 1915.

JOHN HASSELBRING

Brooklyn, New York

See Crown Silver Inc.

Founded about 1890 by John Hasselbring. Purchased by Crown Silver Inc. about 1954-1955 and is now a division of that company in New York. Their products are silver peppermills, bar accessories, silver trimmed salad bowls and silver trimmed cutlery.

Another trademark, containing a deer head, has been reported but not found.

HATTERSLEY & DICKINSON

Newark, New Jersey

William Hattersley is listed as a silversmith 1854-61 and as "Britannia metal works" 1852-53, as a partner in Hattersley & Dickinson 1854-56 and with Hattersley & Son J. britannia metal workers 1856-61. Charles Dickinson is listed under britannia metal 1850-57. The Patent Office records show that they were granted a patent (Design Patent No. 657, July 4, 1854) for the ornamental design for a tea or coffee pot, the type of metal not specified. This tea and coffee service is illustrated in the E. Jaccard catalog of 1856 under Solid Silver Tea Ware.

E.V. HAUGHWOUT & COMPANY

New York, New York

In the 1860s they purchased Reed & Barton wares "in the metal" (unplated) and operated their own plating establishment. According to *Antiques* June 1976) they were already in business in New York and had their own building there.

HAVONE CORPORATION

New York, New York

Listed JC 1915 in sterling silver section. Patents and trademarks taken over by Elgin-American Mfg. Co., Elgin, Illinois.

Elgin-American manufactures match boxes, vanity, photo and cigarette cases, belt buckles, cuff links, traveling clocks, photo lockets and knives.

HAWTHORNE MFG. CO.

New York, New York

Manufacturer of sterling silverware. Listed in JC 1904 as out of business.

HAYDEN MFG. CO.

Newark, New Jersey

See G.W. Parks Co., Inc.

Gold and silversmiths c. 1893. Manufacturers of sterling silverware and jewelry. Succeeded by G.W. Parks Co., Inc. between 1904 and 1909.

WILLIAM W. HAYDEN CO.

Newark, New Jersey

See G.W. Parks Co., Inc.

Listed in JC 1904 in sterling silver section. Out of business before 1909.

HAYES & MCFARLAND

Mount Vernon, New York

See Gorham Corporation

See Mt. Vernon Silversmiths, Inc.

In 1903 merged with the Mauser Manufacturing Company of New York and the Roger Williams Silver Company of Providence, Rhode Island to form the Mt. Vernon

Silversmiths Company which was purchased by the Gorham Corporation in 1913.

J.R. HAYNES
Cincinnati, Ohio

Listed in Cincinnati City Directories 1850-1859 as a silversmith who operated a silverware factory.

HAYNES & LAWTON
San Francisco, California

Silverplaters, not manufacturers. In 1864-65 listed in San Francisco city directory as dealers; in 1869 as agents for electrotyping work; 1870 Benjamin Haynes & Orlando Lawton; 1871 as prop. of Pacific Plate Works; 1874 no longer listed.

"Silverplating under the older methods has been practiced in San Francisco for a number of years, the articles being made of equal quality to the same work imported. During the past year, however, a new branch of the business, viz. electrotyping has been introduced in San Francisco by the Pacific Plate Works, Haynes & Lawton being the agents. By this process excellent work is done, the designs being elegant and the standard coating of metal of a purity and thickness not to be excelled." (Henry Langley, *The Pacific Coast Almanac for 1869*, S.F. 1869, p. 69)

C.E. HAYWARD COMPANY
Attleboro, Massachusetts
See Walter E. Hayward Co., Inc.

HAYWARD & SWEET
Attleboro, Massachusetts
See Walter E. Hayward Co., Inc.

H. ★ S.
H. & S.
STERLING

WALTER E. HAYWARD CO., INC.
Attleboro, Massachusetts

Established in 1851 as Thompson, Hayward and Co., in Mechanicsville. Charles E. Hayward and Johnathan Briggs became partners in 1855. Charles E. Hayward was one of seven children of Abraham Hayward, captain of a privateer during the War of 1812. When Charles was 17 he was apprenticed to Tifft & Whiting to learn jewelry making.

The Hayward and Briggs partnership was dissolved in 1855 and Walter E. Hayward became associated with his father under the name of C.E. Hayward Co.

In 1887 the younger Hayward accepted George Sweet as a partner and the firm became Hayward & Sweet Company. The firm name became Walter E. Hayward Co. before 1904. Frank J. Ryder and Charles C. Wilmarth, both already associated with the firm, purchased the company in 1908.

Ryder bought out Wilmarth's interest in 1917 and remained sole owner until incorporation in 1921. Frank J. Ryder, Sr. died in 1943 and three years later his son, Frank, Jr., became president and part owner; acquiring full ownership in 1949. They are still in business manufacturing religious items of sterling silver and gold and gold-filled jewelry.

HAYWARD

HEADLY & CARROW MFG. CO.
Philadelphia, Pennsylvania

Manufacturers of patented silversmiths' stock. Anton Weber, designer. Patent Office record, April 4, 1892.

HENRY HEBBARD
New York, New York
See Geo. W. Shiebler & Co.

Silversmith, listed New York City directories 1847-51 as Henry Hebbard & Co. Records in the U.S. Patent Office indicate that he was associated with John Polhamus (q.v.) in 1855 when the two obtained design patents for flatware later made by Geo. W. Shiebler & Co. Some later flatware design patents obtained in Hebbard's name from c. 1853 through 1869 were made by the Whiting Mfg. Co.

JACOB S. HECKER & CO.
Philadelphia, Pennsylvania

Manufacturers of silverplated holloware. Purchased by Hartford Sterling Co. in 1900.

HEER BROS. CO., INC.
Baltimore, Maryland

Listed in the Baltimore City Directories 1927-1928 as manufacturers of silverware.

HEEREN BROS. & CO.
Pittsburgh, Pennsylvania

Mentioned as makers of a silver trophy cup. (JC-W 5-9-1900, p. 7)

Adv. (JR 1887) says they are manufacturers of "silver and plated ware."

Their trademark is a cannon with the initials "P. G. H."

HEER-SCHOFIELD CO.
Baltimore, Maryland
See Schofield Co., Inc.

HEINTZ ART METAL SHOP
Buffalo, New York

Listed in JC 1915-1922 in the plated silver section. Became Heintz Bros. Mfg. before 1935. This is the last listing found. Manufacturers of art metal goods and novelty jewelry.

HEIRLOOM
See Oneida Silversmiths

Heirloom is a trademark acquired by Oneida Silversmiths in 1929 through the acquisition of Wm. A. Rogers, Ltd.

HEIRLOOM

HEMILL SILVERWARE INC.
New York, New York

Manufacturers (?) or silverplaters c. 1920-1930.

SHEFFIELD H. S. Co.

SUSSEX

THE HEMMING MFG. CO.
Montreal, Canada

Listed in JC as manufacturers of sterling silverware and jewelry. In business 1903-1912. Succeeded by Canadian Jewellers, Ltd.

GEORGE A. HENCKEL & CO.
New York, New York
See Currier & Roby, Inc.

Manufacturers of small articles in sterling silver for the trade only. Listed in JC 1909-1922. Succeeded by Currier & Roby, inc. before 1943.

HENNEGAN, BATES & COMPANY
Baltimore, Maryland

Established as jewelers and silversmiths in Wheeling, West Virginia, by James T. Scott in 1857. In 1859 William H. Hennegan, a native of Rochester, New York, went to Wheeling from St. Louis and became associated with Scott. The firm's name was changed to James T. Scott & Co. In 1864 they opened a wholesale house in Pittsburgh with Hennegan in charge; Scott remained at the Wheeling store. The Pittsburgh house was known as Scott & Hennegan. This partnership was dissolved in 1869 and Hennegan took over the Wheeling business. In 1866 James O. Bates was admitted to partnership and in 1869 John D. Reynolds joined the firm as jeweler. In 1874 Hennegan and Reynolds moved to Baltimore and opened a jobbing firm; Bates remained in charge of the Wheeling store until it was sold in 1874 to Jacob W. Grubb. Bates then moved to Baltimore where the business was for some time both wholesale and retail. The wholesale business was dropped and only the retail remained. The last listing found in Baltimore City Directories was for c. 1930.

HENNEGAN, BATES & CO.

HERBST & WASSALL
Newark, New Jersey

Listed JC 1904-1922 as manufacturers of sterling silver goods, 14k gold ware and novelties. Last record found was 1931.

JEFFREY HERMAN
Cranston, Rhode Island

Silversmith, jeweler and designer. Studied silversmithing in London, England; silversmithing and jewelry making in Portland School of Art and Southeastern Massachusetts University. Designer, sample and model maker and technical illustrator with Gorham Company.

F.A. HERMANN CO.

Melrose Highlands, Massachusetts

Founded 1908 by F.A. Hermann. Manufacturers of sterling barrettes, brooches, bar pins, baby pins, bracelets, pendants and bookmarks, mostly enameled and hand-painted.

GEORGE E. HERRING

Chicago, Illinois

Registered U.S. Patent No. 59,353 January 8, 1907 for use on imitation silverware. Out of business before 1915.

YOUREX

HIBBARD, SPENCER, BARTLETT & CO.

Chicago, Illinois

Trademark registered May 15, 1906 (No. 52,721) to be used on plated silver holloware, flatware and tableware. Used continuously since April 1, 1905. Application filed by A.M. Graves, secretary.

Trademark registered on August 7, 1906 (No. 55,072) to be used on jewelry, solid and plated, precious metalwares—silver and plated silver holloware. Used continuously since May 1884. Application filed by A.C. Bartlett, president.

This hardware firm took the entire first production of steel traps made by the Oneida Community—the success of this enterprise eventually led to Oneida's silversmithing business.

GEORGE W. HICKOK & CO.

Sante Fe, New Mexico

"Manufacturers of filigree spoons and everything in the filigree line." Century Magazine, April 1892. Montezuma spoon marked "Copyrighted".

HICKOK MATTHEWS COMPANY

Newark, New Jersey

See Eleder-Hickok Co.

See Lebkueker & Co.

Formed by the merger, between 1931-1943 of the Eleder-Hickok Company, manufacturers of sterling silver novelties and the Matthews Company (incorporated in 1901).

They are manufacturers of sterling holloware and presentation pieces.

Purchased in 1965 by Wolfgang K. Schroth from David M. Warren, Jr., president and owner.

Mr. Schroth was born in Frankfort, Germany and received his training under August Bock and Emil Woerner. He formed his own silver company there, but came to this country in 1955 and joined Tiffany and Company as their silversmith. In 1961 he joined Hickok-Matthews as manager and silversmith. One of the country's foremost silversmiths, Mr. Schroth lectures extensively on that subject.

(On novelties)

(On holloware)

HIGGINS, MARCHAND & CO.

Philadelphia, Pennsylvania

Charles E. Marchand, Delaware City, Delaware, was granted a spoon Design Patent, No. 2,788, August 27, 1867, which was assigned to Higgins, Marchand & Co.

HI-GRADE SILVER CO., INC.

New York, New York

Listed in 1927 KJI as manufacturers of sterling silver holloware.

H.M. HILL & CO.

Lynn, Massachusetts

Registered U.S. Patent No. 19,221, March 24, 1891 for manufacture of sterling souvenir flatware.

Herbert H. Hill, native of Barnstead, New Hampshire, moved to Lynn, Massachusetts c. 1889. There, he learned the jewelry and watchmaking business from John M. Humphrey with whom he was in business for about three years. Hill bought the business when Humphrey sold out and continued to operate it until 1914 when he moved to Centre Barnstead.

A. HIMMELLS SILVERWARE MANUFACTORY

New Orleans, Louisiana

"Silverware of all descriptions made to Order at Short Notice. 186 Poydras St." (New Orleans City Directory, 1871)

MAX HIRSCH
Philadelphia, Pennsylvania

Listed as manufacturer of silverplated articles c. 1920. The trademark indicates fittings for leather goods.

M. FRED HIRSCH CO., INC.
Jersey City, New Jersey

In business c. 1920-1945 as manufacturers and jobbers of sterling silverware. Succeeded by Fisher Silver Co.

HIRSCH & OPPENHEIMER
Chicago, Illinois

Manufacturing jeweler and special order work. Listed JC 1904-22 and KJI 1927.

HIPP & COBURN
Chicago, Illinois

S
STERLING HIPP & COBURN CHICAGO
C
(Cameo marks on commemorative spoon)

CHARLES E. HOCHHAUS
Baltimore, Maryland

Listed in Baltimore City Directories 1870-1871 as a silverplater.

F.B. HOFFMAN & CO.
Baltimore, Maryland

Listed in Baltimore City Directories 1870-1871 as silverplaters.

FREDERICK S. HOFFMAN
Brooklyn, New York
See Clarence B. Webster

Listed in JC 1896 in sterling silver section. Other sources indicate that these trademarks were used also on 14 and 18k gold and silver novelties and on silver mountings for leather goods. Succeeded by Clarence B. Webster before 1904.

HOFFMAN MANUFACTURING CO.
Newark, New Jersey

Listed 1927 KJI as manufacturers of sterling silver dresserware, vanity and cigarette cases, tableware and novelties.

MAX HOFFMAN
Newark, New Jersey

Jeweler and silversmith c. 1848-51. Advertised as manufacturer of jewelry, silverware, and metal gilding.

HOLBROOK, WHITING & ALBEE
North Attleboro, Massachusetts
See Frank M. Whiting Co.

HOLBROOK MFG. CO.
Attleboro, Massachusetts

Founded by Harry R. and Charles L. Holbrook. Listed in Attleboro City Directories from 1905-1916 as manufacturers of special machines and novelties.

HOLBROOK & SIMMONS
See Thornton & Company

H. & S.

Successors to Holbrook, Dagg & Co. "Holbrook & Simmons, manufacturing silversmiths, 427 E. 144th Street, New York, have dissolved by mutual consent, Henry B. Simmons retiring. The remaining partners, Eugene C. Holbrook and William H. Thornton, will continue the business as before under the firm name of Holbrook & Thornton later Thornton & Co." (JC&HR 5-2-1896, p. 20)

WILLIAM HOLBROOKE
Baltimore, Maryland

Listed 1850 census as silversmith. Born Maryland.

JOHN HOLIDAY
Baltimore, Maryland

Listed in Baltimore City Directory in 1872 as a silverplater.

HOLMES, BOOTH & HAYDENS
Waterbury, Connecticut

Organized by Israel Holmes in 1853 to roll brass. They made plated silver copper sheets for photography which produced a better and less expensive photograph than copper plate.

During the Civil War they made brass buttons for both military and civil uniforms, brass fittings and kerosene lamps.

After the war they went into the nickel-silver business and turned out huge quantities of knives, forks and spoons for silver-plating.

Bought by Rogers and Hamilton c. 1886, which later became part of International Silver Company.

H. B. & H. A. 1.
SHEFFIELD PLATED CO.
STERLING SILVER PLATE CO.
UNION SILVER PLATE CO.
HOLMES & EDWARDS SILVER CO.
Bridgeport, Connecticut
See International Silver Co.

The Holmes & Edwards Silver Co. was started in Bridgeport, Connecticut in 1882, having taken over a business run under the name of Rogers & Brittin, which had been in existence about two years. At first, their business was largely the making of moderate priced flatware, sometimes producing the blanks, oftentimes buying the blanks from other makers, plating and marketing them. Edwards saw a notice in a newspaper of a new patented idea of inserting a piece of sterling silver in the backs of spoons and forks prior to their being plated. This was patented by William A. Warner of Syracuse. Edwards immediately secured rights to the patent from Warner and put out a line of Holmes & Edwards sterling inlaid flatware in which the idea was utilized. The Holmes & Edwards plant was taken over by the International Silver Company in 1898 though it continued to operate in Bridgeport until moved to Meriden in 1931.

In 1956 the Holmes & Edwards "SILVER — INLAID" trademark was changed to "Holmes & Edwards Deepsilver" and in 1960 changed again to "International Deepsilver."

By 1972 the sterling inlaid feature had been discontinued. It is now marketed by Wallace International Silversmiths, Inc.

HOLMES & TUTTLE MFG. CO.
Bristol, Connecticut
See American Silver Co.
See Bristol Brass & Clock Co.
See International Silver Co.

Organized by Israel Holmes in 1851. Made plated silver knives, forks and spoons. Taken over by Bristol Brass & Clock Co., in 1857 and operated as their silverware department until 1901 when it became the American Silver Company which was bought by International Silver Co. in 1935.

HOLMES & TUTTLE
H. & T. MFG. CO.
WM. HOLMES
ROBERT HOLMES
Baltimore, Maryland

William Holmes, founder of the silver manufacturing business of that name in Baltimore, was born in Sheffield, England July 27, 1816 and died in Baltimore April 7, 1883. Holmes' family had been in the silver manufacturing business in Sheffield and it was there that he learned the trade he established in Baltimore. There is a listing in Baltimore City Directories 1847-1848 as "Wm. Holmes, brass founder, patent, windlass maker, composition and iron caster," which the family feels is a different William Holmes as their records show the silver manufacturer arriving in Baltimore in 1852.

William Holmes and his wife, Ann, had at least six children, four of whom were boys. All four sons learned some branch of the silver manufacturing and plating trade. Samuel specialized in chasing, William, Jr., in buffing and polishing, Robert specialized in spinning, molding and other manufacturing processes and John was listed in City Directories as a gilder.

The manufacturing business established by William Holmes was financially successful for a number of years but failed about 1855 on account of a dishonest bookkeeper. For some years the Holmes' business was dormant until Robert decided to establish a repair, replating and limited manufacturing business (Ledlie I. Laughlin in

XIV

ROLLED PLATE, HOLMES & EDWARDS
ORIENTAL
MEXICAN CRAIG
EDWARDS
B. S. CO.
XIV. HOLMES & EDWARDS

INLAID
HESCO
VIANDE

STRATFORD SILVER PLATE CO.

STRATFORD SILVER CO.   STRATFORD PLATE

ⒺSTERLING INLAID

STRATFORD SILVER CO AXI
STRATFORD SILVERPLATE
WALDO HE

HOLMES & EDWARDS
INLAID

his *Pewter in America*, Vol. II, says that Robert Holmes & Sons were makers of britannia ware in 1853 and 1854.) This new business was started in his home but as the business grew activities were transferred to more suitable locations.

William Holmes was listed in Baltimore Directories from 1865-76 at "over 12 Bank Lane" and at 46 N. Holliday, the latter apparently a factory or business location as the residence was 820 W. Baltimore. Samuel Holmes and George Holmes were listed as electroplater and britannia worker at the N. Holliday address. Other locations and company names listed were Holmes Bros. & Co., 1877-90; Holmes Nickel Plate Co., 1886; Robert Holmes, 1894; Holmes Plating Works., successor to Robert Holmes, 1895-96 and Holmes & Son, 1896-1940.

Robert Holmes had six children, three boys and three girls. All three boys entered the repair establishment with their father. They were Robert Frederick, W. Grover and Morris. Robert Frederick became the plater. Grover inherited the business after the deaths of his father, Robert Frederick and Morris, the youngest. This was carried on principally as a general repair business until Grover retired on account of age in 1960. The business was then placed in the hands of W. Stanley Rauh who had been with the firm for almost forty years. Following Mr. Rauh's death about 1967 the tools and dies were purchased by the Stieff Company of Baltimore.

WM. HOLMES

HOMAN MANUFACTURING COMPANY

Cincinnati, Ohio

Established in 1847 by Henry Homan and Asa F. Flagg.

The Cincinnati City Directories of 1842-1843 and 1846 list Asa F. Flagg as a britannia manufacturer. An English potter, he went to Cincinnati to form a partnership with Homan for the manufacture of pewter. Flagg was so devoted to his work that he was known locally as "Pewter" Flag.

Under the firm name Homan & Co. (pieces are also found marked Flagg & Homan), they made britannia ware until Flagg's retirement in 1854.

M. Miller joined the firm and remained a co-partner until the death of Henry Homan in 1865.

Homan's widow, Margaret, with their sons, Frank (who died in 1880), Louis and Joseph T., managed the firm until her retirement in 1887.

About 1864 the company gradually changed from the manufacture of pewter, britannia and German silver to electroplated silverware. They also advertised that they did gold plating.

Their regular products were ecclesiastical wares, registered U.S. Patent 27,974, March 17, 1896, (chalices, patens, beakers, tankards, baptismal bowls, alms dishes and candlesticks); Ohio-Mississippi river boat equipment (bowls, pewter plates, beakers, trenchers, chargers, tea sets and swivel lamps); bar equipment and articles for domestic use (tea and coffee sets, cups, ewers and basins, warming pans, pitchers, jugs, sugar sifters, pewter combs, special frames, clockweights and buttons).

Around 1896 the name of the firm was the Homan Silver Plate Company which was succeeded by Homan Manufacturing Company between 1904 and 1915. Out of business in 1941.

HOMAN & COMPANY CINCINNATI

(Nickel Silver.)

SICK-CALL

RICHFIELD PLATE CO. QUADRUPLE

(Popular Price Goods.)

HOMAN & COMPANY CINCINNATI

OUTFIT. (Church Goods.)

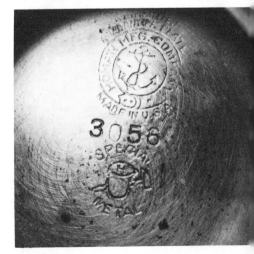

HOME DECORATORS, INC.
Newark, New York

Registered trademarks for use on silver-plated flat and hollow tableware.

Succeeded by Silver Counselors of Home Decorators.

Slate House ⚔ Sterling

PRESTIGE ★ ★ ★ PLATE

(Used since Feb. 4, 1944)

DISTINCTION

(Used since March 20, 1950)

GEO. E. HOMER
Boston, Massachusetts

George E. Homer established a jewelry business with his brother, Joseph J., in 1875. The business grew rapidly and additional stores were opened in Providence, R.I., Portland, Me., and Lowell, Taunton, and Ayer, Mass. These were discontinued after Joseph's death, before 1922. The same year George completed a new building for his store at 45 Winter Street, Boston. The firm is still in business. Many souvenir spoons bear the Homer trademark.

(*Souvenir Spoons.*)

HOPEWELL SILVER COMPANY
See Reed & Barton

HOPEWELL SILVER CO.

HOPKINS & BRIELE
Baltimore, Maryland

Listed in Baltimore City Directories 1879-1886 as gold and silversmiths.

J. SETH HOPKINS & CO.
Baltimore, Maryland

Listed in Baltimore City Directories 1887-1888 under plated silverware.

HORTON & ANGELL
Attleboro, Massachusetts

Manufacturers of gold and silver goods. Listed JC-K 1896. Founded 1870. Now called Horton Angell.

HOTCHKISS & SCHREUDER
Syracuse, New York

David Hotchkiss was first listed as a silversmith in Palmyra, New York, working c. 1840; and advertised with Benjamin R. Norton, also of Palmyra, as jewelers in 1841-1842. Hotchkiss & Andrew B. Schreuder were working c. 1850 in Syracuse, New York where they were listed together until 1871 when Schreuder is listed alone as silversmith. (David Hotchkiss apears in later years to have become a clerk and then the treasurer of an "engine company." Apparently, A.B. Schreuder continued to use the H & S. mark. About 1895-1896 the company was sold to the Syracuse Silver Mfg. Co. (q.v.)

E.V. HOUGHWOUT & COMPANY
New York, New York

In the 1860s they purchased Reed & Barton wares "in the metal" and operated their own plating establishment.

HOUSATONIC MFG. CO.
New Haven, Connecticut

Registered trademark No. 40,725 on July 7, 1903 for use on tableware, spoons, knives, forks, table tongs of plated ware. Used continuously in their business since April 1, 1902. Edgar A. Russsell, Treasurer.

"Articles of association (were drawn for) the Housatonic Mfg. Co., Wallingford, Conn., for the making of 'German silver, brass and other metals, silverware and other goods made in whole or in part of metal, glass, china, queensware, wooden or any other kind of goods to use in combination with above.' by C.A. Hamilton, N.Y., F.W. Carnell and E. A. Russell,

Waterbury; Waterbury Brass Co.; Birmingham Brass Co. and C.E. Minor, New Haven." (JC&HR 9-30-1896, p. 13)

HOWARD & COCKSHAW CO.
New York, New York
See Herbert Cockshaw, Jr.

HOWARD & CO.
New York, New York
Established as silversmiths c. 1866. Last listing 1922.

HOWARD CUTLERY CO.
New York, New York
Manufacturers of plated silver knives and holloware. Successor to E. Magnus before 1896. Out of business before 1909.

(Knives.)

(Holloware.)

HOWARD & SCHERRIEBLE
Providence, Rhode Island
See Howard Sterling Co.
See Roger Williams Silver Co.

HOWARD & SON
Providence, Rhode Island
See Howard Sterling Co.
See Park Bros. & Rogers
The trademark is similar to that used by Parks Bros. & Rogers—a four-leaf clover partially encircled by the word "sterling" in a horseshoe arrangement.
Registered U.S. Patent No. 15,614, June 19, 1888 for useful or ornamental articles made of solid silver.

HOWARD STERLING CO.
Providence, Rhode Island
See S. Cottle

CHRONOLOGY

H. Howard & Co.	1878-79
Howard & Scherrieble	1879-84
Howard & Son	1884-89
The Sterling Co.	1886-91
Howard Sterling Co.	1891-1901

Established January 1, 1878 as H. Howard & Co., with Hiram Howard, A.J. Scherrieble and Arnold Nicoud, to manufacture plated jewelry. January 1, 1879 Arnold Nicoud withdrew and a limited partnership was formed with Sterns Hutchins. The firm name was Howard & Scherrieble until the expiration of the limited partnership on January 1, 1884, when Hutchins retired and Stephen C. Howard, son of the senior member of the firm was admitted as a partner. On February 5, 1884, Scherrieble withdrew and the firm name was changed to Howard & Son. In July 1886 a department was established for the manufacture of sterling silverware and was conducted under the title of The Sterling Company. During the Fall of 1888 the firm discovered that their combined industries had outgrown their limited accommodations, and on January 1, 1889 they moved to a new factory. In January 1891 the concern was incorporated as Howard & Son and continued under that name until December 1891 when they disposed of the electroplated goods branch of the business to Parks Bros. & Rogers, and at the same time the name of the corporation was altered to that of Howard Sterling Co. The company went into receivership about 1901-02. Some of the patterns and dies were sold to the Roger Williams Silver Company and others. Lever cuff and collar buttons were specialties of this company. One, in particular, the "Sensational" collar button, was constructed of rolled gold plate, the shoe and post were drawn from a single piece of stock, while the top or head was made from another piece and firmly secured without the use of solder—all the work being done by a machine invented for the purpose by S. Cottle (q.v.). They also made great quantities of silverware, both table and ornamental.

(used since 1894)

H.G. HUDSON
Amesbury, Massachusetts
Trademarks in 1896-1904 editions of J C-K were parts of the designs used on the souvenir spoons sold by H.G. Hudson honoring John Greenleaf Whittier, "the Quaker Poet," who moved to Amesbury in

1836 after serving in the Massachusetts legislature. U.S. Patent Office also registered No. 19,959, August 4, 1891, for the manufacture of flatware, spoons, knives, forks and ladles. It is doubtful that Hudson did the manufacturing himself as numerous examples of these spoons bear the mark of the Durgin Company, now a Division of The Gorham Company.

J.B. HUDSON
Minneapolis, Minnesota

Founded in 1886 by Josiah Bell Hudson, retail jeweler. Owned by Dayton Co. since 1929. Now a division of Dayton Hudson Jewelers, a part of Dayton Hudson Corporation. Retailers of sterling, silverplate and pewter, holloware, flatware, novelties and importers of their own exclusive line.

J.B.Hudson

JBH

WALTER HUNOLD
Providence, Rhode Island

First listed in Providence City Directory in 1903 as Walter Hunold. About 1920 listed as Nussbaum & Hunold (B. Nussbaum, W. Hunold, J. Nussbaum), manufacturing jewelers. From 1921-1925 the listing was Walter Hunold. This is the last listing.

GEORGE J. HUNT
Boston, Massachusetts

George J. Hunt was born in Liverpool, England in 1865, serving the usual seven years' apprenticeship in one of the leading silversmith concerns of that city. In 1885 he came to the United States and worked in several silver factories. In 1905 he opened his own shop in Boston. His real love was teaching others the craft of silversmithing and this became his major interest. He was also a jeweler.

WM. E. HUNT CO.
Providence, Rhode Island

Listed 1927 KJI as manufacturers of sterling silver and white metal novelties.

HURLY SILVER CO.
Scriba, New York
See Benedict Mfg. Co.

Established in 1890 as John Hurly Silver Co. Purchased by Benedict Silver Co. in 1894.

J.H. HUTCHINSON & CO.
Portsmouth, New Hampshire

Registered U.S. Patent No. 19,770, June 30, 1891, for use on spoons, forks, bells, plates, and holloware of sterling silver and plated silver. This drawing of "Old Constitution" is the trademark registered. It is doubtful if Hutchinson company actually manufactured any of the silverware. Souvenir spoons sold by him bear the Durgin Company mark. Out of business before 1915.

"John H. Hutchinson, B. Nelson, New Hampshire, June 6, 1838. Graduated from Dartmouth College. Took up residence in St. Johnsbury, Vermont where he began the merchant tailoring business and married Mary E. Graham a week before he was commissioned a lieutenant of Co. G, Third Vermont Volunteers and left for the front. Soon after reaching Washington he was commissioned a captain in the signal corps, was later aide-de-camp on the staff of General McClellan.

"After he was mustered out of the service he returned to St. Johnsbury and on May 18, 1878 moved to Portsmouth, New Hampshire and started in the jewelry business under the firm name of Rowell & Hutchinson. Later he purchased the interest of the senior partner and became associated with James R. Connell and so continued for about ten years. Fifteen years ago last January this firm dissolved and each continued in the business, Mr. Hutchinson retaining the old stand and continuing there until two years ago. Last November he removed to the present location. Meanwhile he had associated his daughter and son-in-law with him in the firm. He also established a large florist business. He was active in various civic and charitable organizations. He died Monday morning June 9 at his summer home." (JC&HR 7-16-1896, p. 6)

OLD CONSTITUTION

WM. HUTTON & SONS, LTD.
Sheffield, England

Silversmiths, cutlers and electroplaters established in 1800. Limited, since 1893 in which year they absorbed Fanell, Elliott & Co. Made sterling silverware, nickel spoons and forks and steel cutlery. Last listing in 1922.

Registered U.S. Patent 40,657, June 23, 1903 for silver and plated silver tableware.

Family disagreements in the 1920s caused the firm's demise; its goodwill was transferred in 1930 to James Dixon.

HYDE & GOODRICH
New Orleans, Louisiana

Hyde & Goodrich were in business at least as early as 1816. The earliest New Orleans City Directory available is for 1822 which lists James N. Hyde & C.W. Goodrich, at "15 Chartres Street; jewelry, military and fancy hardware." The firm name Hyde & Goodrich first appears in the 1838 Directory. Their advertisement in the *New Orleans Merchants' Diary and Guide*, 1857-58, says, "The largest importers of jewelry, watches, plated-ware, guns and pistols and the only manufacturers of gold and silverware in the South-West," with the added claim "established forty years in New Orleans." They went out of business in 1866.

I

IDEAL SILVER COMPANY
Portland, Connecticut

A short-lived company, manufacturers of silverware about 1905-06.

IKORA
New York, New York
See Württembergische Metallwarenfabrik

Distributors for Württembergische Mettallwarenfabrik (WMF).

IMC MINT CORP.
Salt Lake City, Utah

No response to inquiries.

J.T. INMAN & CO.
Attleboro, Massachusetts

They were listed in JC 1896-1922 as manufacturers of sterling silver and plated silver cigarette cases, link buttons, buckles, vanity cases, dorines (powder boxes), bar pins, cuff and collar pins and souvenir goods.

Listed in the Attleboro City Directories 1892-1944 as manufacturing jewelers with James McNerney as owner. Listed from 1944-1963 with Roy W. Inman.

When the Watson Company went out of business about 1955, the Inman Company bought some of the souvenir spoon dies (The Wallace Company took over the old Watson business). These dies were used by the Inman Company until 1964 when Whiting & Davis Co. purchased the company and integrated the complete manufacturing facilities into its own plant.

INMAN STERLING

INTERNATIONAL SHEFFIELD WORKS, INC.
New York, New York

Listed in 1927 and 1931 KJI as manufacturers of plated silver holloware, pewterware and pewter lamps.

INTERNATIONAL SILVER CO.
Meriden, Connecticut

The International Silver Company was incorporated in 1898 by a number of independent New England silversmiths whose family backgrounds began with the earliest American settlers. International Silver has become not only world renowned for the quality of its fine silver, it has also become the world's largest manufacturer of silverware.

The history of International Silver Company and its predecessors is a history of America's silversmithing. Early records of this industry started with Ashbil Griswold who in 1808 set up his pewter shop in Meriden, Connecticut, soon expanding his business to include britannia ware. Meriden became the center of pewter, britannia ware and silver manufacturing through the efforts of Griswold and other independent makers who joined together to finance the Yankee peddlers responsible for selling and bartering these wares.

About the same time, the growing demand for coin silver led the three Rogers brothers, Asa, Simeon and William, to open their workshop in Hartford, Connecticut. The high cost of coin silver, as well as its impractical nature for constant use, led to experimentation in the new process of electroplating spoons and forks with pure silver.

In 1847 they perfected this process and marketed their first silverware under the firm name of Rogers Bros. Their fine workmanship and high quality material soon established the name of the Rogers Bros. line throughout the country. This reputation is maintained today.

Britannia, more brilliant, harder and more resistant to wear then pewter, was replacing pewter in many American homes. Several small factories in Meriden turned to the production of this new ware, most of which was marketed by Horace C. and Dennis C. Wilcox under the name of H.C. Wilcox & Co. The Meriden Britannia Company which followed in 1852, offered German silver holloware and flatware for silverplating by 1855.

In 1862, the Rogers brothers, who had been making and selling plated silver ware in Hartford, were moved to Meriden and added to the Meriden Britannia Company. Their 1847 Rogers Bros. trademark was an important addition.

Other silversmiths, who had set up small shops in Connecticut, soon realized they could all work more efficiently and supply the demands of the public better by combining into one organization. The scope of the Meriden Britannia Co. had become international with the establishment of London and Canadian branches and sales offices in New York, Chicago and San Francisco. The Meriden Britannia Co. was the leading spirit in the formation of The International Silver Company in November 1898.

Among the many independent companies which then or later became part of The International Silver Company, either directly or indirectly through Meriden Britannia Co., were the American Silver Co., Bristol, Conn. established in 1901; Barbour Silver Co., Hartford, 1892; Derby Silver Co., Birmingham, 1873; Forbes Silver Co., Meriden, 1894; Hall & Elton Co., Wallingford, 1837; Holmes & Edwards Silver Co., Bridgeport, 1882; Holmes & Tuttle, Bristol, 1851; International Silver Co. of Canada, Ltd., Inc., 1922; La Pierre Mfg. Co., Newark, 1895; Maltby, Stevens & Curtiss, Shelton, 1879; Manhattan Silver Plate Co., Brooklyn, 1877; Meriden Britannia Co., Meriden, 1852; Meriden Britannia Co., Ltd., Hamilton, Ont., 1879; Meriden Silver Plate Co., Meriden, 1869; Middletown Plate Co., Middletown, 1864; Norwich Cutlery Co., Norwich, 1890; Parker & Casper, Meriden, 1867; C. Rogers & Bros., Meriden 1866; Rogers Cutlery Co.,

Hartford, 1871, W. Rogers Mfg. Co., Ltd., Niagara Falls, 1911; Rogers Bros., Hartford, 1847; Rogers & Bro., Waterbury, 1858; Rogers & Hamilton Co., Waterbury, 1886; Rogers, Smith & Co., Wallingford, 1856; Simpson Nickel Silver Co., Wallingford, 1871; Standard Silver Co. of Toronto, Co., Ltd., 1895; Watrous Mfg. Co., Wallingford, 1896; E.G. Webster & Son, Brooklyn 1886; E.G. Webster & Bro., Brooklyn, 1863; Webster Mfg. Co., Brooklyn, 1859; Wilcox Britannia Co., Meriden, 1865; Wilcox Silver Plate Co., Meriden, 1867; Wilcox & Evertsen, New York, 1892 and William Rogers Mfg. Co., Hartford, 1865.

By 1900, the Meriden-Wallingford area of Connecticut had became a center for silver craftsmanship. Almost the peak of production was reached shortly before World War II.

In 1972 the Hotel division of International Silver Company became a subsidiary of that company under the name of World Tableware International (q.v.). This, in turn, was sold to two employees and private investors on October 1, 1983. They organized a new American Silver Company of which World Tableware International is a subsidiary. Their products are flatware and holloware in silverplate and stainless steel, for hotels, restaurants, clubs, ships, institutions and other types of public dining.

In 1984 International Silver Company was sold to Katy Industries, Inc. of Elgin, Illinois which already owned Wallace Silversmiths. The firm name was changed to Wallace International Silversmiths, Wallingford, Connecticut (q.v.). This company markets International Sterling flatware and silverplated flatware trademarked 1847 Rogers Bros., International Deepsilver, International Silverplate and several brands of stainless steel flatware in addition to the Wallace Silversmiths' products.

International Silver Company ceased making sterling holloware in 1976 and in 1981 sold its plated holloware business to Oneida, Ltd., Silversmiths of Oneida, New York (q.v.)

In 1925 the International Silver Company introduced a sterling pattern with an imprint of a pine tree on the back of the handle. The pine tree was similar to that on the pine tree shilling made famous through the tradition that the Mint Master, John Hull, gave his daughter her weight in shillings as a dowry upon her marriage to

Samuel Sewall. When the silver pattern was introduced, the International Silver Company secured permission from the United States Treasury to reproduce in silver, the original pine tree shilling which was first made by John Hull in 1663. The reproductions were distributed for advertising.

International Silver Company weight markings on sterling flatware

The use of letters to indicate the various weights in sterling patterns cannot be answered in a general way as there are some exceptions. Variations occur, depending upon the pattern. For both Wilcox & Evertsen and Simpson, Hall, Miller & Company, in 1899 none of their price lists show what symbols or letters were used. The different weights are listed but not the symbols used.

In 1904 Simpson, Hall, Miller & Company pattern teaspoons were listed as light, medium, heavy, extra heavy and massive. In 1906 there were listed medium, heavy, extra heavy, massive and extra massive (in some patterns). In 1906 the weights were listed as trade, medium, heavy and extra heavy and in 1910 the listing was the same with the addition of massive.

In Wilcox & Evertsen patterns, in 1899 were listed regular, medium, heavy and extra heavy with a footnote to the effect that the regular weight was "small size." (Probably the five o'clock teaspoon size.) In 1901 there were listed medium, heavy, extra heavy and massive and in 1906, regular, medium, heavy and extra heavy.

Not until 1920 did the old price lists show the letters and these were basically for standard patterns. The following seem to be the most commonly used:

Teaspoon (five o'clock)	A
Trade	B
Regular	C
Heavy	D
Massive	E

In some patterns B was sometimes called medium, C was sometimes heavy and A was called regular.

For example:

Deerfield (1913) teaspoons were made in A, B, C and D weights; the 'only other pieces made in different weights were the dessert and tablespoons and the dessert and dinner forks, all made only in A and B weights.

Pantheon (1920) teaspoons were made in B, C, D and E weights; the other four items listed above were made only in B and C.

By 1941 only teaspoons were made in more than one weight with no consistency in the system of marking. The letters R and H were used for Regular and Heavy and also E for Extra Heavy. *Prelude* (1939) and *Gadroon* (1933) teaspoons were made in R and H. *Richelieu* (1935) and *Colonial Shell* (1941) were made just in H and E; *Continental* (1934) was made in R, H and E.

Empress (1932) and *Fontaine* (1924) had teaspoons made in Regular, Heavy and Extra Heavy but these weights were represented by the letters C, D and E. After 1945 extra weight teaspoons were discontinued but some patterns are heavier than others. Patterns are separated into Groups I through IV, all teaspoons within a group being the same weight.

Grade markings for 1847 Rogers Bros. silverplated flatware

The base metal used for these goods is 18% nickel silver—practically indestructible.....The plating on a spoon or fork is .999 pure silver.

There are three grades of plate with marks as follows:

XS
1847 ROGERS BROS. TRIPLE

This is the grade ordinarily sold and more than sufficient for any except especially hard wear. Teaspoons are plated not less than six ounces and table spoons are not less than twelve ounces to the gross (other staple pieces in proportion).

XS
1847 ROGERS BROS. XII TRIPLE

The teaspoons are plated not less than six ounces and table spoons not less than twelve ounces to the gross, and in addition the parts most exposed to wear bear an additional double plating.

xs
1847 ROGERS BROS. Quintuple

This is the heaviest grade of silver plate made and is required only by those who desire something extraordinarily heavy. It is used for the most part by hotels, railroads, etc., where the silver is subjected to constant and hard use. Teaspoons are plated not less

than ten ounces and table spoons not less than twenty ounces to the gross (other staple pieces in proportion).

The above from an early 1900 pamphlet issued by the International Silver Company.

Following the formation of International Silver Company in 1898 they continued to use the trademarks of their predecessors. After 1917, 1847 Rogers Bros. silverplate was made in only one quality and all "quality" marks were discontinued.

The International Silver Company mark was not used until after 1928 on flatware.

BREWSTER
(Pewter holloware)

Insilco sold 1988 to INR Acquisition Corp., Midland, Texas.

Trademarks on silverplate

ALBANY SILVER PLATE
AMERICAN SILVER CO.
AMSILCO
ATLAS SILVER PLATE
AVON SILVER PLATE
BS CO.
CAMELIA SILVERPLATE
CARV-EZE
COURT SILVER PLATE
CROWN SILVER CO.
DEEP SILVER
DEERFIELD SILVER PLATE
EASTERN SILVER CO.
1847 ROGERS BROS.
1865 WM. ROGERS MFG. CO.
EMBASSY SILVER PLATE
GEM SILVER CO.
HOLD-EDGE
HOLMES & EDWARDS
HOLMES & TUTTLE
H. & T. MFG. CO.
INDEPENDENCE TRIPLE
INLAID
INSICO
INTERNATIONAL
INTERNATIONAL SILVER CO.
I.S. CO.
I.S. CO.
KENSICO
KENSINGTON SILVER PLATE
MANOR PLATE
MELODY SILVER PLATE
N.E.S.P. CO.
NEW ENGLAND SILVER PLATE
NO-TARN
OLD COMPANY PLATE
PALLADIANT
R. & B.
R. C. CO.
REVELATION SILVER PLATE
ROGERS CUTLERY CO.
ROGERS & HAMILTON
ROYAL PLATE CO.
SILVER WELD (knives)
SOUTHINGTON COMPANY
STRAND
STRATFORD PLATE
STRATFORD SILVER PLATE CO.
SUPER-PLATE
SUPERIOR

SUPREME SILVER PLATE
VIANDE
VICTOR S. CO.
WILCOX SILVER PLATE CO.
WM. ROGERS MFG. CO.
WM. ROGERS & SON
WORLD
X S TRIPLE

INTERNATIONAL SILVER COMPANY OF CANADA, LTD.
Hamilton, Ontario
See International Silver Co.

Began with the establishment of the Meriden Britannia Co. Ltd. at Hamilton, Ontario in 1879. Organized to take care of the Canadian business of the International Silver Co. Was incorporated in 1925.

The business was sold to Heritage Silversmiths in June 1972.

INTERNATIONAL-COMMON-WEALTH SILVER CO.
New York, New York

Listed in JC 1915-1922 as successor to International Silver Deposit Works, founding date unknown.

POPPY
(Deposit Ware.)

J

D.C. JACCARD & CO.
See Mermod, Jaccard & King

A. JACOBI
Baltimore, Maryland
See Jenkins & Jenkins

Founded in 1879 as manufacturing silversmiths. Company name changed to Jacobi & Co. in 1890.

JACOBI & COMPANY
Baltimore, Maryland
See Jenkins & Jenkins

Successors to A. Jacobi in 1890; reorganized as Jacobi & Jenkins in 1894.

JACOBI & JENKINS
Baltimore, Maryland
See Jenkins & Jenkins

Successors to Jacobi & Co. in 1894; succeeded by Jenkins & Jenkins in 1908.

Members of the firm were A. Jacobi, W. Armour Jenkins and W.F. Jacobi. In 1895

they advertised that they were "the only silversmiths in Maryland making and retailing their own work exclusively—all articles of sterling silver."

RUFUS JACOBY
Silver Spring, Maryland

Silversmith, specializing in hand-wrought liturgical articles. Many of his chalices are a combination of silver and Macassar ebony. Though he fashions all his silver entirely by hand, his work is the essence of modern simplicity and functional design.

JACOBY HANDMADE STERLING

GUY S. JENKINS
New York, New York

Listed JKD 1918-19 as manufacturer of silverplated holloware.

JENKINS & JENKINS
Baltimore, Maryland

CHRONOLOGY

A. Jacobi	1879-90
Jacobi & Co.	1890-94
Jacobi & Jenkins	1894-1908
Jenkins & Jenkins	1908-c. 1915

Originally founded as A. Jacobi in 1879, manufacturing silversmiths; changed to Jacobi & Co., 1890; reorganized as Jacobi & Jenkins in 1895; succeeded by Jenkins & Jenkins in 1908. The tools and dies were purchased c. 1915 by the Schofield Company, Inc. of Baltimore manufacturers of silverware and jewelry. The Schofield Co. was bought by Oscar Caplan & Sons in 1965 and in 1967 sold to the Stieff Co., all of Baltimore.

LEWIS E. JENKS
Boston, Massachusetts

Listed in Boston City Directory 1875 to 1885 at same address as Farrington & Hunnewell. He was also a member of the partnership of Kennard & Jenks which was bought by the Gorham Company c. 1879-80.

JENNINGS & LAUTER
New York, New York

Listed in JC 1896 as Reeves & Sillcocks; succeeded by Reeves & Browne before 1904;

by Browne, Jennings & Lauter before 1915 and by Jennings & Lauter before 1922. Listed in sterling silver section.

JENNINGS BROS. MFG. CO.
Bridgeport, Connecticut
  Manufacturers of silverplated toilet ware, shaving stands, shaving sets, casseroles, table holloware, clocks, lamps, Sheffield reproductions.

1890 JENNINGS BROS. A1

  Trademark J B used on novelties.

JENNINGS SILVER CO.
Irvington, New Jersey
  Manufacturers and jobbers of sterling and plated silver holloware. Listed JC 1915-1943.

J.S.C.

JENNINGS
(On sterling)

JESCO
(On silverplate)

GEORG JENSEN, INC.
Copenhagen, Denmark
  Founded by Georg Jensen (b. 8-31-1866; d. 1935) who opened his first tiny shop at 36 Bregade, Copenhagen, in 1904. Twenty-five years later he had a staff of 250. There are now branches all over the world. Among World War II when silver was not available. Georg Jensen was one of the most influential designers of modern silver.

GEORG JENSEN Inc.
(On base metals)

(On articles made of or plated with precious metals)

Claims use on goods made of bronze since December 1932; on goods made of aluminum since April 1936; on goods made of pewter since October 1936; and on goods made of stainless steel since November 1940.

  The above trademarks all registered in the U.S.

THE JEWELERS' CROWN GUILD
Rockford, Illinois
  The Jewelers' Crown Guild appears to have been successor December 21, 1892 to the Watchmaker's and Jewelers' Guild of the United States which had been formed in 1879. The object of this organization was to combat the "catalogue nuisance," or underselling by firms who sold through catalogs and did not have the expense of maintaining retail outlets—a problem that jewelers still face today. The goods were to be distributed through certain jobbing houses who were bound by Guild restrictons to sell only to Guild members and were required to mark all goods passing through their hands as Guild goods, with certain private marks. The Guild adopted distinctive marks which were to be stamped on all Guild goods. Thus all goods were stamped by both manufacturer and with quality marks, and their course would be easily traced through the various channels of trade in order to fix responsibility. The idea never won complete acceptance and seems to have been of short duration as no record of it has been found after 1904. The old Guild mark was composed of lines, and it was discovered that it broke the plating on certain goods, consequently the Guild adopted as its mark the device used by J.H. Purdy when he was chief distributor for the Guild. The device was adopted by Purdy when two doves flew down and lit on is outstretched hand when he stood in front of a store in Manchester, Iowa, where he had just completed a successful business arrangement for the Guild. Perhaps Mr. Purdy had been recently hearing Lohengrin; at any rate, the incident so impressed him that he accepted it as an omen, and immediately adopted it as his private device until it was later adopted by the Guild.

UNITED STATES
JEWELERS' GUILD.

UNITED JEWELERS' GUILD.

C.C. JOHNSON
Chicago, Illinois
  Listed in 1854-1855 Chicago Directory as a silverplater.

E.S. JOHNSON & CO.
New York, New York
  Listed in 1896-1922 JC in sterling silver and jewelry sections.

JOHNSON & GODLEY
Albany, New York

Samuel Johnson and Richard Godley listed in Albany City Directories 1843-1850 as producing factory-made silver. Their marks consisted of the two surnames in addition to "pseudo hallmarks."

JOHNSON, HAYWARD & PIPER CO.
New York, New York

Listed in JC 1904-1915 in plated silver and jewelry sections. Were probably distributors.

DUTCH SILVER NOVELTIES

J.W. JOHNSON
New York, New York

Founded in 1869 by J.W. Johnson who had as a boy worked for J.A. Babcock & Co. in the plating shop. Johnson was an agent for the Middletown Plate Company after working for Babcock.

By 1919, the J.W. Johnson company was operated by the founder's son, Harry F. Johnson, still under the same name.

They were jobbers who specialized in plating and were also wholesalers of plated silverware. Last listed in 1950.

"There is no longer any Crown Silver Plate Co. but J.W. Johnson stamps this name on plated silverware." (JC&HR 4-17-1898, p. 23)

CONNECTICUT PLATE CO.
(Hollowware.)

CROWN SILVER PLATE CO.
(Flatware.)

ROYAL PLATE CO.
(Flatware.)

J.H. JOHNSTON & CO.
New York, New York

Established in 1844 according to their advertisement in *Harpers Weekly* 1898.

"J.H. Johnston & Co. insolvent. J.H. Johnston, president of the company started in business about 1860, succeeding Many & Lewis. About 1888 he opened the present store at 15th St. and Union Square which he conducted while Albert E. Johnston conducted the Bowery store. The latter store was given up about 1882, and the same year the business was incorporated as J.H. Johnston & Co., with J.H. Johnston becoming president and A.E. Johnston, treasurer." (JC&HR 1-13-1897, p. 17)

"A new corporation, J.H. Johnston Co. formed of creditors of the old company." (JC&HR 3-17-1897, p. 9)

Out of business between 1904 and 1915.

C. B. M. C.
C. P. F.
DUPICATE WEDDING PRESENTS

A.H. JONES CO. INC.
Meriden, Connecticut

Listed as manufacturers of plated silver shakeless cellars and novelties 1918-31.

> JONES, BALL & POOR
> JOHN B. JONES CO.
> JONES, LOW & BALL
> JONES, SHREVE, BROWN & CO.
> JONES & WARD

JONES & WOODLAND
Newark, New Jersey
See Federal Silver Co.

Jones & Woodland owned by Krementz since 1977.

A.R. JUSTICE CO.
Philadelphia, Pennsylvania

The Philadelphia City Directories list the A.R. Justice Company from 1881 (hardware) through 1935-1936. The 1882 listing is in the name of Alfred R. Justice, cutlery. In 1885, the names of F. Millwood & Herbert M. Justice are added. In 1886 is the first reference to plated ware. The 1892 listing is A.R. Justice & Company (with C. Arthur Roberts added to those mentioned), silverware and cutlery. By 1895 there is reference only to silverware and plated ware and in 1899 the reference is to silversmiths. In 1910-1911 silverware and cut glass are mentioned. Further listings mention only silverware. (The name is often spelled Justus.)

(Pearl Handled Knives.)

HICKS SILVER CO.
(Hollowware.)

MEDFORD CUTLERY CO.
(Pearl Handled Knives.)

RIVERTON SILVER CO.
(Hollow and Flatware.)

JUSTIS & ARMIGER
Baltimore, Maryland
See James R. Armiger

First listed in the Baltimore City Directory in 1891 as manufacturers of silverware, solid and plated. Succeeded by James R. Armiger in 1893.

> JUSTIS & ARMIGER
> TRIPLE PLATE
> BALTIMORE

K

THE KALO SHOP
Chicago, Illinois

Founded by Clara Barck Welles in 1900 to become the largest and most influential producer of handwrought silverware and jewelry in the midwest. Mrs. Welles studied at the Art Institute's School of Decorative Designing and after graduation started the Kalo Shop.

Mrs. Welles retired in 1940 at the age of 72. The Kalo Shop continued in operation under the ownership of four employees, Daniel P. Pedersen, Yngve Olsson, Arne Myhre and Robert R. Bower. On the death of Olsson and Pedersen, Bower refused to lower the standards and the shop closed in 1970.

During its early years the Kalo Shop produced some novelty lines. Not until 1915 did they produce silverware exclusively.

Marks:

All Kalo silverware is marked KALO in capital letters. Large items are also marked HAND WROUGHT AT THE KALO SHOPS or THE KALO SHOP. Copper pieces and some early silver was marked only KALO. With the beginning of their silver production, a numbering system was introduced and numbers were impressed in addition to the KALO mark. These numbers soon ran into the thousands and around 1921 a new numbering system was introduced whereby the number represented the design or pattern rather than the order number. The letters S, M and L designated different sizes of a design.

Dating Kalo Shop articles:

Marks: HAND WROUGHT AT THE KALO SHOP, PARK RIDGE, ILLS.   1907-1914
HAND WROUGHT AT THE KALO SHOP, CHICAGO AND NEW YORK   1914-1918
HAND WROUGHT AT THE KALO SHOP, CHICAGO (or no city designation)   1918-

Marks on jewelry:
STERLING/KALO with the letters S, M or L (small, medium, large) appearing on pieces from 1921 on, indicating size of design.

Their Norse line was marked: NS before the number.

KANN BROS. SILVER CO.
Baltimore, Maryland

CHRONOLOGY

Kann & Sons	1870-1885
Kann & Sons Mfg. Co.	1885-1896
Kann Bros. Silver Co.	1899-1913

Originally founded as Kann & Sons. Listed in Baltimore City Directories from 1877 but advertisements say "Established 1870." Succeeded by Kann & Sons Mfg. Co., 1885 and by Kann Bros. Silver Co. 1899.

The firm continued to be listed as silver-platers through 1913.

E.M. KARMEL & CO.
Brooklyn, New York

Listed JC 1915-1922 in sterling silver section.

J. KATZ & CO.
Baltimore, Maryland

Listed in Baltimore City Directories 1901-1904 as silversmiths.

ERNEST KAUFMANN
Philadelphia, Pennsylvania

Listed Philadelphia City Directory only 1855 "brit.—tin." Advertised in *The Watchmaker & Jeweler* June 1870. Adv. has illustration of "Kaufman's (sic!) Patent Butter Dish." Also says "Manufacturers of superior silver plated & Britannia Ware. Established in 1857." Several patents in his name.

C.F. KEES & CO.
Newark, New Jersey

Successor, before 1904, to Henry I. Leibe Mfg. Co. and were succeeded by Archibald, Klement Co. c. 1909. They were manufacturers of sterling silver and gold lorgnettes and related items.

KELLEY & MCBEAN
New York, New York

Listed in the 1900 Niagara Falls City Directory as makers of silver and plated silverware.

"Henry Kelley, senior member of Kelley & McBean, manufacturers of silver plated goods, and inventor of considerable prominence, died a few days ago. He was born in Toulon, Illinois. Fifteen years ago he moved to Niagara Falls where he continued to live. For many years he was superintendent of the Oneida Community mill. In 1892 he launched out with F. Woolworth under the name Kelley & Woolworth in the designing and manufacture of (silver and silverplated) novelties. The firm was changed about a year ago by the retirement of Mr. Woolworth and the succession of H.W. McBean." (JC&HR 3-2-1895, p. 5)

JACK KELLMER CO.
Philadelphia, Pennsylvania

Wholesale and retail outlet for sterling and silverplate and pewter holloware and flatware.

KENNARD & JENKS
Boston, Massachusetts

Mark: An incised dolphin in a shield.

Silversmiths c. 1875-80.

"The Gorham Mfg. Co. have bought out the entire plant and stock of Kennard & Jenks of Boston and will consolidate it with their plant in Providence." (JC&HR Vol. 11, #6, p. 120, July 1880)

MRS. ANNIE KENNEY
Baltimore, Maryland

Listed in Baltimore City Directories 1867-1873 as a goldsmith and silversmith. Her advertisement says "Mfg. of gold pens."

CHARLES KENNEY
Baltimore, Maryland

Listed in Baltimore City Directories 1867-1868 as a silverplater.

AMBROSE KENT & SONS, LTD.
Toronto, Ontario

Established in 1867 as Kent Bros. Merged with Fairweather Ltd. in 1946 and became Kent-Fairweather, Ltd. Kent sold out in late 1953 and the firm name reverted to Fairweather, Ltd. No silverware is sold there now.

KENT SILVERSMITHS
New York, New York

Founded in 1936 by Lewis E. Ellmore and George Fina, now president. Their factory is in Long Island City, New York. Over a period of years they have purchased the tools and dies of several old manufacturers. They are manufacturers, wholesalers and importers of sterling and silverplate, serving pieces, holloware and novelties; also pewter.

KENT & STANLEY CO., LTD.
Providence, Rhode Island

Partners were E.F. Kent and S.W. Stanley. They were successors to Wm. H. Robinson & Co. who began in 1873. The firm changed to Kent & Stanley in 1888 and was incorporated in 1891. The company owned the Enterprise Building and occupied the top floor. Also housed there were Hamilton & Hamilton, Jr., the Howard Sterling Co.

and Parks Brothers & Rogers. Kent & Stanley manufactured silver souvenir articles. An ad in the City Directory says "rolled plate and silver chains as a specialty." The company failed in 1897, went into receivership. The Bassett Jewelry Company, Newark, New Jersey, took over plant and stock in 1898.

STERLING.

WM. B. KERR & CO.
Newark, New Jersey
See Gorham Corporation
(Originally Kerr & Thiery)

Established by William B. Kerr in Newark, New Jersey in 1855. Makers of flat and tableware, gold dresserware and jewelry. Used **fleur-de-lis** trademark in 1892. Purchased by the Gorham Corporation in 1906 and moved to Providence, Rhode Island in 1927.

AMERICAN BEAUTY

H. KESSNER & COMPANY
New York, New York

Listed 1927 KJI as manufacturers of sterling silver, nickel-plated, silver plated, German silver photo frames, mesh bags, and novelties.

KETCHAM & McDOUGALL
New York, New York

Best known as thimble makers. According to JCW 2-5-1919, "The business which is believed to have been founded somewhere between 1802 and 1803 was continued under various names but was developed by the house of Roshore and Wood which began business in 1830."

A different version came from the late Richard McFayden, who at the time of his death in 1969 was President and Chairman of the Board of Directors of Ketcham & McDougall, Inc. of Roseland, New Jersey. According to him, in 1832 John Roshore opened a small silversmith shop in New York City, taking into the business an orphan boy, Edward Ketcham, as apprentice. After the young man had served his apprenticeship, the business became Roshore & Ketcham. Hugh McDougall,

another orphan, was also apprenticed. John Roshore retired in the 1850s and Edward Ketcham brought a member of his family into the business which was then known as Ketcham & Brother. They began to make gold heads for canes and walking sticks, umbrella mounts, ferrules for pipes and similar articles of gold and silver.

In 1875 the brothers took Hugh McDougall into partnership and in 1876 renamed the company Ketcham & McDougall. About this time they built a new and larger factory in Brooklyn. In 1886, Walter McDougall, Hugh's son, started work for the company. In 1894 Hugh McDougall patented a "Device for Securing Eyeglasses," developed by various members of the firm. The device consisted of a fine chain which could be reeled into a decorative case fastened to a coat lapel or lady's dress. The glasses hung on the owner's chest when not in use. This popular device was much copied, but, according to McFayden, it was never equalled.

Even before Edward Ketcham's death in 1894 and that of Hugh McDougall in 1901, Walter McDougall had assumed the major responsibility for the business. In this, he was joined by his brother, Charles McDougall. They developed other automatic holders and continued to make fine jewelry along with these specialty lines. During WWI Ketcham & McDougall made parts of Sperry gyroscopes, parts for early radios and other mechanical devices. The business was incorporated in the 1920s. During the depression of the 1930s sales decreased and they are no longer jewelers but are precision manufacturers of stationary, optical and marine accessories. Their factory is located in Roseland, New Jersey.

CHRONOLOGY
  Successors to;

Prime & Roshore	
Huntington, Long Island	1832
Roshore & Prime	1834
Prime, Roshore & Co.	1848
Roshore & Wood	1850
Roshore & Ketcham	1853
Ketcham & Brother	1854
Ketcham Bro. & Co.	1857
Ketcham & McDougall	1875

KEYSTONE SILVER CO.
Philadelphia, Pennsylvania

Manufacturing silversmiths since 1914. Makers of reproductions in silver and gold; original designing; ecclesiastical goods and restorations.

(On sterling silver)   (On plated silver)

L. KIMBALL & SON
Haverhill, Massachusetts

The business was established by Leverett Kimball in 1840. In 1850 and 1851 Mr. Kimball advertised "burning fluid, lamps, etc." In 1879 his ads were for Christmas gifts. In 1891 his ad in the City Directory states "makers of Hannah Duston (also spelled Dustin) and the Bradford Academy souvenir spoons."

Registered U.S. Patent No. 19,222, March 24, 1891. The firm name is listed until 1927, with F.C. Davis and J.D. Folsom, proprietors and called silversmiths, jewelers and opticians.

KIMBALL & RESTAURICK
Boston, Massachusetts

Listed in sterling silver section of 1904 JC as out of business.

K. & R.

STEPHEN C. KIMBLE
Baltimore, Maryland

Silversmith, listed in 1850 census. Born Maryland.

S. KIND & SON
Philadelphia, Pennsylvania

Silversmiths and jewelers. Advertised free catalog in December 1903 *Ladies' Home Journal*.

Listed directories 1874-1892; JC 1915; K 1922. Their catalogs of 1902 and 1903 indicate that they were "jewelers and silversmiths." The 1902 catalog says they have been selling diamonds since 1872. They designed their own mountings and said they had ample facilities for making jewelry to order. Their "silversmithing" may have been limited to the making of sterling silver brooches and chatelaines, sterling silver charms and lockets, crosses and bracelets.

KING SILVER CO.
Boston, Massachusetts
See Lunt Silversmiths

Founded in 1955. They purchased the Richard Dimes & Co. c. 1956, and in turn were acquired by Lunt Silversmiths about 1957.

KING'S ENAMEL & SILVERWARE, INC.
New York, New York

Listed KJI 1931 as manufacturers of handmade enamel and sterling, bronze, sterling and gold boudoir sets, frames, cigarette boxes, baby sets, etc.

See page 233 for additional information.

H.A. KIRBY
Providence, Rhode Island

Retailer of silverware and jewelry. Established in 1886 as Kirby, Mowry & Co. Incorporated in September 1896. Advertised solid gold and diamond jewelry, earrings, scarf pins, brooches, studs, collar buttons and rings. In 1905 the listing was H.A. Kirby Co. and this listing was continued until the death of Henry A. Kirby in 1920.

KIRK STIEFF CORPORATION
Baltimore, Maryland

ORGANIZATIONAL TITLES

Kirk & Smith	1815-1820
Samuel Kirk	1821-1846
Samuel Kirk & Son	1846-1861
Samuel Kirk & Sons	1861-1868
Samuel Kirk & Son	1868-1896
Samuel Kirk & Son Co.	1896-1924
Samuel Kirk & Son, Inc.	1924-1979
Kirk Stieff Corporation	1979-

Pewter made by Kirk Stieff. (Photo courtesy of Kirk Stieff)

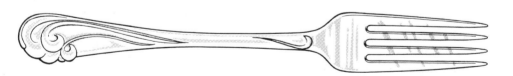

"Dancing Surf" sterling made by Kirk Stieff. (Photo courtesy of Kirk Stieff)

MARKS:
1815-1818	K & S
1818-1821	Kirk & Smith
1821-1846	S. Kirk or Saml Kirk
1846-1861	S. Kirk & Son
1861-1868	S. Kirk & Sons
1868-1896	S. Kirk & Son
1896-1925	S. Kirk & Son Co.
1925-1932	S. Kirk & Son Co. Inc. Sterling
1932-	S. Kirk & Son Sterling

The above were used in conjunction with Baltimore Assay Office marks 1815-1830; with 11/12 or 10.15 1830-1868 (sometimes later); and with 925/1000 c. 1868-1890. Two other curious private marks, one a lion and the other perhaps the figure 11) with embellishment, were used 1829-1830.

In August 1815, 22-year-old Samuel Kirk opened his small shop in Baltimore and founded the oldest surviving silversmithing firm in the United States.

He was born in Doylestown, Pennsylvania in 1793. Through both parents he was descended from English silversmiths of the 17th century: Joan Kirke, registered in Goldsmiths' Hall, England 1696-1697 and Sir Francis Child, Lord Mayor of London in 1669 and founder of the Child Banking House.

At 17, Samuel was apprenticed to James Howell, silversmith of Philadelphia and on completing his apprenticeship moved to Baltimore.

In 1815, Samuel Kirk and John Smith entered into a partnership which continued until 1820. In 1846, Samuel Kirk's son, Henry Child Kirk, became a partner and the firm name was changed to Samuel Kirk & Son. In 1861, Charles D. and Clarence E. Kirk also entered the business and the name was changed to Samuel Kirk & Sons. After the Civil War, the two younger brothers left the firm and the name reverted to Samuel Kirk & Son.

After the death of Samuel Kirk in 1872, his son continued alone until 1890, when his only son, Henry Child Kirk, Jr., joined as a partner retaining the firm name, Samuel Kirk & Son. In 1896, Henry Child Kirk, Sr. formed a corporation and remained as active head until his death in 1914 when his son succeeded as president. Each of these early representatives of the Kirk family served an apprenticeship in the craft and qualified as working silversmiths.

It was Samuel Kirk who introduced the intricate and often imitated Repoussé style of ornamentation to America in 1828. It is often referred to as "Baltimore silver."

Kirk's tradition for fine craftsmanship has brought many famous people to its shop. It is not surprising that when the White House dinner service was in need of repair, Kirk's was selected to renovate the five hundred and fifty pieces of gold flatware that had been in use for state banquets since the administration of President Monroe.

Many famous trophies and presentation pieces have been designed by Kirk's. The most ambitious was the forty-eight piece dinner service commissioned for the old Cruiser **Maryland** in 1905 and now on exhibit at the State House at Annapolis. Nearly two hundred scenes and pictures present a panorama of Maryland's illustrious history.

Kirk silver has always reflected the trends of decorative design. Early pieces were made in the chaste and simple lines of the Georgian era. The China trade is reflected in delicate Oriental lines, and the elaborate ornamentation of the Victorian age produced some magnificent pieces. Contemporary simplicity produces pieces remarkably like those of the very first made by Samuel Kirk.

New techniques, progressive research and new designs have been added to Kirk silver, but, their firm produces prestige merchandise. They pride themselves that hand crafting techniques are still essential in the production of Kirk sterling.

In 1972 the Kirk company added a line of silverplated gift wares.

During recent years the Kirk company has added new lines. Among them are sculptures cast by the lost wax process; new lines in jewelry, some available in 14k gold as well as sterling silver; and numerous functional and decorative articles of pewter.

In September 1979 the Kirk Corp. and the Stieff Company (q.v.) jointly announced their merger. The combined enterprises of the two Baltimore, Maryland makers of silver and pewter, flatware and holloware operate under the name, The Kirk Stieff Company.

YEAR	BALTIMORE ASSAY MARK	DOMINICAL LETTERS
1814		B
	ASSAYER'S AND MAKER'S MARKS	
1815		A
1816		GF

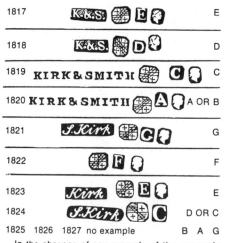

Year	Marks	Dominical Letter
1817	K&S ▦ E ▣	E
1818	K&S ▦ D ▣	D
1819	KIRK & SMITH ▦ C ▣	C
1820	KIRK & SMITH ▦ A ▣	A OR B
1821	S.Kirk ▦ C ▣	G
1822	▦ F ▣	F
1823	Kirk ▦ E ▣	E
1824	S.Kirk ▦ C	D OR C
1825 1826 1827 no example		B A G

In the absence of any example of the assayer's marks for the years 1825 to 1827 and because of the great number of examples in existence bearing the 1824 marks, it is generally conceded that the 1824 marks were continued through the years 1825, 1826, and 1827.

YEAR	ASSAYER'S AND MAKER'S MARKS	DOMINICAL LETTERS
1828	20 11 M'S F SAML KIRK	F OR E
1829	S.KIRK D ▦ ▣ ▣	D
1830	▦ ▦ S.KIRK ▣ KIRK	C

ASSAY MARKS AND DOMINICAL LETTERS WERE NOT USED AFTER 1830

Year	Marks
1830 to 1846	SAML KIRK S.K ▣ S.K 11OZ S.K 11OZ 1015 S.KIRK ▣ S.KIRK SAML KIRK 10.15
1846 to 1861	S.KIRK & SON 11OZ SK & SON S.KIRK & SON 1015 ZO·11
1861 to 1868	S.KIRK & SONS 1015 S.KIRK & SONS 11OZ
1868 to 1898	S KIRK & SON 925/1000
1880 to 1890	S.KIRK & SON S.Kirk & Son 11OZ

YEAR	KIRK'S MAKER'S MARKS
1896 to 1903 flatware	S.KIRK & SONCO 925/1000 S.KIRK & SON CO 925/1000
1903 to 1924 holloware	S.KIRK & SonCo. 925 S.KIRK & SonCo. 925/1000
1907 to 1914 flatware	S.KIRK & SON CO 925/1000 S.KIRK & SON CO 925/1000
1903 to 1907 holloware	KIRKCo 925/1000 S KIRK & SonCo 925/1000 S KIRK & SonCo 925/1000 S.KIRK & Son Co
1925 to 1932 holloware	S.KIRK & SON INC. STERLING
1927 to 1961 flatware	PAT. S.KIRK & SON STERLING
1932 to 1961 flatware	S.KIRK & SON STERLING
1932 to 1961 holloware	S.KIRK & SON STERLING S.KIRK & SON STERLING
1959 to 1961 flatware	S.KIRK & SON STERLING ©

KIRK INTERNATIONAL
New York, New York

A division of The Kirk Corporation, the parent company of Samuel Kirk & Son, the sterling division, and Kirk Pewter (formerly Hanle & Debler) the domestic pewter division. Kirk International was successor to Eisenberg-Lozano in 1970 though the name was not changed until February 1973.

KIRK & MATZ
Danbury, Connecticut

Advertise "cutlery, silverplate, brassware, Sheffield cutlery, etc." Various articles of silverplate illustrated in advertisements.

KIRK PEWTER, INC.
See Hanle & Debler, Inc.

In February 1972 a pilot pewter plant opened in Salisbury, Maryland to work in conjunction with the New York plant until the Salisbury plant could assume the entire work load. In May 1973 this goal was accomplished. Pewter holloware is now all made there. A training course in polishing, soldering and spinning has been underway in Salisbury since February and has proven successful.

JULIUS KIRSCHNER & CO.
New York, New York

Listed JC 1915-1943. Wholesalers of plated silverware and mesh bags.

JULCKO
(Mesh Bags.)

C. KLANK & SONS
Baltimore, Maryland
See Schofield & Co., Inc.

ORGANIZATIONAL TITLES

Klank & Bro.	1872-1891
Conrad Klank & Sons	1892
C. Klank & Sons Mfg. Co.	1893-1894
C. Klank & Sons	1895-1911

First listed in the Baltimore City Directory in 1872-1873 as Klank & Bro., silverplaters. From 1874-1892 they were listed as silversmiths. Conrad, Frederick W. and George H. Klank were listed as members of the firm.

In 1892 the firm name became Conrad Klank & Sons, silversmiths, with Conrad, Frederick and George H. Jr., listed as members of the firm. The 1893 listing was C. Klank & Sons Mfg. Co., with Conrad listed as manager.

In 1895 the listing was C. Klank & Sons, the members of the firm remaining the same until 1899 when the members were listed as Conrad, F. William, and Herbert Klank and James L. McPhail. This listing continued until 1905 when James L. McPhail, who had also been listed as a member of the firm of A.G. Schultz & Co. during the same period, was no longer listed at either. In 1905 or 1906 C. Klank & Sons was purchased by Heer-Schofield, later Schofield & Co. though it continued to be listed under its own name through 1911.

KLANK MFG. CO.
Baltimore, Maryland
See Sterling Silver Mfg. Co.

Listed 1892 Baltimore City Directory as silversmiths and silverplaters. George H. Klank, manager.

"The Klank Mfg. Co. made an assignment for the benefit of creditors to Charles O. Stieff." (JC&HR 11-2-1892, p. 8). "The Klank Mfg. Co. was succeeded by The Sterling Silver Mfg. Co. Baltimore, Maryland (JC&HR 2-14-1894, p. 27)

WILLIAM KLANK
Baltimore, Maryland

Listed in Baltimore City Directories 1895-1899 as a silversmith. Not at the same address as C. Klank & Sons.

KNICKERBOCKER SILVER CO.
Port Jervis, New York

Successor to J(ames) A. Babcock in 1894 under William Tuscano as Knickerbocker

Mfg. Co.; became Knickerbocker Silver Co. before 1904. Taken over by Crescent Silverware Mfg. Co., Inc. in 1962.

Not used after c. 1900

JACOB KNIPE
Baltimore, Maryland

Listed in Baltimore City Directories 1864-1880 as a silverplater.

WM. KNOLL & CO.
New York, New York

Listed JC 1904 in sterling silver section. Out of business before 1915.

J.B. & S.M. KNOWLES CO.
Providence, Rhode Island

In 1852 Joseph B. Knowles formed a partnership with Henry L. Webster (who had been associated with Jabez Gorham, under the firm name of Webster & Knowles) of Boston. The first shop was located near another firm, Farrington & Salisbury which they soon bought out. The business grew steadily and in 1859 Samuel J. Ladd was admitted to the firm. Webster withdrew from the firm in 1864 and died the following year. The firm name was changed to Knowles & Ladd. In 1875 Mr. Ladd retired and Joseph's brother, Stephen M. Knowles, was admitted, the firm name becoming J.B. & S.M. Knowles. In 1891 J.B. Knowles died and that same year the firm was incorporated. In 1905 the Mauser Mfg. Co. leased the plant of J.B. & S.M. Knowles Co. Notices carried in 1905 trade journals stated that "all the articles hitherto made at the Knowles plant will now be produced by the Mauser Mfg. Co."

RED CROSS
(U. S. Design Patent No. 38-096, April 15, 1902 for spoons)

(On coin silver spoons)

KOECHLIN & ENGLEHARDT
Newark, New Jersey

Earliest record found U.S. Patent 56,499, registered October 2, 1906 for use on sterling and plated silver flat and holloware. Out of business before 1915.

GUSTAVE F. KOLB
New York, New York

Manufacturers, manufacturer's representative and importers of sterling silverware at least as early as 1917.

Gustave Frederick Kolb was born in New York City. At the time the Mt. Vernon, New York, Mauser factory was erected Kolb was general superintendent and treasurer of the company. Later he left to establish his own silversmith business in New York City. He retired in 1921 but continued as a director of the George Borgfeldt Corp. of New York City until his death, August 29, 1945 when he was 80 years old.

Kolb was known not only as a manufacturer and industrialist but was prominent in civic and religious activities. While with the Mauser company he was instrumental in persuading the New York New Haven and Hartford Railroad to build the Columbus Avenue station to accommodate commuters to New York City.

KOONZ MFG. CO.
Greenfield, Massachusetts

Listed JC as manufacturers of sterling silver. Out of business before 1922.

CHARLES KRAEMER
Baltimore, Maryland

Listed in Baltimore City Directory 1882 as a silversmith.

CHARLES M. KRAMER
Baltimore, Maryland

Listed in Baltimore City Directory in 1885 as a silverplater.

KRAUS & JANTZEN
New York, New York
See Kraus, McKeever & Adams

KRAUS, KRAGEL & CO.
New York, New York
See Kraus, McKeever & Adams

KRAUS, McKEEVER & ADAMS
New York, New York

First listed in 1896 as Kraus, Kragel & Co.; in 1904 as Kraus & Jantzen and in 1922 as Kraus, McKeever & Adams. Trademarks used on sterling silver frames for handbags; 14k gold mountings and sterling silver mountings for leather articles.

KRIDER & BIDDLE
Philadelphia, Pennsylvania
See Peter L. Krider Co.

PETER L. KRIDER CO.
Philadelphia, Pennsylvania

CHRONOLOGY

Peter L. Krider	c. 1850-60
Krider & Biddle	1860-c. 1870
Peter L. Krider	c. 1870-1903
Simons Bros. Co.	1903-present

Peter L. Krider (b. Philadelphia, 1821; d. there May 12, 1895) at the age of 14 was apprenticed to John Curry, Philadelphia silversmith, whom he served for six years. On Curry's retirement, young Krider's indenture was transferred to R. & W. Wilson, also silversmiths of Philadelphia. Krider worked with them as a journeyman for 15 months and then made a four-year contract with Obadiah Rich, silversmith in Boston. Two years later Rich sold his establishment to Brackett, Crosby & Brown, Boston silversmiths, with Krider in charge of the business. He later served a short time

as foreman in the factory of his old employers, R. & W. Wilson and then went into business for himself. His first order, which was for a tea set, was given by J.E. Caldwell & Co. Krider's business expanded rapidly until he was compelled to find larger quarters and in 1859 took into partnership John W. Biddle, the firm name becoming Krider & Biddle in 1860. During the Civil War Krider served in the army while Biddle maintained the business. Biddle retired five or six years after the War and the firm name became Peter L. Krider Co. About 1888 Krider sold the business to August Weber who later took a partner, W.E. Wood. The business continued to operate under the name Peter L. Krider Co. until 1903 when it was succeeded by Simons Bros. Co., Philadelphia silversmiths established in 1840. The Krider flatware patterns and dies were later sold to the Alvin Mfg. Co. A number of flatware patterns were patented by Krider.

In addition to making a regular line of silverware, flatware as well as holloware, the Krider company was at one time perhaps the largest medal plant in the country. They manufactured medals for the Centennial Commission of 1876; those for the Cincinnati Industrial Exposition; Ohio Mechanics' Institute; National Academy of Design, New York; Georgia State Agricultural Society; Maryland State Agricultural and Mechanical Association; Virginia State Agricultural Society; Massachusetts Humane Society; Pennsylvania State Fair Association; Southern California Horticultural Society; the Agricultural and Industrial Society of Delaware Co., Pa.; Cincinnati High Schools; Industrial Cotton Exposition; the Southern Exposition; the World's Industrial and Cotton Centennial Exposition; Franklin Institute, Philadelphia; the John Scott Legacy, Philadelphia and many others.

KRONHEIMER OLDENBUSCH CO.
New York, New York
Listed in JC 1909-1922 in plated silver section.

LEONARD KROWER & SON, INC.
New Orleans, Louisiana

Established before 1896 as Leonard Krower, wholesalers and jobbers of sterling silver, plated silver, platinum, optical goods, medals, watches, clocks, pearls, diamonds, cut glass and gold jewelry. Listed in JC-K 1943 as Leonard Krower & Son and were incorporated before 1950. Acquired by the Gordon Jewelry Corporation in 1965.

KUEHLER & JANSON
New Orleans, Louisiana
Silversmiths listed in New Orleans City Directory in 1871.

THE FRANK KURSCH & SON CO.
Newark, New Jersey
Listed in JC 1904 in sterling silver section. Out of business before 1915.

Trademark identical to Shoemaker, Pickering & Co.

☆ S   Sterling

L

L'ALLEMAND MFG. CO.
New York, New York

"Ernest A. L'Allemand, doing business as L'Allemand Mfg. Co., manufacturers of electro silver plated ware, N.Y. made an assignment to Oscar L'Allemand. Mr. L'Allemand had bought out his partner, Mr. Stix, two years ago and had not enough capital.

The business was established many years ago and had been carried on by various firms. E.H. Rowley & Co. had it from 1862-1889 when they were succeeded by Stix & L'Allemand, who dissolved on August 31, 1893, since which time Mr. L'Allemand, carried on alone." (JC&HR 7-1-1895, p. 10)

P.W. LAMBERT & COMPANY
New York, New York

"P.W. Lambert & Company, N.Y., mfgrs. of standard goods and introducers of novelties such as pocket books, chatelaine bags, ladies' belts—a complete line of silver novelties. In oxidized and EGYPTIAN GOLD. Established 1867." (Adv. JC&HR 11-18-1896, p. 28)

FERDINAND C. LAMY
Saranac Lake, New York

Registered trademark in U.S. Patent Office No. 21,899, October 25, 1892 for use on spoons, forks, knife handles, etc. of souvenir type. Listed in JC as out of business before 1922.

LANCASTER SILVER PLATE CO.
Lancaster, Pennsylvania

"The Lancaster Silver Plate Company was destroyed by fire September 1893." (JC&HR 2-6-1895, p. 26)

LANDERS, FRARY & CLARK
New Britain, Connecticut

Landers, Frary & Clark began as a partnership in 1842 with George M. Landers and Josiah Dewey; became Landers & Smith Mfg. Co. in 1853 and Landers, Frary & Clark in 1865. They purchased the Meriden Cutlery Co. in 1866 and continued to use the Meriden trademark on some sterling wares. Their newly-built Aetna works held this cutlery division. The factory burned in 1874 and was immediately rebuilt.

The firm's first products were wardrobe hooks. This was later expanded to include other small castings such as drawer pulls, iron coffeepot stands, and sad iron holders. They began the manufacture of cutlery in 1865. They discontinued flatware production c. 1950.

In 1954 they purchased the Dazy Corp. In 1961 control of the firm was taken over by J.B. Williams Co., a subsidiary of Pharmaceuticals, Inc., and now Landers, Frary & Clark are completely liquidated.

LANDERS FRARY & CLARK
ÆTNA WORKS

(Knife blades with solid silver ferrules; Ivoride handles)

AETNA WORKS	
LANDERS, FRARY &	UNIVERSAL
CLARK	(Used after 1897)

R. LANGE
Baltimore, Maryland

Listed in Baltimore City Directory 1864 as a silverplater.

RALPH LANGE
Baltimore, Maryland

Listed in Baltimore City Directories 1872-1889 as a silverplater.

RUDOLPH LANGE
Baltimore, Maryland

Listed in Baltimore City Directories 1884-1885 as a silverplater at the same address as R. Lange who was listed in 1864.

ALPHONSE LA PAGLIA
Meriden, Connecticut

Designer and silversmith associated with the International Silver Company. In 1952 he left New Jersey and settled in Meriden, Connecticut to make handcrafted sterling silver jewelry and holloware. His designs were greatly influenced by Danish designs. He was an experienced silversmith as well as designer. Under the sponsorship of International Silver Company, a small craft shop was equipped in the rear of his home in Meriden. A few silver craftsmen were associated with him in "International Sterling Craft Associates." Practically all the work was done by hand. La Paglia died suddenly and tragically on November 19, 1953 from a bloodclot resulting from a fall at his home.

The business was purchased from his widow by International and manufacturing continued in the same shop for a short while. Eventually, the line was simplified and manufacturing moved to International's regular sterling plant. La Paglia's jewelry line included bracelets, rings, stick pins, earrings, necklaces and brooches, all handcrafted in sterling silver. Much of his output was purchased by Georg Jensen and by a few stores such as J.E. Caldwell, Philadelphia and J.B. Hudson, Minneapolis. The pieces marketed by Georg Jensen are usually marked "Georg Jensen, New York: with La Paglia's initials "L P" or "A. L. P."

Sterling coffee service designed by Alphonse LaPaglia; sponsored by International Silver Company. (Photo courtesy of International Silver Company)

LA PIERRE MFG. CO.
Newark and New York
See International Silver Co.

The La Pierre company started as early as 1888 in New York where Frank H. La Pierre had a small shop at 18 East 14th St. making a variety of novelties and small wares. In 1895 it was incorporated in New Jersey where they had by that time included quite a variety of dresserware. At this time La Pierre was president and G.H. Henckel, secretary. In 1900 the firm was again incorporated by La Pierre and H.C. Brown. In 1929 the La Pierre business was purchased by the International Silver Company and moved to Wallingford, Connecticut where they enlarged the line to cover more designs and pieces in dresserware.

The La Pierre trademark on sterling silver was made up by the letters F and L to represent the conventional pound sterling mark.

(Used before 1896)

LA SECLA, FRIED & CO.
Newark, New Jersey
Listed in JC 1909-1915 in sterling silver section. Out of business before 1922.

WILIAM LAWLER
San Francisco, California

Silversmith and goldsmith who worked in San Francisco c. 1853-1882. He was originally from Missouri and first appeared in San Francisco City Directory in February 1854. His son, Frederick L. Lawler worked with him in the late 1860s to mid 1870s. (Morse papers)

T.B. LEAVENWORTH
Detroit, Michigan

"Silverware manufacturer 1869." (JCW 2-5-1919).

LEBKUECHER & CO.
Newark, New Jersey
See Eleder-Hickok Co., Inc.
See Hickok Matthews Company
-Silversmiths

Silversmiths working c. 1896-1909. Partners were Arthur E. Lebkeucher, Francis (Frank) A. Lebkeucher and Charles C. Wientge, former superintendent and designer for Howard Sterling Company. Name changed by law to F.A. Lester. Taken over by The Eleder Co. in 1918. By 1922 it became the Eleder-Hickok Co., Inc.

TRADEMARK

LEBOLT & CO.
Chicago, Illinois

Registered trademark in U.S. Patent Office No. 70,833-y, October 6, 1908 for manufacture of silverware and jewelry. Listed JC 1915-1922.

LEDIG MFG. CO.
Philadelphia, Pennsylvania

Listed in JC 1896 in plated silver section. Out of business before 1904.

(Solid Plated and Composition Ware.)

LEHMAN BROTHERS SILVERWARE CORP.
New York, New York

Listed 1927 KJI; 1943-73 JCK and 1957-61 JBG as manufacturers of silverplated holloware. No reply to recent inquiry.

LEHMAN SILVER-CRAFT

HENRY L. LEIBE MFG. CO.
Newark, New Jersey
See Archibald, Klement
See C.F. Kees Co.

STERLING

KARL F. LEINONEN
Boston, Massachusetts

Karl F. Leinonen, born in Turku, Finland in 1866. Served the regular seven year apprenticeship there. He came to the United States in 1893 and worked in a commecial repair shop in Boston. In 1901, when Arthur A. Carey, president of the Boston Society of Arts & Crafts, financed the opening of the Handicraft Shop, where a large number of silversmiths had bench space, he placed Leinonen in charge. He was still in this position in 1932. His son, Edwin, became his assistant.

Now listed in the Boston Directory as Karl F. Leinonen & Sons.

THE LENAU CO.
Attleboro Falls, Massachusetts

Listed in JC in sterling silver section in 1896. Out of business before 1904.

L STERLING.

LENOX SILVER INC.
New York, New York

Listed directories c. 1950 as manufacturers of sterling silver.

LENOX

LEONARD MFG. CO.
Chicago, Illinois (?)

Manufactured plated silver spoons to commemorate the World's Columbian Exposition in Chicago, 1892.

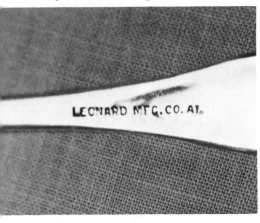

LEONARD, REED & BARTON
Tauton, Massachusetts
See Reed & Barton

LEONARD, REED & BARTON
(On britannia)

LEONARD SILVER MANU-FACTURING COMPANY
Boston, Massachusetts
See Towle Silversmiths

Founded in 1969 by Leonard Florence in Chelsea, Massachusetts, to market silver-plated holloware. Mr. Florence became involved in the silver industry about 1957 through helping to revive the Raimond Silver Company (q.v.) which, in the late 1950s was operating at a loss. Twelve years later the company was sold for $2.1 million with Mr. Florence receiving half the proceeds with which he started his own company.

In 1978 the Leonard Silver Manufacturing Company was acquired by Towle Silversmiths and company headquarters were moved to Boston shortly after the merger.

"The Leonard Silver first operated out of a garage in Chelsea, the rundown Boston suburb that is Mr. Florence's birthplace. The entire staff wrote orders, polished silver and carried boxes to be shipped. When the company built an office building across the street, everyone helped pour concrete." (*The Wall Street Journal*, June 28, 1982, pp. 1 & 13.)

"The Leonard Silver Mfg. Co., manufacturer and distributor, purchased certain assets of Delli Silverplate, San Francisco." (JC-K 3.74, p. 105)

"Leonard Silver Mfg. Co. has entered into a five-year agreement with English Silver Corp., Brooklyn, to market that company's line of silverplated holloware." (JC-K 3-74)

Some of Leonard's products are manufactured by seven different firms in India.

JOSEPH LESHER
Victor, Colorado

Joseph Lesher, a Victor real estate and mining man picked the world's greatest gold mining district as the place to distribute his eight-sided silver dollars which he manufactured in a campaign for the free coinage of silver.

One of the rarest items sought by American numismatists, the silver pieces have achieved real value. But in 1900 and 1901, when Lesher was having the coins minted in Denver, they had a value of $1.25 and were issued to merchants to be handed out and redeemed in merchandise. From the high silver content of the coins, Lesher could not have made any money on the arrangement.

No more than 3,500 of the coins were minted. There was a total of 18 varieties, each differing in some minor detail.

The first dies were made by Frank Hurd of Denver. Later dies were made by Herman Otto. The first type, issued in 1900, was 35mm. across and was stamped one ounce silver, value $1.25. One side had the words, **Jos. Lesher, Referendum Souvenir;** the other side, **A Commodity, Will Give in Exchange for Currency Coin or Merchandise at Face Value.** In order to avoid trouble with the U.S. Government Lesher made his dollars eight-sided, but that did not help. Only a few days after the first coin was issued, government agents called on Lesher to see the dies. Lesher handed them over and then, he reported to the newspapers later, "they pulled out a sack in which they put the dies and walked away, and I never saw them again." The govenment agents claimed that the silver pieces had the function of coins and were contrary to law. Lesher appealed to Senator Teller for help. Teller took it up with the secretary of the treasury and it was finally agreed that with certain changes in the design of the coin, the minting could continue.

The second set was issued for exchange of merchandise at A.B. Bumstead. Others were issued for various firms bearing the legend, Trade Mark Reg. U.S. Patent Office No. 36,192, April 9, 1901 Design Patent April 16, 1901. They also bear the altered inscription "Jos. Lesher's Referendum Silver Souvenir Medal."

REFERENDUM

LESSER & RHEINAUER
New York, New York

"Lesser & Rheinauer, silversmiths now at 427 E. 14th St., N.Y., will move their factory and office about May 1 into the Sterling Building, 14 East 17th St. where they will occupy the entire second loft. A Lesser's Sons, wholesale jewelers of Syracuse, are members of the firm." (JC&HR 4-14-1897, p. 24)

"A. Lesser's Son's business closed by the Sheriff." (JC&HR 3-9-1898, p. 19)

F.A. LESTER COMPANY
See Eleder-Hickok Co., Inc.
See Hickok Matthews Company
-Silversmiths
See Lebkuecher & Co.

S.J. LEVI & CO., LTD.
Birmingham, England

Registered trademarks in the United States. Listed 1927 KJI as manufacturers of silverplated tableware and cigarette cases.

LEVIATHAN
PERFECTA
SQUIRREL BRAND

LEVINE SILVERSMITH CO.
New York, New York

Listed 1927 and 1931 KJI as manufacturers of sterling holloware, carving sets and cutlery.

LESCO

LEVITT & GOLD
New York, New York

Listed in JC 1915-1922 in sterling silver section. The trademark was also used on platinum and gold novelties. Listed c. 1935 as Levitt & Co. (?)

CHAS. J. LEWARD
New York, New York

Listed JC in 1896 in sterling silver section. Out of business before 1904.

TRADE MARK.

LEWIS BROS.
New York, New York

Listed in 1896-1904 JC as manufacturers of sterling silver novelties and jewelry. Address was the same as S.M. Lewis & Co. Out of business before 1915.

S.M. LEWIS & CO.
New York, New York

Listed 1896 JC in sterling silver section. Out of business before 1904. Address was the same as Lewis Bros.

S. M. L. & CO.
STERLING

J.A. L'HOMMEDIEU
Mobile, Alabama

Silversmith and jeweler c. 1839-67. Advertised "SILVER WARE, MADE FROM COIN," in the Mobile Directory in 1859. The brothers, William and John, moved to Mobile from Connecticut about 1840. William apparently left the firm about 1850 while John continued until after the close of the Civil War when he returned North and Zadek & Caldwell took over the business. In 1898 Wm. L'Hommedieu was a traveler for G.I. Mix Co.

L'HOMMEDIEU

J. A. HOMMEDIEU

LIEBS SILVER CO., INC.
New York, New York

Listed in JC 1915 as Liebs Co.; became Liebs Silver Co., Inc. before 1922. The last record found was 1931. Manufacturers of sterling silver holloware.

J. ARTHUR LIMERICK
Baltimore, Maryland

Listed in Baltimore City Directories 1903-1904 as successor to Jacob Gminder who began plating silver in 1867.

WILLIAM LINK CO.
Newark, New Jersey

CHRONOLOGY

Wm. Link	1871-82
Link & Conkling	1882-86
Wm. Link	1886-93
Link, Angell & Weiss	1893-c. 1900
Link & Angell	c. 1900-c. 1910
Wm. Link Co.	c. 1910-c. 1915

Established August 1, 1871 by William Link. In 1875 John D. Nesler was admitted to the firm. Nesler retired in 1882 and Addison Conkling was admitted, the firm becoming Link & Conkling. In 1886 Mr. Conkling retired and the business was continued by Link alone until 1893 when it became Link, Angell & Weiss; Link & Angell about 1900 and finally Wm. Link Co. from c. 1910-c. 1915. Listed out of business in 1915. They were manufacturers of sterling and jewelry.

WILLIAM LINKER
Philadelphia, Pennsylvania

Registered trademark in U.S. Patent Office, No. 55,945, August 21, 1906 for gold and silver flatware, holloware and tableware. Out of business between 1909 and 1915. Wm. Linker was a member of the firm of Davis & Galt in 1896.

THE LINCOLN MINT
Chicago, Illinois

No response to inquiries.

LIPPIATT SILVER PLATE AND ENGRAVING CO.
New York, New York

A few years after the company was established, Samuel F.B. Morse, inventor of the telegraph and founder of the American System of Electro Magnetic Telegraphy, was president. They registered a trademark November 1, 1870 for silver and plated ware. They also owned a patent, dated April 19, 1871, for a process of putting a satin finish on silverplated holloware and planned to license manufacturers to use it. It does not seem to have been much used in the early 1870s and the patent terminated in 1878. Morse died in 1872. The concern failed, indicating that they were not successful. In 1878 the patent was used by a few manufacturers according to the catalogs published at that time, and later a similar "satin" finish was given white metal holloware. Much was sold in the cheaper grades as Satin Engraved and Satin Bright Cut.

L.A. LITTLEFIELD SILVER CO.
New Bedford, Massachusetts

An advertisement in an old (c. 1885-95 and unidentified magazine) Littlefield is called a "manufacturer and silverplater of glassware fittings." The business was established in 1884 by _____ Needham and L.A. Littlefield. Needham retired in 1888. The company was incorporated in 1905 under the name L.A. Littlefield Silver Co. It was consolidated with the Rockford Silver Plate Co. in 1909 and moved to Rockford, Illinois. Littlefield was a manufacturer of trimmings for glassware and electroplate. He supplied the silverplated tops for numerous articles of tableware.

P.H. LOCKLIN & SONS
New York, New York

Manufacturers c. 1920-1930 of sterling silverware, vases, candlesticks, salt and pepper shakers, umbrella handles, canes, riding crops, muffineers, novelties, cigar and cigarette holders, and articles of other materials mounted in 14 and 18k white gold and platinum.

MILLIE B. LOGAN
Rochester, New York

U.S. Patent No. 20,375 registered for Millie B. Logan on November 17, 1891 for

gold and silver tableware. Listed in JC 1896 among manufacturers of souvenir silverware. Rochester city directory lists her as a manufacturer of ladies' fashionable hair work, hair jewelry, etc. from 1871-c. 1908.

V. LOLLO
Brooklyn, New York
Manufacturers of sterling salt and pepper shakers c. 1950.

VL

THOMAS LONG COMPANY
Boston, Massachusetts
Registered trademark for sterling silver, silverplated flatware, holloware and jewelry. Claims use since Oct. 18, 1946.

LONGCRAFT

H. LORD & CO.
Savannah, Georgia
See Black, Starr & Frost Ltd.
In business c. 1805. Partners were Hezekiah Lord, Cornelius Paulding and Isaac Marquand.

LOTT & SCHMITT, INC.
New York, New York
Listed JC 1915 in sterling silver section. Out of business before 1922.

LOW, BALL & CO.
See Shreve, Crump & Low Co. Inc.

DANIEL LOW & CO.
Salem, Massachusetts
Established in 1867 by Daniel Low as a small jewelry store. Low's reputation as a source of unusual gifts and fine gold and silver articles soon earned a reputation for the store and the confidence of his patrons.
In 1887, when souvenir spoons were being introduced in European cities, Daniel Low took a trip abroad and brought back the idea of making a Witch spoon as a souvenir of Salem and the Witchcraft tradition. His son, Seth F. Low, designed

the first Witch spoon. It was made by the Durgin Division of The Gorham Mfg. Co. Its immediate popularity and that of the second Witch spoon which followed shortly afterwards, were largely responsible for the souvenir spoon craze that swept across the country shortly before 1900.
In 1896 Seth F. Low became a partner in the business. On September 1, 1907 the business was incorporated under the name Daniel Low & Co., Inc.
Aware that most of the goods purchased in his store were for gifts, Daniel Low decided to reach out beyond the confines of his own city and in 1893 first published a small catalog to establish a mail order business. The Daniel Low Year Book became a national institution.

WITCH

JOHN J. LOW & CO.
See Shreve, Crump & Low

BENJAMIN F. LOWELL
Malibu Beach, California
Registered trademark for use on hand-wrought sterling silverware—goblets, trays and flatware. Claims use since Feb. 4, 1946.

MRS. LUCKEY
Pittsburgh, Pennsylvania
Woman silversmith who worked in Pittsburgh between 1830 and 1840.

LUDWIG, REDLICH & CO.
See Elgin Silversmith Co., Inc.
See Redlich & Co.
Registered trademark in U.S. Patent Office No. 21,423, July 5, 1892 for solid silverware and tableware.

LUNT SILVERSMITHS
Greenfield, Massachusetts
See Franklin Silver Plate Company
See Rogers, Lunt & Bowlen
Lunt Silversmiths began with the formation of the A.F. Towle & Son Mfg. Co. in 1880 in Newburyport, Massachusetts. Three years later Anthony Towle and his son left the company and built a new factory in Newburyport under the name A.F. Towle & Son Company. They operated

in Newburyport until 1890 when they moved to Greenfield, Massachusetts as a result of the contribution of local financial support. In the early 1890s the firm tried to diversify its operations and went into the manufacture of automobiles and actually manufactured one of the first "horseless carriages" under the name Hertle Horseless Carriages. Lack of proper financing caused the failure of this endeavor and on November 8, 1900 the A.F. Towle & Son Co. failed. George C. Lunt, who had been apprenticed to Anthony Towle as an engraver, obtained financial assistance and established Rogers, Lunt & Bowlen Co., in 1902. Since 1935 the company has used the trade-name LUNT SILVERSMITHS and have trademarked their products LUNT STERLING but the corporate name remains the same.

The Franklin Silver Plate Company of Greenfield, Massachusetts was taken over between 1920-22. With minor exceptions their trademarks have not been used since.

About 1957 the King Silver Company of Boston, including the trademarks and assets of the Richard Dimes Co. was added to the firm. Lunt sterling is noted for fine craftsmanship and good taste in design.

Lunt introduced a line of stainless steel flatware in 1979 and, in 1980, a line of silverplated flatware.

LUNT STERLING

W.H. LYON
Newburgh, New York

Listed in the Newburgh City Directory 1891-1920. His advertisement in the directory stated that Lyon, the Jeweler was sole manufacturer of the Washington Headquarters Souvenir Spoon, in Tea, Coffee, Orange and Sugar Spoons, also Butter Knives, etc. The trademark was the representation of the building known as "George Washington's Newburg(h) N.Y. headquarters." Registered in U.S. Patent Office, No. 18,906, January 17, 1891.

LYONS SILVER PLATE CO.
See Manhattan Silver Plate Co.

"Bel Chateau" sterling flatware by Lunt Silversmiths. (Photo courtesy of Lunt Silversmiths)

M

J.S. MACDONALD CO.
Baltimore, Maryland

J. Stuart MacDonald was listed in Baltimore City Directories under plated silver wares; succeeded by J.S. MacDonald Co. in 1911. Listing continued through 1921.

MACOMBER MFG. CO.
Providence, Rhode Island

Manufacturers of plated siverware c. 1910.

MM Co.

MACFARLANE MFG. CO.
See Bridgeport Silver Plate Co.

R.H. MACY & CO.
New York, New York

Founded by Rowland Hussey Macy of Nantucket Island who went to sea as a whaler when he was only fifteen. At Macy's store he is spoken of as **Captain Macy**—a slight exaggeration.

Nantucketers still speak of "that Macy boy who went to New York and made out all right—even though he did become an off-islander."

He engaged in several business ventures. First, in Boston, where he operated a thread and needle shop—a short-lived venture. His next store was Macy & Company, run in partnership with his brother in Marysville, California, where they were drawn by the Gold Rush.

The family moved back to Massachusetts and in Haverhill he opened the Haverhill Cheap Store.

Finally, in the fall of 1858 he opened his first New York store on 6th Avenue, just below 14th Street.

Macy had some unusual ideas in advertising and believed strongly in the value of this advertising. A distinctive characteristic of this was the introduction of a trademark—a a red rooster—used after June 1851 in the Haverhill Store. In New York he adopted a five-pointed red star in 1862 or 1863.

Silverware was first sold in the store in 1874 and was supplied by L. Straus & Sons, wholesalers. Like other large department stores, Macy's had goods marked with their private brands and trademarks.

Chatsworth

(On plated silver)

E. MAGNUS
New York, New York
See Howard Cutlery Co.

ERIK MAGNUSSEN
Providence, Rhode Island

Erik Magnussen was a designer for the Gorham Company from 1925 until October 1929.

He was born in Denmark May 14, 1884 and became a well known silversmith in his country of birth. His work was principally in what we now term the Art Deco style, an outgrowth of Cubism.

Magnussen's work had been widely exhibited in Copenhagen, Berlin, Paris and Rio de Janeiro.

So radically different were his designs that his association with Gorham's chief designer, William Christmas Codman, apparently was not a happy one.

After leaving the Gorham Company in 1929 Magnussen may have been associated with the shop of August Dingeldein, New York, as the 1931 Keystone shows his mark under that name. In 1932 he had his own workshop in Chicago and from 1932 to 1938 worked in Los Angeles. He returned to Denmark in 1939 and died there on the 24th of February 1961.

ERIK MAGNUSSEN

D.J. MAHONEY
New York, New York

Listed in JC in 1896 in sterling silver section. Out of business before 1904.

M

WM. P. MAHNE SILVER COMPANY
St. Louis, Missouri

Founded 1946 by Mahne and John R. Geddis, formerly of Maschmeyer-Richards Silver Company. (J C-K 2-76)

MAJESTIC MFG. CO.
New York, New York

"The Majestic Mfg. Co. of New York was incorporated to manufacture and sell sterling silver, gold and other metal ware. Directors are: Henry L. Fishel, Louis D. Nessler and Theodore F. Fishel, all of New York." (JC&HR 12-25-1895, p. 18) About 1900 the Majestic Mfg. Co. and Fishel, Nessler & Co. were at the same New York address.

This same trademark with the letters "J.O.-N.Y." replacing the word Majestic has been seen on a tea set. The trademark with the letters "F.N. & Co." replacing the word Majestic is attributed in the 1904 JC to Fishel, Nessler & Co.

MAJESTIC SILVER COMPANY
New Haven, Connecticut

Founded in 1910 as The Regal Silver Manufacturing Company by M.L. Baker. Present president is Milton Baker, son of the founder.

From 1910 till 1942 they manufactured silverplated flatware. In the late 1920s the production of stainless steel flatware was begun.

In the early 1930s a separate related firm, The Regal Specialty Mfg. Co., began the manufacture of silverplate and stainless steel flatware. At the end of World War II silverplated flatware was discontinued and now only stainless steel flatware is made.

In late 1945, through internal corporate changes, The Majestic Silver Co. emerged as the parent company and The Regal Specialty Co. continued as the subsidiary.

MAJESTIC SILVER CO., INC.
New York, New York

Manufacturers sterling silver holloware and pewter novelties c. 1930.

MALTBY, STEVENS & CURTISS CO.
Wallingford, Connecticut
See International Silver Co.

Successor to Maltby, Stevens & Company's spoon factory, Birmingham, Connecticut, the new company was headed by Elizur Seneca Stevens, Chapman Maltby and John Curtiss. They bought and occupied the old Hall, Elton & Co. plant and manufactured flatware for plating about 1890. In 1896 the company was purchased by the Watrous Mfg. Co., which was one of the original companies to become a part of International Silver Co. in 1898.

(On plated silver)   (On sterling silver)

MANCHESTER MFG. CO.
Providence, Rhode Island
See Baker-Manchester Mfg. Co.
See Manchester Silver Co.

Manufacturers of sterling silver fancy flatware, holloware and novelties. Baker-Manchester Mfg. Co. listed in 1922 JC as successors.

MANCHESTER SILVER CO.
Providence, Rhode Island

Founded in 1887 by William H. Manchester, descendent of an English family of silversmiths. Operations started on Stewart Street under the name W.H. Manchester & Co. They moved to Chestnut Street where Mr. Manchester was associated with a Baker family. From 1904 until 1914-1915, the company name was Manchester Mfg. Co. Manchester moved his operation to the present location on Pavilion Avenue in 1914 or 1915, while the Bakers continued for a. time on Chestnut Street under the name Baker-Manchester Co. William Manchester was no longer connected with this operation.

William Manchester had an associate by the name of MacFarland. On his retirement, Frank S. Trumbull, of an industrial family from Connecticut, took his place. When Mr. Manchester and his son retired, the business was owned solely by Frank S. Trumbull until 1947, when E.B. McAlpine and his son, George Wescott McAlpine acquired an interest. Following the death of Mr. Trumbull in 1954 the McAlpine family acquired the entire stock.

Their products are sterling silver flatware and holloware. Everything is marketed under the slogan, "If it's Manchester, it's Sterling."

In 1955 or 1956 they acquired the tools, dies and rights to the flatware patterns formerly produced by Richard Dimes Co.

W.H. MANCHESTER & CO.

Providence, Rhode Island
See Manchester Silver Co.

Manufacturers of sterling silver fancy flatware, holloware and novelties.

"Manchester Silver Co., Inc. maker of sterling silver flatware and holloware, became an early victim of chaos in the silver market. In mid-January, the firm announced it was being liquidated. Causes given: "extremely hazardous market conditions as well as important personal considerations of our president, Mrs. Phebe McAlpine Shepard." There reportedly were several prospective buyers for the company." (J C-K April 1980)

The Manchester Silver Co. was sold, late in 1985 to J.C. Boardman Co., S. Wallingford, Connecticut.

MANDALIAN & HAWKINS

North Attleboro, Massachusetts
See Mandalian Mfg. Co.

Founding date unknown. Succeeded by Mandalian Manufacturing Company before 1922.

M & H

MANDALIAN MFG. CO.

North Attleboro, Massachusetts

Successors to Mandalian & Hawkins before 1922. Last record found in 1935.

Manufacturing jewelers, makers of sterling and nickel silver mesh bags and frames.

DEBUTANTE

MANDIX COMPANY, INC.

New York, New York

Importers and wholesalers of pewterware and glassware with pewter trimming c. 1925-30.

JUST

JUST ANDERSEN

MANHATTAN SILVER PLATE CO.

Lyons, New York
See International Silver Co.
See Hiram Young & Co.

An unconfirmed source says that the company started as a corporation in 1847 but changed to a partnership in 1865, and remained so until 1885 when it was again incorporated with J.W. Young as president, O.F. Thomas as secretary.

According to the *Jewelers' Weekly* (1890) the company was founded in 1872 and incorporated in 1877. In 1889 or 1890 it was moved from Brooklyn to Lyons, New York when it was bought by Orlando F. Thomas. The *Jewelers' Weekly* (3-6-1890) says that the "Manhattan Silver Plate Co. mark is stamped on their best grades of goods of all kinds. A new line is to appear with Lyons Silver Co. as a trademark." The company manufactured electroplated silverwares and exported, mainly to South America and Australia, nearly one-third its production. This was one of the original companies to become part of The International Silver Co. in 1898. The Manhattan trademark was not used after 1904.

There was a Manhattan Plate Co. listed in the New York City Directory in 1865 which may have been this same company.

Identical to a mark used by Roswell Gleason. Perhaps erroneously attributed to Manhattan Silver Plate Co. in 1904 JC.

MANNING, BOWMAN & CO.

Meriden, Connecticut

E.B. Manning, Middletown, Connecticut was a britannia ware maker from 1850-1875.

Robert Bowman was born in Liverpool, England in 1829 and came to this country as a boy. He learned his trade in Middletown, Conn. and after working there a while entered the employ of Samuel Simpson (of later Simpson, Hall, Miller & Co.). He also worked in Baltimore, Md. with Henry Bullard in the silverplating business. At the outbreak of the Civil War he went North again to Middletown and entered into partnership with E.P. Manning and Joseph H. Parsons.

Thaddeus Manning and Manning, Bowman & Company were listed in the Connecticut Business Directory of 1866 as britannia ware manufacturers. The company was founded in 1857 and incorporated in 1887.

117

Company records do not show just when the manufacture of plated silver products began, but, they are listed in JC from 1896-1915 with trademarks for plated silver. One clue lies in the fact that they won an award at an exhibition of the American Institute of New York in 1869 for plated silverware.

Their advertisement (*Keystone* August 1906) says, "For over 40 years makers of the highest grade of wares in nickel and silverplate."

Best known for their manufacture of electrical appliances, the Manning-Bowman Company is now a Division of the McGraw-Edison Company, Boonville, Missouri.

Meriden Britannia Co. was in control c. 1872 and after 1898 the International Silver Company owned more than 50% of the stock.

(Not used after 1898)

MAPPIN & WEBB, LTD.
Sheffield, England

Silversmiths and electroplaters. By appointment to several members of the Royal family and foreign rulers.

John Newton Mappin left the family firm of cutlers Mappin Bros. which he subsequently bought, to found a new firm with George Webb, as his partner. Early in the 1880s they bought the old business of Stephen Smith & Sons (formerly Smith & Nicholson), of Covent Garden, London. In 1896 they bought Heeley Rolling Mills, a high quality foundry started in an old aluminum plant. In 1913 they began the manufacture of a cheaper line under the name Sheffield Silver Plate and Cutlery Company. Now part of British Silverware Ltd.

MAPPIN & WEBB'S
PRINCE'S PLATE

TUSCA

MARCEL NOVELTY CO.
New York, New York

Listed in JC 1896-1904 in sterling silver section. Out of business before 1915.

MARCUS & CO.
New York, New York

There was an I. Marcus, 87 Nassau, New York City in business at least from 1918-27. Manufactured 14K gold and platinum top bar pins, pendants, scarf pins, rings and cuff links.

MARCUS & CO.
New York

(Tentative)

FRED I. MARCY & CO.
Providence, Rhode Island

Frederick I. Marcy (b. Hartland, Vermont 1838; d. Providence, R.I. 1896) was employed for four years with a dealer in tinware, named D. Hoisington. In 1863 he became a traveler with James H. Sturdy, jewelry manufacturer, in Attleboro, and within a year had purchased an interest in the company. In 1867 W.A. Sturdy purchased the business and James H. Sturdy and Marcy moved to Providence where they established the business of Sturdy & Marcy to manufacture jewelry. In 1878 Charles H. Smith became a partner and the name was changed to Fred I. Marcy & Co. Smith retired in 1882 and Marcy continued the business alone. One of their specialties was the "Acme Lever" collar, cuff and sleeve buttons. This type of button was patented August 24, 1881. It was placed on the market and was an immediate success because it "saved time and vexation in dressing." Six thousand different designs were used in their ornamentation—cameos, opals, amethysts, pearls, diamonds, crystal pictures, chasing, engraving and enamel were used on the rolled plate of gold and sterling silver from which they were made. The Marcy trademark is also found on larger silver articles. The business closed shortly before Marcy's suicide in 1896.

MARION MFG. CO.
Salt Lake City, Utah

"The Marion Mfg. Co., Salt Lake City is being organized. They will make a specialty of silverware. The factory is being built like a watch factory so as to have all the light possible. The silverware will be marketed all over the western country." (JW 12-22-1886, p. 716)

MARQUAND & BROTHER
New York, New York
See Black, Starr & Frost, Ltd.

In business 1814-1831. Partners were Isaac Marquand and Frederick Marquand.

MARQUAND & COMPANY
New York, New York
See Black, Starr & Frost, Ltd.

In business 1834-1839. Partners were Frederick Marquand, Josiah P. Marquand and Erastus O. Tompkins. Famed silversmiths and jewelers.

MARQUAND, HARRIMAN & CO.
New York, New York
See Black, Starr & Frost, Ltd.

In business c. 1809-1810. Partners were Isaac Marquand, Orlando Harriman and Cornelius Paulding.

MARQUAND & PAULDING
Savannah, Georgia
See Black, Starr & Frost, Ltd.

Founded c. 1801 and in business until 1810. Partners were Issac Marquand (who had been apprenticed to his uncle, Jacob Jenning, Norwalk, Connecticut) and Cornelius Paulding.

MARQUAND, PAULDING & PENFIELD
Savannah, Georgia
See Black, Starr & Frost, Ltd.

In business c. 1810-1816. Partners were Isaac Marquand, Cornelius Paulding and Josiah Penfield.

MARSHALL-WELLS HARDWARE CO.
Duluth, Minnesota

Began as the Chapin-Wells Hardware Company in 1886. In 1893, Albert M. Marshall, a Saginaw, Michigan merchant bought out the Chapin interest and the company became the Marshall-Wells Co., hardware wholesalers. Old city directory advertisements indicate that the company first distributed only tools, hardware, cutlery and saddlery. Later their merchandise included everything that could be classified as hardware. It was the largest hardware wholesale distributor in the Northwest and Canada.

November 24, 1908 a trademark, No. 71,473 was registered in their name for silverplated knives, forks and spoons. In an advertisement from the *Zenith Magazine*, their monthly publication, it was noted that cutlery was stamped "manufactured exclusively for Marshall-Wells" and bore the Zenith trademark. Branch jobbing houses were located in Winnipeg (1900), Portland (1901), Spokane (1909), Edmonton (1910), Aberdeen, Seattle, Great Falls, Billings, Minneapolis and Vancouver, B.C. They also had warehouses in Moosejaw, Sasketchewan and Calgary, Alberta.

In May 1955, the trustrees of the A.M. Marshall estate sold the controlling interest to Ambrook Industries of New York. At that time Marshall-Wells was the largest wholesale hardware operation in the world. In 1958, Marshall-Wells and Kelly-How, Thompson, a Midwest hardware distributor merged and in August of that same year the company was sold to Coast-to-Coast stores, and in 1959 Marshall-Wells closed its main office and warehouse in Duluth and moved to New York City.

A 1963 newspaper clipping indicated that the Marshall-Wells Co. of Duluth was still in business, having purchased a St. Louis, Missouri furniture company, but no longer operated as a wholesale hardware distributor.

TH. MARTHINSEN SOLVVARE-FABRIKK
Tonsberg, Norway

Established in 1883: now operated by the third generation. Manufacturers of complete lines of sterling and silverplated holloware and flatware. Known especially to collectors in this country through their limited edition enameled and silvergilt Christmas spoons. Products distributed in the U.S. through the Norwegian Silver Corporation.

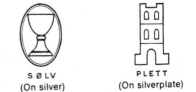

S Ø L V
(On silver)

PLETT
(On silverplate)

MARYLAND SILVER CO.
Baltimore, Maryland

Listed in Baltimore City Directories 1906-1908 as silversmiths.

MARYLAND SILVER PLATE CO.
Baltimore, Maryland

Listed in Baltimore City Directories 1889-1899 under plated silverware.

MASCHMEYER RICHARDS SILVER CO.
St. Louis, Missouri

Listed in 1915 JC and 1922 KJI as importer and wholesaler of silver, glassware, leather goods and ivory.

JOHN MASON
New York, New York

"John Mason, 246 Fifth Avenue, formerly with Tiffany & Co., having his factory and salesrooms manned almost entirely by former employees of the above firm, is enabled to furnish exactly the same quality of goods at a very much lower price. Highgrade Jewelry, Diamonds, Watches, Silverware, Fancy Goods, Cut Glassware, etc." (Adv. in *Harper's Magazine Advertiser,* November 1890)

No record of this business in New York Department of State Corporate Bureau.

MATHEWS & PRIOR
New York, New York

Founding date unknown. Listed in JC in 1904 in sterling silver section as out of business.

N. MATSON
See Spaulding & Co.

Newell Matson was a businessman, not a silversmith. He was born in Simsbury, Connecticut in 1817 and started in business at the age of 15 selling coin silver. He established a small store in Louisburg, Connecticut in 1840. In 1845 he opened a larger store in Owego, New York where he not only sold silverware, but employed several silversmiths whose main output was spoons marked with his name. He started and sold several businesses. One was in Milwaukee, Wisconsin, where he established a partnership of Matson,

Loomis & Hoes with a branch in Chicago. The Chicago store grew so rapidly that he sold the Milwaukee store only to be driven out by the fire in 1871. Soon afterwards he began business again, first in his home and later under the name N. Matson & Co., with George E. Johnson, L.J. Norton and W.E. Higby. They carried a large stock of the usual jewelers' goods—the silver being from the Gorham Mfg. Co. Later the firm name became Spaulding & Co. and then Spaulding-Gorham, Inc. from the 1920s to 1943 when the name reverted to Spaulding & Co.

MATTHEWS COMPANY
Newark, New Jersey
See Hickok Matthews Company -Silversmiths

Incorporated in 1907. Merged with Eleder-Hickok Company between 1931-1943 to become Hickok-Matthews Company. Was purchased in 1965 by Wolfgang K. Schroth and is now known as Hickok Matthews Company—Silversmiths, Montville, New Jersey.

(On sterling holloware)

THE MAUSER MANUFACTURING COMPANY
New York, New York

Frank Mauser, silversmith, began the manufacture of fine sterling silver goods in North Attleboro, Massachusetts in July 1887. In March of the following year Frank O. Coombs became a partner. He was designer and chaser for the growing concern. They made "holloware of every description, stationery and toilet novelties and a large variety of miscellaneous articles and sets." In 1890 they were contemplating a move to New York where they planned to increase the capacity of their production. A note in the JC (1-6-1897) says that the "Mauser Mfg. Co., New York, is successor to Frank Mauser & Co."

In 1903 The Mauser Mfg. Co. merged with the Hayes & McFarland Company of Mount Vernon, New York and the Roger Williams Silver Company of Providence, Rhode Island to form the Mt. Vernon Company Silversmiths, Inc. which was purchased by the Gorham Corporation in 1913.

The diamond-enclosing-an-M trademark is still listed under Mt. Vernon Company Silversmiths.

Some of their flatware patterns were purchased by the Wendell Mfg. Co., c. 1896-97.

MAUTNER MFG. CO.
New York, New York

Manufacturers of jewelry and silver-plated holloware c. 1925-35.

MOREWEAR PLATE
M. M. CO.

MAUTNER FARBER, INC.
New York, New York

Trademark found on 5-piece tea set.

SP ON COPPER

THE MAY DEPARTMENT STORES COMPANY
New York, New York
St. Louis, Missouri

Registered trademark in 1949 for use on silverplated holloware.

FRANK T. MAY CO.
New York, New York and
Rutherford, New Jersey

Manufacturers and distributors of sterling silver bags, 14k vanity and ladies' cigarette cases and novelties and jewelry.

Listed in JC-K in 1904-1943

JOSEPH MAYER & BROS.
Seattle, Washington
See E.J. Towle Mfg. Co.

"Joseph Mayer & Bros. had been in business as Empire Jewelry Company." (JC&HR 9-16-1896, p. 20)

"G.A. Schuman, of Attleboro, left last week for Seattle, where he will establish and manage what promises to be the largest jewelry plant on the Pacific Slope. The firm name will be Joseph Mayer & Bro. Mr. Schuman is a designer and toolmaker who has had experience with Gorham, Whiting and Tiffany, and goes under a year's contract. The arrangements as planned are for a big establishment, capable of turning out a great deal of work." (JC&HR 3-2-1898, p. 32)

In addition to jewelry, the Mayer firm made several patterns of flatware and numerous souvenir spoons. Succeeded by E.J. Towle Mfg. Co., c. 1945.

JOSEPH MAYER & BROS.
Seattle, Washington

Another account of the history of Mayer Bros. is as follows: "Albert and Markus Mayer, emigrants from German's Rhineland, with their older brother, Joseph, started a wholesale and manufacturing business in Seattle in 1897. Seattle, a port city, had attracted throngs of gold hunters headed north, and had become a boom town. The young firm benefitted from that boom business with a government contract assaying northern gold. The lure of the Yukon and adventure drew the two younger brothers who left Joseph to head the firm. They joined the crowded steamship north to Alaska and landed at Skagway. The Mayer brothers staked a claim on the mining town's jewelry business rather than hunting gold on a claim. Business was good. Joseph shipped merchandise north to Dawson, Albert repaired watches and Markus "manufactured" jewelry from gold nuggets. The Klondike left its mark on the company in its trademark: the crossed gold miner's pick and shovel above a rising sun. According to Markus Mayer, Jr., it is stamped on everything they make. By 1900 the company employed 100 craftsmen who manufactured sets of sterling flatware, souvenir spoons, trophies, gold wedding rings, nugget jewelry and jewelers' street clocks. The company made the elaborate silver service for the battle cruiser *Washington* during President Theodore Roosevelt's term of office. They spun brass

binnacles (for ships' compasses) for the U.S. Navy during World War I.

"In 1920 the brothers formed separate companies with Joseph devoting his efforts to manufacturing and Markus and Albert starting the Mayer Brothers Wholesale Jewelry Company. Albert died in 1925 but Markus continued to build up the business to include major watch, diamond and jewelry lines, as well as watch materials and jewelry lines. His son, Markus, Jr., succeeded him in the firm's continued growth. The firm got back into manufacturing in 1970 with the manufacture of nugget jewelry, still one of its biggest sellers. Today Mayer Brothers employs 100 people and covers the western states, including Alaska." (J C-K May 1982)

BENJAMIN MAYO
Newark, New Jersey

Silversmith, 1860-1908. Began business as Smith & Mayo in 1860, gold and silver electroplaters. Other Mayos listed at the same residence as Benjamin in the plating business were Arthur, 1869-71; William G. 1869 (moved to Rochester, N.Y., 1871); John B. 1868-71; and Samuel, 1868-71. Benjamin Mayo was listed in the 1871 Newark Directory as a silver plater and manufacturer of silver ware.

JOSEPH B. MAYO
Newark, New Jersey

"Joseph B. Mayo, an old resident of Newark and a former manufacturer of silver plated ware, but now interested in silver mining, is here (Newark) on a visit to his family." (JC&HR 9-21-1892 supplement)

Joseph B. Mayo was a silversmith, working 1868-96. He was a manufacturer of both plated and sterling wares, including cake baskets, card receivers, castors, waiters, pitchers, forks, etc. Also worked in britannia, white metal and solid silver. The compositions required were alloyed in his own factory.

MAYO & CO.
Chicago, Illinois

Listed in JC in 1896 in sterling silver section. Out of business before 1904.

JAMES EDWARD MAZURKEWICZ
Cleveland, Ohio

Silversmith. Mr. Mazurkewicz was born in Cleveland, Ohio and received his education in the Cleveland and Parma Public Schools, the Cleveland Institute of Arts and the Syracuse University School of Art. He has been awarded numerous scholarships and awards for the excellence of his work. Among these was an award from the National Sterling Silversmiths Guild of America Student Design Competition. Among his most recent exhibits was "The Goldsmith" at Renwick Gallery, Washington, D.C.

Mr. Mazurkewicz was an instructor at the Syracuse University School of Art and is presently instructor of metalsmithing, both beginning and advanced techniques at the Cleveland Institute of Art. He was recently commissioned to make a trophy presentation piece for Scandinavian Airlines.

THE McCHESNEY CO.
Newark, New Jersey
See Gorham Corporation

Samuel D. McChesney, who died Aug. 1, 1926, age 65 had been connected with the silver business more than 35 years. In January 1890 he went with Wm. B. Kerr, his brother-in-law, founder and head of Wm. B. Kerr Co., Newark, New Jersey, for a number of years. After Kerr's death, McChesney was president of the company until he resigned December 1921 and formed the McChesney Co. which manufactured gold and silver wares in a factory in Newark. He continued there until his death.

His brother, Wm. F. McChesney was treasurer and later president of Dominick & Haff (later sold to Reed & Barton).

It appears that after the death of Samuel D. McChesney, his business was taken over by Dominick & Haff. When that company was sold to Reed & Barton in 1928, what

was left of the McChesney business was also taken over by them. The McChesney Company was sold by Reed & Barton in 1931 to the Gorham Company and Wm. F. McChesney went with Gorham. The tools and dies were moved to Providence, Rhode Island.

STERLING

DAVID H. McCONNELL
New York, New York

Earliest record found was registration of U.S. Patent No. 32,828, May 9, 1899 for use on plated flatware. Out of business before 1915.

SO. AM.

H.A. McFARLAND
See Mount Vernon Silversmiths

JOHN M. McFARLANE
See Shreve, Crump & Low Co., Inc.

EDWARD B. McGLYNN
Newark, New Jersey

Listed 1931 KJI as manufacturer of gold and platinum mountings; special order work. In 1950 and 1965 JC-K as maker of sterling silver chalices.

McGLYNN

WALTER H. McKENNA & CO., INC.
Providence, Rhode Island

Established in 1915 as manufacturers of 14k and 10k gold, sterling silver and gold filled jewelry. Also make sterling baby spoons. Still in business.

JOHN O. MEAD
Philadelphia, Pennsylvania

Britannia ware manufacturer of Philadelphia, John O. Mead, laid the foundation for the important 19th century industry of electroplating silver.

Around 1830-1835 Mead was in charge of the silverplating and gilding work at the N.P. Ames Manufacturing Company of Chicopee, Massachusetts, using the old mercury and acid process.

He went to England to learn the new technique in Birmingham and continued his experiments on his return. Reputedly the first successful American electro-silver plater around 1840-1859.

In 1845 he formed a partnership in Hartford, Connecticut with William and Asa Rogers under the name of Rogers & Mead. This company was soon dissolved.

Mead returned to Philadelphia in 1846 (while William and Asa Rogers founded the firm of Rogers & Bro.) and re-established his business under the name John O. Mead, later J.O. Mead & Sons, the partners at that time being John O. Mead, J.P. Mead and Harrison Robbins. About 1850, the firm name became Filley & Mead (or Filley, Mead & Caldwell). Later still the firm name was changed to Mead & Robbins. One account says that John O. Mead died about 1867 and that the firm of Mead & Robbins was dissolved about 1870. However, there is an item (JC&HR 10-19-1892, p. 27) that says "Frederick Robbins, Philadelphia, has withdrawn from the firm of Mead & Robbins and is making preparations for the establishment of a manufacturing and wholesale silverware house. The old firm will be conducted thereafter by Edmund P. Robbins and will be devoted to the retail business." Mead & Robbins was succeeded by Sackett & Co. in 1893.

Mead & Sons had an extensive business. Their plant employed more than two hundred workmen and they turned out about fifty different designs in tea sets alone. Much of their ware was supplied "in the metal" by Reed & Barton, the plating being done in the Mead plant.

MEAD & ROBBINS
Philadelphia, Pennsylvania
See John O. Mead

Harrison Robbins had been with Harrison Robbins & Son of Philadelphia. A business notice of August 1892 refers to him as "the late Harrison Robbins."

MEALY MANUFACTURING COMPANY
Baltimore, Maryland

First listed in the Baltimore City Directory in 1900 as John W. Mealy Son & Company, jewelers. In 1906 John W. was listed as president: Edward H. as treasurer and

Charles A. as secretary. In 1908 Allan B. Crouch was listed as secretary and Charles A. as treasurer.

In 1909 Crouch is no longer listed. The company name was listed through 1956.

All these listings are under the head of silversmiths. This listing, in addition to the type of trademark, indicates hand-wrought silver was made.

HAND /$\frac{925}{1000}$\ WROUGHT

MECHANICS STERLING COMPANY
Attleboro, Massachusetts
See Watson Co.

Listed as sterling manufacturer in Jewelers' Weekly 1896. Mark is identical to Watson-Newell, now part of Wallace Silversmiths—a division of Hamilton Watch Co.

"Mechanics Sterling Co. is the flatware branch of Watson, Newell Co., North Attleboro, Mass." (JC&HR 3-24-1897, p. 17)

STERLING

Flatware.
MECHANICS STERLING CO.

MEDALLIC ART COMPANY
Danbury, Connecticut

The Medallic Art Co., official medalists for the Society of Medalists, grew out of a small lower Manhattan workshop of the French-born Henri Weil, around the turn of the century. He was joined by his brother, Felix Weil, and the two craftsmen acquired the first modern die reducing machine imported into the United States prior to 1905.

The first medals were produced in 1907 and the Medallic Art Company name first appeared in 1909.

Ten years later, in 1919, an Indiana businessman, Clyde C. Trees, joined the two Weil brothers. In 1927 he assumed the presidency and built the flourishing company into the institution it is today. In 1960 Trees died and his nephew, William Trees Louth, was named president.

Medallic Art Co. is noted especially for its introduction into the United States of the diecutting process which allows fine art medals to be reproduced from sculptor's original large size models. The work of many famous 20th century American sculptors has been reproduced by them.

In addition to finely crafted art medals, they also produce tablets, plaques, emblems and the larger medals known as medallions.

Millions of service medals and decorations have been made for the U.S. government.

The key to the production of fine art medals is the Janvier reducing machine. Named after the French engraver Victor Janvier, the device reduces a sculptor's model exactly, cutting a die automatically (rather than by hand) in a pantographic reproduction. It is a little known fact that the Medallic Art Company personnel trained the technicians at the U.S. Mint at Philadelphia after helping that institution obtain its first Janvier machine.

Medalic Art Co. has produced many medals for important occasions, among them are those for the Pulitzer Prize and the inaugural medals for the Presidents Coolidge, Hoover, F.D. Roosevelt, Eisenhower, Kennedy, Johnson and Nixon.

They purchased the medal division of the Aug. C. Frank Co., Inc. of Philadelphia, September 15, 1972. The dies, medal presses and other equipment were incorporated into the Danbury plant soon after that date.

THE MELROSE SILVER CO.
Hartford, Connecticut

Manufactured inexpensive silverplate flatware c. 1900.

⌂ ►M► δΤծ

COLONIAL PLATE CO.
MERIDEN BRITANNIA COMPANY
Meriden, Connecticut
See International Silver Company

Organized in December 1852 by Horace C. and Dennis C. Wilcox of H.C. Wilcox & Co. Other founders were Isaac C. Lewis of I.C. Lewis & Company; James A. Frary of James A. Frary & Company; Lemuel J. Curtis; William W. Lyman of Curtis & Lyman and John Munson.

Organized for quantity production, their first products were britannia hollowares. By 1855 they were also offering plated silver holloware and flatware and German silver articles. Pearl-handled wares were added about 1861.

In 1862 the Rogers brothers who had been making and selling plated silver forks, spoons and other wares were moved to Meriden. Their 1847 Rogers Bros. trademark was an important addition to the Meriden Britannia Company.

In 1896 they ceased stamping their products "Quadruple" plate.

The Meriden Britannia Company officers were among the leaders in the formation of the International Silver Company in 1898.

As early as 1867 the Meriden Britannia Company had a system of stamping nickel silver, silversoldered holloware with a cipher preceding the number and by 1893, nickel silver holloware with white metal mounts had as a part of the number two ciphers. That is, on an article with white metal, 00256, etc. was stamped. This made it quickly understood by the number whether the piece was nickel silver, silver soldered or nickel silver with white metal mounts.

In the production of silverplated flatware one of the biggest improvements was the introduction of sectional plate—depositing an extra amount of silver on spoons, forks, etc., on the parts which are given the hardest wear. A catalog issued in 1871 by MBCo shows a line, more extensive than previously shown, and gives this explanation as to what is meant by "Triple Plate." "A portion of the holloware was on nickel silver base, and a part on white metal, both marketed silverplated. They showed the two trademarks and say "goods carrying these trademarks are warranted triple plate and have at least three times the quantity of silver as on single plate."

In 1895 MBCo bought out a small silversmith's shop in New York being run by Wilcox & Evertsen, successors to Rowan & Wilcox, making a quality line of sterling silver holloware, and moved it to Meriden. This was the start of a representative silver holloware line which in 1898 was taken over by the International Silver Company. In 1897 MBCo produced its first sterling silver flatware pattern, *Revere*. MBCo. marks were used until the 1930s.

MERIDEN BRITANNIA CO., LTD.
Hamilton, Ontario

Established in 1879 for the production of 1847 Rogers Bros. silverplate, sterling silver flatware, silverplated nickel silver and white metal holloware. Merged with International Silver Co. of Canada, Ltd. about 1912.

MERIDEN CUTLERY COMPANY
South Meriden, Connecticut

This firm began in 1834, when G. and D.N. Ropes manufactured cutlery in Maine. A few years later, A.R. Moen of New York manufactured table cutlery in Wethersfield, Connecticut. The business was acquired by Julius Pratt & Co. of Meriden who continued it for about two years. In 1845, these two firms were consolidated as Pratt, Ropes, Webb & Co. Mr. Ropes erected a factory in Hanover where the business continued until 1855, when the joint stock company Meriden Cutlery Company was formed. One of their specialties was pearl handled cutlery which usually carried the date 1855.

The company was purchased by Landers, Frary & Clark in 1866 which was liquidated in the 1960s.

These two trademarks were used on carving knives with sterling silver blades c. 1900.

The Meriden mark was used by Landers, Frary & Clark on some sterling wares.

(On carving knives with sterling ferrules)

MERIDEN CUTLERY CO.

MERIDEN JLY. MFG. CO.
Meriden, Connecticut

Listed in JC 1915. Became Meriden Jewelry Co. before 1922. Manufacturers of sterling silver and plated silver cigarette cases, fancy pieces and flatware.

(On plated silver)

MERIDEN SIVER PLATE CO.
Meriden, Connecticut
See International Silver Co.

Organized in 1869 by Charles Casper and others. George R. Curtis was president. One of the original companies to become part of the International Silver Company in 1898.

"Robert G. Hill, photographer for the Meriden Silver Plate Co., is said to have discovered a new way of photographing on metal. Colors are reproduced and a likeness on the satin-finished silver background is extremely pleasing." (JC&HR 4-5-1893, p. 55)

(On Cheaper Grade.)

EUREKA SILVER PLATE CO.
MERIDEN SILVER PLATE CO.

The "half circle" trademark ws first used in 1921 but not registered until 1923.

MERIDEN STERLING CO.
Meriden, Connecticut

Listed in JC 1896 in the sterling silver section. Out of business before 1904.

MERMOD, JACCARD & KING JEWELRY CO.
St. Louis, Missouri

Established in 1829 by Louis Jaccard who was joined by A.S. Mermod in 1845. In 1848, D.C. Jaccard, relative of Louis Jaccard, joined. In 1865 Goodman King became associated with the firm. In 1901 they absorbed the E. Jaccard Jewelry Co. and Merrick, Walsh & Phelphs Jewelry. In 1905 the name of King was added to the firm name.

In 1917 they became part of Scruggs, Vandevoort & Barney but retain their identity as a separate corporate body.

MERMOD & JACCARD CO.
TRIPLE

THE MERRILL SHOPS
New York, New York

Established March 1893 as J.M. Merrill & Co. Listed 1896 as Merrill Brothers & Co., manufacturers of sterling silver and pewter. By 1922 it was The Merrill Co. and The Merrill Shops before 1931.

MERRIMAC VALLEY SILVERSMITHS

A division of Concord Silversmiths Corp., succeeded by Frank M. Whiting & Co. Dies purchased by Crown Silver Co.

MERRIMAN SILVER COMPANY
Attleboro, Massachusetts

"The Merriman Silver Co., Attleboro, are one of the new companies recently started. Their existence dates from the first week of February. If their anticipations are realized they intend to begin the manufacture of staple goods." (JC&HR 3-17-1897, p. 22)

MERRY & PELTON SILVER CO.
St. Louis, Missouri
See Pelton Bros. Silver Plate Co.

Listed JC 1904 as manufacturers of plated silver holloware and flatware. Out of business before 1909. Not listed in St. Louis City Directories which were checked back to 1840.

SECTIONAL PLATE XII
STANDARD PLATE 4
TRIPLE PLATE 12
(Flatware.)

(Holloware.)   (Holloware.)

MERWIN-WILSON CO., INC.
New Milford, Connecticut

Company established by the Merwin brothers in 1912 as successors to Bennett Merwin Silver Company. Shortly afterwards one brother was killed.

Roy (?) Wilson joined the remaining Merwin. The company made pewter reproductions and plated silver prize cups, trophies and colonial pewter reproductions until 1935 when they sold out to Robert Oliver who operated under the name of Danforth Company. The company and its molds have changed hands several times since that time and are in use now in the manufacture of pewter reproductions by Woodbury Pewterers.

MESICK MFG. CO.
Los Angeles, California

Manufacturers of sterling and silver-plated holloware c. 1950.

METALLURGIC ART CO.
Baltimore, Maryland

Listed in Jewelers' Weekly as manufacturers of sterling silverware in 1896.

First listed in the Baltimore City Directory in 1895 as Victor G. Bloede, Carl Schon, jewelry manufacturers. In 1896 the listing is Metallurgic Art Company. In 1900 Bloede and Carl Schon, Jr. are listed as members of the firm.

In 1901 the Metallurgic Art Company is no longer listed. Bloede is listed as president of Victor G. Bloede, Manufacturing Chemists. Schon is not listed at all, as he moved to Detroit.

METAL PRODUCTS CORP.
Providence, Rhode Island

Manufacturers of plated silverware c. 1920. Out of business before 1922.

METROPOLITAN SILVER CO.
(John Toothill)

New York, New York

Listed in JC in 1896-1904 in plated silver section. Out of business before 1915.

MEYER & WARNE
Philadelphia, Pennsylvania
Silverplaters c. 1859-1880?

WILLIAM B. MEYERS CO.
Newark, New Jersey

William B. Meyers, a noted maker of silver miniatures was born December 1887 at New Brunswick, New Jersey.

His first workshop was set up in 1907 in Maiden Lane, New York but he returned to New Jersey where he established the William B. Meyers Company at 50 Columbia Street. He made reproductions of antiques and ceremonial objects for Jewish temples. He began to make miniatures in 1932. His son, Joseph N. Meyers, joined the firm and also made miniatures.

Meyers was noted for the fine quality, the good design and excellent craftsmanship of his pieces, many of which are unmarked. He died in 1958.

MIAMI SILVER CO.
Cincinnati, Ohio

Listed in City Directories 1903-1912 as silverplaters.

A. MICHELSEN
Copenhagen, Denmark

Anton Michelsen, founder, was born in 1809 and apprenticed to a goldsmith in Odense. He completed his training in Copenhagen, Berlin and Paris. He established his own shop in 1841 and within a few years won approval of the royal court, being designated "Insignia Jeweler"— makers of the official state decorations and Jeweler to His Majesty the King (since 1973 Jeweler to Her Majesty the Queen). The firm has won worldwide recognition for its decorative centerpieces, ornamental goblets, table services and *objets d'art* but is perhaps best known in the U.S. for the annual Christmas spoon and matching fork. Decorative spoons have been among their noted products since 1898 when Michelsen's designed a spoon to commemorate the 80th birthday of King Christian IX. Its success and that of other commemorative spoons led them in 1910 to design and produce the first Christmas spoon, now a yearly tradition.

MIDDLETOWN PLATE CO.
Middletown, Connecticut
See International Silver Co.

One of the early silverware companies that was included in the International Silver Co. The business was first started in 1864 by Edward Payne and Henry Bullard, formerly in the employ of I.C. Lewis, of Meriden, Connecticut, one of the founders of the Meriden Britannia Co. Payne and Bullard formed a partnership doing busi-

ness in the name of the former, in the manufacture of britannia and plated wares in Middletown. In 1866 the Middletown Plate Co. was incorporated and continued in operation until it became part of the International Silver Co. in 1899.

They not only marketed their products under their own name but also sold holloware to Rogers & Bro., New York, who finished it and marketed it with *their* trademark.

The Superior Silver Co. stamp was used by the Middletown Plate Co. on their low priced merchandise. When they moved to Meriden, June 30, 1899, the International Silver Co. was using Gem Silver Plate Co. stamp on the Wilcox low priced merchandise and rather than have the two competitive stamps, they used the Superior Silver Co. stamp on both and eliminated the Gem Silver Plate Co. stamp.

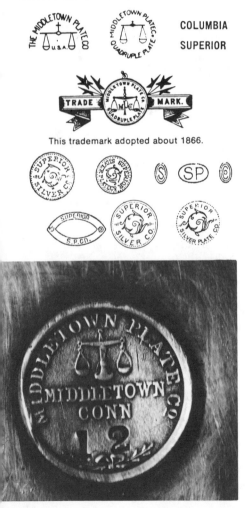

COLUMBIA
SUPERIOR

This trademark adopted about 1866.

MIDDLETOWN SILVER CO.
Middletown, Connecticut

After the business of the Middletown Plate Co. had been taken over by the International Silver Co. in 1899 and moved to other plants, some of the old employees arranged with others to start a new concern, hiring space in the building formerly used by the Middletown Plate Co. The new company went bankrupt, January 6, 1910 but after several reorganizations and changes were still in business as late as 1939. An item in the *Hartford Times* (1-11-1945) indicates that the company was merged with J.A. Otterbein Co. of Middletown. Believed to have been more recently bought by Wallace Silversmiths.

MIDDLETOWN SILVERWARE

(On nickel silver)

(On britannia)

MIDDLESEX SILVER CO.

(On plated nickel silver)

HAROLD A. MILBRATH
Milwaukee, Wisconsin

Founded 1952. An individual maker specializing in sterling silver. Communion service appointments and altar appointments in bronze alloys. Makers of holloware, cast and fabricated articles and special jewelry.

(Used on silver, bronze and pewter)

FREDERICK A. MILLER
Brecksville and Cleveland, Ohio

Silversmith. Mr. Miller was born in Akron, Ohio and is a graduate of Cleveland Institute of Art and Western Reserve University. After his discharge from the Army in 1946 he joined the firm of Potter and Mellen, Inc. and is now president and designer of that firm. He studied silversmithing briefly with Baron Erik Flemming and started working in silversmithing and jewelry following the war. He worked mostly in sterling holloware until recently when he became interested in jewelry.

In 1948 Mr. Miller joined the staff of Cleveland Institute of Art as instructor in silversmithing and jewelry where he is presently teaching.

Mr. Miller's work has been exhibited in the Cleveland May Show from 1948 through 1972, where it has won first prize or a special award each year. He has also exhibited in the State Department Exhibition; the Designer-Craftsman Show, first National Exhibition; Rochester Museum Show; Metropolitan Handwrought Silver Exhibition; Newark Museum Show, 1954; Wichita National Exhibition; Los Angeles County Fair; Brussels World's Fair; Museum of Contemporary Crafts, 1961; the Henry Gallery, Seattle; Objects USA; Ohio Designer Craftsman; American Metalsmiths-DeCordova Museum, 1974 and others.

JOHN PAUL MILLER
Brecksville and Cleveland, Ohio

Silversmith affiliated with the Cleveland Institute of Art. Mr. Miller was born in Huntingdon, Pennsylvania and educated in Ohio Public Schools. He is a graduate of the Cleveland Institute of Art in Industrial Design. He began making jewelry in 1937 and produced holloware in the middle Cleveland Institute of Art in Industrial Design. He began making jewelry in 1937 and produced holloware in the middle 1950s. Almost all of his work is done in gold.

Mr. Miller's work has been shown in many exhibitions in the United States and Europe. Examples are in numerous private and public collections. One man shows have been held in the Museum of Contemporary Crafts, New York; the Art Institute of Chicago; the Henry Gallery, Seattle, Washington; and the Wichita Art Association Museum, Wichita, Kansas.

THE MILLER JLY. CO.
Cincinnati, Ohio

Listed in JC 1915 in the sterling silver section and in jewelry. Last listing in 1922.

M Sterling

WM. J. MILLER
Baltimore, Maryland

Listed in Baltimore City Directories 1904-1920 as a silversmith.

MITCHELL & POOL
Baltimore, Maryland

Listed in Baltimore City Directory in 1889 as silverplaters. Succeeded by B. Pool & Company in 1894.

G.I. MIX & CO.
Yalesville, Connecticut

In 1843 Garry I. Mix began the manufacture of spoons and three years later formed a partnership with Charles Parker of Meriden.

"In 1848 Charles Parker and Garry I. Mix began the manufacture of Britannia and German silverware, continuing until 1854, when Mix retired to establish himself in business at Yalesville. Parker and Jeralds (Thomas and Bennet) continued at the old place as the Parker Mfg. Co. In 1857 the old mill and factory buildings were destroyed by fire and a new factory erected.

"In 1876 the Parker Mfg. Co. discontinued the manufacture of German silverware, but the production of Britannia spoons has since been carried on, in a limited way, by Bennet Jeralds.

"G.I. Mix & Co. at Yalesville, are extensive manufacturers of Britannia goods . . . In 1886 steam power—50 horse—was added to the water motor, and the capacity for production was increased." HISTORY OF NEW HAVEN COUNTY CONNECTICUT, Vol. 1. Edited by J.L. Rockey.

"Garry I. Mix died Saturday (dated New Haven, Aug. 15). He was the leading manufacturer of German silver spoons and tinned ware spoons and edge tools. Some years ago was a State Senator. He built the Baptist Church at Yalesville, mainly at his own expense. In his early business life he manufactured spoons for Russell Hall of Meriden." (JC&HR 8-17-1892, p. 19)

Succeeded c. 1903 by C.I. Yale Mfg. Co., manufacturers of nickle plated copper coffee and tea pots.

CROWN PRINCE
MALACCA PLATED
THE COLUMBIA

JAMES MIX
Albany, New York

The James Mix who designed the James Mix "Albany" souvenir spoon c. 1890 may have been a descendant of James Mix, silversmith in Albany, New York, 1817-1850. His son, James Mix, Jr., was listed in the Albany City Directories as a manufacturing jeweler, 1846-1850.

JAMES MIX

MODERN SILVER MFG. CO., INC.,
Brooklyn, New York

Listed in 1950 JC-K and 1958 JBG as manufacturers of silverplated wares.

HEIRESS

SILVER PLATE

JACOB A. MOLLER
New Rochelle, New York

Listed in 1907 New Rochelle City Directory as a silversmith. No other listing.

MONTGOMERY BROS.
Los Angeles, California

The Los Angeles City Directories list James Montgomery as watchmaker and jeweler from 1883-1886. The first listing for Montgomery Bros. (Jas. A. and Geo. A.) is for the year 1888. The same listing is carried for 1890. No distinction made between retailers and manufacturers in the directories.

On October 27, 1891, Montgomery Bros. registered Patent No. 20,270 for the manufacture of gold, silver and plated articles, flatware and jewelry. Their trademark is listed in JC souvenir section.

MONTGOMERY WARD & CO.
Chicago, Illinois

LAKESIDE BRAND

First used in 1908 on silverplated flatware made by various manufacturers.

MONTGOMERY WARD & CO.,
(First used 1887-1888)
PALACE BRAND
(Used 1886)

MONUMENTAL PLATING WORKS
Baltimore, Maryland

Listed in Baltimore City Directories 1887-1912 as silverplaters. Wm. Focke, proprietor.

MOORE BROS.
Attleboro, Massachusetts

Listed in Attleboro City Directories as manufacturing jewelers with John F. and Thomas H. Moore as owners from 1907-1916 and John F., Thomas H. and Charles E. Moore from 1916-1940.

M.B.

MOORE & HOFMAN
Newark, New Jersey
See Schmitz, Moore & Co.

Successors to Schmitz, Moore & Co. between 1915-1922. Succeeded by Moore & Son (?) before 1943.

Manufacturers of sterling silver dresserware, vanity and cigarette cases, tableware and novelties.

MH

JOHN C. MOORE & SON
New York, New York

John Chandler Moore began the manufacture of silverware in 1827 and was later joined in business by his son, Edward C.

Moore. John Moore was associated from 1832 to 1836 with the firm of Eoff & Moore (Garrett Eoff). He made silverware for Marquand & Co. and also for their successors, Ball, Thompkins & Black. In 1847 John Moore designed and patented a flatware pattern (Design Patent No. 124, May 29, 1847) that is similar to the *Prince Albert* design of Henry Hebbard, N.Y. silversmith (Directories 1847-49), the *Prince Albert* being derived from the *Albert* design made by C.J. Vander, Ltd. London, England makers of hand forged silver. The same design was shown in an Elkington & Mason Co. catalog of 1851 and described as one of the "current styles in silver-plated wares."

Edward C. Moore learned his trade in his father's shop, and was later taken into partnership, finally succeeding his father on the latter's retirement 1851. Before this an arrangement had been effected to manufacture silverware solely for Tiffany & Co., which was continued until 1868 when, Tiffany & Co. becoming a corporation, they bought the entire Moore plant, Edward C. Moore becoming one of the directors. From its beginnings as a small shop the company developed into an industry giving employment to about 500 men.

J. C. M.

MOORE & LEDING, SILVERSMITHS
Washington, D.C.

Listed in the Washington, D.C. City Directories from 1882 to 1902. Listed as Moore & Leding, 1881-1899, jewelers. Listed as Robert Leding (successor to Moore & Leding (1900-1902), jeweler.

Moore & Leding marketed the "Washington City" and "Mount Vernon" souvenir spoons, both made by The Gorham Company. These two spoons were patented in 1890 and 1891, respectively, and were put on the market shortly after the first Witch spoon designed for Daniel Low Company.

R.L. MOOREHEAD & CO.
Providence, Rhode Island

Listed KJI 1918-19 as manufacturers of sterling and plated wares.

MORGAN MORGAN(S), JR.
New York, New York
See Geo. W. Shiebler & Co.

Morgan(s) was a silversmith in New York City who succeeded to the business of Albert Coles (q.v.) and was in turn succeeded by Geo. W. Shiebler & Co. He is listed in the New York City Directories 1879-80. A flatware design patent was obtained in his name February 5, 1878 and was later made by the Shiebler company.

MORGAN SILVER PLATE CO.
Winsted, Connecticut

"The Morgan Silver Plate Co. of Winsted, Conn. recently purchased the building in which its factory is located." (JW 6-8-1892)

"J.T. Morgan of the Morgan Silver Plate Co., Winsted, Conn. has recovered from an illness of several weeks. Arthur H. Morgan left Feb. 25 on a business trip." (JC&HR 3-6-1895, p. 20)

The Morgan Silver Plate Co. was listed as manufacturers of bookends and bridge accessories. (KJI 1931)

H.R. MORSS & CO., INC.
North Attleboro, Massachusetts

Listed c. 1930-1940. Manufacturers of sterling silver flatware, baby goods and hollow-handled knives, salad sets, etc.

MORSS

Trade Mark

MOSSBERG WRENCH COMPANY
Attleboro, Massachusetts

They advertised (*The Manufacturing Jeweler*, October 15, 1894) as manufacturers of novelties. Illustrated were a knife sharpener of silverplate for office or table use. In the advertisement the patent date of February 23, 1892 is stamped on the knife sharpeners, indicating that they were in business at least that early. A brief notice (JC&HR 2-27-1895, p. 22) states that the Mossberg Mfg. Co., Attleboro, Massachusetts, issued a catalog.

Succeeded by Mossberg & Granville Mfg. Co.

MUECK-CARY CO., INC.
New York, New York

Manufacturers of sterling wares in the 1940s and 1950s. The trademark is now owned by Towle Silversmiths.

THE PETER MUELLER-MUNK STUDIO
New York, New York

Advertised in *The Antiquarian* May 1928 that "The Best traditions of the silversmith's art are mirrored in the work

produced under my personal supervision. Here are designed and manufactured candlesticks, tea and coffee sets, tea caddies, bowls, vases, trays, goblets, pitchers, boudoir sets, hand mirrors, perfume bottles, loving cups, brushes, combs and many other miscellaneous items." A teapot with ebony finial and ebony handle is illustrated under the caption "Hand Wrought Silver—individual pieces or sets designed, reproduced or made to order."

MT. VERNON COMPANY SILVERSMITHS, INC.
Mount Vernon, New York
See Gorham Corporation

Organized in 1941 with Harry A. MacFarland as president. It was the successor of Hayes & MacFarland which began in 1903. The Mauser Mfg. Company of New York and Roger Williams Silver Company of Providence, Rhode Island were part of the merger to form the Mount Vernon Company Silversmiths in 1914.

Purchased by the Gorham Corporation in 1923.

MULFORD, WENDELL & CO.
Albany, New York
See Wendell Manufacturing Company

Their history can be traced to William Boyd, silversmith (b. 1775-d. 1840) who entered into partnership with Robert Shepard in 1810, under the name Shepard & Boyd (c. 1810-1830). They were succeeded by Boyd & Hoyt (c. 1830-1842); Boyd & Mulford (c. 1832-1842) and Mulford, Wendell & Co. c. 1843.

John H. Mulford and William Wendell, are listed as silversmiths, as are their predecessors.

Mulford and Wendell were also jobbers who did silverplating about 1855. They published an illustrated catalog in 1859.

MULHOLLAND BROS. INC.
Aurora, Illinois

Successor to Aurora Silver Plate Company between 1915-1922. Continued the manufacture of plated flatware and holloware until 1934 when they went out of business. D.E. Mulholland, president; W.S. Mulholland, vice president.

About 1930 it was called Mulholland Silver Co. Out of business in 1932.

JOHN F. MULLER ASSOC., INC.
New York, New York

Listed JBG 1950s and 1960s as manufacturers and importers of silver goods.

MUSIC CENTER MINT
Nashville, Tennessee
No response to inquiries.

S.F. MYERS & CO.
New York, New York
Wholesale jewelers.

In business about 1860 as specialists in plating. (U.S. Patent, February 8, 1887) for jewelry and silverware, plated silver and clocks. Out of business before business.

MYRICK, ROLLER & HOLBROOK
Philadelphia, Pennsylvania

In business before 1890. Out of business before 1904. Trademark found on souvenir spoons.

N

D. NAGIN MFG. CORP.
East Rutherford, New Jersey

Founded July 1957 by Dan Nagin under his own name. In May 1968 the company became D. Nagin Mfg. Corp. Manufacturers of sterling articles, mostly pendants.

NAPIER-BLISS CO.
Meriden, Connecticut
See Napier Co.

Successor to E.A. Bliss Co. about 1915. Succeeded by the Napier Company in 1920.

NAPIER COMPANY
Meriden, Connecticut

CHRONOLOGY

Carpenter & Bliss	1875-82
Carpenter & Bliss, Inc.	1882-83
E.A. Bliss	1883-90
E.A. Bliss, Inc.	1891-1920
The Napier Company	1922-

The original company started in 1875 by E.A. Bliss and J.E. Carpenter, taking over the Whitney & Rice concern where Bliss had been employed as a traveling salesman. At the start it was called Carpenter & Bliss and in 1882 was incorporated. It became the E.A Bliss Co. by 1883. In 1890 they were offered inducements to move their factory to Meriden, where they incorporated a year later. They were making a variety of jewelry, novelties and staple goods. By 1893 they had added sterling silver novelties.

E.A. Bliss died in 1911 and his son William became active head of the company. In 1915, James H. Napier became associated with the company, and in a reorganization he became general manager. During 1918 they devoted much of their plant to the manufacture of war material. After World War I a large part of their activity was devoted to modern jewelry and many additions to their line of sterling novelties and dresserware. In 1920 Napier was elected president and the name of the company changed to Napier-Bliss Co. Two years later, the name Napier Company was adopted.

NASSAU LIGHTER CO.
New York, New York

Listed JC in sterling silver section in 1915. Out of business before 1922.

NATIONAL SILVER COMPANY
New York, New York

Manufacturers of sterling and plated silverware. Began with Samuel E. Bernstein who was first in business in New York in 1890. Became the National Silver Company before 1904.

Cheltenham & Company, Ltd., Sheffield, England, became a division of National Silver Company before 1950; the F.B. Rogers Silver Company was added in February 1955 and in 1956 they purchased the Ontario Manufacturing Company of Muncie, Indiana.

MONARCH SILVER COMPANY and VICEROY SILVER COMPANY are two tradenames recorded in the Trademark Division of the Patent Office by the National Silver Company in 1943 for use on silverplated flatware and cutlery.

They have not made flatware since 1945.

134

NATIONAL SILVER DEPOSIT WARE CO., INC.
New York, New York

Listed KJI 1918-19. Listed in JC 1922-1950. Manufacturers of silver and gold encrusted glassware, desk sets, ornamental serving trays and silverplated holloware.

T.E. NEILL CO.
Brooklyn, New York

TENCO

NESSLER & CO.
New York, New York

"Nessler & Company was founded in 1869 as Nessler & Redway. It was J.S. & C.L. Nessler in the 70's and Nessler & Bioren later. Still later it was Nessler & Co. It continued until c. 1907 and consisted of father and son. C.L. Nessler died in 1907 and the business was left to his son, Charles F., who continued under the same name. It was incorporated in 1912." (JC-W 2-5-1919)

NEVIUS COMPANY
New York, New York

Registered a trademark, No. 48,036, December 5, 1905 for table utensils made of sterling silver. The application was filed by Benjamin C. Nevius, treasurer, who stated that the trademark had been used continuously by them since 1897.

Out of business before 1915.

NEW AMSTERDAM SILVER CO.
New York, New York
See Knickerbocker Silver Co.

NEW ENGLAND SILVER CO.
Deering, Maine

Founded in 1894 by Joseph S. Dunham, son of Rufus Dunham. Joseph had formerly been associated with Stevens, Smart & Dunham.

NEW ENGLAND SILVER CO.
QUADRUPLE PLATE.

NEW ENGLAND SILVER PLATE CO.
See Adelphi Silver Plate Co.
See American Silver Co.
See Bristol Brass & Clock Co.

Advertised in *St. Nicholas Magazine*, March 1878 that they furnish "first-class articles at a very low price. A set of six SOLID Silver Tea Spoons for $3.50" or "For 85 cents. . . one set of 6 quadruple tea spoons in case. Fine and heavily plated with pure nickel and coin silver, on a new metal, called Alfenide, which is very similar to the finest English white steel. It contains no *brass* or *German silver* in its composition, and consequently *no poison*, or disagreeable taste." The ad was copyrighted in 1877.

NEW ENGLAND SILVER PLATE CO.
Bridgeport, Connecticut

"The New England Silver Plate Co., Conn. has just been organized. The works will be in West End, Bridgeport. Stockholders are S.C. Osborne, Bridgeport; James Dowdle and D.J. Toothill, Orange, New Jersey." (JC&HR 9-18-1895, p. 26). Not the same New England Silver Plate Co. that was in New Haven, Connecticut.

NEW ENGLAND SILVERSMITHS
New York, New York

Makers of sterling silver goods c. 1950.

NEW HAVEN SILVER PLATE CO.
Lyons, New York

The New Haven Silver Plate Company was established at Lyons, New York in September 1891. The business was purchased by the Manhattan Silver Plate Company of that city in November of that same year. They were successors in 1893 to A.H. Towar & Co. silverplaters in Lyons.

The Manhattan Silver Plate Company, the New Haven Silver Plate Company and A.H. Towar & Co. continued manufacturing operations after being taken over by the International Silver Company.

NEW ORLEANS SILVERSMITHS
New Orleans, Louisiana

Manufacturers of sterling and silverplate reproductions. Founded in 1938 by Karl Dingeldein, native of Hanau, Germany, whose family had been silversmiths since 1720. Mr. Dingeldein died about 1966 and the business was purchased by another young German silversmith, Hans Leutkemeier, originally from Darmstadt. Mr. Leutkemeier began his apprenticeship in

Germany in 1952, serving three and a half years as an apprentice. This was followed by five years of working as a jeweler before obtaining full recognition as a goldsmith and silversmith.

(On sterling)

(On silverplate)

NEW YORK SILVER DEPOSIT CO.
Jersey City, New Jersey

Began as New York Silver Deposit Company, founding date unknown. Succeeded by Imperial Art Ware before 1915 and out of business before 1922.

NEW YORK SILVER PLATE CO.
New York, New York

See E. Magnus

"The New York Silver Plate Co., manufacturers of silver plated ware made an assignment. Emil Magnus is president and Stephen C. Duval, secretary. The company was incorporated Sept. 1896 and succeeded to the business carried on at 20 Warren Street by Mr. Magnus who made an assignment July 6, 1896." (JC&HR 8-18-1897, p. 9-10)

NEW YORK STAMPING CO.
Brooklyn, New York

Listed in JC in 1915-1922 in plated silver section.

(Housefurnishing Goods.)

NEWBURYPORT SILVER CO.
Keene, New Hampshire

Manufacturers of sterling silver, flat and holloware. Listed in the City Directory of Keene, New Hampshire 1905-1914. The firm was organized in 1904 with John Currier, President; Geo. E. Stickney, treasurer; Caleb Stickney and Herbert N. Woodwell, managers. Caleb Stickney was once associated with the Towle Silver Company in Newburyport, Massachusetts and was in charge of the machinery of the new company while Mr. Woodwell did the designing and directed the finances. Woodwell had also been with the Towle Silver Company as an engraver in charge of the engraving room—at one time a most important function. John Currier was a prosperous manufacturer of automobile bodies in Amesbury and it is believed that he provided financial backing but took no active part in the management. The firm was unable to obtain loans from the Newburyport banks and moved to Keene, New Hampshire early in 1905. Woodwell died March 1907 and Stickney and his son assumed full charge. Poor management led the firm into bankruptcy in 1914. The silver stock was bought by Rogers, Lunt & Bowler

N S CO
(Sterling Silver Ware.)

N. S. C.

(On plated silver)

WILLIAM F. NEWHALL
Lynn, Massachusetts

First established as a jewelry business by Stephen Cyrus Newhall in 1872. William Frederick Newhall entered the employ of his brother at that time and in 1885, after the death of Stephen, William succeeded to the business. In 1907 he took into partnership his eldest son, Fred Clinton Newhall. The company name became W.F. Newhall & Sons, Inc. before 1922.

Stephen is listed in the Lynn City Directories as a clock repairer, watchmaker and jeweler. William is listed as a clerk, jeweler and optician. Newhall's did special order work, enameling, engraving, die sinking and gold and silverplating.

The 1896-1922 editions of JC carry a trademark (No. 19,751, June 23, 1891 for flat and tableware) that is the handle of a spoon with an old woman and a cat. Newhall's sold many souvenir spoons. Some, at least, carry the Durgin Co. trademark.

There is no record of the shop after 1957.

E. NEWTON & CO.
New York, New York
Listed in JC 1896-1904 in the sterling silver section. Out of business before 1915.

STERLING **N**

NIAGARA SILVER CO.
New York, New York
See Oneida Silversmiths
See Wm. A. Rogers, Ltd.
"The Niagara Silver Company has been incorporated to manufacture and sell silver and silver plated ware." (JW 10-11-1899, p. 25)
"The flatware department of the Pairpoint Mfg. Company has been purchased by the Niagara Silver Company." (JC-W 7-4-1900, p. 8)
Wm. A. Jameson was manager of the company.

R. S. MFG. CO.
COIN SILVER METAL
EXTRA COIN SILVER PLATE
EXTRA COIN SILVER No. 12 PLATE

NICHOLS BROS.
Greenfield, Massachusetts
Listed in 1896 Jewelers' Weekly as manufacturers of plated silverware.

NICHOLS BROS.
Greenfield, Mass.
12 dwt.

THE NICKEL SILVER FLATWARE CO.
Unionville, Connecticut
"The Nickel Silver Flatware Co. is in production, putting out, so they claim, not alone unplated, but silverplated and sterling silver." (JC&HR 6-6-1894)

NEIDERER & MOORE
Baltimore, Maryland
Listed in Balimore City Directory in 1885 as silversmiths.

GEBRUEDER NOELLE
Luedenschied, Germany
Registered trademark U.S. Patent Office, No. 11,800, December 16, 1884 for knives, forks and spoons. Also, No. 50,984, April 3, 1906 for knives, forks and spoons of britannia.

Listed in JC 1896-1922 in the plated silver section. No record after 1922.

(Knives, Forks, Spoons.)

NORBERT MFG. CO.
New York, New York
Manufacturers of sterling goods since c. 1950. No longer listed.

NORTHERN STAMPING & MFG. CO.
Seattle, Washington
See E.J. Towle Mfg. Co.

NORTHAMPTON CUTLERY CO.
Chicago, Illinois
Listed KJI 1918-19 as manufacturers of plated flatware.

NORWEGIAN SILVER CORP.
New York, New York
The Norwegian Silver Corporation is the U.S. distributor of sterling and silverplated holloware, flatware and jewelry made by Th. Marthinsen Solvvarefabrikk a/s, Tonsberg, Norway, established in 1883 and by David Andersen a/s, Oslo, Norway, established in 1876. Both are third generation silversmithing firms.

NORTHWESTERN SILVER WARE MANUFACTURING COMPANY
Chicago, Illinois

Founded shortly after the Civil War. Burned in the Chicago fire of 1871 and not rebuilt. Manufacturers of silverplated wares.

NORWICH CUTLERY COMPANY
Norwich, Connecticut
See International Silver Company
Organized and wholly owned by William H. Watrous, of Rogers Cutlery Company, Hartford, Connecticut.
Made cutlery for plating from 1889. Did not use a trademark because they sold their products to other silver manufacturers.
One of the original companies to become part of the International Silver Company in 1898.

WILLIAM NOST CO., INC.
New York, New York

William Nost was a silversmith in New York before 1915. Succeeded by William Nost Company, Inc. before 1922. They made sterling silver holloware.

NOVELTY PLATING WORKS
Baltimore, Maryland

Listed in the Baltimore City Directories 1890-1915 as successors to Schrier & Protze who began silverplating in 1888.

Anton Protze listed as proprietor 1893-1898. Louis Liepman, proprietor 1899-1915.

NOYES BROTHERS
New York, New York

Wholesalers of silverware and novelties. Begun in New York in 1892 by Pierrepont and Holton Noyes, sons of John Humphrey Noyes, founder of the Oneida Community.

This partnership was dissolved after about two years with Holton going into the restaurant business and Pierrepont Noyes returning to Niagara Falls to develop the Oneida Community silver company.

BENJ. D. NUITZ
Baltimore, Maryland

Listed in 1893 Baltimore City Directory under plated silverware.

NUSSBAUM & HUNOLD
Providence, Rhode Island
See Walter Hunold

O

OLD NEW ENGLAND CRAFTSMEN, INC.
Newburyport, Massachusetts

Makers of Colonial handwrought solid silver and reproductions. Listed in 1931 KJI. Out of business for many years.

PILLSBURY

PORTSMOUTH
(Reproductions)

OLD NEWBURY CRAFTERS
Newburyport, Massachusetts

The largest producer of handwrought silver in the United States, the company began with the partnership in 1915 of Elmer Senior, a spoon maker, and Albert S. MacBurnie, a polisher. Senior had at one time worked with the Frank Smith Silver Company (q.v.) in Gardner, Massachusetts. For four or five years he worked with George Blanchard making handwrought spoons. Apparently, it was from him that he learned silversmithing.

Albert MacBurnie was born in Hantsport, Nova Scotia. From 1895 to 1909 he worked with the Frank Smith company as a polisher. In 1909 he moved to Newburyport and worked with Towle Silversmiths (q.v.) for about 10 years while on evenings and weekends he did finishing of handwrought pieces made by Senior. After four years of part-time work he left Towle and worked full time with Old Newbury Crafters. He remained with them until his death in 1944. Control of the corporation passed to his son, Everett, who, in 1950, sold out to his cousin, Reynold Senior, who operated the business until 1955.

Following the death of Elmer Senior on November 8, 1932, the business was incorporated as "The Old Newbury Crafters."

In September 1955 Reynold Senior sold 100 percent interest to Swift C. Barnes, who had been associated with Towle Silversmiths. Senior remained as Master Silversmith and shop foreman until 1959, when he was succeeded by Chester A. Dow who continued in charge of the shop until his death in 1978.

In 1979 all manufacturing assets and the name Old Newbury Crafters was purchased by a newly formed corporation. It is presently a wholly owned subsidiary of the Michele Silverware and Jewelry Company, Amesbury, Massachusetts, to which city all manufacturing activities have been moved.

From 1915 to 1932 they made handmade holloware and tea ware as well as flatware. The first two patterns they made were *Moulton* and *Old Newbury*. Distribution of their products was largely through arts and crafts societies in major cities, and a few fine jewelry stores.

In 1955 they made seven handwrought flatware designs, all reproductions except *Moderne*. These were *Moulton, Old Newbury, Windsor, Fiddleback, Panel Antique* and *Old English*. In 1978 they began making *Buckingham, Antique* and *Old*

English designs for Shreve & Co. (q.v.), San Francisco which had previously been made in Shreve's own factory.

In 1956, after 25 years in which the company had made only flatware, it resumed making sterling silver holloware. This activity was augmented by the acquisition of Worden-Munnis Co. (q.v.) founded in Boston in 1940, and whose operations were merged with Old Newbury Crafters.

Only sterling silver was used until 1974 when a small pewter holloware division was started, and they also began making sterling silver jewelry and karat gold jewelry.

The mark "HANDWROUGHT" was not stamped on Old Newbury silver before the end of 1955. Since October 1956 all work has been identified by this mark.

The Newbury Eagle, used extensively in their advertising, has never been used on the silver.

The company's *Wilton* pattern has been the official service in Blair House in Washington, D.C., the U.S. State Department's official residence for visiting heads of state and other high-ranking officials.

In 1965 the company started a practice then unique in the American silver industry. Since that time, every handwrought piece has been marked personally by the craftsman who made it. All handwrought pieces made since 1965 bear the maker's signature mark as well as the company marks "O.N.C. HANDWROUGHT," and "STERLING." Work made specifically for certain stores include Cartier, Neiman-Marcus, Shreve & Co., Shreve, Crump & Low and Spaulding & Co. also bears their name.

OLIVER MFG. CO.
Los Angeles, California

Manufacturers of sterling novelties c. 1950.

N. & D. ONDERDONK
New York, New York

N. & D. Onderdonk were silversmiths working in New York c. 1800. They are listed in JC in the sterling silver section. Out of business before 1904.

N. & D. O.

ONEIDA SILVERSMITHS
Sherrill, New York

John Humphrey Noyes and a little association of men first began their experiment in communal living at Oneida Creek about 1848.

Their first products were canned fruits and vegetables which found a ready market. Later their chief support came from the manufacture of steel traps.

In 1877 the Oneida Community embarked on the manufacture of tableware. The Wallingford branch made ungraded, tinned, iron spoons in two patterns called "Lily" and "Oval." These two iron spoons were the direct ancestors of the whole line of Community Plate.

By 1878 the mill was turning out steel spoon blanks sold for plating to the Meriden Britannia Company. In 1880 the factory was moved to Niagara Falls.

Their first silverware could not compete with higher quality silver made by other companies. A decision was made to turn out a better quality and better designed line. Their new design called "Avalon" was exhibited in 1901 at the Buffalo Exposition."

In January 1902 the new line of Community Plate was introduced, but, was not immediately successful. A complete change in advertising methods in high-priced, large-circulation magazines proved enor-

Personal Signature Marks of the
Newbury Crafters

| Fletcher S. Carter | ▲ | Robert H. Bean | | Chester A. Dow | | Chester A. Dow | | James F. Harvey | | James F. Harvey | | Robert H. Lapham | | Robert H. Lapham | | Gayden F. Marshall | | Gayden F. Marshall | | Daniel S. Morrill | | Daniel S. Morrill | | Roger R. Rowell | | Roger R. Rowell | | Reynolds F. Senior | | Reynolds F. Senior | | George R. Woundy | | George R. Woundy | |

In use as of June, 1965   **In use as of May, 1974**

mously effective. It was the first "pretty girl" advertising in America and not only affected the sales of their silver, it also had a profound effect on the whole advertising business. Between 1912-1914 the whole silverware plant was moved from Niagara Falls to Sherrill, New York.

In 1926 they opened a plant, the Kenwood Silver Company, in Sheffield, England and in 1929 bought Wm. A Rogers, Ltd. Besides the main Wm. A. Rogers, Ltd. plant, they acquired four other factories and their brands; 1881 Rogers; Simeon L. & George H. Rogers Company and Heirloom.

On March 1, 1935, the company name was changed to Oneida, Ltd., and is now commonly known as Oneida Silversmiths.

In 1965 they adopted as their symbol of excellence the Roman cube "tessera hospitalis," which was placed in the hands of a visitor as a pledge of hospitality and friendship. Oneida's tessera is a cube of solid silver, engraved with the company name on all planes. Oneida began production of silverplated holloware in 1926. They sold their Canadian subsidiaries in February 1972.

J. Rogers & Co.

A.1. NICKEL SILVER No. 210

CARBON

N. F. SILVER CO., 1877

SILVER METAL

210 NEARSILVER

U. S. SILVER CO.

ALPHA PLATE

COMMUNITY

COMMUNITY PLATE

DURO PLATE

N. F. NICKEL SILVER

NIAGARA FALLS CO., 1877

O. C.

O. C. LUSTRA

ONEIDA

ONEIDA COMMUNITY DIAMOND
  PLATE

ONEIDA COMMUNITY PAR PLATE

ONEIDA COMMUNITY RELIANCE
  PLATE

ONEIDA COMMUNITY SILVER
  PLATE

PURITAN SILVER CO.

REX PLATE

REX PLATE

RELIANCE

RELIANCE PLATE

TRIPLE PLUS

TUDOR PLATE

ONEIDACRAFT

(Used since Dec. 31, 1925)

ONEIDA STERLING
See Oneida Silversmiths

Production of sterling flatware was begun in 1946.

In 1981 the following Webster Wilcox holloware pattern trademarks were purchased from International Silver Company:

WILCOX & DESIGN

CRAFTMETAL

E G W & S & DESIGN

FORBES & SHIELD & DESIGN

FEATHER-CROWN-LIO | & DESIGN

WELLINGTON

STRAFFORDSHIRE

WEBSTER WILCOX

CHIPPENDALE

ROCOCO

JO ANNE

WEBSTER WILCOX, CHIPPENDALE, ROCOCO and JO ANNE are presently in use by Oneida on holloware. In addition, they licensed certain trademarks and of those licensed trademarks, COUNTESS is presently being used on holloware.

"Countess" 5-piece tea and coffee service, Oneida Silversmiths. (Photo courtesy of Oneida Silversmiths)

"Sea Crest" double vegetable dish in silverplate by Oneida Silversmiths. (Photo courtesy of Oneida Silversmiths)

ONODAGO SILVER MFG. CO.
Syracuse, New York

"The Onodago Silver Mfg. Co. of Syracuse have incorporated. Directors are E.P. Goodrich and C.C. Goodrich, of Syracuse, George W. Hills and Frederick W. Chamberlain of Lyons, Elliott M. Tuttle of Munnsville, and S.C. Waterman of Oneida." (JC&HR 4-15-1896, p. 17)

ONTARIO MFG. CO.
Muncie, Indiana
See National Silver Company

Founded 1897. Succeeded by National Silver Company in 1956. Manufactured plated silverware.

HARVEY OSBORN SILVER CO.
Newark, New Jersey

Listed KJI 1918-19 as manufacturers of German silver brushes and mirrors and silver novelties.

OSBORN COMPANY
Lancaster, Pennsylvania
About 1897.

FRANK N. OSBORNE
New York, New York

Listed in JC 1904-1915. May have been wholesale jeweler or distributor.

Also used other trademarks on jewelry sold at the Chicago Columbian Exposition, 1892-1893.

No record after 1915.

XIX CENTURY
HEIRLOOM

No. 23,729 October 24, 1893
For jewelry, spoons, forks, ladles, cutlery, etc.

HEIRLOOM

No. 23,730 October 24, 1893

OVIATT & WARNER
Portland, Oregon

Listed in the Portland City Directory for 1894 and 1895 only. Listed under sterling silver section of the 1896 edition of the JC as out of business in 1896. No information in the Portland newspaper index.

O. & W.

OXFORD HALL SILVERSMITHS, LTD.
New Cassel, L.I. New York

Mentioned in JC-K 1974.

OXFORD SILVERSMITHS CO.
New York, New York

Listed 1918-19 KJI and JC-K 1950 as manufacturers of silverplated wares.

P

PACIFIC PLATE WORKS
San Francisco, California

Working c. 1869-1873. Their plater was William Shepman who, sometime after 1874 moved to Oakland and set up his own business which he called "Pacific Gold and Silver Plate Works." Products were marked "Pacific Plate Works, S.F." or "Haynes & Lawton" (q.v.).

THE PAIRPOINT CORPORATION
New Bedford, Massachusetts

Organized in 1880 as the Pairpoint Mfg. Co., with Edward D. Mandel as president. Thomas J. Pairpoint, for whom the company was named, had most recently been with the Meriden Britannia Company.

Pairpoint served his apprenticeship in Paris and later worked for the prominent firm of Lambert & Rawlings in London. He was chief designer for the Gorham Manufacturing Company from about 1868 until the late 1870s. During this time he designed many pieces of the Gorham Company's regular line as well as special exhibition pieces.

While employed by the Gorham Company, Pairpoint was one of the six artists who submitted designs for the William Cullen Bryant testimonial vase, presented to the poet June 20, 1876. While he lost the competition to James H. Whitehouse,, head designer of Tiffany & Company, his design received favorable press coverage. It was described (*Art Journal*, 1876) as "a poetical work of Grecian character, gracefully elongated to monumental proportions."

Pairpoint was one of the outstanding proponents of the Renaissance Revival. This was clearly illustrated in "The Century Vase" he and George Wilkinson designed for the Gorham Company and which was exhibited at the Philadelphia Centennial in 1876.

Pairpoint was among the first in this country to visualize silver as an art medium. Repoussé figures on his work were often drawn from mythology and other literature. No doubt the literary character of his work may be ascribed to his association with Morel Ladeuil from whom he gained an interest in Renaissance design.

In 1877 Pairpoint left the Gorham Company to become designer and modeler for the Meriden Britannia Company, Meriden, Connecticut. Shortly before leaving the latter, about August 1879, he prepared a series of articles, "Art Work & Silver," (*Jewelers' Circular*, September 1879 through March 1880) in which he discussed silver as an art medium. The esteem in which he was held by that publication is reflected in the editorial comment where Pairpoint is spoken of as "one of the most skillful and artistic designers of the present day, having a reputation that is world wide."

This reputation served the newly formed Pairpoint Mfg. Co. well as it soon commanded favorable attention for the design of its products. In 1882 the *Jewelers' Circular* commented editorially. "The Pairpoint Mfg. Co. is introducing new and more artistic designs by T.J. Pairpoint, a gentleman of rare ability in classical subjects."

On April 1, 1885, Pairpoint severed his connections with the company bearing his name and announced his intention of going into "manufacturing on his own account." There seems to be no record that he really did start a new business. The listing of his name in the Providence, Rhode Island City Directory which had run from 1870 through 1877 and then dropped, reappeared in 1887. The reason for leaving the company is not known. Old-timers there remembered him well but did not know the reason for his leaving.

Pairpoint's obituary (*Providence Journal*, August 30, 1902, p. 3) says that his death came with slight warning. It went on to say that". . .for several years past Mr. Pairpoint had been in poor health, but not of a nature to cause great anxiety. (He is said to have been diabetic.) Mr. Pairpoint was well known locally as an expert silversmith and designer, although he had not been actively engaged in business during recent years."

Although T.J. Pairpoint left the company, the tradition of fine design he had established was maintained by the firm. They became one of the country's largest manufacturers of plated silverware and carried on an extensive export trade, especially with Australia.

In 1894 the Mount Washington Glass Company became part of the Pairpoint organization. This event and their expanded production was noted in the various trade journals.

"The Pairpoint Mfg. Co., owners of the justly celebrated Mt. Washington Glass Co., New Bedford, Mass., contemplate moving their New York business, May 1, from the old stand, 46 Murray St., to Maiden Lane. The new lines of silver plated hollow and glassware and novelties, fine decorated china and glass of this company and their aggregation of rich cut glass tableware, all at popular prices and styles distinctly original, are well calculated to keep this establishment in the front ranks of manufacturers of art wares. An important feature of this establishment is the manufacture from start to finish of special lines of rich cut glass for sterling silver mountings, and manufacturers of sterling silver can avail themselves of the prestige of this company's position to supply designs suited to their requirements and made to the patron's individual suggestions." (JC&HR 3-17-1897, p. 21)

In 1900 financial difficulties of both companies led to their merging to form the Pairpoint Corporation. The combined operations of silverplated wares and glass manufacturing continued successfully until the Depression in 1929, when the company suffered reverses from which it never recovered. Only the glass working part continued under various firm names.

Finally, all operations ceased in 1958. The flatware department was purchased by the Niagara Silver Co. in 1900. Some of the dies and patterns were sold to the Rockford Silver Plate Co. Production of glassware resumed on a limited basis in the 1970s.

PAIRPOINT
FLAT 1880 WARE.
BEST
(Flatware.)

BRISTOL PLATE CO.

(Hollowware.)

TRADE MARK.
(Hollowware.)

(On Sheffield reproductions)

Coffee service designed and patented by Albert Steffin, Assignor to the Pairpoint Corporation (Design Patent No. 36,877; April 12, 1904). (Photo by Roy D. Greaves; courtesy of E.A.P. Evans)

Teapot, creamer and sugar bowl by Pairpoint Corporation. (Photo by Poist's Studio, Hanover, Pennsylvania; courtesy of A. Christian Revi)

PALMER & BACHELDER
Boston, Massachusetts

In the 1860s they purchased Reed & Barton wares "in the metal" and operated their own plating establishment.

PALMER & OWEN
Cincinnati, Ohio

Listed in Cincinnati City Directories 1850-1859 as silversmiths who operated a silverware factory.

PALMER & PECKHAM
North Attleboro, Massachusetts

Listed in JC 1896. Out of business before 1904.

P & P
STERLING.

PARAGON PLATE
A private mail order company (Sears Roebuck & Co.) trademark. Used by International Silver Company c. 1910. In a spiral-bound booklet offered by Follett Studios, Moorhead, Minnesota, there are reprints of pages from various catalogs. On one, there is a teaspoon in the *Royal Oak* pattern "Double Triple Paragon Brand." The ad says it was manufactured by the most renowned firm of silversmiths in the country and will outwear any other brand, including any Rogers brand.

PARKER & CASPER BRITANNIA CO.
See Parker & Casper

PARKER & CASPER CO.
Meriden, Connecticut
See International Silver Co.
See Wilcox Silver Plate Co.

Organized by Charles Casper, John E. Parker, Edmund Parker, Philip S. Pelton and Samuel L. Dodd, Jr. Incorporated St. Louis, Mo., August 6, 1866 with Samuel Dodd, president, under the name Parker & Casper Britannia Co. In May 1867 it became Parker & Casper Co.

They were specialists in silverplated holloware.

The business was sold in 1869 to the Wilcox Silver Plate Co. which became part of International Silver Co. in 1898.

CHARLES PARKER CO.
Meriden, Connecticut
Spoonmakers c. 1887-1907.

PARKS BROS. & ROGERS
Providence, Rhode Island and New York
Established in 1892 by Geo. W. Parks, Wm. C. Parks and Everett I. Rogers who

bought out the American Lever cuff and collar button portion of Howard & Son, the latter devoting all their interests to the silver business. Listed until c. 1930 as manufacturers of 10, 14k gold and gold-filled cuff buttoms, collar buttons, cuff links, dress sets, collar pins and grips, bobbettes, scarf pins, lingerie and tie clasps.

PARKER & WHIPPLE CO.
Meriden, Connecticut

"Parker & Whipple of Meriden has begun the large addition to its factory." (JW 6 July, Vol 14, no 15, p. 12)

G.W. PARKS COMPANY
Providence, Rhode Island

Successors to Hayden Mfg. Co. before 1909. Listed in JC in 1909-1915 as manufacturers of sterling and plated silver. Out of business before 1922.

HOPE SILVER CO.
(On plated silver)

(On sterling silver)

PATENT SILVERWARE MFG. CO.
Buffalo, New York

"The Patent Silverware Mfg. Co. was incorporated for purchasing, selling and manufacturing all kinds of silverware, and to purchase and produce patent rights, etc., patent devices of their own. Frank E. Comstock, Buffalo; B.N. Reynolds, Lakeville, N.Y., and Edith L. Johnston, Wheeling, West Virginia." (JC&HR 11-1-1893, p. 7).

PAUL REVERE SILVER CO., INC.
Boston, Massachusetts

Registered trademark U.S. Patent No. 85,612, March 5, 1912 for plated silverware. Out of business before 1922.

PAUL REVERE

PAYE & BAKER MFG. CO.
North Attleboro, Massachusetts

Successors to Simmons & Paye before 1891. Their first products were souvenir spoons of sterling silver. They also made plated silver table novelties, holloware and Dutch silver reproductions.

Last record found was c. 1935.

Flatware production discontinued c. 1920.

GEO. W. PAYSON & CO.
Baltimore, Maryland

Listed in Baltimore City Directory in 1904 as a silversmith.

C.D. PEACOCK
Chicago, Illinois

Established in 1837 by Elijah Peacock from London whose family tree has been traced back as far as Robert Peacocke, once Lord Mayor of York. He died June 15, 1570. Elijah was born in 1818 and entered the family business of clockmaking and served his apprenticeship. He followed his brother, a former gunsmith, to the United States at the age of 19 and set up business in a wooden shanty on Lake Street in Chicago. His shop antidates Chicago's city charter by several months as it was set up in February 1830 and the city charter was not received until July. So, Peacock's can justly claim that their business is older than the city of Chicago.

Peacock sold trinkets to buckskin-clad trappers and scouts and repaired chronometers for the captains of Great Lakes' sailing vessels before Chicago was linked to the east by telegraph in 1848 or by railroad in 1852. In 1860 Charles Daniel (C.D.) Peacock took charge of the business and later he turned it over to his sons, Charles D. Jr., Robert E. and Walter C. Peacock.

When the Chicago fire in 1871 gutted downtown, everything was lost except the massive Peacock vault. Its steel door saved it from ruin. Because the diamonds, gold and a large quantity of silver had been put away in it for the night, the firm was able to start all over again. That sturdy vault still exists.

Peacock's continued to be managed by family members unti it was sold in 1970 to the Dayton-Hudson Corporation, Minneapolis.

Articles sold there are often stamped with the store name. Peacock's was one of the first retail establishments to market flatware with the store name.

In 1903 they marketed Gorham's *Cambridge* pattern flatware under the name *Crofut.*

PEERLESS SILVER COMPANY
Brooklyn, New York

Listed 1936 Jobber's handbook as manufacturers of plated wares, pewter salts and pepper sets and novelties. Listed through 1960.

 LA FRANCE

PELTON BROS. SILVER PLATE CO.
St. Louis, Missouri

See Merry & Pelton Silver Co.

Listed in St. Louis City Directories, 1872-1900 as manufacturers of plated silverware. Philip S. Pelton was supervisor.

TRIPLE PLATE 12
SECTIONAL PLATE XII
STANDARD PLATE 4

(Flatware.)

(Holloware.)

J. PENFIELD & COMPANY
Savannah, Georgia

See Black, Starr & Frost, Ltd.

In business from 1820-1828. Partners were Josiah Penfield. Moses Eastman and Frederick Marquand.

J.C. PENNEY CO. INC.

The patent number indicates a date of about 1925.

PAT. 72786 J. C. PENNEY CO. INC.

PENNSYLVANIA SILVERWARE COMPANY
Kane, Pennsylvania

Manufacturers of plated silver holloware and soda fountain supplies c. 1920-35.

PEORIA PLATING WORKS
Peoria, Illinois

Found on individual table castor. The company was owned by the Mushard family of Peoria. The company is still in business. It was known for some years as the Central Light & Fixture Company and is presently listed as the Central Fixture Company. Their advertisements now read, "Family owned and operated in Peoria since 1898."

D.C. PERCIVAL & COMPANY
Boston, Massachusetts

David C. Percival was born April 16, 1838 in the Cape Cod town of Sandwich. He was the son of David and Sarah F. Percival. He first planned on attending Harvard but decided to begin a business career and became a salesman for the old Boston jewelry firm of Sackett, Davis & Company. He stayed with them for eight years and then embarked in business as a wholesaler in 1868, the firm name being D.C. Percival, Jr. & Co., and having as partners two young men named Morris & Salisbury. The firm occupied a place near the Old South Church but was burned out at the time of the Boston fire in 1872. After the fire Salisbury retired. The firm was reorganized as Percival & Morris. Later Daniel Morris left the firm and D.C. Percival & Co. was incorporated with D.C. and L.F. Percival entering after their graduation from college.

L.S. PETERSON CO.
North Attleboro, Massachusetts

Manufacturers of novelties of sterling and silverplate c. 1940 to the present.

L. S. P.
L. S. P. Co.

THE PETTERSON STUDIO
Chicago, Illinois

John Pontus Petterson studied silversmithing at the Royal School of Arts and Crafts in Norway and then moved to New York where he worked as a silversmith for Tiffany & Company (q.v.) from 1905 to 1911. He moved to Chicago where he was employed in the shop of Robert Jarvie and then in 1914 established The Petterson Studio. In the 1920s he and his assistants made handwrought silver flatware and holloware, trophies and chalices, jewelry and other items to special order.

J. P. P.

W.H. PEIFFER
Niagara Falls, New York

Listed in the 1890 Niagara Falls City Directory as maker of silver and plated silverware.

F.P. PFLEGHAR & SON
New Haven, Connecticut

The company name first appeared in the New Haven City Directories in 1890. Prior to that Frank P. Pfleghar had been in business alone at that address for a few years. The 1918 Directory lists a change of ownership from Frank P. Pfleghar, Sr. and F.P. Pfleghar to Henry W. Ibelshauser and Max Voight but the business was still operating under the name F.P. Pfleghar & Son. The last listing was in 1919. The type of business was described as "machinists," then "machinists and hardware," or "machinists and hardware mfgrs."

The articles on which the imprint was found are silverplated corn holders. In the Patent Office records Patent #567,284, Sept. 8. 1896 was taken out by Charles W. Stebbins, Hartford, Conn., and assigned to F.P. Pfleghar & Son, New Haven, Conn.

F. P. PFLEGHAR & SON
NEW HAVEN, CONN.
PAT. SEPT. 8 — 96

PHELPS & CARY CO.
New York, New York
See Hartford Sterling Co.
See The Tennant Co.

Listed in JC 1904 in sterling silver section as out of business. Trademark identical to that of Hartford Sterling Co. and The Tennant Co. except for initials in shield. Phelps & Cary business was purchased by the Hartford Sterling Company. H.A. Cary went into business for himself in 1900.

PHILADELPHIA PLATE CO.

Attributed in *Century of Silver*, to a Division of the International Silver Company. Not confirmed by them.

PHILADELPHIA SILVERSMITHING CO.

Philadelphia, Pennsylvania

In business c. 1890. Listed in JC in sterling silver section 1915-1922. Last record found was c. 1935.

THOMAS PHILE

Baltimore, Maryland

Listed in Baltimore City Directories 1871-1872, 1879-1887 as a whitesmith.

PHILLIPS MFG. CO. INC.

Meriden, Connecticut

Listed 1927 and 1931 KJI as manufacturers of plated holloware and pewterware.

ALBERT PICK & CO.

Bridgeport, Connecticut

Manufacturers of plated silver flatware and holloware. Successors to the E.H.H. Smith Silver Company in 1920. Last appeared in the Bridgeport City Directory in 1927. Said to be still in business.

ACORN BRAND

EVERWEAR

STERLINGUARD

J.V. PILCHER

Louisville, Kentucky

Manufacturers of plated compacts and cigarette cases c. 1940.

PILCHER

W.L. & H.E. PITKIN

Hartford, Connecticut

See Eagle Sterling Company

"The creditors of the firm of W.L. & H.E. Pitkin, Hartford, Connecticut, silverware manufacturers, held a meeting to arrange a compromise. Pitkin had been in business for more than 20 years." (JW 5-5, 1886, p. 20)

"W.L. & H.E. Pitkin were related to John Owen Pitkin and Walter Pitkin in the silver business c. 1830-80 under the firm name J.O. & W. Pitkin. "William Leonard Pitkin, senior member of the former firm of W.L. & H.E. Pitkin, silversmiths and silverplaters, died this week.

Mr. Pitkin was one of the oldest silversmiths in the country and a pioneer in this state (Connecticut) to combine the art with the silver plating business. In 1856 he came to this city and bought out the silversmiths and silver plating business then conducted by the late O.D. Seymour. He also bought out a similar business conducted by H.I. Sawyer.

"Early in 1863 Mr. Pitkin's brother, Horace Edward Pitkin, came over from East Hartford and became associated with him in the firm of W.L. & H.E. Pitkin, which continued in existence for more than 31 years. July 1, 1894 they closed out the business and sold the machinery to the Eagle Sterling Company of Glastonbury. Late in the same year both brothers formed a business engagement with the Glastonbury company and have since worked there." (JC&HR 2-27-1895, p. 9)

PITTSBURGH SILVERWARE CO.

Pittsburgh, Pennsylvania

Listed in the Pittsburgh City Directories from 1884 through 1887.

The 1884 directory lists it as the Pittsburgh Silverware Installment Company.

The 1885, 1886 and 1887 directories list it as the Pittsburgh Silverware Company.

The 1887 directory gives the last listing as follows: Pittsburgh Silverware Company, 511 Market St., Manufacturers' Agents for Fine Electro-Plated Ware, Silverware, watches, jewelry leased on easy payments. F.R. Jones, Manager.

No trademark shown.

PITTSBURGH SILVERWARE INSTALLMENT COMPANY

Pittsburgh, Pennsylvania

See Pittsburgh Silverware Co.

Listed in the Pittsburgh City Directory 1884.

GUSTAVUS A. POHLMAN

Baltimore, Maryland

Listed in Baltimore City Directories 1903-1904 as a silversmith.

JOHN POLHAMUS
New York, New York
See Geo. W. Shiebler & Co.

John Polhamus was a silversmith, listed in New York City Directories 1833-40 with the firm of Van Cott & Polhamus, also, Polhamus & Strong, c. 1845 where he made silver for Tiffany & Co. Records in the U.S. Patent Office indicate that he was associated with Henry Hebbard (q.v.) c. 1855 when the two obtained design patents for flatware. This same flatware was later made by the Geo. W. Shiebler & Co. Other flatware design patents obtained in the name of Polhamus from 1860-70 were made by Shiebler and one obtained in 1874 was made by the Whiting Mfg. Co.

POOL & CO.
Baltimore, Maryland

CHRONOLOGY

Mitchell & Pool	1889-94
B. Pool & Co.	1894-99
Pool & Company	1899-1915

Organized in 1889 as Mitchell & Pool, silverplaters; succeeded by B. Pool & Co., 1894; and, by Pool & Company in 1899.

POOLE SILVER CO.
Taunton, Massachusetts

Founded in 1893 in Taunton, Massachusetts with a small two-room factory as manufacturers of plated silverware. Originally called Poole & Roche. Mr. Poole bought out his partner Mr. Roche and was sole owner until his death when his three sons took over the active management. In 1946 they retired and sold the company to an investment group headed by Sidney A. Kane of Providence, Rhode Island. The company has grown rapidly.

In 1946 a sterling silver department was added and in 1964 a brass division.

Today the company operates the Poole Silver Company for plated holloware, the Bristol Silver division, founded in 1950, for popular priced plated holloware as well as the above. Purchased by the Towle Mfg. Co. in 1971.

(On sterling silver) (*Quadruple Plate.*)

PSCo
HAND
HAMMERED

POOLE SILVER CO.
TAUNTON, MASS
NICKEL SILVER

(On plated silver)

TRADEMARK
PEWTER *by* POOLE

BRISTOL SILVER CORP.
POOLE STERLING CO.

POPE'S ISLAND MFG. CORPORATION
New Bedford, Massachusetts

Incorporated in 1890 on the island from which it took its name. Horse bits and harness trimming were manufactured at these works. As the company was listed among manufacturers of silverplated wares by the JC 1896 until 1915, some of these trappings must have been plated silver.

PORTER BRITANNIA & PLATE COMPANY
Taunton, Massachusetts

Organized in 1859. E.W. Porter of Reed & Barton, became superintendent of the new company. Their products were similar to those made by Reed & Barton. In business at least until the 1870s.

FRANKLIN PORTER
Danvers, Massachusetts

Franklin Porter's early artistic training was at the Rhode Island School of Design, followed by technical training at Browne and Sharpe in Providence. For many years his artistic inclinations took second place to the need to support a family. All the while though he made brass and copper pieces and occasionally silver when he could afford the raw material. In 1924 when he reached his fifty-fifth birthday he was released from his factory job without a pension. On that date, May 9, 1924, he purchased a copy of Bigelow's *Historic Silver of the Colonies and Its Makers* and joined the ranks of American silversmiths. In his journal, Porter wrote "January 1, 1925. Beginning this date, I began the practice of attaching my mark to every piece of work executed by me on which it is practicable to attach same, together with 'F. Porter' and 'Sterling' in order to

distinguish my work, should any of it survive, in years to come, from that of F. Porter, Pewterer, of Connecticut."

Sterling   F. Porter   ℞

H L P

(HLP Mark of daughter, Helen Porter Philbrick, used on silver pins made in 1926)

E S D P

(ESDP Mark of adopted son, used April 1927-May 1928 on flatware)

J. POSNER & SONS. INC.
New York, New York
Manufacturers of silver goods c. 1960.

THE POTOSI SILVER CO.
Birmingham, England
Levi and Salaman who were electroplaters and silversmiths in 1870, absorbed the Potosi Silver Company in 1878.

It was succeeded by Barker Bros. Silversmiths, Ltd., Unity Works, Birmingham, England between 1915 and 1922.

On October 19, 1886 they registered a U.S. Patent for plated silver on white metal.

The Potosi Silver Company name was probably derived from the Potosi Mine, discovered in 1545 in the area that was later to be named Bolivia.

(White Metal.)

S.C. POWELL
New York, New York
Catalogs of 1900 in existence showing he was in business by then as manufacturer of sterling silver novelties. Out of business before 1909.

PREISNER SILVER COMPANY
Wallingford, Connecticut
Manufacturers of sterling silver articles c. 1935 to the present.

P S CO.

PREMIER CUTLERY INC.
New York, New York
Manufacturers of plated silver cutlery c. 1920.

PREMIER SILVER CO.
Brooklyn, New York
Manufacturers of sterling silverware c. 1920.

PRESTO CIGARETTE CASE CORP.
North Attleboro, Massachusetts
Manufacturers of gold, sterling and plated silver cigarette cases c. 1920-1930.

JOHN PRICE
Newark, New Jersey
Optician and silversmith working c. 1840-60. Manufacturer of gold and silver spectacles, silver spoons, etc. Succeeded by his son, Henry M. Price, c. 1860-62.

PRILL SILVER CO., INC.
New York, New York
Edward Prill, Inc. listed in 1936-37. Prill Silver Co. successors (?) c. 1940-45. Manufacturers of sterling articles to the present.

J.N. PROVENZANO
New York, New York

In business before 1896. Distributors (?) of sterling silverware, gold and platinum seed pearl and gun metal goods.

Not listed after 1904.

(On Knives.)

PROVIDENCE STOCK CO.
Providence, Rhode Island

Listed in JC 1896-1904 in sterling silver section. Subsequent listings are under jewelry and watch attachments, chains, fobs and bracelets. Last record found was 1950.

TRADE Ⓛ MARK.

PRYOR MFG. CO., INC.
Newark, New Jersey

Listed in JC in 1915 in sterling silver section.

Consolidated with B.M. Shanley, Jr., Co. between 1915-22.

ⓂⓅⒸ

PUTNAM & LOW
See Shreve, Crump & Low Co., Inc.

Q

QUAKER SILVER CO., INC.
North Attleboro, Massachusetts
See Gorham Corporation

Makers of sterling and silverplated holloware, trophies, novelties and pewterware. In business in North Attleboro, Massachusetts at least as early as 1926. Purchased by the Gorham Corp. in 1959.

NARRANGANSETT
(Used on pewter)

QUAKER VOGUE

(On silverplate; used since February 1926)

QUAKER VALLEY MFG. CO.
Chicago, Illinois

Trademark used c. 1900 on silverplated articles used in direct sales.

CUVEE

QUEEN CITY SILVER CO., INC.
Cincinnati, Ohio

Manufacturers of plated silver holloware c. 1888. Liquidated in 1949.

COVENANT
(On pewterware)

QUEEN'S ART PEWTER, LTD.
Brooklyn, New York

Founded in 1920 by Anton Theurer and _____ Bower (now deceased). Mr. Theurer was born in Germany and learned the trade of spinning there. He came to this country and started his own business. He is now retired. John Arcate, with the company since 1960, learned the trade from Mr. Theurer and operates the business today.

QUEEN'S ART PEWTER LTD.

R

RACINE SILVER PLATE CO.
Racine, Wisconsin
See Rockford Silver Plate Co.
See Sheets-Rockford Silver Plate Co.

Founded in 1873 in Racine, Wisconsin. Moved to Rockford, Illinois 1882 and renamed Rockford Silver Plate Co.

"The Guild Stamp Design adopted by the Executive Committee of the United States Guild for flatware, will be used by the Racine Silver Plate Co. on triple plated goods, with ten percent extra weight of silver, without any extra cost. These goods will be sold only to members of the United States and State Associations." (American Jeweler, Feb. 1882, p. 44)

"Mr. Purdy of Purdy & Stein is the originator of the stamp." (American Jeweler, Feb. 1882, p. 44)

"The Racine Silver Plate Co. (Wisconsin) was moved to Rockford, Illinois." (American Jeweler, June 1882, p. 133)

RADAR SILVERSMITHS, INC.
Brooklyn, New York

Manufacturers of sterling lamps and lighters c. 1950.

RA

WILLIAM T. RAE
Newark, New Jersey

Silversmith working c. 1856-64. Successor to A.J. Williams.

RAIMOND SILVER MFG. CO.
Chelsea, Massachusetts

Currently advertise as manufacturers and distributors of sterling and silverplated goods.

"Purchased W. & S. Blackinton Co., Inc. of Meriden, Connecticut, including inventory, materials, existing contracts and tradenames.

"Anthony S. Maisto, independent designer and owner of Maisto Silver, Inc., was named general manager.

"Blackinton was established in 1865 in North Attleboro and moved to Meriden after acquisition by the now defunct Ellmore Silver Co., in 1938." When Ellmore's assets were assigned to creditors in 1960, Blackinton was purchased by Alexander Land of Westport, owners of the present site, who subsequently sold it to a corporation headed by Irving R. Stich, prominent Hartford area builder and developer who backed revitalization of Blackinton in 1961." (*Meriden Journal*, April 26, 1966) Among the products advertised by Raimond's are those of Nils-Johan and Viner's of Sheffield. Sold in 1978.

HARRY S. RAINS
New York, New York

Silverplaters c. 1920.

LA MILITAIRE

RAND & CRANE
Boston, Massachusetts

Successors to C.W. Kennard & Co., Boston in 1886. U.S. Patent registration for HOLMES trademark, May 5, 1891 to be used on solid and plated souvenir spoons and forks.

The company was listed in JC 1896-1922, but the HOLMES trademark was not used after 1903.

HOLMES

THE RANDAHL SHOP
Chicago, Illinois

Julius Olaf Randahl was founder of The Randahl Shop, Park Ridge and Chicago, Illinois. Randahl was born December 21, 1880 in Oëland, Sweden, a small island in the Baltic off the coast of Kalmar. He was apprenticed to a silversmith named J.G. Henshall and after he finished his training he came to the United States in 1901. After working for Tiffany and for Gorham, he worked in his KALO SHOP which made only fine handwrought silver. The shop was first located in Park Ridge and later in Chicago, where it remained until 1971. It closed because of the lack of young silversmiths to enter the business.

In 1910, Randahl, who made only holloware, formed a partnership with Matthias Hanck, a jeweler in Park Ridge. This partnership lasted only one year. The mark used during the partnership was JULMAT, a combination of both their first names.

In 1911 Randahl opened his own business, The Randahl Shop. The early trademark was his initials JOR with a silversmith's hammer drawn through them. Around 1915 the business was moved from Park Ridge to Chicago. It was forced to close during World War I because the men had to go into war work. It re-opened in another location in Chicago in 1919 and in 1930 in still another location closer to the downtown stores, namely Marshall Field's and Peacock's, both of which sold a lot of his silver. Sometime in the 1930s the JOR trademark was dropped and the name RANDAHL was used after that. By 1950, both sons were in business with him and they built a factory in Skokie, a suburb just west of Evanston. Randahl's sons, Julius Olaf Randahl, Jr. and E. Scott Randahl, continued the business until 1965 at which time they sold it to Reed & Barton. It is now their RANDAHL division, using the Randahl trademark. The original founder died April 1972.

Randahl Jewelers in Park Ridge and The Cellini Shop in Evanston, Illinois, are owned by the two sons.

RANDAHL

C. RAY RANDALL & CO.

North Attleboro, Massachusetts

Manufacturers of sterling silver, 10k gold and goldfilled bar pins, brooches, necklaces, belt buckles, scarf pins, links and pin sets.

Listed in JC 1915-1922. Last record found was 1935.

STERLING CRR

RANDALL & FAIRCHILD

See Fairchild & Co.

RAY SILVER CO.

Rockford, Illinois

A division of Sheets-Rockford Silver Co.

RAYMOND MANUFACTURING COMPANY

Muncie, Indiana

Silverplaters. Out of business before 1920.

SOLID YUKON SILVER WARRANTED

DAVID REAY, JR.

Baltimore, Maryland

Listed in Baltimore City Directories 1865-1873 as a silverplater.

REDDALL & CO., INC.

Newark, New Jersey

Listed as John W. Reddall & Co. in 1896 *Jewelers' Weekly*.

Listed in JC 1896-1904 in sterling silver section. Out of business before 1909.

REDFIELD & RICE

New York, New York

See Bernard Rice's Sons

James H. Redfield was born in 1828 according to family genealogy. He died in Boston, Massachusetts on June 24, 1894. According to an obituary published at his death, he was born in 1827 in Clinton, Connecticut, went to New York and was connected with several old concerns in the dry goods district, finally entering into business with E.D. Bray under the firm name of Bray & Redfield, platers and dealers in silverplated ware on John St., near Williams. William Bancroft bought the interest of Mr. Bray about 1862 and at the same time James Rice was admitted to partnership under the name of Bancroft,

Redfield & Rice, manufacturers of silver-plated ware, at 177 Broadway. Upon the withdrawal of Mr. Bancroft the firm became Redfield & Rice and shortly after the change of name moved to 4 Maiden Lane. About 1871 Redfield & Rice were incorporated as Redfield & Rice Manufacturing Company. In 1873 they were forced into bankruptcy and soon afterwards Mr. Redfield retired from active work in that line of business.

NEW YORK

c. 1863-1865

c. 1865

1864-1868

1864-1868

1863-1867

c. 1865-1867

Tentative dates have been assigned to the above trademarks based on stylistic changes. Redfield & Rice purchased the majority of their holloware "in the metal" (unplated) from Reed & Barton but also used at least two other suppliers, Ernest Kaufmann of Philadelphia and Wilcox Silver Plate Company, Meriden, Connecticut. The obliterated company name on the lower left, appears to have been Reed & Barton.

1865-187?

c. 1867

after 1867

1865-1871

c. 1869-1871

1868-1870

after 1867

REDLICH & CO.
New York, New York
See Elgin Silversmith Co., Inc.

Organized February 1890 as Ludwig, Redlich & Co. by Adolph Ludwig, who had for nine years been a designer of silver for Geo. W. Shiebler Co. and A. Alec Redlich, who had been for many years in the diamond business. In the latter part of 1895 Adolph Ludwig sold his interest and the company became Redlich & Co. This firm was taken over in 1846 by the Elgin Silversmith Co. The Redlich trademark is still used. Products are sterling silverware, holloware and 14k gold wares.

REED & BARTON
Taunton, Massachusetts

Isaac Babbitt and William W. Crossman, both of Taunton, Massachusetts, formed the partnership of BABBITT & CROSSMAN in 1824 that led to what is now Reed & Barton.

Babbitt had opened a small jewelry store in 1822. The small workshop in the back held his attention more than selling jewelry and repairing watches. Aware of the public's preference for the new britannia ware, he often discussed its properties with his friend, William Porter, who was also a jeweler.

Early in 1824, after much experimenting, Babbitt hit upon the right combination for producing this new alloy.

William Crossman completed his apprenticeship in the jewelers' trade; became dissatisfied with his job in Castleton, Vermont and returned to Taunton.

Babbitt and Crossman decided to pool their resources and experience in a partnership to manufacture britannia ware, though they did not abandon the jewelry store.

They entered this new industry just at the time when mechanization put many establishments, that continued handwrought production, out of business. Because of the uncertainty of their ability to produce and market britannia, they also turned out a great deal of pewter.

Their business prospered so that in 1826 they were able to build a new shop on Fayette Street, equipped with steam power. New machinery was made by Nathaniel Leonard of Taunton. Babbitt was superintendent; William W. Porter, foreman and it is assumed that Crossman managed the jewelry store and sales of the new factory products.

By 1827, with business increasing, more capital was needed so William Allen West bought into the business and a new partnership was formed under the name BABBITT, CROSSMAN & COMPANY. The jewelry store was apparently sold at this time.

On February 18, 1829, Isaac Babbitt sold his interest in the partnership and Zephaniah A. Leonard bought a one-third interest. The new company of CROSSMAN, WEST & LEONARD was formed.

On August 18, 1830 this partnership was dissolved and a joint-stock company, the TAUNTON BRITANNIA MANUFACTURING COMPANY was formed.

On February 16, 1833 the TAUNTON BRITANNIA MANUFACTURING COMPANY was reorganized. When it failed in November 1834, only three people had faith to continue. They were the company agent, Benjamin Pratt; Henry Reed, a spinner and his friend, Charles E. Barton, the solderer.

Barton, brother-in-law of William Crossman, had moved to Taunton from Warren, Rhode Island and started to work in 1827 at the age of 19 as an apprentice.

Henry Good Reed was the son of a family prominent in Taunton for five generations.

Knowledge of britannia manufacturing was their chief asset. To this, Benjamin Pratt contributed his experience in salesmanship. Once again, April 1, 1835, the TAUNTON BRITANNIA MANUFACTURING COMPANY was under new management.

Reed & Barton rented a few of the tools and equipment of the old company while Pratt sold what he could and tried to collect money owed to the company. By the end of 1836, the business had survived and made slight gains. Horatio Leonard transferred to his son, Gustavus, all rights, title and the stock and tools of the business. Soon afterwards an agreement was drawn up that left ownership of the factory itself in the Leonard family and granted to Reed & Barton one-third ownership each in the tools of the company as well as one-third interest in profits. The Taunton Britannia Manufacturing Company remained in legal existence only in the capacity of a landlord. The operating company was known as LEONARD, REED & BARTON and on February 20, 1837 began business under the new name.

The year 1837 was not an auspicious one for a struggling business. More than 600 banks closed their doors. Nine-tenths of the factories of the eastern states were said to have closed. Once again, they managed to survive.

By 1840, Henry Reed and Charles Barton purchased Leonard's interest in the company. Leonard continued to work for the company as salesman-treasurer and the Leonard, Reed & Barton mark was used on some company wares. However, when the company applied for a renewal of their trademark registration, they claimed that the name "REED & BARTON" had been used since August 26, 1840. Possibly both marks were used from 1840 to 1847.

By 1848, Reed & Barton were turning their attention to plated silverware.

The transition from the 1837 Reed & Barton shops to the 1859 factory was gradual, but, inevitable. Specialization emerged through necessity for business growth. New marketing methods were introduced and were extremely successful.

The 1850s, with its demands far exceeding the producing capacities of some large companies, gave rise to a confusing competitive situation. Started by the Meriden Britannia Company, which purchased large quantities of wares from other manufacturers, other companies soon followed. This often placed the manufacturer in the position of competing with his own goods. Goods manufactured by Reed & Barton might be sent to Hartford for a coating of Rogers Bros. silverplate and a Rogers Bros. stamp, and appear in the market in competition with the Reed & Barton plated line.

In the middle 1860s jobbers, and retailers, who operated their own plating shops purchased two-thirds of the factory output. They purchased quantities of wares "in the metal," plated them and sold them with their own trademarks. Practically none of the britannia or plated silver makers could supply a complete line. Reed & Barton bought most of its flatware from Rogers & Brother and the Hartford Manufacturing Company. They produced little of their own flatware except for the hotel trade until the 1860s. Flatware of almost all manufacturers turned up in many different catalogs and with many trademarks. Rogers & Brother, on the other hand, in 1865 was one of Reed & Barton's largest customers for holloware. That is why it is not unusual to find identical pieces of flatware and holloware bearing the trademarks of either company.

The depression of 1866 and 1867 brought about the failure of many jobbing concerns, a large number of whom abandoned plating and confined themselves to wholesale business.

The extension of the market for solid silver services led Reed & Barton into its production in 1889.

On September 13, 1867, Charles Barton died with Henry Reed at his bedside. In 1868 a new partnership, consisting of Henry Reed, Henry Fish and George Babrook who had long been active in marketing, was formed. Each assumed a third interest. The name of the firm continued unchanged. In February, 1888, the company was incorporated.

As early as 1903 Reed & Barton began to reproduce colonial pewter ware which for more than thirty years was popular and a financial success.

Sterling flat and holloware replaced plated ware in more and more homes so that by 1904 sterling had become the largest selling line produced.

HOPEWELL SILVER CO.

(Registered July 29, 1890)

(On sterling silver)

Viking Brand

REED & BARTON
(Nickel Silver Flatware and Holloware.)

GOLDYN-BRONZ
(On plated silver)

REED BARTON
TRADE MARK

(White Metal Holloware.)

Trade Mark

Sterling

TRADE MARK

STERLING

REED & BARTON
(On pewter)

SILVER ARTISTS CO.

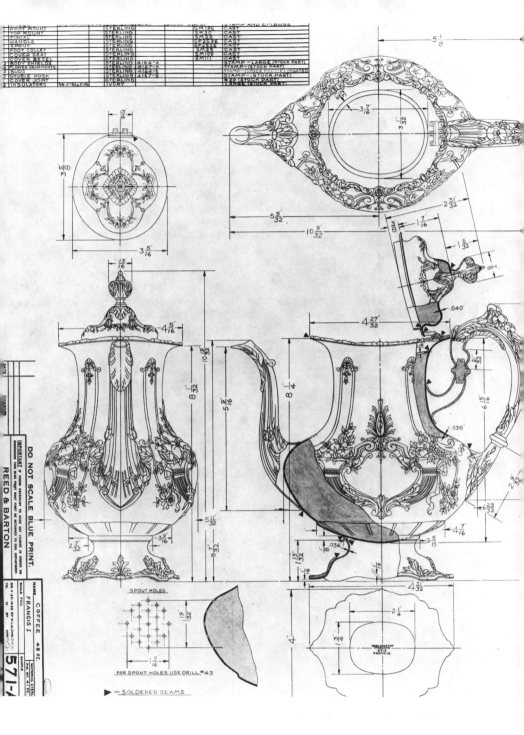

Engineer's working drawing for Reed & Barton's "Francis I" pattern coffee pot. (Photo courtesy of Reed & Barton Silversmiths)

Reed & Barton's "18th Century" pattern sterling flatware. (Photo courtesy of Reed & Barton Silversmiths)

Reed & Barton's hand-chased "Francis I" coffee set in sterling. (Photo courtesy of Reed & Barton Silversmiths)

In 1911 a moderately low-priced line was marketed under the name Reed Silver Company. It passed out of existence in 1913 because the ware did not come up to the standard expected of the Reed & Barton name.

In 1913 the Hopewell Silver Company was formed to marked a high-quality line of small items. They also put out a line of Lenox china with silver and gold deposit. Both lines failed by 1918.

In 1928 Reed & Barton purchased the Dominick & Haff Company of Newark, New Jersey.

In the 1930s the Viking brand of plated holloware was bought out and terminated in 1941 with the revival of a demand for quality wares.

In 1950 the Webster Company became a subsidiary. The newest facility of the Reed & Barton plant is a modern plated holloware department. The new building replaced seven old ones. Great emphasis is placed on the handling of materials. Raw materials come in at one end and with continuous, in-line production, finished products come out at the other. Reed & Barton's first chased designs were produced in 1852. They first made sterling flatware in 1889.

REED & BARTON
YEAR MARKS

1928		1938		1949	
1929		1939		1950	
1930		1940		1951	
1931		1941		1952	
1932		1942		1953	
1933		1943		1954	
1934		1944		1955	
1935		1945		1956	
1936		1946		1957	
1937		1947			
		1948			

From 1928 through 1957 Reed & Barton year-marked all holloware with symbols.

REED, BARTON & COMPANY
Taunton, Massachusetts

Set up in 1886 for electroplating. This short-lived enterprise was managed by Edward Barton, son of Charles Barton, and a Waldo Reed, no relation of Henry Reed, but a son-in-law of Charles Barton. They attempted to capitalize on the reputation of the established Reed & Barton name. Bought out in 1892 by Reed & Barton.

REED SILVER COMPANY
See Reed & Barton

REEVES & BROWNE
Newark, New Jersey
See Jennings & Lauter

REEVES & SILLCOCKS
New York, New York
See Jennings & Lauter

THE REGAL SILVER MFG. CO.
New Haven, Connecticut
See Majestic Silver Co.

(Used 1910 to present)

REGAL SPECIALTY MANUFACTURING COMPANY
See Majestic Silver Company

REIBLING-LEWIS, INC.
Providence, Rhode Island

Manufacturers of sterling holloware and jewelry c. 1950.

GOLDEN WHEEL

OTTO REICHARDT CO.
New York, New York

In Directories from c. 1925 through the 1960s. In 1961 listed at a Brooklyn address. Not listed 1973. Manufacturers of sterling wares.

REICHENBERG-SMITH CO.
Omaha, Nebraska
See A.F. Smith

IMPERIAL SILVER PLATE CO.

RENOMMEE MFG. CO.
Newark, New Jersey

Listed in JC 1896-1904 in sterling silver and jewelry sections.

R. M. CO.

RENTZ BROS.
Minneapolis, Minnesota

Listed in 1896 Jewelers' Weekly as manufacturers of sterling silverware. Also importers of jewelry. Last record found was c. 1935.

REVERE SILVER CO.
Brooklyn, New York
See Crown Silver, Inc.

Successor c. 1960 to Revere Silversmiths, Inc. and now a Division of Crown Silver, Inc., New York. Manufacturers of sterling holloware.

BERNARD RICE'S SONS
New York, New York

CHRONOLOGY

Bray & Redfield	c. 1850-55
Bancroft, Redfield & Rice	1857-71
Redfield & Rice Mfg. Co.	1871-72
Bernard Rice's Sons	1870s-c. 1950

The history of Bernard Rice's Sons can be traced back to Bray & Redfield, established c. 1850-55 by E.D. Bray and James H. Redfield. William Bancroft bought the interest of Mr. Bray about 1857 and at the same time James Rice was admitted to partnership under the name of Bancroft, Redfield & Rice, manufacturers of silverplated ware. On the withdrawal of Bancroft in 1865 the firm name became Redfield & Rice. About 1871 Redfield & Rice was incorporated as Redfield & Rice Mfg. Co.

In 1863 the Hartford Plate Co. was organized by Redfield & Rice in Hartford, Connecticut and operated there until the building was partly destroyed when the foundations gave way in 1865 and the business was moved to Wolcotville. In 1871 the Hartford Plate Co. tools and equipment were sold to the Derby Silver Co.

In 1872 Redfield & Rice went bankrupt. A merger of the Apollo Silver Co., Redfield & Rice and Shepard & Rice formed the company of Bernard Rice's Sons. This took place prior to April 18, 1899 as Patent Office records show the registration of

their trademark to be used on plated silverware, under the company name. The company went out of business before 1959.

DORANTIQUE
(Copper and Brass Novelties.)

L'Aiglon
(On silverplate)

Loraline
"BeauXardt"
"ETCHARDT"
"DUTCHARDT"
(On silverplate)

PATRICIA
(On silverplate)

PEWTER BY RICE

MARION PEWTER

(APOLLO STERLING)
(On sterling)

APOLLO STUDIO
NEW YORK
(On silverplate)

B.R.S. CO.
SHEFFIELD
U. S. A.

JOSEPH T. RICE
Albany, New York
See Mulford & Wendell

Silversmith 1815-1853. John H. Mulford was apprenticed to him.

RICHFIELD PLATE COMPANY
See Homan Manufacturing Company

GEO. S. RICHMOND

A catalog published by L. Boardman & Sons September 1880 says that this is a tradename used on their "second quality Britannia spoons."

RICHTER MFG. CO.
Providence, Rhode Island

Manufacturers and importers of sterling silver deposit ware, novelties, and cut glass c. 1915-1920.

RICKETSON COMPANY
Taunton, Massachusetts

Listed in Directories 1955-61 as manufacturers of silverware.

JOHN H. RILEY
Baltimore, Maryland

Listed in Baltimore City Directories 1876-1883 as a goldsmith and silversmith (gold beater).

GOTTLIEB RITTER
Baltimore, Maryland

Listed in Baltimore City Directories 1895-1899 as a silversmith. Succeeded by Ritter & Sullivan in 1900.

RITTER & SULLIVAN
Baltimore, Maryland

Gottlieb Ritter listed in Baltimore City Directories as a silversmith 1895-1899. Joined by Wyndham A. Sullivan in 1900 in the firm of Ritter & Sullivan which continued in business until 1915.

TRADE ⟨R&S⟩ MARK

CHAS. M. ROBBINS
Attleboro, Massachusetts

What is now The Robbins Company was born during the election year of 1892.

Charles M. Robbins, the company's founder, became so interested in the presidential campaign that he designed and produced campaign buttons for his favorite candidate in his own simple shed workshop. This was the start of a business which now has more than 20 general product lines.

At one time, The Robbins Company's jewelry enameling department was the largest in the world.

Principal products today are emblems, service and safety awards, badges, commemorative materials, medallions, insignia, religious and organization jewelry, advertising specialties, souvenirs, premiums and costume jewelry.

Charles Robbins was joined in 1904 by Ralph Thompson, who acquired ownership of the company in 1910. In 1912, The Robbins Company was formed.

(Used c. 1900-1926)

(Present mark)

(On sterling silver)

(Used before 1900)

(Flatware.)

(On plated silver)

In October, 1961, Robbins acquired a wholly owned Canadian subsidiary, Stephenson, Robbins Company, Ltd., Montreal, Canada.

In July, 1963, The Robbins Company became a wholly owned subsidiary of Continental Communications Corporation of New York. The new owners sold the Canadian subsidiary in 1964. They discontinued the production of plated flatware before 1915.

E.M. ROBERTS & SON
Hartford, Connecticut

"They were manufacturers of silver and silverplated wares, established in East Hartford in 1825. The business failed in 1890 and was reported to be taken by Wm. Rogers Mfg. Co., one of the heaviest creditors." (JW 11-13-1890)

ROBESON CUTLERY CO. INC.
Perry, New York

Manufacturers of silverplated steak knives c. 1950-65.

GOURMET CARVERS
ROBESON "SHUR EDGE"

ROCHESTER STAMPING CO.
Rochester, New York

Silverplaters c. 1920.

ROCKFORD SILVER PLATE CO.
Rockford, Illinois

See Sheets-Rockford Silver Plate Co.

ROCKWELL SILVER COMPANY
Meriden, Connecticut

Organized in 1905 by Lucien Rockwell and James W. Mackay. Prior to his founding of Rockwell Silver, Lucien Rockwell had been a salesman for Chapman Manufacturing Co., which had manufactured saddle hardware and sleigh bells in Meriden.

Rockwell Silver was a manufacturer of sterling silverware, china, glassware and silver deposit ware.

They merged with Silver City Glass Co., in 1978 to form Decorex Industries, Inc. (q.v.)

(For glass candlesticks ornamented with applied silver. Used since August 10, 1914)

RODEN BROS., LTD.
Toronto, Ontario

In business at least as early as 1891 Roden Bros. Listed JC 1904-1922. Became Roden Bros., Ltd. between 1904-1915. Distributors of or jobbers (?) of sterling silverware, plated silver, novelties and cut glass.

JOSEPH RODGERS & SONS
Sheffield, England

Cutlers, silversmiths and electroplaters for more than two centuries. Also manufacturers of silver and plated wares. Their trademark was probably the oldest in continuous use, being granted in 1682. Registered trademark U.S. Patent Office, No. 16,478, April 9, 1889. For the protection of their reputation for high quality, they have acquired the businesses of all cutlery firms in Great Britain bearing the names "Rodgers" or "Rogers." They are today the best known producers of quality cutlery in Sheffield and the oldest in the world.

  RODGERS

(On sterling silver)   (On plated Silver)

ROEDER & KIERSKY
New York, New York

Listed in JC in 1896 in sterling silver section.

R. & K.
STERLING.

ASA ROGERS, JR. & CO.
See Rogers Brothers

Successors to Rogers & Cole on June 4, 1832 when John A. Cole retired from the firm. The business was bought by William Rogers July 28, 1838.

ROGERS & BRITTIN
West Stratford, Connecticut

Trademark registered May 4, 1880 by Rogers & Brittin, West Stratford, Connecticut for britannia, plated silver and solid silverware.

Succeeded by Holmes & Edwards when it was organized in 1882.

(Britannia, Silver Plated and Solid Ware.)

ROGERS & BRO.
Waterbury, Connecticut
See Rogers Brothers

Started as a partnership with Asa and Simeon Rogers, Leroy S. White and David B. Hamilton. Their first goods were stamped (Star) Rogers & Bro. A-1, causing confusion between their stamp and the one used by the Hartford company which was (Star) Rogers Bros. A-1.

Hamilton's eldest son joined the business after the withdrawal of Asa and Simeon Rogers and in 1886 was one of the organizers of Rogers & Hamilton.

What is believed to be the first fancy pattern made in electroplated ware in this country was the *Olive* design, made in the blank, silverplated and finished for marketing from that plant. Earlier, the *Olive* pattern had been sold here, the blanks being imported from England and only the plating being done in this country.

Rogers & Bro. was exclusively a flatware plant for many years, producing German silver blanks for the trade. By 1869 they were also supplying blanks for many other concerns to plate and finish after stamping them with their own trademarks. They are believed to have added holloware to their production about 1874. This was one of the original companies that became part of the International Silver Co. in 1898.

★ ROGERS & BRO., A 1.
(Best Quality Flatware.)

R. & B.
(Second Quality Flatware.)

★ ROGERS & BROTHER,
(H. H. Knives.)

★ ROGERS & BROTHER, 12
(No. 12 Steel Knives.)

★ R & B
(Pearl Knives.)

(Holloware.)

ROGERS & BRO.—GERMAN SILVER
(German Silver Flatware, Unplated.)

MANOR PLATE
(on low priced line)

Silverplated flatware patterns bearing these trademarks discontinued about 1976.

ROGERS BROS.
See Rogers Brothers
In 1847, Asa Rogers, Jr., with his brothers produced and distributed plated silver spoons carrying the ROGERS BROS. trademark.

ROGERS BROTHERS
In 1820 William, the eldest, left the parental farm to become an apprentice to Joseph Church, jeweler and silversmith in Hartford, Connecticut.

In 1825 William became Church's partner in making coin silver spoons stamped, CHURCH & ROGERS. Before 1835, Asa, Jr. and Simeon Rogers were both associated with the firm. William also stamped spoons with his individual (EAGLE) WM. ROGERS (STAR) mark during this time

(1825-1841). His spoons are noted for their symmetrical outline, pleasing proportions and fine finish.

Early in 1830 Asa, Jr. formed a partnership with John A. Cole, in New Britain, ROGERS & COLE, to manufacture coin silver flatware.

When Cole retired on June 4, 1832 the name of the firm was changed to ASA ROGERS JR. & CO. with William Rogers as a partner. In 1834 William left the company and Asa, Jr. continued the business alone, moving to Hartford. William continued his partnership with Church while associated with Asa, Jr. in New Britain. This partnership continued until August 2, 1836 when William moved to his own shop, under the name WILLIAM ROGERS. He was one of the first in this country to advertise and manufacture tableware of sterling silver as it had been the general practice to use coin silver.

On July 23, 1838 William bought the spoon manufactory of Asa, Jr. In 1841 Asa, Jr. advertised that he was once again making spoons.

Simeon learned the trade in William's business and in 1841 was admitted as a partner in the jewelry and silverware store, WM. ROGERS & CO., with the new mark, (EAGLE) WM. ROGERS & CO. (STAR) stamped on their coin silver spoons.

About 1843-1844 Asa, Jr. experimented with electroplating in association with Wm. B. Cowles and James H. Isaacson and on November 13, 1845 the COWLES MFG. CO. in Granby was formed to manufacture German and silverplated spoons, forks, etc. Stockholders were Wm. B. Cowles, Asa Rogers, Jr., Jas. H. Isaacson and John D. Johnson. In 1846 Asa, Jr., William and Isaacson left COWLES MFG. CO. and it went out of business a few years later.

In 1845, William and Asa, Jr. in partnership with J.O. Mead, manufactured electroplated silverware in Hartford as ROGERS & MEAD until 1846.

Early in 1847 Asa, Jr., having returned to Hartford, in cooperation with his brothers, produced and distributed silverplated spoons carrying the ROGERS BROS. trademark. Advertisements of this period read as if WM. ROGERS & CO. (composed of William and Simeon) were the producers.

ROGERS BROS. were unable to handle their increasing volume of business, so in 1853 a new company was organized— ROGERS BROS. MFG. CO. William and Asa, Jr. were large stockholders; William

was president. Simeon did not join the firm except as a stockholder a few months later.

In 1856 William Rogers left ROGERS BROS. MFG. CO. and with George W. Smith, manufacturer of silverplated holloware, organized ROGERS, SMITH & CO. were consolidated with William as president.

In 1862 the MERIDEN BRITANNIA CO. bought the tools and dies of the company. William joined MERIDEN BRITANNIA CO. to direct production of the 1847 ROGERS BROS. line.

In 1865 William became an organizer and partner in the WILLIAM ROGERS MFG. CO. Associated with him was his son, William Rogers, Jr. They manufactured plated silverware. Asa, Jr. and Simeon, still stockholders in ROGERS BROS. MFG. CO., established ROGERS & BROTHER CO. in Waterbury in 1858. It was incorporated the following year.

Asa, Jr., with his nephew, William H. Watrous, in 1871 organized the ROGERS CUTLERY CO. in Hartford. Frank Willson (Wilson) Rogers, brother of William Rogers Jr., was secretary and a director. They manufactured silverplated flatware and became part of INTERNATIONAL SILVER CO. in 1898. William, Asa, Jr. and Simeon were all employed by MERIDEN BRITANNIA CO. when they died.

ROGERS BROS. MFG. CO.
See Rogers Brothers

Organized 1853, by William and Asa Rogers, Jr. Simeon Rogers became a stockholder in a few months. Consolidated with Rogers, Smith & Co., October 1, 1861 because of financial difficulties.

(Used only 1853-61)

C. ROGERS & BROS.
Meriden, Connecticut
See International Silver Co.

Organized February 26, 1866 by Cephas B. Rogers, Gilbert Rogers and Wilbur F. Rogers when they bought the stock in trade of "one Frary," ____probably James A. Frary who had died in December 1865.

Their first products were casket hardware and furniture trimmings. Their use of "C. Rogers & Bros." trademark on silverplated

spoons resulted in court action. They were permitted to use the trademark and continued to do so until the concern was bought by International Silver Co. in 1903. Their products were considered an imitation of the original Rogers brothers and none of their trademarks were ever used by International.

SO. MERIDEN SILVER CO. QUADRUPLE

This tradename was used in a holloware catalog of 1899 with the statement that it is "nicely finished but not standard plate," and "made to supply the demand for a good quality of silver plated ware at moderate prices." This bears out the belief that there was no such thing as a standard quadruple plate.

C. ROGERS & BROS., A 1.

ROGERS & COLE
See Rogers Brothers

Organized in 1830 by Asa Rogers, Jr. and John A. Cole in New Britain to manufacture coin silver flatware. Out of business June 4, 1832.

ROGERS CUTLERY CO.
See Rogers Brothers

Founded in 1871. Consolidated with Wm. Rogers Mfg. Co., Hartford, Connecticut in 1879.

Frank Wilson Rogers, usually known as F. Wilson Rogers, son of William Hazen Rogers and brother of Wm. Henry Rogers (who called himself Wm. Rogers, Jr.) was secretary and a director of Rogers Cutlery Co. and also of Wm. Rogers Mfg. Co. when the two companies consolidated.

One of the original companies to become part of the International Silver Co. in 1898.

R. C. CO. AI PLUS

ROGERS CUTLERY CO.

ROGERS ⬡CO

F.B. ROGERS SILVER CO.
Taunton, Massachusetts

Founded 1883 in Shelburne Falls, Massachusetts. Moved to Taunton in 1886, at which time it was incorporated. Successors

to West Silver Co. before 1896. Still in business.

Became a division of National Silver Co. in February 1955. Sold to J.C. Boardman in 1985.

F.B. ROGERS SILVER CO
TAUNTON, MASS
QUADRUPLE

SHEFFIELD
SILVER METAL
F. B. R.

SHEFFIELD
SILVER ON COPPER
F. B. R.

FRANK W. ROGERS
Hartford, Connecticut

Trademark registered in U.S. Patent Office Dec. 7, 1875 for metal and plated ware, to Frank W. Rogers, Hartford, Connecticut. No record in International Silver Co. that Rogers used this mark.

 WM. ROGERS' SON

(Metal and Plated Ware.)

ROGERS & HAMILTON CO.
Waterbury, Connecticut
See International Silver Co.

Rogers & Hamilton Co. was incorporated February 14, 1886 and produced silverplated flatware, taking over the spoon business of Holmes, Booth & Hayden and occupying their building for eight or ten years. President and a stockholder was Charles Alfred Hamilton, who had traveled for Rogers & Brother, Waterbury, for some time. William H. Rogers was made secretary and was a stockholder. Undoubtedly asked to join the company for the use of his name as he was not a silversmith, but was a cigar dealer in Hartford.

One of the original companies to become part of International Silver Co. in 1898.

ROGERS & HAMILTON.

ROGERS & HAMILTON
(on regular grade)

 ROGERS & HAMILTON, A 1."

HAMILTON.
(on finest grade)

HENRY ROGERS, SONS & CO.
Montreal, P.Q.

Listed in JC in 1909 in plated silver section. No record after c. 1915.

TRADE MARK
H.R.S.&C?

H.O. ROGERS SILVER CO.
Taunton, (Massachusetts?)

Stamped on a soft metal four-piece tea set, two pieces have the Rogers name while the other two are marked Newburyport Silver Co., Taunton.

H. O. ROGERS SILVER CO.
Taunton

J. ROGERS SILVER CO., INC.
See Oneida Silversmiths

ROGERS, LUNT & BOWLEN CO.
Greenfield, Massachusetts
See Lunt Silversmiths

The Pythagorean symbol R L & B Co. was the original Rogers, Lunt & Bowlen Co. registered trademark. Later, they registered the trademark "Treasure" and used it from 1921 to 1954. This has now been abandoned and only the registered LUNT is used. "Little Men and Little Women" was used solely for sterling silver baby goods. "Wee Folks" was used on some pieces of silverplated babyware.

TRADE MARK STERLING

"Treasure" Solid Silver
Little Men and Little Women

ROGERS & MEAD

See Rogers Brothers

In 1845, William and Asa Rogers, Jr. in partnership with J.O. Mead, manufactured electroplated silverware in Hartford under the name Rogers & Mead. This partnership was dissolved in 1846.

ROGERS PARK SILVERWARE CO.

Chicago, Illinois

"The Rogers Park Silverware Co. of Chicago have been closed on chattel mortgages given to the Silver Metal Mfg. Co., Oswego, N.Y." (JC&HR 12-4-1895, p. 26)

ROGERS SILVER PLATE CO.

Danbury, Connecticut

Listed in JC from 1896 through 1922. Founded by Nathaniel Burton Rogers in association with his brothers Cephas B. and Gilbert H. Rogers, who, with another brother, Wilbur F., were principals in the firm of C. Rogers & Bros. of Meriden, Connecticut which later became a part of the International Silver Co.

Rogers Silver Plate Company manufactured silverplated novelties—candlesticks, book ends, pincushions, etc. After the death of the founder, the assets of the company were purchased by Cephas B. (II), who was a manufacturer of electric lighting fixtures and lamps. He continued the manufacture of novelties under his own name until his retirement in the early 1950s.

SIMEON L. & GEO. H. ROGERS CO.

Hartford, Connecticut

See Oneida Silversmiths

In business 1900. Acquired by Wm. A. Rogers Limited in 1918. Purchased by Oneida in 1929.

ACORN

SIMEON L. & GEO. H. ROGERS CO.
☒ S. L. & G. H. ROGERS CO.
S. L. & G. H. R. CO.
☒ ROGERS ☒

ROGERS, SMITH & CO.

See Rogers Brothers

Organized January 1, 1857 by William Rogers, Sr. and George W. Smith. They consolidated October 1, 1861 with Rogers Bros. Mfg. Co. because of financial difficulties.

August 12, 1862, the flatware division was sold to the Meriden Britannia Company and the Rogers brothers went to work for them.

Edward Mitchell, formerly with Rogers, Smith & Co. bought the holloware division and on November 6, 1862 organized the Rogers, Smith Co. of New Haven for the manufacture of holloware.

On January 13, 1863, the Meriden Britannia Company bought the holloware division of the Rogers, Smith & Co. of New Haven. The business continued in New Haven.

In June 1865 the plating shop of the Rogers, Smith & Co. of New Haven was moved to Meriden and consolidated with that of the Meriden Britannia Co. on January 1, 1866.

On May 22, 1876, the Meriden Britannia Co. directors voted to bring the business of Rogers, Smith & Co. to Meriden on January 1, 1877.

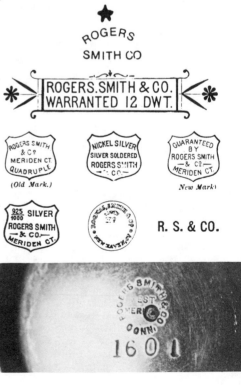

1870's

1870's

1880's

There is merchandise in existence with trademarks bearing the names of Hartford, used from 1857 to 1862; New Haven, 1862 to 1877; West Meriden from 1877 until the early 1880s (when the term West Meriden went out of general use, and Meriden, which was used from that time until about 1918). The Rogers, Smith & Co. as a separate firm was almost non-existent when the International Silver Co. was formed in 1898. It was then simply a trademark that belonged to the Meriden Britannia Co. "Geo. B. White, manager of Rogers, Smith & Co., had been with Young, Smith & Co. which firm had furnished the Rogers brothers with the first imported spoon on which plating had been done." (JC&HR 10-3-1894, p. 18) Rogers, Smith & Co. were in Hartford 1857-62; in New Haven 1862-77 and in Meriden 1877-98.

ROGERS & SPURR MFG. CO.
Greenfield, Massachusetts

On the 14th of February, 1879 David C. Rogers and Geo. E. Rogers of Greenfield, Massachusetts made application to the Patent Office for the registry of the trademark shown here to be used by them in the manufacture of table cutlery, forks, etc. Geo. W. Spurr was listed as president and L.C. Pratt as treasurer. They were successors to George W. Spurr & Co. who started in business c. 1873.

WILLIAM ROGERS
See Roger Brothers

W ROGERS

(On coin silver)

WM. A. ROGERS, LTD.
See Oneida Silversmiths

Wm. A. Rogers as a small storekeeper in New York began to stamp the name Rogers on tinned spoons he sold when he found that they sold better with the name Rogers on them. He soon changed to German silver spoons and lightly silverplated. He was permitted to use Wm. A. Rogers on his goods if the pieces carried the same amount of silver as the well-known Rogers Bros. standard. They succeeded the Niagara Silver Co. before 1904. And, by 1918 took over the business of Simeon L. & Geo. H. Rogers Co. which had started in Hartford, Conn. in 1900. Were succeeded by Oneida Silversmiths in 1929.

According to Oneida records, Wm. A. Rogers, Ltd. was an Ontario corporation with offices in New York City and factories in Niagara Falls, New York and North Hampton, Massachusetts. The company began making plated silverware in 1894.

The (R) Rogers (R) trademark was first used about 1901. The Warren Silver Plate Co. trademark first used in 1901 was apparently derived from the fact that the New York office was at 12 Warren St.

The 1881 (R) Rogers (R) trademark was first used by Wm. A. Rogers, Ltd. c. 1910.

The Niagara Silver Co. and 1877 N. F. Silver Co. are discontinued trademarks which Oneida acquired through the purchase of Wm. A. Rogers, Ltd.

Wm. A. Rogers ® R
(*12 Dwt. Knives and Forks.*)

WM. A. ROGERS A.1. ®

® ROGERS ®
(*12 Dwt. Knives and Forks.*)

® ROGERS 1881 ®
(Popular grade)

NIAGARA SILVER CO.
R. S. MFG. CO.
BUSTER BROWN

R. S. MFG. CO.

(Highest Grade Hollowware.)

WM A ROGERS Special 16 Dwt.

(*Special Knives and Forks Plated with 16 Dwt. Silver.*)

OXFORD CUTLERY CO. WARRANTED NO. 12.

(*Light Plate Knives and Forks.*)

WARREN SILVER QUADRUPLE PLATE COMPANY NEW YORK
(*Medium Grade Hollowware.*)

EAGLE CUTLERY CO. CRESCENT PLATE
(Cheaper grade)

1877 N.F. Co.

OXFORD SILVER PLATE CO.
(Cheaper grade)

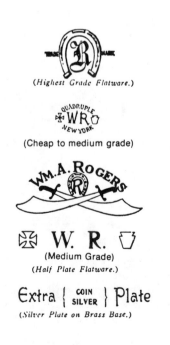

(*Highest Grade Flatware.*)

WRO
(Cheap to medium grade)

WM. A. ROGERS

W. R.
(Medium Grade)
(*Half Plate Flatware.*)

Extra { COIN SILVER } Plate
(*Silver Plate on Brass Base.*)

WILLIAM ROGERS & CO.
See Roger Brothers

Organized in 1841 by William Rogers with his brother, Simeon Rogers who had been apprenticed to him. They used the mark (Eagle) Wm. Rogers & Co. (Star) on their coin silver spoons.

WILLIAM ROGERS, JR.
(William Henry Rogers)

See Rogers Brothers
See Simpson, Hall, Miller & Co.

The original William Hazen Rogers had two sons, William Henry Rogers, and Frank Willson (sometimes spelled Wilson) Rogers. William Henry changed his name to William Rogers, Jr. in order to be more closely associated with his father's well-known name.

In 1868, Wm. Rogers, Jr., together with his father, made a contract with the Meriden Britannia Company for 10 years. Upon the death of his father, in 1873, the contract

was to continue with the son until the expiration—which was in March of 1878. Wm. Rogers, Jr. was not successful in renewing the contract with the Meriden Britannia Co., but in that year he did make a 15-year contract with Simpson, Hall, Miller & Co. to superintend their flatware manufacturing and with his permission to use on the silverplated flatware the trademark (Eagle, WM. ROGERS (Star). The contract with Simpson, Hall, Miller & Co. terminated in 1893 and Wm. Rogers, Jr. died in 1896.

The trademark is a very active one today on moderately priced flatware.

✴ Wm Rogers ★

The above trademark went out of use for flatware in 1976. On silverplated holloware it was first used in 1938 and was also discontinued in 1976.

WILLIAM ROGERS MFG. CO.
Hartford, Connecticut
See Rogers Brothers

Organized in 1865 by William Rogers and his son, Wm. Rogers, Jr. (William Henry Rogers), with Thomas Birch, William J. Pierce and William H. Watrous as members. They were one of the original companies to form the International Silver Company in 1898.

1846 ⚓ ROGERS ⚓ AA

⚓ ROGERS ⚓
**1865. WM. ROGERS M'F'G. CO.
WM. ROGERS & SON.**

**R. C. CO.
ROGERS NICKEL SILVER
ROGERS CUTLERY CO.**

⚓ W. R. & S.   **R. C. CO.**

J S Q

(Jeweler's special quality, used with Anchor Rogers Anchor Warranted)

CUNNINGHAM SILVER PLATE

(On premium flatware made for Ocean Spray Cranberry Sauce)

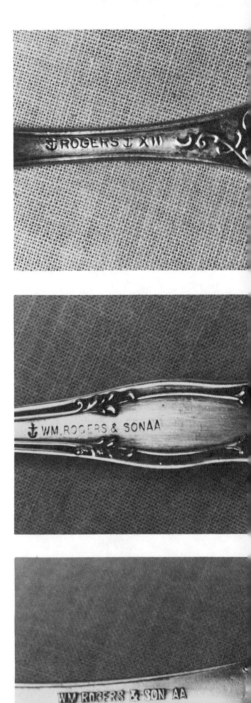

WM. ROGERS MFG. CO., LTD.
Niagara Falls, Ontario

Bought by Wm. Rogers Mfg. Co. (Division of International Silver Co., Meriden, Connecticut in 1905.)

WM. G. ROGERS
Trademark registered U.S. Patent No. 36,147, January 1, 1901 for silverware; knives, forks and spoons.

Listed 1904-1915 in JC plated silver section.

(*Flatware.*)

WILLIAM H. ROGERS
Hartford, Connecticut

Trademark registered U.S. Patent Office, No. 16,007. November 13, 1888 for silver and plated silverware. Out of business before 1915.

ROGERS. A1.

(*Silver and Silver Plated Ware.*)

WILLIAM H. ROGERS CORPORATION
Plainfield, New Jersey

Listed in September 1901 KJI and 1904 JC in plated silver sections. No record in U.S. Patent Office.

ROGERS, WENDT & WILKINSON
New York, New York

A short-lived firm organized January 1860 to make silverware for Ball, Black & Co. Wendt was John R. Wendt, New York silversmith (q.v.) Wilkinson, designer and superintendent of the Gorham Mfg. Co. The partnership was not of long duration, for in August it was dissolved, and Wilkinson returned to the Gorham Co. in Providence, Rhode Island.

HENRY J. ROHRBACH
Chicago, Illinois

"Silversmith and Manufacturing Jeweler." (Adv. JC&HR 9-27-1893, p. 28)

ROMAN SILVERSMITHS, INC.
Brooklyn, New York

Manufacturers of silverplated goods c. 1950.

LIFETIME

ROSE SILVER CO.
New York, New York

Listed 1922 through 1931 KJI as manufacturers of plated holloware.

J.W. ROSENBAUM & CO.
Newark, New Jersey

Listed JC in 1909-1915 in plated silver section. Out of business before 1922.

FRANCIS ROSENDORN
Baltimore, Maryland

Listed in Baltimore City Directories 1864-1869, 1883-1886 as a silverplater.

ROSENTHAL U.S.A. LTD.
New York, New York

The Rosenthal company was founded in 1879 by Privy Councilor Dr. Philip Rosenthal, the third generation of Westphalian potters and china traders. Rosenthal silver flatware was designed to coordinate with existing Rosenthal chinaware and glassware. The first line of flatware was Bjorn Wiinblad's *Romance* in sterling silver. To coordinate with Tapio Wirkkla's *Variation* pattern, two men, Richard Gump, famous San Francisco retailer, and Karl Gustav Hansen, Danish silversmith, worked together to produce flatware with fluted porcelain handles and contemporary sterling cutting and serving ends. To design a flatware in keeping with its *Classic Modern* designed by Raymond Loewy, Richard Latham of Chicago sculpted in high-gloss silverplate a set of tableware cutlery which is also available in matte finish.

ROSLYN SILVER CORP.
Taunton, Massachusetts

Manufacturers of silverplated wares c. 1950.

CHARLES ROUSH
Baltimore, Maryland

Listed in 1891 Baltimore City Directory under plated silverware.

ROWAN & WILCOX
See Wilcox & Evertsen

ROWLEY MFG. CO.
Philadelphia, Pennsylvania

Listed in JC in 1909 in plated silver section. Out of business before 1915.

LUNA METAL

(Seamless Nickel Silver Hollow Ware.)

ROYAL METAL MFG. CO.
New York, New York

Listed in JC in 1909 in plated silver section. Out of business before 1915.

ROYAL SILVER MANUFACTURING CO.
Newark, New Jersey

Listed in KJI 1918-19 as silversmiths. In 1922 JKD as manufacturers of silver novelties and 1931 issue as makers of ladies' handbag frames.

ROYAL SILVERWARE CO.
Detroit, Michigan

"Rev. Robert J. Service, pastor, Turnbull Avenue Presbyterian Church, resigned to become manager of the business owned by Sherman R. Miller (Royal Silverware Co.) Service replaced by Aubrey W. Knowles, who resigned." (Clipping from unidentified newspaper, dated 1899)

A guarantee of quality certificate by the Royal Manufacturing Co., Detroit, Michigan dated November 28, 1900 states: "We, The Royal Manufacturing Co. of Detroit, Mich. do hereby assert and affirm as follows. Our knives are triple plate, 12 dwt. as marked and hand burnished. All hollow ware such as casters, butter dishes, etc., are triple plate, on a white metal base as marked. All plated goods are guaranteed to wear and to give perfect satisfaction to the purchaser for ten years or money refunded.

"All Brazil Silver goods are guaranteed to be the same metal all the way through as shown on the surface and to wear and to give perfect satisfaction to the purchaser for twenty-five years or money refunded. In case any of the goods should fail to prove as represented or should, in any way fail to give perfect satisfaction, we hereby agree to refund all money paid or to replace with new goods as may be desired."

Signed Royal Manufacturing Co.

ROY RUBENS SILVERSMITH
Beverly Hills, California

Listed 1961 JBG as silver manufacturers.

ANTON RUBESCH
Alexandria, Virginia

Anton Rubesch was trained in Budapest. Moved to London in 1956 and later to the United States. His son, Alex Rubesch, joined him in 1968 and uses the mark of "A R" within a shield begun by his father.

While both are trained and skilled silversmiths, a large part of their present business is in repairs.

RUEFF BROS.
New York, New York

Listed in 1922 KJI as manufacturers of silverplated holloware.

C.F. RUMPP & SONS
Philadelphia, Pennsylvania

Carl Frederich Rumpp, born in Nuertingen, Germany, arrived in this country in 1848 at the age of 20. He brought with him little else but an appreciation of this country and its opportunities, the tools of his trade and a determination to make the best leather goods his thorough apprenticeship had taught him.

Only 25 years after its founding in 1850, the fame of the company had spread through the country and is still considered the standard by which leather goods are judged. Many desk sets, belts, writing cases and travel cases they manufacture are fitted with sterling silver mountings.

RUSSELL HARRINGTON CUTLERY CO.
Southbridge, Massachusetts

The present Russell Harrington Cutlery Company was formed in 1932 through the merger of the Harrington Cutlery Co. and the John Russell Co.

Founded in 1834 by John Russell, descendant of an old New England pioneer family, it was first known as J. Russell & Company Green River Works.

The company became well known for an expression used on the American frontier in the two decades preceding the Gold Rush to California in 1849. This expression, "Up to the Green River," had two

meanings—one referred to quality when traders boasted that their goods were "Up to Green River" knives; the other was used when hand-to-hand combat settled personal differences and onlookers shouted, "Give it to him—up to the Green River"—the trademark found near the hilt. (This is the Bowie knife of Texas fame.)

John Russell retired from the firm in 1868, at which time it was incorporated under the name John Russell Mfg. Co. in 1873, it was reorganized and the name was changed to John Russell Cutlery Co. Under this name, in 1881, then located in Turners Falls, they registered a patent for making plated silver knives.

John Russell was the son of the silversmith, also named John Russell, who served his apprenticeship under Isaac Parker. The Parker-Russell Silver Shop in Old Deerfield, Massachusetts, is a tribute to Isaac Parker and the first John Russell. Through Parker and his apprentice, American silver craftsmanship can be traced by way of Russell & Ripply, J. Russell Cutlery, Towle & Sons and Rogers, Lunt & Bowlen to Lunt Silversmiths.

(Used 1881)

J. RUSSELL & CO.
GREEN RIVER WORKS

1834 J. RUSSELL & CO.

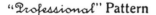 "*Professional*" Pattern

 S   —1

SAART BROS. COMPANY
Attleboro, Massachusetts
   Successors to W.M. Saart Co.
   Founded by William H. Saart, with his brothers, Albert and Herman. Probably in existence for some time prior to its incorporation in 1906. Frank E. Nolan became principal stockholder in 1937. The business

is now conducted by R.J. Nolan, president. Makers of sterling and plated silver holloware, dresserware, cigarette and vanity cases and novelties.

W.H. SAART CO.
Attleboro, Massachusetts
See Saart Bros. Co.

SABEN GLASS CO.
New York, New York
   Registered trademark for sterling coasters, holloware, handles for table knives, carving knives, forks, salad forks, silver bands for glass coasters, drinking glasses and water pitchers. Used since Oct. 16, 1949.

SACKETT & CO., LTD.
Philadelphia, Pennsylvania
   Successors to Mead & Robbins in 1893 as manufacturers of sterling silver. Out of business before 1904.

F.H. SADLER CO., INC.
Attleboro, Massachusetts
   Manufacturers of vanities and compacts c. 1930.

G.T. SADTLER & SONS
Baltimore, Maryland
   Philip Sadtler arrived in this country in 1799 and first opened a shop in Baltimore in 1800. For two years he was in partnership with John William Pfaltz. In 1803 he opened his own shop where he carried a full line of optical goods. While there is some question as to whether he was a

working silversmith, there is a large quantity of silver bearing his initials P S or his full name. The sons and grandsons continued the business until 1923.

"Philip B. Sadtler, founder of the firm, was born in North Germany. He was a painstaking watchmaker and goldsmith, having obtained his training under the apprenticeship days in the finest horological workshops of Europe. On reaching Baltimore, where he came to seek his fortune in the New World, he renounced his German citizenship and embraced the political and civic faith of America. A man of military training he deeply loved his adopted country, and in 1814 when this city was in danger of capture at the hands of the British, and during the same period of time that Francis Scott Key wrote the immortal song of the nation, Sadtler left his shop, organized and drilled the Baltimore Yeagers. He was made captain of the company which participated in the defense of the city when the British, under General Ross, made their fruitless attack.

"Captain Sadtler died in 1860, and the business which was conducted on Baltimore St., near Charles St., was continued by his son, George T. Sadtler. After the death of George T. Sadtler, in 1888, his sons, George W. and C. Herbert Sadtler, formed the firm of George T. Sadtler & Sons. C. Herbert Sadtler died in 1899 and the business was continued by George W. Sadtler and Fernando Volkmar. George W. Sadtler died two years ago, and Mr. Volkmar became head of the firm at that time." (JC-W 2-5-1919, p. 318)

ST. LOUIS METALCRAFTS, INC.,
St. Louis, Missouri

Manufacturers of sterling and silverplate c. 1950.

(On sterling)   (On silverplate)

ST. LOUIS SILVER CO.
St. Louis, Missouri

First appeared in the 1893 St. Louis City Directory as The St. Louis Silver Plate Company at 207 Chestnut Street and in 1904 as the St. Louis Silver Company at 118 Chestnut. No listing after 1912.

SALOSICO WARE

SALES STIMULATORS, INC.
Chicago, Illinois

Registered trademarks for silverplated flatware.

(Claims use since Mar. 5, 1936, on the design; and since Sept. 1, 1948, on the mark in its entirety.)

Queen Esther

(Claims use since Sept. 1, 1948)

SANBORN HERMANOS, S.A.
Mexico, D.F. Mexico

Registered trademark for silverware, including holloware and flatware, made in whole or, in part of, and plated with silver, and ornamental jewelry made of silver.

(Used since Mar. 3, 1931)

SANCRAFT INDUSTRIES
Bronx, New York

Currently doing business in sterling and enameled spoons. Spoons made to order.

SANDLAND, CAPRON & CO.
North Attleboro, Massachusetts

Listed in JC in 1896-1904 in the sterling silver section. Out of business before 1909.

S. C. & Co.
STERLING

J.D. SANFORD & CO.
Granby, Connecticut

Joseph D. Sanford and Lorenzo Peck were in business before 1848 plating and marketing spoons. The business was dissolved c. 1857-58 and Sanford continued at Tariffville. He had some business association with the Cowles Mfg. Co.

PHILIP SAUTER
Baltimore, Maryland

Listed in Baltimore City Directories 1855-1871 as silverplater, manufacturer and dealer in door plates, bell pulls, railing knobs, silver and brass letters and numbers, coffin handles, trimmings, German silver, sheet brass and wire.

P. SAUTER & BRO.
Baltimore, Maryland

Listed in 1864 Baltimore City Directory as silverplaters.

WILLIAM SAUTER
Baltimore, Maryland

Listed in Baltimore City Directories 1865-1886 as silverplaters. Beginning in 1871, coffin trimmings are given special mention.

FREDERICK A. SAWKINS
Baltimore, Maryland

Listed in Baltimore City Directories 1864-1896 as a silverplater.

H.I. SAWYER
See W.L. & H.E. Pitkin

WILLIAM H. SAXTON, JR.
New London, Connecticut

William H. Saxton is listed in the City Directory of New London in 1891 as Collector for port of New London and dealer in watches, clocks and fine jewelry. William H. Saxton, Jr. is listed as watchmaker.

This trademark, No. 20,327 is registered in the name of William H. Saxton, Jr., November 3, 1891, for the manufacture of gold, silver and plated flatware and tableware. The type of trademark would indicate souvenir flatware. Listed 1896 in JC.

MURRAY L. SCHACTER & CO.
New York, New York

Manufacturers (?) of sterling wares c. 1950.

 HAMPSHIRE HOUSE

HARVEY M. SCHADE
Brooklyn, New York

The factory of Henry Schade was established in 1873. The earliest listing found was the 1887 City Directory. Listed 1898-1904 in JC as Schade & Co: and variously as Harry M. Schade and Harvey M. Schade as successor before 1915 and out of business before 1922. In the JW 1890 the name is given as Henry Schade. The Brooklyn

Plate Co. trademark was derived from the company of that name they succeeded before 1904.

BROOKLYN PLATE CO.

SCHAEZLEIN & BURRIDGE
San Francisco, California

Mark found on King Kamehameha Akahi Dala spoon. They were primarily platers and did repair work. Advertised special order work and badges and insignia. The firm no longer exists but descendants in a related business still advertise special order work.

Schaezlein & Burridge was started by Robert Schaezlein who moved to San Francisco in 1879 (d. c. 1932). The business was continued by his son, Robert Frederick (d. 1960) and now by Robert Frederick, Jr. The present Mr. Schaezlein makes everything he sells, mostly silver buckles with gold appliques of initials for Western outfits and special orders. Also, he produces silver (and gold with gold applique) conchos, etc., for belts and saddles. He still has the screw press his father and grandfather saved from the 1906 earthquake and fire and with which they set up shop right after the fire.

S. & B. S. F. CAL.

SCHARLING & CO.
Newark, New Jersey

John H. Scharling first established his business in 1885; incorporated in 1895. The company manufactured sterling, silverplated and pewter holloware and picture frames, novelties, antique gold and plated filigree frames and silver deposit ware.

He first registered a process for producing raised metallic designs (silver deposit) on glassware March 7, 1893; he registered a second on September 26, 1893. The last listing found for the company was 1931.

(On sterling silver, holloware, picture frames and novelties)

(On sterling silver and nickel silver match cases)

SCHARLING SILVER PLATE

(On silverplated holloware.)

(On pewterware)

NIC. SCHELNIN CO.
New York, New York

Listed in JC in 1904 in the sterling silver and jewelry sections. Out of business before 1909.

WM. A. SCHENCK & COMPANY
Newark, New Jersey

Manufacturers of sterling silver and silverplated novelties. Among their products were souvenir spoons with enameling both opaque and transparent, enamel filigree, silver mounted tortoise, pearl and ivory. In *Newark, New Jersey Illustrated*, published in 1893, the Schenck company is **WILLIAM SCHIMPER & CO.**
Hoboken, New Jersey

Successors (?) to William Schimper, listed as a silversmith in New York in 1841. William Schimper & Co. was listed in JC 1896-1927 as manufacturers of dresserware, bonbon baskets, picture frames, match safes, calendars and hair brushes in sterling and plated silver.

JOHN SCHIMPF & SONS
New York, New York
See Adelphi Silver Plate Co.

Made sterling silverware c. 1890-97. Later made silver and gold plated wares as Adelphi Silver Plate Co.

JEROME N. SCHIRM
Baltimore, Maryland

Listed in 1901 Baltimore City Directory as a silversmith.

E. SCHMIDT & CO.
Philadelphia, Pennsylvania

Listed JKD 1918-19 as silversmiths.

SCHMITZ, MOORE & CO.
Newark, New Jersey

Manufacturers of sterling silver dresserware. Listed in JC in 1915. Succeeded by Moore & Hofman between 1915-1922.

SCHOFIELD CO., INC.
Baltimore, Maryland
See Baltimore Silversmiths Mfg. Co.
See Jenkins & Jenkins
See C. Klank & Sons

Founded in 1903 by Frank M. Schofield as the Baltimore Silversmiths Mfg. Co.

Schofield was from a family of silversmiths and worked as a die-cutter. He is said to have cut the dies for the "Baltimore Rose" for The Steiff Company.

Heer-Schofield Co. was the company name from about 1905-1928 when it was changed to Frank M. Schofield Co.

Around 1930 it was changed to Schofield Co. and incorporated a few years later.

Manufacturers of sterling silver flatware and holloware, Schofield Co., Inc. Operated 1948-65 by Berthe M. Schofield, late widow of the founder.

Their trademark has been unchanged except that the letter B in the diamond was changed to an H when the company name was changed to Heer-Schofield.

In 1905 they bought out C. Klank & Sons which continued to be listed under its own name through 1911. Shortly after 1915 they also purchased the tools and dies of Jenkins & Jenkins and also the Farreals Co. Schofield's purchased by Oscar Caplan & Sons in 1965.

Schofield Co. bought by the Stieff Co. in 1967.

MILTON J. SCHREIBER
New York, New York

Registered trademark for use on holloware made in part of, or plated with, precious metal. Used since April 28, 1949.

STERLON

A.B. SCHREUDER
Syracuse, New York
See Syracuse Silver Mfg. Co.

Andrew B. Schreuder was born in Norway, 1828. Listed in Utica, New York City Directories in 1852-1853 as a silversmith and later joined the firm of Hotchkiss & Schreuder in Syracuse. The exact date of the founding of the A.B. Schreuder Company not located.

Succeeded by Syracuse Silver Mfg. Co. in 1895.

H. & S.

SCHRIER & PROTZE
Baltimore, Maryland
Listed in 1888 Baltimore City Directory as silverplaters. Firm name changed to Novelty Plating Works in 1890.

A.G. SCHULTZ & CO.
Baltimore, Maryland
Listed in Baltimore City Directories 1899-1950 as manufacturers of sterling silver holloware.

Successors to Schultz & Tschudy & Co., first listed in 1898. Andrew G. Schultz and Otto Rosenbauer were listed as members of the firm. From 1902-1905, James L. McPhail was also listed as a member of the firm and was listed at C. Klank & Sons during those same years.

(Hollow Ware.)

SCHULTZ, TSCHUDY & CO.
Baltimore, Maryland
Listed in 1898 Baltimore City Directory as silversmiths. Succeeded by A.G. Schultz & Co. in 1899.

SCHULTZ & FISCHER
San Francisco, California

CHRONOLOGY

Fischer & Schulz	1868
Schulz, Fischer & Mohrig	1869
Schulz & Fischer	1874
Schulz, Fischer & McCartney	1883
Schulz & McCartney	1888-1893

William Schulz and Emil A. Fischer were silversmiths with F.R. Reichel in San Francisco, California c. 1857-c. 1867.

Christof Ferdinand Mohrig had been a manufacturing jeweler in San Francisco from c. 1860. After he left Schulz & Fischer he continued to work at their factory address. In 1876 he worked under the name Centennial Mill & Jewelry Manufactory.

Samuel McCartney had been a distiller's agent, an activity he continued after leaving the firm.

The firm of William Schulz and Emil A. Fischer (1868-1886) was one of four early manufacturers of silver flatware in San Francisco. Both men had been employed by Frederick R. Reichel in his San Francisco factory. Like their employer, they were natives of Germany. They were soon joined by Christopher F. Mohrig also from Germany. From 1869 to c. 1873 or 1874 the firm name was Schulz, Fischer & Mohrig. Mohrig was a die maker and may have made the dies for earlier Schulz & Fischer patterns.

In *Commerce and Industries of the Pacific Coast* (San Francisco, 1882) John Hittell described the firm as "the heaviest producers of silverware in the city." Of the approximately fifty coin and sterling silver flatware patterns issued by San Francisco manufacturers before 1900, Schulz & Fischer produced at least seventeen. Patterns identified as theirs include: *Thread, Eureka, Medallion, Pacific, Gem, Olympic, Faralone, Cleopatra, Antique, Occidental, Grecian, Crescent, Oriental, Granny's, Antique Wheat Engraved, Five Star* and *Rococo*. Only *Antique Wheat Engraved* has been found to bear the Schulz & McCartney mark, successor firm (c. 1883-1888) to Schulz & Fischer. Much of their silver is completely unmarked, bearing no maker's name nor COIN or STERLING marks.

Their products included spoons, forks and table silverware as well as presentation pieces. One of their epergnes was 27 inches high—the largest piece of its kind made on the Pacific Coast.

They were also importers and dealers in plated silverware and fine table cutlery.

Berry bowls, cake stands and baskets, dinner castors, goblets, fruit stands, tea kettles, preserve dishes, butter dishes, tea sets, waiters, vegetable dishes, pap feeders, mustard pots, salt dishes and stands, card receivers and pickle dishes were among the great variety of silver holloware offered by Schulz & Fischer. Their offerings were so numerous that one can attribute the following comment only to "eastern establishment" envy. "Wm. Schulz, 230 Kearny St., San Francisco, California, is recorded as a

manufacturing silversmith and probably has a shop on a small scale." (JC&HR 9-8-1897, p. 20)

After the business closed Shreve & Co., San Francisco, acquired part of the Schulz & Fischer flatware dies.

The Schulz & Fischer trademark was based on the California State Seal which is reproduced here also. No matter the size of the piece of silver, the mark is always tiny—no more than 3mm.

SCHWEITZER SILVER CORP.
Brooklyn, New York

Manufacturers of sterling holloware c. 1950 to the late 1960s. A division of Lord Silver, Inc.

SCIENTIFIC SILVER SVC CORP.
New York, New York

Listed JBG 1957 and 1961 as manufacturers.

SCOFIELD & DE WYNGAERT
Newark, New Jersey

Listed 1904 JC in the sterling silver section and in 1915 in jewelry. Became F.P. Scofield & Company before 1922 after which no further listing was found.

SEARS ROEBUCK & CO.
Chicago, Illinois

A number of silverplated flatware patterns were made for them by various silver manufacturers and sold under the tradenames and trademarks illustrated here.

ALASKA METAL
(Used since 1908)

SALEM SILVER PLATE
(First used in 1914)

CAMBRIDGE SILVER PLATE
(First used c. 1909)

FASHION SILVER PLATE

PARAGON

PARAGON EXTRA

HARMONY HOUSE PLATE
(made by R. Wallace & Co.)

JACOB SEEGER
Baltimore, Maryland

Listed in Baltimore City Directories 1864-1869 as a silverplater.

SELLEW & COMPANY
Cincinnati, Ohio

The Cincinnati City Directory lists Sellew & Company as pewterers in 1834. The 1836-1837 Directory lists Enos and Osman Sellew, makers of britannia ware.

About 1860 they discontinued making pewter and devoted their attention to britannia ware.

Out of business in the late 1870s.

SELLEW & CO.
CINCINNATI

(On britannia)

SENECA SILVER CO.
Salamanca, New York

In business about 1900.

Trademark is Seneca Silver Co., Quadruple, Salamanca, N.Y. with an Indian profile in the center.

WILLIAM H. SEYFER
Baltimore, Maryland

Listed in 1884 Baltimore City Directory as a silversmith.

JOS. SEYMOUR MFG. CO.
Syracuse, New York

CHRONOLOGY

Joseph Seymour	1835
Willard & Hawley	1844-c. 1850-51
Norton & Seymour	1850-51
Joseph Seymour & Co.	1851-87
Joseph Seymour, Sons & Co.	1887-98
Joseph Seymour Mfg. Co.	1898-1905

The company was founded by Joseph Seymour, born 1815, near Albany, New York. At the age of 14 he went to New York to apprentice himself to a leading silversmith. He worked there as a silversmith in 1835 and in the early 1840s in Utica. He

became associated with Willard & Hawley (1844-51) in the establishment of a silverware factory in Syracuse, of which he later became owner. About 1850-51 he became a partner in Norton & Seymour (B.R. Norton). The company name was changed to Norton, Seymour & Co., after 1850. Shortly afterwards he went into business for himself under the name of Joseph Seymour & Co. Seymour's sons, Joseph, and E.G., and George F. Comstock, Jr., were admitted to partnership and about 1887 the firm name became Joseph Seymour, Sons & Co. In 1896 the stock was advertised for sale and in 1898 a new company, the Joseph Seymour Mfg. Co., was organized to carry on the manufacture of silverware. This too, went out of business about 1905.

Joseph Seymour patented a process in 1859 for making spoons (Pat. #25,765).

The company manufactured fine silverware. They were one of the first companies to make tableware in patterns, *Cable, Bridal Wreath, Prairie Flower, Corn, Tulip, Cottage, Plain, Thread* and *Prince Albert* being among them. Regrettably, much of their tableware was made by melting down tons of old Hudson Valley silversmiths' work.

J. S. & Co.

(c. 1850-1887)

* S *
(1887-c. 1900)

(c. 1900-c. 1909)

O.D. SEYMOUR
Hartford, Connecticut
See W.L. & H.E. Pitkin

Oliver D. Seymour, silversmith, maker of coin silver spoons was in business in Hartford c. 1845 as a partner in the firm of Seymour & Hollister (Julius Hollister). Their business was succeeded by W.L. & H.E. Pitkin.

The following account appeared in the *Hartford Daily Courant*, December 12, 1848.

NOTES BY A MAN ABOUT TOWN
Number VI

"In our last number we had not completed our exploration of the old jail building and its environs. We will this morning look a little farther among the various colonies which swarm this busy hive. And first we will step into the Spoon Manufactory of Mr. O.D. Seymour—Silversmith.

"The 'raw material' here consists of pure coin, mostly American half dollars—rather a queer article to be sure, and confounding some of our previous notions as to the meaning of the term 'raw material.' Just see those bags of Uncle Sam's precious metal—all of them doomed to be here melted down with as little remorse as the nabob's son usually melts down the dollars of his father.

"Some fifty of those half dollars are run into a bar of about eighteen inches in length. This bar is passed through a steam rolling mill and flattened, and afterwards hammered into a strip of the proper thickness for a spoon, and about half an inch in width, it is now cut into pieces, each piece designed for a spoon, but having no 'spoon fashion' or shape, about it. One end of this then, by a succession of blows skillfully applied with a 'peen' or oval faced hammer, spread out into the shape of a leaf for the bowl, and the other end formed in like manner for the handle. The whole spoon is then smooth hammered or planished upon an anvil, and brought to a uniform thickness and perfectly flat. During this process the silver by repeated heatings has become blackened to the color of iron. By boiling it in vitriol the white color is again restored.

"The bowl is now shaped and the tip formed in a die by 'swedging' or forcing these parts with a steel die into a spoon shaped cavity or matrix, formed in a block of lead. This completes the form. They now go into the hands of the filer, who trims them—next to a brush scouring wheel, which revolves rapidly in a lathe, where they are scoured smooth by a mixture of scotch stone in oil; and thence to the hands of the 'finisher,' who either polishes or burnishes them as the purchaser may direct, or as fancy may dictate.

"That lady who has just entered, you see has a broken spoon in her hand. She very honestly supposes that spoons are run in a mould, and has brought hers to be run over. She is not alone in the error—others are calling in constantly on the same errand, and probably nine tenths of our good citizens who are in the constant use of this now common utensil, entertain a like opinion—block tin, iron or pewter spoons, are indeed cast; but silver ones are always wrought with a hammer, and generally in the mode described.

"The polishing dust and oil, after use, become so imbued with particles, as to sell at the rate of six dollars per pound; and the

very sweepings of the floor and common rubbish of the room are all saved for the filings and impalpable silver dust which they contain, and sold for $25 per hogshead.

"This concern employs from twelve to fourteen hands; feeds some fifty or more persons dependent; and turns off per annum $25,000 worth of silverware, consisting of tea and tablespoons, cream and sugar spoons, dessert knives and forks, etc. &c., &c., which find a market all over the States of New England and New York, and to some extent over other portions of the Union.

"Just examine those elegant silver and pearl handled butter knives. What beautiful things! How finely formed and highly wrought."

B.M. SHANLEY, JR. CO.
See Pryor Mfg. Co., Inc.
Consolidated with Pryor Mfg. Co. between 1915 and 1922. Last record found was c. 1935.

SHAPLEIGH HARDWARE COMPANY
St. Louis, Missouri
Established by A.F. Shapleigh. Their 1915-16 General Hardware Catalog has a photograph of the founder under which there is the statement "Established this Business in St. Louis, 1848." This same catalog illustrated and described "Peerless Silver Flat Ware" under the name Diamond Brand. It is described as "An entirely New Alloy of Metals Containing over 5% Sterling Silver; it is of a Pure White Silver Color Through and Through and will Retain its Luster Until Worn Out. Unlike Silver Plated Ware this Metal May be Scoured without any injury to the Surface."

They also advertised "Lashar Silver Flat Ware" as "Lashar Silveroid Metal is not Plated, but Possesses the Same Color as Pure Silver Through and Through." Nickel silver tea and tablespoons were listed under the trademark "Bridge," and "Bridge Cutlery Co." Among their other offerings were tinned steel spoons and aluminum ones.

GEORGE B. SHARP
Philadelphia, Pennsylvania
Silversmith in Philadelphia c. 1848-1850.

This mark is an example of a type of quality mark used by a few American silversmiths. The American shield was used as a quality mark.

George and William Sharp worked together, perhaps a bit earlier. Their silver was stamped W. & G. SHARP.

George Sharp made silver for Bailey & Co. (later Bailey, Banks & Biddle). A Bailey & Co. advertisement of 1850 includes this mark accompanied by the statement that "All Silver Ware sold by them manufactured on the premises—Assayed by J.C. Booth, Esq., of the U.S. Mint."

George Sharp is recorded as working as a silversmith in Danville, Kentucky c. 1850-70.

CHARLES C. SHAVER
Utica, New York
Charles C. Shaver was born in Germany. He served his apprenticeship under Willard & Hawley (William W. Willard and John D. Hawley) of Syracuse. He moved to Utica in 1854 and was listed there in the City Directories as silversmith and jeweler until 1858.

From 1858-62 he was not listed, but returned in 1863 where he continued in business until his death in 1900.

GEORGE E. SHAW
Putnam, Connecticut
Listed in JC 1896-1922 in sterling silver section.

The Gen. Putnam trademark was registered in U.S. Patent Office, No. 19,736, June 16, 1891, for flatware, solid and plated. This trademark was for two souvenir spoons to commemorate the Revolutionary hero.

GEN. PUTNAM

ALEX SHEARS
Baltimore, Maryland
Listed in the 1850 Census as a silversmith in Baltimore. Born Maryland.

 DIAMOND EDGE

SHEETS-ROCKFORD SILVER PLATE CO.,
Rockford, Illinois

CHRONOLOGY

Racine Silver Plate Co.	1873-82
Rockford Silver Plate Co.	1882-1925
Sheets-Rockford Silver Plate Co.	1925-56

The company was founded in 1873 as the Racine Silver Plate Co., in Racine, Wisconsin. In 1882 the factory there burned. The stockholders decided to rebuild in Rockford, Illinois and erected the new factory there that same year. They made silverwares for the United States Jewelers' Guild (also called Jewelers' Crown Guild) which sold only through jewelry stores. About 1925 the company was bought by Raymond Sheets and became the Sheets-Rockford Silver Plate Co. The manufacture of flatware was discontinued but silverplated holloware was produced. Later Mr. Sheets operated it as a resilvering plant. The stock of the old company was purchased by S.L. & G.H. Rogers and records removed or destroyed. The Sheets-Rockford Silver Co. name appears in the City Directories through 1956.

SHEFFIELD CUTLERY CONCERN
Boston, Massachusetts

Published an illustrated catalog in 1882. Plated silver novelties, including fancy figure napkin rings were illustrated.

SHEFFIELD SILVER CO.
Brooklyn, New York

Registered trademark U.S. Patent Office, No. 107,747, December 28, 1919 for plated silverware and holloware.

Incorporated in the State of New York in 1908. Their basic product is plated silver holloware.

They were moved from New York to Norton, Massachusetts and became a division of Reed & Barton Silversmiths in 1974.

(1908-1950)

THE SHEFFIELD SILVER CO.
MADE IN U. S. A.

(1950-present)

SHELDON & FELTMAN
Albany, New York
See Smith & Company

Britannia workers 1846-1848. Thought to have made a small quantity of plated silver with the mark below. The upper ones most certainly were used only on britannia wares. Succeeded by Smith & Feltman in 1849; and by Smith & Co. in 1853.

SHEPARD MFG. CO.
Melrose Highlands, Massachusetts

Chester Shepard and his son, Chester Burdelle, moved from Connecticut to Melrose, Massachusetts in 1892 or 1893 and established their silversmith business there. For several years they claimed to be the only concern of importance which made a specialty of souvenir spoons, although their products embraced napkin rings and other fancy articles in flatware. The elder Shepard died July 11, 1902. Chester B. continued the business for several years but it passed to a younger brother, Llewlyn in a family disagreement and the factory closed in 1923.

On leaving the Shepard Company, Chester B. worked for several years for the Mt. Vernon Silver Co. In 1918 he founded a second Shepard Mfg. Co. in Detroit, organized for the manufacture of silverplated interior hardware for limousines such as Cadillac, Durant and LaSalle. He sold the business in 1925 and died two years later.

S

SHEPARD & RICE
See Bernard Rice's Sons

SHERIDAN SILVER CO., INC.
Taunton, Massachusetts

Originated in 1944 as the C & C Silver Company by Joseph Caiozzo and Harry Carmody. Incorporated in 1946 as Sheridan

Silver Co., Inc. The largest of the independent silver manufacturers. Their production is limited to plated silver holloware.

SILVER ON COPPER

EMMONS F. SHERMAN
Baltimore, Maryland

Listed in 1868-1869 Baltimore City Directory as a silverplater.

GEORGE W. SHIEBLER & CO.
New York, New York

Geo. W. Shiebler was first employed as a salesman for the firm of Jahne, Smith & Co. in 1867. He remained with them until the deaths of both Jahne and Smith about 1870-71 when the firm was succeeded by Hodenpyl, Tunison & Shiebler, manufacturers of gold chains. In 1873 or 1874 Shiebler purchased the business of Coles & Reynolds, manufacturers of silver spoons. On March 4, 1876, with a force of five men, he began business under his own name. A few months later he bought out the business of John Polhamus, an old and recognized silversmith and merged this plant with his own. A short time later he purchased the factory of M. Morgan, who had succeeded Albert Coles, another silversmith. This plant he merged with the others. The flatware dies of A.&W. Wood and Henry Hebbard and Hebbard & Polhamus were added to his plant. He also succeeded Theo. Evans & Co., probably in the 1870s. A few years later he moved the factory operations to Brooklyn. On January 1, 1892 the firm was incorporated. George W. Shiebler was president and Wm. F. Shiebler, treasurer. It was out of business before 1915. In 1892 there were reported negotiations underway to combine with the Gorham Company but no confirmation has been found.

In the beginning the Shiebler firm made only spoons and forks but this was gradually expanded until they produced the largest line of novelties in silver extant at the time. They were especially noted for their medallion work, inspired by the excavations at Pompeii and Herculanaeum and their transparent enamel work. Raised Greek mottoes appeared on the articles giving them the appearance of the antique. This type of work was applied to brooches, sleeve buttons and bangles and was later extended to forks, spoons and holloware. Oxidized silver had until then been a failure on the market but when introduced by Shiebler met with instant success. Another one of his innovations was silver leaves tinted in all the rich autumn colors. This work was applied to spoons, berry bowls, pitchers and other articles. Shiebler is also credited with the introduction of Renaissance open-work style in jewelry, bonbonnieres, dishes, trays and spoons.

(Old Mark.)

(Mark of an old silversmith named Platt, whose business was acquired by Shiebler. Probably firm of Platt & Brothers, thimble makers, N.Y.C. 1836-46)

SHIELDS, INC.
Attleboro, Massachusetts

Founded c. 1920 as the Fillkwik Company, it was incorporated in 1936 under the present name. In January 1939 the company was bought by Rex Products Corporation of New Rochelle, New York.

During World War II, Shields produced insignia and medals, and now manufactures men's jewelry, fancy display and jewelry boxes.

SHIRLEY METALCRAFT, LTD.
Williamsburg, Virginia

Founded in 1955 by Shirley Robertson. He started working on castings in 1953 in a garage and expanded into the present location in 1955. Only the highest quality, lead-free, heavy gauge pewter is used in the handcrafted Shirley pewter. About a hundred different articles are made and include reproductions and adaptations of old designs as well as his own designs. Among them are bowls, trays, candlesticks, coffee and tea services, mugs, etc.

SHIRLEY
(Intaglio script)

Another mark: Colonial powder horn in Williamsburg with Shirley, Hand Made, Williamsburg, Va.

SHOEMAKER, PICKERING & CO.
Newark, New Jersey

Listed in JC 1896 in sterling and jewelry sections. Out of business before 1915.

Trademark identical to Frank Kursh & Son, Co.

sterling

SHREVE & CO.
San Francisco, California

Two brothers, George C. and S.S. Shreve first opened a jewelry shop in 1852 and were active in its management all their lives. The company was incorporated shortly before 1900.

Ownership and management has remained in the hands of San Franciscans, though since 1912 no member of the Shreve family has been part of the corporation.

Shreve & Co., a San Francisco institution with a history almost as old as the city itself, has made silver services for several battleships and cruisers; the State of California's gift to Queen Elizabeth on her coronation; gifts for the delegates at the founding of the United Nations and has fashioned pieces to the special orders of Kings, presidents, shahs, sheiks and people of the entertainment world. They also produce 20 exclusive flatware patterns.

In 1915 they bought the Vanderslice Company.

Shreve & Co. manufactured their first flatware in 1904.

"Obituary Geo. C. Shreve. B. Salem, Mass. about 65 years ago. He died after an illness of more than a year. He lived in Saco, Maine with his sister, Mrs. Calef, and was in the store of his half-brother, Benjamin, in that town. When a boy he shipped as a sailor aboard a coasting vessel on the Atlantic Coast, with his brother Samuel. After this he was with Kingsley & Shreve, at 22 Maiden Lane, N.Y. He came to California by way of Cape Horn, arriving in San Francisco in 1852. The same year he went into partnership with his brother Samuel S. Shreve, in the jewelry business. While on the way east, a few years later, S.S. Shreve was drowned near the Isthmus of Panama. According to their prior agreement, the surviving brother became sole owner of the business. Some years later George Bonney and Albert J. Lewis were associated with him, the three forming the firm of Geo. C. Shreve & Co." (JC&HR 10-25-1893, p. 13)

"George R. Shreve elected president of Shreve & Co., succeeding the late Al J. Lewis. Bruce Bonney elected treasurer. Mr. Bonney until recently had been manager of the New York wholesale department of Gorham Mfg. Co., in whose employ he had been for about 19 years. Mr. Bonney's uncle, Geo. Bonney is the largest stockholder in Shreve & Co." (JC&HR 10-16-1895, p. 23)

(Little used after 1918)

SHREVE & CO.

(Not used after January 1894)

SHREVE, CRUMP & LOW CO., INC.
Boston, Massachusetts

CHRONOLOGY

John M. McFarlane	1796
Jones & Ward	1809
Baldwin & Jones	1813
Putnam & Low	1822
John J. Low & Co.	1828
John B. Jones Co.	1838
Jones, Low & Ball	1839
Low, Ball & Co.	1840
Jones, Ball & Poor	1846
Harris & Stanwood	1847
Henry B. Stanwood	
Jones, Ball & Co.	1852
Jones, Shreve, Brown & Co.	1854
Shreve, Brown & Co.	1857
Shreve, Stanwood & Co.	1860
Shreve, Crump & Low Co.	1869
Shreve, Crump & Low Co., Inc.	1888

According to tradition, John McFarlane, originally from Salem, proprietor of a modest watchmaker's shop in 1796, was the founder of the company that is now known as Shreve, Crump & Low Co., Inc.

In the early 1800s Jabez Baldwin moved to Boston and formed a copartnership with a neighboring craftsman, and under the title of Baldwin & Jones continued the business begun by McFarlane.

Among the apprentices of Jabez Baldwin in Salem were John J. Low and Edward Putnam, who in 1822 established the firm of Putnam & Low. Three or four years later they separated and in 1839 John J. Low and his brother Francis, joined with George B. Jones, son of Mr. Baldwin's partner. In 1852 Benjamin Shreve was admitted to the firm and 17 years later Charles H. Crump joined. In 1888 the firm was incorporated as Shreve, Crump & Low Company under the law of Massachusetts, with Benjamin Shreve as president.

The Shreve, Crump & Low Company tradition so ably started by the Salem craftsmen and apprentices almost 150 years ago is being carried on today by Richard Shreve, great-grandson of the first Shreve.

The company does no manufacturing, but, has always sold designs made by the finest of American silversmiths; some of the designs being created exclusively for them.

SHREVE, TREAT & EACRET
San Francisco, California

Jewelers and silversmiths. Young George Shreve withdrew from Shreve & Co. and with Treat and Eacret formed the new firm in 1912 around the corner from the old ones and were in business until c. 1940.

The last Directory entry was for 1941 when silversmithing was mentioned. Oddly, in the 1945-46 Directory the name is back in the listing with the note "See Granat Bros." who may have bought the firm but if they did so they did not stay at the same location but moved or located elsewhere. Bought by Granat Bros. in 1941.

VICTOR SIEDMAN MFG. CO., INC.
Brooklyn, New York

Manufacturing silversmiths c. 1920-1930. Makers of sterling silver holloware, picture frames and candlesticks.

A.L. SILBERSTEIN
New York, New York

Successor to Silberstein, Hecht & Co. before 1904.

Succeeded by Griffon Cutlery Works before 1915. Still in business under that name.

(All Above on Cutlery.)

SILBERSTEIN, HECHT & CO.
New York, New York

Founding date unknown.

Succeeded by A.L. Silberstein before 1904. Manufacturers of sterling silverware.

SILBERSTEIN, LA PORTE & CO.
Providence, Rhode Island
New York, New York

"Silberstein, La Porte & Co. importers of cutlery, N.Y. This firm also manufacturers sterling silver cutlery, with a factory in Providence, Rhode Island. Griffen (sic!) trademark." (JC&HR 6-23-1897, p. 36) Probably related to above.

SILO SILVER MFG. CO.
New York, New York

Listed 1927 KJI as manufacturers of silverplated wares.

SILVER BROTHERS
Atlanta, Georgia

Registered trademark for sterling silver and silverplated flatware and holloware and jewelry.

(Used since June 1, 1950)

THE SILVER CITY PLATE CO.
Meriden, Connecticut

"The Silver City Plate Co. has begun the manufacture of Britannia ware in Meriden. Harry Felix, formerly with the Toronto Silver Plate Co., is associated with three others in the enterprise." (JW 1-23-1895, p. 3). Eugene H. Ray, also with the company, had learned his trade from Simons & Miller Co., in Middletown.

In 1908 the International Silver Co. bought from the receivers the business and tools they could use.

SILVER COUNSELORS OF HOME DECORATORS, INC.
Newark, New York

Successors between 1943 and 1950 to Home Decorators, Inc.

State House Sterling

Inaugural   Formality

SILVERART
New York, New York

Listed 1957 and 1961 JBG as manufacturers of silverware.

SILVERCRAFT CO. INC.
Boston, Massachusetts

Listed JC-K 1950 as manufacturers. Owned now by Raimond Silver Manufacturers.

SILVERCRAFT

SILVER METAL MFG. CO.
Lyons and Oswego, New York

"A stock company has been organized to manufacture table ware from a metal recently invented by D.J. Toothill. The new firm will be known as the Silver Metal Mfg. Co. of Lyons." (JW April 1892)

"The Silver Metal Mfg. Co. recently moved from Lyons, N.Y. to Oswego, N.Y. started up last Monday." (JC&HR 8-31-1892, p. 17)

SILVER PLATE CUTLERY CO.
Birmingham, Connecticut

This concern, as the name indicates, made cutlery, and some of it was silver-plated. They were in business as early as 1884 and continued until some time after 1896. Some of their products they sold to other manufacturers, such as Holmes & Edwards, Wm. Rogers Mfg. Co., etc., furnishing lines particularly suitable for the firms doing the marketing.

THE SILVERSMITHS CO.
SILVERSMITHS STOCKS CO.

"The Silversmith's Co. incorporated, the present companies comprised in the new organization... Gorham, Whiting, Dominick & Haff, Geo. W. Shiebler and Towle Mfg. Co." (JC&HR 12-14-1892, p. 22) Nothing ever came of this. A few years later, however, Wm. B. Durgin Co., W.B. Kerr Co., The Mount Vernon Co. and Whiting Mfg. Co. became a part of the Gorham Company.

F.W. SIM & CO.
Troy, New York

Registered U.S. Patent June 6, 1891 for manufacture of souvenir sterling silverware. No other record.

SIMMONS & PAYE
North Attleboro, Massachusetts
See Paye & Baker

"Simmons & Paye, manufacturers of souvenir spoons, etc., will show their goods in Denver in 1898." (JC&HR 12-15-1897, p. 26)

They sold some of their patterns and dies to the Wendell Mfg. Co.

S. & P.

SIMONS, BRO. & CO.
Philadelphia, Pennsylvania

Simons, Bro. & Co. was established in 1840 by George W. Simons, father of John F. Simons, Frederick M. Simons and Edwin S. Simons, who were later members of the firm. Some years subsequent to 1840, Peter

B. Simons joined his brother, the firm becoming George W. Simons & Bro. In 1861 Thomas Maddock was admitted to an interest in the business, and later, S.B. Opdyke, the firm name changing to Simons, Bro., Opdyke & Co. Some years later Mr. Opdyke retired, as did subsequently the elder Simons, the firm continuing under the name of Simons, Bro. & Co. It is now Simons Bros. Co.

George W. Simons was born in Philadelphia in 1819 and learned there the trade of making silver thimbles and pencils. These were the company's first products. Gradually they increased the scope of their activities and produced many exclusive patterns of tea sets and tableware, comb tops, cane and umbrella heads as well as their well-known thimbles. They were successors to Peter L. Krider Co. in 1903. Their flatware patterns and dies and Simons Bros. patterns and dies were sold to the Alvin Mfg. Co. in 1908 and they discontinued flatware manufacturing entirely.

ESTABLISHED 1840

S. B. & CO.

SIMONS & MILLER PLATE CO.
Middletown, Connecticut

Apparently begun by workmen previously associated with the Middletown Plate Co. Listed in the Middletown Directory in 1870. A price list for 1874 is in existence. The New England business directory for 1867 lists Simons, Lawrence & Co. Britannia makers of Middletown, Conn.—probably their predecessors.

SIMPSON-BRAINERD CO.
Providence, Rhode Island

Listed JC 1915-1922 in plated silver section.

ENGLISH SILVER

SIMPSON, HALL, MILLER & CO.
Wallingford, Connecticut
See International Silver Co.

Samuel Simpson was well-known for his britannia ware in Wallingford. In 1866 he organized Simpson, Hall, Miller & Co. to do silverplating. He was extremely successful and in 1878 made a contract

with William Rogers, Jr., to supervise the manufacture and marketing of Simpson, Hall, Miller & Co. Rogers "Eagle" Brand.

In 1895 they started the manufacture of sterling silverware and were one of the original companies to become part of the International Silver Company in 1898. The Wallingford factory became International's sterling center.

Their sterling flatware produced after 1895. The same mark continued by International Silver Co.

Wᵐ ROGERS.

(Flatware.)

SHM&Cᵒ

(Holloware.)

(Cheaper Grade.)

AMERICAN SILVER PLATE CO.

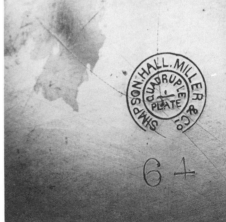

SIMPSON NICKEL SILVER CO.
Wallingford, Connecticut
See International Silver Co.

Incorporated in 1871 by Samuel Simpson, E.W. Sperry, Albert A. Sperry, Alfred W. Sperry and R.L. McChristie. They made nickel silver flatware blanks which were sold to Simpson, Hall, Miller & Co. for plating and marketing. They did not use a trademark because they sold their products to other silver manufacturers. They began the manufacture of sterling silver flatware shortly before the organization of the International Silver Co. The nickel silver operations were moved to other factories after the company became part of the International Silver Co. in 1898.

SINCLAIR MFG. CO.
Chartley, Massachusetts
Listed in 1950 JC-K under sterling.

B. & J. SIPPEL LTD.
Sheffield, England
Registered trademark for flatware.

(Used since August 13, 1934)

JAMES SISSFORD
Baltimore, Maryland
Listed in the 1850 Census as a silversmith. Born in the District of Columbia.

WM. AND GEO. SISSONS
Sheffield, England
Successors to Smith, Sissons & Co. who were makers of Sheffield plate and silversmiths in 1848.

Listed in JC 1909-1922 in sterling and plated silver sections.

W. S.

C. S.

(On plated silver)

(On sterling silver)

A.F. SMITH CO.
Omaha, Nebraska
Founded in 1894 as Reichenberg-Smith Co., wholesale jewelers. A.F. Smith, President, Louis Reichenberg, Vice President and Max Reichenberg, Sec. Last listed under this name in 1905.

The 1906 City Directory carries the listing of the A.F. Smith Co. with Arthur F. Smith as President. They were incorporated in 1932. In 1936 the listing is A.F. Smith & Co. with G.A. Smith as President-treasurer; L.P. Smith, Vice President and A.F. Smith, Secretary.

The 1938 listing is Smith & Co., with Franklin & Gordon A. Smith (sons) listed as owners. The 1941 listing A.F. Smith & Co., Inc. and is the last listing under the Smith name.

It was later known as the Allgaier-Smith Co., Inc. in 1942; Allgaier Jewelry Co. in 1945 and John Byrne Inc. 1948-1964.

SMITH & COMPANY
Albany, New York
Listed in the Albany City Directory 1846-1848 as Sheldon & Feltman, Brittannia (sic) and Argentina Manufactory. Listed 1849-1853 as Smith & Feltman, Argentine and Brittannia Works. Listed 1853-1856 as Smith & Company, Argentine and Brittannia Works.

The Argentina and Argentine are thought to have been britannia ware plated with silver.

C.R. SMITH PLATING COMPANY
Providence, Rhode Island
"The C.R. Smith Plating Company was established in 1890." (JW 3-30-1892)

E.H.H. SMITH KNIFE CO.
Bridgeport, Connecticut

In business in 1899 as manufacturers of plated silver knives. Out of business before 1915.

Probably related to E.H.H. Smith Silver Co. but this could not be established.

(*Knives.*)

E.H.H. SMITH SILVER CO.
Bridgeport, Connecticut
See Albert Pick & Co., Inc.
See Blackstone Silver Co.

The E.H.H. Smith Silver Company was first listed in the Bridgeport City Directory in 1907. Listed in the JC in 1904. U.S. Patent No. 44,191 was issued in their name on February 14, 1905. They were manufacturers of "artistic cutlery and sterling

effects in quintuple plated spoons and forks." They were last listed in the 1919 City Directory and were succeeded by the Albert Pick Company in 1920.

Reorganized as Blackstone Silver Co. in 1914. Sold to Bernstein (of National Silver Co.?) in 1943.

(Flatware.)

SMITH & FELTMAN
See Smith & Company

FRANK W. SMITH SILVER CO., INC.
Gardner, Massachusetts
See The Webster Co.

Frank W. Smith (b. March 13, 1848; d. August 2, 1904), son of Dr. William A. and Susan F. (Durgin) Smith was born in Thornton, New Hampshire. He entered the employ of his relative, William B. Durgin, silversmith in Concord, New Hampshire and remained with him in various capacities until 1886 when the Smith family moved to Gardner, Massachusetts. He established his silversmith's factory that year. He had two sons, William D. and Frank H., the former associated with him in business.

Sterling flatware and holloware were the principal products of the factory. For a time, Arthur J. Stone, expert in hand-wrought silver and designer, was associated with the firm.

In October 1958 all the flatware tools and dies, along with the trade name and trademark, were purchased by the Webster Company and the flatware portion of the business moved to North Attleboro, Massachusetts.

TRADE MARK.
925/1000 FINE

FREDERICK L. SMITH
Denver, Colorado

The business was first listed as the C.H. Green Jewelry Company in 1889 with F.L. Smith as secretary-treasurer and L.H. Gurnsey, manager. In 1890 it was known as the C.H. Green Jewelry Company with the Gurnsey name no longer listed. In 1892 the name was changed to the Green-Smith Watch and Diamond Company. Harper's Magazine, July 1892, carried an advertisement listing them as "manufacturers of souvenir spoons made of Colorado silver." "Protected by letters Patent, dated Feb. 16, 1892." In 1894 the business listing was dropped and the only entry was under Smith. In 1895 the listing was Frederick L. Smith as manager of John W. Knox— successor to Green-Smith Company.

GEORGE W. SMITH
Albany, New York
See Rogers Brothers

Holloware silverplater in Albany, New York before he joined with Wm. Rogers and founded the Rogers, Smith & Co. of Hartford, Connecticut in 1856. Went out of business in 1862.

LAWRENCE B. SMITH CO.
Boston, Massachusetts

Founded in Boston in 1887. Made sterling and plated silverware. Out of business about 1958.

SMITH & MAYO
Newark, New Jersey

Benjamin J. Mayo and Edwin B. Smith were gold and silverplaters c. 1860.

SMITH METAL ARTS COMPANY
Buffalo, New York

Registered trademark for use on trophies, vases, bowls, photograph frames, smoking accessories, desk accessories, etc., all embossed, ornamented or plated with silver.

SILVERCREST

(Used since January 1920)

SMITH, PATTERSON & CO.
Boston, Massachusetts

Founded in 1876, became part of Jordan Marsh, New England's largest department store, in 1956. Agents for "several of the

best manufacturers." Importers of watches, clocks, silverware and jewelry.

RICHARD SMITH
Newark, New Jersey

Richard Smith was a jeweler who sold under the name of the Newark Jewelry Store 1850-1898. He had been with Baldwin & Smith. Advertised in the Newark Directory 1854 a large variety of silverware "manufactured in the best style warranted of the finest quality," and in the 1859 Directory "Not only do I claim superiority so far as artistic design and perfect finish are concerned but every article made is guaranteed to equal the best American coin..."

SMITH & SMITH
Attleboro, Massachusetts
See Wallace Silversmiths

Manufacturers of sterling cigar boxes and novelties.

Specialize in reproductions of early American, English and Dutch pieces in sterling.

A division of Wallace Silversmiths.

W.D. SMITH SILVER CO.
Chicago, Illinois

Rudolph J. Bourgeois, vice-president of the company, registered U.S. Patent No. 148,714 on November 22, 1921 for the manufacture of silverware, particularly holloware, flatware, jewelry and precious metal ware. In applying for this patent registration, it was stated that this trademark had been used continuously since 1913.

The company was incorporated under the laws of Delaware and was located in Chicago.

(Nickel Silver Hollowware.)   *(Plated Flatware.)*

ALBERT SMYTH CO., INC.
Baltimore, Maryland

Listed 1965 JC-K. 1974 listing has no address.

EDWIN V. SNYDER
Philadelphia, Pennsylvania

Listed JKD 1918-19 as a silversmith.

SOCIETE PICARD FRERES
Paris, France

Registered trademarks U.S. Patent Office No. 30,171, June 8, 1897 for table, kitchen, dresserware and utensils of copper and pure silver. No record after c. 1920.

A.M. SOFFEL CO., INC.
Newark, New Jersey

Manufacturers (?) of sterling silverware c. 1920-30.

SOUTHERN SILCO
Hartsville, South Carolina

Name found stamped on silverware.

SOUTHINGTON CUTLERY CO.

Advertised holloware and knives (JC&HR December 1886) "Mfg. fine silver Plated Ware." (Adv. JC&HR March 1887)

"The Southington Cutlery Co. sent out circulars stating that their Britannia department will be reorganized as a separate concern under the name Southington Silver Plate Co." (JC&HR 11-30-1892, p. 4)

SOUTHINGTON CO.
See Barbour Silver Co.
See International Silver Co.

Also used name of company in a circle with TRIPLE.

SOUTHINGTON CO.

SOUTHINGTON SILVER PLATE COMPANY

The Southington Silver Plate Company was bought by Meriden Britannia Company in 1893 but their trademark was never used by Meriden.

A.S. SOUTHWICK & CO.
Providence, Rhode Island

"Established in 1874 as Vose & Southwick." (JW 3-30-1892)

Manufacturers of silverwares.

GEORGE A. SPARKS
Brooklyn, New York
   Manufacturers (?) of plated silver c. 1920.

S-C-A G

J.E. SPARKS
Brooklyn, New York
   Manufacture (?) of sterling silver c. 1920.

$ Spark $

SPAULDING & CO.
Chicago, Illinois
   Founded in 1855 under the name of S. Hoard & Co. In 1888 it was incorporated under the name of Spaulding & Company, Inc., taking over, at that time, the business of N. Matson & Co. (q.v.)
   On November 2, 1888 Levi Leiter of Chicago and Edward Holbrook of New York, representing the interests of the Gorham Mfg. Co. of Providence, and Henry A. Spaulding, formed a corporation to manufacture and retail watches, clocks, jewelry, diamonds, silverware, silverplated ware, objects of art and other related merchandise, with Henry A. Spaulding as its first president. In the 1920s the Gorham Mfg. Co. acquired control of Spaulding & Co. and the name changed to Spaulding-Gorham, Inc. On June 1, 1943 the entire interests of Spaulding-Gorham, Inc. were acquired by Gordon Lang, at which time the name was changed to Spaulding & Company. On October 1, 1973 ownership was acquired by Stewart S. Peacock.
   Spaulding & Co.'s English sterling has its own Guildhall registered London hallmark. They have long been noted for their handforged silver by Fletcher of London as well as flatware by eminent American silversmiths.

REGISTERED LONDON HALLMARK

SPAULDING-GORHAM, INC.
See Spaulding & Co.

D.S. SPAULDING
Mansfield, Massachusetts
   Listed in JC 1896-1922 in sterling and plated silver sections.

(*Sterling Silver Top and Plated Back*)
(On sterling silver)

(On plated silver)

DAVID H. SPEARS
Springfield, Kentucky
   David Huston Spears was born July 5, 1798, the fourth of nine children born to Jacob Spears (1757-1818) and Abigail Huston Spears, at Carpenters Station (Hustonville), Lincoln County, Kentucky. He set up shop in Springfield, Kentucky about 1815. Where he received his training and served his apprenticeship is unknown. He was enroute to New Orleans to set up a shop there but stopped overnight at Gibbons Tavern in Springfield and met and fell in love with Elizabeth Carter Gibbons, daughter of the innkeeper, Arthur E. Gibbons. He stayed in Springfield and hung out his shingle there which read "D.H. Spears, Silversmith and Watchmaker."
   Spears hammered and fashioned beautiful silver items from Spanish dollars obtained from New Orleans trade, and silver coins from the East which were turned in by his customers. He advertised spoons, cups, beakers, pins, brooches, wedding and mourning rings, large and small ladies' watches and clocks. He made silver spectacle frames.
   David H. Spears died February 26, 1876.
   He is said to have designed and made the emblems of the Springfield Masonic Order of which he was a member.

SPENCE, GAVEN & CO.
Newark, New Jersey
   Listed as silversmiths 1859-1916 in Newark City Directories.

SPENCE & CO. STERLING
GAVEN & SPENCE
G. SPENCE (straight line) with pseudo hallmarks, lion, head leopard

G. SPENCE (in half circle) with lion passant, D. Head.
   The business was closed in the autumn of 1918. In 1869 Gaven Spence had operated the Excelsior Jewelry Store.

BEN. SPIER
New York, New York
   Successor to Spier & Forsheim about 1909. Wholesaler (?) of silverware, jewelry and related articles.

SPIER & FORSHEIM
New York, New York
See Ben. Spier Co.
Listed JC 1896. Succeeded by Ben. Spier Co. c. 1909.

WILLIAM SPRATLING
New Orleans, Louisiana
Taxco, Mexico
Spratling had taught architecture at Tulane University, New Orleans. In 1925 he traveled to Mexico and decided to settle in Taxco where he was one of the pioneers in reviving the art of silversmithing there. He started a shop with six boys whom he trained. Incorporating old Aztec designs and *ranchero* motifs the shop turned out fine work, much of it combining wood and metal. In 1944 he was sent to Alaska by the U.S. Dept. of Interior where he trained Alaskan Indians in the art of silversmithing. Spratling left behind a legacy of many silversmiths in both areas, trained in the highest standards of craftsmanship. He himself was killed in an automobile accident in August, 1967.

SPRINGFIELD SILVER PLATE CO.
Springfield, Ohio
"The Springfield Silver Plate Co., Springfield, Ohio, have incorp. to mfg. casket hardware, novelties and to do electroplating. Incorporators are' Ed. N. Lupfer, Charles H. Hiser, W.H. Reania, Paul A. Staley and W.W. Diehl. Lupfer has conducted a successful similar business for three years." (JC&HR 1-22-1896, p. 21)

GEORGE W. SPURR & CO.
Greenfield, Massachusetts
See Rogers & Spurr Mfg. Co.

OLAF SKOOGFORS
Philadelphia, Pennsylvania
"Philadelphia—Olaf Skoogfors, award-winning silversmith and jeweler, died of a heart attack at his home here Saturday. He was 45.
"Best known for his goldplated silver jewelry and wrought silver, he also made hollow ware and ecclesiastical metalwork. His work was exhibited both nationally and internationally. Among his awards were first prize in the Contemporary Jewelry International in 1963 and the $1,000 Tiffany prize in 1967.
"His jewelry and hollow ware are in the permanent collections of the Philadelphia Museum of Art and the Museum of Contemporary Crafts in New York and also are included in museums in Rochester, N.Y.; St. Paul, Minn.; Atlanta, Ga., and Pforzheim, Germany.
"Mr. Skoogfors was born in Bredsjo, Sweden, and came to the United States in 1939 with his family. He trained at the Philadelphia Museum's School of Art and the Rochester, N.Y., Institute of Technology.
"He was professor and chairman of the craft department at the Philadelphia College of Art. He worked in a studio above his garage.
"Mr. Skoogfors is survived by his widow, the former Judy Gesensway, an illustrator and teacher at Moore College of Art; daughters, Kerstin and Mia; a brother, Leif, photography teacher at Moore, and his stepmother, Esther Skoogfors." (Obituary, 12-23-1975 *The Washington Post*)
He was one of the most important goldsmiths of the American craft revival.

S. & S. NOVELTY CO.
Providence, Rhode Island
Manufacturers (?) of plated silver novelties c. 1915-1922.

STANDARD MFG. CO.
Winsted, Connecticut
"The Standard Mfg. Co., Winsted, Conn., who began the mfg. of silverplated table knives, have increased their working capital and are turning out considerable quantities of goods." (JC&HR 3-16-1898, p. 40)

STANLEY & AYLWARD, LTD.
Toronto, Canada
Wholesalers of plated silver holloware c. 1920.

THEODORE B. STARR
New York, New York
In business c. 1900-1924. Succeeded by Reed & Barton.

STANDARD SILVER CO. OF TORONTO
Toronto, Canada
See International Silver Co.
See International Silver Co. of Canada, Ltd.

When the Acme Silver co. of Toronto was liquidated in 1893 it was sold to W.K. George and others who formed the Standard Silver Co., Toronto, Ltd., for the production of silverplated flatware and holloware and hotel ware. Merged with International Silver Co. of Canada, Ltd. about 1912.

(*E. P. on Copper.*)

MONARCH SILVER CO.

STANDARD SILVERWARE COMPANY
Boston, Massachusetts

Retailer and jobber of plated silverware. First appeared in the Boston City Directories in 1883, which probably means that it was founded the previous year. Last listed in 1921. Edward C. Webb was head of the firm and was associated with it from about 1903 through 1921.

NEVADA SILVER METAL

I.J. STEANE & CO.
Hartford, Connecticut and New York
See Barbour Silver Co.

Isaac J. Steane, a watchmaker at Coventry, England, came to America about 1866 to collect a bad debt. He was forced to take over his debtor's stock, which he auctioned off at a profit of $6,000. He continued in the auction business for some time; returned to England, wound up his business affairs and came again to the United States where he formed the firm of Steane, Son & Hall, consisting of Isaac J. Steane, Isaac J. Steane, Jr., and J.P. Hall. Mr. Hall retired in 1886 and the firm name was changed to I.J. Steane & Co.

Mr. Steane bought the Taunton Silver Plate Co., and took stock to New York for auction. He later bought the Albany Silver Plate Co., combining the affairs of these two companies with that of I.J. Steane & Co.

In the early 1880s, Mr. Steane purchased the old silverware stock of the Cromwell Plate Co., of Cromwell, Connecticut. The sale was made by A.E. Hobson, who in 1881 had left the Meriden Britannia Co. to become a salesman for Cromwell.

About this same time, the Barbour Bros. Co. was formed by S.L. Barbour, from Chicago, joined by his brother, Charles, who was in business in New Haven. I.J. Steane & Co. produced the goods that the Barbour Bros. Co. marketed. Mr. Hobson was associated with I.J. Steane at this time. At the suggestion of W.H. Watrous, the business was moved to Hartford and two years later the Hartford Silver Plate Company business was also acquired. Mr. Steane, Sr. retired and returned to England in 1888.

The I.J. Steane Co., the Barbour Bros. Co. and the Barbour Hobson Co., all of Hartford, united to form the Barbour Silver Company in 1892.

Steane introduced many European designs into this country by purchasing silver articles in Europe and bringing them to be copied here.

STEANE, SON & HALL
New York, New York
See Barbour Silver Co.
See I.J. Steane & Co.

THE STEEL-BRUSSEL CO.
New York, New York

Listed in JC 1896 in sterling silver section. Out of business before 1904.

H. STEINACKER
Baltimore, Maryland

Listed in 1868-1869 Baltimore City Directory as a silverplater.

STERLING COMPANY
Derby, Connecticut

Published illustrated catalogs of fine silverware in 1893 and 1898. On the catalogs is the statement, "Established 1866."

STERLING CRAFT
Toronto, Canada

Sterling silver manufacture (?) c. 1920. Related (?) to Spurrier & Co., London.

STERLING SILVER MFG. CO.
Baltimore, Maryland

"The Sterling Silver Manufacturing Company, Baltimore, Md. which by an infusion of new blood and fresh capital, emerged from the Klank Mfg. Co., recently passed the first twelfth month of their existence with a good yearly record. They manufacture solid silver holloware and flatware, and a full line of white metal goods, beside doing considerable repairing and replating. Their new and original designs in holloware have proved very taking. Factory at 110 W. Fayette St., office and salesroom at 17 N. Liberty St." (JC&HR 2-14-1894, p. 27)

THE STERLING SILVER MFG. CO.
Providence, Rhode Island

Listed in the City Directories 1909-1932, Samuel A. Schreiber, president-treasurer; Max L. Jocby vice-president; L.C. McCaffrey, sec. Manufacturing silversmiths. Made sterling flat and holloware and souvenir spoons.

Their flatware dies were purchased by Saart Bros.

STERLING SILVER SOUVENIR CO.
Boston, Massachusetts

In business before 1890. Advertised that they were makers of sterling silver souvenirs. Out of business before 1915.

LOUIS STERN CO., INC.
Providence, Rhode Island

Established in 1871 as chainmakers and silversmiths. Wholesalers of chains, bags, watch bracelets, bracelets, knives, buckles and jewelry. Last record found 1950.

LS. & Co.

S. STERNAU & CO.
Brooklyn, New York and New York, New York

Proprietors were Sigmund Sternau and Charles Nelson.

Listed in 1896 Jewelers' Weekly as manufacturer of plated silver chafing dishes and miscellaneous lines. Last record c. 1920.

(Metal Wares.)

STEVENS & LEITHOFF
Irvington, New Jersey

Listed JC 1915 in sterling silver section. Out of business before 1922.

STEVENS SILVER CO.
Portland, Maine
See Colonial Silver Co.

CHRONOLOGY

Stevens & Smart	1879-1883
Stevens, Smart & Dunham	1884-1886
Stevens & Smart	1887-1890
Stevens, Woodman & Co.	1890-1891
Woodman-Cook Co.	1892-1893
Stevens Silver Co.	1893-1899

The firm of Alfred A. Stevens was listed in 1879 and known as Stevens & Smart (Alfred A. Stevens and Nehemiah Smart), manufacturers of britannia wares until 1883 when it was succeeded by Stevens, Smart & Dunham (Joseph Dunham). It became Stevens, Woodman & Co., (Fred H. Woodman). They advertised that they did silverplating. Woodman-Cook succeeded in 1892. They manufactured silverplated wares. Edward B. Cook was president; C.H. Fessenden, vice president and Fred H. Woodman, treasurer. This was succeeded by the Stevens Silver Co. incorporated in 1893. Alfred A. Stevens was president. He left Woodman-Cook to form the Stevens Silver Company which later became the Colonial Silver Co.

THE STIEFF COMPANY
Baltimore, Maryland
See Kirk Stieff Company

Founded in 1892 as The Baltimore Sterling Silver Company by Charles C. Stieff. In 1904 the corporation name was changed to The Stieff Company.

They are manufacturers of sterling silver flatware and holloware. Their "Rose" pattern is so identified with Baltimore that it is often called "Baltimore Rose." They are the exclusive makers of Williamsburg Restoration, Historic Newport and Old Sturbridge Village sterling silver and pewter reproductions.

Their appointment to make sterling silver holloware and flatware reproductions for Williamsburg was in September 1939.

They began the production of pewter August 19, 1951, after receiving the appointment but because of the tin shortage caused by the Korean war, their first shipments were not made until August 1953.

They bought the Schofield Co. in 1967.

In 1979 the Steiff Company acquired S. Kirk & Son and formed a new corporation called The Kirk Stieff Company.

STIEFF STERLING

"Hallmark" used on Williamsburg Restorations. Used in Virginia in the 17th and 18th centuries as a shipper's or maker's mark. Used in England as early as the 16th century—apparently to indicate the highest quality.

Since 1901 the Stieff Company has used year markings on their sterling silver holloware.

1901	①	1929	𝓎 or 🌿
1902	②	1930	☆
1903	③	1931	♧ or 𝒻
to		1932	➤
1916	⑯	1933	𝒳 or ⚓
1917	▽ or ◇	1934	⌂ or ⊟
1918	△	1935	𝒱 or 𝒱
1919	○	1936	A
1920	⌒ or ◠	1937	B
1921	—	1938	C
1922	+	1939	D
1923	‡ or ++	1940	E
1924	♯	1941	F

1925	⬠	1942	G
1926	⬡ or ◇	1943	H
1927	☾ or ◠	1944	J
1928	卍	1945	K
1946	L	1961	3
1947	M	1962	4
1948	N	1963	5
1949	O	1964	6
1950	P	1965	7
1951	R	1966	8
1952	S	1967	9
1953	T	1968	10
1954	U	1969	11
1955	W	1970	12
1956	X	1971	13
1957	Y	1972	14
1958	Z	1973	15
1959	1	1974	16
1960	2		

STIEFF-ORTH CO.
Baltimore, Maryland

Not listed in Baltimore City Directories which were checked from the 1890s through the 1930s. Listed in JC 1909 sterling silver section. Out of business before 1915.

JAMES H. STIMPSON
Baltimore, Maryland

Listed Baltimore City Directories 1851-1868, variously as "zink works," "chemist" and "manuf'g chemist and patentee of ice pitcher, etc." James H. Stimpson was the son of James Stimpson, inventor of the double-wall ice pitcher. James H. Stimpson

invented and patented a triple-wall ice pitcher and several styles of butter coolers. Though listed as a "chemist" the inventory of his estate revealed that his "chemical works" was actually a silverplating establishment.

G.B. STOCKING
Tacoma, Washington

Jeweler, watchmaker, optician 1893-1896. Registered U.S. Patent No. 22,807, April 18, 1893 for manufacture of jewelry, spoons and other flatware.

RHODODENDRON

ARTHUR J. STONE
Gardner, Massachusetts
See Stone Associates

At least 14 slightly different Stone touch-marks are known. All include a small chasing hammer. Stone's earliest mark consisted of the hammer alone with the word STERLING. This was followed by the hammer with the S incised and then by Stone incised. Around 1908-09 several marks were used simultaneously with much over-lapping of their use. Later marks (1910-1937) have greater uniformity and were cut by die-makers outside the silver shop.

STERLING

STONE ASSOCIATES
Gardner, Massachusetts

Arthur J. Stone, founder, was born in Sheffield, England on the 26th of September 1847. At age 14 he began a seven-year apprenticeship with master silversmith, Edwin Eagle of Sheffield and studied evenings at the National School of Design, Sheffield. From 1868 to 1884 he worked as a silversmith in Edinburgh and Sheffield, work in the latter city being with James Dixon & Sons (q.v.) In 1884 he emigrated to the United States where he worked three years for William Durgin Company (q.v.), Concord, New Hampshire. In 1887 he moved to Gardner, Massachusetts to work for the Frank W. Smith Silver Company (q.v.) as designer and head of the holloware department. During 1895 and 1896 he worked with the J.P. Howard Company

(See Howard Co.) of New York. In 1896 he married Elizabeth Bent Eaton of Gardner and was then self-employed as a designer in that city. In 1901, with the assistance of his young wife, he established his own workshop in Gardner. Five years later he began hiring and training assistants.

Arthur J. Stone was one of the last independent designers and master silver-smiths of New England to employ and train other masters and apprentices. Stone was one of the primary supporters of the Arts and Crafts Movement. He received awards from the Society of Arts and Crafts and others. More than 35 exhibitions have included Stone silver.

Stone retired in 1937 on his birthday and sold the shop to Henry Heywood. He died February 6, 1938.

When Stone began to hire and train apprentices and craftsmen they hammered out the flatware and holloware under his supervision while he did the designing, chasing and other decoration as well as his own forging and raising. When Stone was in charge of the shop he insisted that each craftsman should sign his own work, so that each had his initial stamped under the STERLING mark on holloware and after the STERLING on flatware.

On October 1, 1937 when the shop was sold and renamed "Stone Associates" the mark was temporarily changed to a chaser's hammer crossed by three S's:

Soon the familiar Stone mark was resumed with a lower case "h" in a small shield, added to differentiate it from Stone's 1901-1937 mark:

In 1957 when Stone Associates was dis-banded, Ernest W. Lehtonen. trained in the Stone Associates Shop, bought the Stone mark which he used on flatware, adding a capital "L" in a small shield:

TABLE OF ASSISTANTS:

Date	Initial	Craftsman	Specialty
1906-1907	P	John H. Petty	Holloware
1906-1910	B	George P. Blanchard	Spoonmaker
1907-1911	O	Clinton B. Ogilvie	Holloware
1908-1909	• B •	William Blair	Holloware
1908-1937	T	Herbert A. Taylor	Holloware
1909-1912	L	Sylvanus E. Lamphrey	Spoonmaker, line chaser
1909-1919	C	David Carlson	Holloware
1909-1937	H	Arthur L. Hartwell	Holloware
1912-1937	B	Charles W. Brown	Spoonmaker
1912-1937	H•	Benjamin H. Harrison	Finisher
1912-1914	W	Alfred Wikstrom (or Wickstrom)	Flatware
1914-1916	P	Walter W. Pfeiffer	Flatware
1915-1932	E	George C. Erickson	Flatware
1920-1937	G	Herman W. Glendenning	Holloware, flatware
1921-1927	U	Earle H. Underwood	Holloware
ca. 1921		Thomas Holmes	
1922-1932	C	Magnus Carlberg	Holloware
1923-1933		Lawrence Carlberg	Apprentice
1924-1937	c	Edgar L. Caron	Holloware
1927-1929		Andrew Walker	Chaser
ca. 1929		Benjamin Holmes	Chaser
1928-1929		Charlotte Bone	Designer
1929-1933		Ernest C. Pearson	Finisher
1931-1937	B	Edward Billings	Chaser, designer
	C	Unidentified	Holloware
	B	Unidentified	Holloware

Chasers and designers rarely used initials.

STONE STERLING SILVER CO.
New York, New York

Registered their trademark U.S. Patent Office, No. 28,350, June 4, 1896 for silverware and jewelry. Listed in JC 1896. Out of business before 1904.

MAX H. STORCH
New York, New York

Registered trademarks for use on silverplated and sterling flatware and other tableware.

★Chase★

(Used since 1949)

(Used since 1950)

L.S. STOWE
See H.J. Webb & Co.

Stowe was born August 9, 1834, and orphaned at the age of 12. He was "bound out" to a farmer. When he was 18 he began training in the jewelry trade. He started in business in Gardner, Massachusetts in 1855. He moved to Springfield in 1864. Sold out to Webb in 1900 and died in 1924." (Clipping from unidentified newspaper dated 1924)

A. STOWELL, JR.
Baltimore, Maryland

Silversmith c. 1855. Listed as members of firm Gould, Stowell & Ward in 1855-1856 Baltimore City Directory.

STRATHMORE CO.
Providence, Rhode Island

Manufacturers of sterling flatware and plated silverware, holloware, picture frames and gift shop novelties. Listed 1915 through 1927.

SOLID STRATHMORE SILVER
T.S. CO.
STRATHMORE MESH
DIAMOND MESH

NATHAN STRAUS-DUPARQUET INC.
New York, New York

Tradename filed Sept. 7, 1950 for use on silverplated flatware. Claims use since January 1931.

NASTRAUS

STRAUSS SILVER CO., INC.
New York, New York

Manufacturers and importers of solid and silverplated Dutch silver novelties. Late 1920s and 1930s.

R. STRICKLAND & CO.
Albany, New York

Ralph Strickland listed in Albany City Directories 1857-1884 as manufacturer of plated wares.

Trademark is the company name and Albany, N.Y. in a circle.

STRONG & ELDER CO.
No address.

Listed in JC 1896 sterling section as out of business.

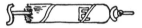

STRONG MFG. CO.
Winsted, Connecticut

In 1856, Markham and Strong of East Hampton, Connecticut made a small line of coffin tacks, screws and handles from white metal. Mr. Markham continued the business while the two Strongs, David and Clark were in the Union service. In 1866 David Strong bought out the company and moved to Winsted, Connecticut. The articles were considered of great beauty and were silver plated. It is reported that General Grant's casket was adorned with gold handles made by them. Also, handles and plates were furnished for the caskets of ex-president Harrison and Cornelius Vanderbilt. The company is last listed in 1934 city directory. No trademark has been located.

ARTHUR STUART COMPANY
Albuquerque, New Mexico

The company was established in 1949 and operated, according to the 1959 Albuquerque City Directory, by Arthur H. Spiegel. The above trademark and the sterling flatware pattern names *Empress Carlotta* and *Fidelity* were registered on the same date. Four additional sterling silver flatware pattern names, *Queen of Scots*, *Ceremonial*, *Crescendo* and *Breath of Spring*, were registered November 10, 1949.

The designs originated in Albuquerque and were sold on a direct mail basis from there. The silver was manufactured in Meriden, Connecticut by the Amston Company. When Amston went into bankruptcy in 1960, the Arthur Stuart Company was dissolved.

(No. 598,123, filed May 25, 1950; claims use since August 15, 1949.)

ROBERT STUART
Cincinnati, Ohio

Listed as manufacturers of hand-made silverware. (1931 Keystone)

STUDIO SILVERSMITHS
Division of Hannon & Smith Co., Inc.
Hawthorne, New Jersey

Founded in 1950 as Hannon & Smith Co. by Jack Hannon and Elmer Smith, both deceased. Now owned by Elmer Smith's widow, since remarried, Margaret Smith Gunster. Manufacturers of 24k gold plate, silverplate, crystal combined with gold and silverplate. Products include holloware, salad bowls, salad servers, gold and silver footed crystal bowls, candelabra, centerpieces, etc.

SSS

STURDY & MARCY
See Fred I. Marcy & Co.

SUCKLING, LTD.
Birmingham, England

Successor to Wm. Suckling & Sons between 1915-1922. Manufacturers of plated silverware.

WYNDHAM A. SULLIVAN
Baltimore, Maryland

Listed in Baltimore City Directories 1900-1915 as a silversmith in the firm of Ritter & Sullivan.

SUMMIT SILVER INC.
New York, New York

Advertised 1965-74. Advertising says "two-tone decorative silverplate that never needs any polishing...From the famous HOKA silversmiths in Western Germany." Distributors (?) only.

SUNDERLIN COMPANY
Rochester, New York

This silversmithing business began with three Burr brothers; Albert, who was apprenticed to Erastus Cook, and died shortly after starting his jewelry business; Alexander J., who was Albert's apprentice and Cornelius. The business went through a series of partnerships from 1838 and was known as C.A. Burr & Company after the death of the two brothers. In 1864 it was sold to Sunderlin & Weaver; became Sunderlin & McAllister; L. Sunderlin & Company and in 1944 was the Sunderlin Company. Out of business in 1952.

SUPERIOR SILVER COMPANY
See Middletown Plate Co.
See Wilcox Silver Plate Co.

The Superior Silver Co. marks were used by the Middletown Plate Co.

The Superior marks first read "Superior Silver Co." and later read "Superior Silver Plate Co." This change may have been after the Middletown Plate Company moved to Meriden and the Superior line was transferred to Wilcox Silver Plate Company.

(Registered April 3, 1906; first use claimed February 6, 1906; renewed in 1926)

SUPREME SILVER CO.
New York, New York

Manufacturers of sterling silver holloware and repair work c. 1930.

SUTTON HOO JEWELERS
Colorado Springs, Colorado

Founded November 1972 by Bob Newell and Charles Lamoreaux. They make one-of-a-kind jewelry and holloware of sterling silver and gold. The firm was joined in 1974 by Lewis Ridenour, silversmith, who concentrates on holloware and flatware. Bob Newell (b. December 6, 1940) received his education at the New Mexico Military Institute and studied the art of *ciré de perdue* with the master technician from New Gold Company. Charles Lamoureaux (b. December 26, 1950) received his education at the University of Kansas. Lewis Ridenour, (b. July 8, 1949) was educated at Northwest Missouri State College and the University of Kansas.

Bob Newell   Charles Lamoreaux   Lewis Ridenour

(Shop stamp)

THE SWEETSER CO.
New York, New York

Gold and silversmiths c. 1900-1915.

CHAS. N. SWIFT & CO.
New York, New York

Listed JC 1904 sterling silver section. Out of business before 1915.

SYRACUSE SILVER COMPANY
Syracuse, New York

First listed in Syracuse City Directory in 1940 as manufacturers of silverplated holloware, novelties, trophies, also plating. Ernest Kauer, owner. The 1946-56 Directories list Mrs. Edith O. Kauer as owner and the 1965-66 telephone directory lists only her home address.

SYRACUSE SILVER MFG. CO.

Syracuse, New York
See Lesser & Rheinauer
See A.B. Schreuder

"The sterling silver manufacturing plant of A.B. Schreuder, which has been in existence for 40 years, goes into the hands of the Syracuse Silver Mfg. Co. The latter is a new organization formed by the partners in the firm of A. Lesser's Sons, wholesale jewelers. Members of the company are Simon Lesser, S. Harry Lesser and Benjamin Lesser. They will manufacture sterling silver novelties. Benjamin Lesser will be manager." (JC&HR 2-20-1895, p. 10)

Listed 1896-1904 in JC as manufactures of sterling silverware. Syracuse Silver Mfg. Co. listed in Syracuse, New York City Directories 1895-1900. Under the first listing, J. Barton French was president and business manager, A. Hubbs, Secretary and E. Elmer Keeler, treas. in 1896-1897, Benjamin F., Simon and Solomon H. Lesser were listed as owners. In 1898-1900, it was listed as Silverware Manufacturers, A. Lesser's Son. In 1900, the listing was A. Lesser Son, watch materials.

T

TABER & TIBBITS, INC.

Wallingford, Connecticut

Listed in the City Directory 1919-1941. Makers of silverplated hollowares and novelties. Trademark was a tabor (small drum).

The firm was started in 1919 by Charles H. Tibbits and R.H. Taber, his son-in-law. They were succeeded by Silvercraft Co.

TALBOT MFG. CO.

Providence, Rhode Island

Manufacturers of cigarette cases in the 1920s.

TALCO

H.H. TAMMEN CURIO CO.

Denver, Colorado

In business from c. 1881 to 1962. Was purchased by Con Becker in 1957 and is now the Thrift Novelty Company.

First begun by H.H. Tammen as a curio shop, the business was expanded to include the manufacture and wholesaling of souvenir novelties and jewelry. Among their widely distributed souvenirs were sterling silver spoons depicting people and places of the West. By 1887, after several moves for expansion, a museum established in connection with the business, advertised that "it was lighted by electric light," and was considered a place no traveler should miss. The business managed to survive the panic of 1893 and went on to become the largest of its kind in the West.

TAUNTON BRITANNIA MANUFACTURING COMPANY

Taunton, Massachusetts
See Reed & Barton

The Taunton Britannia Manufacturing Company was the successor to Crossman, West & Leonard when the need for additional capital for expansion brought about the establishment of this joint-stock company on August 18, 1830.

There were eight shareholders in the new company. Of these, only William Crossman, Haile N. Wood, Daniel Cobb and William West were experienced in the britannia business. James Crossman had been a merchant tailor, real estate investor and was at that time a director of the Cohannet Bank in Taunton. Haile Wood, Sr., dealt in real estate and Horatio and Z.A. Leonard were prominent in the metal and textile trades.

Immediately a new factory at Hopewell, on the Mill River, was built. Water was planned as the main source of power, but the old steam engine from the Fayette Street shop was installed for power during summer droughts.

By 1831, the manufacturing of britannia ware had all been shifted to the new factory. Throughout that year, many additions to their product line were added. Among them were castor frames, tankards, church cups, christening bowls, soup ladles and candlesticks. In 1832, toast racks, soda

dispensers and fruit dishes were added. Sales of the tea sets, that had been the backbone of the business, dropped after 1831.

The Taunton Britannia Manufacturing Company was noted for the production of some of the most beautiful lamps made in America. New designs in these lighting devices and an increased supply of whale oil on the market promoted their popularity.

Castor sets were to be found on every dining table in America; many of them were made by this company. Their revolving sets were considered the epitome of luxurious living.

In 1832, William Crossman, William West and Zephaniah Leonard sold their interests in the company to Horatio Leonard and in 1833, Isaac Babbitt, superintendent of the plant, left the company.

On February 16, 1833, a new corporation, with Horatio Leonard, James Crossman, Haile Wood, Daniel Cobb and Haile N. Wood was formed under the same name—the Taunton Britannia Mfg. Company. General business uncertainty of the period, competition from other britannia ware establishments, as well as a strong preference for foreign articles brought about the total failure of the company in November, 1834.

Three people still had great faith in the enterprise. They were the company agent, Benjamin Pratt; Henry Reed, a spinner; and his friend, Charles E. Barton, the solderer. On April 1, 1835, they reopened the factory and eventually formed what is now Reed & Barton.

T. B. M. CO.
TAUNTON BRIT.
MANFG. CO.

TAUNTON SILVERSMITHS

A subsidiary of Lenox, Inc. The Taunton Collection, a line of silverplated holloware, is offered only to Lenox dinnerware dealers. Introduced late in 1974.

TAUNTON SILVERPLATE COMPANY
Taunton, Massachusetts

Founded in 1853 and stayed in business until 1859. They stamped their pieces with that name and also used the name Taunton Britannia and Silver Plate Co. since the base metal was britannia. George B. Atwood was president with Thomas Furness and John Fletcher being directors. These men had been brought from England to begin

the silverplating of britannia. Their shop was on Cohannet Street in Taunton but they moved to a large building on Winthrop Street.

ANDREW A. TAYLOR
Newark, New Jersey

Listed from c. 1930 to 1973 as manufacturer of sterling silver holloware. No longer listed.

DAVID TAYLOR JEWELRY CO.
New York, New York

Registered trademark for use on flatware, holloware, insignia, service medals and costume jewelry made of or plated with gold, silver, or other precious metals, all for use of officers and enlisted men of the Armed Forces of the U.S.

(Used since April 15, 1945)

F.C. TAYLOR & CO.
Baltimore, Maryland

Listed in 1881 Baltimore City Directory as silverplaters.

T.C. SHOP
Chicago, Illinois

Founded by Emery W. Todd (?) and Clemencia C. Cosio (?) 1910-1913. Todd had been employed by the Kalo Shop. He incorporated Clara Welles' styles into his handmade silver flatware and other domestic wares. He executed the designs of his partner, Clemencia Cosio, or had them

made by Matthias Hamch, a Park Ridge craftsman. Todd also taught jewelry making at the Art Institute of Chicago 1927-1930.

Mark: THE SHOP

THE TENNANT COMPANY
New York, New York
See Hartford Sterling Co.
See Phelps & Cary Co.

Silversmiths before 1896. Makers of holloware and dresserware in sterling silver only. Trophies, presentation pieces. Succeeded (?) by Hartford Sterling Co. c. 1901. Trademark is identical to one used by Hartford Sterling Co. and by Phelps & Cary Co., with the exception of the initials in the shield.

THIERY & CO.
Newark, New Jersey

Listed JC as jewelers; out of business before 1909. Trademarks found on souvenir spoons.

THE THOMAE CO.
Attleboro, Massachusetts

Chas. Thomae & Son, Inc. was established August 1, 1920 by the late Charles Thomae and his son, Herbert L. Thomae. They make novelty goods of 14k gold and sterling silver, religious medals, photo etching on gold and silver and make bronze memorial plates and signs.

Charles Thomae was superintendent of the Watson Co. for several years and developed enameling and a line of novelties and dresserware till it reached the importance of a separate business. The Thomae Co. was formed as a division of the Watson Co. In 1920, Charles Thomae resigned from both firms and started a new business with the name of Chas. Thomae & Son.

The firm's founder died in 1958. It is now run by his two sons Herbert L., President and Charles G. Thomae.

The trademark 𝕿 has been used with little change since 1920 and was a personal

mark used by Charles Thomae to mark his own work before that.

THOMPSON, HAYWARD & CO.
Mechanicsville, Massachusetts
See Walter E. Hayward Co., Inc.

THOMPSONS
ERNEST THOMPSON, JR.
Damariscotta, Maine

A husband and wife team, trained as silversmiths and jewelers in both the craft and design. They have a second generation joining their forces. They are involved primarily in silversmithing in the traditional manner but are also equipped for small productions.

They make reproductions of historical and domestic as well as ecclesiastical articles—monstrances, croziers, processional crosses, chalices, ciboria, pectoral crosses, candlesticks, pyxes, etc., in both traditional and contemporary designs. Their work is primarily handwrought.

The Thompsons also do designing to order, chasing, enameling, inlay and encrustation, engraving, spinning and finishing, and the other processes necessary to a complete silversmithing operation.

E.T. Thompson (intaglio; single or double line)

E.T. Thompson (cameo; single line)

Also Reproduction and Sterling Silver (cameo)

THORNTON BROTHERS
New York, New York

"The Thornton Brothers were established in 1877." (JW 4-6-1892) Listed 1927 JKD as manufacturers of emblems.

THORNTON & COMPANY
New York, New York

"William H. Thornton, salesman for Krementz & Co. (1892) started on the road for Rogers & Bro., then at 690 Broadway, N.Y. William H. Thornton was born near Louisville, Kentucky of English parents,

on April 14, 1859. After graduating from Notre Dame College, Notre Dame, Indiana, at about 19 years of age, he engaged with a retail jeweler in Louisville, acting as salesman and manager. Subsequently, he went to N.Y. and became house salesman for J.T. Scott & Co. At the end of two years he accepted the position of traveling salesman for Rogers & Bro. covering territory for them for 5 years. He left this house to go with Krementz & Co. for whom he has traveled 8 years, going west as far as San Francisco and south to New Orleans. He makes two trips a year to the Pacific Coast. Mr. Thornton is unmarried, and can thus accept all the advantages of the Manhattan Athletic Club, of which he is a member. He is an all-round athlete, being especially fond of yachting." (J-C 9-28-1892, p. 24)

"Receivers appointed for Thornton & Co., silversmiths. Action was brought by Wm. H. Thornton against Henrietta Williams, his partner. Thornton & Co. who started May 26, 1896, are the successors of Holbrook & Simmons and Holbrook & Thornton. Mrs. Williams was a special partner in the former, and a general partner in the latter firm, and Thornton & Co. their successors." (J-C 9-16-1896, p. 20)

H. & S.

Old Mark of
Holbrook & Simmons.

TIFFANY & CO., INC.
New York, New York

CHRONOLOGY

Tiffany & Young	1837
Tiffany, Young & Ellis	1841
Tiffany & Company	1853
Tiffany & Co., Inc.	1868-

Founded by Charles L. Tiffany in 1837 with John B. Young under the name Tiffany & Young. They first stocked their store with stationary, Chinese bric-a-brac, fans, pottery, umbrellas and desks. They purchased almost all of their silverware from John C. Moore (q.v.) who had begun the manufacture of silverware in 1827 and who was later joined in business by his son, Edward C. Moore. Tiffany bought the Moore business in 1868.

During the 1850s Tiffany & Co. produced some electroplated wares but their greatest production came after the Civil War. Electroplated wares were discontinued after 1931.

In 1852 Tiffany introduced the English sterling silver standard to America for Tiffany silver. This standard was later adopted by the U.S. Government and made into Federal law determining the minimum amount of fine silver required for articles marked "Sterling Silver."

In 1868 when Tiffany was incorporated and the silverware factory of the Moores became part of the organization with Edward C. Moore becoming one of its directors, the silverware made in the factory bore not only the mark "Tiffany & Co." but also the latter "M." Following the death of Edward C. Moore in 1891, the surname initial of the incumbent president was included as part of the Tiffany trademark. This practice was discontinued after 1965.

According to the findings of the Carpenters (see *Tiffany Silver*) the Adams & Shaw (q.v.) firm was absorbed into Tiffany & Co., probably in the 1880s, with Mr. Shaw becoming superintendent of the Tiffany plant.

For the almost 20 years (c. 1850 to 1869) before Tiffany made their own flatware, they retailed the flatware of other makers. This was usually marked with the maker's mark and Tiffany, Young & Ellis prior to 1853 or Tiffany & Co. after 1853.

Marks on electroplated wares have tended to follow the tradition of euphism, euphemism, and sometimes downright confusion. Tiffany was no exception. One finds the term "silver-soldered" which has nothing to do with the electroplating process but means that silver solder was used rather than the softer lead solder. Tiffany used a variety of marks on their electroplated wares ranging from simply the company name to more complex marks which bear some resemblance to those on their sterling products.

Tiffany holloware and a few flatware marks include two numbers—the pattern number and the order number. The pattern number refers to the original drawing or pattern. These are roughly in consecutive order. The order number is an assigned number for a particular order. These numbers are beyond the scope of this volume and the reader is referred to *Tiffany Silver* by Charles H. Carpenter, Jr. and Mary Grace Carpenter for a full discussion.

TIFFANY YOUNG & ELLIS
J.C.M

20

(Used 1850-52.)

TIFFANY&CO
271 BROADWAY

TIFFANY&CO
271 BROADWAY

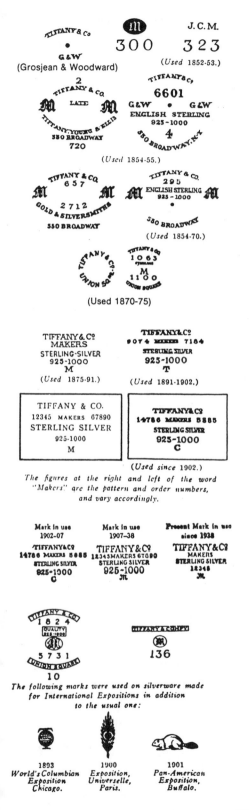

TIFFT & WHITING

North Attleboro, Massachusetts
See Gorham Corporation

Founded in 1840 in North Attleboro, Massachusetts. Succeeded by Whiting Manufacturing Company, Newark, New Jersey in 1866. Purchased by the Gorham Corporation in 1905.

TILDEN-THURBER CO.

Providence, Rhode Island

Roots of Tilden-Thurber Company go deep into the history and business development of Rhode Island. In 1856, when the doors of the new firm opened, the sign above the window read GORHAM CO. AND BROWN. Gorham Thurber, great-grandfather of today's president, was listed as one of the officers. An unusually active man in business, in addition to his interest in Gorham Co. & Brown, he formed a co-partnership with John Gorham, forming the firm of Gorham & Thurber, one of the predecessors of the Gorham Manufacturing Company.

In 1878, Gorham Co. & Brown moved across the street from its first location and changed its name to Henry T. Brown & Co. Members of the board were Mr. Brown, Henry Tilden and Gorham Thurber. The firm remained there until 1895 when it moved into the present Tilden-Thurber building. Gorham Thurber died shortly afterwards.

In March, 1880, the name of the firm was changed to Tilden-Thurber & Co. In the same year, William H. Thurber, grandfather of the present officers and son of Gorham Thurber, joined the firm, becoming a partner in 1885.

On June 23, 1892, the company became incorporated under the present name Tilden-Thurber Corporation. At this time Henry Tilden was elected President and William H. Thurber, Treasurer. William H. Thurber's contributions to the development of the company were an increased volume of business and addition of a number of new departments added to the original line of jewelry and silverware. Following Mr. Tilden's death in 1907, Mr. Thurber was elected President and Treasurer.

Henry C. Tilden, son of Henry Tilden, joined the firm and became manager of the sterling silver department. In 1915, he moved to Chicago and joined Spaulding & Co., leading jewelers and eventually became president of that firm.

In 1956, when the company celebrated its 100th anniversary, Frederick B. Thurber was President and William Gorham Thurber, Treasurer. Tracy Gorham Thurber, son of W.G. Thurber, joined the company in 1951. Another son, William H. Thurber, is currently President.

Since 1878, Tilden-Thurber has been noted as the source of rare and beautiful importations. Fine paintings and etchings are displayed in the Tilden-Thurber Art Galleries.

Working with the Gorham Manufacturing Company, Tilden-Thurber furnished a complete sterling silver service for the Battleship **Rhode Island,** later placed on display in the State House. They also furnished the silver service for the Cruiser, **Providence,** later exhibited at Brown University.

Service to the community and active interest in its employees have been outstanding characteristics of this company. This has been demonstrated in the establishment of a Brown University scholarship for a local student; assistance in the establishment of a rigorous educational and training program for jewelers; a company-paid pension plan and, most recently, a profit-sharing plan for employees.

TILLINGHAST SILVER CO.
Meriden, Connecticut

Manufacturers of sterling silver hollow handle serving pieces. In business c. 1920-1935.

TILLINGHAST SILVER CO.

EDWARD TODD & CO.
New York, New York

Edward Todd & Co. began as Smith & Todd in 1851, as successors to Bard Brothers & Co. The changes have been from Smith & Todd to Mabie, Todd & Co. and then to Edward Todd & Co. They were manufacturers of sterling silverware and gold pens.

Another account reads: "The Edward Todd Co. was formed in 1869. He had previously been with E.G. Bagley, which company was founded in 1843. It continued until 1851. C.F. Newton succeeded in 1859 and was succeeded by Newton, Kurtz & Co. which continued for 10 years when Edward Todd & Co. was formed. The company was incorporated in 1897." (JC-W 2-5-1919) It was still listed in business in 1927 JKD.

EUGENE S. TONER CO.
New York, New York

Manufacturers (?) of sterling silverware. Listed JC 1909 as out of business.

Note similarity of trademark to that of Depasse Mfg. Co.

JOHN TOOTHILL
See Metropolitan Silver Co.

TOOTHILL & McBEAN SILVER CO.
Ottawa, Illinois

Listed JC 1898 in plated silver section. Out of business before 1904.

QUADRUPLE PLATE

TORONTO SILVER PLATE COMPANY
Toronto, Canada

Founded in 1882 by James A. Watts, formerly sales representative of the Meriden Britannia Co. of Connecticut, and others to manufacture a complete line of silver-plated and sterling wares in Canada. Around 1885 they began the production of Holmes & Edwards flatware under license. In addition to their own productions they had some silver made for them by Henry & Leslie, silversmiths in Montreal. This silver bears the marks **STERLING⊕☐T.S.P.**

The Toronto Silver Plate Co. was absorbed by the Wm. A. Rogers Co. about 1914 and when that company was sold to Oneida in 1929 the Toronto company marks were no longer used.

STERLING

STERLING T.S.P.

(On sterling silver)

Sterling marks not used after 1915.

(On plated silver holloware)

TORONTO SILVER PLATE CO.

(Flatware.)

TORSIL METAL
TORSIL STEEL
TORSIL E. P.—N. S.

(Knives.)

JOHN TORSLEFF
Boston, Massachusetts

John Torsleff first appears in the Boston City Directory of 1857; at that time associated with Thomas Barker & Co., silverplated ware, along with one Charles Anthes. From 1858 through 1860 Torsleff and Anthes were in business together, and from 1861 through 1863 (the last listing) John Torsleff, silverplated ware, was in business at 334 Washington St. He lived in Chelsea, Mass. Either this John Torsleff or John Torsleff, Jr., died about 1869.

Some pieces of his manufacture are of thin sterling with decorative elements of cast brass, silverplated.

J. TOSTRUP
Oslo, Norway

Founded in 1832 by Jacob Ubrich Holfeldt Tostrup, great-grandfather of the present manager. Makers of all kinds of flatware and holloware. The firm has won many international awards for the excellence of its work. They were influential in 19th century revival of filigree work and were especially noted for their *plique à jour* enamels.

(Both marks for use on flatware and holloware, made of or plated with precious metal. Registered in the U.S. in 1949. Norwegian registration 1947.)

A.H. TOWAR & CO.
Lyons, New York
See New Haven Silver Plate Co.

A.F. TOWLE & SON CO.
Greenfield, Massachusetts
See Lunt Silversmiths
See Rogers, Lunt & Bowlen
See Towle Silversmiths

A.F. Towle & Son, successors to Towle & Jones, were the links between the Moultons, of Newburyport, and the Towle Silversmiths. Anthony F. Towle was an apprentice to William Moulton IV and bought his business and that of Joseph Moulton IV in 1873. In 1882, with others, the business was incorporated as Towle Silversmiths. Anthony F. Towle & Son moved to Greenfield, Massachusetts in 1890 and operated until 1902. At that time their business was taken over by Rogers, Lunt & Bowlen, now known as Lunt Silversmiths.

They were manufacturers of both sterling and plated silverware. Registered trademark, U.S. Patent Office, No. 27,286, November 19, 1895 for electroplated ware.

"Anthony F. Towle, b. Newburyport, Dec. 12, 1816. He learned silversmith trade with the late firm of N. & T. Foster, and in 1855 established the firm of Towle & Jones, jewelers and silversmiths. Subsequently the firm name was changed to Towle, Jones & Co. and A.F. Towle & Son. Under the last firm name, in 1880, the manufacture of silverware was established in this city (Newburyport) by the deceased. Mr. Towle retired from active business in 1892. He leaves three children. Mrs. E.B. Horn of Boston, and Edward B. and William A. Towle of Newburyport." (JC&HR 4-7-1897, p. 19)

E.J. TOWLE MFG. CO.
Seattle, Washington

Began as Joseph Mayer & Bros. 1898; Jos. Mayer, Inc. before 1922; Northern Stamping & Manufacturing Co. (still used for some items) and was succeeded by E.J. Towle Manufacturing Company c. 1938.

Were wholesalers of diamonds, watches, jewelry, sterling silverware, plated silver goods, cut glass and optical goods.

Medals and other presentation pieces have been and are still made. Some of the finest die work in the country is still done by this company.

Their work is now mainly the designing and manufacturing of silver jewelry, charms, religious goods and souvenir silverware.

E. J. T. Co.

In 1980 the company was sold to Raoul Le Blanc.

TOWLE SILVERSMITHS
Newburyport, Massachusetts

William Moulton II, born in 1664 settled in old Newbury, later Newburyport, to become the first silversmith in a long lineage of craftsmen now the Towle Silversmiths. He was succeeded by Joseph I, William III (who moved to Marietta, Ohio and became not only the first silversmith in The Northwest Territory, but, also one of the founders of Marietta), Joseph II, Joseph III, Ebenezer, William IV, Enoch, Abel and Joseph IV—all silversmiths.

Anthony F. Towle and William P. Jones, apprentices of William IV, began business under the name Towle & Jones in 1857, later buying the business of William IV and Joseph IV. Anthony F. Towle and Edward F., his son, engaged in business as A.F. Towle & Son in 1873, and this partnership was the germ of the A.F. Towle & Son Co., Inc. in 1880, which in 1882 became the Towle Manufacturing Company, Anthony F. Towle and Edward F. Towle retiring. The company is now known as the Towle Silversmiths.

About 1890 the familiar "T enclosing a lion" was first used as a trademark. It is said to have been designed by Anthony Towle from the family coat of arms.

In 1890 the manufacture of holloware began at the Towle company under Richard Dimes who later went to Frank W. Smith, Gardner, and finally established his own business in Boston.

The Towle firm made plated flatware from 1906-1909. It was gradually discontinued, the last pattern was *Chester*. The stock was sold to Samuel Weare.

They have been leaders in establishing an exhibit gallery where artist-silversmiths skills are presented to the public. Other exhibits of silver craftsmanship have been prepared in cooperation with musuems.

In the 1940s Mueck-Cary Co. was purchased by Towle and the trademark now belongs to them. Carvel Hall, a subsidiary manufacturing fine cutlery, is in Crisfield, Maryland.

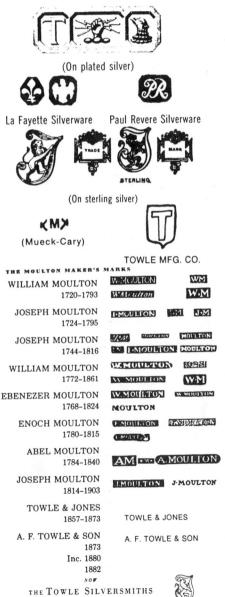

(On plated silver)

La Fayette Silverware   Paul Revere Silverware

STERLING

(On sterling silver)

(Mueck-Cary)

TOWLE MFG. CO.

THE MOULTON MAKER'S MARKS

WILLIAM MOULTON 1720–1793	W.MOULTON W.Moulton	WM W·M
JOSEPH MOULTON 1724–1795	I.MOULTON I·M	J·M
JOSEPH MOULTON 1744–1816	I.M MOULTON I·MOULTON MOULTON	
WILLIAM MOULTON 1772–1861	W.MOULTON W.MOULTON	W·M
EBENEZER MOULTON 1768–1824	W.MOULTON W.MOULTON MOULTON	
ENOCH MOULTON 1780–1815	E.MOULTON E.MOULTON E.MOULTON	
ABEL MOULTON 1784–1840	AM A·M A.MOULTON	
JOSEPH MOULTON 1814–1903	J.MOULTON J·MOULTON	
TOWLE & JONES 1857–1873	TOWLE & JONES	
A. F. TOWLE & SON 1873 Inc. 1880 1882 NOW	A. F. TOWLE & SON	

THE TOWLE SILVERSMITHS

In 1978 the Leonard Silver Manufacturing Company was acquired by Towle and company headquarters were moved to Boston. Leonard Florence, founder of the Leonard company became chairman and instituted sweeping changes in the Towle organization. Diversification has brought spectacular growth but has brought charges by other silver manufacturers that the quality of Towle's products has declined.

IRA STRONG TOWN & J. TOWN
Montpelier, Vermont

Advertised 1830-1838 as clockmakers and silversmiths—"silver work of every description manufactured to order on short notice."

IRA S. TOWN & ELIJAH B. WITHERELL
Montpelier, Vermont

Successors to Ira Strong Town and J. Town. Formed a partnership that took

"Candlight" sterling flatware by Towle Silversmiths. (Photo courtesy of Towle silversmiths)

"Old Master" sterling flatware by Towle Silversmiths. (Photo courtesy of Towle Silversmiths)

over the business until it was dissolved in 1845. Advertised that "they made all the silverware bought at their shop and it was warrented to be the best quality."

THE TOWNSEND, DESMOND & VOORHIS CO.

New York, New York

Listed JC 1896-1904 in sterling silver section. Out of business before 1909.

T. D. & V. CO. STERLING.

TRINAC METALCRAFTS INC.

Brooklyn, New York

Manufacturers of pewterwares. In business now.

J.W. TUCKER

San Francisco, California

John William Tucker arrived in San Francisco August 1849 from New York on board the ship **Panama**. He had trained as a carpenter, sold watches and made a fortune. He set up shop in August 1850 as "J.W. Tucker & Co., importing jeweler." In April 1874 the listing was changed to "Tucker Jewelry Manufacturing & Commercial Co." Many pieces bear his name though no known pieces can actually be attributed to his workmanship or to his shop.

Tucker died in July 1876 but the business was continued under his name for another ten years. The last listing being in 1886. Occasionally, directory entries mention "mfgr." before and after his death but may refer only to repair work or possibly special orders.

TUCKER & PARKERHURST CO.

Ogdensburg, New York

Successors to Bell Bros. in 1898. Out of business before 1904.

JAMES W. TUFTS

Boston, Massachusetts

Trademark registered February 2, 1875 for plated silverware by James W. Tufts, Medford, Massachusetts. Incorporated 1881. Out of business before 1915.

Tufts started his business career as an apprentice in the apothecary store of Samuel Kidder in Charlestown, Massachusetts. He soon went into business for himself and became the proprietor of a chain of three pharmacies. His interest in the concoction of syrups and other products sold at the soda fountain led to the manufacture of these products. His next step was to branch out into the manufacture of the apparatus used in drugstores. The soda fountain of that time was a magnificent piece of equipment. Many were of Italian marble and the metal parts were silverplated. From the silverplating of fountain parts, Tufts branched out in 1875 into the manufacture of an extensive line of silverplated items such as pitchers, dishes and bases. The business, which had been conducted under Tufts' name, was consolidated in 1891 with other soda fountain companies and became the American Soda Fountain Company, the largest in its field. By 1895 Tufts turned the active management of his business over to others because of his health. In search of a more healthful climate and atmosphere, he purchased 5,000 acres in the sandhills of North Carolina and founded the resort town of Pinehurst. He died there February 2, 1902.

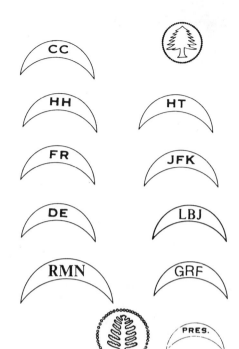

TUTTLE SILVER CO.
Boston, Massachusetts
See Tuttle Silversmiths

TUTTLE SILVERSMITHS
Boston, Massachusetts

In 1890, Boston silversmith Timothy Tuttle was first commissioned by wealthy families to copy old English silver. His original pieces were dated in the English custom with the crest of the reigning monarch. During the term of office of President Calvin Coolidge, Tuttle adopted this custom, marking each piece with a crescent and the initials of the incumbent President of the United States. Today this date mark is unique with Tuttle.

The figure II below the initials of Ronald Reagan indicate a second term of office.

Timothy Tuttle used the Pine Tree Shilling symbol as his trademark. The Pine Tree Shilling was one of the earliest silver coins minted in the American colonies by Hull and Sanderson in 1652. Used as the Tuttle trademark it is the stamp of quality and prestige appearing on all Tuttle sterling pieces, including authentic reproductions of Early American, European and modern design.

In 1915, the company was listed as Tuttle Silver Co. By 1922, it was incorporated.

In 1955 Tuttle Silversmiths was purchased by R. Wallace & Sons Mfg. Co. (now Wallace Silversmiths) and became an acquisition of the Hamilton Watch Company of Lancaster, Pennsylvania when Hamilton purchased Wallace Silversmiths in December 1959. Every piece of Tuttle silver is sterling. They make no plated silver.

Depending on the shape of each flatware piece, either pine tree is used.

TYSON, TRUMP & CO.
Baltimore, Maryland

Listed in 1867-1868 Baltimore City Directory as silverplaters.

U

UNGER BROS.
Newark, New Jersey

CHRONOLOGY

Unger Brothers	1872-1879
(William, George, Frederick, Herman and Eugene)	
Unger Brothers	1879-1904
(Herman and Eugene)	
Unger Brothers, Inc.	1904-1919
(Herman and Eugene; Philemon O. Dickinson)	

William Unger was a partner of Thomas A. Edison from 1870 to 1872 in the Newark Telegraph Works. This firm was dissolved that year and the five brothers organized Unger Brothers for the manufacture and sale of pocket knives and hardware specialties. They began the manufacture of silver jewelry in 1878. Three of the brothers, William, George and Frederick died that year and the two surviving brothers, Herman and Eugene reorganized the business, retaining the name Unger Brothers.

FINE STERLING
TUTTLE SILVERSMITHS

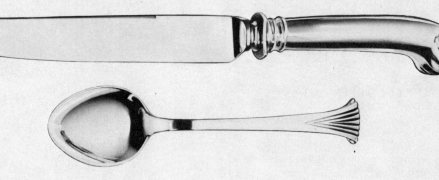

"Onslow" sterling flatware by Tuttle Silversmiths. (Photo courtesy of Tuttle Silversmiths)

"Hannah Hull" sterling flatware by Tuttle Silversmiths. (Photo courtesy of Tuttle Silversmiths)

"Beauvoir" sterling flatware by Tuttle Silversmiths. (Photo courtesy of Tuttle Silversmiths)

When Eugene Unger married Emma L. Dickinson, daughter of Philemon Dickinson, in 1880, a new dimension was added to the firm. It was Dickinson who was the designer of the extensive line of Art Nouveau articles made by the Unger firm and now so avidly sought by collectors.

January 21, 1904 the firm was incorporated. The last of the Unger brothers died in 1909 and by 1910 the dies for the Art Nouveau patterns were no longer used; a simpler, more rectilinear line being produced. In 1914 the firm ceased production of silver articles entirely to manufacture airplane parts. In 1919 the business was sold.

The trademark of the Unger Brothers, an interlaced U and B, was stamped on all Unger silver with the exception of some jewelry made after 1910. This jewelry is of light weight and of lesser quality than the original work.

UNITED STATES SILVER CO., INC.
New York, New York

Manufacturers of plated wares. First listing found was 1948. Still listed.

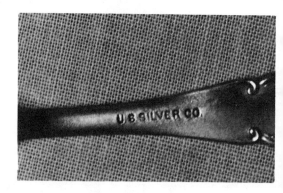

UTOPIAN SILVER DEPOSIT & NOVELTY CO.

New York, New York

Listed JC 1915 in sterling silver section. Out of business before 1922.

V

THOMAS J. VAIL

Connecticut

See American Sterling Co.
See Curtisville Mfg. Co.
See Williams Bros. Mfg. Co.

During the Civil War Thomas Vail produced war materials. Between 1865 and 1869 Vail probably was in the silver plating business as in the Hartford Directory for 1869 he is listed as manufacturer of German Silver and plated ware, etc. In 1871, The American Sterling Company took over the property from the trustee, Leavitt Hunt.

VALENTINE LINSLEY SILVER CO.

Wallingford, Connecticut

See Wallace Bros. Silver Co.
See The Wallingford Co.

Listed in the City Directory 1895-1899. Makers of plated silverware. Succeeded by The Wallingford Co. in 1899.

V. L.

(Silver Plated Hollowware.)

MADE AND PLATED BY WALLACE BROS. SILVER CO.

VAN BERGH SILVER PLATE CO.

Rochester, New York

Founded 1892 by Frederick W. Van Bergh and Maurice H. Van Bergh, who were President and Secretary, respectively. A third brother is said to have joined the firm in 1898 (not confirmed). The company was incorporated July 1, 1904. In 1925 all assets were transferred to a new corporation, the Van Bergh Silver Plate Company, Inc., set up by Oneida Community Limited. This new corporation was merged into Oneida Community Limited in 1926 and moved from Rochester to Oneida, New York.

BRITANNIA METAL CO.

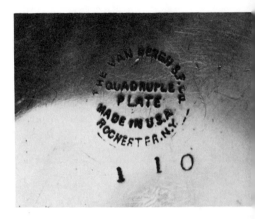

W.K. VANDERSLICE

San Francisco, California

William Keyser Vanderslice learned silver-smithing in Philadelphia and began business there in 1857. He arrived in San Francisco in May 1858 bringing with him equipment he had brought around Cape Horn. He set up shop in 1860 and took his brother-in-law, Charles Henry Sherman, into the business in 1862. Late in 1868 Lucius M. Thompson, formerly with Shreve & Co. (q.v.), joined the firm as a partner. They employed about 20 men at that time and used around 1,500 ounces of silver each month. They introduced their patented flatware patterns about this time. William Melrose joined the firm as an engraver in 1875. Thompson left the firm in 1880 and Melrose became a partner by 1882. The business was incorporated as W.K. Vanderslice & Co. in March 1897 with Melrose as vice president. Following Vanderslice's death in March 1899 Melrose became president. The firm was sold to Shreve & Co. in 1908. (Morse papers)

CLARENCE A. VANDERBILT
New York, New York

Manufacturers of sterling silverware, baskets, salt and peppers, cups, candlesticks, cigarette cases, vanity cases, picture frames, napkin rings and flasks from c. 1909-1935.

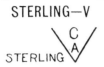

JOHN T. VANSANT & BROTHER
Philadelphia, Pennsylvania

Vansant & Co. was listed as silversmiths in 1850. John T. Vansant Mfg. Co. listed around 1887 to 1905.

"John T. Vansant & Brother, manufacturers of silverware, Philadelphia, who have been in financial difficulties recently were sold out by the sheriff." (JW 8-18-1886, p. 984)

ERSKINE V. VAN HOUTEN
White Plains, New York

Listed 1931 to 1950 as manufacturers of table glassware (apparently silver deposit-ware).

VAUGHAN PEWTER SHOP
Taunton, Massachusetts

Lester H. Vaughan was a manufacturer of pewterware c. 1930-1950. Originally L.H. Vaughan; later Vaughan Pewter Shop.

P.M. VERMASS
Minneapolis, Minnesota

Successors to F.L. Bosworth before 1921. They were jobbers who bought wares "in the metal" and plated them in their own shop. No record after 1922.

VERNAY & LINCOLN
Attleboro, Massachusetts

Silver manufacturers. "Vernay & Lincoln are doing quite a business. Their facilities for turning out work are excellent and their prices reasonable." (*Jeweler, Silversmith & Watchmaker*, Oct. 1877)

VICTOR SILVER CO.
See International Silver Co.

Trademark of Derby Silver Co. on less expensive line. Variation used after 1922 by International on silverplated flatware for hotels, restaurants, etc.

VICTOR S. CO.

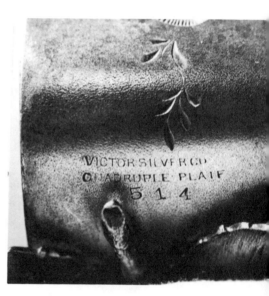

VINEGAR BROS.
New York, New York

Listed 1927 KJI as manufacturers of silverware.

VINER'S OF SHEFFIELD
Sheffield, England

Founded in 1907. Britain's largest silver trade's manufacturer. The plant is almost entirely automated. Their 1960 cutlery was 85% electroplate and in 1967 75% stainless steel. They have factories in Hong Kong and in Japan. They bought two fine old Sheffield firms of cutlers, Thomas Turner and Harrison Bros. and Howson. They manufacture 60% of the current lightweight sterling tableware, mostly traditional designs. These are distributed in the United States through Raimond Silver Mfg. Co., Inc.

GEO. L. VOSE MFG. CO., INC.

Providence, Rhode Island

Successor to Geo. L. Vose & Co. between 1904-1915. Manufacturing jeweler. Last listed c. 1920.

W

J. WAGNER & SON, INC.

New York, New York

CHRONOLOGY

Central Sterling Company	1909
Weber-Wagner Co.	Before 1915
Weber-Wagner & Benson Co.	1915
A.L. Wagner Mfg. Co., Inc.	1927
A.L. Wagner & Son, Inc.	1931
J. Wagner & Son, Inc.	1950

No longer listed. They were manufacturers of silverplated and sterling silver holloware.

Used since 1909

THE WALDO FOUNDRY

Bridgeport, Connecticut

Listed in JC 1896-1904. Out of business before 1915. Manufacturers of aluminum-gold flat and tableware.

Note similarity to trademarks of the W.H. Glenny & Co. and H.H. Curtis & Co.

(*Aluminium-Gold Flat and Table Ware.*)

WALDORF SILVER CO.

See Woodman-Cook Co.

Trademark of Woodman-Cook Co.

WALDORF SILVER CO.

WALLACE BROS. SILVER COMPANY

Wallingford, Connecticut

See Wallace Silversmiths

ESSEX SILVER CO.
ESSEX SILVER CO.
QUAD PLATE

(Silver plated britannia)

MADE AND PLATED BY WALLACE BROS. SILVER CO.

R. WALLACE & SONS. MFG. CO.

Wallingford, Connecticut

See Wallace Silversmiths

Successor to Wallace, Simpson & Co. in 1871. Name changed to Wallace Silversmiths in 1956.

"The first spoons made in this country of German or nickel silver were manufactured by Robert Wallace in 1835. From that date to January 1, 1897, we manufactured more than 5 million dozen nickel silver spoons, forks, etc...and not one single one bore our name or trademark—these goods having been made for other firms who have built up on our skill and workmanship a world-wide reputation for the quality and durability of such wares. On January 1, 1897, we began to place our nickel silver flatware on the market bearing our name, which is a guarantee of both the quality and durability of the goods so stamped. They are plated with FINE SILVER, in the following grade: EXTRA or STANDARD which we plate 20 PER CENT heavier than the regular standard. TRIPLE and

SECTIONAL PLATES. The stamps and trademarks are:

    1835 R. Wallace A1 for Extra Plate
    1835 R. Wallace XII for Sectional Plate
    1835 R. Wallace 6, 9 or 12 for Triple Plate"

(Adv. JC 7-2-1898, p. 6)

TRADE **1835** MARK
R·WALLACE
(*Flatware.*)
(Used since 1897)

900
(Steel Flatware.)

(Hollowware.)

(Nickel Goods.)

Trade Mark.

R·W·&·S·
Sterling.

(On sterling silver knives about 1898)

R. WALLACE
(Silver Soldered.)

SILVER SOLDERED

LUXOR PLATE
FORTUNE SILVER PLATE
ANDOVER SILVER PLATE CO.

ADAMS MANUFACTURING CO.
WALLINGFORD CO. SECTIONAL
WALLINGFORD CO. AI

MELFORD
SILVERPLATE
ON COPPER

M ELFORD
SILVER PLATE

**MELFORD   MELFORD
E.P.W.M.   E.P.N.S.**

LUXOR PLATE—WALLACE

The Wallace silverplate flatware dies were sold to the International Silver Co. in 1954.

WALLACE SILVERSMITHS, INC.
Wallingford, Connecticut

CHRONOLOGY
Robert Wallace	1834
Robert Wallace & Co.	1855
Wallace, Simpson & Co.	1865
R. Wallace & Sons Mfg. Co.	1871
Wallace Silversmiths	1956
Wallace Silversmiths, Inc.	1984

ROBERT WALLACE was born in Prospect, Connecticut in 1815. He was the grandson of James Wallace, who had come from Scotland and settled in Blandford, Mass., late in the 18th Century. At 16, Robert was apprenticed to Captain William Mix of Prospect to learn the art of making britannia spoons. Two years later, in 1833, he set up shop in an old grist mill to make spoons on his own. About a year later he saw a German silver spoon, made by Dixon & Sons of Sheffield, England. He recognized its superior strength and color and with Deacon Almer Hall (later head of Hall, Elton & Co.) began the manufacture of German silver spoons—the first in this country.

From 1834 to 1849 he made these spoons for Deacon Hall, for Hall, Elton & Co. and in 1849 entered into a co-partnership with J.B. Pomeroy to manufacture them on contract for Fred R. Curtis Co. of Hartford and made britannia spoons for Hall, Elton & Co. and Edgar Atwater of Wallingford.

In 1854, Robert decided to take up farming, but soon returned to Wallingford to continue the manufacture of German silver forks, spoons and similar articles with Samuel Simpson of Wallingford. This ten-year partnership was formed May 1, 1855, under the name of R. WALLACE & CO.

On May 15, 1855, Simpson's partners in the Meriden Britannia Co., H.C. Wilcox, W.W. Lyman and Isaac C. Lewis, were admitted, with the firm name remaining the same. This contract was terminated in 1865 when a new contract was made and the corporation WALLACE, SIMPSON & CO. was organized.

In 1870, Wallace purchased two-thirds of Simpson's interest and in 1871 bought the remainder. On July 17, 1871 the corporate name was changed to R. WALLACE & SONS MFG. CO. with his two sons, Robert B. and William J. and a son-in-law, W.J. Leavenworth members of the firm.

In 1871 Wallace introduced three sterling flatware patterns, *Hawthorne, The Crown* and *St. Leon.*

They made silverplated flatware from 1877 to 1941; production was resumed in 1981. The manufacture of silverplated hotel flatware continued until 1953.

In July 1875, Robert Wallace with his sons, Robert B., William J., Henry L., George H., Frank A. and sons-in-law W.J. Leavenworth and D.E. Morris formed a co-partnership under the name of WALLACE BROTHERS for the manufacture of silverplated flatware on a base of cast steel. Manufacture of silverplated holloware also began at this time. The manufacture of holloware ceased in 1986. On June 23,

1879, the corporation of R. WALLACE & SONS MFG. CO. acquired and took over the business and good will of WALLACE BROTHERS.

New machinery and mass production methods made possible great expansion. All types of flatware, holloware, dresser silver and practically all lines of articles in which silver is a component, as well as stainless steel, were added.

In 1924 a Canadian plant was opened in Cookshire, Quebec, for production of tinned spoons and forks. In 1944 sterling flatware was added to the line. In 1945 the Canadian branch was incorporated as R. WALLACE & SONS OF CANADA, LTD. It was sold in 1964.

In 1934, William S. Warren, designer for the company, conceived the idea of three-dimensional flatware patterns—for which the Wallace Company is noted. The Watson Company of Attleboro, Mass. was bought by Wallace in 1955, moving to Wallingford in 1956. The name R. WALLACE & SONS MFG. CO. was changed to WALLACE SILVERSMITHS in 1956. The Tuttle Silver company and Smith & Smith were acquired by Wallace and moved to Wallingford.

Wallace Silversmiths, in 1959 was purchased by the Hamilton Watch Company of Lancaster, Pennsylvania but in 1971 became a division of H.M.W. Industries and a Subsidiary of Katy Industries, Inc., Elgin, Illinois in 1983. Bought by Syratech in 1986 and moved to Syracuse, New York.

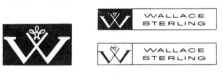

THE WALLINGFORD CO., INC.
Wallingford, Connecticut
See Wallace Bros. Silver Co.

The Wallingford Co. was listed in the City Directory 1903-1941.

ESSEX SILVER CO.
(Quadruple Plate.)

QUADRUPLE PLATE

V. L.
(Silver Plated Hollowware.)

MADE AND PLATED BY WALLACE BROS. SILVER CO.

ESSEX SILVER CO. QUADRUPLE PLATE

JOHN WANAMAKER
Philadelphia, Pennsylvania

Founded 1861 as Wanamaker & Brown. Became John Wanamaker in 1870. It was the first American system store—actually a collection of exclusive stores under one roof.

Like Marshall Field's, Macy's and others, they sold silverware stamped with their own trademark.

(On silverplate)

ANDREW E. WARNER, JR.
Baltimore, Maryland

Listed in Baltimore City Directories as a goldsmith and silversmith from 1864 till 1893. Listed as Andrew E. Warner & Son, 1867-1870. Andrew E. is listed alone from 1874-1889. The listing from 1890-1893 is A.E. Warner.

ANDREW E. WARNER, SR.
Baltimore, Maryland

Andrew Ellicott Warner was born in 1786 and died in 1870. He was listed as a goldsmith and silversmith from c. 1805 till his death.

Andrew and Thomas H. Warner (1780-1828) worked together c. 1805-1812.

GEORGE C. WARNER
Baltimore, Maryland
Listed in 1855-1856 Baltimore City Directory as a silver chaser.

WARNER MFG. CO.
Greenfield, Massachusetts
Manufacturers of silverplated flatware c. 1905-1909. They were among the first manufacturers to supply retail outlets with flatware stamped with private brand names.

WARNER SILVER MFG. CO.
Chicago, Illinois
Incorporated in March 1894 with Augustus Warner, P.B. Warner and Cassius C. Palmer. Out of business before 1915.

THOMAS H. WARNER
Baltimore, Maryland
Thomas H. Warner c. 1780-1828. He and Andrew Ellicott Warner worked together c. 1805-1812. From 1814 to 1824, and perhaps longer, Thomas H. Warner was assayer for the city of Baltimore. His duty was to "test silverwares to see that they were of no less fineness than eleven ounces pure silver to every pound troy."

WARREN MANSFIELD CO.
Portland, Maine
An advertisement in Leslie's Magazine, November 1904 carried the statement that they were goldsmiths and silversmiths, established in 1867. They are not listed in the Portland City Directories.

They published an illustrated catalog with price list of jewelry, spoons, tableware, watches, etc. in 1900. Another catalog, dated 1907, illustrated an extensive line of silverware. No trademark is shown.

WARREN SILVER PLATE CO.
New York, New York
See Oneida Silversmiths
See Wm. A. Rogers, Ltd.
Warren Silver Plate Company was a trademark first used in 1901 by Wm. A. Rogers Company on their medium grade holloware. The name apparently was based

on the fact that the New York Office was located at 12 Warren Street.

(*Medium Grade* Holloware.)

WARWICK STERLING CO.
Providence, Rhode Island
John F. Brady, treasurer of the company, registered the lower trademark, U.S. Patent Office No. 97,038 on May 19, 1914 to be used on sterling silver, flatware, holloware, tableware, dresserware, desk articles, sewing articles, silver trimming for leather, glass, wood, metal, fabrics and jewelry. He stated that this trademark had been used continuously since January 1, 1913. No record after 1922.

GEORGE WASHINGTON MINT
New York, New York
Out of business.

WATROUS MFG. CO.
Wallingford, Connecticut
See International Silver Co.
Started as Maltby, Stevens & Company, later Maltby, Stevens and Curtiss. Incorporated as Watrous Mfg. Co. in 1896.

The largest part of their business had been the making of German silver spoon blanks which they had sold to others, where they were plated and trademarked for the market. When the Watrous Co. was organized in 1896 most of the product was furnished to the Wm. Rogers Mfg. Co. in Hartford. After 1898 the spoons they made were distributed among several of the International Silver factories and they also added smaller articles and novelties which they made in sterling. Among these were vanity cases, dorine boxes, match boxes, belt buckles and small holloware. These were distributed through regular trade channels.

They were one of the original companies to become part of the International Silver Co. in 1898.

The "half circle" trademark was first used in 1921 and registered in 1923.

(Silver Plated on Nickel Silver Hollowware.)

ALEXANDRA SOLOWIJ WATKINS
Brunswick, Maine
Listed as a silversmith in the "Handcraft Trails in Maine," 1966 edition.

THE WATSON & BRIGGS CO.
Attleboro, Massachusetts
In the 1934 dresserware catalog Watson & Briggs is given as the successor to the Thomae Co.

WATSON COMPANY
Attleboro, Massachusetts
See Wallace Silversmiths

CHRONOLOGY

Cobb, Gould & Co.	1874-1880
Watson & Newell	1880-1886
Watson, Newell & Co.	1886-1895
Watson, Newell Co.	1895-1919
Watson Company	1919-1955

The company began with the partnership of Cobb, Gould & Co. in 1874. With these two were associated Clarence L. Watson and Fred A. Newell.

By 1894 and continuing through 1919, C.L. Watson and Fred A. Newell were in control. At first they produced jewelry principally but soon began the production of souvenir spoons. A little later they added silverplated flatware, holloware and novelties. Later the business was confined to sterling flatware and holloware.

About 1900 they made a line of sterling holloware for Wilcox & Wagner which was sold under the Wilcox & Wagner trademark. When Wilcox & Wagner gave up operating as selling agents about 1908, Watson continued the line and took over their New York office. Wilcox & Wagner started business after being associated with the Wilcox & Evertsen line which business had been sold to the Meriden Britannia Co.

J.T. Inman, also of Attleboro, bought the souvenir spoon dies from the Watson Co. The balance of the business was purchased by R. Wallace & Sons (now Wallace Silversmiths). In 1964 these same souvenir spoon dies were sold to Whiting & Davis who are producing the spoons stamped with their own trademark.

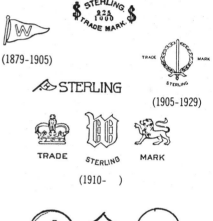

(1879-1905)

(1905-1929)

(1910-)

The above trademark was found on some souvenir spoons.

JULIUS R. WATTS & CO.
Atlanta, Georgia
Established in 1888 and listed in the Atlanta City Directories through 1958-1959. They are listed as watchmakers and more recently as jewelers and watch inspectors. The Uncle Remus trademark was stamped on souvenir spoons.

(On Souvenir Spoons.)

218

JOHN WAUBEL
Baltimore, Maryland

Listed in the 1864 Baltimore City Directory as a silverplater.

WAYNE SILVER CO.
Honesdale, Pennsylvania

"The Wayne Silver Co. of Honesdale, Pa. was incorporated. Directors are: L.J. Dorflinger, Thomas B. Clark, Wm. B. Holmes, Walter A. Wood and Grant W. Lane. They manufacture fancy and useful articles of silver, not plated, with the possible exception of knives and forks." (JC&HR 3-13-1895, p. 14)

"Operations began in the Wayne Silver Co.'s factory. The building is completed and mechanics are making models, dies, etc. Tea sets, berry sets, cake baskets and fancy and useful articles of various kinds will be made of sterling silver. E. Newton, formerly with Tiffany & Co., N.Y., is the manager of the factory." (JC&HR 9-25-1895, p. 14)

Listed out of business before 1904.

WAYNE SILVERSMITH, INC.
Yonkers, New York

Makers of handwrought sterling silver articles from c. 1950 to the present.

J.P. WEATHERSTONE
Chicago, Illinois

Advertised in the *American Jeweler*, Sept. 1892, p. 3, as a manufacturer of sterling and coin silverware. He advertised that special pieces in silver could be made on short notice. Prices for making over old silver were quoted at 45¢ per ounce, an extra charge for hand engravings.

WEB SILVER COMPANY, INC.
Philadelphia, Pennsylvania

Successors to the Web Jewelry Manufacturing Co. between 1950-1965. In 1952 they acquired the sterling flatware dies and patterns formerly used by the Weidlich

Sterling Spoon Company, Bridgeport, Connecticut.

GEORGE W. WEBB
Baltimore, Maryland

George W. Webb was born in 1812 and died in 1890. The earliest record found for his goldsmithing and silversmithing was an advertisement stating that his business was established in 1850. He is listed in the Baltimore City Directories as George W. Webb until 1865-1866 when the name was changed to Webb & Company. G.W. Webb, A. Remick and W.H. Sexton, partners. This listing continued until 1877 when it changed to Geo. W. Webb & Co. The latter listing continued through 1886.

H.J. WEBB & CO.
Springfield, Massachusetts

Successors to L.S. Stowe & Co. between 1896 and 1904. Jobbers and retailers of silver and jewelry. Out of business before 1915.

JOHN WEBB
Baltimore, Maryland

John Webb is listed by Pleasants and Sill (see bibliography) as a silversmith in Baltimore c. 1827-1842. In the Baltimore City Directories John Webb is listed 1855-1856 as a goldsmith. The 1864 listing is in the name John Webb, Sr. The 1865-1866 listing is John Webb, jeweler.

WEBER-WAGNER & BENSON CO., INC.
See J. Wagner & Son, Inc.

WEBER-WAGNER CO.
See J. Wagner & Son, Inc.

A.A. WEBSTER & CO.
Brooklyn, New York

Silversmiths, jewelers and opticians, c. 1886. Succeeded by Clarence B. Webster before 1904.

Their trademark was the company name and address in concentric circles.

The principal product has always been articles made of sterling silver. They are mostly baby goods, dresserware and picture frames.

In October 1958 they purchased the Frank W. Smith Silver Co. Inc. and all the tools and dies, along with the tradename and trademark. The flatware portion of this business was moved to North Attleboro from the original location in Gardner, Massachusetts.

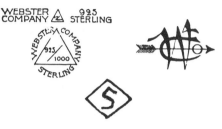

Trademark now owned by the Webster Co. Division of Reed & Barton Silversmiths.

CLARENCE B. WEBSTER
Brooklyn, New York

CHRONOLOGY
Frederick S. Hoffman
Webster Brother & Co.
A.A. Webster & Co.
Clarence B. Webster

The company began as Frederick S. Hoffman (q.v) founding date not known; succeeded by Webster Brother & Co., and then by A.A. Webster & Co. in 1886; became Clarence B. Webster before 1904. A.A. Webster was formerly with E.G. Webster & Bro.

Manufacturers of sterling silver goods, 14k and 18k gold novelties and leather goods with silver mountings.

E.G. WEBSTER & SON
Brooklyn, New York
See International Silver Co.

CHRONOLOGY

Webster Mfg. Co.	1859-1873
E.G. Webster & Bros.	1873-1886
E.G. Webster & Son	1886-1928

In 1859 Elizur G. Webster (1829-1900) bought Henry L. Webster's (formerly with Jabez Gorham) store and with his brother, A.A. Webster, started a small manufacturing business in Brooklyn in the early 1860s under the name of Webster Mfg. Co. In 1873 the firm name became E.G. Webster & Bros. and with the retirement of his brother in 1886, he took in his son, Fred H. Webster under the name E.G. Webster &

WEBSTER COMPANY
North Attleboro, Massachusetts
See Reed & Barton
See Frank W. Smith Silver Co., Inc.
See G.K. Webster Co.

Founded by George K. Webster in 1869 in North Attleboro under the name of G.K. Webster and Company. As the business grew, Mr. Webster purchased the interest of his partners. It operated under his direct supervision throughout his lifetime.

On January 1, 1950 it became a subsidiary of Reed & Barton of Taunton, Massachusetts. It continues its independent operation as The Webster Company.

Son. After his father's death, Fred H. Webster continued the business until it was sold to the International Silver Co. in 1928 and moved from Brooklyn to Meriden, Conn.

Their main line was silverplated holloware, much of it on German silver. It is well known for its highly chased holloware and English reproductions. The business was combined with the Barbour Silver Co. factory "A" plant in Meriden. Fred H. Webster continued with the firm, but retired a few years before he died in 1941.

In 1961 the trademark was changed to Webster-Wilcox which continued to 1981 when the business was sold to Oneida Silversmiths.

(On sterling silver)

Brooklyn S.P. Co. Quadruple Plate
(On napkin rings)

G.K. WEBSTER

North Attleboro, Massachusetts
See Reed & Barton
See Webster Co.

"G.K. Webster, North Attleboro, Born Wentworth, N.H., 1850. Attended common schools there until old enough to attend academy at Newbury, Vt. from which he graduated. In 1868 he went to New Jersey and worked for the then Raritan and Delaware railroad in the office of the repair shop. Later he went to Lawrence, Massachusetts and worked at the drug business for three years and in Boston for two years for a wholesale drug concern. He then moved to N. Attleboro and engaged in the drug business for himself. In 1879 he sold out and began manufacturing and making a general line (sterling and jewelry) and also novelties." (Obit. *Manufacturing Jeweler*, 10-2-1894, p. 60)

The company was succeeded by the Webster Co. soon after his death.

H.L. WEBSTER & CO.

See J.B. & S.M. Knowles
See Gorham Corporation

W.E. WEBSTER CO.

Providence, Rhode Island
Registered trademark U.S. Patent Office, No. 27,241, November 19, 1895 for sterling silver, rings, pins and ornamental jewelry. Out of business before 1904.

WEE CHERUB MFG. CO.

Houston, Texas
Manufacturers (?) of sterling novelties c. 1950.

WEE CHERUB

THE WEIDLICH BROS. MFG. CO.

Bridgeport, Connecticut
Founded in 1901 in Bridgeport, Connecticut. Specialized in sterling and plated trophies. Went into voluntary dissolution in 1950. No connection with Weidlich, Inc. 140 Hurd Avenue, Bridgeport, Connecticut.

POMPEIAN GOLD

THE WARNER SILVER CO.

FVFR DRY
(On salt & pepper sets)

AVON
(On sterling)

MAYFLOWER
(On pewter)

WEIDLICH STERLING SPOON CO.

Bridgeport, Connecticut
Related to Weidlich Bros. Mfg. Co. of Bridgeport. Made sterling silver souvenir spoons and sterling silver flatware (U.S. Patent 103,304, March 30, 1915). In 1952 the Web Jewelry Mfg. Co., now the Web Silver Co., Inc., silversmiths in Philadelphia, acquired the sterling flatware dies and patterns. No connection with present Weidlich, Inc., 140 Hurd Avenue, Bridgeport, Connecticut.

E.M. WEINBERG & CO.
New York, New York
Listed JC 1915 in plated silver section. Out of business before 1922.

Note similarity of trademark to that of F.G. Whitney & Co., Attleboro, Massachusetts.

WEINMAN CO.
Philadelphia, Pennsylvania
Manufacturers of plated silverware in Philadelphia c. 1900-1915.

BRAZIL SILVER

WEIZENNEGGER BROS.
Newark, New Jersey
Listed JC 1909-1922 in sterling silver section, manufacturers of mesh bags, dealers in diamonds.

WELLS, INC.
Attleboro, Massachusetts
Wells manufactures charms and other fine jewelry.

In 1977 they were combined with Benrus to form Wells Benrus Corp. And, in 1978 Wells Benrus made the decision to leave the jewelry industry.

Successors to Canfield Bros. & Co.

"Welsh & Bro. of Baltimore designed and manufactured the Communion service presented by the Altar Guild of Mt. Calvary Protestant Episcopal Church to the Rev. Geo. A. Leakin." (JC&HR 4-20-1898, p. 28)

WENDELL MANUFACTURING COMPANY
Chicago, Illinois
See Mulford & Wendell
Founded by Charles Wendell c. 1850. Became the Wendell Mfg. Co. by 1885; incorporated May 1889. Manufacturers of sterling silver badges. Around 1896-97 they acquired some of the flatware patterns and dies of the Mauser Mfg. Co. Retail or wholesale outlet in New York listed as Wendell & Co. 1904-1909. Not listed in Chicago City Directories.

They made sterling wares for Marshall Field & Co., some of which were marked with trademarks of both. Discontinued flatware productions c. 1900.

J.R. WENDT & CO.
New York, New York
In business c. 1855-1870. John R. Wendt had a shop in the building erected at Broadway & Prince Street, New York, in 1859 by Ball, Black & Co., then the largest jewelry store in America. The factory occupied the two upper floors, and they worked on orders from the jewelry firm below.

The firm was, during and immediately following the Civil War, the most prominent maker of silver flatware in the country being well-known throughout.

For a brief period—January to August 1860—Wendt was one of the partners in Rogers, Wendt & Wilkinson (q.v.)

Wendt's business was sold in two parts, one part going to the Whiting Mfg. Co. and the other to Adams & Shaw Co. and later to Dominick & Haff.

THE WESSELL SILVER CO.
New York, New York
"The Wessell Silver Co. of 1945 Park Avenue, N.Y. made an assignment Wednesday. The company began business in July 1893. W. Emlen Roosevelt, president and Charles Wessell, secretary. The original incorporators were C.A. Wessell, R.A. Mead and Arthur Cristodoro. The company manufactured a composition metal called Wessell silver, which they recently began to make into spoons, forks and other tableware." (JC&HR 5-5-1896, p. 18)

WEST SILVER CO.
Taunton, Massachusetts
Founded in Taunton, Massachusetts in 1883. F.B. Rogers successors before 1896.

WESTBROOK BRITANNIA COMPANY
Portland, Maine
Listed in 1869-1885 City Directories. William Wallace Stevens, owner.

WESTERLING COMPANY
Chicago, Illinois
Founded in 1944 by Jack Luhn, Les Hedge and Glenn Olmstead as the Easterling Co. A direct sales company handling only sterling silver flatware. Tableware lines were diversified to include china, crystal, cook-and-serve wares and others. The sterling inventory and pattern rights were sold to the Westerling Co. in March 1974. These six patterns are manufactured by the Gorham Company for Westerling.

WESTERN SILVER WORKS, INC.
New York, New York
Listed 1927 KJI as manufacturers of silverplated ware.

WESTMORLAND STERLING CO.
Wallingford, Connecticut
Westmorland was created in 1940 through the cooperative efforts of Wearever Aluminum Inc. and Wallace Silversmiths. Wartime priorities made it necessary to diversify hence the idea of selling sterling flatware on a direct-to-consumer basis was developed. Wearever developed the marketing programs and Wallace Silversmiths manufactured five sterling silver flatware patterns, exclusive to that organization. In 1966, Wallace assumed the marketing responsibility for Westmoreland and reorganized the marketing program by establishing franchised dealers and continues to manufacture the same five patterns.

C.A. WETHERELL & CO.
Attleboro, Massachusetts
Listed in Jeweler's Weekly, 1896 as manufacturers of sterling silverware. Listed in Attleboro City Directories 1892-1897 as manufacturing jewelers.

WHITE SILVER CO.
Taunton, Massachusetts
Manufacturers of plated silver holloware, prize cups and pewterware c. 1900-1930.

H.L. WHITE & CO.
Providence, Rhode Island
In business c. 1852. Succeeded by J.B. & S.M. Knowles in 1891.

WHITING & DAVIS CO., INC.
Plainville, Massachusetts
Began as a small chain manufacturing company c. 1876. Operated by William Wade and Edward P. Davis. C.A. Whiting, while still a young boy, entered the business as an unskilled worker. He worked as an artisan, salesman and partner, finally becoming owner in 1907.

Years of experimenting led to the development of the first chainmail mesh machine shortly after 1907. Whiting & Davis is now the world's largest manufacturer of mesh products including such items as safety gloves and aprons, mesh handbags and purse accessories, and jewelry. They also produce an outstanding line of antique reproduction jewelry—many pieces copies of museum masterpieces.

In 1964 they purchased the J.T. Inman Company and integrated the complete manufacturing facilities into their main plant. The souvenir spoon equipment, dies and tools were bought from the Watson Company by J.T. Inman. The balance of the business was sold to the Wallace Company. These dies are now used to make souvenir spoons. There are approximately 3,000 designs, according to the Executive Vice President, George J. LeMire. They will be stamped, whenever possible, with the Whiting & Davis registered trademark.

W. & D.   **WHITING & DAVIS CO**

FRANK M. WHITING CO.
North Attleboro, Massachusetts
See Ellmore Silver Co.

CHRONOLOGY

Holbrook, Whiting & Albee	-1878
F.M. Whiting & Co.	1878-1891
F.M. Whiting	1891-1895
F.M. Whiting Co.	1895-1896
Frank M. Whiting & Co.	1896-1940

Frank M. Whiting, son of William D. Whiting, founder of the Whiting Mfg. Co. had been associated with his father in that company. Prior to 1878 he left the company and formed the firm of Holbrook, Whiting & Albee, who began the manufacture of silverware in North Attleboro, Massachusetts. In 1878, Frank M. Whiting bought out his two partners and continued business under the firm name of F.M. Whiting & Co. In 1881 his father, William D. Whiting, became a partner, the firm name remaining the same until his father's death in 1891, when it was changed to F.M. Whiting. The following year Frank M. Whiting died and the business was continued by his widow, mother and two sisters. In 1895 it was converted into a stock company under the name F.M. Whiting Co. About 1940 it became a division of the Ellmore Silver Co. which went out of business c. 1960. The sterling flatware dies were bought by the Crown Silver Co., New York. It is believed that they are no longer being used.

Action brought by the Whiting Mfg. Co. against the F.M. Whiting Co. in 1896 resulted in F.M. Whiting agreeing to change their name to Frank M. Whiting & Co. The suit was to restrain the defendant company from using a griffin trademark which testimony showed led to confusion with the mark of the Whiting Mfg. Co. trademark.

(Not used after 1896)

WHITING MANUFACTURING COMPANY
Providence, Rhode Island
See Gorham Corporation

Originated by Albert T. Tifft and William D. Whiting in 1840 as Tifft & Whiting, to manufacture jewelry. They later added ladies' silver combs and small holloware. For a brief time, prior to 1858, the firm was Whiting, Fessenden & Cowan (W.B. Fessenden (q.v.)) located in North Attleboro, Massachusetts. It became Whiting Mfg. Co. in 1866. After the factory in North Attleboro was destroyed by fire, one unconfirmed account states that they moved to Newark, New Jersey. In 1910 the

company was moved to Bridgeport, Connecticut where a large modern plant was erected, and a complete line of silverware was produced. The company was purchased by the Gorham Company in 1926 and moved to Providence, Rhode Island where the original trademark continued to be used.

WHITING M.F.G. CO
YEAR MARKS

Mark	Year	Mark	Year
♣ ·	1905	大 ·	1915
⚶ ·	1906	⅄ ·	1916
⚵ ·	1907	⊐ ·	1917
⚶ ·	1908	⅂ ·	1918
◇ ·	1909	□ ·	1919
⚶ ·	1910	X ·	1920
⚶ ·	1911	⊔ ·	1921
人 ·	1912	⅃ ·	1922
△ ·	1913	⊏ ·	1923
⚶ ·	1914	∟ ·	1924

CHARLES WHITLOCK
Baltimore, Maryland
Listed in the 1850 Census as a silversmith in Baltimore. Born in Maryland.

F.G. WHITNEY & CO.
Attleboro, Massachusetts
Trademark registered July 12, 1881 for use on jewelry. Note similarity to trademark of E.M. Weinberg & Co. of New York.

WHITNEY JEWELRY COMPANY
Boston, Massachusetts
First listed in the Boston City Directories in 1883; probably founded the previous year. It was first listed as Whitney Brothers, jewelers. The brothers were: Edwin A. Whitney of Watertown, Massachusetts, and later of Newton, Massachusetts, and Albert E. Whitney of Fitchburg, Massachusetts. Albert E. was not connected with the firm

by 1894, when it was listed as E.A. Whitney Company, watches and jewelry. Was in business through 1911.

U.S. Patents No. 19,778 through 19,992 were registered in the name of Edwin A. Whitney, June 30, 1891, for use on gold, silver and plated flatware Barbara Frietchie No. 19,788.

Signing the Emancipation Proclamation, January 1, 1863, No. 19,787

Columbus Before the Queen
No. 19,778

Barbara Frietchie
No. 19,788

Columbus and the Egg
No. 19,779

Fort Smith
No. 19,790

Monitor & Merrimac
March 9, 1862
No. 19,791

Antietam, September 17, 1862,
No. 19,992

Gettysburg, July 1863,
No. 19,789

The Santa Maria, No. 19,780

The March to the Sea
No. 19,781

Appomattox, April 9, 1865
No. 19,782

July 4, 1776, No. 19,784

Sheriden's Ride
No. 19,783

General Stonewall Jackson,
No. 19,785

"The Seven Days" battle used in spoon bowl, General Robert E. Lee is the trademark, No. 19,786

There is a discrepancy between the historical scenes listed in the trademark description and those actually shown. Numbers 19,784 and 19,790 are listed as "July 4, 1776" and "Fort Smith." The two scenes shown are actually of Harpers Ferry, Oct. 17, 1859 and Fort Sumpter, April 12, 1861.

H.F. WICHMAN
Honolulu, Hawaii

Designers and manufacturing jewelers and retail outlets. They began in 1887 as Gomes & Wichman. Became H.F. Wichman in 1891 and continues business under that name.

His Majesty, King David Kalakaua, ruler of the Kingdom of Hawaii, gave an order for heroic medals to H.F. Wichman. This order provided the financial base for the beginning of the first jewelry store in the islands. Their craftsmen select the finest diamonds, sapphires, zircons, opals, cultured pearls and other precious stones and set them in distinctive mountings.

The original store and manufacturing facilities were in downtown on Fort Street. Following a disastrous fire, the main store was moved to Kalakaua Avenue. There are now branches in major hotels. The factory is located on Olohana Street.

H. F. WICHMAN

HENRY WIENER & SON
New York, New York

Distributors (?) of sterling silver mesh bags c. 1920. PICADILLY

CHAS. C. WIENTGE CO.
Newark, New Jersey

Charles C. Wientge designed silverware for the Howard Sterling Co. Providence, Rhode Island, c. 1891-93 and was a silversmith working for himself in Newark, 1893-96; employed by Lebkuecher & Co., Newark in 1896.

WILCOX BRITANNIA CO.

See International Silver Co.
See Wilcox Silver Plate Co.

WILCOX & EVERTSEN

New York, New York
See International Silver Co.

Successors to Rowan & Wilcox, who started under that name the latter part of 1889. Became Wilcox & Evertsen in 1892 with Robert M. Wilcox and Henry H. Evertsen as partners. They were makers of sterling silver holloware. In 1896 the company was purchased by the Meriden Britannia Co. and moved to Meriden, Connecticut.

They made a beautiful line of sterling holloware and started a sterling flatware line. After the formation of the International Silver Co., in 1898, the tools and equipment for flatware were moved to Wallingford, Connecticut and used space in the Simpson Nickel Silver plant while the holloware was made in Meriden. When more room became necessary they consolidated in 1929 in Wallingford with other sterling lines in the old Simpson, Hall, Miller & Co. buildings.

For their flatware markings see the International Silver Co.

H.C. WILCOX & CO.

Meriden, Connecticut
See International Silver Co.
See Meriden Britannia Co.

Organized in 1848 by Horace C. and Dennis C. Wilcox to market the products of Meriden's britannia ware. A forerunner of Meriden Britannia Co.

WILCOX-ROTH CO.

Newark, New Jersey
Listed in JC 1909 in sterling silver section as out of business.

WILCOX SILVER PLATE CO.

Meriden, Connecticut
See International Silver Co.
See Superior Silver Co.

Organized in 1865 by Jedediah and Horace Wilcox, Charles Parker, Aaron Collins and Hezekiah Miller and others to make holloware as Wilcox Britannia Co. In 1867 the name was changed to Wilcox Silver Plate Co. In 1869 they purchased the Parker & Casper Co. They were one of the original companies to become part of the International Silver Co. in 1898.

In 1941 because of a metal shortage during World War II, the factory was closed. After the war, Wilcox Silver Place Company designs were made in other International Silver Company factories. In 1961 the trademark was changed to Webster-Wilcox.

The "half circle" trademark was first used in 1921 and registered in 1923.

WILCOX & WAGONER

New York, New York
Listed in JC 1904 in sterling silverware and cut glass sections. Bought by the Watson Co. before 1905.

WILEY-CRAWFORD CO., INC.

Newark, New Jersey
Manufacturers of gold and sterling silver

novelties, card trays and jewelry c. 1915-1922.

WILKINSON SWORD CO.
London and Sheffield, England
  Manufacturers of plated silver swords. Listed JC 1909-1922.

WILLIAMS BROS. MFG. CO.
Naubuc, Connecticut
See American Sterling Co.
See F. Curtis & Co.
See Curtisville Mfg. Co.
See Thomas J. Vail

  James B. and William Williams bought the American Sterling Company and founded the Williams Bros. Mfg. Co., in 1880. Manufacturers of plated silver spoons, forks and a general line of flatware. They went out of business in June 1950.
  American Sterling Co. used as a brand name on some of their silverplated ware.

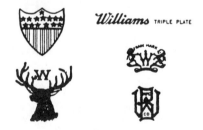

ROGER WILLIAMS SILVER CO.
Providence, Rhode Island
See Gorham Corporation
See Mt. Vernon Co. Silversmiths, Inc.

  The Roger Williams Silver Co. was successor c. 1900 to Howard Sterling Silver Co. It was merged in 1903 with the Mauser Mfg. Co. of New York and Hayes & McFarland of Mount Vernon, New York to form the Mt. Vernon Company Silversmiths, Inc. which was bought by the Gorham Corporation in 1913.
  For a brief time c. 1911 control of the Roger Williams Silver Co. was transferred to the Silversmiths' Co. of New York, under the management of Theo Bender, Wm. Linker, from David & Galt, silversmiths of Philadelphia, was associated

with the firm. U.S. Patent No. 36,769, July 16, 1901 for certain named metalwares—whole or in part of silver.

 R & W

  Trademark used continuously since June 1, 1901.

JAMES A. WILLIG
Baltimore, Maryland
  Listed in the 1850 Census as a silversmith. Born in Pennsylvania.

JOHN W. WILLSON
Baltimore, Maryland
  Listed 1867-1869 Baltimore City Directories as silverplaters.

WILMORT MFG. CO.
Chicago, Illinois
  Manufacturers of sterling and plated silverware and novelties c. 1920-1930.

Wilmort   W̄ilmort

(Silver Plated Hollowware)
  Dissolved March 21, 1930.

WM. WILSON & SON
Philadelphia, Pennsylvania
  Patent Office records show the registration of two trademarks by William Wilson & Son in 1883. They were also listed in JC in 1896 and 1904 and were out of business before 1909.
  Robert Wilson was listed in New York City Directory in 1805 and Philadelphia City Directories 1816-1846. Robert Wilson and William Wilson (R. & W. Wilson) listed in Philadelphia Directories 1825-1850. Wm. Wilson & Son, silversmiths, Philadelphia, listed in *Jeweller, Silversmith & Watchmaker*, 1877.

  U.S. Patent No. 9,949, January 9, 1883 for sterling silverware.

  U.S. Patent No. 9,950, January 9, 1883 for electroplated wares.

WILTON BRASS FOUNDRY
Columbia, Pennsylvania

Manufacturers of articles that are "hand-cast in sand, hand-polished. The beauty and weight of pewter...(made of) a secret fusion of 10 metals..."

WINDSOR SILVER CO., INC.
Brooklyn, New York

Listed 1966-1973 JC-K under sterling and plated holloware. No reply to recent inquiry.

WINNIPEG SILVER PLATE CO., LTD.
Winnipeg, Manitoba

Listed JC 1915-1922 in plated silver section.

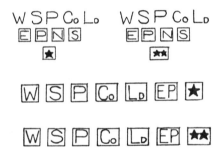

WOLF & KNELL
New York, New York

Manufacturers and importers c. 1900 of antique silver in Dutch, French and English designs. Decanters, tea and coffee sets, vases, spoons, tea strainers, etc. O. Buchholz, U.S. and Canadian representative. Factory at Hanau, Germany.

WOLFENDEN SILVER COMPANY
North Attleboro, Massachusetts
See Crown Silver, Inc.

Successor to J.W. Wolfenden Corp. Founded in 1919 by John W. Wolfenden and now a Division of Crown Silver Inc., New York. Dies and equipment were moved to the Crown factory in New York in 1955.

(Used since May 24, 1949)

WOOD & HUGHES
New York, New York
See Gorham Corporation
See Graff, Washbourne & Dunn

CHRONOLOGY
Gale, Wood & Hughes	1833-1845
Wood & Hughes	1845-1899

In 1833 William Gale formed a partnership with Jacob Wood and Jasper H. Hughes, under the name Gale, Wood & Hughes. Wood and Hughes had both served apprenticeships under Gale. Jacob Wood and Jasper H. Hughes remained in the partnership until 1851, the year of the death of the founder. Then Charles Hughes and Stephen T. Fraprie entered the business. Jasper H. Hughes retired in 1856, the business being continued by the three remaining partners until 1865. In that year Henry Wood and Dixon G. Hughes were admitted and succeeded to the business as equal partners after the death of Charles Wood in 1881, Charles H. Wood in 1883 and S.T. Fraprie in 1889. They manufactured a general line of sterling silverware and were noted for the excellence of their work. Succeeded by Graff, Washbourne & Dunn in 1899.

(*Used* 1833 *to* 1871.)   (*Used since* 1871.)

Muffineer by Wood & Hughes (Photo courtesy of Diana Cramer, Editor SILVER)

N.G. WOOD & SONS
Boston, Massachusetts

Registered trademark U.S. Patent Office, No. 20,515, December 29, 1891 for spoons, gold, silver and plated.

Listed JC 1896-1922 in sterling silver section. The trademark illustrated was for souvenir spoons made to commemorate the Boston Tea Party and was discontinued before 1922.

MRS. SARAH B. DICKINSON WOOD
Niagara Falls, New York

The House of Dickinson, well-known jewelry firm of Buffalo was founded by Thomas V. Dickinson in 1849. Associated with him were his wife, Elizabeth, and later his son, Alfred; his grandson, Alfred. Now the great grandson Alfred Dickinson is in charge of the business.

The founder was granted a patent on July 21, 1891 for the manufacture of silver, flat and tableware, using the buffalo head trademark that his daughter (later Mrs. Sarah B. Dickinson Wood) used on souvenir silverware. According to Alfred III, they have no records that the Dickinsons actually manufactured these items themselves. They were probably made for them by one of the many companies who did this sort of work and stamped it with the trademark of the wholesaler or retailer.

WOODBURY PEWTERERS
Woodbury, Connecticut

Founded in 1952 by R.C. Holbrook and L.R. Titcomb when they acquired the tools, etc. of the Merwin & Wilson Co., New Milford, Connecticut and the Danforth

(Under each mark)

Pewter Co., Woodbury, Connecticut and used them as the nucleus for developing a product line of early American pewter reproductions, later expanded to include a separate line for the Henry Ford Museum.

The ATC Hallmark on Pewter indicates that the finest quality metal has been used in its manufacture. The Hallmark guarantees that the metal contains only tin, and very small percentages of copper and antimony, as hardening agents. It is the quality mark of Pewter!

WOODMAN-COOK CO.
Portland, Maine
See Stevens Silver Co.

Began as Stevens & Smart 1879-1883. Manufacturers of britannia ware. Became Stevens, Smart & Dunham 1884-1886; Stevens & Smart, 1887-1890; Stevens, Woodman and Company, 1891-1892 and Woodman-Cook Company 1893-1914. Manufacturers of plated silverwares. Edward B. Coon, president; C.H. Fessenden, vice-president; Fred H. Woodman, treasurer.

"Fred H. Woodman, of Woodman-Cook Co. Born Palmyra, Maine, December 28, 1855. At the age of 18 taught school and soon after he was engaged in the business department of a cotton mill. Later he bought an interest in the business of Stevens & Smart, manufacturers of silver plated ware, Portland. The business was founded in 1878 by Rufus (?) Dunham, who had been making Britannia ware since 1837. Later the firm became Stevens, Woodman & Co. and finally it was incorporated as Woodman-Cook Co." (JC&HR 3-1-1897, p. 19)

WALDORF SILVER CO.

WOODS & CHATELLIER
New York, New York

Successor to Stephen Woods before 1904. Manufacturers of sterling cases, novelties, boxes and jewelry. Listed JC 1904-1922.

STEPHEN WOODS
Newark, New Jersey
See Woods & Chatellier

RICHARD M. WOODS & CO.
New York, New York

Successor to Woodside Sterling Company c. 1920. Makers of sterling silver holloware,

dresserware and novelties. Around 1940 also listed as wholesalers.

WOODSIDE STERLING CO.
See Richard M. Wood & Co.
Listed 1896 Jewelers' Weekly. Listed 1904 JC. Succeeded by Richard M. Woods & Co. c. 1920.

JAMES T. WOOLLEY
Boston, Massachusetts
James T. Woolley was born in Providence, Rhode Island in 1864. He learned the silversmithing craft in The Gorham Company. For eighteen years he was foreman at Goodnow & Jenks (q.v.) in Boston. For two years he shared bench room with George J. Hunt at 79 Chestnut St. though they worked independently. Around 1908 he opened his own shop in the Studio Building in adjacent Lime Street. Many of his pieces are excellent adaptations of colonial silver.

WORDEN-MUNNIS CO., INC.
Boston, Massachusetts
Silversmiths and goldsmiths, founded in 1940. Makers of early American, English and Irish reproductions. The company was purchased in 1964 by Old Newbury Crafters who are producing the sterling holloware line.

WORLD HAND FORGED MFG. CO.
New York, New York
Manufacturers of silverplated wares c. 1950.

WORLD TABLEWARE INTERNATIONAL
Wallingford, Connecticut
See American Silver Company
In 1972 the Hotel Division of International Silver Company became a subsidiary of that company under the name of World Tableware International. This, in turn, was sold to two employees and private investors on October 1, 1983. They organized a new American Silver Company of which World Tableware International is a subsidiary. Their products are flatware and holloware in both silverplate and stainless steel, for hotels, restaurants, clubs, ships, institutions and other types of public dining.

World Tableware International Trademarks

International® Stainless (Flatware & Holloware)
International® Silverplate (Flatware & Holloware)
International® Silver Co. (Nickel Silverplated Holloware)
Victor S. Company (Nickel Silverplated Holloware)
World® Stainless (Flatware & Holloware)

INTERNATIONAL

WORTZ & VOORHIS
New York, New York
Listed in JC 1896 in sterling silver section. Out of business before 1915.

Trademark identical to D. C. Bourquin

WURTTEMBERGISCHE METALLWARENFABRIK (WMF)
Geislingen, Germany
Founded in 1853 by Daniel Straub (1815-1889), a miller who had been repairing tools and railway construction equipment. Under the name Straub & Schweizer they produced tableware from silverplated copper sheets. In 1880 Straub & Schweizer joined with A. Ritter & Co. of Esslingen which had been founded in 1871 for the manufacture of silverplated wares. In 1883 a glass works was added and in 1897 WMF took over Schauffler & Safft of Göppingen, makers of light holloware. They advertised under the WMF-IKORA name "The original tarnish-resistant silverplate."

"King George" International Silverplate by World Tableware. Their products are distributed only in the food service industry. (Photo courtesy of World Tableware International)

"Silhouette" International Silverplate by World Tableware. Their products are distributed only in the food service industry. (Photo courtesy of World Tableware International)

Extra heavy hotel plate by World Tableware International. (Photo courtesy of World Tableware International)

Stainless steel tableware, multicolored ikora: metal and bronze castings were 20th century introductions. The company was especially noted for its Art Nouveau styles c. 1900. Still in business. Distributed in this country through WMF-IKORA.

WYMBLE MFG CO.
Newark, New Jersey

About 1886 a new method of depositing silver on non-metallic articles was discovered. Among the companies founded for the purpose of decorating articles by this process was the Wymble Mfg. Co. organized

in September 1890. Justus Verschuur, artist and designer, was one of the founders. The firm set up a handsome and extensive display of its wares in the American jewelry and silverware exhibit at the World's Columbian Exposition held in Chicago in 1893-94. The company went into receivership in March 1895 and the Alvin Mfg. Co. purchased the entire stock and fixtures.

Y

YORK SILVER CO.
New York, New York

PAT JANE

Listed 1950 JC-K under sterling.

HIRAM YOUNG & COMPANY
New York, New York

In the 1860s they purchased Reed & Barton wares "in the metal" and operated their own plating establishment.

In 1860-62 the firm was listed at 20 John St., New York, at the same address as the Manhattan Plate Co. In 1868, the *Jewelers' Weekly* says that the Manhattan Plate Co. was a trademark used by Henry Young and Henry C. Reed, whose factory was at 227 6th St.; showroom at 8 Maiden Lane. In 1870-72 this Henry C. Reed is identified as the one connected with Reed & Barton Co. In 1879 there is a reference to "the old Manhattan Plate Co. now owned by Hiram Young."

OTTO YOUNG & COMPANY
Chicago, Illinois

Established in 1865. Importers, manufacturers and wholesalers of all types of silverware and jewelers' merchandise.

Successors in 1880 to William B. Clapp, Young & Co.

An illustrated catalog of 1893 (courtesy of the Whittelsey Fund, Metropolitan Museum of Art) depicts silverware, jewelry, optical goods, clocks and watches.

Succeeded by A.C. Becken Co. c. 1924.

Z

ZELL BROS.
Portland, Oregon

Listed in 1950 JC-K under sterling. They advertise Reed & Barton collector's limited edition Damascene plates. These are made of sterling or silverplate.

C.H. ZIMMERMAN & COMPANY
New Orleans, Louisiana

Silverware manufacturers listed in New Orleans City Directory 1871.

ADDITIONAL INFORMATION

See page 36
CODMAN & CODMAN
Providence, Rhode Island

Photocopy of an undated advertisement. Codman & Codman were probably William Christmas Codman and son William W.C. Codman was chief designer for the Gorham company 1891-1914 and was succeeded in that position by William. W.C. Codman was best known for his art nouveau designs which were executed by Gorham silversmiths. William's design interests are characterized by his *Colonial* coffee service with its clean undecorated lines.

See page 100
DAVID & EDWARD KINSEY
Cincinnati, Ohio

David (b. 1819, d. 1874) (w. 1840-1870) and Edward (b. 1810, d. 1861) (w. 1834-1861) were sons of Thomas & Ann Kinsey. Edward learned silversmithing from Thomas and, in turn, taught David. They worked together until 1861 when Edward retired. Their silverware manufacturing plant produced the bulk of the homemade holloware and flatware of Cincinnati of their time. Said to have been the most prolific of the Cincinnati silversmiths of the pre-Civil War period. (Beckman, E.D. *An In-depth Study of the Cincinnati Silversmiths, Jewelers, Watch and Clockmakers.* B.B. & Co., Cincinnati, Ohio. 1975)

Unascribed Marks

 STERLING

 STERLING

SILVER ON COPPER

 B STERLING

SILVER PLATED
JF
TRADE MARK

STERLING
WEIGHTED

Mary C. Knight listed as a designer, metalworker and silversmith in The Society of Arts and Crafts, Boston Exhibition Record 1897-1927. *She worked between 1902 and 1927.(Photo courtesy of John R. McGrew)*

LEXINGTON S. P. CO. in a circle. Quadruple Plate underneath. Location unknown.

Patent
Sterling
W. MOIR

Found on a Victorian pattern dessert set of flatware. Location unknown.

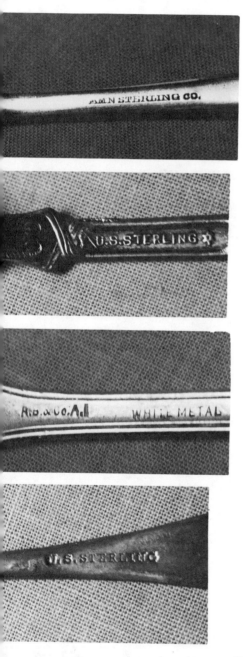

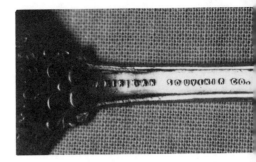

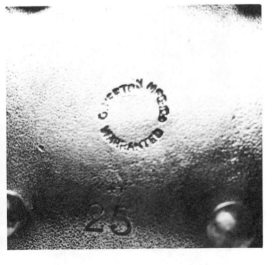

Alphabetical Listing of Trade Names

A. 1. NIKEL SILVER No. 210 . . . . .ONEIDA
ACORN BRAND . . . . .ALBERT PICK & CO.
ALASKA METAL . . . . .SEARS ROEBUCK & CO.
ALBANY SILVER PLATE . . . . .INSILCO
ALDEN . . . . .DERBY SILVER CO.
ALPHA PLATE . . . . .ONEIDA
ALUMINUM SILVER . . . . .DANIEL & ARTER
AMERICAN SILVER CO. . . . . .INSILCO
AMERICAN SILVER PLATE CO. . . . . .SIMPSON, HALL, MILLER & CO.
AMSILCO . . . . .INSILCO
ANDERSON, JUST . . . . .MANDIX CO.
APOLLO . . . . .BERNARD RICE'S SONS
ARGENLINE . . . . .DANIEL & ARTER
ARMETALE . . . . .WILTON BRASS FOUNDRY
ARROW PLATE . . . . .GLASTONBURY SILVER CO.
A. S. Co. . . . . .AMERICAN SILVER CO.
ATLANTIC SILVER PLATE CO. . . . . .RUEFF BROS.
ATLAS SILVER PLATE . . . . .INSILCO
AVON SILVER PLATE . . . . .INSILCO
AZTEC COIN METAL . . . . .HOLMES & EDWARDS CO.
BALTCO . . . . .BALTES-CHANCE CO.
B. B. & CO. . . . . .BARDEN BLAKE & CO.
BANQUET PLATE . . . . .GORHAM
BEACON SILVER CO. . . . . .AMERICAN SILVER CO.
BEACON SILVER CO. . . . . .F. B. ROGERS SILVER CO.
BEAUXARDT . . . . .BERNARD RICE'S SONS
B$_N^E$ . . . . .BENJAMIN F. LOWELL
BENGAL SILVER . . . . .DANIEL & ARTER
BERKELEY . . . . .BENEDICT MFG. CO.
BREWSTER . . . . .INSILCO
BRIDGE . . . . .SHAPLEIGH HARDWARE CO.
BRISTOL CUTLERY CO. . . . . .AMERICAN SILVER CO.
BRISTOL PLATE CO. . . . . .PAIRPOINT MFG. CO.
BRISTOL SILVER CORP. . . . . .POOLE SILVER CO.
BRITANNIA ARTISTIC SILVER . . . . .M. T. GOLDSMITH
BRITANNIA METAL CO. .VAN BERGH SILVER PLATE CO.
BROOKLYN PLATE CO. . . . . .SCHADE & CO.
B. R. S. CO. SHEFFIELD, U.S.A. .BERNARD RICE'S SONS
B. S. CO. . . . . .BIRMINGHAM SILVER CO.

```
BS CO. ...................................................INSILCO
B.S. Co. ............................HOLMES & EDWARDS SILVER CO.
BURMAROID...................................DANIEL & ARTER
CAMBRIDGE SILVER PLATE ...................SEARS ROEBUCK & CO.
CAMELIA SILVERPLATE ....................................INSILCO
CARAVELLE.................................SUMMIT SILVER CO.
CARBON..............................................ONEIDA
CARLTON SILVERPLATE .................................ONEIDA
CARVEL HALL........................CHAS. D. BRIDELL, INC.
CARV-EZE ...........................................INSILCO
THE CELLAR SHOPS ....................RAYMOND BRENNER
CENTURY STERLING ................................INSILCO
CHASE .................................MAX H. STORCH
CHATSWORTH .........................R. H. MACY & CO.
CHICAGO SILVER PLATE CO. .............ELGIN-AMERICAN MFG. CO.
COLONIAL PLATE CO. ......................MELROSE SILVER CO.
COLUMBIA ...........................MIDDLETOWN PLATE CO.
COLUMBIAN SILVER CO. .....................QUEEN SILVER CO.
COMMUNITY .........................................ONEIDA
CONNECTICUT PLATE CO. .............ADELPHI SILVER PLATE CO.
CONNECTICUT PLATE CO. ....................J. W. JOHNSON
COURT SILVER PLATE .................................INSILCO
CRESCENT SILVER CO......................ALBERT G. FINN SILVER CO.
CROSBY ...............................A. COHEN & SONS
CROWN GUILD ................ROCKFORD SILVER PLATE CO.
CROWN GUILD ...............JEWELERS' CROWN GUILD
CROWN PRINCE...........................G. I. MIX & CO.
CROWN SILVER CO. ..................AMERICAN SILVER CO.
CROWN SILVER CO. ...................................INSILCO
CROWN SILVER PLATE CO. ..............AMERICAN SILVER CO.
CUNNINGHAM SILVER PLATE CO. ..........WM. ROGERS MFG. CO.
CUVEE ..........................QUAKER VALLEY MFG. CO.
DEEP SILVER ........................................INSILCO
DEERFIELD SILVER PLATE .............................INSILCO
DEKRA .............................ARGENTUM SILVER CO.
DEPOS-ART ........................CANADIAN JEWELERS
DIAMOND EDGE .....................SHAPLEIGH HARDWARE CO.
DISTINCTION .........................HOME DECORATORS
DORANTIQUE .......................BERNARD RICE'S SONS
DOUBLE-TESTED SILVERPLATE ...............NATIONAL SILVER CO.
DU BARRY ..............................NAPIER COMPANY
DUNGEON ROCK .........................H. M. HILL & CO.
DUNKIRK ...............GOLD RECOVERY & REFINING CORP.
DURO PLATE ........................................ONEIDA
DUTCH SILVER NOVELTIES ............JOHNSON, HAYWARD & PIPER CO.
EAGLE BRAND....................SIMPSON, HALL, MILLER & CO.
EASTERN SILVER CO......................AMERICAN SILVER CO.
EASTERN SILVER CO. ................................INSILCO
1847 ROGERS BROS. ................................INSILCO
1847 ROGERS BROS. ................MERIDEN BRITANNIA CO.
1857 WELCH-ATKINS .................AMERICAN SILVER CO.
1865 WM. ROGERS MFG. CO. ..........................INSILCO
```

```
ELMWOOD PLATE ..............................................GORHAM
EMBASSY SILVER PLATE ........................................INSILCO
EMPIRE ART SILVER .......................................E. & J. BASS
EMPIRE SILVER COMPANY ..........................BENEDICT MFG. CO.
EMPRESS WARE ...............................NEW YORK STAMPING CO.
ENGLISH SILVER ..................................SIMPSON-BRAINERD CO.
ENGLISH STERLING ...........................................TIFFANY & CO.
ESSEX SILVER CO. .....................................WALLINGFORD CO.
ETCHARDT ........................................BERNARD RICE'S SONS
EUREKA SILVER PLATE CO. ....................MERIDEN SILVER PLATE CO.
EVERWEAR ..........................................ALBERT PICK & CO.
EVOLUTION ...........................................NAPIER COMPANY
FASHION PLATE ...................................SEARS ROEBUCK & CO.
FASHION SILVER PLATE ............................SEARS ROEBUCK & CO.
FORTUNE SILVER PLATE ...................R. WALLACE & SONS MFG. CO.
GEE-ESCO .....................................GLASTONBURY SILVER CO.
GEM SILVER CO. ...............................................INSILCO
GEORGIAN ...........................................BENEDICT MFG. CO.
GERMAN SILVER.....................................HOLMES & EDWARDS
GOLD ALUMINUM ...................................HOLMES & EDWARDS
GOLDYN-BRONZ ............................................REED & BARTON
GONDOLA SILVER ...................................CARLBERT MFG. CO.
GOPHER BRAND.....................................F. L. BOSWORTH CO.
GUILDCRAFT .......................................NATIONAL SILVER CO.
HAMPSHIRE HOUSE ..........................MURRAY L. SCHACTER & CO.
HAR-MAC ...................................HARPER & MACINTIRE CO.
HARMONY HOUSE PLATE AA + .....................SEARS ROEBUCK & CO.
H. B. & H. A1 .............................HOLMES, BOOTH & HAYDENS
HARMONY HOUSE PLATE .......................SEARS ROEBUCK & CO.
HARVEST .........................................ELLMORE SILVER CO.
HICKS SILVER CO. .....................................A. R. JUSTICE CO.
HOLD-EDGE ...................................................INSILCO
HOLMES & EDWARDS ...........................................INSILCO
HOLMES & TUTTLE .............................................INSILCO
HOPE SILVER CO. ..................................GEO. W. PARKS CO.
H. & T. MFG. CO. .............................................INSILCO
IMPERIAL PLATE .....................................NATIONAL SILVER CO.
IMPERIAL SILVER PLATE CO...............................A. F. SMITH CO.
INDEPENDENCE BRAND ..........................AMERICAN SILVER CO.
INDEPENDENCE TRIPLE ........................................INSILCO
INDIANA BRAND .............................ANCHOR SILVER PLATE CO.
INDIAN SILVER .........................................DANIEL & ARTER
INLAID .....................................................INSILCO
INSICO .....................................................INSILCO
INTERNATIONAL ...............................................INSILCO
INTERNATIONAL SILVER CO.......................................INSILCO
I.S.C.O. ....................................................INSILCO
I.S. CO.....................................................INSILCO
JAPANESE SILVER .....................................DANIEL & ARTER
J (CROWN) G ..........................ROCKFORD SILVER PLATE CO.
J. ROGERS & CO. ..........................................ONEIDA
KENSICO ...................................................INSILCO
```

KENSINGTON SILVER PLATE . . . . .INSILCO
KIRBYKRAFT . . . . .MIDDLETOWN SILVER CO.
KRANSHIRE . . . . .A. COHEN & SONS
LADY BERKSHIRE . . . . .NATIONAL SILVER CO.
LAKESIDE BRAND . . . . .MONTGOMERY WARD & CO.
LASHAR . . . . .INSILCO
LAXEY SILVER . . . . .DANIEL & ARTER
LESCO . . . . .LEVINE SILVER CO.
LEVIATHAN . . . . .S. J. LEVI & CO.
LIFETIME . . . . .ZELL BROS.
LORALINE . . . . .BERNARD RICE'S SONS
LORD BERKSHIRE . . . . .NATIONAL SILVER CO.
LULLABY STERLING . . . . .ALVIN
LUNA METAL . . . . .ROWLEY MFG. CO.
LUXOR PLATE . . . . .R. WALLACE & SONS MFG. CO.
MALACCA PLATED . . . . .G. I. MIX & CO.
MANOR PLATE . . . . .INSILCO
MARIE LOUISE . . . . .R. BLACKINTON
MARION PLATE CO. . . . . .BERNARD RICE'S SONS
MARION SILVERPLATE . . . . .INSILCO
MEDFORD CUTLERY CO. . . . . .A. R. JUSTICE CO.
MEDFORD SILVER CO. . . . . .R. WALLACE & SONS MFG. CO.
MELODY SILVER PLATE . . . . .INSILCO
MEXICAN CRAIG . . . . .HOLMES & EDWARDS SILVER CO.
MEXICAN SILVER . . . . .HOLMES & EDWARDS SILVER CO.
MIDDLESEX SILVER CO. . . . . .MIDDLETOWN SILVER CO.
MILDRED QUALITY SILVER PLATE .NATIONAL SILVER CO.
M. M. CO. . . . . .MACOMBER MFG. CO.
MONARCH SILVER CO. . . . . .STANDARD SILVER CO.
MONARCH SILVER CO. . . . . .KNICKERBOCKER SILVER CO.
MONARCH SILVER CO. . . . . .NATIONAL SILVER CO.
MOREWEAR PLATE . . . . .MAUTNER MFG. CO.
MONTAUK SILVER CO. . . . . .J. W. JOHNSON
NACO . . . . .NAPIER COMPANY
NARRAGANSETT PEWTER . . . . .QUAKER SILVER CO.
NASCO . . . . .NATIONAL SILVER CO.
NATIONAL CUTLERY CO. . . . . .ROCKFORD SILVER PLATE CO.
N. E. S. P. CO. . . . . .INSILCO
NEVADA SILVER . . . . .DANIEL & ARTER
NEVADA SILVER METAL . . . . .STANDARD SILVERWARE CO.
NEW ENGLAND SILVER PLATE . . . . .INSILCO
NEW ENGLAND CUTLERY CO. . . . . .AMERICAN SILVER CO.
NEWFIELD SILVER COMPANY . . . . .BRIDGEPORT SILVER PLATE CO.
NEWPORT STERLING . . . . .GORHAM
N. F. NICKEL SILVER CO., 1877 . . . . .ONEIDA
NIAGARA FALLS CO., 1877 . . . . .ONEIDA
NICKELITE SILVER . . . . .GOLDSMITH'S CO. OF CHICAGO
NOBILITY PLATE . . . . .EMPIRE CRAFTS CORP.
NORMAN PLATE . . . . .STANLEY & ALYARD
NORTH AMERICA . . . . .JAMES J. DAWSON CO.
NO-TARN . . . . .INSILCO
N.S.C. . . . . .NATIONAL SILVER CO.

O.C. ....ONEIDA
O.C. EXTRA ....ONEIDA
OHIO SILVER PLATE CO. ....QUEEN SILVER CO.
OLD COMPANY PLATE...INSILCO
OLD ENGLISH BRAND B ....AMERICAN SILVER CO.
ONEIDA...ONEIDA
ONEIDA PAR PLATE ....ONEIDA
ONEIDA RELIANCE PLATE ....ONEIDA
ONEIDA SILVERPLATE ....ONEIDA
ONEIDACRAFT ....ONEIDA
OXFORD SILVER PLATE CO. ....WM. A. ROGERS LTD.
PALACE BRAND ....MONTGOMERY WARD & CO.
PALLADIANT ....INSILCO
PALM BEACH ....NAPIER COMPANY
PARAGON ....SEARS ROEBUCK & CO.
PARAGON EXTRA ....SEARS ROEBUCK & CO.
PEQUABUCK MFG. CO. ....AMERICAN SILVER CO.
PERFECTA ....S. J. LEVI & CO.
PERMA-BRITE ....NATIONAL SILVER CO.
PILGRIM ....FRIEDMAN SILVER CO.
POMPEIAN GOLD ....WEIDLICH BROS. MFG. CO.
PONTIFEX ....R. BLACKINTON
POPPY ....................INTERNATIONAL-COMMONWEALTH SILVER CO.
PRESTIGE PLATE ....HOME DECORATORS
PRINCE'S PLATE ....MAPPIN & WEBB
PROVIDENCE SILVER PLATE CO.................AURORA SILVER PLATE CO.
PURITAN SILVER CO. ....ONEIDA
QUEEN ESTHER ....SALES STIMULATORS
R. & B. ....INSILCO
R. C. CO. ....INSILCO
R. COIN ....A. DAVIS CO.
R. COIN ....M. C. EPPENSTEIN
RELIANCE ....ONEIDA
RELIANCE PLATE ....ONEIDA
R SPECIAL ....A. DAVIS CO.
REVELATION SILVER PLATE ....INSILCO
REVERE ....BENEDICT MFG. CO.
REV-O-NOC.........................HIBBARD, SPENCER, BARTLETT & CO.
REX PLATE ....ONEIDA
RICHFIELD PLATE COMPANY ....HOMAN MFG. CO.
RIVERTON SILVER CO. ....A. R. JUSTICE
ROGERS CUTLERY CO. ....INSILCO
ROGERS & HAMILTON ....INSILCO
ROYAL CREST STERLING ....EMPIRE CRAFTS CORP.
ROYAL FAMILY ....SABEN GLASS CO.
ROYAL PLATE CO..INSILCO
ROYAL PLATE CO. ....AMERICAN SILVER CO.
ROYAL PLATE CO.......................................J. W. JOHNSON
ROYAL SILVER ....LEDIG MFG. CO.
R. S. MFG. CO. ....NIAGARA SILVER CO.
SALEM SILVER PLATE......................SEARS ROEBUCK & CO.
SALOSICO WARE ....ST. LOUIS SILVER CO.

```
S. E. B. ...........................................NATIONAL SILVER CO.
SHADOARDT ....................................BERNARD RICE'S SONS
SHEFFIELD H. S. CO. ........................HEMILL SILVERWARE INC.
SHEFFIELD PLATED CO. ...................HOLMES, BOOTH & HAYDENS
SHEFFIELD PLATED CO. .................................INSILCO
SILVER ARTISTS COMPANY ......................REED & BARTON
SILVER CREST ..........................SMITH METAL ARTS CO.
SILVER CRAFT ..................................FARBER BROS.
SILVERGRAMS ....................CHICAGO MONOGRAM STUDIOS
SILVER HARVEST..........................ELLMORE SILVER CO.
SILVEROIN ..................................BRISTOL MFG. CO.
SILVER METAL ..........................................ONEIDA
SILVER WELD (knives) .................................INSILCO
SKYSCRAPER......................................BERNARD RICE'S SONS
SO. AM. .....................................DAVID H. MCCONNELL
SOCIAL SILVER ...............................DELLI SILVERPLATE
SOLID YUKON SILVER WARRANTED ...................RAYMOND MFG. CO.
SO. MERIDEN SILVER CO. QUADRUPLE ................C. ROGERS & BROS.
SOMERSET ........................................W. BELL CO.
SOUTHINGTON COMPANY ................................INSILCO
SOVEREIGN PLATE ....................................P. W. ELLIS
SQUIRREL BRAND .................................S. J. LEVI & CO.
STANDISH.......................................BENEDICT MFG. CO.
STAR CUTLERY CO. ...................ELGIN-AMERICAN MFG. CO.
STATE HOUSE STERLING ......................HOME DECORATORS
STERLING B ....................................BATTIN & CO.
STERLING G ....................................F. S. GILBERT
STERLINGUARD .............................ALBERT PICK & CO.
STERLING PLATE ◁ B ▷ .....................AMERICAN SILVER CO.
STERLING SILVER PLATE CO. ..........HOLMES, BOOTH & HAYDENS
STERLING SILVER PLATE CO. ...........................INSILCO
STERLON ..................................MILTON J. SCREIBER
STRAND.................................................INSILCO
STRATFORD SILVER PLATE CO. ..........................INSILCO
STRATFORD PLATE .......................................INSILCO
STRATFORD SILVER CO. ................................INSILCO
SUFFOLK SILVERPLATE ..................................GORHAM
SUPER-PLATE............................................INSILCO
SUPERIOR ..............................................INSILCO
SUPREME SILVER PLATE ................................INSILCO
SUREFIRE ..........................................NAPIER COMPANY
SUSSEX .....................................HEMILL SILVERWARE CO.
TABARD SILVER.................................BENEDICT MFG. CO.
TAUNTON SILVER PLATE CO. ........................I. J. STEANE & CO.
THE COLUMBIA ..................................G. I. MIX & CO.
JOHN TOOTHILL .........................METROPOLITAN SILVER CO.
TORSIL METAL ..........................TORONTO SILVER PLATE CO.
TORSIL E. P. - N. S. .....................TORONTO SILVER PLATE CO.
TRIPLE PLUS ...........................................ONEIDA
TUDOR PLATE ...........................................ONEIDA
TWINKLE STERLING ......................................GORHAM
210 NEARSILVER ........................................ONEIDA
```

243

UNION SILVER PLATE CO. .HOLMES, BOOTH & HAYDENS
UNION SILVER PLATE CO. . . . . .INSILCO
UNITED JEWELERS' CROWN GUILD . . . . .JEWELERS' CROWN GUILD
UNIVERSAL . . . . .LANDERS, FRARY & CLARK
U. S. SILVER CO. . . . . .ONEIDA
VIANDE . . . . .INSILCO
VICTOR S. CO. . . . . .INSILCO
VOGUE . . . . .GORHAM
WARNER SILVER COMPANY .WEIDLICH BROS. MFG. CO.
WARWICK . . . . .W. BELL CO.
WEARWELL . . . . .GOTHAM SILVER CO.
WMF . . . . .WÜRTTENBERGISCHE METALLWARENFABRIK
WELCH SILVER . . . . .AMERICAN SILVER CO.
WILCOX SILVER PLATE CO. . . . . .INSILCO
WM. ROGERS MFG. CO. . . . . .INSILCO
WM. ROGERS & SON . . . . .INSILCO
WORLD . . . . .INSILCO
X S TRIPLE . . . . .INSILCO
YOUREX . . . . .GEORGE E. HERRING
Y STERLING . . . . .W. F. CORY & BRO.
YUKON SILVER . . . . .CATTARAUGUS CUTLERY CO.
ZENITH . . . . .MARSHALL-WELLS HARDWARE CO.

Key to Unlettered Marks

ADELPHI SILVER PLATE CO.

E. & J. BASS

ERNST GIDEON BEK, INC.

BENEDICT MFG. CO.

E. A. BLISS CO.

BRISTOL MFG. CO.

ADELPHI SILVER PLATE CO.
and
J. SCHIMPF & SONS

OTTO G. FABER

J. H. HUTCHINSON & CO.

BARBOUR SILVER CO.

MULHOLLAND BROS. INC.

JACOBI & JENKINS

TH. MARTHINSEN

MT. VERNON COMPANY SILVERSMITHS, INC.

ELLIS-BARKER SILVER COMPANIES

SUCKLING, LTD.

 E. & J. BASS

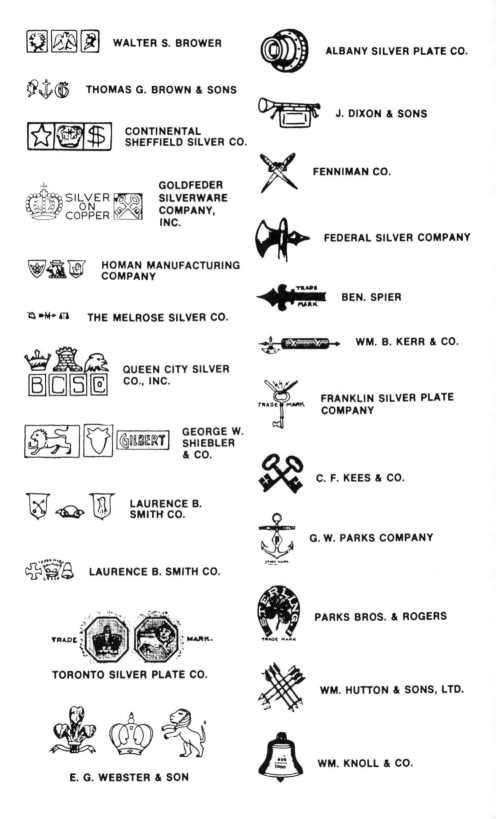

WALTER S. BROWER

THOMAS G. BROWN & SONS

CONTINENTAL SHEFFIELD SILVER CO.

GOLDFEDER SILVERWARE COMPANY, INC.

HOMAN MANUFACTURING COMPANY

THE MELROSE SILVER CO.

QUEEN CITY SILVER CO., INC.

GEORGE W. SHIEBLER & CO.

LAURENCE B. SMITH CO.

LAURENCE B. SMITH CO.

TORONTO SILVER PLATE CO.

E. G. WEBSTER & SON

ALBANY SILVER PLATE CO.

J. DIXON & SONS

FENNIMAN CO.

FEDERAL SILVER COMPANY

BEN. SPIER

WM. B. KERR & CO.

FRANKLIN SILVER PLATE COMPANY

C. F. KEES & CO.

G. W. PARKS COMPANY

PARKS BROS. & ROGERS

WM. HUTTON & SONS, LTD.

WM. KNOLL & CO.

ST. LOUIS METALCRAFTS, INC.,

 REDDALL & CO., INC.

 WM. AND GEO. SISSONS

 SOCIÉTÉ PICARD FRERES

 TH. MARTHINSEN

 DAVIS & GALT

 POOLE SILVER CO.

 WM. B. KERR & CO.

 ELLIS-BARKER SILVER COMPANIES

 WILLIAM LINKER

 J. TOSTRUP

 JOSEPH MAYER & BROS.

 THE POTOSI SILVER CO.

 TOWLE SILVERSMITHS

FINE ARTS STERLING SILVER COMPANY

 INTERNATIONAL SILVER CO.

KENT & STANLEY CO., LTD.

OLD NEW ENGLAND CRAFTSMEN, INC.

BROWN & WARD

 SOCIÉTÉ PICARD FRERES

 MERMOD, JACCARD & KING JEWELRY CO.

DOMINICK & HAFF

 MERRIMAC VALLEY SILVERSMITHS

 H. H. CURTIS & CO.

 STERLING

MECHANICS STERLING COMPANY and WATSON COMPANY

 THE MAUSER MANUFACTURING COMPANY

 BACHRACH & FREEDMAN

 REDLICH & CO.

 C. E. BARKER MFG. CO.

 SACKETT & CO., LTD.

 MISS SARAH B. DICKINSON and MRS. SARAH B. DICKINSON WOOD

 THE MERRILL SHOPS

 JACK BOWLING

 A. L. SILBERSTEIN

 ALBERT FELDENHEIMER

 A. L. SILBERSTEIN

ELLIS-BARKER SILVER COMPANIES

 TILDEN-THURBER CO.

 MAX HIRSCH

 BARKER BROS. SILVER CO., INC.

 LEHMAN BROTHERS SILVERWARE CORP.

 POTOSI SILVER CO.

 S. J. LEVI & CO., LTD.

 BLACK, STARR & FROST, LTD.

 THORNTON & CO.

MAYO & CO.

 MERIDEN BRITANNIA COMPANY

 MANNING, BOWMAN & CO.

 OLD NEWBURY CRAFTERS, INC.

 A. G. SCHULTZ & CO.

 WM. B. DURGIN CO.

 J. T. INMAN & CO.

  STERLING
WILLIAM C. FINCK CO.

BARKER BROS. SILVER CO.

 SHREVE, CRUMP & LOW CO., INC.

 J. W. ROSENBAUM & CO.

 H. J. WEBB & CO.

 COLONIAL SILVER COMPANY, INC.

 HENRY C. HASKELL

 TUTTLE SILVERSMITHS

 MAJESTIC SILVER COMPANY

 TIMOTHY TUTTLE

 GENOVA SILVER CO., INC.

HAWTHORNE MFG. CO.

MERIDEN BRITANNIA COMPANY

 CHARTER COMPANY

CHARTER COMPANY

 CHARTER COMPANY

 ECKFELDT & ACKLEY

 LOTT & SCHMITT, INC.

 SIMEON L. & GEO. H. ROGERS CO.

 ELLIS-BARKER SILVER COMPANIES

 STANDARD SILVER CO. OF TORONTO

 NORBERT MFG. CO.

 WATSON COMPANY

 MATHEWS & PRIOR

HANLE & DEBLER, INC.

 PRILL SILVER CO., INC.

 ST. LOUIS METALCRAFTS

 GEBRUEDER NOELLE

 NEW ORLEANS SILVERSMITHS

 NEW ORLEANS SILVERSMITHS

 W. E. WEBSTER CO.

 J. J. COHN

 GALT & BRO., INC.

 MT. VERNON COMPANY

 GALT & BRO., INC.

 GALT & BRO., INC.

SCHULZ & FISCHER

MEDALLIC ART COMPANY

MILLIE B. LOGAN

UTOPIAN SILVER DEPOSIT & NOVELTY CO.

WITCH

DANIEL LOW & CO.

ROGER WILLIAMS SILVER CO.

E. A. BLISS CO.

AUG. C. FRANK CO., INC.

FERDINAND C. LAMY

R. GLEASON & SONS

WILLIAM F. NEWHALL

HARRIS & SCHAFER

WILLIAM H. SAXTON, JR.

N. G. WOOD & SONS

ROMAN SILVERSMITHS, INC.

SUTTON HOO JEWELERS

H. G. HUDSON

MONTGOMERY BROS.

MERIDEN BRITANNIA COMPANY

STERLING FINE

L. KIMBALL & SON

WILCOX & EVERTSEN

H. G. HUDSON

H. H. TAMMEN CURIO CO.

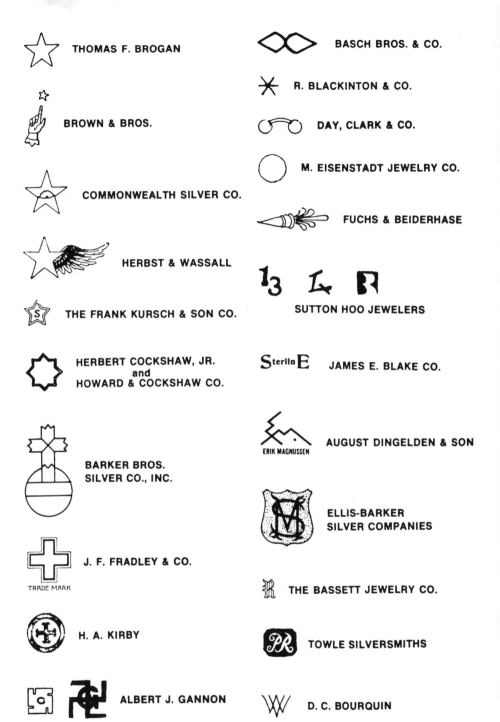

THOMAS F. BROGAN

BROWN & BROS.

COMMONWEALTH SILVER CO.

HERBST & WASSALL

THE FRANK KURSCH & SON CO.

HERBERT COCKSHAW, JR.
and
HOWARD & COCKSHAW CO.

BARKER BROS.
SILVER CO., INC.

J. F. FRADLEY & CO.

TRADE MARK

H. A. KIRBY

ALBERT J. GANNON

BASCH BROS. & CO.

R. BLACKINTON & CO.

DAY, CLARK & CO.

M. EISENSTADT JEWELRY CO.

FUCHS & BEIDERHASE

SUTTON HOO JEWELERS

JAMES E. BLAKE CO.

ERIK MAGNUSSEN

AUGUST DINGELDEN & SON

ELLIS-BARKER
SILVER COMPANIES

THE BASSETT JEWELRY CO.

TOWLE SILVERSMITHS

D. C. BOURQUIN

Glossary

Acanthus: A form of ornamentation taken from the acanthus leaf, originally used extensively on the Corinthian capital throughout the Renaissance period, 16th–17th centuries.

Ajouré: A French term applied to metalwork which is pierced through, perforated or openwork.

Alaska Silver: Base metal of secret composition. According to contemporary ads, "Its purpose is to imitate solid silver at a fraction of the cost." It is subject to damage if left 12 hours or more in acid foods, fats or grease. It is also a tradename used on silverplated flatware sold by Sears Roebuck & Co., c. 1908. In the 1908 catalog was the statement that Alaska Metal was their special formula of composition metal made to imitate solid silver. Contains no silver.

Albata: Alloy of nickel, copper, and zinc, forming a silvery white metal.

Alchemy: A superior pewter used in the 16th and 17th centuries for making spoons and plates; an alloy of tin and copper.

Alcomy: An alloy of various base metals.

Alfenide: "Spoons made of alfenide similar to finest English white metal. Contains no brass or German steel." (Clipping dated March 18, 1878, *St. Nicholas Magazine.*)

Alloy: A substance composed of two or more metals intimately united, usually intermixed when molten.

Alpacca: German silver and nickel silver; are synonymous trade names of an alloy of copper, nickel and zinc.

Aluminum Silver: A composition of aluminum and silver which is much harder than aluminum. It takes a high polish. Air does not affect the color. The proportion of ingredients varies. One of three parts silver and ninety-seven parts aluminum makes an alloy similar in appearance to pure aluminum but is much harder and takes a better polish.

Annealing: Reheating of silver to keep it malleable while it is being worked.

Anvil: An iron block on which metal is hammered and shaped.

Apocryphal: Classical term for a fake.

Applied: Certain parts, such as spouts, handles, covers, et cetera, are sometimes made separately and applied with solder.

Apprentice: One who is bound by indentures to serve another person with a view of learning a trade.

Argentine: An alloy of tin and antimony used as a base for plating; nickel silver; German silver; also "British plate"; known in China as Paktong. Bradbury says, "Credit [is] due to W. Hutton & Sons, of Sheffield, for being the first firm to manufacture spoons and forks from the newly-invented metal called Argentine, in the year 1833."

Assay: The test made to prove that the metal is of the required quality.

Baltimore Assay Marks: Starting in 1814, silver made in Baltimore was marked at a hall and identified by a date letter; this compulsory marking was abolished in 1830.

Base Metal: An alloy or metal of comparatively low value to which a coating or plating is normally applied.

Bat's-wing Fluting: Gadrooning, graduated and curved to resemble the outline of a bat's wing and encircling holloware.

Beading: A border ornament composed of small, contiguous, bead-like, half-spheres. Popular in late 18th century.

Beakhorn: A sharply pointed anvil.

Bell Metal: A variety of Sheffield Plate consisting of an unusually heavy coating of silver, introduced in 1789 by Samuel Roberts.

Black Pewter: An alloy of 60 per cent tin and 40 per cent lead. Used for making organ pipes and candle molds.

Bleeding: The technical term applied to pieces of plate whereon the copper base is exposed.

Bobêche: Flat or saucerlike rings placed around candle bases to stop wax drippings.

Bright-cut Engraving: A particular form of engraving popular about 1790, in which the metal is removed by bevelled cutting tools.

This gives a jewel-like, faceted sparkle to the surface.

Bright Finish: Highly polished, mirror-like finish produced by use of jeweler's rouge on a polishing wheel.

Britannia: A silver-white alloy composed largely of tin hardened with copper and antimony. Closely akin to pewter, yet differing in the higher proportion of tin, the addition of antimony and the omission of lead, resulting in a more silvery appearance than is possible with the pewter mixture. It often contains also a small quanitity of zinc and bismuth. A common proportion is 140 parts of tin, three of copper and ten of antimony.

Bronze: An alloy chiefly of copper and tin.

Buffing: Removal of the outer layer of metal with a flexible abrasive wheel or a soft mop, exposing a shiny undersurface but imparting no additional hardness.

Burnisher: Tool with hard, polished working surface such as agate, for burnishing gold and silver.

Burnishing: Electro deposits consist of a multitude of small crystals, with intervals between them, and with facets reflecting the light in every direction. The deposited metal is hardened by burnishing and forcing into the pores of the underlying metal. The durability is thus increased to such an extent that, with the same amount of silver, a burnished article will last twice as long as one which has not been so treated.

Butler's Finish: Satin finish produced by a revolving wheel of wire which makes many tiny scratches, giving the article a dull appearance. Patented by James H. Reilly, Brooklyn Silver Co.

C: (See Coin.)

Cable: Molding like twisted rope, derived from Norman architecture.

Cast: Formed in a mold, i.e., handles, ornaments, et cetera are often cast separately.

Chafing-dish: One dish or vessel within another, the outer vessel being filled with hot water and in direct contact with the heat source and an inner container for food.

Chamber-candlestick: A tray candlestick in the form of a circular dish stand with a handle.

Champleve: Enameling by cutting troughs in the metal into which the frit is melted; the surface is ground flush and polished.

Chasing: A cold modeling process of ornamenting metal by hammers. Also called embossing.

Cloisonné: Enameling by melting the frit into areas defined by wire soldered to surface to be decorated.

Coin: By 1830, COIN, PURE COIN, DOLLAR,

STANDARD, PREMIUM or C or D were used to indicate 900/1000 parts of silver.

Coin Silver: 900/1000 fine, with 100/1000 of copper. Used by early silversmiths to whom sterling was not available.

Commercial Silver: 999/1000 fine or higher.

Craig Silver: Similar to German silver. Used for making knives.

C-scroll: Usually applied to the shape of a handle in the form of the letter C; also called 'single scroll'.

Cut-cardwork: Silver work in which conventional designs of leaves and flowers are cut from thin sheet-silver and applied to a silver surface.

Cutler: One who makes, deals in, or repairs utensils or knives.

Cutlery: Knives having a cutting edge.

D: (See Coin.)

Date Letter; Date Mark: Proper assay marks on English silver, the date being indicated by a letter of the alphabet. Some American silver is date marked. (See Gorham, Kirk, Tiffany, and Tuttle.)

Dish Cross: An x-shaped support for a dish, some with spirit lamps for warming food.

Dish Ring: A silver stand particularly identified with Irish silver, and sometimes called a potato-ring.

Dollar: (See Coin.)

Dolphin: The sea dolphin used as a sculptured or carved motif.

Domed: Spheroid form of cover, first used in 1715 on tankards, teapots and coffeepots.

Domestic Plate: Silverware for home use.

Double-scroll: A sinuous line of S-shape, or composed of reverse curves, used especially in design of handles.

Drawing Irons: Metal parts of a drawing bench, through which silver is drawn.

Electrolysis: Conduction of an electric current by an electrolyte of charged particles.

Electroplate: Articles consisting of a base metal coated with silver by the process of electrolysis.

Electrotype: Copy of art object produced by electroplating a wax impression. Much used in the nineteenth century to reproduce antique objects. Now employed in the production of facsimile plates for use in printing.

Electrum: A natural pale-yellow alloy of gold and silver. Also, an imitative alloy of silver, 8 parts copper, 4 nickel, and 3½ zinc.

Embossing: Making raised designs on the surface of metal from the reverse side, strictly applicable only to hammered work (Repoussé).

Engraving: Cutting lines into metal with a scorper or graver.

EPC: Electroplate on copper.

EPBM: Electroplate on britannia metal.

Epergne: An elaborate centerpiece, especially for a dining table; an ensemble of cups and vases for holding fruits, flowers, et cetera.

EPNS: Electroplate on nickel silver.

E.P.N.S. — W.M.M.: Electroplate on nickel silver with white metal mounts.

EPWM: Electroplate on white metal.

Etching: Surface decoration bitten-in with acid.

Ewer: A jug or pitcher having a wide spout and a handle.

Feather Edge: Decoration of edge of spoon-handle with chased, slanting lines. An engraved, decorative design.

Fine Pewter: Eighty per cent tin and 20 per cent brass or copper. Used for making plates because of the smooth surface, attractive color and strength.

Fine Silver: Better than 999/1000 pure. It is too soft for practical fabrication, and is mainly used in the form of anodes or sheets for plating.

Flagon: Large vessel for serving wine or other liquors.

Flash Plate: Unbuffed, cheap plated ware.

Flat Chasing: Surface decoration in low relief. Popular in England in early 18th century, and widely used in America, 1750–1785.

Flatware: Knives, forks, spoons and serving pieces.

Fluted: A type of grooving.

Foreign Silver: Other than English sterling, is sometimes of uncertain silver content, in some instances running considerably below the coin standard. The fineness is often stamped on the article. In the Scandinavian countries and Germany solid silver tableware 830/1000 fine has been standardized, and the stamp "830" signifies this silver content.

Forging: The shaping of metal by heating and hammering.

Fusion: An act or operation of melting, as the fusion of metals. Usually accomplished by the application of intense heat.

Gadroon: A border ornament radiating lobes of curved or straight form. Used on rims and feet of cups, plates and other vessels from late 17th century.

German Silver: A silver-white alloy consisting principally of copper, zinc and nickel. During World War I this name was dropped by many and the term nickel silver used.

Gold Aluminum: A solid alloy used for flatware made by Holmes & Edwards Silver Co., Bridgeport, Connecticut. Marked with a trademark WALDO HE preceded by a symbol used by the Waldo Foundry which probably made the metal. Flatware made only in *Rialto* pattern which was also made in silverplate.

Gold Plating: The covering of an article with gold.

Goldsmiths' Company: The organization under whose jurisdiction and regulation the English silver industry has been conducted.

Graver: Tool used to engrave silver.

Hallmark: The official mark of the English Goldsmiths' Company used on articles of gold and silver to indicate their genuineness.

Hollow Handle (H. H.): Handles made of two halves soldered together. Knives, especially, need the thickness provided for comfortable use, controlled handle weight and balance.

Holloware: A general term for articles in the form of hollow vessels, such as mugs, ewers, teapots, coffeepots, bowls and pitchers also includes trays, waiters, meat and chop plates and flat sandwich trays.

Holloware Pewter: Eighty per cent tin and 20 per cent lead, used for making teapots, tankards, coffee pots and liquid measures.

Ingot: A bar of silver or other metal.

Katé: A Malayan weight equal to 11.73 ounces. Tea was sold by the kate (pronounced katde). It became "caddy" — hence tea caddy. Also spelled kati.

Lashar Silver: A process invented by Thomas B. Lashar of the Holmes & Edwards Silver Co., whereby the copper and zinc from the surface of nickel alloy was removed, leaving only the nickel exposed.

Latten: An alloy of copper and zinc; brass.

Limoges: Enamel painted on metal, covering the surface.

Maker's Mark: The distinguishing mark of the individual goldsmith.

Malleable: Capable of being extended or shaped by beating with a hammer; ductile.

Matted-ground: A dull surface made by light punchwork, to secure contrast with a burnished surface.

Metalsmith: One versed in the intricacies of working with metals.

Nickel Silver: An alloy of nickel, copper and zinc.

Niello: Deep-line engraving on gold or silver with the lines filled with copper, lead and sulphur in borax, forming a type of black enamel which is fired and polished.

Non-tarnishing Silver: Produced by alloying silver with cadmium or by the application of a thin plating of rhodium or palladium on the surface.

N.S.: Nickel silver.

Onslow Pattern: Design for flatware shaped as a volute scroll.

Ormolu: "Ground gold," literally. Ground gold leaf used as a gilt pigment. Also, brass made to look like gold.

Oxidizing: Accented beauty of ornamentation by the application of an oxide which darkens metal wherever applied. Shadows and highlights are created which give depth and character.

Patina: Soft luster caused by tiny scratches that come with daily use.

Pewter: An alloy of tin and copper or any alloy of the low-melting-point metals, including tin, lead, bismuth and antimony. Sad pewter is the heaviest, but not the best. The higher the tin content, the better the pewter.

Pinchbeck: An alloy of copper or zinc used to imitate gold. Invented by Christopher Pinchbeck (1670–1732), London. Also called "Chapman's" gold or Mannheim gold.

Pit Marks: Minute holes usually found on lead or soft metal borders.

Planishing: To make smooth or plain. Oval-faced planishing hammers are used to conceal hammer marks used in forming a piece.

Plate: Used in England and on the Continent when referring to articles made of precious metals.

Plique-à-jour: Translucent enamel without a metal backing, enclosed within metal frames, giving a stained glass or jewel-like effect

Premium: (See Coin.)

Pricking: Delicate needle-point engraving. Pricked initials were often used on early pieces.

Pseudo Hall-marks: Devices used to suggest English hall-marks.

Pure Coin: (See Coin.)

Raising: Formation of a piece of holloware beginning with a flat circle of silver. It is hammered in concentric circles over a succession of anvils with frequent annealings.

Rolled Plate: (See Sheffield Plate.)

Rope-molding: A type of gadroon bordering made up of reeds and flutes slightly spiralled.

R.P.: Rolled Plate.

Repoussé: Relief ornament hammered from the under or inner side of the metal. Usually given added sharpness of form by surface chasing of detail and outline. Has been practiced from early times. Introduced to this country by Samuel Kirk in 1828.

Satin Finish: (See Butler's Finish.)

Scorper: Small chisel for engraving. The blades are of various shapes.

Sheffield Plate: True Sheffield plate was produced by fusing, with intense heat, a thin sheet of silver to one or both sides of a thick sheet of copper. The composite metal was then rolled down to the proper thickness for fabrication. Invented by Thomas Boulsover about 1743 Frequently called "Old Sheffield Plate" to distinguish it from electroplate.

Silver Edge: An ornamental border of solid silver.

Silverite: "A combination of tin, nickel, platinum, etc." according to advertisements.

Silverplate: A base metal, usually either nickel silver or copper, coated with a layer of pure silver by electroplating.

Spinning: Process used for forming holloware. A metal plate is cut to proper size, placed against a chuck in a lathe, where pressure against it with a smooth revolving instrument produces the desired form.

Stake: An iron anvil or tongue, on which a silver object is formed.

Stamping: Impressing of designs from dies into the metal by means of heavy hammers. Often followed by hand chasing to sharpen up design details.

Stamping Trademarks and Stock Numbers: As early as 1867, the Meriden Britannia Co. had a system of stamping nickel silver, silver soldered holloware with a cipher preceding the number, and by 1893, nickel silver holloware with white metal mounts had as a part of the number two ciphers. That is, on a waiter with white metal, 00256, etc. would be stamped. This made it quickly understood by the number whether the piece was nickel silver, silversoldered or nickel silver with white metal mounts.

Standard: (See Coin.)

Sterling II: Flatware whose hollow handles are of sterling silver but tines, bowls and blades are stainless steel. Developed by Wallace Silversmiths.

Sterling Silver: 925/1000 fine, with 75/1000 of added metal, usually copper, to give it strength and stiffness. This is the standard set by the United States Government in the Stamping Act of 1906, and any article stamped "sterling" is of assured quality. It appears on Baltimore silver, 1800–1814, and after 1860, elsewhere.

Stoning: Polishing of silver with an emery-stone.

Swaged: Shaped by the process of rolling or hammering.

Tempering: Strengthening of metal by heat.

Touch: Maker's mark, impressed with a punch.

Touchstone: A hard siliceous stone or modern square of Wedgwood on which a piece of silver or gold of known quality can be rubbed to compare its mark with that of a piece being assayed.

Town Mark: The mark assigned to a city and applied as a hallmark to denote the location of manufacture.

Trademark: Symbol or tradename by which a manufacturer may be identified. Widely used in this country as a guarantee of quality. A distinction should be made between a trademark and a hallmark, as required by English and other European countries. Because the United States has never had a goldsmiths' or silversmiths' hall, there are no true hallmarks on American silver.

Trifle Pewter: Sixty per cent tin and 40 per cent lead. Of a darker color and softer than better grades of pewter, it was short lived. The alloy was altered to 83 parts tin and 17 parts antimony and was made into spoons, saltshakers, buttons and similar articles which could not be finished on a lathe. Workers in this alloy were called "triflers."

Vermeil: Gold plating process developed in France in the mid 1700s. France banned production of vermeil early in the 19th century because the process involved the use of mercury. Present-day vermeil is produced by a safe electrolytic process.

Victorian Plate: Plated silver ware made during the period c. 1840–1900 by the process of electrolysis.

Waiter: A tray on which something is carried; a salver.

White Metal: An alloy usually containing two or more of the following elements — tin, copper, lead, antimony and bismuth. The color depends on whether lead or tin predominates. The more tin the whiter the color.

Whitesmith: A planishing smith; superior workman in iron, comparable to the armorer. Also a worker in pure tin of the "block" variety, not cast, but hammered and battered, planished and "skum." Originally "whitster."

Silverplate Specifications

When plated silver production first began, some manufacturers either ignored indicating the quality or marked their products "Triple" or "Quadruple" plate. About this, the JEWELERS' CIRCULAR had this to say:

SILVER PLATED WARE

NOTE: — Manufacturers of silver plated flatware, in addition to their trade-mark, stamp the quality upon their goods, almost all of them adopting the same signs and figures. These quality signs and figures are as follows:

A.I. ....represents standard plate
XII ....represents sectional plate
4 ....represents double plate, tea spoons
6 ....represents double plate, dessert spoons and forks
8 ....represents double plate, table spoons
6 ....represents triple plate, tea spoons
9 ....represents triple plate, dessert spoons and forks.
12 ....represents triple plate, table spoons.

There is an amount of cheap plated ware on the market stamped with the names of fictitious companies, such as "Quadruple Silver Plate Co." "Royal Sterling Plate Co.," etc. These goods are furnished, bearing no stamp, to department storekeepers, conductors of gift enterprises and jobbers of cheap merchandise, who stamp the goods themselves with such names as suit their fancy. It is, therefore, practically impossible to trace these stamps.

FOR FLATWARE

Half plate: 1 troy oz. per gross of teaspoons
Standard plate: 2 troy oz. per gross of teaspoons
Double plate: 4 troy oz. per gross of teaspoons
Triple plate: 6 troy oz. per gross of teaspoons
Quadruple plate: 8 troy oz. per gross of teaspoons
Federal specification: 9 troy oz. per gross of teaspoons

These specifications produce a thickness whose range is from 0.00015 to 0.00125 in. — the latter equivalent to 1 troy oz. per square ft. Federal specifications call for an average of 0.000125 in. thickness to be reinforced by silver to a minimum of 0.00180 in. on the backs of spoon bowls and fork tines.

FOR HOTELWARE – HOLLOWARE

Federal specification plate: 20 dwt. per sq. ft.
Extra heavy hotel plate: 15 dwt. per sq. ft.
Heavy hotel plate: 10 dwt. per sq. ft.
Medium plate: 5 dwt. per sq. ft.
Light plate: 2 dwt. per sq. ft.

The Federal specification is for 0.00125 in., the same thickness required for flatware. Light plate is 0.000125 in., slightly less than the half plate under flatware.

Table of Equivalents

TROY WEIGHT

POUNDS		OUNCES		PENNYWEIGHTS (dwts.)
1	=	12	=	240
		1	=	20

1 oz. avoir. = .91146 Troy oz. = 28.3495 gms.
1 oz. Troy = 1.0971 oz. avoir. = 31.035 gms.
1 lb. avoir. = 14.58 oz. Troy
1 lb. Troy = 13.165 oz. avoir.

SILVER STANDARDS

$.896 = 10.15$ (Used in Maryland c. 1840–c. 1860) $= \dfrac{10.75}{12}$

.892 Standard for U.S. coins 1792–1837

$.900$ (Standard for U.S. coins after 1837) $= 10.8 = \dfrac{10 \text{ oz. } 16 \text{ dwts.}}{12}$

$.917 = 11 = {}^{11}/_{12}$ Baltimore standard during Assay Office period. 1814–1830. Midway between coin and sterling.

$.925 = 11.1 = \dfrac{11 \text{ oz. } 2 \text{ dwts.}}{12}$ The sterling standard. Used often in Baltimore c. 1800–1814. Not used consistently elsewhere in the U.S. until c. 1865.

$.958 = 11.5 = \dfrac{11 \text{ oz. } 10 \text{ dwts.}}{12}$ The Britannia standard.

Bibliography

Abbey, Staton. *The Goldsmiths and Silversmiths Handbook.* New York: Van Nostrand, 1952.

Albany Silver. Albany, New York: Albany Institute of History and Art, 1964.

Alexander, S. E. "Tiffany's Sterling: History and Status," *National Jeweler,* June, 1963.

American Church Silver of 17th and 18th Centuries Exhibited at the Museum of Fine Arts, July to December, 1911. Boston: Boston Museum of Fine Arts, 1911.

"American Silver," *American Magazine of Art,* August 1919, v. 10, p. 400.

Antiquarian Magazine. 1924–1933.

Antiques Digest. Frederick, Maryland: Antiques Publications, Inc., 1951–1952.

Antiques Magazine. New York: 1922–1975.

Attleboro Daily Sun, Anniversary Edition. Attleboro, Mass.: 1964.

Avery, Clara Louise. "New York Metropolitan Museum of Art, American Silver of the 17th and 18th centuries." *Metropolitan Museum of Art Bulletin.* 1920.

Avery, Clara Louise. "New York Metropolitan Museum of Art, Exhibition of Early American Silver." *Metropolitan Museum of Art Bulletin.* December, 1931.

Avery, Clara Louise. *Early American Silver.* New York: The Century Company, 1930.

Bartlett, W. A. *Digest of Trade-Marks. (Registered in the U. S.) for Machines, Metals, Jewelry and the Hardware and Allied Trades.* Washington, D.C.: Gibson Bros., Printers, 1893.

Bent, Dorothy. "A Fascinating Biography of Knives and Forks." *Arts and Decoration.* Vol. 25, June, 1926.

Bigelow, Francis Hill. *Historic Silver of the Colonies and its Makers.* New York: The Macmillan Company, 1917.

Biographical History of the Manufacturers and Business Men of Rhode Island at the Opening of the Twentieth Century. Providence, Rhode Island: J. D. Hall & Co., 1901.

Bishop, J. Oleander. *A History of American Manufacturers from 1808–1860,* 2 vols. Philadelphia: Young & Co., 1861.

Boger, H. Batterson and Boger, Louise Ade. *The Dictionary of Antiques and the Decorative Arts.* New York: Charles Scribner's Sons, 1957.

Bolles, Albert S. *Industrial History of the United States from the Earliest Settlements to the Present Time.* Norwich, Conn.: 1879.

Bradbury, Frederick. *History of Old Sheffield Plate.* J. W. Northend, Sheffield, England, 1912; reprinted 1968.

Brix, Maurice. *List of Philadelphia Silversmiths and Allied Artificers, 1682–1850.* Philadelphia: Privately printed, 1920.

The Bromwell Story. Washington, D.C.: D. L. Bromwell, Inc., pamphlet, no date.

Buck, J. H. *Old Plate, Its Makers and Marks.* New York: Gorham Manufacturing Company, 1903.

Buhler, Kathryn C. "Silver 1640–1820," *The Concise Encyclopedia of American Antiques.* New York: Hawthorn Books, Inc., Vol 1., no date.

Burton E. Milby. *South Carolina Silversmiths 1690–1860.* Charleston: The Charleston Museum, 1942.

Bury, Shirley. *Victorian Electroplate.* Country Life Collectors' Guides. The Hamlyn Pub. Group, London, 1971.

Carlisle, Lilian Baker. *News and Notes.* Vermont Historical Society, no date.

Carlisle, Lilian Baker. *Vermont Clock and Watchmakers, Silversmiths and Jewelers, 1778-1878.* Burlington, Verkmont, 1970.

Carpenter, Charles H., Jr. *Gorham Silver.* Dodd, Mead & C., New York. 1982.

Carpenter, Charles H., Jr. & Mary Grace Carpenter. *Tiffany Silver.* Dodd, Mead & Co., New York. 1978.

Carpenter, Ralph E. Jr. *The Arts and Crafts of Newport.* Rhode Island: Preservation Society of Newport County, Pittshead Tavern, 1954.

Catalog of an Exhibition of Paintings by Gilbert Stuart, Furniture by the Goddards and Townsends, Silver by Rhode Island Silversmiths. Rhode Island School of Design, Providence, Rhode Island: 1936.

Chickering, Elenita C. "Arthur J. Stone, Hand-

wrought Silver, 1901-1937." Boston Athenaeum, 1981.

"A Cincinnati Industry, Homan & Co., the largest manufacturers of fine silver-plated ware in the city," *The Watch Dial*, July 1888.

Clarke, Hermann Frederick, *John Coney, Silversmith 1655-1722*. Boston: Houghton Mifflin Company, 1932.

Clarke, Hermann Frederick and Foote, Henry Wilder. *Jeremiah Dummer, Colonial Craftsman and Merchant 1645-1718*. Boston: Houghton Mifflin Company 1935.

Clarke, Hermann Frederick. *John Hull, Builder of the Bay Colony*. Portland, Me.: The Southworth-Anthoensen Press, 1940.

Clark, Victor S. *History of Manufacturers in the United States*. New York: Carnegie Institute of Washington, 1929.

Clearwater, Alphonso T. *American Silver, List of Unidentified Makers and Marks*. New York: 1913.

A Collection of Early American Silver. New York: Tiffany and Company, 1920.

Colonial Silversmiths, Masters & Apprentices. Boston Museum of Fine Arts, 1956.

Comstock, Helen. "American Silver," *The Concise Encyclopedia of Antiques*. New York: Hawthorn Books, Inc.

"The Craft of the Spoonmaker." *Antiques*, 1929.

Crosby, Everett Uberto. *Books and Baskets, Signs and Silver of Old Time Nantucket*. Nantucket, Mass.: Inquirer and Mirror Press, 1940.

Crosby, Everett Uberto. *95% Perfect*. Nantucket, Island, Mass.: Tetaukimmo Press, 1953.

Crosby, Everett Uberto. *The Spoon Primer*. Nantucket, Mass.: Inquirer and Mirror Press, 1941.

Currier, Ernest M. *Early American Silversmiths, The Newbury Spoonmakers*. New York: 1929.

Currier, Ernest M. *Marks of Early American Silversmiths, List of New York City Silversmiths 1815-1841*. Portland, Me.: The Southworth-Athoensen Press. 1938; reprinted 1970 by Robert Alan Green.

Curtis, George Munson. *Early Silver of Connecticut and Makers*. Meriden, Conn.: International Silver Company, 1913.

Cutten, George Barton. *Silversmiths of Georgia*. Savannah, Ga.: Pigeonhole Press, 1958.

Cutten, George Barton, *Silversmiths of Northampton, Massachusetts and Vicinity down to 1850*. Pamphlet.

Cutten, George Barton. *Silversmiths of North Carolina*. Raleigh, N. C.: State Department of Archives & History, 1948.

Cutten, George Barton and Cutten, Minnie Warren. *Silversmiths of Utica*. Hamilton, New York: 1936.

Cutten, George Barton. *Silversmiths, Watchmakers and Jewelers of the State of New York Outside New York City*. Hamilton, N. Y.: Privately printed, 1939.

Cutten, George Barton. *Silversmiths of Virginia*. Richmond, Va.: The Dietz Press, 1952.

Cutten, George Barton. *Ten Silversmith Families of New York State*. Albany, New York: State Historical Assoc., 1946.

Danbury (Conn.) News-Times, December 2, 1938.

Davis, Charles H. S. *History of Wallingford, Connecticut*. Published by author, 1870.

Davis, Fredna Harris and Deibel, Kenneth K. *Silver Plated Flatware Patterns*. Dallas, Texas: Bluebonnet Press, 1972.

Day, Clive. *Rise of Manufacturing in Connecticut, 1820-1850*. Yale University Press for Tercentenary of Conn.

Depew, Chauncey M. *One Hundred Years of American Commerce*. D. O. Haynes & Co., 1895, Vol. 2.

Descriptive Catalogue of Various Pieces of Silver Plate forming Collection of the New York Farmers 1882-1932.

Detroit Historical Society Bulletin. Detroit, Mich.: November, 1952.

Dreppard, Carl W. *The Primer of American Antiques*. Garden City, N. Y.: Doubleday & Company, Inc., 1954.

Duhousset, Charles. *l'Art Pour Tous*. Paris: 1879.

Durrett, Colonel Reuben T. *Traditions of the Earliest Visits of Foreigners*. (Filson Club Publications No. 23) Louisville, Kentucky: John P. Morton & Co., 1908.

Dyer, W. A. "Early American Silver," *Arts and Decoration*. VII (May 1917)

Early American Spoons and Their Makers. Editor and Publisher, Golden Anniversary Issue, July 21, 1934.

Early Connecticut Silver 1700-1830. Gallery of Fine Arts. New Haven, Conn.: Yale University Press, Connecticut Tercentenary Commission, 1935.

Early, Eleanor. *An Island Patchwork*. Boston: Houghton Mifflin Company, 1941.

Early New England Silver lent from the Mark Bortman Collection. Northampton, Mass.: Smith College Museum of Art, 1958.

Eaton, Allen H. *Handicrafts of New England*. New York: Harper & Brothers Publishers, 1949.

Eberlein, H. D. "Early American Silver," *Arts and Decoration*. XI (August 1919).

Eberlein, Harold D. and McClure, Abbot. *The Practical Book of American Antiques*. Garden City, New York: Halcyon House, 1948.

Edmonds, Walter D. *The First Hundred Years, 1848-1948*, Oneida Community. Oneida, N.Y. : Oneida Ltd., 1958.

Ellis, Leonard Bolles, *History of New Bedford and its Vicinity, 1602-1892*. Syracuse, New York: D. Mason & Company, Publishers, 1892.

Ensko, Robert. *Makers of Early American Silver*. New York: Trow Press, 1915.

Ensko, Stephen. *American Silversmiths and Their Marks*. New York: Privately printed, 1927.

Ensko, Stephen. *American Silversmiths and Their Marks II*. New York: Robert Ensko, Inc., Privately printed, 1937.

Ensko, Stephen. *American Silversmiths and Their Marks III*. New York: Robert Ensko, Inc., Privately printed, 1948.

Exhibition of Old American and English Silver. Pennsylvania Museum and School of Industrial Art, 1917.

Evans, Paul. *Shreve & Co. of San Francisco*. Parts I & II. No date. Privately printed.

Fisher, Leonard Everett. *The Silversmiths*. New York: Franklin Watts, Inc.

Flynt, Henry N. and Fales, Martha Gandy. *The Heritage Collection of Silver, Old Deerfield, Massachusetts:* The Heritage Foundation, 1968.

Forbes, Esther. *Paul Revere and the World He Lived In*. Boston: Houghton Mifflin Co., 1942.

Freedley, E. T. *Philadelphia and its Manufacturers*, 1857.

Freeman, Larry and Beaumont, Jane. *Early American Silversmiths and Their Marks*. New York: Walpole Society, 1947.

French, Hollis. *Jacob Hurd and His Sons Nathaniel and Benjamin, Silversmiths*. Printed by the Riverside Press for the Walpole Society, 1939.

From Colony to Nation, Exhibit. Chicago, Illinois: Chicago Art Institute, 1949.

Galt & Bro., Washington, D. C.: Pamphlet, no date.

Gibb, George S. *The Whitesmiths of Taunton, A History of Reed and Barton*. Cambridge, Mass.: Harvard University Press, 1946.

Gillespie, Charles Bancroft. *An Historic Record & Pictorial Description of the Town of Meriden*. Meriden, Conn.: Journal Pub. Co., 1906.

Gillingham, H. E. "Silver," *Pennsylvania Magazine of History and Biography*, 1930–1935.

Gorham Silver Co. *The Gorham Manufacturing Company Silversmiths*. New York: Cheltenham Press, 1900.

Goyne, Nancy A. "Britannia in America, the introduction of a new alloy and a new industry," *Winterthur Portfolio II*, Winterthur, Delaware, The Henry Francis Dupont Winterthur Museum, 1965.

Graham, James Jr. *Early American Silver Marks*. New York: James Graham Jr., 1936.

Greene, Welcome Howard. *The Providence Plantations for Two Hundred and Fifty Years*. Providence, R.I.: J. A. & R. A. Reid Publishers, 1886.

Grimwade, A. G. "Silver, " *The Concise Encyclopedia of Antiques*. New York: Hawthorn Books, Inc.

Halsey, R. T. Haines. *New York Metropolitan Museum Catalogue of Exhibition of Silver Used in New York, New Jersey, and the South*. Metropolitan Museum of Art, 1911.

Hardt, Anton. *Souvenir Spoons of the 90's*. New York: Privately printed, 1962.

Harrington, Jessie. *Silversmiths of Delaware 1700–1850*. Delaware: National Society of Colonial Dames of America, 1939.

Heller, David. *History of Cape Silver, 1700–1750*. 1949.

Hiatt, Noble W. and Lucy F. *The Silversmiths of Kentucky*. Louisville, Ky.: The Standard Printing Co., 1954.

"Highlights of the House of Kirk," *Hobbies*. August, 1939.

Hill, H. W. *Maryland's Silver Service*. Baltimore, Maryland: Waverly Press, Inc., 1962.

Hipkiss, E. J. *Boston Museum of Fine Arts Philip Leffingwell Spaulding Collection of Early American Silver*. Cambridge, Mass.: Harvard University Press, 1943.

Historical and Biographical Sketch of the Gorham Manufacturing Company. Reprint of booklet issued, 1878.

History of New Haven County, Connecticut. Edited by J. L. Rockey, Vol. One

History of the Spoon, Knife and Fork. Taunton, Mass.: Reed & Barton, 1926.

Hittell, John S. *Commerce and Industries of the Pacific Coast of North America*. San Francisco: A. L. Bancroft & Co., 1882.

Hoitsma, Muriel Cutten. *Early Cleveland Silversmiths*. Cleveland, Ohio: Gates Publishing Co., 1953.

The House of Kirk, Our 150th Year, 1815–1965. Baltimore: Samuel Kirk & Son, Inc., 1965.

Hoving, Walter. "The History of Tiffany," *Christian Science Monitor*. April 9, 10, 11, 1959.

"How America's $400 Million-a-Year Silver Manufacturing Industry Grew," *The Jewelers' Circular-Keystone*, Directory Issue. Philadelphia, Pa.: 1965.

Hower, Ralph Merle. *History of Macy's of New York, 1858–1919*. Cambridge, Mass.: Harvard University Press, c. 1943.

Hughes, G. Bernard. "Sheffield Plate," *The Concise Encyclopedia of Antiques*. New York: Hawthorn Books Inc., Vol. Two.

Hughes, Graham. *Modern Silver*. New York: Crown Pub., Inc., 1967.

Humphreys, Mary Gay. "Maiden Lane of the Past and Present," *Jewelers' Circular & Horological Review*, Nov. 28, 1894.

Hungerford, Edward. *The Romance of a Great Store (Macy's)*. New York: Robert M. McBride & Co., 1922.

Index of Trademarks Issued from the United States Patent Office, 1881.

Jacobs, Carl. *Guide to American Pewter*. New York: McBride, 1957.

James, George B., Jr. .*Souvenir Spoons*, Boston, Mass.: A. W. Fuller & Co., 1891.

Jayne, H. F. and Woodhouse, S. W., Jr. "Early

Philadelphia Silversmiths," *Art in America*. IX (October 1921).

Jeweler Buyers' Guide, A McKenna Publication. New York: Sherry Publishing Co., Inc., 1957, 1958, 1960.

The Jewelers' Circular & Horological Review. New York: D. H. Hopkinson, no date.

The Jewelers' Circular-Keystone. Philadelphia Pa.: Chilton Publication, 1869–1975.

The Jewelers' Circular-Weekly, 50th Anniversary Number. New York: Jewelers' Circular Pub. Co., 1919.

The Jewelers' Dictionary. New York: The Jewelers' Circular-Keystone, no date (c. 1950).

Jobbers' Handbook. 1936–1937.

Johnson, J. Stewart. "Silver in Newark, A Newark 300th Anniversary Study," *The Museum*, New Series, Vol. 18, Nos. 3 & 4. The Newark Museum, 1966.

Jones E. Alfred. *Old Silver of Europe and America*. Philadelphia: Lippincott Co., 1928.

Keddell, E. Avery. "Romance of the Spoon," *Art Journal*. January 1907.

Keir, Robert M. *Manufacturing in Industries of America*. Roland Press, 1928.

Kelley, Etna M. *The Business Founding Date Directory, (1687–1915)*. Scarsdale, N.Y.: Morgan & Morgan, 1954.

"Kentucky Silversmiths before 1850," *Filson Club History Quarterly*. XVI, No. 2, April 1942, 111–126.

Kerfoot, J. B. *American Pewter*. Boston and New York: Houghton Mifflin Co., 1924.

The Keystone Jewelers' Index. Phila.: The Keystone Publishing Co., 1922, 1924, 1927, 1931.

Kirk in U. S. Museums. Baltimore, Maryland: Samuel Kirk & Son, Inc., 1961.

Kirk Sterling—A Complete Catalog of America's Finest Sterling by America's Oldest Silversmiths. Baltimore: 1956 (?).

Knittle, Rhea Mansfield. *Early Ohio Silversmiths and Pewterers 1787–1847*. (Ohio Frontier Series.) Cleveland, Ohio: Calvert-Hatch Company, 1943.

"Knives for a Nation," *Industry September*, 1961.

Kovel, Ralph M. and Kovel, Terry H. *A Directory of American Silver, Pewter and Silverplate*. New York: Crown Publishers, 1961.

Lambert, Isaac E. *The Public Accepts; Stories Behind Famous Trademarks, Names and Slogans*. Albuquerque, N. M.: Univ. of N. M. Press, 1941.

Langdon, John Emerson. *Canadian Silversmiths & Their Marks, 1667–1867*. Lunenberg, Vermont: The Stinehour Press, 1960.

Langley, Henry. "Silverplating in California," *The Pacific Coast Almanac for 1869*, San Francisco, 1869.

Lathrop, W. G. *The Brass Industry in the United States*. Mt. Carmel, Conn.: Wilson H. Lee Co., 1926.

Laughlin, Ledlie I. *Pewter in America*. Boston: Houghton Mifflin Co., 1940.

Macomber, Henry P. "The Silversmiths of New England," *The American Magazine of Art*. Oct. 1932.

The Magazine SILVER (formerly Silver-Rama). 1968–1975.

Masterpieces of New England Silver 1650–1800. Gallery of Fine Arts, Yale University, 1939.

May, Earl Chapin. *A Century of Silver 1847–1947*. New York: Robert McBride Co., 1947.

Mazulla, Fred M. and J. *The First Hundred Years, Cripple Creek and the Pikes Peak Region*. Denver, Colorado: A. B. Hirschfeld Press, 1956.

Meeks, E. V. *Masterpieces of New England Silver*. Cambridge: Harvard Univ. Press, 1939.

"Men Who Developed the Silver Plated Ware Industry," *The Jewelers' Circular & Horological Review*, Oct. 3, 1894.

Meriden, the Silver City. Connecticut Tercentenary Committee, 1935.

The Meriden Daily Journal, 50th Anniversary Number. April 17, 1936.

Miller, V. Isabelle. *Silver by New York Makers, Late Seventeenth Century to 1900*. New York: Women's Committee of the Museum of The City of New York, 1938.

Miller, William Davis. *The Silversmiths of Little Rest*, Rhode Island. D. B. Updike, The Merrymount Press, 1928.

Morse, Edgar W. *San Francisco Silverware, A Preliminary List of Makers & Retailers*. 1977. Privately printed.

National Jeweler's Speed Book, No. 11, National Jeweler, c. 1930.

The National Jewelers' Trade and Trade-Mark Directory, 1918–19. Chicago: The National Jeweler, 1918.

Nationally Established Trade-Marks. New York: Periodical Publishers Assoc. of America, 1934.

"New England Silversmiths, news items gleaned from Boston newspapers, 1704–1705." *Art in America*, (February 1922), 75.

The New England States. William T. Davis, Ed. Vol. II: 832,833.

New York State Silversmiths. Eggertsville, N. Y.: Darling Foundation, 1965.

New York Sun. Antiques section.

Okie, Howard Pitcher. *Old Silver and Old Sheffield Plate*. New York: Doubleday, Doran and Company, 1928.

"Old American Silver," *Country Life in America*. February 1913–January 1915.

Ormsbee, Thomas H. *Know Your Heirlooms*. New York: The McBride Co., 1956

Parke-Bernet Galleries catalogue. January 1938–1975.

Elias Pelletreau, Long Island Silversmith and his Sources of Design. Brooklyn, N.Y.: Brooklyn Institute of Arts and Sciences, Brooklyn Museum, 1959.

"Pennsylvania Museum and School of Industrial Art Loan exhibition of Colonial Silver, special catalogue." *Pennsylvania Museum Bulletin.* No. 68, June 1921.

Percy, Randolph T. "The American at Work, IV: Among the Silver-Platers," *Appleton's Journal*, New Series, No. 30. (Dec. 1878).

"Philadelphia Silver 1682–1800," *Philadelphia Museum Bulletin*, LI, No. 249 (Spring 1956).

Philbrick, Helen Porter. "Franklin Porter, Silversmith (1869–1835)" *Essex Institute Historical Collections, Annual Report, 1968–69*, Salem, Massachusetts.

Phillips, John Marshall. *American Silver.* New York: Chanticleer Press, 1949.

"Pioneers of the American Silver Plate Industry," *Hobbies.* April, 1947.

Pleasants, J. Hall and Sill, Howard. *Maryland Silversmiths, 1715–1830.* Baltimore: The Lord Baltimore Press, 1930; reprinted 1972 by Robert Alan Green.

Porter, Edmund W. "Metallic Sketches," *Taunton Daily Gazette.* March 19, 1906–Sept. 28, 1907.

Prime, Alfred Coxe. *The Arts & Crafts in Philadelphia, Maryland and South Carolina, 1721–1785.*

Prime, Alfred Coxe. *The Arts & Crafts in Philadelphia, Maryland and South Carolina, 1786–1800.*

Prime, Mrs. Alfred Coxe. *Three Centuries of Historic Silver*, Philadelphia: Pennsylvania Society of Colonial Dames of America, 1938.

Purdy, W. Frank. "Developments in American Silversmithing," *The Art World*, May 1917.

Rainwater, Dorothy T. *Sterling Silver Holloware.* A Catalog reprint, American Historical Catalog Collection. Princeton, New Jersey: The Pyne Press, 1973.

Rainwater, Dorothy T. and Felger, Donna H. *American Spoons, Souvenir & Historical.* Nashville, Tennessee: Thomas Nelson Inc., and Hanover, Pennsylvania: Everybodys Press, 1968.

Rainwater, Dorothy T. and Rainwater, H Ivan. *American Silverplate.* Nashville, Tennessee: Thomas Nelson Inc., and Hanover, Pennsylvania: Everybodys Press, 1972.

Randolph, Howard S. F., "Jacob Boelen, Goldsmith of New York and his family circle," *New York Genealogical and Biographical Record.* October, 1941.

Report of the Eighth Industrial Exhibition of the Mechanics Institute, 1871. San Francisco, 1872.

Retrospect, A publication of the Historical Society of Glastonbury, Conn. No. 10, Feb. 1948.

Revi, Albert Christian. *Nineteenth Century Glass.* New York: Thomas Nelson & Sons, 1959.

Roach, Ruth Hunter. *St. Louis Silversmiths.* Privately printed, St. Louis, 1967.

Robertson, Constance, *The Oneida Community.* Pamphlet, no date.

Roe, Joseph Wickham. *Connecticut Inventors.* Tercentenary Commission of Connecticut, N.Y. Press, 1935.

Rogers, Edward S. *The Lanham Act and the Social Function of Trade-Marks, in Law and Contemporary Problems.* Durham, S. C. Quarterly, pub. by Duke Univ. School of Law, V. 14, No. 2, 1949.

"The Rogers Manufacturing Company," *The American Jeweler*, March 1882.

William Rogers and his Brothers in the Silverware Industry. Philadelphia: Keystone, Keystone Publishing Company, August and September, 1934.

Romaine, Lawrence B. *A Guide to American Trade Catalogs, 1744–1900.* New York: R. R. Bowker Company, 1960.

Rosenbaum, Jeanette. *Myer Myers, Goldsmith.* Philadelphia: Jewish Publication Society of America, 1954.

Rumpp, Leaders for a Century in Fine Leather Goods. Philadelphia: C. F. Rumpp & Sons, Inc., 1950.

Sabine, Julia. *Silversmiths of New Jersey.* Proc. of the New Jersey Historical Society, July–October, 1943 (Newark, 1943).

Schild, Joan Lynn. *Silversmiths of Rochester.* Rochester, N. Y.: Rochester Museum of Arts and Sciences, 1944.

Seeger and Guernsey. *Cyclopaedia of the Manufacturers and Products of the United States.* New York: 1890.

Selwyn, A. *The Retail Jeweller's Handbook.* New York: McBride Company, 1947.

Semon, Kurt M. *A Treasury of Old Silver.* New York: McBride Company, 1947.

"Silver by New York Makers," *Museum of the City of New York.* New York: 1937.

"The Silversmiths of New England," *American Magazine of Art.* October, 1932.

"The Silverware Industry in America," *The Jewelers' Circular-Keystone.* New York: November and December 1946.

"The Silverware Industry, Early Workers in Silver," *The Keystone*, November, 1899.

Sniffen, Philip L. *A Century of Silversmithing.* Reed & Barton Silversmiths. Taunton, Massachusetts: 1924.

Snow, Wm. G. "Early Silver Plating in America," *Metal Industry*, New York: June 1935.

Snow, Wm. G. "Silverplating in Connecticut, Its Early Days," *United States Investor*, May 18, 1935.

Souvenir Spoons of America. New York: The Jewelers Circular Publishing Co., 1891.

The Spinning Wheel. Hanover, Pa.: 1945–1975.

The Spoon from Earliest Times. Meriden, Conn.: International Silver Company, 1915.

Sterling Flatware Pattern Index. N. Y. and Phila.: Jewelers' Circular-Keystone, 1949.

Stieff Sterling Silver, The Stieff Company. Balti-

more: Barton-Gillet, c. 1930.

The Story of Daniel Low. Salem, Mass.: Daniel Low & Co., Catalog for 1917.

The Story of Sterling. Newburyport, Mass.: The Towle Silversmiths, 1954.

The Story of Sterling. New York: Sterling Silversmiths Guild of America, 1937.

The Story of the House of Kirk. Baltimore: Samuel Kirk & Son, Inc., 1914 and 1939.

Stow, M. *American Silver*. New York: Barrow & Co. 1950.

Stutzenberger, Albert. *The American Story in Spoons*. Louisville, Ky.: Privately printed, 1953.

"Tammen Curio Company of Denver," *Denver Post*. January 29, 1957.

"Tammen's Curio Shop," *Rocky Mountain Life*. Denver, Colorado: March 1949.

Taylor, Emerson. *Paul Revere*. New York: Dodd, Mead & Co., 1930.

Taylor, Gerald. *Silver*. London: Unwin Brothers, Ltd. 1956.

Thorn, C. Jordan. *Handbook of American Silver and Pewter Marks*. New York: Tudor Publishing Company, 1949.

Those Green River Knives. Russell Harrington Cutlery Company (Reprinted in part from Indian Notes, Vol. IV, No. 4 Museum of the American Indian, Heye Foundation, New York: October, 1927.

"Three Centuries of European and American Silver," *M. H. de Young Memorial Museum Bulletin*. San Francisco: October 1938.

"Charles L. Tiffany and the House of Tiffany & Co.," *Jewelers' Circular & Horological Review*, February 7, 1894.

Tilton, George P. *Colonial History* (catalogues of Benjamin Franklin, La Fayette, Paul Revere, Newbury and Georgian flatware patterns in addition to the histories of the persons and places.) Newburyport, Mass.: Towle Manufacturing Company, 1905.

Trade Marks of the Jewelry and Kindred Trades, New York and Philadelphia: Jewelers' Circular-Keystone Publishing Co., 1869, 1896, 1898, 1904, 1910, 1915, 1922, 1943, 1950, 1965, 1969, 1973.

Tryon, R. M. *Household Manufactures in U. S.* Chicago: University Press, 1917.

Turner, Noel D. *American Silver Flatware, 1837–1910*. Cranbury, New Jersey: A. S. Barnes & Co., Inc., 1972.

Twyman, Robert W. *History of Marshall Field & Co., 1852–1906*. Philadelphia: University of Pennsylvania Press, 1954.

U. S. Bureau of the Census, *Digest of Accounts of Manufacturing Establishments in the United States and of Their Manufacturers*. Washington, D.C.: 1823.

U. S. Tariff Commission. *A Survey of the various types of silverware, the organization of the industry and the trade in silverware, with special reference to tariff consideration*. Washington, D. C.: U. S. Gov't Printing Office, 1940. Report No. 139, Second Series.

Wallace, Floyd, Sr. *Wallace News*. June 1947. Credit to Miss Emma Dray.

Wardle, Patricia. *Victorian Silver & Silver Plate*. Victorian Collector Series. Thomas Nelson & Sons, 1963.

Wendt, Lloyd & Kogen, Herman, *Give the Lady what She Wants*. History of Marshall Fields, Chicago: Rand McNally, c. 1952.

Wenham, Edward. *Practical Book of American Silver*. New York and Philadelphia: J. B. Lippincott Co., 1949.

Westman, Habakkuk O. "The Spoon: Primitive, Egyptian, Roman, Medieval & Modern," *The Transactions of the Society of Literary and Scientific Chiffoniers*. New York: 1844.

White, Benjamin. *Silver, its History and Romance*. New York and London: Hodder & Stoughton. 1917.

White, Richard L. "A Century of Inventions for the American Home," *The Newcomen Society in North America*, lecture, 1955.

Williams, Carl Mark. *Silversmiths of New Jersey 1700–1825*. Philadelphia: G. S. McManus Co., 1949.

Woolsey, Theodore S. "Old Silver," *Harper's Magazine*, 1896.

Wroth, Lawrence C. *Abel Buell of Connecticut, Silversmith, Typefounder, and Engraver*. 1926.

Wyler, Seymour B. *The Book of Old Silver*. New York: Crown Publishers, 1937.

Wyler, Seymour B. *The Book of Sheffield Plate, Including Victorian Plate*. New York: Crown Publishers, 1949.

Magazines

Anonymous news note in *Science News*, November 23, 1974, Vol. 106, No. 21.

Claremont, Chris and Byrne, John. *The Uncanny X-Men*, Marvel Comics, May 1981.

Love, Martin. "Painting from the Past," in *Aramco World Magazine*, January-February 1983.

Sagan, Carl and Drake, Frank. "The Search for Extra-Terrestrial Intelligence" in *Scientific American*, May 1975, Vol. 232, No. 5.

Sears, Peter. "Learning Language by Invention," in *Teachers & Writers*, September-October 1982, Vol. 14, No. 1.

Snow, Dean R. "Rock Art and the Power of Shamans," in *Natural History*, February 1977.